Brontë Transformations

For Catherine and Marianne, who have grown up
with this book in their attic

Brontë Transformations

The Cultural Dissemination of Jane Eyre and Wuthering Heights

Patsy Stoneman

University of Hull

PRENTICE HALL
HARVESTER WHEATSHEAF

London   New York   Toronto   Sydney   Tokyo   Singapore
Madrid   Mexico City   Munich

First published 1996 by
Prentice Hall/Harvester Wheatsheaf
Campus 400, Maylands Avenue
Hemel Hempstead
Hertfordshire, HP2 7EZ
A division of
Simon & Schuster International Group

Typeset in 10/12pt Ehrhardt
by Hands Fotoset, Leicester

Printed and bound in Great Britain by
Hartnolls Limited, Bodmin, Cornwall

Library of Congress Cataloging-in-Publication Data

Stoneman, Patsy.
    Brontë transformations : the cultural dissemination of Jane Eyre
and Wuthering Heights / Patsy Stoneman.
      p. cm.
    Includes bibliographical references and index.
    ISBN 0-13-355561-5
    1. Brontë, Charlotte, 1816–1855. Jane Eyre. 2. Women and
literature—England—History—19th century. 3. Brontë, Charlotte,
1816–1855—Criticism and interpretation—History. 4. Brontë, Emily,
1818–1848—Criticism and interpretation—History. 5. English
fiction—Women authors—History and criticism—Theory, etc.
6. Brontë, Emily, 1818–1848. Wuthering Heights. 7. Brontë,
Charlotte, 1816–1855—Adaptations. 8. Brontë, Emily, 1818–1848—
—Adaptations. 9. English fiction—Appreciation. 10. English
fiction—Adaptations. I. Title.
PR4167 J5S75   1995
823'.8—dc20   95–495
                                             CIP

British Library Cataloguing in Publication Data

A catalogue record for this book is available from
the British Library

ISBN 0-13-355561-5

1 2 3 4 5   00 99 98 97 96

Contents

List of Figures

Note on references and abbreviations

References broadly follow the Harvard system in which a brief reference in the text (author date: page) can be fully identified by turning to a list at the end of the book. The system has, however, been adapted here to cope with three different categories of reference:

1. References to *Jane Eyre* and *Wuthering Heights* will always appear in the form (*JE*) and (*WH*) and refer to the following editions:

   Brontë, Charlotte ([1847] 1993) *Jane Eyre* (The World Classics), Margaret Smith (ed. and intro.), Oxford: Oxford University Press.
   Brontë, Emily ([1847] 1995) *Wuthering Heights* (The World's Classics), Ian Jack (ed.), Patsy Stoneman (intro.), Oxford: Oxford University Press.

   Note: these editions number the chapters in accordance with the original division into volumes; chapter references will therefore take the form I i (vol. I ch. i).

2. References to works of criticism, biography, etc. appear in the text in the form (Brooks 1976: 10) and can be fully identified in the general bibliography which lists works alphabetically by author.

3. Derivatives of *JE* and *WH* referred to in the text can be fully identified by reference to the two chronological lists of derivatives which are each arranged by year, subdivided by genre and within that by alphabetical listing of author, painter, etc. Where there is a page reference in brackets in the text this is distinguished from references to the general bibliography by the abbreviation *JE* or *WH* followed by the date and author, e.g. (*JE* 1856 Brougham: 10). Where an edition other than the original is cited in the chronological list, the reference will take the form (*JE* 1898 James [1964: 10]). In discussions of performances, some brief reviews are identified only by a date (e.g. 5.12.90); more details will usually be found in the chronological list.

Derivatives of *JE* and *WH* can also be traced by means of the index, which will list the author or director, etc. and sometimes other details such as the name of a principal actor. In the index, page references to the chronological lists of derivatives are distinguished from ordinary textual references by bold type.

Common abbreviations are:

BPM   Brontë Parsonage Museum.
BSG   *Brontë Society Gazette.*
BST   *Brontë Society Transactions.* I have adopted the convention of reference recommended by the Brontë Society, namely *BST* 15.77.143 (1967), which gives volume, part, page number and date.

Preface

This book arose from my interest in the phenomenon of *famous* texts – what happens to literary texts when they become so well known that they are common property within the culture. *Jane Eyre* and *Wuthering Heights* have been disseminated by repeated reproductions in a variety of media from the date of their first publication to the present day. Few of these reproductions are simple facsimiles of the original written text. Apart from the scholarly 'framing' provided by the education system – introductions, notes, critical essays, biographical sketches and so on – there are editions with illustrations, stage, film and television adaptations, musical, operatic and ballet versions, picturebook and comicbook versions, parodies and, most interesting of all, a variety of 'reworkings' of the famous texts by subsequent creative writers. These reproductions are not limited to Britain or even to the English-speaking world; a stage melodrama based on *Jane Eyre* was performed in New York in 1856, and *Wuthering Heights* featured in a Tokyo trade fair in 1991.

My interest extends, moreover, beyond editions, adaptations and illustrations to incidental references and also to structural parallels which may not even refer to their Brontë originals. This means that individual examples elude systematic methods of bibliographical searching and it is thus impossible to be exhaustive. Although I have been collecting material for over ten years, the only source which I can claim to have covered comprehensively is the material held by the Brontë Parsonage Museum at Haworth, and I must record here my enormous gratitude to Kathryn White and Ann Dinsdale who have made that task so easy and pleasant. I also owe thanks to the Brontë Society itself for making available to me the resources of their library, especially their unique collection of ephemera, which has contributed richness, variety and humour to my book.

The older material held by the BPM is itself, however, not systematically collected, being the result of voluntary contributions and having a strong local bias. Moreover, although the previous paragraphs distinguish between different categories of derivatives of *Jane Eyre* and *Wuthering Heights*, I have not attempted precision in such distinctions. Especially where parallels rather than reproductions or allusions are concerned, the criterion for a text being included in this book may be no more rigorous than that someone other than myself has perceived it to be a 'Brontë derivative'. Among other effects, this means that I have had to rely to a much greater extent than is normal in academic work on chance findings and on the generous participation of dozens of voluntary informants.

First in this category come members of the Northern Network, whose enthusiastic response to a paper delivered in 1990 confirmed me on the path which has led to this book. In particular, Shirley Foster, Gill Frith, Judie Newman and Helen Taylor have generously shared their knowledge about Victorian women novelists, Jean Rhys and popular romances. I am also extremely grateful to Donna Marie Nudd for making available to me in draft form her paper on stage and film adaptations of *Jane Eyre* (Nudd 1992), as well as for her PhD thesis on the same subject (Nudd 1989). In the case of some American stage plays, I have had no access to a text and am thus especially indebted to Professor Nudd's account. Helen Hughes's MA thesis on adaptations of *Wuthering Heights* has also been very valuable (Hughes, H. 1991). I would also like to thank my 'Erasmus' colleagues, Vita Fortunati, Gabriella Morisco, Nicole Rowan, Liz Russell and Aranzazu Usandizaga, for bearing with me in a series of trial Brontë papers, some of which have been published in Erasmus symposia (Fortunati and Morisco 1993; Russell and Usandizaga 1995; Rowan 1995). Material which appears in Chapters 4, 5 and 7 was published in a different form in Richard Andrews's book, *Rebirth of Rhetoric* (Stoneman 1992b).

I am also grateful for specific finds: Richard Andrews passed on valuable material from the Bradford Museum of Photography, Film and Television. Sarah Cheesmond first alerted me to the manuscript plays in the Lord Chamberlain's Collection. John and Margaret Crompton have been indefatigable in 'turning up' parallels and allusions and I owe a special debt to John Crompton for introducing me to Elizabeth Taylor. Sarah Fermi has found some particularly amusing American parodies. Mike Forsyth was generous enough to make photocopies of rare texts by Julia Kavanagh. Chris Greenhalgh suggested Muriel Spark's *Not to Disturb* and Debra Hicks suggested Doris Lessing's *The Four-Gated City*. Sue Hamilton led me to the 'Rawhide' version of *Wuthering Heights* and, more importantly, to Jane Urquhart. Marie C. Hennedy was kind enough to send me an audiotape of some songs from Ted Davis's musical of *Jane Eyre* (1984) and Catherine Constable sent me a copy of *Good Housekeeping* containing a *Jane Eyre* competition. Siv Jansson gave me the words to Kate Bush's 'Wuthering Heights' and a programme for Toothill's *Brontë Follies* (1988); Maureen Reddy told me about Michael Penn's *No Myth*. Nodge Jones and Marilyn Ribbands have both found poems. Angela Leighton told me about Charlotte Mew. Lynne Pearce alerted me to the *Jane Eyre* references in Jeanette Winterson's *Oranges Are Not the Only Fruit* and Penny Summerfield described to me Judith Rowbotham's talk on missionary texts (which I have not been able to locate). Anne Powell introduced me both to Sarah Grand and to her own mother, Twinks Kenyon, who played the child Catherine in the 1920 silent film of *Wuthering Heights*. Jim Thompson provided some useful information about early railways. Kathryn White not only gave me a copy of her article on *Jane Eyre* and Conan Doyle (White 1992), but has entered into my project to the extent of volunteering to check details of my typescript, for which I am very grateful. Responsibility for any remaining errors is, of course, mine.

Collecting the material is one thing; making it into a book is another. It was Sue Roe who had faith enough to sign me up for this book; Jackie Jones kept me going and Christina Wipf has galvanized me into finishing it. Along the way, I am grateful to Elaine Jordan for timely encouragement and to Stevie Davies for a cheering stream of letters. Closer to home, I owe an enormous debt to my friends and colleagues Angela Leighton and Marion Shaw, who have, in their different ways, stood by me during the long gestation of this book.

Finally, there is my husband Colin, who has been there, as always, from start to finish, and has helped me in more ways than I can record – as instant encyclopedia, as supplier of delicious meals and strategic gins and tonics, as mediator between me and a succession of word-processors, and as someone who always believed the book would be good. If it measures up to the faith he has always had in me, it will be a good book indeed.

Introduction

This book has a deliberately ambiguous title. *Brontë Transformations* is meant to indicate both the ways in which people transform texts and the ways in which texts transform people; it even suggests that texts transform themselves. My title gestures towards the general Brontë phenomenon but I have chosen to focus on *Jane Eyre* and *Wuthering Heights*, not only because they are powerful texts which make an impact on their readers but also because they are *famous* texts which are widely handled in different ways; literally 'broadcast', they have fallen on various soils and have borne various fruits. My interest is not in a possible ultimate meaning but on the process of change: I want to read these texts in history and to suggest how and why transformations occur.

This book itself has had a long history, and has been subject to change. It was inspired by the Essex conferences of the late 1970s, which created an atmosphere in which traditional notions of literary value were challenged and upset. In place of a canon of great works, distinguished by their timeless truths and artistic originality, post-structuralist theories encouraged us to see high and low culture as a continuum of textuality in which texts were determined by an intersection of cultural forces rather than the inspiration of genius. As well as changing our perception of how texts are produced, however, this new climate alerted us to the way in which texts are received and transmitted. It no longer seemed irrelevant whether you read *Henry V* in a school text, saw it acted at Stratford, or watched Olivier's film in your local cinema. Literary texts were ceasing to be 'verbal icons', fixed objects for admiration, and were becoming part of a historical process which did not cease with their production.

At Essex, I discovered Pierre Macherey (1978), who, 'instead of treating the text as a "creation" or self-contained artifact, regards it as a "production" in which a number of disparate materials are worked over and changed in the process' (Seldon 1985: 40). Macherey also argues that literary 'value' is not inherent in the text but is produced by the institutions of society, especially the education system. Thus the text is not only 'produced' by its writer, it is 're-produced' by society. Five years later, at a Higher Education Teachers of English (HETE) Conference in Leicester, I heard two demonstrations of Machereyan criticism. Peter Widdowson showed how the literary commodity known as 'Thomas Hardy' had been produced by the education system (Widdowson 1983), while Terence Hawkes argued that Dover

Wilson's famous book *What Happens in Hamlet* was produced in 1917 as a desperate patriotic reaction to the combined threats of the Kaiser and the Russian Revolution. It began to seem possible to analyze the reproduction of the famous Brontë texts in such a way as to give an ideological history of the culture which goes on reproducing them. It was with this intention that in 1982 I signed a contract for a book which was to be called *The Brontë Texts: Production and Re-production*. Very soon, however, I realized that my proposed topic was too big, and it is only the 're-production' of the texts which forms the basis of the book which follows.

Both Widdowson and Hawkes have long since completed their respective projects in book form. Terence Hawkes describes the kind of literary criticism which follows from Machereyan theory in *That Shakespeherian Rag*. It invites us, he says, to confront 'not the "great" works of art in themselves . . . but the ways in which those works of art have been processed . . . as part of the struggle for cultural meaning '(Hawkes 1986: 123). Peter Widdowson's stated aim in *Hardy in History* (1989) is also to investigate the 'production and reproduction of meaning, status, and value', this time in the case of Thomas Hardy. In some ways Widdowson's book offers a model for my own, but where Widdowson's priority is class relations I intend to privilege gender. Moreover, Widdowson's account is confined to what Althusser called 'ideological state apparatuses' – particularly the education system. I want to allow space for what Jean Bethke Elshtain calls the 'unpredictable and surprising possibilities' for transforming an existing text through imaginative writing (Elshtain 1982: 143). Where Widdowson takes vertical slices through history, I hope to take horizontal slices as well, relating all the various media of reproduction at any one date.

This project has, in fact, outlived its theoretical beginnings. In 1982, Macherey's approach seemed obvious; since then I have discovered, for instance, Derrida's writing on 'iterability' – 'a text's . . . capacity to be constantly "re-read" and "re-written", with "diverse meanings" and "plural effects"' (Bennett 1982: 226–7); I have also discovered discourse theory, the new work around rhetoric and Kristeva's work on intertextuality (1986: 37). Finally, my theoretical procedures have been eclectic, and I have been encouraged in this by Terry Eagleton, who writes,

> It is not a matter of starting from certain theoretical or methodological problems: it is
> a matter of starting from what we want to *do*, and then seeing which method and
> theories will best help us to achieve these ends. (Eagleton 1983: 210)

This book is, therefore, different from its original conception. As I engaged with particular texts, it emerged that what I wanted to *do* was to bring to the foreground the specifically textual effects of various plays, poems, films, pictures and novels, and I found that my planned 'ideological history', which I had conceived as closely deriving from economic and social history, had become a relatively autonomous textual history. In this, too, however, I have received encouragement, this time from Antony Easthope, who in *Literary into Cultural Studies* argues that signifying practice cannot be collapsed into a discussion of economic practice precisely because 'textuality is characterised by what Derrida names as "dissemination"' – the transformation, not of raw materials but of *meanings* (Easthope 1991: 111, 110). On the other hand, Easthope argues that the processes of reading which have traditionally formed the basis of literary study can no longer be reserved for what has traditionally been called 'literature' but must be extended to cover all forms of discourse. The premise of his book, in fact, is that the challenge represented by Macherey and Derrida among others to the paradigm of literary studies has now gone so far that 'the old paradigm has collapsed, that the moment of crisis symptomatically registered in concern with theory is now passing, and that a fresh paradigm has emerged' (Easthope 1991: 5).

When I began this book about cultural process, I did not anticipate that the process of producing it would itself fit so neatly into cultural history. It seems, however, that, beginning from a position within literary studies, I have ended in the 'new paradigm'. Because I hope that my readers will come from both literary and cultural studies, it is perhaps important to state that although the new paradigm challenges traditional notions of literary value, it need not have a levelling effect. Famous texts such as *Jane Eyre* and *Wuthering Heights* emerge from my book powerfully distinguished from the rest, just as in traditional criticism, though by different criteria. Easthope here confirms my own conclusion that the only reliable way of measuring literary value is by the extent to which a text 'has exceeded the conjuncture of its production, has engaged with altered ideological contexts and been reproduced in different contemporary readings' (1991: 57). Maria Corti, with reference to Umberto Eco's writing on dissemination, writes:

> the more artistically complex and original a work of art, the higher it rises over the works that surround it, the greater is its availability to different readings on both the synchronic and the diachronic levels . . . Every era applies its own reading codes, its changed vantage points; the text continues to accumulate sign possibilities which are communicative precisely because the text is inside a system in movement. (in Easthope 1991: 58–9)

Studying a 'system in movement' is both exciting and daunting. Marxist, feminist and cultural theories all stress the importance of making large connections between text and context. Griselda Pollock, for instance, argues that an

> understanding of what specific artistic practices are doing, their meanings and social effects, demands . . . a dual approach. First the practice must be located as part of the social struggles between classes, races and genders, articulating with other sites of representation. But second we must analyse what any specific practice is doing, what meaning is being produced, and how and for whom. (Pollock 1988: 7)

This means that in studying, say, a stage version of *Jane Eyre* from 1856, I should on the one hand put it in the context of its age, but on the other hand put it also in the generic context of stage plays from 1936 or 1994. Multiplied across genres and discourses, and across the one hundred and fifty years since the publication of the Brontë texts, the potential field becomes vast. Dissemination, moreover, is an unsystematic process which may take the form of almost exact reproductions (editions), versions in other media (stage plays, films), selective reproductions or versions (dramatized scenes, visual illustrations), parodies, allusions, structural parallels (which may not even mention the original text) and what Christopher Richards calls 'incremental' writings (sequels, prequels, etc.) (Richards, C. 1989). These derivatives, moreover, interact with one another, so that post-war versions of *Wuthering Heights*, for instance, often derive more closely from the 1939 film than from Emily Brontë's text, and recent versions of *Jane Eyre* have included material from Jean Rhys's *Wide Sargasso Sea*. Not only the gathering of material, but also its analysis, becomes problematic.

Traditional literary criticism, based on the assumption that the text is the outcome of the author's intention, has only been able to deal with the relationship between literary texts by means of such concepts as influence, imitation or critique. Post-structuralist ideas, however, have introduced a more open and less deliberate notion of textual construction and interdependence. Roland Barthes, writing in 1973, argues that

> What founds the text is not an internal, closed, accountable structure, but the outlet of the text on to other texts, other signs; what makes the text is the intertextual. We are beginning to glimpse . . . the fact that research must little by little get used to the conjunction of two ideas which for a long time were thought incompatible: the idea of structure and the idea of combinational infinity; the conciliation of these two postulations is forced upon us now because language, which we are getting to know better, is at once infinite and structured. (in Lodge 1988: 174)

Julia Kristeva, following Mikhail Bakhtin, also argues that all literature is 'intertextual' in that 'any text is constructed as a mosaic of quotations; any text is the absorption and transformation of another' (1986: 37). Famous texts like *Jane Eyre* and *Wuthering Heights*, which are repeatedly plundered, however, acquire a different status, rather like that of a fairytale, which we might describe as mythological. This status depends partly on some inherent significance in the original text, and partly on the process of reiteration itself. In his book on *Frankenstein*, Chris Baldick argues that such 'modern myths prolong their lives not by being retold at great length, but by being alluded to . . . This process . . . reduc[es] them to the simplest memorable patterns' (Baldick 1987a: 3). Thus the plot of *Jane Eyre* – the Cinderella-type heroine, the older man with a mysterious past, and the haunting presence of the hero's first, striking, mad, bad wife – has become a staple of popular romance.

There are two questions we can ask ourselves about such modern myths. One is, 'what is it in the original story which gives it such enduring interest?', and we might answer this question in structural or Freudian terms. Such an answer to the endurance of the myth only, however, begs more questions, such as, why does the Oedipus complex itself endure? Barbara Herrstein Smith, in fact, writing on the Cinderella myth, concludes 'that there is no single *basically* basic story subsisting beneath it, but, rather, an unlimited number of other narratives that can be *constructed in response* to it or *perceived as related* to it' (Smith 1980: 221). Such a response derives, again, from Roland Barthes, who wrote in 'The Death of the Author' (1968) that

> We know now that a text is not a line of words releasing a single 'theological' meaning
> (the 'message' of the Author-God) but a multi-dimensional space in which a variety
> of writings, none of them original, blend and clash. The text is a tissue of quotations
> drawn from the innumerable centres of culture . . . but there is one place where this
> multiplicity is focused and that place is the reader, not, as was hitherto said, the author.
> (in Lodge 1988: 170–1)

If, however, the reader is the place where the meanings of a text meet, he or she
is also the place where new meanings may be generated. Every writer (or painter
or film-maker) is also a reader who transforms previous texts into new shapes. This
book will, therefore, look neither for an origin or final cause for a particular textual
manifestation, nor for a final reading. Rather it will look at the process of reading
and writing and ask 'how has the generative text been transformed in the course of
its reproduction, and what relationship do these transformations have to the
societies that made them?' My perception of this relationship is less deterministic
than that of more thorough-going cultural materialists, and I would agree with
Annette Kuhn that 'a society's representations of itself . . . may be seen as a vital,
pervasive and active element in the constitution of social structures and formations'
so that 'interventions within culture have some independent potential to transform'
them (Kuhn 1982: 5, 6). Like Baldick and Kuhn, Eagleton also suggests that
discursive practices are relatively autonomous, since 'discourses . . . shape forms
of consciousness and unconsciousness, which are closely related to the maintenance
or transformation of our existing systems of power' (Eagleton 1983: 210).

The potential for transformation lies to a significant extent within the medium
of representation. Because versions of the same myth share elements such as
characters and incident, any comparative study throws emphasis on their formal
differences, both of medium (novel to film or picture) and of signifying structures
('plot' and 'style'). Although, therefore, part of my aim is to describe the great variety
of transformations of *Jane Eyre* and *Wuthering Heights*, I shall also deal with some
examples in detail in order to suggest how our reading of different versions of the
same originating text is conditioned by formal changes, both of medium and of
internal rhetoric. This focus on form does not, however, divert my study from its
historical intentions; in fact Barthes insists that 'the more a system is specifically
defined in its forms, the more amenable it is to historical criticism' (1981: 112).

The structure of this book is broadly chronological, and its two bibliographies
of primary material also take the form of chronological lists. This reflects my
continuing conviction that there is a significant relationship between economic,
political and social history and the evolution of texts. I now feel, however, not only
that this relationship is less close and less 'readable' than my original hypothesis,
but also that there is no hierarchy of causation which makes economic change
more 'basic' than any other. The references which I had intended to make to
changes in social formations have, for various reasons, become slighter than I had
envisaged, and although I hope that my structure will make my material amenable
to analysis from a more thoroughly materialist position, my own current position is
that textual transformation, though itself a material practice, and though evidently

linked with the other material changes of history, is as much constitutive as constituted.

The content of the chapters, which appears uneven, has been dictated by the material which has emerged. Chapter 1 is wholly devoted to *Jane Eyre* because it was *Jane Eyre* which made an immediate impact; I have discovered no derivatives of *Wuthering Heights* before the 1880s, when it was Emily rather than her novel which seized the *avant garde* imagination (see Chapter 2 below). Although, on the whole, I have tried to restrict the book to derivatives of the two famous texts, it was impossible to avoid biographical treatments altogether and from time to time these became dominant. Thus Chapter 3 is 'mainly biographical' and steps somewhat outside the chronological sequence to deal with the mythification of the Brontë lives and the ways in which this interacted with the treatment of the novels, particularly in the inter-war period. The production in 1939 of William Wyler's film of *Wuthering Heights* formed a watershed in popular perception, not only establishing Emily's novel belatedly as equivalent in value to Charlotte's, but fixing the way in which the novel has predominantly been read until the present day. Readings of *Jane Eyre* have been consistently produced in the context of women's liberation from roles of servitude, and the fluctuations of these processes are recorded in Chapters 4 and 5. Although perceptions of Jane have evolved with the historical situation of women, however, the major innovation in the reading of Charlotte's novel has concerned not its heroine but her 'other' – the imprisoned wife who has, in the past thirty years, been read as representative of the repressed in terms of sexuality, rationality and race. *Jane Eyre*'s 'other' thus forms the separate subject matter of Chapter 6. The final chapter gives some sense of the extent to which these novels have now become common currency and are regularly used in the formation and testing of individual subject-positions as well as in commercial enterprises. I have tried to suggest that this 'system in movement' offers the possibility of active self-definition as well as for ideological petrifaction. If the beginning of the book is dominated by *Jane Eyre*, *Wuthering Heights* takes prominence towards its end, and I have given the last word not to a formal conclusion but to a treatment of *Wuthering Heights* which at last seems to rise to the challenge of the 'death of the author'.

One of the hardest parts of writing this book has been to decide that it is, in any sense, finished. In many ways it is *not* finished; I am aware of its gaps and inadequacies, of the examples not found or analyses imperfectly developed. More basically, it can never be finished, since *Jane Eyre* and *Wuthering Heights* go on being read, and 'the lonely hour of the final reading never comes' (Easthope 1991: 33). Moreover, to claim that a book of this kind is definitive would be a contradiction in terms, appealing to that tradition of mastery which the new paradigm aims to unseat. I offer the book, therefore, as a contribution to a process in which you are invited to partake.

Chapter 1

The nineteenth century

Jane Eyre and *Wuthering Heights* were not born to blush unseen. Miriam Allott's anthology, *The Brontës: The Critical Heritage* (1974), testifies to the abundance of material available to anyone wishing to investigate early critical opinions of the Brontë novels. All the novels were extensively reviewed in the periodical press, making it relatively easy to construct what Widdowson calls a 'critiography' – an account of the critical history – of *Jane Eyre* and *Wuthering Heights* (1989: 6). In particular, these early reviews provide us with a context in which to consider two of the main channels through which *Jane Eyre* made its impact on the world beyond its immediate readers: the stage melodrama and the 'woman's' novel.

'Tableaux of astonishment': Jane Eyre *on the stage, 1848–56*

Jane Eyre impressed its original readers as nothing less than revolutionary. An anonymous reviewer writing in 1848 – the 'year of revolutions' – finds that 'every page burns with moral Jacobinism. "Unjust, unjust," is the burden of every reflection upon the things and powers that be' (in Allott 1974: 90). Lady Eastlake, in the same year, confirms that

> there is throughout it a murmuring against the comforts of the rich and against the privations of the poor, which, as far as each individual is concerned, is a murmuring against God's appointment – there is a proud and perpetual assertion of the rights of man . . . [a] pervading tone of ungodly discontent . . . We do not hesitate to say that the tone of the mind and thought which has overthrown authority and violated every code human and divine abroad, and fostered Chartism and rebellion at home, is the same which has also written Jane Eyre. (in Allott 1974: 109–10)

Interestingly, a French reviewer in 1848 saw the novel not as revolutionary but as radical in a 'completely English' way, the product of a race who 'firmly implant in the hearts of their children the feeling for freedom and responsibility; who have given the world not Saint-Simon and Fourier, but William Penn, Daniel Defoe and Benjamin Franklin' (Eugène Forçade, in Allott 1974: 101). England, of course, though it feared revolution, experienced it only in terms of constitutional change.

The first Reform Bill of 1832, extending the franchise to the wealthier middle classes, gave political form to the economic shift in the class structure which had been effected by the Industrial Revolution. The reaction to *Jane Eyre*, however, suggests that the more conservative middle classes were well aware of the dangers of revolution at the level of discourse. Early reviewers react not so much to what Jane does as to her insubordinate thoughts, and it is possibly for this reason that *Jane Eyre* was immediately perceived as appropriate material for the popular stage melodrama, since Peter Brooks finds the assertive rhetoric of the melodrama 'in all cases radically democratic' (1976: 15). Although Martha Vicinus (1981: 129) assumes a seventeenth-century origin for stage melodrama, Brooks is confident that

> The origins of melodrama can be accurately located within the context of the French Revolution and its aftermath. This is the epistemological moment which it illustrates and to which it contributes: the moment that symbolically, and really, marks the final liquidation of the traditional Sacred . . . Melodrama . . . comes into being in a world where the traditional imperatives of truth and ethics have been violently thrown into question, yet where the promulgation of truth and ethics, their instauration as a way of life, is of immediate, daily, political concern. (1976: 15)

In the newly bourgeois world in which Charlotte Brontë wrote, 'truth and ethics' were no less under question than in post-revolutionary France, and although the *Athenaeum* in 1849 tried to pass off its effect as 'yet one more expression of aching discontents and vague ambitions' (in Allott 1974: 122), *Jane Eyre* was still able to agitate the English middle class. Mrs Oliphant, however, having frightened her readers with revolutionary imagery, then applies it to a domestic rather than a class revolution:

> Yes, it is but a mere vulgar boiling over of the political cauldron, which tosses your French monarch into chaos, and makes a new one in his stead.
>   Here is your true revolution. France is but one of the Western Powers; woman is the half of the world. (1855: 558)

Forty years later, in 1887, Oliphant still identifies the success of *Jane Eyre* as lying in its 'impassioned revelation' of 'feminine distresses' (in Allott 1974: 41). If the 'revolutionary' fervour of *Jane Eyre*, with its individualism and assertion of the rights of the poor and disconnected, lends itself to the form of popular melodrama as defined by Peter Brooks, its extension to the cause of women creates problems. According to Brooks, 'the word melodrama . . . appears to have first been used . . . by Rousseau' to describe one of his own plays in 1770 (1976: 14). Now although Rousseau was one of the inspirers of the French Revolution, a radical supporter of the rights of the individual, we know (from Mary Wollstonecraft, for instance) that his radicalism stopped short at the emancipation of women. The education of his ideal 'natural' man, Émile, includes a wife whose mission in life is to serve him (*Émile* (1762) book 5). Similarly, the form of melodrama as it later evolved in England depended on conventional gender relations to stabilize its alternative, bourgeois 'truth and ethics'. The stage melodrama versions of *Jane Eyre* which appeared almost immediately after the novel's publication, therefore, altered the emphasis of the novel in two, almost opposite ways. On the one hand, they gave exaggerated vocal expression to Jane's sense of class oppression and victimization; on the other, they recuperated the radical implications of her relationship with Rochester into conventional comic nuptials.

John Courtney's play, *Jane Eyre, or The Secrets of Thornfield Manor* (1849), was produced in London within a year of the novel's publication, and by the early 1880s there had been at least eight different adaptations performed in England and America. John Brougham's melodrama, first performed in 1856, demonstrates the contradictory treatment of Charlotte Brontë's material. The drawing-room scene, for instance, where Jane is forced to listen silently while Rochester's upper-class guests make fun of governesses (*JE* II ii), is in this play transformed into dialogue between Jane and her tormentors. The effect is to make transparently explicit the class basis of her victimization. For this purpose, Mary Ingram is separated from her relations by her sympathy for Jane; Jane thanks her, but replies, 'The mind that's conscious of its own superiority stands on too high an eminence to be reached by the petty shafts of pride and ignorance'. When Lord Ingram makes a clumsy pass at her – 'do you know, Jane, that you're devilish pretty?' – Jane replies by asking what he would think if anyone addressed one of his sisters like that. He is dumbfounded: 'I can't imagine; it's a very different thing – '. Jane continues with what Ingram describes as 'a regular sermon, by Jupiter', and deals coolly with his angry response:

> *Jane:* Pray calm yourself, my Lord. I shall retire, not out of dread of your contumely, but from very pity of your infirmities: and it may be, that the poor, lowly-nurtured drudge, whom you sent for to bring you unworthy amusement, will have given you a wholesome, though unwelcome lesson.
> *Lord Ing:* Snubbed, by Jove!
> *Col. Dent:* Prodigiously.
> *Tableaux of astonishment.*
> *End of Act I.* (I ii 10–11)

Although it is such *coups de théâtre* that make melodrama laughable by naturalistic standards, Brooks argues that the dramaturgy of melodrama is focused on such moments, which

> can perhaps best be characterised as the admiration of virtue. Confrontation and peripety are managed so as to make possible a remarkable, public, spectacular homage to virtue . . . and the language has continual recourse to hyperbole and grandiose antithesis to explicate and clarify the admirableness of this virtue'.
> The heroine is 'femme étonnante' . . . because her demonstration, her representation, of virtue strikes with almost physical force, astounding and convincing. The melodramatic moment of astonishment is a moment of ethical evidence and recognition. (Brooks 1976: 25–6)

It is not, however, only in dialogue that Jane is given her voice. If, as Brooks contends, plays such as this depend on 'the dramaturgy of virtue misprized and eventually recognized' (27), it is the audience as much as the other characters who provide the vindicating jury. What in the novel are Jane's private thoughts in the melodrama become either dialogue or direct address to the audience. Immediately on her first entrance, for instance, against the background of the Lowood schoolroom, Jane faces the audience and says:

> Ah, aunt, aunt! you do not, you cannot know the bitter slavery to which your hate has doomed me: eight long years of joyless, hopeless, pitiless imprisonment – life dragged along in one unvarying level, in the very springtime of my youth – with heart and brain astir, and yearning for the love of kindred, full of bright thoughts and glorious impulses, the world and all its chances, changes, forever closed against me – it is terrible. Oh, for freedom! freedom! My heart bounds like an imprisoned bird against its wiry barrier, at the mere thought – freedom – blessed freedom; those only, who lose thee, know thy worth. (*throws open window*) Oh, I have prayed for liberty until my loud cry seemed scattered on the passing wind. I cannot rest – I cannot think – my tortured brain, in wild confusion, whirls. Heaven send me a change, no matter what – a break to this heart-cankering monotony – a change, or I shall go mad. (*JE* 1856 Brougham: 5–6)

Now this is even more impassioned than Jane's inner reflections in I x of Charlotte Brontë's novel, and as an utterance it changes in character by being, in one sense, part of a dialogue, in present tense, with a sympathetic audience. In spite of the artificiality of the style, Jane appears not as a silenced, marginal figure but as an articulate rebel, holding the centre stage; the auditorium is full of listeners to her cry of 'Unjust! – unjust!' (*JE* 15).

According to Brooks, 'the desire to express all seems a fundamental characteristic of the melodrama mode . . . the characters stand on stage and utter the unspeakable, give voice to their deepest feelings' (1976: 4). One curious effect of these stage adaptations of *Jane Eyre*, in fact, is that their conventions seem to step behind the relatively naturalistic modes of Charlotte Brontë's published novel, reaching back to the emotional intensities of the Brontë juvenilia, which are full of Romantic complaints from youthful prisoners like the young princes and princesses in the dungeons of the Palace of Instruction (Alexander 1983: 46). Behind both again are perhaps the democratic and Romantic impulses of the French Revolution. Peter Brooks instances *Latude*, the last play of the famous French melodramatist Pixérecord, produced in 1834, in which the hero and heroine, locked in dungeons by evil monks and nuns acting for a corrupt aristocracy, are liberated by a republican mayor. 'The play suggests', Brooks argues,

> the connection of the claustral space to the Gothic on the one hand, to the Revolution on the other: the Revolution as an opening up of and liberation from the claustral, the victory of democracy as virtue and innocence.
>   The word *liberty* echoes throughout the play . . . (1976: 50)

Brougham's play, however, has to shift the emphasis of Jane's distress and her plea for liberty to place it in a class context. In the novel, Jane's discomfiture in the drawing room is at least partly due to her sense of sexual inferiority to Blanche Ingram, who snubs her in Rochester's presence. In the play, however, the scene between her and the Ingrams takes place soon after her arrival at Thornfield, before the scene where Rochester falls from his horse. This means that Jane is alone with her aristocratic tormentors, and her reaction to the drawing-room scene provides material for an unhappy soliloquy immediately before Rochester's appearance, which is somewhat like her lament at the inactivity of her life in I xii of the novel immediately before the meeting with Rochester. In the novel, nothing ails her but ennui: the wish for 'incident, life, fire, feeling' (114). In the play, however, her torment is attributed to class victimization:

> Shame, shame upon their cruelty: the pride that blazed within me is quenched in the flood of my great disappointment . . . Better, a thousand times better, my solitary cell once more, than be gibed and mocked at by the vulgar-wealthy; to have the badge of servitude engraved upon my very heart, and know that tyrant circumstance has placed me in a world all prison, where every human being is a watchful jailor, and where you must endure the unceasing lash of insolence, the certain punishment of that statuteless but unforgiven crime, poverty. (*JE* 1856 Brougham: 12)

Gilbert Cross points out that although 'hatred of the aristocracy was in part an importation from abroad', nevertheless its representation persisted because it came to symbolize all unjust power. For the audience, almost all of whom had been born in the country, even if they now lived in a town, the memory of a local aristocracy would persist as 'the only human power that could significantly affect men's lives' (Cross, G. 1977: 198–9). It is from this explicit distress that Rochester rescues Jane when in Act III he rebukes Lord Ingram, saying, 'The instructress of my child, my lord, ranks among the foremost of my friends; my acquaintances surely need not blush to be in such society' (*JE* 1856 Brougham: 17). The Ingrams, still in attendance at the hastily arranged wedding, are horrified: 'Marry the governess? revolting!', to which Rochester replies, 'Yes, *the governess*! one pure instant of whose companionship were worth a whole eternity with such as ye . . .' (27).

In Brougham's play the marriage is prevented only by the fire which destroys the obstacle to it; Bertha is mentioned only as matter for a little light comedy between the servants in Act II, and never appears. The whole focus of the play is on Jane's sufferings at the hands of the aristocracy, and of Rochester's rescue of her from this situation. When we remember that in England, the melodrama, though written and promoted by the middle class, was scarcely a respectable amusement for any but the lower classes, it is easier to see why such a transformation should appeal to audiences of similarly humiliated people.

Stage melodramas frequently intensified the victim status of their heroines by making them orphans, and here, of course, *Jane Eyre* provides ready-made material. Charlotte Birch-Pfeiffer's very influential play, first performed in New York, in German in 1854 and in English in 1870 (and in eight productions up to 1882), is entitled *Jane Eyre, or The Orphan of Lowood*, and the subtitle was adopted as the only title for a Hungarian film made in 1920, a German film made in 1926, and also for a bowdlerized printed edition for children produced in Hungarian in the 1960s. It is notable, in this context, that the conventions of melodrama survived in silent film when they had been overtaken by Edwardian naturalism on the live stage, while melodramatic polarization of good and evil is also characteristic of much writing for children.

The pathos of Charlotte Brontë's orphan heroine is immediately appealing. Bessie's song, 'The Poor Orphan Child', in I iii of *Jane Eyre*, was itself within the genre of popular pathetic ballads, and was quickly seized to be set to music in 1848. Eric Bentley, in *The Life of the Drama*, identifies tears as a major acknowledged response to Victorian melodrama – 'the tears shed by the audience at a Victorian melodrama . . . might be called the poor man's catharsis' (Bentley, E. 1964: 198) – and Thackeray and G. H. Lewes, among others, recorded that they wept when they read *Jane Eyre* (in Allott 1974: 68, 70, 83, 94, 95). The reading of fiction and viewing of melodrama legitimized the 'childish' expression of emotion which was normally repressed in adult life, and this can be seen as one of the main functions of melodrama, whose plot, according to Brooks, follows 'the dynamics of repression and the return of the repressed' (1976: 201). Bentley also argues that the production of tears, as an important release of repressed emotion, justifies 'exaggeration', or what *Jane Eyre*'s reviewers called 'improbability'. 'Modern psychiatry begins', he argues, 'with those *Studies on Hysteria* in which Freud and Breuer try to explain what happens when emotional impressions are not allowed to wear themselves out' (1964: 199). Naturalism in art, like 'controlled' social behaviour, is not 'natural'; on the contrary, it is a sophisticated concept, 'an ideal standard, and what we all have are the magnified feelings of the child, the neurotic, the savage' (216). It is easy for us to see that the 'exaggeration' of the dream life is not foolish, because it is not empty of feeling; thus, Bentley argues, 'intensity of feeling justifies formal exaggerations in art, just as intensity of feeling creates the "exaggerated" forms of childish fantasies and adult dreams' (199). In melodrama, 'expressive language acts as a carrier or conduit for the return of something repressed, articulating those very terms that cannot be used in normal, repressed psychic circumstances' (Brooks 1976: 42). If literary naturalism is an understated mode dedicated to the reality principle, melodrama can be conceived as '*the Naturalism of the dream life*' (Bentley, E. 1964: 204–5).

Pathos – sob stuff – is already important in Charlotte Brontë's novel, though in this more naturalistic mode, the articulation of basic emotion is confined to interior monologue. Jane Eyre's orphan status is also important, however, for a rather different reason: namely, that in the realistic context of Victorian family structures, the untrammelled status of orphan becomes a necessary social condition for any effort towards female self-determination. I have more to say about this in the next section, but we might note here that once again we can see the early stage melodrama as reaching back to the childish antecedents of Charlotte Brontë's novel – to uncover not, this time, its intense self-pity, but its urge towards power.

In biographical terms, *Jane Eyre* was Charlotte Brontë's attempt to move out of the world of melodrama into the world of realism. Critics have on the whole reacted with embarrassment to the extravagant intensities of Charlotte's 'early imaginary world', and have seen her devotion to it, persisting well into adulthood, as 'hindering her progress as a writer'. In this context *Jane Eyre* appears as the fruit of Charlotte's 'self-discipline . . . in the journey from her Angrian fantasies towards a more ordered and complex achievement' (Allott 1973: 35). Q. D. Leavis finds in the early writings 'a feverish imagination . . . drawing on no first-hand experience whatever' (1966: 9). Kathleen Tillotson congratulates Charlotte Brontë on 'her moral emancipation from the world of Angria', finding *Jane Eyre* 'disinfected of feverish emotion' (in Allott 1973: 183–4).

It is, however, possible to argue that the 'realism' of *Jane Eyre* is purchased at the price of a loss of imaginary power, because in the juvenilia the author identified with powerful male figures who had access to the world of politics, commerce, high culture and autonomous sexuality. What we find in Christine Alexander's descriptions of the juvenilia is Charlotte's textual facsimile of metropolitan society. Her models were all men: the Duke of Wellington; Wellington's eldest son Douro, who eventually became Charlotte's central Angrian character, the Duke of Zamorna; Wellington's second son Charles Wellesley who became Charlotte's habitual mouthpiece; the poet Byron, who turned the later juvenilia into an 'orgy of Byronism' (Ratchford 1941: 84); the Romantic painter John Martin, whose engravings suggested Charlotte's original conception of Glass Town (Alexander 1983: 235–7); journalists and newspaper editors (48); and the local men who figured in the industrial disputes of Yorkshire (83). In almost all the early writings Charlotte uses a masculine persona. When all her knowledge of literature came from men, it was inevitable that she should perceive writing as a male domain (227). Alexander argues that the early writings of Charlotte and Branwell were very similar and that 'as she grew older, Charlotte saw that to write as a man allowed her to exercise the same freedom she had wielded as a child' (96, 228).

Christine Alexander, like Leavis and Tillotson, sees Charlotte's progression from 'romance' to 'realism' as an unquestionable improvement (209). From a different point of view, however, we can see the early stories as Charlotte's expression of competence to operate in the public world and to practise sexual autonomy – expression which becomes stifled as she accepts her 'proper sphere'. Charlotte herself recognized that her move from the world of Glass Town to the real world made her 'a stranger in a distant country, where "every face was unknown and the character of all the population an enigma"' (245). Alexander takes this as Charlotte's recognition that she has remained too long a child and must now grow up, but it is also a moving statement of the position of nineteenth-century women in relation to the real public world – a world in which they were aliens, strangers in a distant country, remote from the centres of knowledge and power. At the time when Charlotte was confidently writing *High Life in Verdopolis*, she wrote to her friend Ellen Nussey that London was 'almost apocryphal as Babylon or Ninevah, or ancient Rome' (116).

If the juvenile 'romances' of high life are a more powerful expression of Charlotte Brontë's ambition and ability than her published work, which is realistic about the options socially available to nineteenth-century women, then oddly, the early stage melodrama restored to Charlotte's heroine something of the articulate self-assertion of her juvenile writing. Peter Brooks concludes an extensive survey of stage melodrama in France by reassessing the value of various 'infantile' modes of expression:

> We may now advance the hypothesis that melodramatic rhetoric, and the whole expressive enterprise of the genre, represents a victory over repression . . . social, psychological, historical, and conventional: what could not be said . . . within the codes of society. The melodramatic utterance breaks through everything that constitutes the 'reality principle' . . . Desire cries aloud its language in identification with full states of being. Melodrama partakes of the dream world, as Bentley and Booth suggested, and this is in no wise more true than in the possibility it provides of saying what is in 'real life' unsayable. To stand on the stage and utter phrases such as 'Heaven is witness to my innocence' . . . is to achieve the full expression of psychological condition and moral feeling in the most transparent, unmodified, infantile form. Desire triumphs over the world of substitute-formations and detours, it achieves plenitude of meaning. (Brooks 1976: 41)

The word 'melodrama' conveys to most people primarily a set of dramatic conventions or stylistic features. Brooks lists common connotations of 'melodrama' as 'the indulgence of strong emotionalism; moral polarization and schematization; extreme states of being, situations, actions, overt villainy, persecution of the good, and final reward of virtue; inflated and extravagant expression, dark plottings, suspense, breathtaking peripety' (11–12). We have seen that stage adaptors were quick to seize on *Jane Eyre* as suitable material for melodrama, and several original reviewers found 'melodramatic' features in the novel itself (in Allott 1974: 68, 72, 850). Its events are 'improbable' though 'striking' (68); the heroine 'is too outrageously tried, and too romantically assisted in her difficulties' (72).

Charlotte Brontë's novel, published in 1847, occupies an interesting position in the relative histories of melodrama and Realism. Bentley cites the year 1850 (near enough the date of *Jane Eyre*) as the watershed between an age for which melodrama had provided an appropriate rhetoric, and an age in which Realism (later the Naturalism of Zola) became the acknowledged norm. Naturalism, he says, insisted on the banalities of life as a reaction to the perceived inadequacies of the melodramatic vision. Although melodramatic rhetoric aimed at heightened emotion,

> the effect of removing 'banalities' from the Victorian melodrama . . . had been to reduce the spectator's anxiety by relieving him of contact with his own life. By such a reduction, melodrama was becoming ever more boring and silly. What Zola is really doing is recharging the battery of fear which had been allowed to run down. The substitution of a banal . . . milieu for a 'romantic' . . . milieu is to play on the spectator's anxieties. (Bentley, E. 1964: 211)

Jane Eyre is neither boring nor silly – one early reviewer called it 'a book to make the pulses gallop and the heart to beat' (in Allott 1974: 67) – and this must be, as G. H. Lewes recognized, because its melodramatic appeal to infantile emotion is closely linked to the realistic anxieties resulting from Jane's recognition of her 'proper sphere' as a woman. The female persona of *Jane Eyre* is perhaps its most striking difference from the juvenilia, but because Charlotte Brontë had been since childhood in the habit of writing as a man, the subject-positions of the characters in *Jane Eyre* are all complicated.

In the early juvenilia Charlotte's identification with masculine power includes conventional attitudes to women. Her early heroines, like Henrietta Percy (Alexander 1983: frontis.), or Lily Hart (109), are described as 'transcendently fair and inaccessibly sacred beings' (176). As she copied her female portraits from biographies of Nelson or Byron, so she copied the attitudes of Nelson, or of Byron, or their male biographers, or their male illustrators. As Charlotte began to experience life as a woman in the real world, however, her heroines became more complex, and in *Jane Eyre*, the complex heroine learns to negotiate public restraints. The novel attempts a new negotiation of 'masculine' and 'feminine'; it also engages with the anxieties of accommodating 'melodramatic' emotions within the 'banalities' of social existence. Although Jane never reaches the 'busy world' which she yearns for, within the carefully circumscribed world of the country house she and Rochester attempt a utopia in which some of the normal social expectations of marriage are evaded. The image of Rochester as a blasted tree both supporting and deriving comfort from Jane as a winding plant suggests a mutual dependence (468), so that within the novel, Jane can say, 'I am my husband's life as fully as he is mine' (475). The pact between them, however, is a fragile, inward affair, vulnerable to social readings outside their control. The stage adaptations, for instance, pull the novel back into a world where 'anxieties' are dispelled by the conventions of a happy ending in which masculine and feminine roles are defined by a long social tradition.

In John Courtney's play, although the relationship between Jane and Rochester is taken fairly faithfully from the novel, there is extended extraneous material providing comic business between characters called Betty Bunce, Joe Joker, Sally Suds, etc. In the final scene, Richard Mason runs mad and attacks the happy couple, making an opportunity for them to be rescued by Carter (the surgeon), Briggs (the lawyer), all the comic characters, farm servants, etc., and the play ends with cheers from the whole company.

The social placing of Jane and Rochester's marriage is even more pronounced in John Brougham's play. We have seen that, early in this play, Jane's cry for freedom is appropriated to a class meaning and manipulated to provide a typical melodramatic climax in which 'a poor persecuted girl can confront her powerful oppressor with the truth about their moral conditions' (Brooks 1976: 44), and as soon as Jane and Rochester finally agree to marry, they are joined by troops of cheering, dancing peasants bringing gifts and garlands of flowers. Martha Vicinus argues that 'the central paradox of melodrama is that it defends the domestic ideal against a malign society under the belief that a larger moral order will prevail, yet in fact this moral order is a reflection of current social values' (Vicinus 1981: 134). Brougham's play consolidates current values in just this way. Jane announces that her husband's ambition 'is to be the kind landlord', and the garland which forms their wedding canopy bears the words, The Farmer's Friend (*JE* 1856 Brougham:

32). The effect is compatible with an increasing bourgeoisification of class relations, but it also reincorporates Charlotte Brontë's text into an older tradition of comic romance typified by Shakespeare's plays or many comic operas in which, after the 'madness' of courtship, marriage represents the reintegration of young people into the existing community. Brougham's 'merry peasant' ending, despite its democratic aspects, thus compromises both the vocal independence of his own heroine and the challenge to gender conventions in Charlotte Brontë's text, where Jane and Rochester's marriage is markedly isolated from a larger society. Peter Brooks argues that although 'the social structure of melodramas often appears inherently feudal – landed gentry or bourgeoisie and their faithful yeomanry', this is less important than the democratic effect of its 'making the world morally legible' (1976: 44, 42). In the case of *Jane Eyre*, however, its 'legible' class meanings are bought at the expense of more subtle negotiations of gender relations – a vivid instance of the text as 'a site of the struggle for meaning' (Bennett 1982: 227, 229).

Jane Eyre *and the woman's novel, 1850–70*

Charlotte Brontë's novel lent itself to the stage melodrama because of the intensity of its emotional drive, which draws on what Bentley calls the 'magnified feelings of the child'. Bentley argues that melodrama 'correspond[s] to that phase of a child's life when he creates magic worlds . . . when thoughts seem omnipotent, when the distinction between *I want to* and *I can* is not clearly made, in short when the larger reality has not been given diplomatic recognition' (Bentley, E. 1964: 205, 217; original emphasis). In the previous section I drew attention to some specific aspects of Charlotte Brontë's own 'magic world' of childhood – its appeal to pathos and its drive towards power. What seems to be at issue in Bentley's description of melodrama, however, is the imaginative process itself. At the age of nineteen, Charlotte was still deeply involved with the heroic people of Angria:

> Succeeding fast and faster still
>   Scenes that no words can give,
> And gathering strength from every thrill
>   They stir, the[y] breathe, they live.
> (in Alexander, 1983: 141)

Yet three years later she renounced that 'magic world'. Her voluntary self-repression belatedly follows the advice given to her in 1837 by the ageing Romantic poet Robert Southey, who wrote:

> The daydreams in which you habitually indulge are likely to produce a distempered state of mind; and, in proportion as all the ordinary uses of the world seem to you flat and unprofitable, you will become unfitted for them without becoming fitted for anything else. Literature cannot be the business of a woman's life, and it ought not to be. The more she is engaged in her proper duties, the less leisure will she have for it.
> (Gaskell [1857] 1975: 173)

Charlotte replied to this that although her first letter 'was all senseless trash from beginning to end', she was 'not altogether the idle, dreaming being it would seem to denote'. She describes her life as a governess, claiming that she has 'endeavoured not only attentively to observe all the duties a woman ought to fulfil, but to feel deeply interested in them' (174–5). What we see here is the superimposing, on to the Brontë's dream-life, of the new Victorian notion of duty, the idea that, as Mrs Ellis puts it, a woman's 'highest duty is so often to suffer and be still' (Ellis 1845: 126). It is this acceptance of duty that makes Charlotte's novel seem, to modern readers, more conventional than Emily's, but it also enabled her to speak accurately for and to a large body of Victorian women.

Florence Nightingale, for instance, in 1852, describes the kind of middle-class family who would make the bulk of the novel-reading public. In such a family, notions of 'duty' require the daughters to be around, but gives them nothing substantial and fulfilling to do. The result is that they live a double life, outwardly conforming but inwardly devoted to the wildest daydreams. 'Many', Nightingale comments,

> struggle against this as a 'snare' . . . We fast mentally, scourge ourselves morally, use the intellectual hair-shirt, in order to subdue that perpetual day-dreaming, which is so dangerous! . . . Never, with the slightest success. By mortifying vanity we do ourselves no good. It is the want of interest in our life which produces it; by filling up that want of interest in our life we can alone remedy it. (Nightingale 1978: 397)

The split which Florence Nightingale describes, between the outwardly enforced observation of domestic duties and the highly-coloured daydreams, is basic to Charlotte Brontë's own mentality and to that of her heroines. At the beginning of I xii of *Jane Eyre*, when Jane is established as governess at Thornfield Hall, she expresses precisely this sense of restless dissatisfaction:

> Who blames me? Many no doubt; and I shall be called discontented. I could not help it: the restlessness was in my nature; it agitated me to pain sometimes. Then my sole relief was to walk along the corridor of the third story, backwards and forwards, safe in the silence and solitude of the spot, and allow my mind's eye to dwell on whatever bright visions rose before it. (114)

Charlotte Brontë the author has thus reproduced in her heroine both the sense of domestic confinement and the daydream compensation which Florence Nightingale identified as characteristic of Victorian women. But *as* author Charlotte Brontë had the power to give her heroine slightly more room for manoeuvre than she herself had, so that Jane Eyre represents both the constraint of her author and the expanded freedom of a daydream heroine. Here again Florence Nightingale sees that fiction, as well as private daydreams, serves this need for an expanded field of imaginary action. Immediately after the passage quoted above, she goes on:

> What are novels? What is the secret of the charm of every romance that ever was written? The first thing in a good novel is . . . romantic events . . . The second is that the heroine has *generally* no family ties (almost *invariably* no mother), or, if she has, these do not interfere with her entire independence.

These two things constitute the main charm of reading novels. (Nightingale 1978: 397)

Crude as this may sound, Florence Nightingale's analysis is supported by modern feminist critics. Sally Mitchell associates the whole genre of the 'woman's novel' in the 1860s with the daydream (1977: 32), and Florence Nightingale's second point is echoed by the Marxist–Feminist Literature Collective in 1978. These writers claim that in three of Charlotte Brontë's novels and Elizabeth Barrett Browning's *Aurora Leigh* 'the devised absence of the father represents a triple evasion of . . . class structure, kinship structure and Oedipal socialisation' (188). The child without parents, in other words, whether mother, father or both, is able to slip between the roles and definitions which confine the middle-class daughter at home.

As soon as *Jane Eyre* was published, its readers recognized that its heroine was such a child, and many 'were visited by a distressing mental epidemic, passing under the name of the "Jane Eyre fever"' (in Allott 1974: 97). Mrs Oliphant's 1855 review article is particularly interesting for our purposes, since it takes as its main theme the impact which *Jane Eyre* had, not just on readers but also on contemporary novelists, in particular Julia Kavanagh, Dinah Mulock Craik and Elizabeth Gaskell. As always, the question of influence is difficult to prove. If we were to look before *Jane Eyre* as well as after, we would undoubtedly see the novel as part of a continuous flux of literary production and reproduction. Shirley Foster, however, in *Victorian Women's Fiction: Marriage, Freedom and the Individual*, argues that, 'it is possible to talk of a "sisterhood" of women writers, sharing similar preoccupations and techniques' (Foster 1985: 16), and she lists as relevant to her theme only three novels published before *Jane Eyre*, as opposed to more than fifty published after it (230–4). An *Athenaeum* review of Julia Kavanagh's *Nathalie* (1850), says bluntly that

> Whatever the world's verdict on *Jane Eyre* (or *Mrs Rochester*), about whom people have quarrelled almost as if she were a living woman, – whether she be rated as among the brazen disturbers of our social system whose deeds every one belonging to the families of *Grundy* and *Graveairs* is bound to discourage for the interests of decorum, or be canonized by the 'strong-minded' as a *Judith* who has given a stab to the *Holofernes* of conventionalism, – certain it is, that she has been the foundress of a family; and we cannot but think that "Nathalie" would hardly have been born had not Currer Bell's daughter been her ancestress. (*Athenaeum* 16.11.1850: 1184)

Foster, moreover, dissents from the influential feminist critical position advanced by Gilbert and Gubar and Nina Auerbach. Because, she says, these critics

> argue from the premise of the writers' deviousness and their 'covert/overt' strategy, they tend to play down the fact that puzzlement, as much as anger and rebellion, constitutes the female literary response to contemporary ideologies. Although it is true that Victorian women novelists often had to resort to obliquity in order to voice their dissent, it is also the case that many of them quite consciously articulate in their novels their ambivalence about sexual roles . . . writing in the context of growing protest about the position of their own sex, [they] echo the anxieties, anger, and ambivalence which . . . constitute the voice of mid-century feminism. (Foster 1985: 14–15)

One striking similarity between *Jane Eyre* and *Nathalie* which supports this view is *Nathalie*'s repeated expression of the stultifying inactivity of women's lives. Most of *Nathalie* is set in a French château where the heroine experiences a restlessness very similar to I xii of *Jane Eyre*, before the arrival of Mr Rochester at Thornfield. Looking through the park gates, or at the view from the roof, Jane longs to reach

> the busy world, towns, regions full of life I had heard of but never seen . . . more of practical experience than I possessed; more of intercourse with my kind, of acquaintance with variety of character, than was here within my reach . . . Then my sole relief was . . . to open my inward ear to a tale that was never ended – a tale my imagination created, and narrated continuously; quickened with all of incident, life, fire, feeling, that I desired and had not in my actual existence.
>
> It is in vain to say human beings ought to be satisfied with tranquillity: they must have action; and they will make it if they cannot find it. (114)

Nathalie protests,

> Among the 'wrongs of women', few are really more heavy and insupportable than the forced inactivity to which they are condemned in all the life, fire, and energy of youth : . . They are social prisoners, and, like the enchanted princesses of fairy tales, they look down from the high and inaccessible tower of their solitude on the life and action ever going on beneath them, but in which they must never hope to join. (*JE* 1850 Kavanagh: II 104–5)

In this condition of restless imprisonment, Nathalie

> listened invariably to the wonderful and endless romance, which her own thoughts had framed from the dreams that haunt the brain and trouble the heart of longing and ardent youth . . . (II 138)

'Women are supposed to be very calm generally', Jane Eyre goes on, and Nathalie replies,

> Believe me, we are not calm; calmness is not human; life is a running stream . . . Hide it as we will, we carry within us the germ of restless longings; a fever of the heart which nothing can satiate or appease. (III 7)

Neither Jane nor Nathalie is, at this point, longing for romantic love but for a more fulfilling daily activity. Dinah Mulock Craik, unmarried herself until middle age, particularly addressed herself to the problem of unmarried women's inactivity in the absence of the 'normal' claims of wife- and motherhood. Her practical book, *A Woman's Thoughts About Women* (1856), begins with a chapter called, 'Something to do' (Rossetti and Craik 1993). Although these women novelists, like Charlotte Brontë, believed that to be a wife and mother was the natural and therefore most desirable lot for women, they are fierce in defence of the dignity and necessity of self-dependence for the single woman. Like Helen Huntingdon, several of their heroines have artistic abilities and some utilize these to earn a living. The heroine of Craik's *Olive* (1850) is an artist who comes to perceive her ability as more than useful – even 'Promethean' (Showalter 1975: 16); and in *The Head of the Family*

(1852), the heroine, having been abandoned by her husband, supports herself as an actress. Craik's *Bread Upon the Waters: A Governess's Life* (1852), has a passage reminiscent of Jane Eyre's self-congratulation at having escaped 'a fool's paradise at Marseilles – fevered with delusive bliss . . . to be a village school-mistress, free and honest, in a breezy mountain nook' (*JE* 379). Craik's governess heroine finds that: 'the very thought of toil gives me strength. It is like plunging into a cold bath, after being suffocated with foul vapoury streams' (in Foster 1985: 59).

Margaret Oliphant, however, is more concerned at Jane's impact on accepted attitudes to love and marriage, characterizing her as 'a dangerous little person, inimical to the peace of society'. After a brief outline of the relationship between Jane and Rochester, she concludes, 'such was the impetuous little spirit which dashed into our well-ordered world, broke its boundaries, and defied its principles – and the most alarming revolution of modern times has followed the invasion of *Jane Eyre*' (1855: 557). It seems that despite the decorum of Jane's outward deportment, her readers had no difficulty in identifying her restless imagining of change as 'the new generation nailing its colours to the mast'. For Oliphant, the core of this revolution lies in the novel's 'furious love-making', which she describes as 'but a wild declaration of the "Rights of Woman" in a new aspect'. She is perceptive enough to see that it is not the outcome, but the process of courtship which is at issue. To the new heroine,

> the man who presumed to treat her with reverence was one who insulted her pretensions; while the lover who struggled with her as he would have struggled with another man . . . was the only one who truly recognised her claims of equality. 'A fair field and no favour', screams the representative of womanhood. 'Let him take me captive, seize upon me, overpower me if he is the better man – let us fight it out, my weapons against his weapons, and see which is the strongest . . .' Whereupon our heroine rushes into the field, makes desperate sorties out of her Sebastopol, blazes abroad her ammunition into the skies, commits herself to be ignominiously captured, and seized upon with a ferocious appropriation which is very much unlike the noble and grand sentiment which we used to call love . . .
>
> These are the doctrines, startling and original, propounded by Jane Eyre; and they are not Jane Eyre's opinions only, as we may guess from the host of followers or imitators who have copied them. (557–8)

Oliphant sees the same tendencies in Julia Kavanagh, a writer 'whose books are all so many reflections of *Jane Eyre* . . . from *Nathalie* to *Grace Lee*, she has done little else than repeat the attractive story of this conflict and combat of love or war – for either name will do' (559). *Nathalie*, published in 1850, has as heroine a pretty, vivacious Provençale who earns her living as a teacher. Her sister Rose, subdued, resigned and devout, acts as a foil for Nathalie's restless search for happiness. Some improbable turns of the plot bring Nathalie into the household of an austere older man who proposes marriage in the second of three volumes. The match is acceptable to her, but the novel is protracted by misunderstandings and *éclaircissements* which go far beyond mere devices for suspense. It is as if Jane Eyre's doubts, during the 'month of courtship', were stretched to be a major feature of Kavanagh's novel.

The legal disabilities of married women, in these years before the Matrimonial Causes Act (1857) and the Married Women's Property Bill (first proposed in 1857), were well known and widely debated. Barbara Leigh Smith summarizes them succinctly in 1854:

> A man and wife are one person in law: the wife loses all her rights as a single woman, and her existence is entirely absorbed in that of her husband. He is civilly responsible for her acts; she lives under his protection or cover, and her condition is called coverture. (in Pykett 1992: 58)

In this legal context it is hardly surprising that a woman with any means of self-sufficiency should consider long and hard before committing herself to the bond of matrimony, nor that it should present itself in rather dramatic colours. Charlotte Brontë uses the imagery of the grand Turk's seraglio to picture the over-possessive Rochester during his courtship (*JE* II ix), and the final pages of *Nathalie* include her godmother's anxious advice that her prospective husband should 'behave to her like a Christian and a gentleman; not like a Turk' (III 298). The relatively conservative Oliphant, however, cannot tolerate what she sees as sexual antagonism. Oliphant sees even the sober heroine of Gaskell's *North and South* as part of a movement in which 'all our love-stories [shall] be squabbles'. 'Here is again the desperate, bitter quarrel out of which love is to come; here is love itself, always in a fury, often looking exceedingly like hatred, and by no means distinguished for its good manners, or its graces of speech' (Oliphant 1855: 560, 559).

Dinah Mulock Craik is another author of the 1850s perceived by Mrs Oliphant as influenced by *Jane Eyre*, though in this case the long courtships are not so antagonistic. Craik's *Olive*, published in 1850, has a heroine who supports herself as an artist and does not expect to marry because of a slight deformity. She is happy with a pupil/master relationship with her teacher, and refuses to marry him because there is no love between them. She then suffers long unrequited love for another man who is eventually softened by being injured in a fire, after which Olive gives him her support and is rewarded by his love. According to Sally Mitchell, the sick or crippled hero was almost a standard feature of women's novels during the 1860s:

> he is both a manageable object for the heroine's affections and an alternate persona, who provides the daydreamer with a gender role in which more interesting adventures are possible . . . But what we are apt to overlook in the twentieth century is that suffering also has a positive moral and religious meaning. Women novelists could make use of suffering in order to develop traits in their characters which express an alternate, feminine value system: compassion, sensitivity, consideration, expression of the emotions, and most importantly – in an increasingly competitive, individualistic society – the sense of human weakness and dependence on each other. (Mitchell, S. 1977: 40)

Elizabeth Barrett Browning's *Aurora Leigh* (1857) is another text of this period in which the blinding of the hero in a fire brings him and the heroine together. Barrett Browning claimed that she had not had *Jane Eyre* in mind when she wrote her ending

(Kenyon 1897: II 245–6), which supports Sally Mitchell's suggestion that the repeated plot device was a response to a social necessity rather than a question of influence.

Craik is one of several women novelists who extend what Foster calls 'the courtship theme of *Jane Eyre*' to analyze how marriage itself 'may easily prove a delusory paradise' (Foster 1985: 16, 18). By giving her hero the name of the notorious seventeenth-century debauché, the Earl of Rochester, Charlotte Brontë invited debate about the old saw that 'a reformed rake makes the best husband', and it is possible that Anne Brontë's novel, *The Tenant of Wildfell Hall* (1849), is intended as an answer to *Jane Eyre*'s implication that such men are susceptible to women's virtuous influence. Its heroine, Helen Huntingdon, finds that she has neither personal influence nor legal power to resist the debauched tastes of her husband, and in order to save her infant son from his corrupting influence she has no option but to flee the matrimonial home – an illegal act – and support herself by painting (see Reiss 1934: 6–7).

Even with a civilized husband, marriage can appear like a prison. Contemplating marriage with St John Rivers, Jane Eyre fears the self-repression which would make her life 'a rayless dungeon' and 'an iron shroud' (*JE* 425). In Craik's novel, *Agatha's Husband* (1853), the heroine, married at nineteen, similarly feels the duty of obedience to her husband

> like a chain of iron wrapped round her; however she writhed and dashed herself against it, there it was . . . his very love seemed to hang over her like a cloud . . . She did so long to dash out into the sunshine of her careless, girlish life. (*JE* 1853 Craik: 211, 186)

Julia Kavanagh's later novel, *Adèle* (1858), also examines the situation which ensues when the sixteen-year-old heroine accepts marriage from an older man whom she hero-worships; the couple spend the final two volumes of the novel in a kind of soap-opera of emotional shifts, painfully negotiating the imbalances of power, incompatible needs and misunderstandings which arise even between two well-disposed, unneurotic and articulate people. At one point Adèle wishes she were dead: 'it makes me mad to be married – because I feel like one that is bound hand and foot – stifled like one that has not air to breathe' (*JE* 1858 Kavanagh: II 107). She records her dread of her husband's 'tenderness' in a context which makes it seem possible that this is a euphemism for sexual attentions (II 322). At the opening of the final volume, the stages of her wifedom – oppression, resignation, jealousy – are recapitulated in a way that makes it clear that this is the major theme of the novel (III 9), though their difficulties are compounded by scheming and unsympathetic relatives. Several other unhappy marriages provide an ominous prophecy of what may be to come, and this novel also has recourse to the devices of fire and major illness to 'prove' the marriage, before the wicked are confounded and the good hasten together to perfect felicity.

Even with a freely-chosen, much-loved husband, Jane Eyre is apprehensive:

> For a little while you will perhaps be as you are now, – a very little while; and then

you will turn cool; and then you will be capricious; and then you will be stern, and I shall have much ado to please you: but when you get well used to me, you will perhaps like me again, – *like* me, I say, not *love* me. I suppose your love will effervesce in six months or less. I have observed in books written by men, that period assigned as the furthest to which a husband's ardour extends. Yet, after all, as a friend and companion, I hope never to become quite distasteful to my dear master. (*JE* 272–3)

This cool prognosis is, of course, touchingly revised by Jane's retrospective judgement on her marriage after ten years:

I know what it is to live entirely for and with what I love best on earth. I hold myself supremely blest – blest beyond what language can express; because I am my husband's life as fully as he is mine. No woman was ever nearer to her mate than I am: ever more absolutely bone of his bone, and flesh of his flesh. (475)

Shirley Foster reads Craik's and Kavanagh's conclusions, like that of *Jane Eyre*, as drawing back from the more radical implications of their explorations of married life, and Craik at least is much more conservative. In *Agatha's Husband* (1853), the plot is manipulated so that the young heroine is forced to 'trust' her husband, who is bound by a promise not to explain that his apparently harsh and unreasonable decisions are made necessary by the loss of her fortune. The growth of love between them, although it involves the heroine's moral growth, is predicated upon the 'divine and unalterable law given with the first human marriage – "*He shall rule over thee*"' (119). Foster points out that in *Agatha's Husband*:

the advice given by an older woman to a young bride has authorial resonance: the husband is a tree upon which the wife can lean, but she must 'always remember that it is a noble forest-oak, and that you are only its dews or its sunshine, or its ivy garland. You never must attempt to come between it and the skies'. This image, unlike the similar one at the end of *Jane Eyre*, gives little suggestion of mutual support. (Foster 1985: 51)

Even here, however, there is some role-reversal at the end, when the young wife conquers her fear of the sea to search for her husband, adrift in a small boat after a shipwreck by fire. The novel ends with a mutual recognition of need and a mutual confession of past faults.

Sally Mitchell summarizes some common features of this school of women's writing as it persists in the 1860s:

They remake society not through revolution but by magic. The idealized marriage takes place in a patently unreal world in which the desired social order already exists. Marriage is a partnership, not a dependent relationship. Woman's power is recognized; man's pride is humbled. There is some explicit physical or financial or moral basis of equality between the partners. The weakening of the male figure is so central to the happy ending, that it can hardly be seen as other than a symbolic codification of an emotional perception that a partnership-marriage is impossible unless men are forced to give up some of the power which law and social conditioning have embedded in their characters. The achievement of that weakening through suffering embodies a world view which takes feminine qualities, as understood by the

authors and readers of the time, as the desirable norm for the human character.
(Mitchell, S. 1977: 43–4)

One interesting novel in this category is Emma Warboise's *Thorneycroft Hall*,
published in 1865. Emma Warboise refers explicitly to *Jane Eyre*, notably because
she herself attended the Clergy Daughters' School some ten years after Charlotte
Brontë, when it had been reformed and removed from Cowan Bridge to Casterton;
her pseudo-autobiography contains extended and eulogistic defences of the school
and of the Reverend Carus Wilson. The novel is intensely religious in tone; there
are five saintly deaths and much suffering which is attributed to God's will. The
orphan heroine learns to subdue her hot temper with the aid of kindly friends,
especially Marshall Cleaton, her 'red-cross knight', who eventually marries her.
Cleaton, who explicitly prefers Tennyson to Byron, is feminized not only by his
religion but also by a close relationship with his saintly mother. The ending, in
keeping with Mitchell's analysis, is idyllic, combining the Cleatons' vocation as
dissenting minister and wife with the virtue of not claiming an inheritance (and,
like Mr Brocklehurst's infant saint, being rewarded with another) and the joys of
a country cottage (much enlarged by inherited wealth). Interestingly, although the
main thrust of this novel is to negate the rebellious features of *Jane Eyre*, there is
one section where Warboise, perhaps unconsciously, repeats some of its most
spectacular imagery. In *Jane Eyre*, Jane describes her feelings after the failed
wedding in terms of fierce oppositions of cold and heat, life and death:

> A Christmas frost had come at midsummer: a white December storm had whirled
> over June; ice glazed the ripe apples, drifts crushed the blowing roses . . . My hopes
> were all dead . . . they lay stark, chill, livid – corpses that could never revive. (310)

Warboise's heroine, Ellen, suddenly relieved from her belief that her beloved
Cleaton had married another woman, reverses this imagery:

> My soul had been benumbed in icy regions of perpetual winter; an everlasting snow-
> line had seemed the horizon of my thoughts; a cold grey sky was over my head, a
> barren soil beneath my feet, mists and spectral shadows on and over all. And now –
> now I rose as one who has been dead, and is alive again. The winter was past and
> gone. Spring, with all her buds, and flowers, and tender green, and sunny skies, and
> woodland songs, was around me once more – nay, it bloomed as it had never bloomed
> before . . .' (274–5)

Even the virtuous heroine, it seems, is not immune to connubial bliss, and this
emphasis, though muted here, was characteristic of the 1860s. Where Kavanagh
and Craik echoed *Jane Eyre*'s fierce independence, her desperate daydreaming and
her apprehensions about the state of marriage, this new generation take up her
recognition of physical desire.

In 1867, the year of the second Reform Bill and of J. S. Mill's women's suffrage
amendment, Mrs Oliphant declares that freedom has gone far enough:

> women's rights and women's duties have had enough discussion, perhaps even from
> the ridiculous point of view. We have most of us made merry over Mr Mill's crotchet
> on the subject, and over the Dr Marys and Dr Elizabeths . . . (Oliphant 1867: 258, 275)

Oliphant is not, however, primarily concerned here with 'rights and duties'; she finds a major, and worrying, shift of emphasis in women's novels of the 1860s. Many original reviewers of *Jane Eyre* commented on its disturbing 'fleshliness'. J. G. Lockhart, though finding Jane Eyre 'worth fifty Trollopes and Martineaus rolled into one counterpane, with fifty Dickenses and Bulwers to keep them company', nevertheless calls her 'rather a brazen Miss' (in Allott 1974: 82). *The North American Review* was simply scandalized, complaining of scenes 'given to the exhibition of mere animal appetite . . . scenes of passion, so hot, emphatic, and condensed in expression, that we are almost sure we observe the mind of the author of *Wuthering Heights* . . .' (in Allott 1974: 99). For *The Christian Remembrancer*, 'the love-scenes glow with a fire as fierce as that of Sappho' (in Allott 1974: 88). Just as the melodramatists seem to have reached behind Charlotte Brontë's text to recognize its repressed desire for power, these reviewers, over-reacting by modern standards, seem to have recognized an unorthodox sexual freedom which is more nakedly expressed in the juvenilia. According to John Maynard in *Charlotte Brontë and Sexuality*, the later juvenilia formed 'a workshop in which Brontë, free from public restraints and norms, could imagine, draft, and articulate her intuitions of sexual experience' (Maynard 1984: 41). By 1867 Oliphant is seriously alarmed; 'a singular change has passed upon our light literature' which 'began at the time when Jane Eyre made what advanced critics call her "protest" against the conventionalities in which the world clothes itself' (258). She insists, though, that 'things have gone very much further since' then:

> We have grown accustomed to the reproduction, not only of wails over female loneliness and the impossibility of finding anybody to marry, but to the narrative of many thrills of feeling much more practical and conclusive. What is held up to us as the story of the feminine soul as it really exists underneath its conventional coverings, is a very fleshly and unlovely record. Women driven wild with love for the man who leads them on to desperation before he accords that word of encouragement which carries them into the seventh heaven; women who marry their grooms in fits of sensual passion; women who pray their lovers to carry them off from husbands and homes they hate; women, at the very least of it, who give and receive burning kisses and frantic embraces, and live in a voluptuous dream, either waiting for or brooding over the inevitable lover, – such are the heroines who have been imported into modern fiction . . . Now it is no knight of romance riding down the forest glades, ready for the defence and succour of all the oppressed, for whom the dreaming maiden waits. She waits now for flesh and muscles, for strong arms that seize her, and warm breath that thrills her through, and a host of other physical attractions, which she indicates to the world with a charming frankness. (259)

Sir Leslie Stephen, writing in 1879, confirms that

> Mr Rochester . . . is probably responsible in part for some of the muscular heroes who have appeared since his time in the world of fiction . . . He is in reality the personification of a true woman's longing (may one say it now) for a strong master. (418)

The 'sensation' novelists of the 1860s to whom Oliphant specifically refers are

Annie Thomas, Mary Elizabeth Braddon, Rhoda Broughton and 'Ouida'. Not only did they deal with sensational material – such as was being reported from the proceedings of the new Divorce Court – they also caused a sensation. Lyn Pykett argues that their very publicity meant that

> their representation of women and of women's lot became part of the current meaning of 'woman'. Repeatedly throughout the 1860s . . . commentators on the contemporary scene used the sensation novel . . . as evidence or symptom of social movements. Sensation heroines . . . entered the general discourse as representative types of modern femininity. (Pykett 1992: 21)

The link between these and the more sober novels of the 1850s is the analysis of marriage; as Justin McCarthy noted in 1864, 'the institution of marriage might almost seem to be . . . just now upon its trial' (in Pykett 1992: 55). According to Pykett,

> sensation fiction engages in an intense focus on the domestic space of the marital home – the desired goal of the domestic heroine – which becomes in the sensation novel . . . the locus of passion, deception, violence and crime. This is one of the key areas in which sensation fiction represents and (variously) negotiates the contradictions of the domestic ideology. The home, in Ruskinian orthodoxy, 'the shelter, not only from all injury but from all terror, doubt and division' . . . becomes instead the site of terror, doubt and division. However, in the sensation novel . . . it is a woman who tends to be the origin of the terror, doubt and division. (74)

In these novels, the orphan heroine becomes a rather different creature from the plucky victim of the early melodramas or the self-reliant heroines of *Jane Eyre*'s first imitators. Dinah Mulock Craik, in one of her later novels, *Christian's Mistake* (1865), attributes her heroine's 'powerfulness [to] her youthful exclusion from the normal feminine world of "small sillinesses, narrow formalities, and petty unkindnesses", an exclusion which saved her from "women's smallnesses"' (quoted in Foster 1985: 60). Two years later, however, Oliphant is complaining that 'ill-brought-up motherless girls, left to grow anyhow, out of all feminine guardianship, have become the ideal of the novelist' (1867: 265).

Her complaint seems particularly to apply to the heroine of Rhoda Broughton's *Cometh Up As a Flower*, which, published in 1867, may well have been the immediate occasion for Oliphant's review article. Even by modern standards, Nell Le Strange has a free-and-easy manner and a slangy diction, referring to her baronet father as 'my old dad', and making no objection when a young man refers to him as a 'lucky old beggar' for living with Nell. This heroine cannot understand why daughters should regret the loss of their mothers:

> It was to me a matter of unfeigned and heartfelt gratulation that my mother had died in my infancy, [sic] As often as I came in contact with well-drilled daughters, nestling under the wing of a portly mamma, I hugged myself on my freedom; my father was more to me than ten mothers. If my mother had lived, thought I, I should have been only second in his affections . . . an idea almost too bitter to be contemplated . . . I should have had to mend my gloves, and keep my hair tidy, and practice on the piano, and be initiated into the mysteries of stitching. (40)

At first Nell's rejoicing in freedom from feminine restraint seems admirable, just as we sympathize with Aurora Leigh's wish for freedom from her aunt's petty regime. Like Kavanagh's Adèle, she is an attractively active heroine, who can climb walls, hedges and ladders (4, 62, 91), and is alert to bodily sensations. Lying in a summer meadow, Nell records how

> I clasp my hands at the back of my head and lie very still, so still that a little blue butterfly settles on my breast, and opens and closes its white-lined wings slowly in the sun; and green dragon flies go whirring confidently past, almost brushing my nose as they sail gauzily by. (142)

After a road accident, she lies 'feeling nothing much, wishing nothing much, thinking of nothing much except myself as a mere animal; my headache, my vertigo, and my heat' (231). Lyn Pykett argues that in a context where literary realism, with its minute observations of domestic life, was perceived as a proper field for women writers,

> the sensation novel was . . . assigned to the domain of the improper feminine because of the way it *read* the body, or *produced a reading* in the body, by its 'appeal to the nerves rather than to the heart' (*Christian Remembrancer* 1863, p. 210), to the animal passions rather than to the reason. (Pykett 1992: 35)

Nell's first-person narrative makes very free reference to the assumption that women expect 'to make men's hearts ache, and their hot blood surge' (*JE* 1867 Broughton: 19) – and the novel is best-known for its explicit treatment of the marriage market in physical terms. *Jane Eyre* can tell the over-amorous Rochester to go 'to the bazaars of Stamboul without delay; and lay out in extensive slave-purchases some of that spare cash you seem at a loss to spend satisfactorily here', and he knows that she means 'so many tons of flesh and such an assortment of black eyes' (282), but any application to their own situation remains implicit. In *Cometh Up As a Flower*, Nell is explicit that the bargain made between her and Hugh involves: 'so much young flesh and blood for so much current coin of the realm' (312). *Jane Eyre* refuses a loveless marriage which would require her to 'keep the fire of my nature continually low, to compel it to burn inwardly and never utter a cry, though the imprisoned flame consumed vital after vital' (429), but Nell Le Strange agrees 'to give my shrinking body to Sir Hugh's arms, and my abhorring soul into his custody, though both body and soul cleave still with desperate, ineradicable passion to that other' (*JE* 1867 Broughton: 307).

Among modern feminist critics, working in the light of psychoanalysis and the knowledge of repression, there is a general tendency to approve of 'writing the body' as subversive of oppressive codes of silence, and in this context it is tempting to dismiss Oliphant's objections to this 'fleshly' school of writing as mere Victorian prudery. Rhoda Broughton's writing, however, has an unpleasant tone of self-indulgence, self-dramatization, without the 1850s emphasis on self-reliance. When her heroine makes assignations, out of doors and late at night, with a young man she hardly knows, and indulges in passionate and protracted kissing (48, 105, 154,

170), this could be seen as refreshingly independent. She does not, however, act simply from impulse or desire; despite her parade of youthful spontaneity she is fully aware of the spectacle she makes in various affecting stances. She speaks of her own 'two full soft lips begging with such pretty humility' (75) and says, 'I really believe that I was not aware that my big blue eyes looked rather well . . .' (80). Describing a protracted farewell at the garden gate, she says, 'there we pose ourselves in the attitude of the famous "Huguenot" picture' (170). She is in fact complicit in the bargain she makes with her prospective husband, knowing the value of her 'flesh'. Forced to spend the night with him, before their marriage, after a road accident, she writes,

> I pull down my sleeve, and consider my maimed limb. What is there in nature or art so pretty, so appealing to the senses as a beautiful arm? Mine was beautiful, round and firm, and polished like marble, that some god had kissed into warm life; with dear little nicks and dimples about elbow and wrist. I find a big black bruise . . . 'It hurts', I say, looking up rather ruefully at my companion, somewhat in the manner that a dog does that has got a thorn in his foot . . .

When Hugh rises to the bait and kisses the arm, she rounds on him, 'fierce as a young huntress, looking volumes of outraged virtue at him; "will you never understand that I *hate* you?"' (226–7).

With hindsight, it is distressing to find *Jane Eyre* identified as the fount of this kind of writing. There is certainly physical passion in *Jane Eyre*. In the scene where Jane is tempted to become Rochester's mistress,

> He seemed to devour me with his flaming glance: physically, I felt, at the moment, powerless as stubble exposed to the draught and glow of a furnace – mentally, I still possessed my soul, and with it the certainty of ultimate safety. (335)

Nell, contemplating an assignation, excuses herself with what looks like a sneering reference to this scene:

> really, I don't think that English women are given to flaming, and burning, and melting, and being generally combustible on ordinary occasions . . . Foggy England is not peopled with Sapphos. (*JE* 1867 Broughton: 58)

This might be amusing if she did not repeatedly describe herself as 'passion-drunk' (269); moreover, Nell does not 'possess her soul', nor is she prepared like Jane to 'hold to the principles received by me when I was sane, and not mad – as I am now'. Where Jane believes that 'laws and principles are not for the times when there is no temptation: they are for such moments as this, when body and soul rise in mutiny against their rigour' (*JE* 334), Nell's notions of morality are unpleasantly self-serving. Tardily remembering that her father would not approve an assignation she has made with Richard, she concludes easily that, 'if it is a sin to disobey a parent, it is also a sin to break one's word, and when one must commit one of two sins, one may as well choose the pleasantest' (*JE* 1867 Broughton: 157).

Her 'immorality' goes much further than sexual unconventionality. While she is indulging her rather foolish love affair with Richard, who cannot afford to support her, and her 'dear old dad' is dying from worry as the estate crumbles towards bankruptcy, she wanders through the garden wondering what to do to pass the time.

> There was a little book came out some years ago, which I believe had a great run among the spinsters of Britain, entitled 'Work: plenty to do, and How to do It' . . . I had no work to do, and should not have done it if I had. How would the ingenious author have dealt with me? (*JE* 1867 Broughton: 141)

The 'little book' sounds very much like Dinah Mulock Craik's *A Woman's Thoughts About Women* (1856), and in 1882 Craik was to offer some *Plain Speaking* which would answer Nell's insouciance, advocating education so that 'every unmarried woman who does not inherit an income ought to owe it to neither father, brother, nor any other male relation, but to earn it' (quoted in Foster 1985: 46). There is in general a disturbing slippage in *Cometh Up As a Flower* between freedom from undue restraint and freedom from proper responsibility. Nell does not, for instance, recognize debt as an injury; when the butcher, after waiting a year, asks for payment for the ninth time, she calls him a 'wretch' and 'a "greasy kill-cow"' and longs for 'those fine old days . . . when the Sieur Le Strange might take twenty lances and transfer as many fat kine as seemed good in his mind's eye from his low-born neighbours' premises to his own' (11, 177–8). Nell's conception of her financial situation is that she is the innocent victim of her father's creditors, who are, it seems, by definition Jewish: 'greasy Jews – the offscouring of the earth (my one point of sympathy with the barbarians of the middle ages is their loathing and maltreatment of the accursed Israelitish dog) – have been prowling about, trading, as is their wont, on the miseries and weaknesses of poor humanity' (355; see also 307, 329). Using images which recall Brontë and Craik, she foresees life with Hugh as 'the fetid stifling air of an eastern dungeon'; for Nell, however, the contrasting 'free gales rioting under the blue April heavens' lie not in sturdy self-reliance but in those other 'strong arms where I may yet find Heaven' (329). Given that she has the free choice to marry Hugh, but lacks the courage to 'defy the might of Israel', her representation of her wedding (oft-quoted in feminist contexts) is unpleasantly self-dramatizing:

> There is a great sacrifice to the fore; a hecatomb offered at the altar of filial affection; a pretty white lamb is being led out, be-laced, be-ribboned, be-filleted to the slaughter. Pipe and tabor go too-tooing before her, and the butcher, with his sharp knife gleaming, walks behind her. But the lamb knows that she is going to the sacrifice, and she bleats very piteously. (330)

The overblown rhetoric of such passages suggests the word 'melodramatic', and Pykett argues that:

> This concern with the domestic scene and the dynamics of the family is . . . one of sensation fiction's many points of connection with the popular melodrama, from which many of its plot situations, character types and rhetorical devices were borrowed. Indeed the women's sensation novel seems to display most of the characteristics which Peter Brooks discerns in melodrama. (Pykett 1992: 74)

There are, however, important differences. Whereas the melodrama versions of *Jane Eyre* emphasized her misprized virtue, the sensation novelists emphasized her unconventionality. Nell is scornful of the 'melodrama' code of polarized good and evil; when Richard reappears after she is married she begs him to take her away with him, though he refuses, for her sake. Later she comments on a novel (which sounds like Ellen Wood's *East Lynne* (1861)),

> about a married woman, who ran away from her husband and suffered the extremity of human ills in consequence. I have made several steps in morality of late . . . but even now, I can hardly imagine that I should have been very miserable if Dick had taken me away with him. (*JE* 1867 Broughton: 389)

To do justice to Oliphant, she does not object to the scene in which Nell, overcome with passion, begs Richard to take her away. This, like the temptation scene in *Jane Eyre*, is justified by its intensity of feeling and its atmosphere of moral struggle. What Oliphant finds 'disgusting' (1867: 268) is precisely that self-regarding complicity, that willingness to use her own physical charms, which makes Nell a manipulator rather than a self-reliant feminist heroine.

Nell is not, however, a heroine of the Becky Sharp school who consciously sizes up the extent to which the economic odds were stacked against women. The more thorough-going sensation heroines were fully conscious that a plucky little governess might, like Jane Eyre, keep her 'own soul', but not much else. In *Cometh Up As a Flower*, Nell is an innocent compared with her sister Dolly, who prompts her to cry:

> Where, where is my story-book code of morality? . . . Here is a young woman who has told lies, has forged, has wrecked the happiness of her sister's whole life, and she is punished; how? – why by marrying a lord with £80,000 a year. (391)

Pykett argues, in fact, that

> In the female sensation novel the family was not simply a refuge from change (as Vicinus argues in relation to stage melodrama), but also, more emphatically, the site of change. It was not only an arena in which an abstract moral 'struggle between good and evil' . . . was played out, it was itself both the cause and the site of a struggle in which those abstract moral categories were destabilized. (Pykett 1992: 76, quoting Vicinus 1981: 131)

The heroine of Mary Elizabeth Braddon's bestseller, *Lady Audley's Secret* (1862), does not, like Nell Le Strange, just take the line of least resistance; she is a positively active schemer, liar, bigamist and murderer. Oddly, however, the spectacle is less distasteful than *Cometh Up As a Flower*. The difference lies partly in the quality of the writing; the first-person moralizing of Broughton's heroine is both tedious and self-contradictory. With complete access to her own motivations, she claims both the impunity of 'innocence' (according to contemporary standards) and the freedom to express conscious passion; both the dignity of outraged virtue and a worldly calculation of its price. The result is not clear-cut enough to be either hypocrisy or challenge; it is merely an ethical muddle. Braddon's representation of Lady Audley, on the other hand, radically questions the nature of the feminine. Because *Lady Audley's Secret* is narrated by a male observer, the element of self-display which was disingenuous in *Cometh Up As a Flower* assumes a mysterious fascination. Lady Audley's beautiful appearance explicitly evokes the clear-cut virtue of melodrama while the text as a whole reverses this signification. She has 'the most wonderful curls in the world . . . making a pale halo round her head when the sunlight shone through them' (*JE* 1862 Braddon [1985: 7]); 'wherever she went she seemed to take joy and brightness with her. In the cottages of the poor her fair face shone like a sunbeam' (5). Her portrait, however, gave

> a lurid brightness to the blonde complexion, and a strange, sinister light to the deep blue eyes . . . It was so like, and yet so unlike . . . it seemed as if the painter had copied mediaeval monstrosities until his brain had grown bewildered, for my lady, in his portrait of her, had the aspect of a beautiful fiend. (60)

The portrait, in other words, is an indicator of my lady's doubleness of nature. The spectacle of a rebellious girl, like Nell Le Strange, might be 'disgusting' but was comprehensible; what was really disturbing was the suggestion that the 'signs' of impeccable womanhood might not mean what they seemed.

Victorians knew that crime and vice existed, but they liked to think that they were practised by those whom Stephen Marcus has called 'The Other Victorians' – those who frequented brothels, drank, gambled, cheated and sold children into prostitution. The awful effect of the sensation novels was to make the readers feel that 'we have met the Other Victorians and they are us' (Showalter 1976: 2). Elaine Showalter thus argues that 'the power of Victorian sensationalism derives' not 'from its revelation of particular scandals', but 'from its exposure of secrecy as the fundamental and enabling condition of middle-class life' (Showalter 1978: 104). A Victorian journal commented that:

> It is on our domestic hearths that we are taught to look for the incredible. A mystery sleeps in our cradles; fearful errors lurk in our nuptial couches; fiends sit down with us at table; our innocent-looking garden walks hold the secret of treacherous murders. (quoted in Hughes, W. 1980: 44)

The image of the caged bird, which in *Jane Eyre*, in the melodramas and the domestic novels of the 1850s suggested a pitiful or brave victim, in the reviews of the 1860s sensation novels becomes a caged animal. Pykett cites reviewers whose vision of women is:

> as 'so many wild beasts', whose lusts and licentiousness run riot 'when you have unbarred [their] cages'. In other words, the improper feminine could only be contained within the patriarchal family, an institution which it also constantly threatened to dissolve or destroy. (1992: 56)

The early readers of *Jane Eyre* were, of course, affected by the 'sensational' elements of its plot – especially the madwoman in the attic – though interestingly, both Thackeray and Chorley state that they have met the plot before, both in fiction and in real life (in Allott 1974: 70, 72). Winifred Hughes, in her book on the 1860s sensation novels, notes, in the aftermath of *Jane Eyre*,

> an inordinate proliferation of domestic secrets and maniacs under lock and key. But in the authentic sensation novel . . . Jane no longer runs away from the would-be bigamist; she is much more likely to dabble in a little bigamy of her own. (Hughes, W. 1980: 9)

Nor was bigamy the only crime these latter Janes would contemplate. '"Jane Eyre's Mr Rochester"! exclaimed a sensation heroine in 1861. "If I had been Jane Eyre I would have killed him"' (quoted in Showalter 1976: 1). The effect of these novels is to deconstruct the socially-important oppositions between virtue and vice, legality and crime. While exploiting the sensational aspects of insanity, they did not, like the later melodramas, reinforce the opposition between sanity and madness. Lady Audley's departures from the proper feminine are so gross that at the end of the novel they have to be explained by hereditary insanity. The explanation, however, is not adequate to dispel the doubts raised by her appearance of normality. The doctor called to comment on her mental state at the end unwittingly demonstrates that duplicity and crime is the only sane response to the normal condition of Victorian women:

> She ran away from her home, because her home was not a pleasant one, and she left in the hope of finding a better. There is no madness in that. She committed the crime of bigamy, because by that crime she obtained fortune and position. There is no madness there. When she found herself in a desperate position, she . . . carried out a conspiracy which required coolness and deliberation in its execution. There is no madness in that. (*JE* 1862 Braddon [1985: 319])

Mary Wollstonecraft, writing in 1792, had already recognized that 'it is vain to expect virtue from women till they are in some degree independent of men . . . Whilst they are absolutely dependent on their husbands they will be cunning, mean, and selfish' (Wollstonecraft [1792] 1929: 154–5). As Showalter drily comments, 'Lady Audley is devious and perfidious not because she is a criminal and mad, but because she is a lady and sane' (1978: 113).

The sensation novels destabilized Victorian notions as thoroughly as the Gothic novels had done in a previous age. The *Christian Remembrancer* in 1863 recognized that 'realistic' material such as 'bigamy . . . is sensational as fully . . . as are ghosts and portents; it disturbs in the same way the reader's sense of the stability of things, and opens a new, untried vista of what may be' (quoted in Boyle 1983: 93). In particular, sensation readers were forced to confront the fleshly nature of women. Thomas F. Boyle argues that

> what was unacceptable . . . in these works of fiction, was much the same as what outraged traditional morality in Darwin's work, and, later, in Freud's: the suggestion that the passionate instincts are as human as they are bestial, and that such subconscious drives . . . could triumph over reason . . . even in the best families. (95–6)

In *Jane Eyre*, the heroine's first-person narrative reveals an iron integrity which prevents her from enlarging very greatly the cage which contains her restless spirit, and the leap from her to Lady Audley may, to modern readers, seem so great that the connection lacks conviction. Here, I think, we must accept contemporary opinion. The readiness with which women writers of the 1850s and 1860s took advantage of Jane's small beginning may be taken as a sign of the pressure within the cage, and it was this pressure which allowed an 'impetuous little spirit' to broach 'the most alarming revolution of modern times' (Oliphant 1855: 557).

'Protected by this strong arm': Jane Eyre *on the stage, 1867–1909*

It is no accident that the sudden flowering of the sensation novel should coincide with an intensification of ideological prescriptions of femininity, as if, when the 'wild beasts' appeared, the 'bars of their cages' had to be reinforced. Ruskin's 'Of Queens' gardens' and Coventry Patmore's 'The Angel in the House' are both texts of the 1860s. The stage versions of *Jane Eyre* from the 1860s onwards are also focused on the question of proper womanhood. In contrast to the women's sensation novels, the stage plays, produced in the theatre, which was of course dominated by men, increasingly emphasized Jane's saintly virtue and her vulnerability, which calls out manly goodness.

Interestingly, although G. H. Lewes, among other early reviewers of *Jane Eyre*, had noted its 'melodramatic' features, he is convinced by the 'truth' of Jane herself because 'we never lose sight of her plainness; no effort is made to throw romance about her'; she is 'a creature of flesh and blood, with very fleshly infirmities, and very mortal excellencies; a woman, not a pattern' (in Allott 1974: 85). Once those 'fleshly infirmities' had given rise to the progeny of the sensation heroines, however, they had to be suppressed in stage representations of Jane herself.

One of the most radical shifts to the original story is to be found in Charlotte Birch-Pfeiffer's *Jane Eyre*, first produced in New York in German in 1854 and in English in 1870; an anonymous English play, probably a plagiarized version of Birch-Pfeiffer's, was produced in London in 1867. It may not be an accident that 1867 is the year not only of *Cometh Up As a Flower* and Oliphant's alarmed review of the sensation novels, but also of John Stuart Mill's unsuccessful Women's Suffrage Amendment to the Second Reform Act. Birch-Pfeiffer's play sets about reinforcing the conventional notions of gender roles within the home, especially that of the man as protector. In the first of the two acts Jane is discovered making a virtual shrine of her Uncle Reed's portrait, honouring him with 'the poor orphan's tears' (*JE* 1867 [Birch-Pfeiffer]: 4v). Aunt Reed confirms that her 'weak minded' husband had taken in not only the orphan Jane but her mother who 'brought shame on our house. Eloped with a poor officer – married him – . . . returned here a beggared widow' (5). When Aunt Reed announces her intention to send Jane to Lowood, Jane foretells how

At another tribunal you will meet my uncle again – He will say ? [sic] Where is the
orphan girl I confided to y^r care . . . – Answer I have persecuted – beaten her, banished
her from my roof, – to the stranger bequeathed her as a pauper homeless and friendless
– (7)

Comparing Jane's speech with the first soliloquy in John Brougham's play ten years
earlier, we find that the emphasis has shifted from spirited self-defence to an appeal
in the later play for a strong protector. In the 1870 play, Jane tells Mrs Harleigh
(Fairfax) that she will sleep well after Rochester returns to Thornfield, because
'now we have a severe but reliable protector – now we have a MAN in the house!'
(*JE* 1870 Birch-Pfeiffer: 23). The treatment of orphans and widows becomes a
moral touchstone for those in authority in these plays. Judged by this criterion
Rochester (elevated to Sir Rowland in 1867 and Lord Rowland in 1870) is notably
distinguished, since he has taken in not only the orphan Adèle, but also her mother,
the 'maniac' (so called in all these plays), who is in all these versions not Rochester's
wife but his first love, married in his absence to his elder brother. She went mad
when her husband shot a subsequent lover – Adèle's father – in a duel. The brother
on his deathbed besought Rochester's forgiveness and he agreed to succour the
widow and orphan. Rochester is thus not only blameless but ennobled; Jane has no
moral struggle except what arises from her belief that he is to marry the widowed
Lady Claremont ('Clarens' in 1870; alias Georgina [sic] Reed, who in these versions
takes the place of Blanche Ingram). Rochester controls the whole plot, revealing
that he has used Georgina to provoke Jane into a confession of her love. The play
ends with his presentation of Jane to the assembled company as

> 'my future wife Lady Rochester.'
> *Omnes:* 'His wife!' . . .
> *Sir Rowland:* 'Yes my wife, protected by this strong arm and heart from all
> persecuting and envious foes.' (1867: 17)

This curtain-line goes further than the 'merry peasant' ending of the Brougham
play, asserting the peculiarly Victorian ideology of the home as the place where 'the
man . . . guards the woman . . . from all danger and temptation' (Ruskin [1865]
1905: 136). Interestingly, this virtuous, manly Rochester re-emerges in Paul West's
1918 film, *Woman and Wife*, where he only begins courting Jane in the belief that
his wife is dead.

In 1877 the Theatre Royal, Coventry, performed another plagiarized version of
Charlotte Birch-Pfeiffer's *Jane Eyre*. This play shows a curiously double response
to the prevalent atmosphere of the 'sensation' novels, intensifying both the 'fleshly'
responses of its characters and their conventional virtue. On the one hand there
are extensive stage directions which focus on the physical representation of
emotion. When Jane rescues Rochester (in this version *Lord* Rowland) from the fire
in his bedroom, 'his head rests on her shoulder' and she 'has put one of her arms
round his waist, to support him'; Rochester comments aside, 'My pulse is
hammering, and I'll be bound the blood does not flow one bit faster through her
veins' (*JE* 1877 von Hering: 55). After Jane's 'equal as we are' speech, Rowland,

'whose chest heaves violently . . . suddenly throws his arms round her, and presses her to him' (77v). He reveals the trick whereby Jane has been led to believe that he will marry Georgina (in this play Lady Clarence):

> 'obstinate girl! I intended that jealousy should help me! . . . I will have you!
> Poor and insignificant, forlorn and orphan as you are, I will have you, and no
> other!'

Jane: 'Ah Rowland, my lord – my world – I am yours!'
> (Throws herself into his arms)
> (Music to end of Act) (79–79v)

On the other hand, despite these displays of passion, the virtue of both protagonists reaches new heights. Judith Harleigh (Mrs Fairfax) tells Jane that since Rochester's return from the West Indies, 'he has been quite a father to all the poor and distressed in the whole county' (22). As in the 1867 play, after Rochester's rescue from the burning bed, Jane's calling 'Grace Poole' 'a perfect fiend' prompts him to call Jane 'a perfect angel' (54); Jane in turn thinks Rochester's rescue of the maniac (and Adèle) 'more than noble, it is sublime!' (76) The finale to this play is all but an apotheosis:

> *Scene the last:* All enter.
> *Lord Rowland . . .* (embraces Jane): Yes, my bride, my wife, my treasure which my
> strong arm hereafter shall protect – and God who has caused the hand of hatred
> to lead the Orphan to the embrace of love, will protect two beings who require,
> for their happiness, nothing but themselves (embracing Jane with one arm and
> stretching the other towards heaven) and His blessing.
> *Tableau:* Jane has clasped her hands, and seems to pray. (79v)

Three later stage versions, from 1879 and 1882, dilute Rochester's virtue by allowing the maniac to be his wife, but shift the emphasis to Jane's saintliness by contrasting her with scheming or fallen women and/or showing her resisting unwanted attentions. T. H. Paul's adaptation, written for the Adelphi Theatre, Oldham, in 1879, opens at Lowood where Jane has been a teacher for two years. The Reeds arrive en masse, already impoverished by John's debaucheries, knowing of Jane's legacy, and hoping to recoup their fortunes by patching up their relationship. In this version Rochester appears at Lowood as its benefactor, and takes Jane in when Broklehurst [sic] is provoked by the frustrated Reeds into dismissing her. Rochester's general kindliness is emphasized as he owns Adèle as 'my own child' and calls her 'darling' as she sits on his knee and calls him 'Papa' (32). John Reed, having failed in his plan to marry Jane for her money, now plots with Mason to blackmail Rochester. John, assured by Mason that Rochester's 'indomitable will and nerve of iron you will not conquer or shake', vents his spite by interrupting a full-scale village wedding with flowers, cheering children and so on (66). This play has the most sensational treatment so far of the 'maniac', who first appears outside a window in the snow brandishing a burning stick, intensifying the contrast with Jane, who is the one to insist that Rochester try to save his wife from the final fire (57, 68). This super-scrupulous Jane will not stay with the blind

Rochester because of 'respect for the dead as well as duty to myself' (73); his explanation of his marriage, in this version delayed to this point, is necessary to overcome these pronounced susceptibilities. Mason then reveals Jane's legacy and she immediately applies it to what Rochester calls her 'angel work' of helping her Reed cousins, who receive it as 'coals of fire' (76).

The adaptation by James Willing and Leonard Rae, performed in London in 1879, further intensifies Jane's 'angelic' aspect. The young Jane in a Gateshead 'Prologue' is shown entering 'meekly' and telling her aunt, 'I've been trying to be good' (3). Although her defiant speech is rendered as in the novel, she follows it with an appeal to her Uncle Reed and dead mother and father to witness that she forgives Aunt Reed: 'And though you wish me dead and won't say goodbye – I say it to you, Good Bye, and when I say my prayers – I'll still say Heaven bless Aunt Reed' (10). In the earlier plays, the polarization of the 'angelic' Jane and 'fiendish' maniac was a major device in establishing Jane's virtue; in the Willing version, however, the major contrast is with Blanche Ingram. In this play, when Rochester reveals his relative poverty to Blanche, she elopes with John Reed, persuading herself that 'a reformed rake generally makes the most devoted of husbands' (27). Jane, after discovering the existence of the mad wife, also leaves Thornfield, after a very explicit statement of her motivation: 'Mr Rochester I love you – but you see before you a Woman who prizes honour as the noblest gift' (51). To underline the worth of this 'gift', she then resists the suit of a now-comic and widowed Brocklehurst and establishes herself in a village school, where Blanche appears, having been abandoned by John Reed, begging for food and shelter. He has, she says,

> robbed me of the choicest jewel of a woman's life – & then flung aside the empty casket... The woman, who suffers all the degradation, losing position, friends, station, is an outcast whose momentary sin, no repentance can pallate [sic], no reparation condone – The man the betrayer whose base passions has [sic] ruined the heart he should have cherished Society receives with open arms – He is free to ruin other homes, and send more innocent souls to perdition [etc.] (52–3)

Like Blanche, Jane has been tempted, but, Blanche points out, 'Not, fallen . . . The Workhouse – a Pauper's grave are all I pray for' (53). The physical appearance of Blanche, a 'fallen' woman outside Jane's door in a 'tract of snow', recalls Richard Redgrave's emotive painting 'The Outcast' (1851), and creates an iconographically unambiguous contrast with Jane, secure within her house (Roberts 1974: 63–4). The sharp moral certainties of this pictorial scene in turn contrast with Charlotte Brontë's novel, where Jane herself, though moved by the purest of motives, places herself in a 'fallen' position outside the door of Moor House.

The stage melodramatists were very conscious of pictorial effects, and most of the plays end acts with 'tableaux' or 'pictures' intended to convey meaning without words. Such meanings depend, however, on unambiguously shared values in the audience, and are not a good medium for conveying complex motives. Norman Bryson argues that even paintings which offer a richly realistic complexity are open to social recuperation, since their very redundancy of information permits viewers to 'read' them in terms of simple, orthodox meanings (Bryson 1983: 154). Though most of the illustrated editions of *Jane Eyre* are later in date than the stage plays, it is interesting in this context to look at printed illustrations of the scenes of Jane's exile. The message conveyed by these pictures is that by putting herself outside the house, outside the woman's 'proper sphere', Jane has lost the claim to social respectability. In Ethel Gabain's 1923 edition, for instance, Jane's shapeless garments seem to deprive her of any class status while a furtive backward look makes her seem guilty (*JE* 1923 Gabain: 182). Her low and often horizontal position, whether in 1897 (*JE* Townsend: 323) or 1943 (*JE* Eichenberg: 252), is the classic pose of the 'fallen woman'. Another Gabain illustration shows Jane's body sunk into and echoing the line of a low hill, while both Jane and the hill are pressed down in the picture by a very low horizon (*JE* 1923: 189). The picture is similar to George Watts's early Victorian painting of a fallen woman – even though, ironically, Jane has run away from Rochester in order to avoid being morally 'fallen'. The apparent meaning of Jane's 'fallen' state in book illustrations is, of course, offset by the printed text, but stage adaptors have little motive to reproduce the long verbal exchanges between Jane and Rochester which, in Charlotte Brontë's novel, implicate the reader in the irony between Jane's outer disgrace and inner virtue. Even in the plays of the 1870s and 1880s the evidence is that the dramatists were still devoted to what Brooks calls the duty of making the world 'morally legible'. Instead of representing Jane's painfully ambiguous stance, therefore, Willing's play sharply divides the signifiers of fallen woman, which it gives to Blanche, from those of virtuous woman, which remain with Jane.

Helena Michie uses Willing's play as a starting point for an examination of Victorian 'sisterhood as a structure for the containment and representation of sexual differences among women', arguing that 'the poignant play of sameness and difference between Jane and Blanche . . . is quickly transformed . . . into an idiom that seems to repress and rewrite the distinction between the fallen and the unfallen woman so crucial to Victorian culture'. This transforming idiom is 'the idiom of family', especially 'the capacious trope of sisterhood, which allows for the possibility of sexual fall and for the reinstatement of the fallen woman within the family' (Michie 1989: 405, 402–4). While Charlotte Brontë's renegotiated marriage in *Jane Eyre* is an intensely private affair, defined by Jane's feeling that 'no woman was ever nearer to her mate than I am' (*JE* 475), Willing's play has 'Jane and Blanche embrace in a tableau of sisterly love that works spectacularly against the psychological grain of the novel' (Michie 1989: 402). The final presence of Blanche in this play allows Jane to be recuperated into the role of Ruskin's queen, or socially responsible woman, who, from the stronghold of her 'garden', reaches out to the 'feeble florets' who 'are lying, with all their fresh leaves torn, and their stems broken' to 'set them in order in their little fragrant beds, [and] fence them, in their trembling, from the fierce wind' (Ruskin [1865] 1905: 177). Willing's Jane not only takes Blanche into her home and calls her 'sister' but offers her a share of her fortune (of which John Reed has so far failed to cheat her). Blanche, overcome, cries, 'I came here to curse you – and I stay – to bless – to adore you'; they leave together 'To help the cripple – To give sight to the Blind!' (54–5). Rochester, having heard Jane's avowal of love, reveals that he is not really blind but only testing her devotion – a deception which enables him also to detect John Reed's intention of stealing Uncle John Eyre's will. Rochester, despite his culpability in plotting bigamy, is thus left, as in von Hering's play, in control of the plot and still relatively powerful at the end. Both he and Jane finally appear as social benefactors, she sharing her fortune with Blanche and he promising to endow Brocklehurst's school. In Miron Leffingwell's play (1909) Jane's self-sacrifice is pressed even further as she cares for Rochester for three months after his accident, posing as a deaf mute nurse (Nudd 1989: 54).

A rather different emphasis informs the version by W. G. Wills performed at the Globe Theatre, London, in 1882. Wills increases Jane's virtue yet further but weakens her independence by giving her good friends – a clergyman called Prior and his mother – whom she leaves to go to Thornfield. She has left because she does not want to be more than a friend to Mr Prior, but he is entirely honourable, so that her wanderings are from one place of safety to another. Unlike all the others, this play begins at Thornfield and has no childhood scenes; the 'social problem' aspects of the Lowood episodes have vanished and Jane's orphan status is less important. The emphasis in this play is less on social responsibility and the proper use of inherited wealth, and much more on sexual morality. Jane is surrounded by people who warn her against Mr Rochester's suspected profligacy – Mr Prior, Mrs Fairfax, Grace Poole, the Ingrams – while we also see Rochester battling, in great emotion, with his conscience. Even 'the maniac' in this version seems to be a guardian of Jane's virgin state, since she attacks Jane 'with horrible menaces' immediately after she and Rochester have confessed their mutual love (50).

Jane is rescued from this attack by Rochester, thus reversing the obligation which Rochester has to Jane in the bedroom scene of the novel and creating a contradiction between his general reliability and his sexual deception; this play does, in fact, seem prepared to debate the question of Rochester's responsibility to his first wife and to Jane. Jane, working from a general knowledge of his character, defends Rochester when Blanche Ingram calls him 'a dishonourable, despicable, unprincipled man whose life has been one system of hypocrisy' (58), but after learning the truth about his wife she reproaches him in similar terms: 'I have been a poor truthful vain fool, and you have purposed to destroy me, without pity or warning' (66). In Chapter 2 we see how the debate over the Contagious Diseases Acts throughout the 1870s and 1880s altered people's perceptions so that women's chastity became important not just to the man who might possess her, but to herself, as a safeguard against the diseased inroads of unscrupulous men. In this context Wills's 1882 *Jane Eyre* can be read not just as a heightening of the conventional melodramatic valuation of 'virtue' threatened by villainy, but as a recognition of the threat of disease posed by men in general.

The shifts in representation of *Jane Eyre* on the stage during the forty years after its publication can be well shown by their various treatments of the image of a snared bird. In John Courtney's play of 1848, Jane's speech appears, very much as in the novel, as an assertion of emotional independence; believing Rochester about to marry, she cries, 'I am no bird, no net ensnares me – my will is free, which I now exert to leave you' (615v). In John Brougham's play (1856) the image has become one of a spontaneous, generalized wish for 'freedom' from class oppression. In the later plays, however, it becomes an image of Rochester's deliberate plot to ensnare Jane. In the 1867 and 1877 plays, this plot is a relatively blameless device to provoke Jane into declaring her love by making her jealous. In the 1867 play, Jane cries, 'Unloose me, Sir Rowland, you are betrothed unloose me', to which he replies, 'No, Jane the net encompasses you' (16v). In the 'fleshly' version of 1877, Lord Rowland literally 'throws his arms round her' before announcing 'the net is around you – now you are caught' (78v). In the Wills version of 1882, however, the 'plot' is more serious, involving Rochester's deception about his wife, and Jane reproaches him, 'you spread your net well'. Although Rochester's great emotion prompts her to forgive him, and they are finally reconciled more or less as in the novel, interestingly both lovers in this version end relatively poor, Rochester being impoverished by the fire and there being no mention of Jane's legacy. The emphasis has moved from Jane's spirited independence in the 1840s and 1850s through the saintly social benefactions of the 1860s and 1870s to a more personal and sexual morality.

Chapter 2

The turn of the century

Versions of Bertha, 1892–1917

Chapter 1 included two different types of reproduction of *Jane Eyre*. The stage plays appropriated the title, characters and plot of Charlotte Brontë's novel and *re-presented* it with varying ideological emphases. The women novelists, on the other hand, often made no mention of *Jane Eyre*, but were recognized by contemporary readers as *imitating* the novel in some way. Chapter 1 also showed that the revolutionary aspects of *Jane Eyre*, which made a tremendous impact at the time of publication and took a new direction with the sensation novels of the 1860s, were resisted by the stage versions of the 1870s and 1880s, which reasserted the conventional virtue of the protagonists.

The reputation of Charlotte Brontë herself had also become progressively sanctified following Elizabeth Gaskell's *Life* (1857), which aimed to 'make the world honour the woman as much as they have admired the writer' (Chapple and Pollard 1966: L241). By the end of the nineteenth century *Jane Eyre* had lost its revolutionary impact and its author was enshrined as a noble though homely woman. Brontë bibliographies include titles like *An Hour with Charlotte Brontë or Flowers from a Yorkshire Moor* (Holloway 1882), or *Charlotte Brontë at Home* in the Literary Hearthstones series (Harland 1899); but she also figures in *Heroines of our Time: Being Sketches of the Lives of Eminent Women with examples of their benevolent works, truthful lives and noble deeds* (Johnson [1860]), *Stories of the Lives of Noble Women* (Adams 1891), and *Queens of Literature of the Victorian Era*, including 'Charlotte Brontë, the moorland romancist' by the authors of 'Our Queen', 'Life of General Gordon' etc. ([Hope] 1886). This biographical hagiography reinforces what Eric Bentley and Peter Brooks called the 'desacralization and sentimentalization of ethics' characteristic of the stage melodramas, which produced an increasingly bland surface text which did not engage with the reader's or viewer's anxieties (Brooks 1976: 19; Bentley, E. 1964: 211).

In the 1890s, therefore, Charlotte Brontë's text was being read in a context which included both 'tamed' versions of itself and its author, and also the more challenging 'new woman' fiction of the period, which made Charlotte Brontë's cautious modifications to marriage seem outdated. Miriam Allott, in fact, finds that one of the remarkable features of 'the Brontës' critical reputation during the later part of the nineteenth century . . . [was] the movement of feeling which gradually swept Charlotte's novels from the centre of the stage' (Allott 1973: 26).

It is, therefore, interesting that the following four texts, identified by various readers as 1890s derivatives of *Jane Eyre*, are neither representations nor imitations of the originating text but bear an oblique, allusive and critical relationship to it. It is also interesting that each of these texts is outside the canonical range of genres. One is a detective story, one a mystery, one a ghost story and one a school story. In each of these texts the focus is on the relationship not between Jane and Rochester but between Jane and the mad, confined or uncanny 'other' represented by the 'maniac'. Moreover, where the melodramas had exploited the contrast between Jane and the maniac (so called in all those plays), these later texts suggest that there are links between Jane and some 'hidden self'. Now that Darwin had introduced unsettling ideas about the animal origins of the human race, and various studies on hysteria were beginning to reveal the existence of the unconscious mind (Showalter 1987), the melodramatic certainties about the polarization of sanity and insanity, humanity and bestiality, were being replaced by fascinated explorations of human duality in texts such as *The Strange Case of Dr Jekyll and Mr Hyde* (1886) or *The Picture of Dorian Gray* (1891). Readers and reproducers are no longer certain what Bertha 'means'. Illustrations, for instance, show markedly different views of Bertha's death by fire; Edmund Garrett suggests that she becomes a kind of transcendent spirit (*JE* 1897 Garrett: 280), while F. H. Townsend shows her as eminently material – flattened on the stones to be peered at by domestics (*JE* 1897 Townsend: 413). It was with some of this curiosity that readers must have approached the texts discussed below.

In Conan Doyle's story, 'The Copper Beeches' (1892), Sherlock Holmes and Dr Watson are visited by Violet Hunter, a self-sufficient young woman who has been a governess and is now offered a suspiciously large sum to look after a little boy in the country. She is worried because her employer has asked her to cut off her hair, to wear a particular worn dress and to sit in a particular chair. Holmes at first suspects that Mrs Rucastle, her employer's wife, is a lunatic with strange whims, but this proves not to be the case. When Violet arrives at the Copper Beeches, however, she does find a locked wing with a locked door within it. As Holmes and Watson travel down from London, Holmes philosophizes on the potential for violent crime in lonely country houses, isolated from the safeguards of community; his comments recall Henry Tilney in *Northanger Abbey* (Austen 1953 [1818]: 152) or Marlow in 'The heart of darkness' (Conrad no date [1902]: 127–30). Eventually Holmes deduces that Mr Rucastle has locked up his grown-up daughter to prevent her money falling into the hands of her suitor; Violet was to have unwittingly impersonated the daughter to throw the suitor off the scent. When, however, they break into the locked room they find that the daughter has already escaped; Mr Rucastle is then savaged by his own terrible dog. The daughter marries her lover, while Violet goes on to become the successful head of a private school.

The similarities with *Jane Eyre* lie in a particular plot motif, in which a governess goes to a remote country house at the behest of an employer around whom a mystery hangs, possibly involving a mad wife, and finds there a locked apartment with an unknown occupant. These similarities are reinforced by contextual evidence. Kathryn White, librarian of the Brontë Parsonage Museum and Sherlock Holmes enthusiast, points out that Conan Doyle's grandmother let lodgings to governesses, that his mother lived near Cowan Bridge School (famous as the origin of Lowood in *Jane Eyre*) and that his sisters were governesses (White 1992: 7). The suggestions of horror in the story, however, are rapidly dispelled. As Kathryn White points out, the detective work in this story is so slight that Sherlock Holmes has nothing to do but 'witness the story unfold' (6). Violet is a refreshing innovation of the suffragette era – a 'brave, sensible girl' whose ambition is to earn her living, not to fall in love. Otherwise, the story offers us only the moral certainties of an old-fashioned melodrama. Mr Rucastle proves an unambiguous villain; Violet is what she appears to be – 'a young lady who is very well able to take care of herself' (*JE* 1892 Doyle: 233). Most puzzling and disappointing of all is that the *doppelgänger* in the locked wing proves to be an untroubling mirror-image of Violet – another brisk, resourceful, modern young woman, who does not need to be rescued either by her lover or by Sherlock Holmes but effects her own deliverance. The text thus invites us to admire an 1890s version of Jane Eyre as independent woman, and while gesturing towards mysteries, effectively denies their existence. Villainy is concentrated in a conventional authority figure who is appropriately punished and contained, and the story closes all possibilities of further trouble except the reproduction of patriarchal tyranny *via* an infant Rucastle whose pleasure lies in 'giving pain to any creature weaker than himself' (237). In this rational universe the secrets of all hearts are open, and the idea that the Jane figure herself might conceal hidden depths is never even broached.

E. Nesbit's *The Secret of Kyriels* (1899), like *Jane Eyre*, begins from the perspective of a child. Nesbit is now, of course, mainly known as the writer of children's stories, a genre from which, as Julia Briggs explains, 'the dangerous area of sexuality had been rigorously excluded'. *The Secret of Kyriels*, Nesbit's second novel, is, nevertheless, 'the novel in which she makes her closest approach to the forbidden topic' (Briggs 1987: 193, 192). Again, *Jane Eyre* is never explicitly mentioned, but the plot similarities proliferate so as to call attention to their own excess: the heroine, whose mother is supposed dead, is scared as a child by a 'ghost' from a locked-up part of the ancient house in which she lives, which is divided between the mainland and an island lake. Later we are told how she discovered

> a tall woman with a face white as death. In her hand she held a candle. Her long hair streamed over her white dress . . . the dead-white face lit up with a glad look of recognition . . . 'My child', said a strange low voice. (*JE* 1899 Nesbit: 51)

Esther's father, Nicholas Kyriel, explains that the woman is his dead wife's sister, who is of unsound mind (54). Meanwhile, Esther makes friends with an enterprising Cuban girl called Bertha (59) and a Mr Talbot from India; there are a number of conversations about 'niggers and planters' (34, 58). Like Violet Hunter, Esther Kyriel inhabits a rational universe; her active life and common-sense attitudes sort oddly with the continuing mystery of the madwoman, so that Esther wishes she lived in 'a brand-new red-brick beast of a place' with

> no room for a mystery, and I could live a reasonable, cheerful, commonplace life, like other girls. It's awful to feel as though one were a princess in a fairy-tale, shut up in a magician's palace waiting for the story to go on. (105–6)

The story does, however, go on. By Book 3 (of eight books) they are suspecting that the madwoman is Esther's mother, but Mr Talbot, in a speech reminiscent of Rochester, declares that she is '*my wife*' (130). Nicholas Kyriel had apparently run away with her and returned with her and Esther, suggesting that she should live in seclusion to avoid scandal. Esther blames her father for Mrs Talbot's melancholy, since 'her life was chosen for her' (178). Eventually, after many exciting incidents, it emerges that Mrs Talbot had never been unfaithful to her husband and that Esther is Mr Talbot's legitimate child. Her mother had, however, had several periods of madness, attributable to various deceptions imposed on her, and Kyriel had locked her up to avoid her being sent to an asylum. The novel ends, after Kyriel's death, with the fragile Talbot family re-established, and Esther taking her place as daughter, wife and mother.

Julia Briggs's analysis of the novel focuses on its symbolism, through which, she argues, Nesbit 'found a way of expressing what could not be expressed elsewhere – her sense of what it meant to be a woman in a world dominated by men'. The novel not only 'abounds in images of female imprisonment', but offers a topography which is nakedly meaningful to the post-Freudian reader:

> The New House [which is actually older than the 'Old House'], with its hidden courtyard and secret passages, is at once female, and associated with the mysterious power of the id, while the Old House faces the outer world, and, with its library of authoritative books, is at once masculine and perhaps stands for the superego . . . There is a further layer of topographical symbolism in the second island on which stands a tall round tower . . . from the base of which a secret underwater passage leads to a subterranean entry to the New House . . . Kit finds that he must enter this secret passage in order to save Esther . . . The trapdoor at the passage's end only yields to the greatest pressure, and after Christopher's forced but necessary entry, the sluice gates open and the passage is flooded. (Briggs 1987: 194–5)

Esther is unlike Jane in being a tomboyish and independent heroine, and various characters in the story emphasize the modern quality of their attitudes, which contrast amusingly with the Gothic, fairytale or melodramatic aspects of the plot in which they find themselves. These brisk modern characters are, nevertheless, embroiled in complications and threats which derive, as the symbolism of the house demonstrates, from an environment of unacknowledged sexuality. Although Esther's surface self is not unlike Violet Hunter in 'The Copper Beeches', the novel presents us with a different *alter ego* in the Caribbean Bertha de Lisle, a character who is far from mad, but is, like *Jane Eyre*'s Bertha, passionate and wilful. We last see her on a stolen bicycle, in 'bicycling knickerbockers and her skirt twisted round her waist', riding 'at racing speed' to save the man she loves (354). The bicycle was, of course, a potent symbol of the 'new woman's' emancipation from housebound immobility (see Rubinstein 1986).

The Secret of Kyriels, however, separates this energetic Bertha from the madwoman, who proves to be more like the Lady of Shalott, the epitome of languid Victorian female virtue, imprisoned on her island by false notions of propriety and male domination. This beautiful and pathetic figure is sympathetically treated and her intermittent madness attributed explicitly to her dependent situation, which lays her open to deceptions. Perhaps most interesting of all, Esther's trust in her beloved 'father' proves misplaced, while a conspiracy of silence keeps her in ignorance of her maternal inheritance. While the later Victorian melodramas showed Jane reliant on the 'strong arm' of masculine protection, Nesbit's story casts doubt on this solution to female insecurity. Esther's feeling that 'mystery . . . seemed to encompass her like an enchanted wall' (*JE* 1899 Nesbit: 107) is surely a foreboding that, despite the freedom and security of her childhood and education, masculine protection eventually entails feminine imprisonment. It is her father who urges her to marry the unpleasant Bertram, who, in a childhood game, had played the part of a fairy prince who wakes a princess with a rose. When Bertram later attempts to rape her, an uncomfortable relation is established between the fairytale myths of unawakened womanhood and the realities of sexual politics.

The story has a resoundingly happy ending. Esther and her friend Kit, who collaborate as children to act out 'quest' stories from Scott and Malory, survive all vicissitudes to become well-adjusted man and wife. As a revision of *Jane Eyre*, however, the most significant feature is that the 'secret' at the heart of the Gothic mansion is the heroine's mother, who is neither dead, bad nor thoroughly mad but only ill-used and neglected. Where the 'other woman' in *Jane Eyre* occupies the Oedipal role of 'bad mother' as obstacle to heterosexual fulfilment, *The Secret of Kyriels* gives us a co-operative, quasi-sibling Bertha and a sweet, maternal madwoman. Where Florence Nightingale had identified the absence of the mother as the *sine qua non* of romance ([1852] 1978: 397), *The Secret of Kyriels* reinstates the mother at the centre of an extended happy family. Nesbit has thus implicitly denied the monstrosity of the female 'other' and divided the 'Bertha' of *Jane Eyre* into the repressed, constrained woman of the past and the sexually active woman of the future. The process of moving from one to the other, however, was by no means problem-free, as Henry James demonstrates in *The Turn of the Screw* (1898).

With *The Turn of the Screw* we move for the first time into 'high culture' and an area of extensive literary criticism, though James himself was overtly dismissive of this short piece, which he described as 'essentially a pot-boiler and a *jeu d'ésprit*' (in *JE* 1898 James [1964: viii]). Once more, though many readers have noted its relation to *Jane Eyre*, there are no explicit references in the text; there are, however, circumstantial details relating the two. Oscar Cargill points out that, shortly before writing *The Turn of the Screw*, James had dealings with Clement Shorter, whose important book on Charlotte Brontë appeared in 1896, and that this may have prompted him to reread *Jane Eyre* (Cargill 1963: 249 n. 53). William S. Petersen confirms that James had an extensive argument with Mrs Humphrey Ward, the editor of the Haworth Edition of the Brontë works, in 1897 (Petersen 1971: 919). Adeline Tintner points out that the governess in James's story is thirty, as was Charlotte Brontë when she wrote *Jane Eyre*, and suggests that Blanche Ingram's story of a governess who had an 'immoral' relationship with the tutor may have been its germ (Tintner 1976: 42).

Tintner's essay predates that of Alice Hall Petry, who claims to be first to notice this possible origin (1983: 63). Petry, arguing that *The Turn of the Screw* is 'a remarkably clever . . . parody of *Jane Eyre*' (76), provides a relentlessly detailed list of similarities between the two texts, not all of which are convincing. There are, however, obvious broad similarities: a young governess goes to live in a remote house in order to care for orphan children; her immediate contact is a housekeeper, and her employer is a single man who feels his guardianship of the children to be a burden. The governess takes a pride in discharging her duties well and independently, and cares more than she acknowledges for 'the master'. In each case there is a mystery, and in *The Turn of the Screw* the first hint of this prompts an implicit reference to *Jane Eyre*: 'Was there a "secret" at Bly'? the governess asks herself, 'a mystery of Udolpho or an insane, an unmentionable relative kept in unsuspected confinement?' (*JE* 1898 James [1964: 33]). Despite Petry's insistence that the parody is 'not merely . . . for the sake of comedy' (1983: 62), she is not able to suggest much in the way of motivation for the particular shape of this revision of Charlotte Brontë's story, beyond a monitory perception that it is dangerous to confuse fiction with reality: 'the governess's confusion of her reality and the Jane Eyre model is ghastly – and it is all the more ghastly in that she comes to realize (and ultimately to write down) exactly what was happening to her at Bly' (76). There are, however, plenty of critics who would dispute that the governess ever realizes 'exactly what was happening to her', or, indeed, that anyone can finally say what that was.

Shoshana Felman, in her brilliant essay, 'Turning the screw of interpretation', argues that 'the illusion of total *mastery*, of "seeing all", is in reality a counterpart to the act of "shutting one's eyes"', since

> to *master* . . . is . . . to become *like the Master* . . . [who] is indeed the incarnation of the very principle of *censorship* and of the imposition of a *limit*, as constitutive of authority . . . To 'master', therefore, to understand and '*see it all*' . . . is . . . to occupy the very place of *blindness*. (Felman 1977: 168)

The demonstration which supports this assertion is long and complex and deserves to be read in full. From the perspective of our interest in *Jane Eyre*, however, Felman's essay allows us to perceive how *The Turn of the Screw* functions to question the status of first-person narrative and of moral heroism. Like Jane Eyre, James's governess takes the moral high-ground, but the consequences of her actions are so debatable that most modern readers see her as deranged. Because, however, she takes her stand on rationality – her ability to observe, analyze and draw deductions from what she sees – it is impossible for us to adopt a position of rationality in order to declare her mad, without implicating ourselves in the precise form of her 'madness'. *The Turn of the Screw* thus, Felman argues, 'succeeds in *trapping* the very analytical interpretation it in effect *invites* but whose authority it at the same time *deconstructs*' (196). A comparison with *Jane Eyre*, moreover, provides a historical dimension absent from Felman's discussion which allows us to see more clearly that what passes for reason and sanity is socially constructed.

For at least twenty years after publication, *Jane Eyre* was perceived as the voice of revolution, and the early melodramas presented Jane projecting her own indignant words without mediation to a receptive audience. By the 1890s, the young woman who occupies Jane's social space as governess has instead become the object of investigation. In *Jane Eyre*, the unmediated autobiographical form grants the heroine's voice the authority of a final moral arbiter. *The Turn of the Screw*, on the other hand, is more like *Wuthering Heights* in its elaborate frame structure, which allows us to arrive at the governess's narrative only through the mediation of an unnamed narrator and another character called Douglas, who knew the governess and possesses her manuscript. These men discuss the governess's story, situation and motivation with a group of mainly male listeners who eventually form the audience for a reading of the governess's manuscript. Before we hear her words, therefore, the governess is subjected to an intense male scrutiny.

Although *The Turn of the Screw* was written fifty years after *Jane Eyre* and its frame is apparently set in present time, the events described in the governess's narrative took place 'forty years' ago (*JE* 1898 James [1964: 7]), so that the ideological context in which the governess operates is roughly that of *Jane Eyre*'s time of writing. The frame structure of *The Turn of the Screw* thus involves not only a male/female scrutiny, but also historical hindsight; both throw into question the status of the female narrator. The narrative situation of *The Turn of the Screw*, in which a woman's story of her past life is discussed by later male listeners, is mirrored in the 1890s (as several commentators have noticed) by the new methods of analysis being developed by male experts to investigate the largely female disorder called hysteria. Freud and Breuer in particular developed what one of Breuer's patients called 'the talking cure' (Freud and Breuer [1893–5] 1991: 83), in which the woman patient was encouraged to tell stories about her past so that the male therapist could assign her symptoms to their traumatic origin. Barbara Ehrenreich and Deirdre English make a link between hysteria and that sense of being socially stifled which *Jane Eyre* expresses so vividly and which so appealed to the imaginations of Craik and Kavanagh: 'the hysterical fit, for many women, must have been the only acceptable outburst – of rage, of despair, or simply of *energy* – possible' (Ehrenreich and English 1979: 124). Although the popular understanding of hysteria is of an undisciplined display of emotion, the analysts of the late nineteenth century identified an astonishing variety of hysterical symptoms, including pain, paralysis, nervous 'tics', hallucinations and phobias. 'Anna O', the woman who gave the 'talking cure' its name, was, among other things, afflicted by an inability to speak her native language.

Henry James was well placed to act as a focus for the older, more political, manifestations of 'the woman question' (which he had explored in *The Portrait of a Lady* (1881) and *The Bostonians* (1886)), and for the newer psychiatric investigations of female disorders. His brother William had studied with Charcot, the pioneer investigator of hysteria, and in a lecture in 1896 refers to Freud's 'relief of certain hysterias by handling the buried idea' (quoted in Cargill 1963: 247). Henry and William's sister Alice was herself a hysteric, and because of this personal interest, Cargill speculates persuasively that Henry James may himself have read Freud and Breuer's *Studies on Hysteria*, which appeared in 1895.

In the first case study in this volume, the case of 'Anna O', Joseph Breuer makes explicit the link between hysteria and social inactivity. This twenty-one-year-old patient

> was markedly intelligent, with an astonishingly quick grasp of things and penetrating intuition. She possessed a powerful intellect which would have been capable of digesting solid mental pabulum and which stood in need of it – though without receiving it after she had left school . . . Her will-power was energetic, tenacious and persistent; sometimes it reached the pitch of an obstinacy which only gave way out of kindness and regard for other people.
>
> One of her essential character traits was sympathetic kindness . . . Her states of feeling always tended to a slight exaggeration . . . The element of sexuality was astonishingly undeveloped in her . . .
>
> This girl, who was bubbling over with intellectual vitality, led an extremely monotonous existence in her puritanically-minded family. She embellished her life in a manner which probably influenced her decisively in the direction of her illness, by indulging in systematic day-dreaming, which she described as her 'private theatre' (Freud and Breuer [1893–5] 1991: 73–4).

This collection of characteristics had already been identified as stereotypical by Florence Nightingale in 1852 (Nightingale [1852] 1978: 397). What was new in Freud and Breuer's analysis was a detailed understanding of the mechanism whereby this social syndrome could result in psychiatric disorder. The rationality, intelligence and social decorum which Anna O shares with Jane Eyre and James's governess, are revealed as precisely the recipe for madness in a society where 'solid mental pabulum' is withheld (see also Cohen, P. 1986: 79).

Oscar Cargill identifies another of the *Studies on Hysteria* as the probable germ of *The Turn of the Screw* (1963: 244). This is the case of 'Lucy R', which Freud uses as his primary *exemplum* for the process of repression. Like James's governess and Charlotte Brontë in 1847, Lucy R is thirty years old. She is an English governess to two motherless children in a Viennese family (Freud and Breuer [1893-5] 1991: 170) who feels that the children's father and grandfather fail to support her as they should; her primary allegiance, however, is to their dead mother:

> Their mother was a distant relation of my mother's, and I had promised her on her death-bed that I would devote myself with all my power to the children, that I would not leave them and that I would take their mother's place with them. (179)

Her hysteria takes the form of an olfactory hallucination; she is 'haunted' by smells, particularly that of cigar-smoke (the 'warning fragrance' by which Jane recognizes

Mr Rochester (*JE* 260)). Freud, proceeding on the principle that 'before hysteria can be acquired . . . an idea must be *intentionally repressed from consciousness*' (Freud and Breuer [1893–5] 1991: 180), argues that Lucy's smells remain as a 'physical symbol' of an idea which is incompatible with the ego. In this case, Freud proposes that the repressed idea is that 'you are in love with your employer'. The mother's plea that the governess should 'take her place' in terms of protecting the children has become a hope that she will 'take her place' as their father's wife. This hope, encouraged by a confidential talk with her employer, had been suddenly damaged in a scene where he berated her for allowing a lady visitor to kiss the children on the mouth. His unexpected hostility was the 'incompatible idea' which was subsequently represented by the smell of the cigar he was smoking at the time. Freud explains that 'the hysterical method of defense . . . lies in the conversion of the excitation into a somatic innervation; and the advantage of this is that the incompatible idea is forced out of the ego's consciousness . . .' (187). Freud's identification of the traumatic scene as the source of the governess's hysteria is persuasive, particularly since her symptoms disappeared after the diagnosis. He seems not to have noticed, however, that there is in the same scene a second potential source of trauma in her recognition that she had failed to protect the children from 'contamination', and it is this, quite as persuasively as her incipient love for the 'Master', which could explain her repression and, incidentally, make a more specific link with *The Turn of the Screw*.

Lucy R readily agrees with Freud's diagnosis that she was in love with her employer, but when he asks why she didn't volunteer this information, she replies, 'I didn't know'. Speaking of 'the strange state of mind in which one knows and does not know a thing at the same time', Freud gives an example from his own experience, in which 'I was afflicted by that blindness of the seeing eye which is so astonishing in the attitude of mothers to their daughters' (181 & n.). Peter Cominos, in his pioneering essay, 'Innocent femina sensualis in unconscious conflict', explains that this blindness is not at all astonishing, but systematic. Whereas Victorian boys were encouraged strenuously to struggle against the snares of the flesh, girls were perceived as childlike innocents and denied the basic information which allows responsible adults to make informed choices.

> Moral responsibility presupposed freedom of choice as well as the knowledge of moral alternatives. Victorian culture and the genteel family withheld the knowledge from their daughters and their responsibility for choosing. Innocent daughters were spared the awareness of conflicting motives. Hence there was no conscious conflict for innocent daughters; no conscious choice to be made. A conscious struggle was waged on behalf of their moral purity by overprotective parents and chaperons who were forever cognizant of danger. As a state of repressed consciousness, innocence absolved daughters from the exercise of responsibility. (Cominos 1974: 161)

The problem with governesses is that they are both daughters and surrogate mothers, though they are daughters without parents and mothers without husbands. The dangerous knowledge of sexuality thus continually threatens to surface along the borderline between childlike purity and adult responsibility. The case of Lucy R demonstrates how repression acts as an escape from this difficulty.

We have seen that Freud takes as 'a *sine qua non* for the acquisition of hysteria that an incompatibility should develop between the ego and some idea presented to it'. Lucy R's case enables him to conclude that 'the actual traumatic moment . . . is the one at which the incompatibility forces itself upon the ego and at which the latter decides on the repudiation of the incompatible idea' (Freud and Breuer [1893–5] 1991: 187–8). If we accept my addition to his account of the 'incompatible idea', and see that it is not only the loss of her employer's approval which is traumatic, but also its cause – her failure to 'take the mother's place' by protecting the children – it becomes significant that James's governess first sees the ghost on the tower at the moment, after receiving the letter announcing Miles's expulsion from school, when she is imagining her employer's approval of her handling of the situation in a way which preserves the children's purity (chapter 3). The letter thus simultaneously provokes her zeal to protect the children, and her resistance to the knowledge of infant sexuality, which, like any Victorian mother, she has and does not have.

There are many psychoanalytic accounts of *The Turn of the Screw* which turn on the notion of repressed sexuality, but they have all followed the hint that, like Lucy R and Jane Eyre, James's governess is in love with her employer, so that the repression is of her own focused desires (e.g. Wilson 1934: 88; Cargill 1963: 245; cf. Cohen, P. 1986: 80). The case of Lucy R, however, suggests that the primary repression involved may well be of the recognition of the sexuality of infants. The question of what Miles did at school is in a way immaterial – Lucy R's employer's reaction to the lady visitor's kiss shows that it is sexuality itself which is 'unmentionable' rather than any gross practice, so that even the slightest evidence can be projected as 'horrors'. Shoshana Felman points out that the 'horrors' are what is missing from the letters in *The Turn of the Screw*; the ghosts are also described as 'horrors'; so that 'the ghosts are in reality nothing other than the letters' *content*' (1977: 150). The governess herself is, moreover, implicated: when she and Mrs Grose first discuss the possibility of Miles's 'badness', the housekeeper asks, with 'an odd laugh', 'Are you afraid he'll corrupt *you?*' (22), and when Peter Quint appears for the second time, she responds in a way which confirms Freud's later definition of the 'uncanny' as 'the return of the repressed', since she finds him both 'strange' and familiar, 'as if I had been looking at him for years and had known him always' (*JE* 1898 James [1964: 38]). It has seemed odd to some readers that the title phrase, 'the turn of the screw', is used by Douglas to describe the manufactured horror of a ghost story (4), and by the governess to describe moral heroism; the link is provided, however, by the concept of repression. In chapter 12 the governess herself analyzes the link between 'ordinary human virtue' and 'the hideous obscure'; for our purposes, try substituting 'accepted social codes' for 'nature' and 'repression' for 'virtue':

I felt afresh . . . how my equilibrium depended on the success of my rigid will, the

will to shut my eyes as tight as possible to the truth that what I had to deal with was,
revoltingly, against nature. I could only get on at all by taking 'nature' into my
confidence and my account, by treating my monstrous ordeal as a push in a direction
unusual, of course, and unpleasant, but demanding after all, for a fair front, only
another turn of the screw of ordinary human virtue. (146–7)

In chapter 15 she confirms that 'the horrors' are by definition that which cannot be
spoken, especially to the 'Master' who occupies the place of social arbiter:

> my fear was of having to deal with the intolerable question of the grounds for [Miles's]
> dismissal from school, since that was really but the question of the horrors gathered
> behind. That his uncle should arrive to treat with me of these things was a solution
> that, strictly speaking, I ought now to have desired to bring on; but I could so little
> face the ugliness and the pain of it that I simply procrastinated. (105)

The extreme tension of *The Turn of the Screw* thus derives from the governess's
simultaneous compulsion and reluctance to abandon the Victorian notion of infant
purity and with it, the idea of pure womanhood as a kind of extended infancy.

Jane Eyre appears to deal with this problem by adopting the strategy of feminine
oppositions which Cominos defines as hegemonic:

> the respectable ideal of purity represented unadulterated femininity; her opposite
> represented the *projection* of those rejected and unacceptable desires and actions that
> must be destroyed to keep women pure beings. If those thoughts and actions could
> not be totally suppressed inside the womanly woman, they had to be destroyed in the
> projected outside version of herself. (1974: 168)

Modern feminist critics have accepted this as the psychological explanation of
Bertha Mason and of what is now identified as the 'hysterical text', the 'double-
voiced discourse' of the nineteenth-century woman writer, so extensively
demonstrated in *The Madwoman in the Attic* (see Gilbert and Gubar 1979 *passim*;
Mitchell, J. 1984: 101; Showalter 1982: 31). The theory behind the idea of
'hysterical texts' is that certain unacceptable ideas are repressed by the text as a
whole (not by characters within the text). The angel/monster dichotomy elaborated
by Gilbert and Gubar is the most notable strategy of this kind; it was a social
phenomenon, reproduced across a range of contemporary texts.

    If we turn to Jane Eyre as a character, therefore, we find that her author has, as
it were, done some of her psychological work for her by projecting her unacceptable
desires into a monstrous other whose existence and evaluation is confirmed by other
people. This projection, therefore, does not require an individual effort of
repression by Jane herself and does not involve her hysterical trauma. It is notable
that Jane lacks anxiety about her own 'purity', and does not share the quasi-maternal
fervour of the later governesses. In her dream on the eve of her wedding, the wailing
child is a burden: 'I might not lay it down anywhere, however tired were my arms
– however much its weight impeded my progress'. This dream may indicate her
apprehension about crossing the border from a state of 'innocence', in which she
is a fit guardian for the infant purity she shares, to 'experience', a state in which the

'burden' of purity will drop from her (*JE* 296). Jane, however, accepts no conscious responsibility for her dream and is therefore able to tell it simply to Rochester. Moreover, when her reason tells her that continued 'innocence' would 'impede her progress', she lets it roll from her. She answers Rochester's plea to be his mistress not as 'innocent femina sensualis in unconscious conflict', but as an adult cognizant of the necessary information.

Despite the shock of the failed wedding, Jane is not traumatized into 'demonizing' her 'other', but is able to stand 'grave and quiet at the mouth of hell' (308). She knows that she is watching what everyone would agree to be a madwoman, and her security within a general evaluation enables her to be relatively independent, reproaching Rochester: 'you are inexorable for that unfortunate lady . . . It is cruel – she cannot help being mad' (317). Her analysis of what constitutes rational behaviour is externally endorsed; Rochester, for instance, confirms that on Jane's forehead, 'Reason sits firm and holds the reins, and she will not let the feelings burst away and hurry her to wild chasms' (211). Guided by that 'still small voice', she is thus able to recognize and articulate both the 'furnace' of masculine desire and the 'running fire' of her own. Confronting the 'insanity' of her desire, Jane invokes 'the law given by God; sanctioned by man' (334–5), and makes, not a hysterical defence, but a rational retreat. In *Studies on Hysteria*, Freud confirms that 'hysterical symptoms . . . are not left behind if the original excitation has been discharged by abreaction or thought-activity' (Freud and Breuer [1893–5] 1991: 146); it is, therefore, appropriate that Jane explains her flight by saying, 'I knew what I had to do' (*JE* 338). Freud and Breuer's major innovation in the analysis of hysteria was, of course, to listen to what their patients said, instead of trying, like earlier psychiatrists, to derive a diagnosis from their physical appearance (see Rose 1983: 12–16). Remarkably, Jane's self-analysis survives, without repression, even her experiences as 'fallen woman' and she is able to analyze accurately why she cannot marry St John: 'to compel [the fire of my nature] to burn inwardly and never utter a cry . . . – *this* would be unendurable' (*JE* 429).

The sharp dichotomy between reason and passion which is found throughout Charlotte Brontë's work finds an interesting echo in the case of Anna O. Summing up her case, Breuer reports that, 'even when she was in a very bad condition . . . a clear-sighted and calm observer sat, as she put it, in a corner of her brain and looked on at all the mad business'. Breuer concludes with 'the astonishing fact' that 'all the mad business' was 'permanently removed by being given verbal utterance' (Freud and Breuer [1893–5] 1991: 101–2), and we may note here that Rochester's analysis of Jane leads him to conclude that her mouth 'was never intended to be compressed in the eternal silence of solitude' (*JE* 211). The conclusion to which I am leading is that although we may accept the modern feminist analysis of *Jane Eyre* as hysterical text, Jane Eyre the character avoids hysteria not by challenging the assumptions of her culture about dichotomies of vice and virtue but by claiming the right to speak them; not by disputing the existence of infant purity, but by claiming adult status for herself. Her reaction to Rochester's seduction can, for instance, be usefully contrasted with Margaret Hale's response, in Gaskell's *North and South* (1855), to Thornton's proposal of marriage. Instead of acknowledging that her actions have produced a sexual response in him, Margaret attempts to preserve her 'maiden virtue' by repressing this recognition; notably, in relation to the 'horrors' of *The Turn of the Screw*, it is projected as a loathsome external presence:

> The deep impression made by the interview, was like that of horror in a dream; that will not leave the room although we waken up . . . It is there – there, cowering and gibbering, with its fixed ghastly eyes, in some corner of the chamber. (*JE* 1855 Gaskell [1970: 257])

Although *North and South* was identified by Mrs Oliphant as one of the 'family' of *Jane Eyre* (1855: 559), it is clear that Margaret Hale has applied another turn of the screw of female self-surveillance which was to produce 'The Angel in the House' in the 1860s and the hysterics of the 1890s. Margaret's problem is not so much controlling her own behaviour, but knowing how to respond to the outside world, which was both adult and predominantly masculine. Her role as 'Christian hero' conflicts with that of 'Victorian heroine' (see Stoneman 1987: 130–1), and as the century wore on, it became increasingly apparent that the codes of 'innocent femina sensualis' could not cope with external reality.

Freud's Lucy R and James's governess aspire to both heroism and heroinism, and like Margaret Hale and Anna O, they have impressive personal qualities. Both governesses show an energetic self-reliance and an exaggerated determination to carry out their 'mission' to protect the children; James's governess hopes that

> by offering myself bravely as the sole subject of such experience, by accepting, by inviting, by surmounting it all, I should serve as an expiatory victim and guard the tranquillity of the rest of the household. The children in especial I should thus fence about and absolutely save. (*JE* 1898 James [1964: 48])

In view of this claim to heroic self-sacrifice, it is ironic that Freud describes the hysteric mechanism as 'an act of moral cowardice' (Freud and Breuer [1893–5] 1991: 188). Crucially, both governesses falter at the point where they are required to take 'adult' responsibility. Lucy R has to recognize that she should have seen the sexual threat involved in the lady's kiss; James's governess has to decide how to respond to Miles's expulsion from school. The situation of the governess thus throws into relief the contradictions inherent in the Victorian ideology of femininity. In a sense, the whole rationale of being a governess was to 'take the place of the mother', and thus epitomizes the sexual double bind of Victorian women in general: that they must protect themselves and their children tirelessly against a knowledge which they must have, in order to see its danger, and which they must not have, in order to remain pure. What would constitute 'an act of moral cowardice' in a man, therefore, is in a woman educated in the code of 'purity' merely another turn of the screw of a virtue defined as voluntary blindness. In James's revision of *Jane Eyre*, therefore, the 'insane . . . unmentionable relative kept in unsuspected confinement' appears to be the knowledge of sexuality itself (*JE* 1898 James [1964: 33]).

The particular problem encountered by James's governess is that of a little boy, who inhabits both the world of childhood (and therefore imputed innocence) and the world of masculinity (and therefore potential corruption). When the letter from the headmaster arrives, Mrs Grose declares that a boy who is never 'bad' is not a boy at all, or at least 'no boy for *me*!' (22). Cargill notes that Alice James's journal also reveals a 'lively curiosity for sexual matters, such as . . . the vices of the Eton boys' or the 'osculatory relaxations' of a waiter and a chambermaid. When Alice's journal came into his hands, Henry described it as 'heroic in its individuality, its independence – its face-to-face with the universe for and by herself' (1963: 248). Alice herself, however, speaking of her hysterical afflictions, writes, 'it used to seem to me that the only difference between me and the insane was that I had all the horrors and suffering of insanity, but the duties of doctor, nurse, and strait jacket imposed on me too' (in Cargill 1963: 246). It is surely arguable that this duty of self-restraint was as much cause as effect of her illness.

James's governess, unable, despite the evidence of the letter, to accept 'the obtrusion of the idea of grossness and guilt on a small, helpless creature', decides that her heroic act must be to take the whole burden of 'the law' upon herself: 'seeing and facing what I saw and faced, to keep the boy himself unaware' (*JE* 1898 James [1964: 152, 154]). Willing to play an 'adult' role, but without access to either the language or the audience which would authenticate her action in the larger world, she falls back upon the mechanisms of repression, inviting the charge of insanity by projecting her fears into 'horrors' visible only to herself. Unable to communicate with her 'master', she sends him a blank page and writes her narrative for an unimagined reader; it remains in a locked drawer for twenty years until Douglas and his friends investigate it as an example of 'general uncanny ugliness and horror and pain' (4). The narrative is her account, which she is forbidden to reveal, of her simultaneous recognition and repression of the knowledge which is necessary to protect 'innocence'. Shoshana Felman thus argues that 'the whole story springs from the impossibility, as well as from the necessity, of writing *a letter about what is missing in the original letter*' (1977: 144). The ending of the story, in which Miles is 'saved', presents the ultimate 'turn of the screw' of virtue defined as repression: 'by my success, his sense was sealed and his communication stopped' (*JE* 1898 James [1964: 155]). The governess's 'personal triumph' is that he now perceives 'nothing' (156), the most vivid demonstration possible that, as Mrs Grose had warned, a boy who is never 'bad' is 'no boy' (22) – that is, a dead boy (160).

If *Jane Eyre* is a hysterical text within which the heroine offers an inspiring model of rationality, *The Turn of the Screw* is a rational text in which the inspired heroine is defined as hysterical. Since both heroines are heroic and virtuous, the effect of the comparison is to emphasize the importance of the control of discourse. *Jane Eyre* shows us a society inimical to women, within which Jane achieves (relative) independence because she can articulate her (limited) choices. *The Turn of the Screw* gives us a situation where the governess conducts her heroic fight without adequate linguistic tools and is later 'framed' within a metanarrative which, however we analyze her story, diminishes its autonomy. In *Jane Eyre* the madwoman in the attic represents an ideology, however misguided by present standards, to which the heroine has access; in *The Turn of the Screw* the letter functions for the governess only as a signpost to what others are presumed to know. Given what we now know about the ideological climate, and about the process of repression, James's version of a mid-century governess who attempts heroism is, historically and psychologic-ally, more probable than *Jane Eyre*. Since *Jane Eyre* is, however, an authentic product of its age, a comparison with *The Turn of the Screw* confirms the extraordinary independence of the earlier text and explains its subsequent status as an inspiration to women. It does, however, raise disturbing questions about the education of children.

In Walter de la Mare's *Henry Brocken: His Travels and Adventures* (1904), Henry is about to leave Ferndean, where he has been entertained by Jane and Rochester in the flush of their marriage, when he is arrested by the sight of a child sitting on a wall.

> And she raised changeling hands at me, and laughed and danced and chattered like the drops upon a waterfall; and clear as if a tiny bell had jingled I heard her cry.
> And my heart smote me heavily since I had of my own courtesy not remembered Adèle. (*JE* 1904 Ramal [1944: 40])

The Victorian melodramas, though ready enough to exploit the pathos of Jane's status at Gateshead, accept without question that Jane herself will make a benign stepmother. Moreover, they ignore Lowood, with its panoply of alternative 'mothers' – Helen, Miss Temple, Miss Scatcherd. These texts from the turn of the century, however, open up the question of mother/child relationships where the place of the lost mother is taken by women who are not themselves accorded adult status. The figure of Rochester recedes as a new triangle presents itself, between child, (lost) mother and stepmother (governess). Since we see Jane as both child and teacher, the relationship between *Jane Eyre* and these later texts is complex, but they present the child as vulnerable to the reproduction of (substitute) mothering, in a society where women are less than adult. Esther, in *The Secret of Kyriels*, has a governess who is also a friend, but Clemence Dane's novel, *Regiment of Women* (1917), shows the destructive power of women who acquire the status of mentors without emotional maturity. Just as De la Mare's Adèle is excluded from the too-absorbing love of Jane and Rochester, so, in Clemence Dane's novel, thirteen-year-old Louise is the victim of emotional power struggles between her teachers, Clare and Alwynne.

Although *Regiment of Women* makes no reference to *Jane Eyre*, and as far as I know no-one has recognized the connection, Clemence Dane was later to write a play about the Brontë sisters (*Wild Decembers* (1932)). Clare, Alwynne and Louise are, moreover, notably well-read; their conversation at best sparkles with allusion. In a book which is partly about books as a mode of education, it seems probable that *Jane Eyre*, as a famous text for women, provides some of the imagery – in particular the topography – for this analysis of women's education. Unlike Jane, Clare and Alwynne are teachers in a girls' school which enters candidates for public examinations and has the air of serious scholarship. It is, however, a 'patch-work' institution, in which twentieth-century teaching methods have been superimposed on the relational structures of a Young Ladies' Seminary of the 1870s (*JE* 1917 Dane [1927: 207]). The book takes as its topic the emotional fitness of such young ladies to be educators, and the theme is investigated from the point of view of the child and of the teacher.

Louise Denny, situated like Jane Eyre in the household of a stepmother, discovers her dead mother's books and reads them in the attic. The mother, who is described as 'elusive . . . shy and unawakened' with 'pale, wood-sorrel beauty', becomes for Louise 'Mother, the shadow of the attic'. By voracious reading, Louise constructs for herself 'a gorgeous world inside my head' where her mother lives with 'all my special friends . . . Elizabeth Bennett, and the Little Women, and Garm, and Amadis of Gaul . . .', and eagerly submits to educational 'forcing' from her teacher Clare, whose influence affects her 'like being in the attic' (*JE* 1917 Dane [1927: 42, 47, 87, 52]). On the morning of an important examination, however, her stepmother announces her intention of clearing the attic. In the examination hall,

> A hideous picture rose up in Louise's mind. With photographic clearness she saw the attic and the faint shadow of her mother wavering from visibility to nothingness as the sunlight caught and lost her impalpable outlines: there was a sound of footsteps – Louise heard it: the faint thing held out sweet arms and Louise strained towards them; but the door opened, and Mrs Denny and the maids came in. Mamma [the second Mrs Denny] pointed, while the maids laughed and took their brooms and chased the forlorn appearance, and it fled before them about the room, cowering, afraid, calling in its whisper to Louise. But the maids closed in, and swept that shrinking nothingness into the dark corner behind the old trunk: but when they had moved the trunk, there was nothing to be seen but a delicate cobweb or two. So they swept it into the dustpan and settled down to the scrubbing of the floor. (144)

In growing delirium, Louise tries to imagine Mother in heaven, but confuses her throned figure with that of the examiner on the dais, the representative of Clare:

> There was Mother – and the Other – one was shape and one was shadow – but which was real? There was Mother – and the Other – who was Mother? No, who was – who was – The Other was not Mother – but if not, who? – who? – who? – (145)

Clare, who plays upon the incipient lesbian feelings of staff and pupils in order to maintain her position in the school, is a frightening picture of irresponsible female power. The eighteen years which elapsed between *The Secret of Kyriels* (1899) and *Regiment of Women* (1917) had, of course, seen the militant suffrage campaign, with its heady comradeship and its assumption that the end justifies the means. There were plenty of women in the non-militant campaign who were unhappy about the emotional intensities exploited by the WSPU, but they were probably most vividly shown by Mary Augusta Ward, a leading member of the Women's Anti-Suffrage League, in her novel, *Delia Blanchflower* (1915), where Delia falls under the influence of a charismatic but embittered feminist who has no respect even for human life. Clare, in *Regiment of Women*, has no political motivation, but her management of the school shows a similar lack of scruple.

Louise fails the examination but, in an attempt to retrieve her favour with Clare, gives an inspired performance of Prince Arthur in *King John*. As she says Shakespeare's words,

> 'I would that I were low laid in my grave' . . . it was not Arthur that spoke, nor Louise
> . . . It was the voice of childhood itself, sexless, aloof; childhood the eternal pilgrim,
> wandering passive and perplexed, an elf among the giants; childhood, jostled by the
> uncaring crowd, swayed by gross energies and seared by alien passions. (167)

After the performance, imitating Arthur in the play, Louise jumps to her death. As elsewhere in this novel, *Jane Eyre* here functions to indicate the cyclic element linking introspective child, stifled governess and incarcerated (m)other. Louise, like Jane, 'was fond of curling up in the window-seats with her books' (249), but Louise's final window-seat is on the third storey, and it is from here that she leaps to her death. Moreover, just as Jane, stifled by the schoolroom, 'raised the trap-door of the attic, and . . . looked out afar over sequestered field and hill, and along dim skyline' (*JE* 114), so Louise, as she stands on the schoolroom windowsill before leaping, looks to 'the horizon, above the faint line of hills', and thinks, 'So there was a world beyond the school!' (*JE* 1917 Dane [1927: 174]). Jane 'longed for a power of vision which might overpass that limit', and although her eventual escape is not spectacular, she does achieve the one route possible to emotional maturity; she neither stays locked in the schoolroom nor leaps from the leads. Louise's emotional focus is, by contrast, fatally narrowed. After her death, Clare and Alwynne discover an essay in which Louise imagines one of King John's tortures:

> You dream you are free and people love you . . . and the one you love most kisses your
> forehead. But then the kiss grow so cold that you shrink away, only you cannot . . .
> and you wake up and it is the stone. It is the sinking stone that is pressing you, pressing
> you, pressing you to death – (196)

For Louise, Clare occupies the position not only of the (m)other, but also of Rochester. Although it is made plain that Louise does not understand sexual difference, there is no doubt that her feeling for Clare is sexual (124). Alwynne, who herself receives 'passionate kisses' from Clare (73), explains 'innocently' that, 'If she had been grown-up it would have been like being in love' (250). Clare, selfish and manipulative, shifts the guilt for Louise's suicide on to Alwynne, who suffers nightmares and hysterics before a sympathetic male confessor allows her a 'talking cure'. Because Clare is a villain, Roger is an advocate of co-education, and Alwynne eventually escapes to a conventional marriage, the novel presents itself as anti-lesbian, seeing women's feeling for each other as, at best, a phase, and at worst, dangerously perverse. The psychology of the three women is, however, persuasively rendered through the literary intertext which forms their common consciousness. The novel gives us a nightmare confusion of *Jane Eyre*'s certainties of topography and identity, so that Jane's window-seat becomes the point from which the madwoman leaps, and 'the shadow in the attic' changes from the benign and beautiful 'Mother' into Clare, the negligent governess and unsustaining lover.

The novel ends with Alwynne rescued by Roger/Rochester and a 'healthy' heterosexuality, and Clare 'thinking – thinking – ' (345) about where she went wrong. The relief with which Alwynne, this new woman of the suffragette era, sinks into marriage is disappointing, but the claustrophic atmosphere of the school is shrewdly analyzed. These women have claimed intellectual and economic independence, but are in no way integrated into the public world. Twenty years later, Virginia Woolf was to describe the 'daughters of educated men' as

> between the devil and the deep sea. Behind us lies the patriarchal system; the private house, with its nullity, its immorality, its hypocrisy, its servility. Before us lies the public world, the professional system, with its possessiveness, its jealousy, its pugnacity, its greed. (Woolf [1938] 1977: 42)

Roger, in *Regiment of Women*, suspects Clare's attraction and hopes that Alwynne will 'prefer my deep sea to her devil' (*JE* 1917 Dane [1927: 289]). Clare, however, is not part of the public world. The school teaches only the difficult climb from the window-seat to the attic; its danger lies in its self-perpetuation and its impact on vulnerable children. In Elizabeth von Arnim's *Vera* (1921), an insensitive husband sees his wife fall from her room on the third storey, past his window, to her death. He is upset, but he is to blame. In *Regiment of Women* it is one of the younger children – 'a baby' (252) – who sees Louise fall.

Emily Brontë and the New Women, 1883–1904

The fact that this book is so far almost entirely devoted to *Jane Eyre* is not an accidental imbalance on my part. The early reviews of *Wuthering Heights*, though ready to testify to its 'power, splendour and wildness' (in Allott 1974: 330), showed puzzlement and apprehension. It was not a novel which readers took to their hearts, in an era when literature was valued for the truth of its representations and the inspiration of its moral stance. The Bradford Mechanics' Institute, for instance, when it cautiously admitted some English novelists to its library in 1870, drew the line at Emily Brontë, 'whose *Wuthering Heights* was at that time considered as a very wicked book' (Federer 1906: 640). Abroad, although the promptness of the first German translation in 1851 'testifies to the spontaneous reception of the novel outside England', nevertheless 'the interest in *Wuthering Heights* in German-speaking countries remained sporadic rather than general and continued' (Ganner 1980: 375). The first French translation was not made until 1892 (BST 17.86.20–34 (1976)). In Britain, there seems to have been no popular 'school' of *Wuthering Heights*. No-one, it seems, tried to reproduce the novel in other media. I have traced no stage plays based on *Wuthering Heights* during the nineteenth century; Helen Hughes cites an American stage play published in 1914 but otherwise a silent film of 1920 seems to have been its first dramatic representation.

In 1883, a new wave of interest was created by Mary Robinson's *Emily Brontë*, the first full-length biography. Robinson played dramatically upon the previous neglect of *Wuthering Heights* (though even she, apparently, did not envisage West Riding censorship!):

> Here and there a mill-girl in the West Riding read and re-read the tattered copy from the lending library; here and there some eager, unsatisfied, passionate child came upon the book and loved it, in spite of chiding . . . or some strong-fibred heart felt without a shudder the justice of that stern vision of inevitable, inherited ruin following the chance-found child of a foreign sailor and seaport mother. But these readers were not many: even yet the book is not popular. (Robinson, A. 1890: 2)

It is, therefore, curiously appropriate that the first 'transformation' of *Wuthering Heights* identified by many later readers should be, not a public adaptation, but an echo, distant in several ways. *The Story of an African Farm* (1883), like *Wuthering Heights*, was a first novel by an unlikely author. Olive Schreiner, who grew up on a remote farm in Basutoland, was precisely such an 'eager, unsatisfied, passionate child' as Robinson describes, who grew into a 'strong-fibred heart'. Like Emily Brontë, Olive Schreiner was passionately attached to the bleak landscape of her early home and in her novel tries to wrest from its hostile beauty a philosophy to replace the unsustaining Christian creeds of, her education. Moreover, she recognized her kinship with the earlier writer. R. D. Haynes asserts that

> Olive Schreiner referred to Emily Brontë as the greatest woman writer of genius whom the English-speaking people have produced and that she included Emily Brontë in her list of the world's twelve greatest women. (Haynes 1981: 60)

The Story of an African Farm is a more self-consciously intellectual book than *Wuthering Heights*, and the ideas developed in it were to define Schreiner as one of the most radical thinkers of her time. Later she became a prominent member of the Men and Women Club, formed to debate a 'new sexuality' (see Showalter 1992: 47). Nevertheless there are more than passing similarities between the two novels. Showalter notes that 'the central situation of the persecuted orphan, Waldo, who falls in love with his childhood ally, Lyndall, has reminded many readers of *Wuthering Heights*', and Haynes cites several critics who have made the same comparison (Showalter 1977: 199; Haynes 1981: 60). Haynes's project is to present Schreiner's novel in a broad tradition of literary Romanticism, but he also notes 'striking' parallels in the plot and characterization of the two novels.

> Like Heathcliff and Cathy, Waldo and Lyndall are first indulged by a kindly father-figure, and subsequently persecuted by an authoritarian tyrant under whose regime hell-fire religion is the standard Sabbath fare. As Cathy forsakes the uncouth Heathcliff and her 'roots' in the moors for a life of manners and social graces, so Lyndall leaves Waldo and the farm to seek fulfilment in a more urbane and cultured sphere. Waldo, like Heathcliff, disappears for a time from his natural milieu to return only when it is too late to win the woman he loves, while Gregory Rose, with his gentle, half-feminine nature, his extraordinary tenderness towards the unresponsive Lyndall and, not less, his petulance is almost a parody of Edgar Linton. Lyndall, like Cathy,

dies of pneumonia, self-induced, after the birth of a child, although of course Lyndall's child dies while Catherine Linton lives . . . In each novel the male protagonist dies, apparently of grief after the death of the beloved woman and, in each case, a kind of serenity is restored at the end although in effect it does not approach the intensity of emotion evoked during the time of tumult. (60)

There are, however, some problems with too simple an identification. Waldo's sympathy with nature is much more explicit and meditative than Heathcliff's, and the speeches which are most reminiscent of Heathcliff's passion are given, not to Waldo, but to Gregory Rose. Haynes identifies Gregory with Edgar, but when he first appears and falls in love with Lyndall's cousin Em, his expressions of love are not only more extravagant than anything Edgar Linton says, they are also undercut by his evident self-dramatization. In a letter to his sister, he writes, 'It is a choice between death and madness. I can endure no more . . . Tell mother to take care of my pearl studs' (*WH* 1883 Schreiner: 182). In his mouth the conventions of Romantic 'oneness' become suspect: 'If you were dead, though my body moved, my soul would be under the ground with you . . . If every relation I had in the world were to die tomorrow, I would be quite happy if I still only had you!' (187). Having transferred his devotion to Lyndall, his rhetoric remains unchanged, and he is desolate when she deserts him: 'You can forget all the world, but you cannot forget yourself . . . How can I forget her when, wherever I turn, she is there, and not there? I cannot, I will not, live where I do not see her' (274–5). Although Gregory gains in stature as the story progresses, the effect is still as if Lockwood were to speak Heathcliff's lines. The text thus exposes the discourse of Romantic oneness as a convention which can, indeed, engross the speaker and shape his whole existence, but which is in a way chosen, not inevitable.

The fact that Gregory attains something like tragic stature only at the end, when he adopts woman's clothing in order to nurse Lyndall through her last illness, suggests that the rhetoric of love has been one of the ways in which women have been constrained and sustained within their serving role, achieving, like Gregory, an ecstasy of self-renunciation. These scenes of devotion contrast oddly with the death of Catherine Earnshaw, in which Heathcliff, despite his despair, can find access only to the 'masculine' language of savage abuse and the prospect of revenge. It is notable that even on the night of Catherine's death Heathcliff's exaggerated notion of masculine pride will not let him simply grieve, lest this should seem a sign of weakness. Nelly observes how

> he held a silent combat with his inward agony, defying, meanwhile, my sympathy with an unflinching, ferocious stare . . . 'Poor wretch!' I thought; 'you have a heart and nerves the same as your brother men! Why should you be so anxious to conceal them?' (*WH* 166)

It is possible to read Catherine's haunting of Heathcliff in *Wuthering Heights* as her reproach to him for effectively cutting her out of his consciousness by translating his grief into revenge (*WH* xxxviii). Gregory's story in *The Story of an African Farm* also suggests that our culture regards tenderness as effeminate, endorsing in men only self-sufficiency. Lyndall's part in these scenes is also different from Catherine's – reserved and self-contained. Haynes sees her as 'arrogant' and believes that she 'despises' Gregory; it seems that our culture not only endorses in men only self-sufficiency, but also endorses self-sufficiency only in men.

Haynes, in fact, does not mention the more original sections of the plot, in which Lyndall leaves the farm, driven by the desire for knowledge and experience, and gives herself to a lover who appears only briefly in the story. Despite the prospect of bearing his child, Lyndall refuses to marry him, 'because I cannot be tied' (*WH* 1883 Schreiner: 264). Instead she dies from pneumonia contracted while grieving in the rain on her dead child's grave. The novel is clearly offering a critique of the Romantic duality of love presented in *Wuthering Heights*. Lyndall is not to be drawn into the position in which Catherine says, 'I *am* Heathcliff', but coolly reasons about the nature of love:

> There is a love that begins in the head, and goes down to the heart, and grows slowly; but it lasts till death, and asks less than it gives. There is another love, that blots out wisdom, that is sweet with the sweetness of life and bitter with the bitterness of death, lasting for an hour; but it is worth having lived a whole life for that hour. (251)

She does not, however, make the mistake of believing that the love 'that blots out wisdom' can be the basis of a life.

Haynes sees both Lyndall and Catherine as 'self-centred' and as lacking in self-knowledge: 'Both Cathy and Lyndall think they wish to dictate to men, but really desire to be mastered, to adore a superior man' (1981: 60). Such a reading is inappropriate for *Wuthering Heights*, whether we stress Catherine's sense of 'oneness' with Heathcliff, or accept the reading which I have argued elsewhere that Catherine is prepared to find pragmatic solutions to her difficulties, conceiving it as a viable life-plan to live amicably with both her lovers, and only forced into a tragic impasse by their non-cooperation (*WH* xxxvii). It is, however, much more obviously inappropriate for *The Story of an African Farm*. It discounts the long feminist statement in part II, chapter IV, in which Lyndall complains that women 'fit our sphere as a Chinese woman's foot fits her shoe' (*WH* 1883 Schreiner: 199), although 'the mightiest and noblest of human work is given to us' (205). More particularly it discounts Lyndall's refusal to marry her lover. She agrees that she loved him 'because you are strong', but also 'because I like to experience, I like to try' (264). She refuses to marry him, however, because 'I must know and see, I cannot be bound to one whom I love as I love you' (317). We might think that 'as I love you' means with the Romantic intensity of Catherine and Heathcliff. The unnamed lover, however, refuses this kind of avowal:

> It is all very well to have ideals and theories; but you know as well as anyone can that they must not be carried into the practical world. I love you. I do not pretend that it is in any high, superhuman sense; I do not say that I should like you as well if you were ugly and deformed, or that I should continue to prize you whatever your treatment of me might be, or to love you though you were a spirit without any body at all. That is sentimentality for beardless boys. Every one not a mere child (and you are not a

child, except in years) knows what love between a man and a woman means. I love you with that love. (262)

The danger which Lyndall sees in marriage is thus the bondage of physical passion, strong enough to enslave her so that she can no longer 'know and see', and unreliable enough to leave her unsustained when she grows unattractive. The stranger does not occupy the position of Heathcliff any more than Waldo or Gregory; the novel, in fact, divides the qualities of Heathcliff between the three men: his nature mysticism goes to Waldo; the sentiments of Romantic oneness to Gregory; and the force of physical passion to 'Lyndall's stranger'. None of these men alone has the qualities of a life-companion, though Lyndall considers Waldo for friendship, Gregory for stability and service, and her stranger for the love they know. Moreover, none of them has the power which Catherine and Heathcliff find in each other, to mirror each other's existence. Waldo, returning after his abortive search for experience, writes a letter to Lyndall expressing his 'sudden gladness' in recognizing that 'You are my very own; nothing else is my own so' (295). But the letter, which, as Rachel Blau du Plessis notes, 'recalls the passionate outcries in both Charlotte and Emily Brontë', is written after Lyndall is already dead (du Plessis 1985: 25). This is not a world of poetic fitness but one in which, as Schreiner's preface says, 'when the crisis comes the man who would fit it does not return' (*WH* 1883 Schreiner: viii).

After her interview with her stranger, Lyndall looks into the mirror but she sees only herself. The first thought provoked by the mirror is conventional: 'One day I will love something utterly, and then I will be better'. This, however, is swiftly followed by a more realistic recognition; looking at her own eyes, she says, 'We are all alone, you and I, . . . no one helps us, no one understands us; but we will help ourselves'. Soon this becomes more positive: 'We shall never be quite alone, you and I . . . We shall always be together, as we were when we were little . . . We are not afraid . . . Dear eyes! we will never be quite alone till they part us' (269). As she dies, 'the dying eyes on the pillow looked into the dying eyes in the glass; they knew their hour had come' (324).

Lyndall's ideal of self-sufficiency founders because 'the unaddressed problem of the legitimacy and care of children put women at much greater risk of abandonment' (Showalter 1992: 50), but her bodily weakness is sharply distinguished from her mental strength. In this she differs from the historical women who attempted a similar independence. Showalter points out that both Schreiner and her friend Eleanor Marx

> suffered most of their lives from crippling psychosomatic diseases and nervous symptoms like those of the hysterical women Freud and Breuer were treating in Vienna . . . Thus, for all their greatness, both were tragic feminist intellectuals of the *fin de siècle* whose lives revealed the huge gap between socialist-feminist theory and the realities of women's lives. (1992: 53)

The Story of an African Farm is in tune with this tragic situation; its heroine is an outspoken, brave but ultimately powerless woman, seeing the trap in which

Catherine Earnshaw perished, but unable to do more than die in a trap of her own making. According to Showalter,

> Schreiner came to believe that her generation of feminists had been called upon to sacrifice their sexuality and their opportunities for love in order to secure the future freedom of other women. Until New Men were educated to appreciate the love of free women, the most advanced women would be doomed to celibacy and loneliness. (56)

By coincidence, it was in the same year as *The Story of an African Farm* that Mary Robinson's biography of Emily Brontë appeared. Robinson perhaps exaggerates the neglect under which she had hitherto lain, arguing that 'in 1848, the peals of triumph which acclaimed the success of "Jane Eyre" had no echo for the work of Ellis Bell' ([1883] 1890: 207; cf. Allott 1974: 29–30). The image of a lonely and unappreciated genius was, however, congruent with that of the feminist heroine described by Showalter, enabling Robinson to present Emily Brontë as a voice for the time. It is significant, moreover, that where *Jane Eyre* had appealed immediately to mainstream imitators and the popular stage, *Wuthering Heights* was adopted by *avant garde* writers a generation later. Robinson acknowledges that it was

> Mr Swinburne [who], so to speak, blew the dust from 'Wuthering Heights' . . . Until then, a few brave lines of welcome from Sydney Dobell, one fine verse of Mr Arnold's, one notice from Mr Reid, was all the praise that had been given to the book by those in authority. ([1883] 1890: 2)

Appropriately, it was Swinburne who reviewed Robinson's biography. Comparing Charlotte's work with Emily's, he asserts that because Emily's gift is poetic, rather than realistic, 'it was therefore all the more proper that the honour of raising a biographical and critical monument to the author of *Wuthering Heights* should have been reserved for a poetess of the next generation to her own.' (Swinburne 1883: 762–3) There is a serious point under this mutual congratulation; Swinburne and Robinson are signalling that Emily Brontë is 'one of us'. Swinburne, of course, was well known as a rebel against Victorian convention and religion, an intense admirer of Shelley. Mary Robinson, however, also moved in 'advanced' circles; her parents entertained Oscar Wilde, and she herself had already published 'exotic, melancholy, *fin de siècle*' poems for her close friend, Vernon Lee (Blain *et al.* 1990: 914). However, while Swinburne led an alcoholic and generally dissipated life, Robinson identified with the deliberate self-contained chastity eventually prescribed by Schreiner, which was to become so characteristic of the *fin de siècle* woman, whether 'aesthete' or suffragette.

Her characterization of Emily Brontë rests on a strong contrast between her and Branwell, justified because to pass over Branwell's

> follies and failures . . . would have been to leave untold the patience, the courage, the unselfishness which perfected Emily Brontë's heroic character; and to have left her burdened with the calumny of having chosen to invent the crimes and violence of her *dramatis personae*. Not so, alas! They were but reflected from the passion and sorrow

that darkened her home; it was no perverse fancy which drove that pure and innocent girl into ceaseless brooding on the conquering force of sin and the supremacy of injustice. ([1883] 1890: 6)

In the same way, she sketches a picture of Anne, 'gentler, dearer, fairer, slowly dying, inch by inch, of the blighting neighbourhood of vice' (154). Superficially, this extolling of female purity sounds like the conventional ideology of the madonna/magdalen dichotomy. Even in the last of the *Jane Eyre* plays (1882), however, we saw that Rochester's claim to be a reformed rake was regarded with suspicion (see Chapter 1 page 38 above), and modern commentators have recognized that 'the Victorian insistence on female purity, hysterical as it sounds at times, is in part a reaction against the masculine impurity imposed by the economics of middle-class sexuality' (Schneewind 1970: 115). In 1883, when the debate over the second Married Women's Property Act (1882) and the campaign to repeal the Contagious Diseases Acts (1864–86) had publicized the domestic sufferings of women at the hands of debauched men, Emily Brontë could be offered to the world as a heroine who looked at depravity and was not defiled. Branwell is presented as the cause why 'this quiet clergyman's daughter, always hearing evil of Dissenters, has therefore from pure courage and revolted justice become a dissenter herself' (Robinson, A. [1883] 1890: 157). The strength of *Wuthering Heights* is that it reveals

the unlikeness of life to the authorised pictures of life; the force of evil, only conquerable by the slow-revolving process of nature which admits not the eternal duration of the perverse; the grim and fearful lessons of heredity. (158)

Believing the Brontës to be Calvinists, Robinson goes on:

From this doctrine of reward and punishment she learned that for every unchecked evil tendency there is a fearful expiation; though she placed it not indeed in the flames of hell, but in the perverted instincts of our own children. Terrible theories of doomed incurable sin and predestined loss warned her that an evil stock will only beget contamination: the children of the mad must be liable to madness; the children of the depraved, bent towards depravity; the seed of the poison-plant springs up to blast and ruin, only to be overcome by uprooting and sterilisation, or by the judicious grafting, the patient training of many years . . .

From thistles you gather no grapes.

No use, she seems to be saying, in waiting for the children of evil parents to grow, of their own will and unassisted, straight and noble. The very quality of their will is as inherited as their eyes and hair. Heathcliff is no fiend or goblin; the untrained doomed child of some half-savage sailor's holiday, violent and treacherous. And how far shall we hold the sinner responsible for a nature which is itself the punishment of some forefather's crime. (158–9)

Emily Brontë's chastity, Robinson argues, is the requisite for her appraisal:

none but an inexperienced girl could have treated the subject with the absolute and sexless purity which we find in 'Wuthering Heights' . . . That purity as of polished steel, as cold and harder than ice, that freedom in dealing with love and hate. (163–4)

By the 1890s, however, 'that purity' was being adopted as a political stance by those other than inexperienced girls. Sarah Grand, for instance, was the daughter of an alcoholic and the wife of 'a doctor who serviced an institution for the incarceration of prostitutes with venereal disease'. Her third novel, *The Heavenly Twins* (1893), dealt with 'women's desire for emancipation, with double sexual standards and, especially, with knowledge gained by her support of Josephine Butler's crusade to repeal the Contagious Diseases Act'. Unlike *Wuthering Heights*, 'it caused a sensation, selling 20,000 copies in one year' (Blain *et al.* 1990: 451; the Contagious Diseases Act was finally repealed in 1886). Grand nevertheless adopts precisely the position which Mary Robinson saw as Emily Brontë's: 'that purity as of polished steel, as cold and harder than ice, that freedom in dealing with love and hate' (Robinson, A. [1883] 1890: 164). Her novel is unusual in having three heroines, one of whom, ironically named Angelica, has a male twin with whom she exchanges clothes in order to pursue a friendship without sexual complications.

No-one, so far as I know, has heard echoes of *Wuthering Heights* in *The Heavenly Twins*; its small-town setting, exuberant humour, explicit feminism and proliferation of characters all distinguish it from the earlier novel. The brother-and-sister twins, however, give Grand an opportunity to explore the idea of mirrored likeness in a context free from Romantic intensity, and some such conscious reference is suggested in the dialogue where the young Angelica insists that she and her brother should exchange their tutor and governess because '*I* am Diavolo and *he* is me' (*WH* 1893 Grand: 124). The exchange lacks all the urgency of Catherine's 'I *am* Heathcliff' and prompts us instead to consider just what are the essential differences between children identical in all respects but that of sex (for the purposes of the novel, Grand ignores the fact that opposite-sex twins are always 'fraternal' rather than identical). The issue at point yields to logic, and both children are allowed to share the same tutor, but Angelica's later friendship with 'the Tenor' proves to owe much of its intimacy and sweetness to her disguise as 'the Boy'; when her identity is revealed, social codes of behaviour immediately rule out almost everything which had distinguished their rapport, innocent though it was. Disguised as 'the Boy', Angelica defines genius in a way that looks forward to Virginia Woolf, as 'the attributes of both minds, masculine and feminine, perfectly united in one person of either sex' (403), but as in *Wuthering Heights*, the decorum of adult life precipitates the children in opposite directions. When her brother leaves her for Sandhurst, Angelica laments, 'Why had Diavolo ceased to be all in all to her?' (492). She learns to wish she was a girl again, as does Catherine in I xii, when she too laments the loss of 'my all in all, as Heathcliff was at that time' (*WH* 125).

Angelica's education in the ways of the world is, however, more extensive than Catherine's. It includes seeing her cousin Edith die from the venereal disease which she contracted from the husband approved for her by her clerical father. The reader is also invited to weigh the decision of her friend Evadne, who, discovering on her wedding day that her husband had led a debauched life, insists on living celibate, though in his house. The strain of this existence leads to hysteria, in the form of paranoia that somehow the children of her second marriage to a blameless man will inherit the 'taint' of her first. These elements of the plot are distant from *Wuthering Heights*, yet Evadne's position of 'absolute and sexless purity', the position attributed to Emily Brontë by her 1883 biography, forms the context in which Angelica investigates the possibility of uniting 'the attributes of both minds, masculine and feminine', not in an abandonment of love, but in a child-like freedom.

Robinson and Schreiner were not the only women of the *fin de siècle avant garde* to be fascinated by Emily Brontë. May Sinclair's close friend Charlotte Mew, who lived at the centre of the 1890s literary scene, is described by her modern editor as being 'infatuated' with Emily Brontë (Mew 1981: xix). Like Sarah Grand, Charlotte Mew had only too much experience of the possible 'taint' of heredity; she lived in fear of hereditary madness and refrained from marriage to avoid passing it on. Her essay on 'The poems of Emily Brontë' identifies in the earlier writer the heroism of renunciation which she needed for her own life:

> Everywhere . . . the note of pure passion is predominant, a passion untouched by mortality and unappropriated by sex . . . Through the mist and sorrow of an ever-unsatisfied desire, she looked out upon the world, which the sad circumstances of her environment, together with the gloomy bias of her nature, showed so dark, with a curious indifference and mistrust. (Mew [1904] 1981: 358)

Mew takes as her text Charlotte Brontë's words about Emily: 'her nature stood alone', and with them conjures Emily into near-apotheosis:

> Her nature stood alone. That was the awful fact – the tragedy of her life.
> Alone in its negation of all that other mortals hold most dear: alone in its unwavering pity for frailty and error – no touch of which could ever mar the righteousness and vigour of this one woman's heart; alone in suffering and achievement; in the dark uncompanied vigils of its life and the triumphant conflict of its death . . . She lived long enough to lift such a cry for liberty as few women have ever lifted. (368)

Like Angelica in *The Heavenly Twins*, Mew sees in this singularity the conditions of genius:

> It is said that her genius was masculine, but surely it was purely spiritual, strangely and exquisitely severed from embodiment and freed from any accident of sex. Never perhaps has passion been portrayed as she portrayed it – wayward and wild as storm, but pure as fire, as incorruptible as life's own essence – deathless in the face of death. (363)

According to Warner, Mew's 'most intractable figure of renunciation' is to be found in Elinor, the heroine of the short story bearing her name, whom Warner identifies as 'Charlotte Mew's fictionalized picture of Emily Brontë' (xix). Elinor is the elder of two orphan sisters who live with an old servant in an isolated house; the story is told by Jean, the younger and more conventional sister. Elinor is strangely strong and remote; her philosophy is expressed on a slip of paper found by Jean:

> Man shapes his destiny alone . . . No deity surveys his work. He alone sanctions his own slavery or wrests his spirit free . . . his soul is bound with curious chains . . .; the

subtlest suffering, and the deadliest – that which caressing while it strangles – men call love. (285)

Elinor does not go to church, and quarrels with the rector who, it appears later, wished to marry Jean. She talks, however, with 'brilliant freedom' to a massive but courtly stranger who speaks of her 'great work' (288). Speaking of religion, she says, 'Can *no* man summon strength to stand alone!', to which he replies, 'It is your mission to persuade them'. Jean comments, 'It must have been my fancy that falsely detected a lurking ring of mockery in his tone'. 'Remembering . . . the words on that slip of paper', Jean goes on, 'the fact that they were lovers seemed at first incredible, but soon I found it one impossible to doubt' (289, 291). Without explanation, however, the lover is soon dismissed, though Jean is allowed to marry. When she presses her sister, Elinor is unable to reply:

> 'I cannot tell . . . I was not made to yield to any tyrant – no, not even to the world's sublimest despot . . .' '"All souls were made for happiness" was my last plea'.
> '"Rather for victory", was her reply' . . .
> Love came simply to me . . . but she confronted it . . . with desperate revolt. I could not view that terrible rebellion against a power to which Nature has bade us yield, without a certain horror and dismay. (293–5)

Elinor grows thin and gaunt but denies her illness – the narrative clearly echoes Gaskell's account of Emily Brontë's death – pointing to a pile of manuscript as evidence that 'the work is done' (296). Later she burns the manuscript and writes to the lover to come to her, but 'the agony of this enforced submission had cast a dreader shadow over her face than ever resistance had laid there'. She burns the letter before it is sent. Unhappily Jean has anticipated her request; when the lover appears, Elinor takes as weapon a biblical quotation:

> Standing erect and motionless, she pressed both hands across her eyes and lifted one fierce, ringing and revulsive cry: her voice – a spot of anguish – dropped and flickered, then burst again to a living flame.
> 'Thou has not yet resisted – unto blood.'
> It was her final utterance.
> Till dawn we watched with her.
> At dawn she died. (297)

Charlotte Mew's recreation of Emily Brontë's death by implication assigns to her suffering a precise source: sexual renunciation. The story, read in isolation, is melodramatic, but in the context of women's *fin de siècle* experiences it has a painful poignancy. Despite her suffering, Elinor retains neither her 'great work', nor her lover, nor, finally, even the dignity of unbroken resistance. She found, however, 'the strength to stand alone'.

The American poet Harriet Prescott Spofford echoes this identification of Emily Brontë as a heroine of renunciation in her 1897 poem 'Brontë':

> There are two ghosts without the door, –
> One lofty as when first she wore

The purple of her youth, and bore
Her state like some young queen. Full white
And icy as the northern light
The death-mask on her face. And see,
A cold flame where her heart should be!
Calm, bitter calm, and fair and frore,
There are two ghosts without the door. (Spofford 1897: 39)

It is notable that the New Women who looked back to Emily Brontë identified with the writer rather than her heroine. *Wuthering Heights* is not, like *Jane Eyre*, the kind of text which invites identification with its characters, and this is doubtless one reason why it was left for literary women to see the strength and audacity of Emily Brontë's writing. After Swinburne and Robinson, however, her reputation rapidly advanced. By 1898 Angus Mackay was writing that 'it is scarcely too much to say of Emily Brontë that she might have been Shakespeare's younger sister' (in Allott 1974: 102).

Chapter 3

Mainly biographical

'The blank page called for the scribble', 1904–32

At the beginning of Chapter 2 I noted a tendency, towards the end of the nineteenth century, to enshrine Charlotte Brontë. Rebecca West's essay on Charlotte, published in 1932, still appeared in a volume entitled *Great Victorians*, but it begins by saying, 'this generation knows that Charlotte Brontë's own generation gave her too high a place in the artistic hierarchy . . .' (47). With the turn of the century, a distinctly less reverent attitude appeared in Brontë biography and pseudo-biography. Volumes began to appear with titles like *The Key to the Brontë Works* (Malham-Dembleby 1911) and *The Secret of Charlotte Brontë* (Macdonald 1914). In 1917 C. L. Graves, in a poem addressed 'To Charlotte Brontë', wrote:

> Sensation-mongers, strident and voracious,
>   Must needs explore your inner life anew,
> Clutching with fingers ruthlessly tenacious
>   At the remotest semblance of a clue;
> Raking the rag heaps for unprinted matter,
>   And prodigal of cheap and tasteless chatter. (Graves 1917: 79)

By 1912, May Sinclair, who had been writing a series of introductions to the Brontë works since 1908, was moved to indignation on Charlotte Brontë's behalf:

> No woman who ever wrote was more criticised, more spied upon, more lied about, than Charlotte. It was as if the singular purity and poverty of her legend offered irresistible provocation. The blank page called for the scribble. The silence that hung about her was dark with challenge; it was felt to be ambiguous, enigmatic. Reserve suggests a reservation, something hidden and kept back from the insatiable public with its 'right to know'. (1912: 47)

When May Sinclair wrote *The Three Brontës* in 1912, she defined her main task as 'the humble day-labour of clearing away some of the rubbish that has gathered round them' (2). In the event, Sinclair is anything but humble, making a spirited defence of the Brontë sisters against the insidious and growing assumption that they were motivated mainly by frustrated sexuality:

> There are no words severe enough for Mrs Oliphant's horrible portrait of [Charlotte] as a plain-faced, lachrymose, middle-aged spinster, dying, visibly, to be married,

obsessed for ever with the idea, for ever whining over the frustration of her sex. What Mrs Oliphant, 'the married woman', resented in Charlotte Brontë, over and above her fame, was Charlotte's unsanctioned knowledge of the mysteries, her intrusion into the veiled places, her unbaring of the virgin heart. (21)

Sinclair, a member of the Women Writers' Suffrage League, had already written two novels on 'the destructive influence of the Victorian ideal of marriage', and in 1910 her book *The Creators* 'exposed the way men denigrate women's creativity and showed the difficulty for a woman of sustaining her art against the demands of a family' (Blain *et al.* 1990: 987). *The Three Brontës* appeared in the same year as her pamphlet, 'Feminism'. It is, then, hardly surprising that Sinclair also takes to task Clement Shorter, whose book *Charlotte Brontë and Her Circle* (1896) is still an important source of biographical information. According to Sinclair, Clement Shorter 'has a theory that Charlotte Brontë was a woman of morbid mood, "to whom the problem of sex appealed with all its complications"'. To this she opposes the evidence of Charlotte's letters to Ellen Nussey, which reveal 'a mind singularly wholesome and impersonal' (Sinclair 1912: 65–6). Sinclair was also one of the earliest English women to be professionally engaged in psychoanalysis, and thus able to bring something more than social convention and personal emotion to bear on the subject. Interestingly, she recognizes that Patrick Brontë's role had not been that of a repressive parent: 'Why, the average evangelical parson would have been shocked into apoplexy at the idea of any child of his producing *Wuthering Heights* and *Jane Eyre*'; instead, of course, 'he was profoundly proud of his daughters' genius' (9). On the other hand, overstating her case (as we know with hindsight), she protested against Angus Mackay's picture of Charlotte passing through a 'furnace of temptation' in Brussels: 'it was', Sinclair asserts, 'self-development, and not passion . . . that she went to Brussels for' (74–5).

Sinclair's most interesting insight is that in the writers she attacks what seems to be biographical comment may derive from a displaced response to Charlotte's writing. Although Charlotte's life was blameless, there was something in *Jane Eyre* that 'made Charles Kingsley think that Currer Bell was coarse'. 'Jane offended', Sinclair argues, in that

> she sinned against the unwritten code that ordains that a woman may lie till she is purple in the face, but she must not, as a piece of gratuitous information, tell a man she loves him; not, that is to say, in so many words. She may exhibit every ignominious and sickly sign of it; her eyes may glow like hot coals; she may tremble; she may flush and turn pale; she may do almost anything, provided she does not speak the actual words. (111–12)

What Sinclair describes here is, of course, the recipe for hysteria discussed in Chapter 2 (above), so that when Jane says to Rochester in the garden that she will regret being far 'from *you*, sir' (*JE* 263), she lays herself open to charges of indelicacy, but she preserves herself from hysteria by availing herself of speech. In a delightful piece of reverse discourse, Sinclair takes the conventional charge, that Charlotte 'glorified passion', and shows that, indeed, she did: 'she clothed it in light and flame; she showed it for the divine, the beautiful, the utterly pure and radiant thing it is . . . It was thus that Charlotte Brontë glorified passion' (Sinclair 1912: 118–19).

Elaine Showalter points out that 'many feminists had been attracted to psychoanalysis from its earliest years' precisely because they saw it 'as a theory that accepted female sexuality and freed women from the shackles of a puritanical Darwinian science' (1987: 196). The Medico-Psychological Clinic in London, funded by Sinclair from 1913, was, however, eclectic in its methods and Sinclair was clearly impatient with a too easy attribution of all ills to either sexual frustration (the new theory) or hereditary tendencies (the old). In *The Three Brontës* she thus rejects not only the 'frustrated spinster' theory about Charlotte, but also Mary Robinson's view of *Wuthering Heights* as demonstrating a pessimistic theory of hereditary corruption: 'the passion that consumes Catherine and Heathcliff, that burns their bodies and destroys them, is nine-tenths a passion of the soul. It taught them nothing of the sad secrets of the body' (Sinclair 1912: 213, 215). Addressing both the early critics who found Ellis Bell obsessed with 'the depravity of human nature' (in Allott 1974: 247) and the New Women who took Emily Brontë as a heroine of inspired celibacy, Sinclair answers, 'the moral problem never entered into Emily Brontë's head' (1912: 224).

Two years after *The Three Brontës*, Sinclair published a novel entitled *The Three Sisters* (1914). Its title, together with the situation of its three sisters, who live with their parson father in a remote moorland village, invites comparisons – indeed the Virago edition of the novel bears the Brontë group portrait on its cover. There is, however, a curious dissonance between the two works. *The Three Brontës* presents the Brontë sisters as articulate heroines, escaping the prevalent repression of Victorian women by a combination of fortunate upbringing and heroic clearsighted-ness. *The Three Sisters*, on the other hand, reads like a demonstration of Freud's comments on the difficulty, for women, of negotiating the Oedipus complex. Mary, Gwendolen and Alice Carteret are like object lessons in Freud's three possible outcomes of the feminine Oedipus process. Mary achieves 'normal' femininity, focusing her existence on husband, home and children; the independent Gwendolen shows us a 'masculinity complex'; the fragile Alice resorts to defensive hysteria.[1] All are condemned to less than full humanity by their repressive father, himself subject to unacknowledged drives. Gwendolen and Alice, who attempt self-sacrifice in each other's interest, fall joint victims to the 'normal' Mary, who takes the man who is the object of all their desires. It is, however, the lucid Gwenda, who bravely invokes a range of sublimatory strategies, who is finally left desolate when the 'hero' succumbs to middle-aged contentment and forgets the shared Romantic yearning which had offered an attenuated reason for Gwenda's continuing life.

The co-existence of *The Three Sisters* and *The Three Brontës* demonstrates the contradictory need in early twentieth century feminists for rational analysis of women's psychological disabilities on the one hand and, on the other, for feminist heroines who would rise triumphant above them. It is a problem which has not gone away. Assessing the uneasy relationship between psychoanalysis and (feminist) politics in 1983, Jacqueline Rose writes,

> nor does the concept of the unconscious sit comfortably with the necessary attempt by feminists to claim a new sureness of identity for women, or with the idea of always conscious and deliberate political decision-making and control. (Rose 1983: 19)

The fundamental idea of psychoanalysis – the existence of the unconscious – was too easily assimilated to existing ideas of femininity as a state of diminished responsibility for psychoanalysis to be the progressive force that early feminists had hoped for. Elaine Showalter notes that

> Freudian ideas became immediately popular with the literary avant-garde after the war. 'All literary London discovered Freud', the novelist Bryher (Winifred Allerman) recalled; 'the theories were the great subject of conversation wherever one went at that date' . . . Yet the real effect of these changes was disappointing . . . The postwar period . . . was one of renewed conservatism about sex roles and gender issues. (1987: 196–7)

Throughout the first three decades of the century, therefore, where unconscious desire was recognized in the Brontë lives it was likely to reinforce, rather than dispel, the cruder nineteenth-century analysis of the Brontë sisters as women who wrote because they lacked 'normal' satisfactions. Some writers invoked the unconscious as vindication of the eccentric behaviour of social victims; others as evidence of a shameful or derisory failing.

It is not always clear whether Rosamond Langbridge's highly coloured *Psychological Study* of Charlotte Brontë (1929) is meant as vindication or accusation. Langbridge complains that biographers adopt an 'attitude of adoration' based on a mistaken evaluation of martyrdom:

> there are two kinds of self-sacrifice: the first . . . deliberately embraced as something imperatively needful for the general good; the second placidly incurred through morbid inability for criticism or self-protection. The large community of martyred mothers, wives and daughters come second under this head, and to this band of compulsory saints Charlotte belonged. (3–5)

By such words as 'placidly' and 'morbid', Langbridge betrays her impatience that Charlotte failed to rebel against 'filial piety, that stagnant blight on character and judgment which mildewed the Victorian era . . . Every agony she endured may be traced back directly to . . . her revered Papa' (5). Langbridge is no scholar, and repeats, together with a great many other errors, all the most sensational stories about Patrick Brontë's misogyny, but it is difficult to tell whether she applauds or deplores the use of Brontë history to excuse the sisters' behaviour: 'What a feast of exploration for the modern psycho-analyst is here in these harrowing records of suppressed and crippled childhood!' (27). Despite assertions that various temperamental qualities were 'in their blood' (e.g. 40), however, Langbridge does accept the theory of repression:

I am sure that the three Brontës longed, in the sultry little closets of their corseted Victorian hearts for lovers, passionate, vehement, dark and brooding as their own Yorkshire moors.

But . . . in those days of 'Papa, potatoes, prunes and prisms' young ladies learned to close their lips upon the subject of 'such things'. 'Such things' were not to be breathed or hinted at, unless Passion came, top-hat-in-hand, to the front door, wearing the mask of tepid Respect, or of depressed 'esteem'. (84–5)

Her conclusion, moreover, is sympathetic; Charlotte's life

was only too easily summed up: *Charlotte had nothing that she wanted in her life* . . . The result was, that Charlotte Brontë, born witty, independent, gay, was gradually changed from a bright moth into that dull grub, the well-meaning woman . . . The whole secret of Charlotte Brontë's miseries, her sicknesses of mind, her sicknesses of body, the sickness of her Fate, is that she was suffering from *suppressed Personality*. (254)

As this last phrase shows, Langbridge does not understand psychoanalytic terminology, and her book is an ill-informed and opinionated muddle; it does, however, represent the mixture of exasperation and fascination with the Brontës which was characteristic of the interwar period. Although more sophisticated writers were becoming impatient with the Brontë cult, moreover, it persisted. A poem reproduced in *Brontë Society Transactions* for 1946, for instance, reads as follows:

With book in hand – fade out, dividing years! –
I live your life, I share your hopes and fears,
And feel myself grow cold in a warm room
When your white corpse is lowered to the tomb. (Mair 1946: 39)

Brontë ghosts conjured and confronted, 1855–1946

Titles of other pseudo-biographical writings suggest that writers of this period were struggling to come to terms with figures who were admirable without being exemplary in modern terms. A Brontë play from *c*.1926 was called *The Tragic Race* (Linton [1926]), and the *Radio Times* in 1930 carried a feature entitled 'The three demon-haunted sisters' (25 July). The purchase of the parsonage by the Brontë Society in 1927 and its subsequent opening as a museum stimulated interest in the physical circumstances of the Brontë lives, which became a metaphor for their emotional confinement. Some of these works had titles suggesting repression, such as *Three Virgins of Haworth* (Romieu 1930), *The Parson's Children* (Sheridan 1933) and *The Brontës of Haworth Parsonage* (Davison 1934). E. and G. Romieu's *The Brontë Sisters* (1931) tells us that 'no sufferings can compare with the slow expiration of those disheartened hours in which hands are folded inert and the contracted knees press together against unappeased desire' (Romieu 1931: 20–1). E. T. Cook's *They Lived: A Brontë Novel*, published in 1935, presents Charlotte as starving for love of M. Heger, but also gives her all the most feminist speeches from *Jane Eyre* and *Shirley*, and shows her calling 'hysterically' for a 'way out' of her feminine trap (78, 85). It was the contrast between inner fire and outward ice which fascinated writers, and by contrast during the same period there were plays and biographies with titles drawn from the wild Yorkshire setting as metaphor for wild emotions: *Storm-Wrack* (Mackereth 1927); *Wild Decembers* (Dane 1932); *Empurpled Moors* (Firkins 1932); *Moor Born* (Totteroh 1934); and *Stone Walls* (Moorhouse 1936).

This topographical imagery has a long history in relation to the Brontë lives. In 1942 it contributes to Edith Sitwell's page-long account of Emily Brontë in *English Women*: 'The life of this woman of genius is like that of the wind and rain, knowing no incidents and but few landmarks . . . She was not a creature of this warm human life, her home was not built with hands.' (35–6) Already in the year of Charlotte Brontë's death, however, Matthew Arnold had written his elegy, 'Haworth Parsonage' (1855), placing the Brontë sisters in the Romantic tradition which was their primary source. Ending with a calm, restorative picture of the moors in summer, Arnold adds, as if involuntarily, an epilogue in which the angry Muse disdains his easy conclusion and reinstates the real weather of the Yorkshire moors:

> Stormy, through driving mist,
> Loom the blurred hills; the rain
> Lashes the newly-made grave,
> Unquiet souls!
> – In the dark fermentation of earth,
> In the never idle workshop of nature,
> In the eternal movement,
> Ye shall find yourselves again. (ll. 131–8)

Harriet Spofford, writing in 1897, continues this tradition:

> On wintry driving of the sleet,
> Between those graves whose furrows meet,
> She sees a yearning face and sweet.
> All night she hears the great winds blow,
> And sees the wild, white, whirling snow
> Sweep up the black vault of the sky,
> And sees a shadow fleeting by
> That treads the storm with royal feet, –
> There are two ghosts upon the sleet. (40)

In a lecture delivered in 1905, Henry James expresses extreme irritation with the confusion of 'life' and 'works' which followed Arnold's elegy and Gaskell's *Life of Charlotte Brontë* (1857), revived by Mary Robinson's *Emily Brontë* (1883) and reaching a peak with Clement Shorter's *Charlotte Brontë and her Circle* (1896) and the foundation of the Brontë Society in 1893. *Jane Eyre* and *Wuthering Heights* were, James argues,

> stories of a lively interest, [but] the medium from which they sprang was above all itself a story, such a story as has fairly elbowed out the rights of appreciation, as has come at last to impose itself as an expression of the power concerned. The personal

e three sisters, of the two in particular, has been marked, in short, with
accent that this accent has become for us the very tone of their united
1. It covers and supplants their matter, their spirit, their style, their talent,
e; it embodies, really, the most complete intellectual muddle, if the term be
ravagant, ever achieved, on a literary question, by our wonderful public. The
on has scarce indeed been accepted as belonging to literature at all. Literature
is an objective, a projected result; it is life that is the unconscious, the agitated, the
struggling, floundering cause. But the fashion has been in looking at the Brontës, so
to confound the cause with the result that we cease to know, in the present [sic] of
such ecstasies, what we have hold of or what we are talking about. They represent,
the ecstasies, the high-water mark of sentimental judgment. (quoted in Petersen
1971: 919)

James's position depends on his assumption that the literary text can and should be
separated from the context of its reception. The purpose of this present study,
however, is precisely to situate texts '*in history*', a process which, in Peter
Widdowson's words, 'implies . . . a displacement of the apparently neutral
"primary" material from the central focus in favour of the constitutive social
discourses which make it available in a determinate form as a present cultural fact'
(1989: 15). One such 'social discourse' was the rise of English studies, described
in Chris Baldick's book, *The Social Mission of English Criticism* (1987b). From Arnold
to Leavis, Baldick argues, the process which James perceives as a 'muddle' can be
traced to social determinants. After the First World War in particular, the 'ecstatic'
apotheosis of writers such as Shakespeare and Wordsworth can be seen as part of
a more or less systematic attempt to repair the damage done to national morale by
stressing the 'national heritage'. George Gordon, an early professor of English
literature at Oxford, ironically summarized a growing body of feeling to the effect
that 'England is sick, and . . . English literature must save it. The Churches . . .
having failed, and social remedies being slow, English literature [must] . . . save our
souls and heal the State'. Terry Eagleton comments: 'as religion progressively
ceases to provide the . . . basic mythologies by which a socially turbulent class-
society can be welded together, "English" is constructed as a subject to carry this
ideological burden . . . ' (Eagleton 1983: 23). In the troubled inter-war years British
educators believed that the study of English literature could encourage 'humane
values' which would transcend 'narrow' class sympathies; Peter Widdowson's book,
Hardy in History, demonstrates in detail how this process involved not just reading
literary texts, but producing a literary icon in the figure of 'Hardy the novelist'
(1989: 6). How successfully this was achieved with the Brontë sisters is illustrated
by James Hilton's novel, *Lost Horizon* (1933), in which an aged lama in Shangri-
La, the mythical Tibetan land of eternal youth, is writing a book about the Brontës.
After long meditation he has discovered that 'the really big moment in his entire
life occurred when he was a young man visiting a house in which there lived an old
parson and his three daughters' (quoted in Cunliffe 1950: 332).

J. A. Mackereth's poem *Storm-Wrack: A Night with the Brontës* (1927) also clearly
aims to place the Brontës in a position of inspiring transcendence. Since Baldick

sees the rise of English studies as beginning with Matthew Arnold, it is appropriate that Mackereth appears to take his theme from Arnold's 'Haworth Parsonage'. Mackereth, however, maintains the intense nature-imagery of Arnold's 'Epilogue' for twenty-seven pages, elevating Branwell's suffering to a Christ-like passion, and Emily's devotion to him into 'a challenge to Eternity' (27). The story of *Storm-Wrack* is very slight; Patrick, Charlotte, Emily and Anne sit waiting for Branwell to come home from the Black Bull; eventually Emily goes out in the storm to bring him back. The elevated language, however, in which the physical storm functions as metaphor for mental distress, aims to raise this trivial event to epic status:

> In that grim life-prisoning shell,
>   Fevered of heart and brain,
> Mortals, tossed betwixt heaven and hell,
> Leap to the flame-flash, starkly plain,
> And into the blackness plunge again
>   Shudderingly, and, tortured, tell
>   Their pain to ease their pain. (3)

Emily in particular is presented as 'one with the storm-stress . . . Storm, to the storm she is gone – ' (3):

> Captive, and rebel, meekly great,
> Spurning the terms of fate,
> Waiting, watching, hounded there,
> With senses straining, with tortured hair,
> Flashes to sight by the flame-struck stone
>   Emily Brontë, flesh and bone. (8)

She is also, however, presented as motivated by an intense affinity with Branwell:

> Softly the angel-guardian word,
> Childhood's closest fondest word,
> Flies toward his lips like a spirit-bird:
>   *Em – i – ly !* –
> Echo of innocence, plaintive and wild,
> Innocence – gone with the dreams of the child:
> 'Tis the sob of a soul, by flesh unheard . . .
> Was it a wraith on the howling moor
>   That *Branwell! Branwell!* cried?
> Pitying, passionate, startling shame,
> Was it a sister called his name,
>   Called like an angel-bride? (12)

Eventually,

> She with frail enfolding arm
> Shields that torn Brother-soul from harm . . .
> Sister-heart, mother-heart, tenderer than God!
>   Closer than God! (27)

While recognizing Emily Brontë's religious unorthodoxy, Mackereth invokes orthodox terminology of crucifixion and redemption. Similarly, while celebrating her as 'rebelliously innocent' (27), he manages to recoup her into a maenadic version of the angel in the house. While Mackereth's verse is technically accurate and inventive, its atmosphere of unrelieved anguish makes me sympathize with Flora Poste in *Cold Comfort Farm*, who

> felt as though she were at one of Eugène O'Neill's plays; that kind that goes on for hours and hours and hours, until the R.S.P.C. Audiences batters the doors of the theatre in and insists on a tea interval. (Gibbons [1932] 1978: 178)

Clemence Dane's play, *Wild Decembers* (1932), occupies an uneasy position in this tradition. A detailed biographical play, it covers the Brontë lives from the death of Aunt Branwell to the death of Charlotte, with scenes from *Villette* providing an account of Charlotte's relationship with M. Heger. The dominant strand of the play, however, is the relationship between Branwell and Emily. As in E. T. Cook's later novel, *They Lived* (1935), Branwell is shown as having conceived the idea for *Wuthering Heights* but as unable to carry it out (see Morgan 1932: 66 for the sources of this idea). It is because Emily sees herself as having 'taken it on' for him, that she is so fiercely resistant to her own name being associated with the novel (Cook 1935: 71). The picture of Emily presented by this play is a strong one, and she and Branwell are shown inhabiting a world very like that of *Wuthering Heights*, in which love and cruelty are close together and life is lived at extremes. Nevertheless the real authorship of *Wuthering Heights* is transferred from Emily to Branwell. Clemence Dane was the pen-name of Winifred Ashton, a novelist and playwright who was active in the Society of Women Journalists and whose essays, in *The Woman's Side* (1926), establish her as a feminist. It is at first puzzling why such a writer should have chosen to give such prominence to Branwell, but there is perhaps a clue in Clemence Dane's first novel, *The Regiment of Women* (1917). If we accept Eagleton's argument that in the early years of the century 'English' was in the process of taking over the ideological burden previously carried by religion, then it follows that an unexpected responsibility is suddenly perceived as being in the hands of the previously undervalued teachers of English, many of whom were women. *The Regiment of Women* deals intensively with two such teachers and one of their pupils in a girls' school. Clare Hartill, who cares primarily about power, first feeds her young pupil's omnivorous hunger for literature and then confirms her religious doubts in the process of weaning her from another teacher's influence. Contemplating her handiwork, she reflects:

> After all, for an insignificant spinster, she had a fair share of power – real power – not the mere authority of kings and policemen. Her mind, not her office, ruled a hundred other minds, and in one heart, at least, a shrug of her shoulders had toppled God off His throne; and the vacant seat was hers, to fill or flout as she chose. (Dane [1917] 1927: 97)

In *Storm-Wrack*, Emily Brontë takes the place of bride, sister, mother, becoming for Branwell 'closer than God'; just so Clare Hartill takes the place of God by abusing her pupil's tendency to associate her teacher with her mother (47). The power of women is uniquely entwined with childhood needs, and it is perhaps fear that the icons of female power would be used unscrupulously which reduces Clemence Dane's Emily from a toweringly independent producer to a kindly helpmeet. Her hint, however, fell on fruitful soil. By 1948, the dust-jacket to Martyn Richards' play, *Branwell* announces:

> Although 'Wuthering Heights' is attributed to Emily Brontë, it is considered by the author of this play and others that it was really the work of Branwell Brontë. This play is written with a view to doing him tardy justice. (Richards, M. 1948; see also Purchase 1937)

Whether or not Branwell was attributed with the authorship of *Wuthering Heights*, writers began to see him as a crucial factor in the lives of his sisters. Dan Totheroh's play *Moor Born* (1934) deals with the 'ironical sacrifice made by the three talented sisters . . . for their dissolute brother, Branwell' (jacket blurb). Kathryn MacFarlane's 'life' of Emily Brontë, *Divide the Desolation* (1936) intensifies the myth of this 'brilliant, tempestuous family' by differentiating sharply (and unwarrantably) between the sisters, writing of

> Charlotte, whose conventional tastes and preference for writing about pretty-pretty heroines (who never spoke or acted 'coarsely') resulted in *Jane Eyre*; of Emily's love and understanding of diffident, mouselike sister Ann [sic]; of her adoration of the one who did most for her, meteoric brother Branwell. (MacFarlane 1936: jacket blurb)

The tradition of Emily's devotion reached its height with the Warner Brothers' film, *Devotion* (1946) in which 'much of the drama of the film story turns [round] Branwell Brontë' and the sisters are sanctified by their devotion to him and to one another (*Yorkshire Post* 20.1.1943). *Devotion*, written by James Hilton, the author of *Lost Horizon* (1933), was described in *Brontë Society Transactions* as a 'vulgar distortion of the life story of the Haworth immortals' which embroiders Emily's self-sacrifice as follows:

> Emily (played by Ida Lupino) is passionately in love with the Reverend A. B. Nicholls (Paul Henreid), a 'Boyaresque' clergyman, but he is in love with Charlotte (Olivia de Havilland), and so, out of devotion to her sister, Emily leaves the way clear for the lovers by going into a decline, while the celestial choir bursts into song and the ghostly 'Dark Horseman' from 'Wuthering Heights' puts in an appearance. (no author; *BST* 16.56.38–9 (1946) 38; the 'dark horseman' is, of course, apocryphal)

As Emily dies, she tells Charlotte that 'loving is the only thing that really matters', and the film ends with Charlotte, hand in hand with Mr Nicholls, whispering 'You were right, dear Emily . . . I have found the meaning now . . .' (Mannon 1946: 84, 86). Charlotte Brontë's 'hunger, rage and rebellion' begins to be seen as the 'natural' desire of a woman for a husband.

Both Charlotte and Emily were thus ambiguously transmitted into the 1930s; Charlotte as both feminist heroine and dutiful daughter, and Emily as martyr both of *fin-de-siècle* feminist renunciation and of post-war sisterly devotion. The combined prominence and ambiguity of the Brontë inheritance meant that coming to terms with the Brontës, like killing the Angel in the House, 'was part of the occupation of a woman writer' (Woolf 1979: 60). We have seen that many women novelists of the nineteenth century, such as Elizabeth Gaskell, Margaret Oliphant, Augusta Ward and Edith Nesbit, also wrote critical or biographical commentaries on the Brontës. The same is true in the early twentieth century of Edith Sitwell, May Sinclair, Virginia Woolf, Alice Meynell, Rachel Ferguson, Rebecca West, E. M. Delafield, Elizabeth Goudge, Phyllis Bentley, and Elizabeth von Arnim – and their interest in the Brontë texts reflects contemporary debates about femininity.

As early as 1867 Bret Harte had got tired of the cult of Charlotte Brontë, producing a tale which Sandra Gilbert and Susan Gubar describe as

> a parody of *Jane Eyre* that the American humorist reinterprets as a muddled and melodramatic farce in which the smugly virtuous heroine leaves her childhood home at 'Minerva Cottage' forever to enter the service (and the arms) of 'Mr Rawjester', the polygamous master of 'Blunderbore Hall', who bears a 'remarkable likeness to a gorilla'. (Gilbert and Gubar 1988: 211)

Emily Dickinson, on the other hand, 'celebrated the achievements of such foremothers as . . . Charlotte Brontë with a kind of ecstasy' (211 – The relevant poems are Dickinson 1955: Nos 312, 593 and 1562). A poem written in 1883 reads:

> Her losses make our Gains ashamed –
> She bore Life's empty Pack
> As gallantly as if the East
> Were swinging at her Back.
> Life's empty Pack is heaviest,
> As every Porter knows –
> In vain to punish Honey –
> It only sweeter grows. (No. 1562)

The very first piece of work that Virginia Woolf had accepted for publication was entitled, 'Haworth. November 1904'. It describes a pilgrimage to the parsonage whose pleasure 'had in it an element of suspense that was really painful, as though we were to meet some long-separated friend' (Woolf 1979: 122). But, Gilbert and Gubar argue,

> the existence of a series of autonomous authorial mothers inspired feelings of intense ambivalence in turn-of-the-century, modernist, and contemporary women writers. On the one hand . . . female artists, looking for literary mothers and grandmothers . . ., have been delighted to recover the writings of their ancestresses. On the other hand, we are now convinced that female artists, looking at and recovering such precursors, are also haunted and daunted by the autonomy of these figures. In fact, we suspect that the love women writers send forward into the past is, in patriarchal culture, inexorably contaminated by mingled feelings of rivalry and anxiety . . . the autonomy of the mother is frequently as terrifying as it is attractive, for – as Woolf's comments about Charlotte Brontë suggest – it has been won at great cost. (1988: I 144)

Twenty years after 'Haworth. November 1904', Woolf wrote an essay called 'Indiscretions: "Never seek to tell thy love, love that never told can be" – but one's feelings for some writers outrun all prudence'. Here she further examines her excitement at approaching the women writers of the past:

> inevitably, we come to the harem, and tremble slightly as we approach the curtain and catch glimpses of women behind it and even hear ripples of laughter and snatches of conversation. Some obscurity still veils the relations of women to each other. A hundred years ago it was simple enough; they were stars who shone only in male sunshine; deprived of it, they languished into nonentity – sniffed, bickered, envied each other – so men said.

But, Woolf goes on, in what seems a deliberate critique of Freud's theory of penis envy,

> it is by no means certain that every woman is inspired by pure envy when she reads what another has written. More probably Emily Brontë was a passion of her youth; Charlotte even she loved with nervous affection; and cherished a quiet sisterly regard for Anne . . . (Woolf 1979: 75–6)

Gilbert and Gubar point out that Woolf's strategy here is to 'transform[] her precursors first into characters, then into ancestresses'; Gaskell appears as a maternal figure and George Eliot as an Aunt (1988: I 197–8).

Even among women writers who celebrate a female tradition, however, the figures of the past are not unproblematic. The American poet Harriet Spofford, who 'treats the domestic novel as an organ of sisterhood', believing that '"the proper study of womankind is woman"' (Blain *et al.* 1990: 1017), can still conceive of the lure of lost sisterhood denying life to those who remain:

> What memories nestling in her heart
> With wild, sweet wings of longing start!
> The things they touched – with awful art –
> The clock's dull tick, the walls, the doors,
> The very shadows on the floors,
> The old smiles, wake an aching fret.
> Barbed with the poison of regret
> Each moment gives a keener smart, –
> There are two ghosts within her heart!
> There are two ghosts upon the stair.
> Long since Fame spread his splendid snare;
> Love came and camped about her there.
> Oh, love was sweet, and life was dear, –
> But, hark! those voices, strong and clear,
> They wail, they call, she must not stay –
> Out to the open, and away!
> Oh, love past death and death's despair,
> There are three ghosts upon the stair! (Spofford 1897: 42)

It is this lure which Rachel Ferguson addresses in her novel, *The Brontës Went to*

Woolworth's (1931). Like Woolf, she eventually adopts the strategy of making her Victorian ghosts into part of the family, yet the first sentence of this brittle, whimsical book announces its distrust of family sagas:

> How I loathe that kind of novel which is about a lot of sisters. It is usually called *They Were Seven*, or *Three – Not Out*, and one spends one's entire time trying to sort them all, and muttering, 'Was it Isobel who drank, or Gertie? . . . (Ferguson [1931] 1988: 3)

Deirdre Carne, however, is very much ensconced in her family, which consists of two sisters (one a child), her mother and her young sister's governess. They have various peculiarities, including believing in ghosts and nature spirits (e.g. 21), but the most significant is their compulsive habit of 'making out' – constructing stories about people who may have passed through the margins of their lives, but whom they endow with a rich particularity of existence. Deirdre is a voracious reader but takes down *Jane Eyre* only in a fit of depression, since 'the only possible book for these occasions' is one 'about people whose spirits were even "lower" than mine' (42). When, shortly afterwards, they spend a holiday in Yorkshire, and pass the time in 'table-turning', it does not occur to any of them that the 'Charlotte, Anne and Elizabeth' who contact them, and the 'red-haired boy [who] was frightfully squiffed again' (71) might be Brontë ghosts. Nevertheless they take fright at the spirits' threat to carry Sheil, the youngest daughter, 'back in time', and decamp to London. Lord and Lady Toddington, who begin as part of their fantasy and become real friends, are similarly unimpressed with the Brontë books, and look forward to having 'good times' with the Carne girls, 'not all Brontës and highbrowism' (166). When Lady Toddington says she's 'bored stiff' with Gaskell's *Life*, her husband calls her 'a very plucky woman to admit it. Confound the Brontës!' (167).

Ferguson's emphasis is on the possibility – the necessity in fact – of later control over figures of the past. Two years later, she published a play called *Charlotte Brontë* (1933), with a prologue in present time set in the Brontë Parsonage Museum (the Brontë Society had purchased the parsonage in 1927) which dramatizes some of the prevailing positions about the Brontë cult. The Englishwoman and her daughter are bored and anxious for their lunch (1933: 13); the American is very well informed but over-inclined to reverence: his 'heart swells' as he stands 'right where . . .', and his 'blood boil[s]' to 'picture those motherless kiddies . . .' (15–16, 20–21). Ferguson, however, reveals her own biases through the clergyman: Emily 'was a force of nature . . . Too big for human loves' (22). The prologue ends with the debate raised by May Sinclair, about whether Charlotte 'worshipped Heger's brain', as the clergyman thinks, or 'was in love with him', as the English girl thinks. The last words of the prologue emphasize the plasticity of this material: 'we shall never know now. We shall never know . . .' (23). So the play proceeds to give us one more version.

It is notable that the Carne family, in *The Brontës Went to Woolworth's*, is like a latterday Brontë family without its male members, since in Ferguson's *Charlotte Brontë*, Branwell is a male chauvinist boor and Patrick an arbitrary tyrant. Unlike the selfless sisters in *Storm-Wrack* and *Wild Decembers*, moreover, Ferguson's

Charlotte learns to say, 'One has always been taught that sisters must give way to their brothers. But I see now that this is a false idea, so false that I think, one day, the world will look at the matter very differently' (1933: 47). Ferguson accepts without irony the nature-spirit tradition about Emily; before her death she throws open the window and cries, 'My love! . . . I see. That is your help. You are killing me with your bitter cold. You want me! You long for me! We've never failed each other . . . The moors! The moors!' (66). On the other hand, Ferguson's Emily is impatient with Charlotte's infatuation with M. Heger:

> when I see you, you with your spirit and your brain, transfigured because of a letter: behaving like any whimpering fool of a woman not fit to tie your shoelace . . . Throwing your fineness, your vision and your very personality overboard like any servant girl – faugh! it makes me afraid. (44)

Charlotte, however, tells Mr Nicholls that she doesn't know if she is in love with Heger, and in other ways she is shown to be independent. The timing of Nicholls's proposal is in this play altered so that Charlotte can refuse him until after the success of *Jane Eyre*: 'I couldn't have come to you penniless', she says, 'I don't believe in wives being a drag on their husbands' (59). In the author's note to the play, Ferguson simply attributes this change to 'the purposes of the theatre', but *The Brontës Went to Woolworth's* allows us to see Ferguson as conscious of her, and everyone's, power to reconstruct the past.

In George Moore's *Conversations in Ebury Street* (1924), he meditates writing a story about the scene when Thackeray invited Charlotte Brontë to dinner: he imagines 'a dozen pompous men standing before the fire, their coat-tails lifted, their eyes fixed on the timid girl who had discovered bigamy and written it out all by herself' (226). In Ferguson's play, however, Thackeray sets quite a different tone: 'It seemed as if the Brontë girls were unable to go on living; as if the burden of life, or their own genius, was too heavy' (1933: 73). This Romantic assessment of Emily and Anne, however, is immediately followed by a 'little thing' composed for Miss Brontë by a Miss Chute:

> Sing to us, wildflower of the Northern moor
> Your natural lays we have not heard before . . .
> And oh, believe wherever you may roam
> There is a place for you inside our home
> As honoured guest, and so, whate'er your lot
> Be always welcome with us, dear Miss Charlotte. (74)

The moral of this scene seems to be that the 'authentic presence' of the writer provides no defence against the reader's reception; Moore's Thackeray is not Ferguson's and Ferguson's Thackeray and Miss Chute each construct their own Charlotte Brontë even in her presence.

Similarly, Ferguson's apparently whimsical novel shows intertextuality not as an academic concept but as a battlefield where writing subjects struggle for control. Deirdre Carne, the first-person narrator, is a bright young thing who, like Ferguson herself, earns her living as a journalist (the original title page attributed the novel to '"Rachel" of Punch'). She seems to have achieved *Jane Eyre*'s dream of reaching 'the busy world, towns, regions full of life' (*JE* 114). Yet she and her sisters, like many Victorian women, 'live[] with visions . . . instead of men and women' (Browning 1850). Their fantasy life is much more 'real' than the office she never describes. Virginia Woolf describes women of this period as historically 'on the bridge' between the private house of the past and the public world of the future. It is not a comfortable position 'between the devil and the deep sea' ([1938] 1977: 86). For the Carne sisters, the Brontës represent 'the devil' which they must and cannot escape. Judith Kegan Gardiner argues that 'twentieth-century women writers . . . often . . . communicate a consciousness of their identity through paradoxes of sameness and difference' (1981: 354), and *The Brontës Went to Woolworth's* is paradoxical in this way; the Carne sisters copy the Brontë sisters by inventing 'a tale that was never ended' (*JE* 114), but they also fear them as spinsters whose lives were ruled by love. It is, perhaps, significant that Deirdre is named after the Irish heroine who learns through her storytelling nurse of the tragic love in store for her. (Yeats's *Deirdre* (1907) and Synge's *Deirdre of the Sorrows* (1910) were published soon before Deirdre Carne's putative birth.) It is the modern women's fear of regression to lives ruled by hopeless desire which allows the Brontës to figure as spectres in a text which also mirrors their fantasy lives; they threaten to occupy the position which, in more recent women's fiction, is taken by a 'bad mother'. Gardiner argues that 'the mother-villain is so frightening because she is what the daughter fears to become' (1981: 356 n. 18). In intertextual terms, the Carne sisters fear being 'characters' in a story in which the 'bad mother' is their 'author'.

Sheil's governess, Miss Martin, although she writes love-letters to herself and generally suffers from 'repression' (158), tries to wean her away from what seems to her their irresponsible communal fantasizing. At this crisis, the house is visited by Charlotte and Emily Brontë; the elder Carnes return home to find the house 'simply humming with alien personalities' (191) and Miss Martin gone. Miss Martin, it seems, has gone to join a charitable settlement to help a curate called Arthur, to whom she is privately devoted. 'How had one found the courage to do it?' she asks herself (198); the implication is that it came from the hour when, Sheil tells us, 'the spectacles one [Charlotte] went into Miss Martin's bedroom and they talked' (194). Lord Toddington, when Deirdre tells him this story, speculates that the Brontë sisters were 'drawn to you, as a family, by a happiness they never had themselves' (211). In Ferguson's play, *Charlotte Brontë*, the clergyman points out that we never hear of the Brontës giving or receiving Christmas presents or 'having a little tree' (1933: 21). *The Brontës Went to Woolworth's*, however, ends with a family Christmas during which the Toddingtons receive presents from Charlotte and Emily. Lady Toddington completes their domestication by reporting that she has seen them in Woolworth's; what they bought there becomes matter for communal speculation.

The Carnes' solution to the Brontë threat is thus simply to '*bag*' them' (Ferguson [1931] 1988: 213). The Brontës become part of their fantasy lives. Lady Toddington announces that 'Emily's writing a new book called *Swithering Depths*'

(230). The Brontë 'visitations', however, also suggest that the Carnes' fear has been based on a misunderstanding of the Brontë lives; their practical impact on the family is quite positive. Already, in Yorkshire, Deirdre had discovered Charlotte's annotations on her rejected novel; now these acerbic comments give her the courage to 'rend [it] in twain' (246). In the play, Ferguson shows Charlotte herself as part of an intertextual chain, being strengthened during her death scene by discovering 'No Coward Soul is Mine' (86). *The Brontës Went to Woolworth's* shows its modern characters as continuing this chain, in which dead sisters can give us the strength to do the things which may not be ideal, but are just within our reach. Charlotte need not die feeling herself a coward; Miss Martin can seek a new servitude; Deirdre can write a better novel. The Carne sisters' fantasies are thus more vital in gaining control over their lives than the work they do in the 'busy world'. Refusing the Brontës as authors, they use them in ways dictated by their own necessities. The Brontës go to Woolworth's because only in that way can the Carne sisters be authors of their own lives.

As with *The Three Brontës* and *The Three Sisters*, Ferguson shows a less critical attitude to the Brontës in her biographical play than in her fiction; but the prologue to her play is decidedly irreverent. The Englishwoman is sure that the Brontës would have 'spoiled' Christmas by 'some matter-of-fact remark' or 'some brainstorm. Oh! what a relief it is . . . to admit that Charlotte was sometimes enraging!' (1933: 21). This need to 'debunk' the myth can be seen in several very amusing efforts to confront Victorian ghosts in the 1930s. One wonders whether Ferguson, who wrote for *Punch*, had a hand in the full-page doggerel cartoon by F[rancis] B[ickley] which appeared in that journal on Christmas Day, 1935. Like Mackereth's *Storm-Wrack*, the drawing shows 'five chairs drawn round . . . And one that is vacant speaks/ Of a lad who knows what wild hearts know,/ Who seeks what the sick heart seeks' (Mackereth 1927: 3). Bickley's version, however, gives us the 'matter-of-fact remark' and the 'brainstorm' rather than the epic strain:

Emily:	Pleasure? What is it? Man is born to grief.
Mr Brontë:	This bird is very tough. Is there no beef?
Charlotte:	No Sir; I thought the turkey would suffice.
	Anne, eat a little: really, it is nice.
Anne:	I cannot eat when Branwell is not here.
Mr Brontë:	Name not that name, I say; but pass the beer.
	[Anne bursts into tears.
Emily:	Tears, idle tears, I know not what they mean.
Charlotte:	You would not. I could weep the might-have-been.
Emily:	She broods on Brussels.
Mr Brontë:	Emily, the sprouts.
Anne:	And Branwell roistering with village louts.
Emily:	Seeking oblivion. Would that I were he –
	Free as the wind is and the moors are free,
	Not cribbed and cabined in this narrow room,
	My cradle and my prison and my tomb.
	[She totters to the window and draws back the curtain.

	Listen! The birds of night are on the wing!
Anne:	How she goes on!
Charlotte:	She is but wuthering.
Anne:	Charlotte, I sometimes wish we had a mother,
	For then perhaps our sister would not wuther.
	(B[ickley] 1935)

Like Ferguson, Bickley holds Patrick responsible for the sisters' misery. When he leaves the table, they respond in counterpoint:

Anne:	He's gone.
Emily:	Thank God!
Charlotte:	His dinner barely tasted.
	Just like our lives – hard, underdone and wasted.

Where Mackereth shows Emily as 'meekly great' (1927: 8), and Clemence Dane shows her responding to Branwell's despair over finishing *Wuthering Heights* with 'I'd help you, Branwell' (Dane 1932: 51), Bickley shows Branwell having stolen 'No Coward Soul is Mine':

Emily:	That is not yours!
Branwell:	Of course it is.
Emily:	You swine!
	You stole it from me – liar, drunkard, thief!
Branwell:	My dear, your language staggers all belief.
	[Emily swoops upon him and cuffs him violently several times.
Emily:	Take that, you brute, and that, and that, and that!
	[She rushes from the room. Anne dissolves in renewed tears.
	Branwell subsides into a chair and goes to sleep.
Charlotte:	I somehow felt this party might fall flat.

In 1931 Emilie and Georges Romieu had published *The Brontë Sisters*, a joint biography which represents the sisters as having desires which

> exceed human realizations. The waiting lips will never receive the charity of one kiss. No lover will spring to their side or will press them against a heart that beats only for them. Their arms embrace only the void, and no form emerges for them to press frenziedly to their ripening breasts . . .
> Blessed misery!
> Deep within life will burn with an unexampled heat – unappeased. The white page is the needful outlet; thereupon in words of flame they will write an immortal utterance! (Romieu 1931: 10)

Emily is singled out as the lonely genius who courts the storm,

> bareheaded, her brow affronting the bite of the wind and the gash of the hail . . .
> When the farm people glimpse the weird form in the distance, they rush in and lock their doors and fold trembling hands in prayer. (11)

It was in response to this kind of romantic excess that Stella Gibbons wrote *Cold Comfort Farm* (1932). Set 'in the near future', it is the story of Flora Poste, who, like the heroines of Gothic romances and Victorian domestic novels, is left orphaned and not-quite-penniless (but 'a hundred pounds a year won't even keep you in stockings . . .' ([1932] 1978: 15)) at the age of nineteen, and goes to live on a remote farm with unsympathetic kin. Unlike her predecessors, however, she is armed with a modern education and a copy of the Abbé Fausse-Maigre's *The Higher Common Sense*. With this help she completely 'sorts out' her tragic cousins; Elfine makes a county marriage ('Flora was pleased to see that the wild-bird-cum-dryad atmosphere which hung over Elfine like a pestilential vapour was wearing thin' (127)); Cousin Seth (a latterday Heathcliff) goes off to be a Hollywood film star; Cousin Judith, who is in the habit of referring to herself as a 'Used Gourd', is given a course of psychoanalysis which transfers her obsessions to 'something harmless' like 'olt churches' (201–2); Cousin Amos, the hell-fire preacher, goes on a gospel tour of America; and Aunt Ada Doom, who never recovered from seeing something nasty in the woodshed when she was 'very small' (113), departs in a black leather flying suit to spend a comfortable old age in Continental hotels (221–2). Flora, who is of a generation to be '*miserable* if you haven't got a job, when all your friends have' (15), nevertheless ends the novel by flying into a moonlight night with Charles, 'unutterably moved' by mutual declarations of love.

Like Rachel Ferguson, Stella Gibbons was a professional journalist, and her wildly funny book has a self-consciously literary frame of reference. In the foreword, Gibbons contrasts herself, tutored in the 'meaningless and vulgar bustle of newspaper offices' (a phrase repeated four times in two pages, so that one suspects some private reference), with her dedicatee, Tony Pookworthy, whose books are 'records of intense spiritual struggles, staged in the wild setting of mere, berg or fen'. One wonders if she had in mind the twenty-seven pages of *Storm-Wrack* (dealing with a journey of perhaps a hundred yards to bring home the drunken Branwell), when she congratulates Pookworthy because 'you can paint everyday domestic tragedies (are not the entire first hundred pages of *The Fulfilment of Martin Hoare* a masterly analysis of a bilious attack?) as vividly as you paint soul cataclysms' (8). 'Purple passages' in *Cold Comfort Farm*, marked on the Baedeker model with one, two or three stars, recall Mary Webb (32–3) or D. H. Lawrence (36), but the literary figure within the novel is a Mr Mybug (properly Meyerburg), whose response to nature is decidedly Freudian ('God! those rhododendron buds had a phallic, urgent look!' (121)). According to the publican's wife, Mr Mybug (like Edward Purchase, Martyn Richards and Clemence Dane) is writing about a

'young fellow who wrote books, and then his sisters pretended *they* wrote them, and then they all died of consumption, poor young mommets'.

'Ha! A life of Branwell Brontë', thought Flora. 'I might have known it. There has been increasing discontent among the male intellectuals for some time at the thought that a woman wrote *Wuthering Heights*. I thought one of them would produce something of this kind, sooner or later. Well, I must just avoid him, that's all.' (75–6)

Unfortunately it proves not so easy to avoid Mr Mybug, and we eventually come in for the whole story of how Branwell 'secretly . . . worked twelve hours a day writing

Shirley and *Villette* – and, of course, *Wuthering Heights*' – in order to finance his sisters' drink dependency (102). Flora reflects that

> one of the disadvantages of almost universal education was the fact that all kinds of persons acquired a familiarity with one's favourite writers. It gave one a curious feeling; it was like seeing a drunken stranger wrapped in one's dressing-gown. (105)

There is ample evidence of this rude familiarity during the 1930s. Modern young people resisted the lure of the Brontës, seeing them perhaps as eminent Victorians, outdated and either dangerous or uninteresting. In a novel by Margaret Flowerdew called *The Lonely Road* (1933), someone points out that they are travelling through 'the Brontë country . . . It was here that Charlotte Brontë wrote her famous books'. After a paragraph of description, '"Oh, really", said Alison, rummaging violently in her leather handbag. "Aubrey – where *is* my powder-puff? How very interesting – about the Brontë person, I mean"' (32). There is no further Brontë reference.

Note

1. This formulation derives from Freud's essay, 'Femininity', which appeared in 1933, but his 'Three contributions to a theory of sexuality' was translated into English in 1910.

Chapter 4

The inter-war period

Jane Eyre *between private and public worlds, 1921–38*

Almost all of Chapter 3 was concerned not with the Brontës' famous texts but with the Brontës themselves. It has seemed necessary to plot the various ways in which the authors were reproduced – elevated, domesticated, parodied – because of what Henry James called the 'complete intellectual muddle' which has in the case of the Brontës 'confounded the cause [the lives] with the result [the works]' ([1905]; quoted in Petersen 1971: 919). Throughout this period, however, *Jane Eyre* and *Wuthering Heights* – but particularly *Jane Eyre* – were themselves being 'bagged', especially by inter-war women attempting to come to terms with their new situation.

As Emily's reputation grew among the *avant garde*, *Jane Eyre* maintained its popular interest. Between 1872 and 1946 there were at least ten illustrated editions and several popular and comicbook editions. Silent films were produced in Italy in 1909, 1910, 1915 and 1918, in Hungary in 1920 and in Germany in 1926; at least four silent films were produced in the United States between 1910 and 1921 and sound pictures were made in 1934 and 1944. At least ten different stage versions were produced between 1910 and 1945; the novel was performed on British radio four times between 1930 and 1946, and on television in Britain in 1937 and America in 1939. The culmination of this popularity came in 1944 when Orson Welles appeared as Mr Rochester in a Hollywood film. Ivor Brown's 1936 preface to Helen Jerome's play brackets Charlotte Brontë and Jane Austen as 'writers almost canonised by their faithful. Year after year, decade after decade, they continue to hold the intense devotion of many readers' (Brown 1936: 7), and we may guess that many of these devotees were women. Despite the changes in women's lives during the century since the publication of *Jane Eyre*, this Victorian novel evidently still had some central relevance to the lives of women. By this time most Victorian legal wrongs had been righted. Women even looked different, with short hair and more practical clothes; they were entitled to free state education, were much more likely to undertake paid work and they had the vote. Both legal and social constraints, however, prevented most married women from working, and large numbers of unmarried daughters were still living a life which Winifred Holtby, in 1924, describes as one of desperate vacuity – little different from Florence Nightingale's. Despite apparent improvements in the position of women, therefore, it is clear that the relationship of power between men and women had changed little, so that a novel like *Jane Eyre* which dealt with gender relations in 1847 was still highly relevant in this period.

Some reproducers used it, in fact, to try to recreate a Victorian frame for gender relations. Marjorie Carleton's stage play, produced in America in 1936, is intensely religious, showing Jane repeating the twenty-third Psalm to give her strength to confront Bertha; it also shows her as unconditionally loyal to Mr Rochester (unlike the novel where Jane promises to 'dare censure' if he 'deserved my adherence' (*JE* 215)) – while unable to rise to a crisis, remaining 'half-conscious' throughout Rochester's explanation of his intended bigamy. What Donna Marie Nudd calls 'stand-by-your-man' speeches and scenes of swooning dependence were common in the nineteenth-century melodramas; their persistence in a woman's play on the eve of the Second World War suggests that *Jane Eyre* is playing a curious part in a struggle for the definition of gender roles.

In my introduction, I suggested that the continued interest in *Jane Eyre* might be explained in Freudian terms. The little heroine's desire for the love of the strong hero represents what Freud defines as 'normal' femininity: the process in which women recognize their own inferiority and choose to attach themselves to a powerful male figure modelled on the father (see Freud [1933] 1973). If you read *Jane Eyre* in this way, the figure of the mad wife becomes a warning of what happens to women who are 'abnormal' – 'intemperate and unchaste' in Rochester's description (*JE* 323). Charlotte Brontë's presentation of gendered subject positions is, however, more complicated than this; one reason that the novel continues to fascinate readers, illustrators, playwrights and film-makers is that its meanings are unstable and ambiguous. One clue to this ambiguity lies in Charlotte Brontë's early, unpublished writings, which adopt a masculine point of view and deal with topics which are conventionally regarded as masculine – politics, industrial relations, painting, literary debate (see page 13 above). When Charlotte Brontë's experience in nineteenth-century society convinced her that she could not wield masculine power in the real world, her response was divided. In part she had no choice but to write as Jane Eyre – poor, obscure and dependent – and to take as her goal a strong, masculine lover, thus conforming to what Freud would identify as normal behaviour for a woman. As well as these normal desires, however, Jane shows symptoms of what Freud would have called a masculinity complex; rather than attaching herself to a powerful male, she at least partly wants to wield that power herself. She defends herself against those who mistreat her as a child, and argues that 'when we are struck at without a reason, we should strike back again very hard' (60). She is restless with her calm life as a governess in a country house and longs for more of life and experience than she had there (114). She resents Mr Rochester's attempts to attach her to himself like a possession and imagines herself as a revolutionary liberator of harem slaves (282). At the same time, however, she wants to *be* Mr Rochester, whose experience was 'quickened with all of incident, life, fire, feeling, that [Jane] desired and had not in [her] actual existence' (114).

Mr Rochester is in many ways like the heroes of the early writings, especially

Charlotte's central character, the Duke of Zamorna (see Stoneman 1989). He has freedom of action and movement; he is decisive and authoritative; he has wealth and independence; he has experience of multiple relationships, and retains the right to autonomous action such as his attempt at bigamous marriage. Like Zamorna, Rochester has a fiery horse (Alexander 1983: 182) and his drawing room at Thornfield is crimson, which in the juvenilia represents Zamorna's decadence (Alexander 1983: 238); in II ix, like Zamorna, he is likened to a Sultan with his seraglio (Alexander 1983: 118). Rochester is, however, different from Zamorna in two significant ways as a result of being seen from Jane's point of view. In the first place, Zamorna's military and political power has shrunk to Rochester's management of a country estate and a spirited horse, which represent masculine power in forms most likely to be encountered by nineteenth-century women. Secondly, because Jane is the object and not the subject of Rochester's power, that power appears threatening as well as invigorating: the country house is a place of confinement as well as of safety, and the horse a potential threat – an illustration of 1897 has as a caption Jane's words, 'I was mortally afraid of its trampling fore feet' (*JE* 1897 Townsend: 106).

If Jane Eyre is ambiguous in her response to masculine power, Bertha Mason has been seen as expressing more directly the rage and frustration experienced by a woman who felt herself to be a combination of Lord Byron and the Duke of Wellington, yet who had to live the life of a lady in a country house (e.g. *JE* 1897 Townsend: 273). Sandra Gilbert and Susan Gubar, in *The Madwoman in the Attic* (1979), take the figure of Bertha Mason as representative of the nineteenth-century female imagination, forced to divide itself between a compromising heroine like Jane Eyre, and an outrageous figure like Bertha Mason who, by her very presence in the text, registers the anger which is also experienced by the heroine. There are, therefore, a number of different emphases which can be placed even on the basic triangle of *Jane Eyre* (Jane–Rochester–Bertha), and it is not surprising that illustrators and dramatists have repeatedly taken up those scenes from the novel which seem emblematic of their power struggle. One such scene is Rochester's appearance on horse-back – dramatically represented in Fritz Eichenberg's 1943 woodcut (84); another is the contrast between Jane as an acceptable type of womanhood and Bertha as the unacceptable – an 1897 illustration, for instance, illustrates the scene where Rochester says, of Bertha, 'that is *my wife*' and, of Jane, 'This is what I wished to have' (Figure 4.1: *JE* 1897 Townsend: 281); and a third is the destruction of Thornfield, representing the 'kingdom' of the modern man – the 1943 woodcut gives a particularly stark representation of the ruin (*JE* 1943 Eichenberg: 322). Because these significant situations are emphasized in illustrations, plays and films, they become known even by people who have not read the novel, and pass into the general culture.

In these representations, however, the point of view and the arrangement of the figures differ from one version to another, and even such crude differences as which figure is high and which low, which vertical and which horizontal, produce different effects of power and subjection. The French artist Ethel Gabain (1923), for

Figure 4.1   'That is *my wife*': F. H. Townsend's illustration to the 1897 Service and Paton
edition of *Jane Eyre*, p. 281.

instance, chooses to emphasize the relative equality of Jane and Rochester after his
fall from the horse (*JE* 1923 Gabain: 64), though it is much more common for
illustrators to stress his dominance, and even the fact that he wears riding dress
carries some echoes of a Zamorna-like authority in the *Picture Post* still from Orson
Welles's film (15.1.1944: 23).

    These variations in reproduction nevertheless work within a set of binary
oppositions between active and passive, public and private, outside and inside,
which are conventionally aligned with masculinity and femininity (see Cixous 1981:

90). Charlotte Brontë's text itself tries hard to resolve these oppositions and thus, despite the initial contrast between Jane and Rochester, Jane soon finds that he is as 'familiar to me as my own face in the glass' (*JE* 212), just as Rochester finds in her 'my equal . . . and my likeness' (267). It is, however, difficult to find visual representations of this final equality. In one 1897 edition, for instance, Jane stands higher than Rochester when she first finds him blinded (*JE* 1897 Townsend: 422), but when he begins to see again their positions are reversed (435); even Ethel Gabain suggests a change in relative status from Jane standing behind the seated Rochester to them standing together, but with Jane bending to kiss his hand (*JE* 1923 Gabain: 248, 254). In all versions of a final embrace, the simple fact that Rochester is taller than Jane tends to undermine any sense of the equality of the lovers. In Helen Jerome's play, as soon as Jane has accepted Rochester's final proposal, the stage instruction reads, 'Rochester *rises*'. A playbill for the 1937 performance in Leeds emphasizes this point, which also applies to the Orson Welles film of 1944 (see *Picture Post* 15.1.1944: 23). The effect of these pictures is to minimize the distance travelled by Jane and Rochester between the first proposal scene and the painfully achieved marriage.

Within the carefully circumscribed world of the country house, Charlotte Brontë attempts a utopia in which 'I am my husband's life as fully as he is mine' (*JE* 475), but the pact between Jane and Rochester has the 'precariousness' which Pierre Macherey sees as characteristic of all such 'fictive resolution[s] of ideological conflicts' ([1966] 1978: 155–6). Because *Jane Eyre* provides such striking emblems of shifting gender balance, however, it became a uniquely fruitful 'site of the struggle for meaning' in the first half of this century, in which women tested their ability – and their desire – to move from private to public worlds.

As early as 1904 Walter de la Mare was trying to imagine the marital utopia with which the novel ends. In *Henry Brocken: His Travels and Adventures*, Henry, on his mare Rosinante, wanders into Ferndean after, as Jane puts it, 'I married him'. He finds a taciturn Rochester, still maimed and blind, and a sparkling, witty Jane. When Rochester is suspicious at finding a stranger in his garden, Jane asks, 'Shall I count the strawberries, sir'? (Ramal [1904] 1944: 28). Henry admires 'the exquisite cleverness of her mouth and chin, the lovely courage and simplicity of that yet childish brow . . .' (30), and yet, despite the apparent contrast between the two, he also appreciates their closeness. After the extremities of *Storm-Wrack* (Mackereth 1927; see Chapter 3 pages 74–6 above) there is something very delicate, as well as intense, about de la Mare's appreciation of this peculiar love:

> They sat, try as I would not to observe them, hand touching hand throughout the meal. But to me it was as if one might sit to eat under a great mountain ruffled with pines, and perpetually clamorous with torrents. All that Mr Rochester said, every gesture, these were but the ghosts of words and movements. Behind them, gloomy, imperturbable, withdrawn, slumbered a strange smouldering power. I began to see how very hotly Jane must love him, she who loved above all things storm, the winds of the equinox, the illimitable night skies. (Ramal [1904] 1944: 32)

Yet despite her intelligence and appearance of being in control, their boasted equality is eroded by romantic conventions. Jane sings that 'bonds are life to me' (37) and says, 'I see him as the moon the sun, never weary of gazing. I borrow his radiance to observe him by' (35). This brief, oblique story suggests both the rewards and the penalties of love lived to exclusion.

Elizabeth von Arnim's *Vera* (*JE* 1921 von Arnim) concentrates on the penalties, especially for the women. Unlike *Henry Brocken*, *Vera* does not refer explicitly to *Jane Eyre*, but implicitly evokes its triangular structure. Like the later *Rebecca*, *Vera* takes its name from the dead wife whose place our heroine now inhabits, and its macabre atmosphere rises from Lucy's 'uncanny sensation that the past is repeating itself through her'. This phrase is taken from Tania Modleski's discussion of modern 'female Gothic', in which she distinguishes Gothic from romance fiction (Modleski 1982: 69). Whereas, she says, the feelings of the romance heroine 'undergo a transformation from fear to love, . . . for the Gothic heroine, the transformation is from love into fear' (60). Because 'the structure of the Western family, with its unequal distribution of power, almost inevitably generates . . . feminine conflicts and anxieties', we can see 'Gothics [as] expressions of the "normal" feminine paranoid personality, just as [romance fictions] are in some ways expressions of the "normal" feminine hysterical character' (81). *Jane Eyre* is widely accepted as a paradigmatic romance, but the madwoman in the attic introduces into the novel suggestions of female suffering and injustice at male hands, while the parallels between her and Jane are sufficiently plain for some later readers to reproduce the text as Gothic. In Chapter 5 I investigate this phenomenon further; but here we may note that *Vera*, like *The Secret of Kyriels*, conforms to Modleski's picture of the modern Gothic, rather than to Gilbert and Gubar's nineteenth-century madwoman:

> There are some striking differences between the typical popular Gothic plot and the plot which Sandra Gilbert and Susan Gubar take to be the 'paradigmatic female story'. For Gilbert and Gubar, this is the story of the imprisoned madwoman whose anger and rebelliousness represents the heroine's own repressed rage and whose forced confinement functions paradoxically both as a metaphor for . . . the feminine role and as a warning against stepping outside [it] . . . The imprisoned woman in our stories, by contrast, is presented not as a rebel, but almost wholly as a victim . . . and it is against assuming the victim's role that the heroine desperately struggles. (Modleski 1982: 72)

Lucy Entwhistle, the heroine of *Vera*, does not in fact even 'struggle', but her story is presented in such a way that anger is provoked in the reader. Lucy, left desolate at the age of twenty-two by the death of her father, accidentally meets Everard Wemyss, left desolate at the age of forty-five by the death of his wife, Vera. In the circumstances they become very close very quickly, are married and return to the house where Vera met her death by falling from her window in the third storey. At first afraid of Vera's memory and clinging to her husband, Lucy soon finds that it is he who is the source of her unhappiness. In a series of blackly comic scenes, Wemyss is revealed as a domestic tyrant of the most petty and egotistical kind. For

Lucy, Vera's room becomes a refuge and Vera's books a way of understanding her mind. The triangular plot, superficially reminiscent of *Jane Eyre*, rapidly undermines the expected angel/monster division to yield us an alliance of the two women (whose names mean truth and light). With faint echoes of Browning's 'My Last Duchess', Lucy thinks of her own portrait: 'How very odd it would be if she were hung up next to Vera . . .' (*JE* 1921 von Arnim [1983: 164]). Echoes of the Brontë novels are also faint but telling:

> Early in their engagement, Wemyss had expounded his theory to Lucy that there should be the most perfect frankness between lovers, while as for husband and wife there oughtn't to be a corner anywhere about either of them, mind, body, or soul, which couldn't be revealed to the other one.
>
> 'You can talk about everything to your Everard', he assured her. 'Tell him your innermost thoughts, whatever they may be. You need no more be ashamed of telling him than of thinking them by yourself. He *is* you. You and he are one in mind and soul now, and when he is your husband you and he will become perfect and complete by being one in body as well'. (139)

His words, deriving from the Anglican *Book of Common Prayer*, also recall both Jane Eyre's paraphrase of the Solemnization of Matrimony ('bone of his bone, and flesh of his flesh' (*JE* 475)) and Catherine Earnshaw's more radical 'I *am* Heathcliff' (*WH* 82)), yet with alarming ease he assimilates the idea of 'oneness' to existing power structures. When he discovers Lucy reading *Wuthering Heights* in Vera's room, he is displeased: 'he hadn't read it, but he fancied he had heard of it as a morbid story' (210). We may guess that Vera read it, like her collection of Baedekers and travel books, for its contrast with her actual imprisonment, but we must also feel that its message is not a helpful one in her situation, since in Wemyss's mouth it becomes 'my wife and I are one, and I am he' (see Strachey [1928] 1978: 15). Von Arnim's novel, in fact, reverses the romance paradigm offered by the Brontë texts; the hero proves to be not the mirror but the enemy of the vulnerable heroine, and his house not a haven but a prison.

Vera, moreover, unlike modern Gothics, does not have a happy ending. Lucy's intrepid Aunt Dot, who tries to warn Wemyss that Lucy will last much less than Vera's fifteen years, is simply put out of the house, and the book ends with Lucy turning placatingly to the man who is her real enemy. Modleski draws on a study of the paranoid process to explain why the female victim of such domestic situations does not easily rebel:

> since an imbalance in the power structure – with the male dominant – is considered the ideal familial situation in our culture, and since the aim of our socialization process is to get the child to identify with the parent of the same sex, the female is more likely than the male to retain the (feminine) 'victim' introject and to deny (project) feelings of aggression and anger. At this point, we can see how Gothics, like [romances], perform the function of giving expression to women's hostility towards men while simultaneously allowing them to repudiate it. Because the male appears to be the outrageous persecutor, the reader can allow herself a measure of anger against him; yet at the same time she can identify with the heroine who is entirely without malice and innocent of any wrongdoing. (Modleski 1982: 66)

In the popular Gothics which Modleski refers to, the 'outrageous persecutor' often proves to be wrongly suspected; in *Vera*, however, although Lucy remains free of 'malice', Wemyss does not change his ways. The effect of the story for the reader, therefore, is extremely chilling, since we recognize a dangerous syndrome without being able to help its immediate victim. Elizabeth von Arnim, who was first cousin to Katherine Mansfield, based her story partly on her experiences as the wife of Francis, Lord Russell (Bertrand Russell's elder brother). She was well known in literary circles and, unlike Vera and Lucy, she had the courage to leave her husband. Her story, which was praised by Rebecca West for its 'rare success in the macabre' (Blain *et al.* 1990: 1116), forms the first link in a chain of *Jane Eyre* derivatives including *Rebecca* (1938) and Elizabeth Taylor's *Palladian* (1946), suggesting that the hysterical text of the nineteenth century was giving way, among more thoughtful women, to the paranoid text of the twentieth.

It is tempting to place in this tradition a novel which Jean Rhys described as 'a horrible and sinister thing called Harriet. It has a certain power but is awful awful awful – a shocking book and true' (Rhys 1984: 68). Elizabeth Jenkins's *Harriet* (1934) is described by Rhys's editors as

> based on a true Victorian scandal, about a family who keep their rich relation locked up, half starved, in an attic. Harriet's fate has obvious affinities with that of 'the first Mrs Rochester' in *Jane Eyre* and *Wide Sargasso Sea*. (69)

Beyond the fact of her imprisonment, however, Harriet's story has little in common with *Jane Eyre*; her relationships with her captors, their motivation, the class structure and physical surroundings are all very different. Perhaps its interest lies mainly in its confirmation, in the 1930s, of that acceptable incarceration of women which Thackeray and others had described as commonplace in the 1840s (see Chapter 1, page 31 above). Although, as a structure, *Harriet* seems independent of *Jane Eyre*, the circulation of this sensational tale may well have predisposed some readers to take a paranoid view of Charlotte Brontë's text.

Even for those who saw *Jane Eyre* primarily as a love story, modern developments in the expression of love raised painful comparisons with the earlier text. In Chapter 1 we saw how, in the 1860s, *Jane Eyre* was thought to be the source of sensual daydreams for women. Charlotte Mew, writing in 1899 on 'The governess in fiction', is still sharply aware of this effect:

> It is instructive to remember nowadays, when nothing, it seems, is impermissible to youth, that to the young person of that period *Jane Eyre* was a forbidden book; we doubt, however, if it was a closed one. We suspect that many a young mentor, while zealously withholding from her pupils that too unfettered, too fervid romance, pored over it in secret, burning her candle low over its pages, weaving from them dreams that were to be the realities of the magic future – that dim, yet brilliant, and all-possible future, the saddest and happiest fallacy of youth. How many Rochesters loomed there, as unsubstantial as that sorry hero himself, hidden only by the veil of the prosaic present, waiting to storm the easy fortress of their hearts! (Mew 1981: 336)

Charlotte Mew, although writing fifty years after *Jane Eyre*, was still a Victorian; for the governesses in her essay, the kind of paid work available to women cannot compete with the dream of a lover. Forty years later still, Virginia Woolf looks back on the changes in women's lives since the First World War and thinks that the most significant advance has been

> the right to earn one's living . . . conferred upon us less than twenty years ago, in the year 1919, by an Act which unbarred the professions. The door of the private house was thrown open . . . in imagination perhaps we can see the educated man's daughter, as she issues from the shadow of the private house, and stands on the bridge which lies between the old world and the new, and asks . . . 'What shall I do with it? What do I see with it?'. (Woolf [1938] 1977: 19)

In the decades following women's suffrage and the unbarring of higher education and the professions, there was intense debate about 'what they would do with it'. Helen Jerome, whose stage version of *Jane Eyre* was first produced in 1936, also contributed to this debate with *The Secret of Woman* (1923), written in response to a book called *In Defense of Women*, by the outrageous American journalist, H. L. Mencken. Where Mencken delights in attacking convention, Jerome unexpectedly counters by affirming that women *are* 'emotional', and hence 'impossible on a jury, improbable and ludicrous as a judge, quite unreliable as a surgeon . . . There are periods when it is practically impossible to rely on her – when she is at the mercy of her nerves' (Jerome 1923: 17, 26). She concedes, in fact, one after another of the points made by the opponents of women's emancipation, agreeing that the role of housewife and mother is a noble and satisfying one and that women are 'by nature' engrossed by things of the body rather than the intellect. Having apparently ceded the whole case, however, she then rounds on men for their tyranny, insincerity and insensitivity to women, who are forced into deception and self-repression in order to maintain the illusion of a viable relationship. Like Lucy in *Vera*, her particular grievance is that women are 'never, day or night, an instant off duty' (*JE* 1921 von Arnim [1983: 128]), forced to submit to unwanted sexual demands, while being denied the friendship from men which would make domestic life fulfilling. Although Jerome derides Freudian explanations, she nevertheless quotes Ouida as rightly saying, 'As well expect a house to resist an earthquake as a soul to resist passion' (Jerome 1923: 174), and insists that this dictum applies to women as well as men: '"when the white flower of chastity has been more enforced upon one sex than another, it means the degradation of marriage. Men find a way of escape": women, bound in the coils, stay and waste!' (176). Jerome's complaints lack political force because although she sees that economic imbalance is at their root, she will not contemplate actions which might change that; her method is to appeal to men's better nature. Moreover, although her analysis is the same as that of the New Women discussed in Chapter 2 above – namely that women's self-sacrifice perpetuates the selfishness of men – she does not endorse their separatist solutions. Her position is thus an interesting one for the 'woman on the bridge'. She has no desire to come out of 'the private house', but has courage to complain that things are not well within. She looks forward to 'the possible end to hypocrisy and the dawn of an era of equal standards of chastity. It is in this that I see the hope for any possible equality between men and women' (185).

It is understandable that while Emily Brontë appealed as the austere heroine of the New Women, to a woman like Jerome, *Jane Eyre* would appeal as the testimony of a woman who wishes for marriage, but wishes for marriage to be different. Jerome's immensely successful stage version of *Jane Eyre*, first performed in 1936 and televised in 1937, thus shares some of the ambiguity of its original. Despite its subtitle, 'A Drama of Passion', the play is curiously neutral; although much of the dialogue is taken from the novel, the absence of Jane's inner commentary robs the play of some of the novel's urgency. The emphasis of *The Secret of Woman* is on the torture of unwanted sex, rather than of thwarted desire, and perhaps for this reason the play exploits neither Jane's fevered response to Rochester's temptation nor her refusal of St John Rivers, with its semi-explicit reference to 'the fire of my nature'. It is clear, moreover, from photographs of the first production, that the text allowed the triangle structure to be interpreted in a sensationally conventional way. Rochester's masculinity is emphasized by his riding gear, worn inside the stage-set house. The first Mrs Rochester, as in the Victorian melodramas, is named in the cast list as 'The Maniac' and appears in publicity stills framed in a Gothic arch (see Figure 4.3). The two women are shown facing each other over the sleeping figure of Rochester as in the Victorian angel/monster dichotomy (*Play Pictorial*: 4, 9). A Bradford reviewer clearly saw it as a period piece, mentioning the 'beauty of the courtly language' (*JE* 1938 [Jerome]). Another performance, on the other hand, seems to have revived some of *Jane Eyre*'s original impact. A review in the *Liverpool Echo* begins by outlining the 'stereotypical' aspects of the plots, but goes on:

> The novel shocked many of its writer's contemporaries by dealing with love between the sexes from the woman's rather than the man's point of view, by discarding the then conventional assumption that woman was always the desired and never the desiring, and by portraying a heroine consumed by passion and not afraid of admitting it: indeed, glorying in it. (*JE* 1938 [Jerome])

In the American touring production, moreover, the part of Jane was played by Katharine Hepburn, thus associating the play with the outspoken feminism of many of Hepburn's screen roles (*JE* 1936–7 [Jerome]). Donna Marie Nudd points out that Jane's 'feminist' speech from I xii is represented in Jerome's 1937 printed play, though the whole scene was removed from subsequent editions (Nudd 1989: 197). It is lamentable that Hepburn's production never got to New York and never became a film. Laurence Olivier, who was to have played Rochester, was not available, and Hepburn thought the third act 'hopeless'. The third act includes scenes at Moor House and at Ferndean, but rather compressed, showing little of Jane's 'imprisoned flame', and while Jerome does not scruple to make Jane speak fragments of her thoughts about how 'white December has whirled over June' to Hannah, she finds no way of conveying the 'bone of his bone' atmosphere of her marriage, which is arrived at with conventionally perfunctory joy. If Hepburn found insufficient substance here for her spirited concept of Jane, Jerome refused to change it. Tony Miner, however, confirms that

Kate's interpretation of *Jane Eyre* was fascinating. She played the role with a quiet wit, a delicate charm and sense of gaiety and exuberance. Joan Fontaine, in the film, showed the governess as mousy, beaten, shy, yet bold. Kate played the part with spirit, she *confronted it*, she dealt with Rochester, her employer, with a certain sharp intelligence. It was the very best portrayal of the role I have seen, on stage or screen. (in Higham 1975: 82–3)

The photograph of Hepburn in costume for *Jane Eyre* shows her characteristic flashing eye, raised chin and humorous mouth. One can imagine this Jane asking whether she should count the strawberries, but not seeing with borrowed light.

In her extremely useful thesis on stage and film adaptations of *Jane Eyre*, Donna Marie Nudd provides a thorough survey of eight adaptations by women between 1929 and 1959 and concludes that the plot of seven of these plays 'uncannily resembles' the '"truncated and abridged"' version of *Jane Eyre*, focused almost exclusively on Thornfield, which Adrienne Rich describes as 'the one commonly remembered'. The reason offered by Nudd is that 'they were intent on presenting their own views on what constitutes an "ideal" heterosexual relationship' (Nudd 1989: 142). Despite the focus on love and marriage, Nudd points out that, by contrast with male adaptors, the women place emphasis on Jane's education and her artistic ability, and they show her in command of the situations where she rescues Rochester in Hay Lane and in the bedroom fire. All the women see the climax of the plot not in the interrupted wedding but in the following scenes of discussion, which are given full emphasis, and five of the plays are explicit about Jane's inheritance. On the other hand, these adaptors also respond to some of Charlotte Brontë's original phrases which are more 'melodramatic' and conventional than more modern feminists would like. Nudd points out, for instance, that Adrienne Rich, quoting from the garden scene, omits the clauses where Jane asks if Rochester thinks she can bear 'to have my morsel of bread snatched from my lips, and my drop of living water dashed from my cup?' (255). Most of the plays under discussion render this intensity of emotional need by some device such as fainting or sobbing (Rich 1979: 89–106; Nudd 1989: 168–9). Nudd concludes that what these women were looking for was not so much independence but recognition; Rochester's role in these plays is that of the '"great Recogniser"' (Thurman 1989: 122 in Nudd 1989: 199).

In the same year that Jerome's play was produced in London, Rosamond Lehmann published *The Weather in the Streets* (1936), a novel which deals notably with 'the woman on the bridge'. Like Virginia Woolf, Rosamond Lehmann consciously saw herself in the tradition of the nineteenth-century women novelists. Judy Simons identifies 'George Eliot, the Brontës and Mrs Gaskell [as] . . . "great ancestresses, revered, loved and somehow intimately known"' (Simons 1992: 20, quoting Lehmann [1967] 1982: 69). Many readers have noticed that *The Weather in the Streets* repeats the *Jane Eyre* plot in so far as its heroine, Olivia Curtis, falls in love with an older, richer man, Rollo Spencer, whose invalid wife spends much of her time in her room. Lehmann's novel is, however, a painfully modern book. Olivia, an 'educated man's daughter', has assumed some of the new freedom, but is still asking, 'What shall I do with it?'. Despite the legal advances in the position of women, she has access to no satisfying or lucrative work, and exists on the fringes of a bohemian group, sharing a London flat with her cousin Etty. The passage describing this aimless life has a bleak futility by contrast with which Jane Eyre's 'new servitude' seems crisp and purposeful:

> the book taken up, the book laid down, aghast, because of the traffic's sadness, which was time, lamenting and pouring away down all the streets for ever; because of the lives passing up and down outside with steps and voices of futile purpose and forlorn commotion: draining out my life, out of the window, in their echoing wake, leaving me dry, stranded, sterile, bound solitary to the room's minute respectability, the gas-fire, the cigarette, the awaited bell . . . (*JE* 1936 Lehmann [1981: 77])

In this context, the 'big house' existence of the Spencer family, despite its decay, has the attraction of a foundation in time, of structures of kinship, of social rituals. Like Mrs Ramsay, Lady Spencer knows how to draw her guests towards her, then 'to relinquish them with care and set them in motion towards one another. For the millionth time in this drawing-room, by such a fire, effortlessly, she was designing the social process . . . ' (70). Olivia, however, draws no sense of identity from either the private house or the public world, and drifts through life as if eternally condemned to sit in the window-seat. Without a strong sense of self, she acquiesces in Rollo's definition of their affair as the conventional triangle of modern domestic drama. Whereas in *Jane Eyre*, the unseen wife is clearly the abjected 'other' to Jane's rational and virtuous identity, in *The Weather in the Streets* it is unclear who is the 'other'. Olivia is our centre of consciousness, and in the pattern provided by *Jane Eyre*, Nicola occupies the place of the 'madwoman'. Socially, however, it is Olivia who is the 'other woman'; legitimacy and fecundity still belong to Nicola. In this novel, moreover, Olivia cannot make common cause with her predecessor, as Lucy does in *Vera*, because Nicola is still alive and in possession of her place; the women are forced into the antagonism which Freud saw as part of the Oedipal process. More sadly, *The Weather in the Streets* exposes the rewards of love, even when consummated, as etiolated by deception and all but destroyed by its own physical consequences. This novel was the first in English to show without evasion the experience of pregnancy and abortion for a single woman; it makes Jane Eyre's determination 'to keep the law . . . sanctioned by man' (*JE* 321) seem less arbitrary. Most haunting, however, is the erosion of Olivia's sense of connection with the world. At Thornfield, Jane is forced to live at a mental distance from her love, but her consciousness of difference and of categories sharpens her sense of identity and provokes her to draw her own portrait (163). Olivia, absorbed into the life of her lover, finds herself in a time

> when there wasn't any time. The journey was in the dark, going on without end or beginning, without landmarks, bearings lost . . .
>   Beyond the glass casing I was in, was the weather, were the winter streets in rain, wind, fog . . .
>   In this time there was no sequence, no development. Each time was new, was

different, existing without relation to the before and after; all the times were one and the same. (*JE* 1936 Lehmann [1981: 144–5])

If *Jane Eyre*, with its sharp dichotomies and its articulate heroine, is the hysterical text of a woman forced to participate in a discourse which separates her from her 'other', and *The Turn of the Screw* is the metanarrative of a male observer who can 'place' his hysterical heroine in a discourse to which she has no access, then *The Weather in the Streets* is a text in which the heroine, no longer excluded from knowledge of her own condition, is nevertheless confronted with the symbolic realities of a public world which she is powerless to change.

Olivia, as we have seen, has a private yearning to return to the 'big house' of the Spencers; in Charlotte Brontë's novel, however, Jane's miseries are ended by the simultaneous destruction of Thornfield Hall and the first Mrs Rochester, and many transformations of *Jane Eyre* in the 1930s focus on the country house as an outdated symbol of woman's domestic imprisonment. Even a Women's World edition of *Jane Eyre* shows a subtly smiling Jane superimposed on the ruin, giving the strong impression that her final triumph depends on the destruction of the country house. Two bestselling novels which are almost contemporaneous with Jerome's play and *The Weather in the Streets* share this focus on the house, while producing very different meanings from the textual 'site of struggle'. These are Winifred Holtby's *South Riding* (1936) and Daphne du Maurier's *Rebecca* (1938).

Because the plot of *Rebecca* so clearly echoes that of *Jane Eyre*, the later novel seems to be looking back and asking what has changed. The young heroine (who has no name until she marries Maxim de Winter) is like Jane Eyre in being an orphan, 'humble, shy and diffident' (*JE* 1938 du Maurier [1975: 78]) and her occupation, as companion to a rich lady, is similar in status to that of a Victorian governess. The hero, Maxim de Winter, is like Mr Rochester in being rich and independent, the owner of a country house, and in having an unhappy secret which makes him moody and inward-looking. The two secrets are also similar – both have had first wives who were brilliant but immoral, and both have attempted to rid themselves of their wives by illegal means. In both cases the country house becomes oppressive to its owner because of its association with the mad, bad wife. Rochester, after the encounter with Richard Mason, already feels the house to be 'a mere dungeon'; after the failed wedding, his language becomes extreme:

> this accursed place – this tent of Achan – this insolent vault, offering the ghastliness of living death to the light of the open sky – this narrow stone hell, with its one real fiend, worse than a legion of such as we imagine. (*JE* 316)

In *Rebecca*, Maxim's feelings are suggested by contrast with the speaker's naive suppositions: '"I'm told it's like fairyland . . . it looks perfectly enchanting . . . I wonder you can ever bear to leave it." His silence was now painful . . .' (*JE* 1938 du Maurier [1975: 19]). In spite of being haunted and oppressed, however, by the houses which contain evidence of disastrous first marriages, both Mr Rochester and Maxim de Winter, like Everard Wemyss in *Vera*, try to establish their new, young wives in the same houses and the same domestic roles. In all these novels there is a strong sense of past events shaping the present, creating an uncanny inevitability. When Lucy approaches The Willows, she can feel Vera 'waiting for her' (*JE* 1921 von Arnim [1983: 145, 148]), and the role of wife becomes horrific by association with its dead occupant. When the young heroine of *Rebecca* first speaks the words, 'your wife', she feels as if she had said 'something heinous and appalling' (*JE* 1938 du Maurier [1975: 42]), just as Mr Rochester makes the word sound like an insult when he points to Bertha and says, 'That is *my wife*' (*JE* 308). The repetition of words, both within and between texts, implies that the suffering in these stories comes, not from individual actions, but from social structures – the institution of marriage as it is lived in the country house which allots to men and women separate spheres and imposes on both, but especially the women, the duty to repeat the lives of previous generations.

Du Maurier's novel links past, present and future only to suggest that nothing really changes. Its title, *Rebecca*, is the name of a woman who is dead, and yet she seems alive because her habits and her belongings are still preserved in the house; the young heroine finds herself wearing Rebecca's clothes, sitting in Rebecca's chair, following Rebecca's routine. As soon as she takes on the name of wife, of Mrs de Winter – a name that has belonged to someone else before her – and occupies the house, Manderley, she becomes nothing but a function, the 'mistress of the house'. In Virginia Woolf's essay, 'Professions for women' (1931), she argues that a professional woman in the 1930s 'had to do battle with a certain phantom' which she calls, after Coventry Patmore's poem, 'The Angel in the House'. Rebecca was no angel, but she does haunt Manderley with the spectre of woman's domestic role. Virginia Woolf claims that 'Killing the Angel in the House' is 'part of the occupation' of a professional woman, and, she adds, 'it is far harder to kill a phantom than a reality' (Woolf 1979: 60).

The second wives in these stories have no option but to repeat the roles their husbands impose on them. The reason that the men return to the scene of their former errors, however, is that the country house is more than a place to live. In *Vera*, it is a middle-class status symbol, a retreat from work in the city, but Thornfield and Manderley are, for their masters, places of work, the administrative centres of large estates. Jane Eyre comments on the difference between Thornfield Hall before Mr Rochester's arrival, when it was 'silent as a church', and after, when 'a rill from the outer world was flowing through it' (123–4). This separation of masculine and feminine spheres is repeated in *Rebecca*, where the young heroine is dismayed to discover how much business her husband has to attend to (*JE* 1938 du Maurier [1975: 73, 84). The first Mrs de Winter, however, refuses to accept a passive role. Her desk has labelled compartments, like that of a man of business, and she makes her position as mistress of Manderley into a kind of public office, with house parties and the famous fancy dress dance. Like Rochester, she controls spirited horses; she claims the right to her own private life and, like him, has many lovers; she plants blood-red rhododendrons whose sensual colour recalls Zamorna's and Rochester's crimson furnishings, and there is a kind of splendid defiance in the way she brings about her own death. She is selfish and cruel, but all her actions can be seen as a defiant response to being the mistress of a house, a role which Maxim and Manderley impose on her.

Despite the lapse of time between *Jane Eyre* and *Rebecca*, in some ways the first and second Mrs de Winters are more polarized than the two Mrs Rochesters. The young heroine of *Rebecca* is even worse prepared for life than Jane, because she has 'no qualifications of any kind', and is less independent in spirit. (Joan Fontaine, who strikes one critic as 'sadly vanilla-flavoured' as Jane Eyre (in Halliwell 1986), seems apt as the unnamed heroine of *Rebecca*.) She is almost effaced by Rebecca: when someone asks for 'Mrs de Winter', she replies, 'Mrs de Winter has been dead for over a year' (*JE* 1938 du Maurier [1975: 91]). Many recent readers respond to *Rebecca*, in fact, as a revision of *Jane Eyre* which makes us feel primarily the energetic and attractive force of the first Mrs de Winter, who was beautiful and efficient; who felt the desperate vacuity of domestic life but instead of sinking into madness asserted herself to make something of her role as mistress of the house.

In 1847 there was little real alternative to marriage for women, and the best that Charlotte Brontë could imagine was a companionate marriage which would wipe out the memory of the madwoman in the attic. In 1938, as Virginia Woolf points out, the door of the private house had opened, and we might expect, in *Rebecca*, to see the young heroine emerge from its shadow. In fact she seems less able to do so than Jane Eyre herself. Although *Rebecca* begins with a description of Manderley as a ruin, the young heroine is ruled by her memory, where Manderley still exists because 'it is far harder to kill a phantom than a reality'. She still lacks what Virginia Woolf sees as the weapons for killing the angel in the house – education and the right to earn her own living.

Both Thornfield Hall and Manderley are destroyed by fire. In *Three Guineas* (1938), Virginia Woolf also imagines a fire which would destroy the system that sends men to universities, and keeps women in private houses. She encourages 'the daughters of educated men [to] dance around the fire . . . And let their mothers lean from the upper windows and cry "Let it blaze! Let it blaze!"' (Woolf [1938] 1977: 42). She then imagines a procession of professional men wearing the hats, badges, wigs and gowns which are the signs of their professions, and says, 'We who have looked so long at the pageant in books . . . need look passively no longer. We too can leave the house, can mount those steps, pass in and out of those doors' (71). (It is pleasant to remember that Dorothy Sayers' novel, *Gaudy Night* (1935), takes place in an Oxford which includes a 'Brontë College'.) Woolf, however, reminds us that 'We are here, on the bridge, to ask ourselves certain questions . . . do we wish to join that procession . . .? Above all, where is it leading us, the procession of educated men?' (72). She concludes

> that we, daughters of educated men, are between the devil and the deep sea. Behind us lies the patriarchal system; the private house, with its nullity, its immorality, its hypocrisy, its servility. Before us lies the public world, the professional system, with its possessiveness, its jealousy, its pugnacity, its greed. The one shuts us up like slaves in a harem; the other forces us to circle, like caterpillars head to tail, round and round the mulberry tree, the sacred tree, of property. It is a choice of evils. Each is bad. Had

we not better plunge off the bridge into the river; give up the game, declare that the whole of human life is a mistake and so end it? (86).

Rebecca ends with both husband and wife still dithering on the bridge; they are together, but they have left the private house without entering the public procession. *South Riding*, on the other hand, is able to leave the bridge because it redefines the public world.

Like *Rebecca*, *South Riding* makes deliberate references to *Jane Eyre* which invite us to compare and contrast. Its heroine, Sarah Burton, is like Jane in being, again, an orphan, obscure, plain and little, but the novel, unlike *Rebecca*, emphasizes the social changes which have given women access to higher education. Sarah has an Oxford degree – granted to women in 1920 – and has taught at a fictional version of the North London Collegiate School for Girls, a landmark institution in women's education, founded in 1850 by Mary Buss (where Stella Gibbons, author of *Cold Comfort Farm*, was educated). She has thus the means of earning her own living not at subsistence level, in a position of degrading dependence, like a governess, nor in the enclosed atmosphere of a private school, like the teachers in *Regiment of Women*, but with some style and a good deal of social benefit as the headmistress of a County High School.

Robert Carne, the central male character, is like Mr Rochester in being a landed gentleman, his status symbolized by his management of horses. The film of *South Riding* which was made in 1937 seizes this point, unwittingly endorsing the nostalgia for England past which the novel questions. The film's opening sequence of ploughing horses and thatched cottages shows a landscape quite unlike the East Riding original of Holtby's novel; the hunt which figures in Book 2, chapter 1 was also enthusiastically represented in both film versions (1937, 1974). In the novel, however, Carne's horsemanship represents a cluster of qualities to do with 'big house' management which the text presents for a scrutiny in which intertextual strategies are explicitly used. When Sarah, out for a walk on a snowy day, meets Carne on his 'big, dark horse', the effect is quite as dramatic as Rochester's appearance on Mesrour:

> So startled was she that for a moment she could say nothing, aware only of the tossing black neck of the horse, flecked by white foam, its white, rolling eyeballs, its black, gleaming, powerful flanks, and the dark eyes challenging her from the white face of the rider. It was as though some romantic sinister aspect of the snow-scene had taken heroic shape . . . Into Sarah's irreverent and well-educated mind flashed the memory of Jane Eyre and Mr Rochester. (*JE* 1936 Holtby [1974: 137–8])

The encounter is as inconclusive as that in Hay Lane, but the explicit reference to *Jane Eyre* does not, as it might in *Rebecca*, imply a compulsion to repeat. Sarah has already demonstrated her ability to subvert culturally encoded meanings: on her arrival in Kiplington she promises herself (anticipating Mary Daly by half a century), 'I was born to be a spinster, and by God, I'm going to spin' (67). The reference to *Jane Eyre*, therefore, is ironic rather than uncanny. This is not a plot in which 'we know what happens next'.

Carne is certainly like Rochester: he owns a country estate, he is older than the heroine, and he has a mad wife. Unlike Maxim de Winter, however, Carne is subject to real historical forces. His estate is burdened with debts and the cost of keeping his wife in an expensive nursing home is crippling. Whereas Manderley is a flourishing symbol of patriarchal power, Maythorpe (in a novel written two years earlier than *Rebecca*) is already perceived as 'crumbling to pieces' (26). In 1932 Winifred Holtby published a book on Virginia Woolf, and a passage in *South Riding* vividly recalls, even in the cadence of its sentences, the 'Time Passes' section of *To the Lighthouse* (1927). In *To the Lighthouse* the decay of the holiday house takes the foreground during a time in which the war happens and people die; *South Riding* is similarly permeated with the aftermath of war, in which the crumbling of Maythorpe has much larger resonances:

> The neglected lawns grew tall as a watered meadow. The unpruned roses straggled across the paths and dripped from the leaning archways. Apples rotted as they fell below the orchard trees. No callers came, but as human life receded from the old house it seemed to take to itself its own non-human populace. Mice scratched and whimpered under the bedroom floors; bats hung in the attic; earwigs and spiders ran up the window curtains. (320)

In a text which works extensively through intertextual reference, from Milton to 'Tipperary', the ruin of Maythorpe, described in the style of Woolf, declares itself historically situated, different from the adventitious ruin of Thornfield or Manderley.

As in *Rebecca*, the characters of *South Riding* do recall the past splendours of Maythorpe and of its mistress, Muriel, and her room, like Rebecca's, is kept ready. *South Riding*, however, does not endorse this nostalgia. Rebecca's room is preserved as if it could live again:

> I had expected to see chairs and tables swathed in dust-sheets, and dust-sheets too over the great double bed against the wall. Nothing was covered up. There were brushes and combs on the dressing-table, scent, and powder. The bed was made up ... There were flowers ... A satin dressing-gown lay on a chair, and a pair of bedroom slippers beneath. For one desperate moment I thought that something had happened to my brain, that I was seeing back into Time, and looking upon the room as it used to be, before she died ... In a minute Rebecca herself would come back into the room ... (*JE* 1938 du Maurier [1975: 172–3])

Muriel's room also lies 'awaiting her return':

> The curtains were drawn; their green taffeta, faded and rotting at the folds, left only a whispering light ... On the dressing-table, the creams cracked in their jars, and the nail polish crumbled to powder, the scents evaporated from cut-glass bottles among the rusting files and pins and scissors. In the wardrobes hung Mrs Carne's deserted dresses ... (*JE* 1936 Holtby [1974: 36])

In *South Riding* time does not pass without effect. Mrs Carne is seen, like the house, as an extravagant left-over from a pre-war age, and Maythorpe, stricken by the depression, cannot support a Mrs Danvers to preserve her kingdom or transmit her legend.

As in *Vera*, so in *Rebecca*, one result of the heroine's 'uncanny sensation that the past is repeating itself through her' is the collapsing together of categories of femininity which were expected to be opposed (Modleski 1982: 33). *Jane Eyre* itself maintains the conventional opposition: Jane contrasts her own portrait with that of Blanche Ingram, who somewhat resembles the first Mrs Rochester (*JE* 169–70), and after her engagement she resists Rochester's taste in clothes, which would have effaced this difference (281). Victorian illustrators of *Jane Eyre* accepted current taxonomies of women, and much later popular representations, like a comicbook version which I think dates from the 1920s, still make much of the contrast between Bertha and Jane. Ethel Gabain's 1923 illustration (Figure 4.2) is the only one to suggest a common perspective, showing the veil-tearing scene with a back view of Jane and of a relatively distant Bertha, a focus ending in the mirror which might well reflect them both (*JE* 1923 Gabain: 160).

Both *Rebecca* and *South Riding* also use visual episodes to suggest parallels between apparently opposed types of womanhood, as well as uncanny 'hauntings' from one generation to the next. In *Rebecca* the new wife appears dressed in Rebecca's costume, which is itself copied from an earlier Mrs de Winter. Just as Jane fails to recognize herself when dressed as a bride (*JE* 300), so the second Mrs de Winter in the costume of the first 'did not recognize the face that stared at me in the glass' (*JE* 1938 du Maurier [1975: 221]). Jane's reflection, however, shows her someone who 'would not be born till tomorrow' (*JE* 288), whereas the second Mrs de Winter is the only person at the ball who does not recognize her as a facsimile of the first. In *South Riding*, Muriel's clothes and 'lovely terrifying portrait' (*JE* 1936 Holtby [1974: 32]) similarly threaten to impose a pattern both on Sarah and on her own daughter, Midge. We first see Midge trying to 'bring back to Maythorpe its legendary happiness' by assuming her mother's clothes and praying:

> 'For Christ's sake! For Christ's sake! For Christ's sake!' she screamed, on her feet, beating away from her in maniacal horror her father who stood, seeing his wife, in 1918, frenzied, in her gallant highwayman's costume, beating him off in the outburst of hysteria with which she accompanied her announcement that she was going to bear his child. (38–9)

It is a pattern repeated in Elizabeth Taylor's *Palladian* between the haughty, dead Violet and her daughter (*JE* 1946 [1985: 55]). In *South Riding*, Sarah, after birthing the calf with Carne, is similarly confronted by the portrait of 'Miss Sedgmire. A hunting beauty. Shut away, insane' (*JE* 1936 Holtby [1974: 185]). In the 1937 film of *South Riding* the echoed clothes are changed to evening dress, which allows Sarah (who does not ride) also to take her place in the chain of women attached to Carne – a suggestion followed through in the 'happy ending' to this film, which unites Sarah and Carne. In the novel, when Sarah meets Carne in Manchester, her reaction, made uncharacteristic by desire, is defined by parallels both inside and outside the text:

Figure 4.2 Bertha tears the veil: Ethel Gabain's lithograph for *Jane Eyre*, Editions du Souvenir et de l'Amitié, 1923, p. 160.

> Big and black and white Carne stood before her, solid as a cliff. Into her mind flashed that vision of him in the snow on his big black horse . . . Perhaps, she thought, if he hardly notices me he'll think I'm Muriel. (366)

The implication is that women who place themselves primarily in relation to a man are defined by that relationship, and become 'haunted' by previous incarnations of wives and daughters.

South Riding confronts the problem of sexual love for a woman who is not content to repeat old patterns, yet the novel cannot present us with a solution to this problem;

Sarah would have become Carne's mistress if he had not been taken ill. Eventually he dies, symbolically from a fall from his horse, and Maythorpe is demolished to make way for an institution for mentally defective children. Sarah remains alone, but the novel has none of the ghostliness of *Rebecca*. It contains an element entirely missing from *Jane Eyre* and *Rebecca* which means that Maythorpe is really dead and the future is really a future, not a pale version of the past.

The new element is the public world – not the 'pageant' imagined by Virginia Woolf, but the less ceremonial world of education and local government. *South Riding* also contains a new character. In place of Mrs Danvers, the professional housekeeper who 'worshipped Rebecca', *South Riding* gives us Mrs Beddows, a character based on Holtby's own mother, a wife and mother who is also an alderman, a woman who sits in council and on committees, who makes decisions and is effective in the public world. This world represents Sarah's future, and it is significant that *South Riding* ends with a public occasion which includes the girls from her school, 'the citizens of the future' (506), who assemble with the rest of the town for King George V's jubilee celebrations. The celebration, unlike Charlotte Brontë's early writings, is not to do with councils of war or political intrigue. On the other hand, unlike *Regiment of Women*, it is not entirely enclosed within the school. It shows us the corporate spirit of a small town where local government is, as Winifred Holtby puts it, 'the first line defence thrown up by the community against our common enemies – poverty, sickness, ignorance, isolation, mental derangement and social maladjustment' (6). And for the first time, women were taking their place in this struggle. Instead of Virginia Woolf's procession of wigs and gowns, Sarah Burton looks back on 'a procession of past generations submitting patiently to all the old evils of the world' (206), and in place of Emily Brontë's plea for 'courage to endure', she wants courage 'not so much to endure, as to act' (206). While Charlotte Brontë's model for public assemblies was something like John Martin's painting 'Satan addressing the Infernal Council' (Martin 1964: 16) – grandiose and exclusively masculine – Sarah's public world is symbolized by Mrs Beddows, with 'gaiety . . . kindliness . . . valour of the spirit, beckoning her on from a serene old age' (*JE* 1936 Holtby [1974: 510]). Where Rebecca and Muriel Carne tried to imitate masculine power by whipping their horses, Sarah takes possession of new technology, driving her own car and surveying her 'kingdom' from a plane.

Because the heroine in *Rebecca* has no public role, the structure of that novel repeats the *Jane Eyre* triangle (Jane–Rochester–Bertha) as if nothing had changed in the meantime, though the changed circumstances introduce a muted note into the ending. John M. Stahl's 1939 film *When Tomorrow Comes* not only denies the heroine a happy ending but also refuses the note of tragedy. In this film 'Jane' sees 'Rochester' depart without visible emotion. As Molly Haskell points out, although the heroine is still in a context where self-sacrifice is demanded, her attitude is 'resolute and brave, an act of strength rather than helplessness' (1974: 184). *South Riding* is also tempted by the triangle and abandons it with pain, but its conclusion is more like that hoped for by Woolf: Sarah and Mrs Beddows share a committee room. Where *Jane Eyre* and *Rebecca* make room for their heroines by destroying Mr Rochester's first wife, *South Riding*'s more painful solution is to destroy Mr Rochester.

'The world's great love stories': Brontës recuperated, 1920–44

While writers from Elizabeth von Arnim to Winifred Holtby were developing the *Jane Eyre* plot to meet new historical circumstances, other reproducers were eroding even the challenge of the original. We have seen how illustrators tended to return emblematic scenes of *Jane Eyre* to a culturally recognized norm, and surviving stills suggest that the same is true of even the earliest film-makers. Hugo Ballin's *Jane Eyre* (1921) includes a carefully composed shot of Bertha tearing the veil which exploits space and perspective to emphasise the difference between them. We see Bertha from the back, large in the foreground, her hands raised; at some distance, centre shot, Jane lies small and horizontal in her bed. The alignment of the figures contrasts sharply with Ethel Gabain's almost contemporaneous illustration (1923) for an expensive quarto edition, in which Jane and Bertha are aligned in a perspective ending in the mirror (Figure 4.2: *JE* 1923 Gabain: 160). An undated comicbook of this period may derive from Ballin's film, since its Jane is represented as wearing 'ear-muff' plaits, a hair-style worn by Mabel Ballin in the film. Whatever the date, the comic endorses conventional gender positions. Rochester is stern and authoritative; Bertha bestial and aggressive; Jane timid and shrinking. The penultimate frame, where Rochester delivers his 'sightless block' speech, looks as if Rochester is reproving a recalcitrant housemaid, and the final picture shows Jane sitting on his knee like a tolerated child. An undated retelling of the story which seems to come from this period is entitled *I Take This Woman* – it is hardly possible to diverge further from Jane's 'Reader, I married him'.

Although radio adaptations generally receive less publicity than films, there were almost nine million radio receivers in Britain in 1939 (Beauman 1983: 229), and one contemporary account suggests that the four British radio broadcasts of *Jane Eyre* between 1931 and 1946 'introduced "Jane Eyre" . . . to a public far wider than that already reached by the book, the play or the films' (Raleigh [1946]: 36). Although this Brontë Society reviewer finds it 'impossible to speak too highly' of Barbara Couper's adaptation for radio, nevertheless there were features of the broadcasts which tended to incorporate them into the growing commercial consensus. Milton Rosmer, for instance, who read the part of Rochester in 1932, had appeared as Heathcliff in A. V. Bramble's silent film (1920), which had reproduced the moral certainties of the old melodramas. Similarly, the 1946 broadcast used Reginald Tate, who had played both Rochester (1936) and Heathcliff (1939) on the stage. These voices, for those who had seen the film or plays, would tend to define the radio broadcast as belonging to the same genre. Almost from the moment of publication in 1847, commercial promoters like the publisher Newby had tried to confuse the authorship of the Brontë sisters' works, exploiting the success of *Jane Eyre* to sell *Wuthering Heights* (Gérin 1967: 349–50, 357–8). In the twentieth century, this phenomenon has continued, though the relative popularity of the two works has shifted. Over the next decades we shall see that actors regarded Heathcliff and Rochester as a kind of 'double bill', while the moorland setting of *Wuthering Heights* is regularly transposed to provide additional atmosphere for *Jane Eyre* (see Chapter 7 page 205, below).

Ann Wilton, who played the part of Jane in Phyllis Birkett's version of *Jane Eyre* in 1929 and 1931, wrote to a friend that the stage

> is the only way of interesting the young people of today. They will not be 'bothered' to read 'Victorian Literature', but they *will* seek amusement, and there is more thrill and mystery, combined with vital humanity and beauty of thought and language in Charlotte Brontë's works, than in all the modern sex and physicological [sic] plays put together. (Wilton 1929)

A Bradford reviewer, however, thought that Phyllis Birkett's play, as staged in 1931,

> must be the nearest approach that London has recently seen to the Old Lyceum melodrama . . . and . . . sets out to exploit the thrills . . . This is a Jane Eyre with the mysterious shrieks and thuds exaggerated to such incredible proportions that the house seems inhabited by a squad of policemen and a kennel full of dogs . . . ([Bradford] *Observer* 25.9.1931)

Although, as I argue in Chapter 5, the play itself may not have intended this focus, nevertheless this is the impact it made on its first audiences. Helen Jerome's 1936 version (which was still being performed in 1993) also exploits a sensationalist interest in the first Mrs Rochester (see Figure 4.3). These stage Berthas were shown, as in the melodramas, simply as an obstacle to the 'true love' of Jane and Rochester, without the recognition offered in contemporary novels that to occupy her place was to risk sharing her fate. In Charlotte Brontë's novel, as in *Rebecca* and *South Riding*, Jane's future depends on the destruction of the 'big house'; the 'maniac' of Jerome's play, however, inhabits not the third storey but the 'west wing', and Jane at the end slips smoothly into place as mistress of a Thornfield Hall unchanged apart from the destruction of this wing and its inconvenient 'ghost'. (It is interesting to note that Rebecca, in the novel written two years after this play, also lives in the 'west wing'; but there seems also to be an older tradition from Victorian sensation plays.)

Adèle Comandini's 1934 film is more restrained about the madwoman, but its representation of Jane is extremely domesticated and conventionally feminine. Stills show Jane as very blonde, in gingham and pantaloons or, in another shot, in a low-cut silk dress with jewels. This tendency to show Jane as the unthreatening girl-next-door, ready to be transformed into a decorative wife, seems to intensify with the threat of war. In 1943 Jacques Tourneur produced *I Walked with a Zombie*, a reworking of the *Jane Eyre* plot in a Caribbean setting including a voodoo background which means that the first, mad wife is unable to die because she is 'possessed'. In this film she is a modern *femme fatale*, blonde and beautiful in a

Figure 4.3   Dorothy Hamilton as Bertha in Helen Jerome's 1936 stage play, *Jane Eyre*; picture from *Play Pictorial*, vol. 69 (143).

sophisticated style contrasting with the more homely dark prettiness of the heroine. Despite its sensational elements, the plot is basically a triangle in which the first wife is an obstacle to the 'natural' love of 'Rochester' and 'Jane', who in this version is the madwoman's nurse.

In the same year (1943) Fritz Eichenberg produced a set of wood-cuts for what is probably the most famous illustrated edition of *Jane Eyre*. It is interesting to compare its iconography with that of the Hollywood film issued a year later. If, as seems probable, there was no direct influence, the two texts demonstrate a curious ideological consensus. Eichenberg's strong, rather repellent illustrations emphasize Jane's vulnerability and Rochester's power. The meeting in Hay Lane finds Rochester controlling his rearing horse with one hand, while Jane looks on from a corner (*JE* 1943 Eichenberg: 84). The representation of Rochester as a rake, huge, cloaked and striding through a bevy of available beauties, is rather like those medieval religious paintings where the more important people (like God) are proportionately bigger than the rest (234). When Bertha comes to Jane's bedroom, Eichenberg illustrates the moment in claustrophic close-up; the repeated lines of the two women's heads and shoulders suggest that Bertha could be a grotesque emanation of Jane's unconscious mind; but Jane's defensive hand and shrinking frown, and Bertha's aggressive snarl and dangerously dripping candle present Jane as in need of protection (212). The final illustration shows Rochester blind and anguished in expression, but still dominating the page, still with striding gait, aligned with one of his own knotty trees and with hand hidden in his bosom in a gesture reminiscent of Napoleon (328). Because Jane does not appear in this final picture, we are forced to reconstruct the scene of their final rapprochement from the visual material provided for the first proposal scene (see Figure 4.4), which shows Rochester's tall figure completely enveloping a diminutive Jane amidst massive trees which represent both his physical strength and his ownership of property (190).

   The process of gender polarization reaches a climax in Robert Stevenson's film of *Jane Eyre*, starring Orson Welles as Rochester, produced in 1944. Like the Eichenberg woodcuts, many aspects of this film strain after Gothic effects. Lowood Institution, which 'haunts the spectator like Old Newgate Gaol' (Andrews 1944); the castle-like Thornfield with flagstones and Gothic arches, reached by a journey over bleak moors; Rochester's sudden apparition on horseback; the omnipresent whirling mist and eerie music; Bertha's turret – 'the mystery in the tower' – ; all create an atmosphere combining the more 'stagey' kinds of Gothic with the more ethereal effects of *Wuthering Heights*. Bernard Herrmann, who wrote the music for the film, was to go on to write an opera based on *Wuthering Heights* in 1965, and his music is one of the more original features of this film. On the other hand, the *Picture Post* review was entitled '"Jane Eyre" as a film melodrama', and a still from the film was captioned, 'The mysterious affray in the old wing of Thornfield Hall' – stressing the continuity of the film with the melodrama tradition (15.1.1944: 22). Within this framework, Jane, played by Joan Fontaine, appears in the character of the 'girl-next-door longing to marry', who is prepared to pour water into Rochester's foot-bath at their first meeting. In a curious intertextual involution, this film of *Jane Eyre* strikes Geoffrey Wagner like 'a remake of *Rebecca*', which was, of course, itself a *Jane Eyre* derivative (Wagner 1975: 250–1). It is disappointing that the film should not be more challenging, since Aldous Huxley was one of the adaptors (the other was John Houseman), and Orson Welles, who influenced the direction as well as acting Rochester, had already made his reputation as an original film-maker with *Citizen Kane* (1941) and *The Magnificent Ambersons* (1942).

Figure 4.4 Jane and Rochester in the garden: Fritz Eichenberg's wood engraving for the
1943 Random House edition of *Jane Eyre*, p. 190.

Stevenson (the director), Huxley and Houseman all 'claimed that the screenplay
was a close approximation of the novel' (Higashi 1977: 15), but the film ends with
Joan Fontaine's Jane apparently 'destined for the task of that character sacred
to soap-opera, the nurse' (Wagner 1975: 250). This is, of course, the actual

occupation of the Jane-figure in *I Walked with a Zombie* (1943), and we must allow for the emotional charge carried by such figures in wartime productions.

The relation of the film to its wartime background has been variously theorized. Sumiko Higashi explains the attraction of the film, which was publicized as 'the most powerful love story of all time!', by suggesting that 'changes in the daily routine of women's lives began to accelerate under the impact of war so that daydreams of a romantic hero were all the more necessary to preserve the psychological status quo'. The reason for this, she argues, was that women in wartime found themselves doing paid work in addition to housework, placing a strain on traditional notions of male dominance. It was a situation in which women either had to capitalize on their new economic power to force increased equality within the family, or to reinforce traditional concepts of dependence by recourse to the 'narcotic' of romance, aimed at perpetuating 'the Cinderella psyche in women'. Given the commercial basis of Hollywood films, it was almost inevitable that a Hollywood version of *Jane Eyre* should lean to the latter course of action; film-makers 'relied upon proved formulas to ensure a standardized product with predictable mass appeal' (Higashi 1977: 28). Although one reviewer saw that the film Jane becomes 'a sort of bloodless Trilby from the time that Rochester sweeps upon the scene', others described her as 'forlorn', 'gently obeisant', 'shy' and raising 'tear-drenched eyes' to her master, as if these were appropriate qualities of the romantic heroine. A contemporary *Picture Post* article does contrast the film with the normal Hollywood scenario, in which the plain Jane would be shown 'falling in love with a handsome young man, inspired by love to take a course of beauty treatment or psychoanalysis, and emerging from it as a glamour girl fit for the embraces of Clark Gable' (15.1.1944: 21). Most reviewers, however, did not see the difference between this and the 'diluted' version of Charlotte Brontë's novel which Stevenson's film offered them. As Higashi observes,

> the film industry and reviewers were unable to conceptualize a heterosexual relationship in terms other than those which continue to be popularized by true romance magazines. As a film, *Jane Eyre* simply reenforced standardized formulas about heterosexual love and thus became ordinary. (25)

Kate Ellis and Ann Kaplan's analysis of the film, though more recent and more sophisticated than Higashi's, rather oddly sites its production in the 'post-World War II period' in which women, 'having played active roles in the public sphere during the war, . . . were now being told to go back into their homes and care for their husbands and children'. A clue to this oddity is perhaps provided by the mistaken citation of the date as 1946 at one point, but it is difficult to accept a historical analysis based on this mistake (Ellis and Kaplan 1981: 86, 91).

If there is some disagreement about the causes, there is large consensus about the effects of the film's emphases. Geoffrey Wagner deplores what he calls 'the total and quite unnecessary suppression of Jane's intellect in the role played by Joan Fontaine' (245). Higashi, Ellis and Kaplan, and Donna Marie Nudd have all commented on what Ellis and Kaplan call the film's 'dilution of Jane's rebellious spirit' (83). They all note one or more of the following points. Jane's defiant speech, delivered in the novel to her Aunt Reed, is in the film shouted at the outside of the gate as she leaves. Miss Temple's place as Jane's friend and mentor at Lowood is largely taken, in the film, by a kindly doctor called Rivers (St John and his sisters do not appear in the film). This change, as Ellis and Kaplan note, removes a strong female model for Jane (87); moreover, Dr Rivers's 'role is essentially to teach her her place'. In the meeting between Jane and Rochester in Hay Lane, Rochester is not sufficiently injured to need Jane's assistance, and filmic techniques of sound, lighting and cutting are exploited to reinforce his romantic aura (Higashi 1977: 16–18). Jane's 'equal, – as we are!' speech is shortened and the vocabulary conventionalized so as to 'rob[ ] it of its bite' (Higashi: 19), and it is accompanied by romantic string and woodwind music which assimilates it to a romantic norm.[1] During the speech, Jane stands higher than Rochester, silhouetted against the sky, which gives her a commanding stance while it lasts. Immediately afterwards, however, Rochester rises so that he is very much above her, lowering down to insist on her promise of marriage. During the engagement, Rochester offers Jane 'scarlet' satin, not 'pink' as in the novel, and Jane's resistance is 'ineffectual'. In the fire, Rochester is not scarred and does not lose a hand, which means that the promise of restored sight brings him back to his original strength (Higashi: 21, 23). The scene where Jane brings Rochester his tray and teases him out of his gloom is simply omitted (Lemon 1944). Welles 'limps through the ruins but is hardly the mellowed, chastened Rochester . . . of Brontë's closing chapters. Their coming together simply represents the typical lovers' reunion' (Ellis and Kaplan: 91). A contemporary reviewer confirms that it was received as such: 'the back breaking kiss given the heroine by the hero along with a blast of trumpets or something, at the finale, brought the type of yell from the audience lately developed by the manifestation of Frank Sinatra' (quoted in Higashi: 23).

Ellis and Kaplan provide a more specifically cinematic analysis than Higashi, attributing the changed impact of the film to the fact that 'Jane is seen, for the most part, from a male point of view' (84). By this, they do not mean that, as in many films, Jane is the object of the male gaze:

> We retain Jane's point of view, but her gaze is fixed on Rochester as object of desire, an odd reversal of the usual situation in film where the male observes the woman as object of desire in such a way that the audience sees her that way too. Interestingly, the reversal of the look does not give Jane any more power: Rochester comes and goes, commands and manages, orders Jane's presence as he wishes. Jane's look is of a yearning, passive kind as against the more usual controlling male look at the woman. (89)

As for Welles as Rochester, a contemporary comment in *Brontë Society Transactions* calls him

> a strange monster born of the movies. He rants and bullies; in the steamy half-light of the moor he towers like the Spectre of the Brocken and there is a gleaming of the whites of his eyes in his wild swarthy face, but under the glittering chandeliers of his

drawing-room he sheds these gigantesque attributes and becomes a sort of noisy frontier lout. (Andrews 1944)

Wagner also calls him a 'bully', and finds in the film the story 'of the governess governed' (250, 251). Nevertheless W. L. A[ndrews], for the Brontë Society, reports that by 1951 this film had been seen by 180 million people.

While the 'archetypal' triangular structure and happy ending of *Jane Eyre* had from the beginning found both adaptors and imitators, *Wuthering Heights* at best seemed to inspire glancing reference. Its author, it seems, was more fascinating than her work. The early illustrated editions of *Wuthering Heights* suggest some of the reasons why this should be so. In the realist style of the nineteenth century, with eighteenth-century costume and a graphic clarity of detail, these early engravings present us with a world altogether too defined, intelligible and fixed to render the ambiguity of *Wuthering Heights*. The scene of Catherine's 'I *am* Heathcliff' speech, which particularly attracted illustrators, becomes curiously mundane in representation with settle, rafters and domestic details (*WH* 1893 Greig: 104; 1920s Buckland: 161). Some editions contented themselves with scenic views of places in the vicinity of Haworth (e.g. *WH* 1873; 1900 Ward; 1907; 1924).

Jeanne Delbaere-Garant, however, points to parallels between *Wuthering Heights* and Virginia Woolf's *The Voyage Out* (1915), arguing that 'both heroines are mystics dissatisfied with the dualities of the world but over-estimating their own capacities to transcend them'. Delbaere-Garant also situates Woolf's response to *Wuthering Heights* in the context of sexual crisis discussed in Chapter 2 (above), which had produced 'the hypersensitive and sexually inhibited Virginia Woolf for whom to fall in love must have been a terrifying and perilous experiment'. Although for Rachel Vinrace love opens her eyes to

> the fundamental division and imperfection of the everyday world . . ., the tone of challenge and passionate affirmation of *Wuthering Heights* is conspicuously absent from *The Voyage Out* which ends on a note of resignation and hopelessness. When Rachel dies Terence does not howl like 'a savage beast' [*WH* 167] but sadly reflects that 'they had now what they had always wanted to have, the union which had been impossible while they lived'. (Delbaere-Garant 1979: 702)

The first extended treatment of *Wuthering Heights* in another medium was the silent film directed by A. V. Bramble 1920. According to a contemporary report, the film aims

> to reproduce the story as nearly as possible in the actual scenes in which Emily Brontë set it. '"*Wuthering Heights*" was hewn in a wild workshop', wrote Charlotte Brontë, and Mr Bramble has gone to that 'wild workshop' of the moors above Haworth in order that the film version of the tragic tale shall be topographically authentic. (*Yorkshire Observer* 5.5.1920)

There is no known copy of the film in existence, but surviving stills show Milton Rosmer as a young Heathcliff who visibly smells of the cowshed, while Catherine's death-scene shows her pale and sweaty, with matted hair. The film was clearly very different from the sanitized Hollywood versions of the 1930s. Interestingly, it was not billed as a great love story but as 'Emily Brontë's tremendous Story of Hate', and much is made of Rosmer's lowering brows. Catherine's death scene (see Figure 4.5) shows Heathcliff, wearing a heavy greatcoat, and looking much older than Catherine, standing before the bed and half-lifting her with one hand, so that her head falls back, while his other arm is thrust backwards in a melodramatic gesture towards the audience. The scene has the atmosphere of a nineteenth-century 'tableau' (though with Heathcliff in the role of villain rather than *jeune premier*), and we may guess that the whole film intensified the emotions in the same way. There were, however, factors which might have interfered with authenticity and intensity. The film carried an 'A' certificate, which allowed children to watch if accompanied by an adult; this is a new consideration in adaptations of the Brontë novels. Jonas Bradley, quoted in the *Yorkshire Observer* for 1920, approves of the way in which 'the more gruesome elements of the story have been minimised. "They are hardly fit for children to know much about", he declared'. The film also included an unusual number of child actors.

In January 1995, I was lucky enough to meet 'Twinkles' Hunter, who at the age of five had played the child Catherine in Bramble's film, and her recollections of this experience reorientated the assumptions I had made on the basis of the stills. Personally, she stressed the impact which Yorkshire made on her as a London child, sitting in costume, often for hours together, in an alien landscape; we may assume that its filmed impact was similar on a largely urban audience. She stressed the dedication of the cast and crew and the pains they took to keep 'in character'; she also confirmed the attention to detail which is evident in the stills. There were careful interior scenes, shot in the London studios, including one of the young Heathcliff (aged five) being scrubbed in a wooden wash-tub. A complimentary programme provided for the film provides further evidence of the care taken. There were, for instance, no fewer than three actors for Heathcliff, to ensure that he 'grew up' convincingly. Even more surprising, given that this was a standard six-reel film lasting no more than an hour and a half, is that the cast includes the second generation characters, including two actresses for the second Catherine. Hindley, Edgar and Hareton also had child and adult actors. Twinkles, at five years old, played the scene where Heathcliff first arrived – she remembers being asked to show resentment, which she did very thoroughly! – but the later childhood scenes seem to have been taken by Anne Trevor, who carried the part to adulthood.

The programme includes a synopsis of the plot which makes it clear that the 'hate' which motivates the story is finally 'overthrown': after seeing the love of young Catherine and Hareton, 'Heathcliff's face lost its hardness and became beautified with hope and faith'. He dies in the moment of kissing the phantom Catherine: 'For the evil in him had perished utterly, and in all-conquering love – the love of the woman he had now rejoined – he had found the real Power, and the only happiness'. If the gestures of melodrama are still traceable in the silent film, so, it seems, is the 'moral universe' of the Victorian stage, where all must be restored to a knowable and 'right' stasis, even though the 'story of hate' may be what we remember. It is

Figure 4.5   Catherine's death scene, from the 1920 silent film, *Wuthering Heights*, directed by A. V. Bramble, with Milton Rosmer as Heathcliff and Anne Trevor as Catherine.

interesting that despite the location filming, none of the surviving stills give us the 'hilltop lovers' motif which later became inseparable from popular ideas of the story. Publicity for this film focused on Heathcliff, and the film's movement towards closure has more of a Christian than a pantheistic feeling. Some indication of the persistent influence of Bramble's film is given by an article in the *Radio Times* in which Barbara Couper describes her 1934 radio adaptation of *Wuthering Heights*. The article is accompanied by a photograph 'of Milton Rosmer as Heathcliff . . . actually taken on the Haworth Moors, scene of the play'. Rosmer, who played the part in Bramble's film, also read the radio part fourteen years later. The photograph carries the caption, 'The monster Heathcliff', and Couper (who was praised for the accuracy of her adaptation of *Jane Eyre*), describes all the characters of *Wuthering Heights* as 'puppets struggling in the grasp of this monster Heathcliff'.

In 1933 *Wuthering Heights* was adapted for the stage in an influential version by Mary Pakington and Olive Walter. Helen Hughes describes the play as 'aiming at a faithful, realistic rendering of the novel. Dialogue is condensed . . . with very little change' (1991: 257–8). A review of the Leeds Little Theatre production in 1934, however, describes the play as 'powerful melodrama', praising the performers for 'a convincing production of this incredible thriller' (*Yorkshire Post* 25.10.1934). This play, which was produced in a number of separate productions between 1933 and 1947 and an English Touring Production in 1935 and 1937, seems to have perpetuated a *Wuthering Heights* in the tradition of nineteenth-century melodrama, with intensified emotion and ethical polarization. Like the old melodramas also, its acts were interspersed with music, seemingly of a light romantic kind: The Manchester Repertory Theatre production of 1934 (which shows Miss Joan Littlewood as Assistant Stage Manager) used ballads such as 'I Love You Truly' and 'Just A-Wearying for You', together with 'Serenade', 'Tales by Moonlight', 'April Bloom' and so on; the Theatre Royal, Huddersfield, in 1937 used 'Here Goes', 'Girl in the Train', several tangos, an Irish and an American medley, and so on.

Alongside these indications that *Wuthering Heights* was being assimilated to an old popular tradition, however, are contrary indications that theatre companies were beginning to take seriously their role as educators entrusted, as Professor Gordon had put it, with the job of 'saving our souls and healing the State' by promoting Eng. Lit. (in Eagleton 1983: 23; see Chapter 3, page 74 above). A programme for a production of *Wuthering Heights* at the Little Theatre, Sheffield, was printed by the Sheffield Educational Settlement. This play appears, from the division of scenes, not to be Pakington's adaptation, and the programme adopts an explanatory tone, including a family tree with dates and quotations from Charles Simpson's *Emily Brontë* (1929). The management of the Manchester Repertory Theatre also addressed itself explicitly to the young, offering a prize for the best essay on the play. Their programme included a note to the effect that

> 'Wuthering Heights' is a play which every boy and girl should see, because it will go a long way towards increasing their interest in English Literature, particularly in that period of literature which has always wrongly been regarded as rather dull. (*WH* 1934 Pakington and Walter)

Amid these mingled strains of popular sensationalism and educational sobriety, Clare Leighton's illustrations for the 1931 Random House edition of *Wuthering Heights* break upon the scene like a breath of fresh air. Clare Leighton was the sister of the Roland Leighton who was engaged to Vera Brittain, died in the First World War and became widely known through Brittain's *Testament of Youth*. Her woodcuts for *Wuthering Heights* differed from all previous representations partly because of their clean, simple lines and partly because she chose to focus on unusual scenes, such as the death of Mr Earnshaw, Isabella feeding the pigeons, or young Catherine making tea for Mr Lockwood (*WH* 1931 Leighton: 42, 110, 270). Notably, however, she shows the famous scenes from the point of view of a woman of the 1930s. Her costumes, though appropriate to the period, are not insisted upon so as to distance her figures from the viewer in present time. Her picture of Catherine's illness, for instance, shows Catherine as a lithe, long-limbed girl with loose, shoulder-length hair, half-supporting herself in bed on both arms behind her, wearing a sleeveless shift whose wide armhole suggests freedom of movement. Nelly, facing her with compressed mouth and half-raised, disapproving hand, seems like a figure from another age in collar, cameo brooch and apron (126). The picture of young Catherine as a child, exploring Penistone Crags with Hareton, shows them both wearing simple country straw hats which, with loose hair for Cathy and easy breeches and waistcoat for Hareton, again make them possible figures of the present day, just as the picture of them as young adults digging in the garden shows Catherine with a fur-edged wrap which might easily be of the 1920s (190, 294). The picture of young Catherine meeting Heathcliff on the moor, like that of her mother's illness, has the effect of two ages meeting; the little girl wears loose hair and puffed sleeves of a kind common for children in the inter-war period; the bottom of her dress is hidden so that it does not appear long. Towering over her, Heathcliff wears top-boots, double-breasted waistcoat and many-caped overcoat, a style of dress which places him at the turn of the eighteenth century (206).

The most challenging frame is the frontispiece, which shows Catherine and Heathcliff on the moors, against a background of wide, empty hills and turbulent sky (cover illustration to the present volume). Shockingly, Catherine is shown surmounting a peak, leaving a mere touch of the hand to Heathcliff, who looks up from below. Her physique is strong; strong jaw, strong shoulders and above all, strong legs, clad in wrinkling socks that inescapably suggest the hiker or the hoyden. Her stance is that of the conqueror, one elbow rested lazily on her knee, the foot raised on a stone, her wide-spread legs disregarding decorum. It is a particularly masculine position, adopted for instance by the mountaineering boy scouts in a contemporary *Geographic Magazine* (vol. 14, 1934: 644), reminding us that girls were for the first time joining the Girl Guides, going camping, and at least in fantasy stories, living gypsy-like, adventurous lives free from parental control and chaperonage (Drotner 1983: 41–4). On the other hand, Catherine's dress, though short, is low-cut and the shape of her hair, flowing out to the wind, is a quotation from Botticelli's *Birth of Venus*; she therefore represents both strong, independent womanhood and the beauty and sexuality of traditional woman. The conjunction of 'timeless' landscape, Victorian text and 1930s illustration suggests the analysis of young girls' 'nature-worship' made by Simone de Beauvoir in *The Second Sex*:

> At home, mother, law, customs, routine hold sway, and she would fain escape these aspects of her past; she would in her turn become a sovereign subject . . . seated on the hilltop, she is mistress of all the world's riches, spread out at her feet, offered for the taking. (de Beauvoir [1949] 1970: 104)

Interestingly, the Regal Films International Poster for William Wyler's 1939 film of *Wuthering Heights* has an inset showing Heathcliff, in 'boy-scout' posture, leaning down towards a Catherine who looks up with outstretched arms in a direct reversal of Leighton's picture.

Clare Leighton's illustrations, like Ethel Gabain's for *Jane Eyre*, were presented as collector's items, not for general purchase. They were printed in a limited edition of four hundred and fifty copies, and only twelve years later were superseded by 'the' Random House edition, illustrated by Fritz Eichenberg. It is interesting to compare the two sets of pictures. The most striking feature of Leighton's illustrations is their humanity. Earlier illustrators had attempted a laboured realism, largely in interior scenes, which had the effect of pegging the novel to its surface meanings. The stage plays, on the other hand, exploited the sensationalism of the plot to suggest that the characters were 'monsters' or 'puppets', in the grip of almost supernatural forces. Leighton's pictures are different from both of these. Many of the scenes are out of doors, and suggest, by the restlessness of the sky, the flowing lines of the hills and the frequent presence of birds, the largeness of the open world. The figures, on the other hand, are neither stereotyped nor grotesque, but seem motivated by recognizable emotions, mundane but poignant. The figure of Heathcliff in particular is far from monstrous. In the scene where he learns of Catherine's death, Leighton's Heathcliff, head bowed and hand gripping the tree, has clearly been 'standing a long time in that position' (WH 165), but the landscape around him seems to have put out spears, goads and traps, from the pointed buds of the ash tree to the engulfing hollows in its trunk (WH 1931 Leighton: 162). Eichenberg's landscapes are also animated; his strength lies in his representation of wind and the ribbed sinews of trees. By contrast with Leighton, however, his Heathcliff is a grotesque; it is impossible to imagine him a young man, separated by only a few years from a shared childhood with Catherine (WH 1943 Eichenberg: cover). In the scene where Heathcliff digs up Catherine's grave, Leighton represents him as calmly resolute, with only a certain ghastliness suggested by the lighting from a low-placed lantern; Eichenberg's Heathcliff digs with a glaring, bestial snarl (Leighton: 246; Eichenberg: 182). The unambiguously repellent nature of his Heathcliff is particularly evident in contrast with his Catherine. Eichenberg shows Catherine alone on the night when Heathcliff disappears, looking small and rather helpless in face of the empty moor; during her illness, moreover, she is shown lying with compressed brow and hands clutching her temples, low down in a frame which is hugely occupied by a frowning Heathcliff, lines deeply etched in a face which looks middle-aged next to her childish features (54, 80). Someone who had not read the novel would, I think, take it as a picture of a child haunted by some oppressive evil force, not as a lover remembering her childhood and lamenting the absence of her 'other soul'.

It is possible to explain the polarization of Eichenberg's lovers, however, by reference to the kind of reading of the novel developed by Gilbert and Gubar in *The Madwoman in the Attic*, where they see *Wuthering Heights* as a parable of a young girl's fall into the grace of social respectability (1979: 255). Catherine's education in femininity at Thrushcross Grange includes an enforced recognition of her place in the social order. All the authority figures in *Wuthering Heights* are, of course, men, because only men had legal power, owned property and had the right to interpret religion. If we take Catherine and Heathcliff as a rebellious twin soul, united against authority, then that authority is represented by Mr Earnshaw, Joseph and the Bible, and later by Edgar Linton. Although Heathcliff, with his powerful physique, seems more obviously masculine than the weak, fair Edgar, Gilbert and Gubar point out that this does not affect their relative power in a social sense:

Edgar does not need a strong, conventionally masculine body, because his mastery is contained in books, wills, testaments, leases, titles, rent-rolls, documents, languages, all the paraphernalia by which patriarchal culture is transmitted from one generation to the next. (1979: 281)

As children, Catherine and Heathcliff are equally excluded from this patriarchal power; specifically from education and from inheritance. At puberty, however, a dramatic breach occurs between Catherine and her 'other self', Heathcliff. With apparent perversity, she rejects Heathcliff and chooses instead to marry Edgar Linton. The whole action of the novel turns on this choice, and the conventional interpretation has been to attribute it to an accidental weakness in Catherine's character, a tragic 'fatal flaw' like Othello's jealousy, which makes her susceptible to social status and wealth at the expense of 'true' feeling.

Wuthering Heights, however, operates not simply at the level of Romantic intensity, but also at the level of solid social structures. Catherine and Heathcliff are not just airy spirits, disembodied forces, but have 'a local habitation and a name'. The novel shows us quite literally the difference between being inside a house and outside it; rain wets and snow freezes; hearth-fires are desirable, so are cups of tea, bread and butter, bacon, potatoes and porridge. Catherine's dilemma is quite real; Penistone Crag may represent sublimity, but it also represents starvation; she must eat to live, and, since as a woman she can possess nothing in her own right, she must marry someone who can (see Reiss 1934 for women's legal disabilities). In Romantic terms Catherine may seem perverse and self-destructive in choosing Edgar, but in economic terms she has no other choice.

The split which thus develops between Catherine and Heathcliff uncannily reflects the divergent processes which Freud later identified as the Oedipal pattern in girls and boys. Whereas girls reach what society defines as normal maturity by recognizing their own inferiority and powerlessness, and compensate for this by *attaching* themselves to a powerful male, boys transcend the powerlessness of their youth by *identifying* themselves with a powerful adult male and competing with other men for the possession of women. Thus, when Catherine takes the normal female role, attaching herself to the lord of the manor as a way of coping with her childish lack of power, Heathcliff takes a 'normal' masculine route to acquiring power in his own right. Offstage, he acquires education and possessions. By gambling with Hindley, and manipulating the younger generation, he accumulates exactly that kind of power which distinguishes Edgar Linton as a patriarchal figure – power which lies in 'wills, testaments, leases, titles, rent-rolls, documents'.

From the 'twin soul' of childhood, therefore, Catherine and Heathcliff are forced into a kind of parody of 'normal' gender role polarization. As 'Mrs Linton, the lady of Thrushcross Grange', Catherine becomes a prisoner of gentility, starving herself, gnashing her teeth and showing in an extreme form the symptoms of hysteria which were to become characteristic of Victorian women as the century progressed (see Ehrenreich and English 1979; Showalter 1987). Heathcliff, on the other hand, by combining his real legal and financial power with physical violence and sadistic tortures, exposes the hidden violence which underlies all power, however polite. The ultimate fulfilment for a Victorian lady was supposed to be that of wife and mother, yet Catherine dies in childbirth. Correspondingly Heathcliff dies in the empty, solitary state of alienation from human relationships which was necessary for his acquisition of wealth and domestic power.

Eichenberg's childish Catherine and aggressive Heathcliff are in line with this reading; he also, however, allows us a sublime recapitulation of childish 'oneness' in his illustration of Catherine's death scene (Figure 4.6), where she is shown sitting in a chair, while Heathcliff kneels before her and clasps her to him (*WH* 1943 Eichenberg: 102). Their faces are on a level and pressed together, facing the viewer, and every aspect of their bodies seems repeated. The line of their noses, the curl of their hair, the closed eyes and frown of concentration, the downward-curving mouth, the crooked elbow – even the tendons of the hand – all these features are seen in both figures as if one were a mirror of the other. To complete the picture, the window curtain blows in the wind behind them, suggesting a turbulence absent from their frozen embrace. In this plate, Catherine seems older, Heathcliff younger, than in the other pictures I have described, and both seem more simply human and less childish or demonic.

Although Eichenberg does not 'minimise the more gruesome aspects of the novel', his illustrations are nevertheless 'fit for children'. The set of drawings made for *Wuthering Heights* by Balthus, however, explicitly raises issues of sexuality in a modern class context. Balthus, though of Polish origin, lived most of his life in France and is thought of as a French artist. From 1933 to 1935 he produced a series of fourteen drawings to illustrate *Wuthering Heights*, one of which – *La Toilette de Cathy* – became an oil painting, now displayed in the Pompidou Centre in Paris. These pictures are quite unlike either Leighton or Eichenberg. In style they are odd, sketchy-looking, the characters in stiff, unlifelike stances and with distorted body-shapes. John Rewald's catalogue of *Drawings by Balthus* (1963) shows that most of his other drawings are naturalistic, and John Russell's introduction to the 1968 Tate Gallery exhibition of Balthus drawings confirms that

> the trenchant penmanship of the *Wuthering Heights* drawings is like nothing else in Balthus' work. It is as if he was possessed by . . . Heathcliff the lost boy, the foundling, the human animal toughened by continuous unkindness, the classic outsider. Heathcliff, in the *Wuthering Heights* drawings, is manifestly Balthus himself. (in Lemon 1969)

An unidentified introduction to the drawings held by the Brontë Society confirms that the 'defiant and handsome features' of Balthus's Heathcliff 'are those of the artist himself', while Catherine is 'a portrait of Antoinette de Watteville, a young Swiss woman with whom Balthus was in love'. What gives these identifications more than personal interest is that Balthus, as 'a poor and unknown painter', came to identify with Heathcliff as 'the romantic outsider who battles against defeat'. Although these drawings show the characters in modern dress, the sympathetic treatment of Heathcliff gives us, therefore, something like the Byronic hero who was one of Emily Brontë's sources. The scene which Balthus chose to develop into

Figure 4.6   Catherine's death scene: Fritz Eichenberg's wood engraving for the 1943 Random House edition of *Wuthering Heights*, p. 102.

a painting, *La Toilette de Cathy*, is the one where Catherine, still at the Heights, prepares to receive a visit from Edgar Linton (Figure 4.7). In the novel, Heathcliff asks 'Why have you that silk frock on . . .?', and eventually provokes her into saying that his company 'is no company at all', since he 'might be dumb or a baby for

Figure 4.7   'La Toilette de Cathy': 1933 oil painting by Balthus, Musée National d'Art Moderne, Centre Georges Pompidou, Paris. © DACS 1995.

anything you say to amuse me' (*WH* 68–9). In William Wyler's 1939 film, Merle Oberon appears in this scene with elaborately dressed ringlets and a silk evening dress trimmed with bows and ruffles. Balthus has translated the scene to make visible its underlying sexual tensions; the strained technique of the painting presents Heathcliff as neutral and therefore somehow blameless, while Catherine is in an artificial stance of display. The well proportioned, well moulded figure of Heathcliff, with its naturalistic pose, handsome features and suffering expression, contrasts startlingly with the flatly-lit figure of Cathy, who is taller and has a much larger head than the pursed-up, cartoon-like Nelly who is combing her hair. Cathy, in high-heeled slippers, adopts a model-like pose, with advanced hips, one slightly bent leg in front of the other; with wry neck and rapt, narrowed eyes, she looks away from the other two, apparently oblivious of the way her housecoat falls open to reveal naked, sharp, outward-pointing breasts, an elongated torso and improbably narrow hips. The effect is of different genres juxtaposed within one frame: Catherine, it seems, is deliberately putting herself into a different kind of story from the one Heathcliff represents.

John Rewald claims that unlike his paintings, Balthus's drawings reveal 'no mystery . . . no voluptuousness, no suggestion of precocious perversity' (1963). Although the drawings give us a clothed version of this scene, I would argue that as a whole they do give precisely a sense of adolescent sexuality. Catherine and Heathcliff on the moors are presented as lying together, her head in his lap and his arm across her breast. Escaping from the wash-house, Catherine displays a bare leg to the top of her thigh. Caught by the Lintons' bulldog, she lies on the ground with her skirt dragged between her legs. She delivers her 'I *am* Heathcliff' speech supine on the ground, with legs spread wide, the thin fabric of her skirt showing the outline of her body. In almost every drawing, Heathcliff's clothes conceal the shape of his body, while Cathy's reveal hers; she, moreover, is often shown in an active pose, while he stands or sits, observing, suffering. The overall effect is to suggest that Cathy uses her sexuality to reinforce the power over Heathcliff given by her class.

The various 1930s reproductions of *Wuthering Heights* show a movement from the melodramatic assumption that the story is motivated by 'the monster Heathcliff' to a more modern fear that the ambitious woman is the source of all its trouble. Unlike *Jane Eyre*, however, *Wuthering Heights* seems to lend itself to fragmentation rather than development. Although, as we have seen, *Jane Eyre* was ambiguous enough to become a much-populated 'site of the struggle for meaning', its triangular structure was widely intelligible, and later versions of the text tended to focus around recognizable debates about marriage and the position of women. Inter-war versions of *Wuthering Heights*, by contrast, give the impression of a battleground 'swept with confused alarms', in which the monstrous Heathcliff of the melodramas contends with the brief challenge of Leighton's tomboy Cathy or the *vagina dentata* of Balthus (Figure 4.7). Apart from the remarkable Eichenberg picture (Figure 4.6), there seems to be little attempt to reproduce the 'oneness' of the original pair; yet Emily Brontë's reputation, based on her character as a 'mystic', was steadily gaining ground in the academic world and shedding faint echoes in commercial lip-service to literature. *Wuthering Heights* was, moreover, now tardily beginning to be popular. Randolph Carter's American stage play, first performed in 1933, was produced almost annually during the 1930s and was still being performed in 1990, and in 1937 John Davison adapted the novel for the British stage – a version that was still being performed in 1986.

Davison's play, like the Balthus drawings, gives us a Catherine who is aware of her sexuality and is prepared to use it. The stage directions present her as 'attractive, passionate, ruthless and vital, stormy yet tender and feminine'; she wears 'an expensive silk dress of the period'. She sounds like Scarlett O'Hara, and, as if *Gone With the Wind* (1936) had given the clue, this play, like *Jane Eyre*, is structured as an explicit love triangle, though with the genders reversed, so that Heathcliff competes with Edgar for Catherine in the way that Jane competes with Bertha for Rochester, with Isabella, like St John Rivers, as an afterthought. It may seem an obvious structure, but the (incomplete) indications are that earlier versions had not had quite this emphasis, presenting Heathcliff in a more villainous role. In Davison's play, Edgar, as might be expected, is 'well-dressed, and handsome in the finery of a gentleman of the period', but Heathcliff is no longer the monster of earlier plays. In order to make the competition in love plausible, he is 'young, dark and handsome, yet not sinister' (*WH* 1937 Davison: 1). In the first scene, where Catherine and Heathcliff appear to be young adults, they play a chasing game during which class and gender differences are clearly established: when Heathcliff warns her that she might tear her dress, she replies that she has 'plenty more' (1–2). The relationship between them is explicitly sexual (the game involves kissing) and Catherine uses her sexuality to goad Heathcliff into rebellion against Hindley; she is impatient with his waiting strategy and calls him a 'fool' (3). As in the Balthus drawings, Davison's Heathcliff is more spiritual than Catherine; when he offers her his soul, she asks, 'And what of your body?' (4). The story has been transformed into a conventional competition between rival suitors, and this change is well demonstrated by the scene in which Catherine and Heathcliff escape from the Heights and look into the windows of the Grange. In the novel, this scene is described in two brief passages. The first, from I iii, is simply two sentences from Catherine's diary, written as a child, describing how her 'companion' – presumably Heathcliff – is impatient for 'a scamper on the moors' since they 'cannot be damper, or colder, in the rain than we are here' and they will, moreover, escape from the house and the 'surly old man', Joseph (*WH* 20). The second passage is part of Nelly's narrative in I vi, describing how the two children 'promised fair to grow up rude as savages' because Catherine's brother Hindley didn't take proper care of them. Her description includes some of Heathcliff's direct speech, describing how he and Catherine 'escaped from the wash-house to have a ramble at liberty' and how they 'ran from the top of the Heights to the park, without stopping – Catherine completely beaten in the race, because she was barefoot' (44–6).

In Davison's play, this episode becomes a weapon in the sex war. All the 'framing' devices of the novel are dispensed with, so that Nelly's mediation of the scene is missing. Moreover, in this version Catherine speaks not to her diary but to Edgar, and her description is turned to a specific purpose – to make Edgar jealous. When Edgar hears that Catherine and Heathcliff 'strolled' to the park gates last night, he is 'amazed':

> *Edgar:*   Why, the lodge gates . . . are quite three miles from here. Heavens, weren't you tired out?
> *Cathy (easily):*   Oh, Heathcliff carried me part of the way back. It was a glorious night.
> *Edgar (a shade annoyed):*   Heathcliff! carried you?
> *Cathy:*   Oh yes, he often does . . .

> *Edgar:*   Catherine, you shouldn't allow the fellow to be so familiar. To carry you,
>   indeed; I hope no one saw you.
> *Cathy:*   I don't know whether they did or they didn't. I had my eyes closed most of
>   the time.
> *Edgar:*   Why?
> *Cathy:*   Don't you ever close your eyes in moments of ecstasy, Edgar?
> *Edgar:*   Is it such ecstasy, then, to be carried over the moors by that Heathcliff fellow?
>   Really, Catherine!
> *Cathy:*   Oh, don't be absurd, Edgar. I was weary and . . . and footsore. (*WH* 1937
>   Davison: 8)

Edgar here is acutely conscious of the class difference between Catherine and 'that fellow', while Catherine seems to intend to make him jealous, because later she says she might let Edgar carry her if he did not let her fall. In order to set up this triangle situation, however, Davison has had to weaken Catherine. She agrees with Edgar that 'three miles' is enough to tire her so much that she needed to be carried, although, in the novel, there is no sign that she feels fatigue any more than Heathcliff. We have seen how Clare Leighton works on this suggestion of strength to create her feminist Catherine: in her version of the relationship it is Heathcliff who appears to be struggling with the climb. In the novel, Catherine is beaten in the race because she is 'barefoot' (in rough country). In the play this becomes 'footsore', suggesting the delicate lady not fit for much exertion. The rhetoric of Davison's passage therefore works on our recognition of signs of both class distinction, in words like 'fellow', and conventional gender distinctions, based on words like 'tired' and 'footsore'. Speaking of William Wyler's 1939 film, George Bluestone was to say that Wyler had transformed *Wuthering Heights* into 'the story of the stable-boy and the lady' (in Wagner 1975: 234). As in the film, so in Davison's play, the motivation of Catherine in particular has been altered, making her manipulative instead of merely capricious. After Catherine's death, Nelly offers a hesitant explanation, that 'Cathy and Heathcliff were . . . were different. They were like creatures of the wild; to confine them, to try to tame them only meant . . . a sure way of killing them' (*WH* 1937 Davison: 56): but we have seen nothing to give substance to this 'difference'.

Two years later, in 1939, William Wyler produced his famous film starring Laurence Olivier as Heathcliff. Here too, there are indications that *Gone With the Wind*, a novel of the 1930s, played a role in the interpretation of Emily Brontë's Victorian novel. Olivier apparently wanted Vivien Leigh to play Catherine; in the event, she took the part of Scarlett in the film of *Gone With the Wind* which appeared in the same year as Wyler's *Wuthering Heights* (Hawkins 1990: ch. 4 n. 3). Viewers have also noticed a similarity in the music of the two films. Issued on the outbreak of war, Wyler's film had an unprecedented success, drawing on a kind of cultural nostalgia (the costumes, for instance, were brazenly drawn from the 1840s because the director thought the fashions more attractive than the eighteenth century) and a kind of factitious high-mindedness. Sam Goldwyn, the producer, apparently intended to call the film 'He Died For Her'

(*BSG* 5: 1), a title which would have stressed what film critics now call the 'feel good factor'.

In 1989, the *Guardian* carried an obituary for Sam Goldwyn; it was accompanied by a half-page drawing by cartoonist Steve Bell, headed 'Withering Heights' and showing Catherine and Heathcliff on Penistone Crag. The only odd thing about the drawing is that both Catherine and Heathcliff have the face of Sam Goldwyn; the cartoon is a visual allusion to the famous publicity still for the film showing Laurence Olivier as Heathcliff and Merle Oberon as Catherine, alone on Penistone Crag (Figure 4.8). Unlike the stage versions, the film had the freedom to represent the landscape and the weather with something like the insistence of the novel; unlike Eichenberg's 'mirror' illustration (Figure 4.6), moreover, which is situated indoors, the lovers-on-the-hilltop image of the film combined for the first time the intensities of romantic oneness with the intensities of the place. The Regal Films International Poster advertises the Wyler film as providing 'Yearning . . . incessant as the pounding sea! Love . . . stormy as the windswept moors!'

There is, as we have seen, very little description of Catherine and Heathcliff out of doors in *Wuthering Heights* itself. Even the passages quoted above in relation to Davison's play have some features which are worth recalling. First, although they are themselves very brief, they still include less about Catherine and Heathcliff on the hilltops than about what they have left behind – the 'surly old man', the curate who 'reprimanded' them for not going to church, the 'young master' who would order 'Heathcliff a flogging, and Catherine a fast', Nelly herself, who 'cried to [her]self to watch them growing more reckless daily', and the Linton children in their drawing-room. Secondly, both passages refer to the period of childhood; the only time Catherine and Heathcliff are referred to out of doors together as adults, they are accompanied by Isabella (*WH* 101). Thirdly, neither of these episodes is recounted directly to the reader: Catherine's diary is reported to us by Mr Lockwood and Heathcliff's story is related by Nelly, together with her own feelings, to Mr Lockwood. This means that the image of Catherine and Heathcliff 'scampering on the moors' is 'framed' for us by the judgements of Joseph, Hindley, the curate and Nelly, who find the children 'savage', 'naughty' and 'reckless', as well as 'unfriended'.

Nevertheless, in the film, the picture of Catherine and Heathcliff together, as adults, on the hilltop, silhouetted against the sky which represents their mutual aspiration, has become a visual emblem of what the novel 'means'. By 1989 it was so well known that Monty Python's Flying Circus could assume that two lovers on a hilltop constituted a cultural icon to which a mass audience would respond (*WH* 1989 Chapman). Umberto Eco, in his essay on 'Casablanca', explains how an image like that of Olivier and Oberon on the hilltop, which becomes a repeated motif in the film, and was also extracted from it for publicity purposes, becomes what he calls an 'intertextual archetype' – it has the 'magic' quality of a frame which, when separated from the whole, transforms the movie into a cult object (1988: 448). Eco is concerned with the separation of frames from a whole film; in dealing with *Wuthering Heights* we have the added separation of film from written text. The still

Figure 4.8   Catherine and Heathcliff on the hilltop, from the 1939 film, *Wuthering Heights*, directed by William Wyler, with Laurence Olivier and Merle Oberon. © MCMXXXIX by Samuel Goldwyn. All Rights Reserved.

photograph (Figure 4.8) transforms the original text in significant ways; it gives visual shape to the image which remains implicit in the novel, of Catherine and Heathcliff out of doors as adults, and it presents them in a pose and a physical situation which invites our direct participation in their experience and implicitly denies the existence of the framing, judging voices of the novel.

In her book on feminism and cinema, Annette Kuhn uses Lacanian psychoanalysis to argue that 'one of the central ideological operations of dominant cinema' – which would certainly include this Hollywood version of *Wuthering Heights* – 'is precisely the positioning of the viewing subject as apparently unitary' (1982: 210). What she means is that as we watch the film, the technique of the camera is to persuade us that we are the camera, looking directly at the figures who appear on the screen, without any such mediation as appears in Emily Brontë's novel in the form of a variety of narrators. Moreover, what she calls 'classic narrative codes' – the characteristic structure of the film plot – encourages us to identify with the characters (157; see also Hawkins 1990: 35). Even more crucially, she argues that this activity of looking at a human object on the screen repeats the important moment in our childhood when we begin to construct an identity for ourselves by looking at our own image in a mirror or the image of another child (Kuhn 1982: 47–9). The operation of dominant cinema is, according to Kuhn, ideologically powerful because it repeats the process by which we 'recognize' who we are. This image of Catherine and Heathcliff, the lines of their bodies and the direction of their gaze repeating each other against the sky, offers us a picture of our own ideal identity, as one half of an inseparable pair who together take on sublimity. It is a picture of romantic love as a kind of heaven.

We have seen that certain 'mythic' texts become reduced, in the process of retelling, to their 'simplest memorable patterns' (Baldick 1987a). For the wide audience who recognize the Goldwyn cartoon or the Monty Python semaphore sketch, the 'simplest memorable pattern' of *Wuthering Heights* derives more from this Hollywood film than from the original text. This might be explained by the fact that more people go to the cinema than read books; but the image itself clearly answers a need in the viewing public to which there are clues in contemporary texts. Although Sam Goldwyn may not have known it, William Wyler's visual image (Figure 4.8) matches a metaphor in an academic essay written five years earlier by Lord David Cecil, Professor of English Literature at Oxford. In his book *Early Victorian Novelists*, Cecil wrote that Catherine and Heathcliff 'loom before us in the simple epic outline which is all that we see of man when revealed against the huge landscape of the cosmic scheme' (Cecil 1934: 150–1). It was Charlotte Brontë who began the association of the novel with the landscape; in her preface to the 1850 edition of *Wuthering Heights* she writes of how her sister 'found a granite block on a solitary moor' and 'wrought [it] with a crude chisel . . . with time and labour, the crag took human shape; and there it stands colossal, dark, and frowning, half statue, half rock' (*WH* 370–1). Critics of the 1920s and 1930s, however, seem particularly devoted to the notion that the novel represented something at once human and superhuman. Virginia Woolf, writing in 1925, speaks of the novelist's 'struggle . . . to say something through the mouths of her characters which is not merely "I love" or "I hate", but "we, the whole human race" and "you, the eternal powers . . ."' (1979: 126–32). Ernest Baker, in his standard *History of the English Novel* (1937), makes a value judgement more clearly in line with Wyler's film:

> Emily has not merely grasped the modern idea of the supreme value of the individual soul, which realises itself in its personal life and in mutual understanding, complete harmony, virtual identity with its destined mate; she sees the personality and the consummated union as eternal facts, which mortality itself cannot annul. (in Lettis and Morris 1961: 50)

Behind Wyler's film, therefore, is an ideology which puts great value on epic grandeur and cosmic scale which is nevertheless related to 'the supreme value of the individual soul, which realises itself in its personal life'. It is an ideology which lends itself well to the interwar project identified by Chris Baldick and Terry Eagleton, of utilizing an elevated English literature to supply the cohesion no longer offered by a national church (Eagleton 1983: 23). In this climate, literature was valued not for its realistic depiction of specific societies, but for its 'universality'.

Nevertheless the intensifying need for such an ideology can be located in history. The *New York Times* for 16 April, 1939 describes how, in the Goldwyn studio,

> Heathcliff was peering out across the moors and screaming, 'Cathy, come in to me! Cathy, my own!' while there beyond, in a corner of the stage, muted when the set's microphone was alive, a tiny radio was tuned to one of Hitler's more portentous harangues. Between each take, between Heathcliff's heartbreaking cries and the corn-flake flurries of the studio-made gale, cast, director and crew were sprinting to the radio corner where a little property man with a knowledge of German was standing in newfound dignity, haltingly translating phrases that might have spelled a war, but did not. Truly, 'Wuthering Heights' was hewn in a wild workshop, in the literature of the screen as in literature.

In 1930s accounts of *Wuthering Heights*, the word 'epic' figures prominently, and although 'epic' and 'universal' seem to suggest infinite openness of meaning, Mikhail Bakhtin claims that epic discourse is peculiarly dogmatic, the fitting vehicle of ideology (Moi 1986: 41). Although Emily Brontë's novel does not in itself conform to Bakhtin's definition of an epic, both Cecil and Wyler are attempting to transform it into just that. It was precisely in 1939 that the Brontë sisters were accepted into the pantheon of the great by being given a memorial in Westminster Abbey. *The Times* endorsed this recognition, finding 'two of the sisters . . . among the highest ornaments of the literature that is common to the English-speaking world'.[2] In the tense pre-war atmosphere, Baker's emphasis on 'the supreme value of the individual soul' takes on a new intensity, so that, by obscure emotional processes, the political rhetoric of the 'free world' lies behind the picture of Catherine and Heathcliff on Penistone Crag, a visual image of 'consummated union as eternal fact'.

Jay Clayton, in his book, *Romantic Vision and the Novel*, argues that *Wuthering Heights* itself, by contrast, fascinates because it refuses to provide this image:

> We continue to believe in the visionary existence of their bond, even when they have been divided from one another, precisely because the bond itself has never been represented . . . If we [look] . . . for a place in the text that records an authentic moment of union, we can locate nothing but a gap, a hole in the narrative beyond which the topic of union becomes prominent . . . The representational void is so great that William Wyler, making his movie of *Wuthering Heights*, felt required to fill it both with a place – Penistone Crags, where the lovers meet even after their death – and with an action, a sexual embrace. (1987: 93, 83, 84)

Wyler, who must, in a visual medium, present a visual image of his lovers, thus confronts a problem which Cecil and Baker, in written texts, can evade. The recognizable figures of Laurence Olivier and Merle Oberon (e.g. Figure 4.8) are clearly not simply, as Cecil suggests, 'manifestations of natural forces', who function in relation to a 'cosmic scheme' rather than to 'human civilizations and societies and codes of conduct' (1934: 165, 150). The image of real human beings must prompt us to question their relationship with codes of conduct, and in what sense their union is consummated.

Ernest Baker, in the passage quoted above, slides from the 'mutual understanding' to the 'virtual identity' of 'destined mate[s]' as if there were no problem in this conflation, but Juliet Mitchell, in a very persuasive analysis, makes a clear distinction between these two kinds of love. One is legitimate or married love, which she sees as 'the triumph of sexuality over death, the species over the individual'. The other is romantic love, which represents 'the triumph of death over life'. She is using the word 'romantic' in its academic sense, as relating to the Romantic poets, for instance. Romantic love is a model of love which 'does not have a sexual object that is ultimately different from itself' (1984: 111). The object of the Romantic poets' search is the sister-muse, the alter ego, the epipsyche, not the wife, the helpmate, the little woman. It is clearly Romantic love which animates Emily Brontë's novel: Catherine declares that she *is* Heathcliff, while Heathcliff '*cannot* live without [his] soul' (*WH* 82, 167). It is a concept of love which is both sublime and retrogressive in that it looks back to childhood and tries to deny adult separation and responsibility; but for these reasons it is hardly a concept which contributes to social cohesion. Its promise of ontological security is attractive to the needy child in all of us, and in this sense it gives form to 'universal' desires. It is not, however, an ideal to be adopted *en masse* by readers and viewers who need to live in society, where desire is normally channelled into marriage and sexuality does, on the whole, triumph over death.

We have seen that in the passages I have quoted from *Wuthering Heights* itself, what Cecil calls 'societies and codes of conduct' are very much present (1934: 150). Catherine and Heathcliff are framed by other people's behaviour (going to church and sitting in the drawing room) and other people's judgements (they are savage or naughty). In relation to the frame, Catherine and Heathcliff stand together; mutually excluded from society, they assert their own centrality to a different code of values. In the novel, the meaning of their escape to Penistone Crag is that 'society' doesn't matter. According to the psychoanalytic model which I described earlier, they derive their sense of identity and worth not from the judgements of society but precisely from looking at each other; as Nelly says, 'they forgot everything the minute they were together again' (*WH* 44). In order, though, for *Wuthering Heights* to be presented as a great love story of a type which will confirm rather than reject social codes of conduct, Catherine and Heathcliff must be brought within society and must, above all, relate to one another as *heterosexual* lovers who could, potentially, marry.

Emily Brontë's early Victorian novel draws on a rhetoric in which consummation is a matter of souls, not bodies. This discourse of Romantic love was perhaps the only challenge to 'legitimate or married love' available to a woman writer at that time. Wyler's film, like Davison's play, however, was a product of a different age, the inter-war period which in Britain and America was one of rapid social advance for women in society. Women were for the first time able to participate in previous male enclaves such as the law, higher education, big business. In America this development is reflected in the series of films with strong public heroines played by Katharine Hepburn, and Annette Kuhn confirms that one of the major projects of 1930s cinema was to 'recuperate' the image of woman into the dominant ideology (1982: 34). The problem posed by *Wuthering Heights* to William Wyler is, therefore, the problem of Catherine, who must be presented to the viewing public not as Heathcliff's *alter ego* but as the object of his desire.

Wyler's solution to this problem is to keep the 'epic sublimity' of the image of Catherine and Heathcliff on Penistone Crag (Figure 4.8), but to offer as an explanation for their exile not their own mutual scorn of 'societies and codes of conduct', but a different myth – the myth of star-crossed lovers, who would willingly conform, by marrying, if only society would let them. Wyler's version of the myth, like Davison's, is based on class – 'the story of the stable-boy and the lady' (Wagner 1975: 234), and in order to give substance to this reading he presents Catherine in ringlets and silks, with chandeliers and grand pianos (quite beyond the rural gentry of Yorkshire) and exaggerates the class difference between Edgar and Heathcliff in order, eventually, to emphasize the power of love to transcend class. In the meantime, however, as she vacillates between the two men, Catherine appears as 'a vulgar tease and common snob, the bitch-heroine luring her helpless male to destruction'. Geoffrey Wagner thus argues that Wyler structured his film to fit 'the quick social climbing and class mobility of America in the Thirties' (240). To this end, the film inserts a scene which is not in the novel at all, showing Catherine and Heathcliff out of doors as children; significantly, however, it emphasizes not their identity with one another, but their gendered difference. At first the scene seems to follow the feeling of the novel well, showing the children, aged about twelve, dressed simply and mounted on rough farm ponies galloping across moor and rough pasture, exhilarated by speed. There seems to be neither class nor gender distinction between them until they speak. Catherine's first words, however, are, 'Heathcliff, I'll race you to the barn. The one that loses has to be the other's slave'. The introduction of a power-relationship here is quite foreign to the novel's sense of the *identity* of the two children. (As Heathcliff says in the novel, 'When would you catch me wishing to have what Catherine wanted?' (*WH* 46).) The 'stable-boy and the lady' myth, however, requires a complex adjustment of power in terms of class and gender. Heathcliff must be low enough in class terms for Catherine's love to represent a triumph over social convention, but strong enough in gender terms to be a protective husband.

In the novel, while Mr Earnshaw is alive, Heathcliff is able to dominate Catherine's brother Hindley, the legitimate son of the house. In Wyler's film, however, Heathcliff is beaten by Hindley, confirming his class inferiority, so that Catherine needs to be suddenly feminine to restore his masculine pride. Her reason for wanting to go to Penistone Crag is no longer to beat him in a race but to 'pick bluebells' (a flower, incidentally, that grows only in sheltered woodlands), and she is prepared to be servile to get him to agree, curtseying and saying, '*Please*, m'lord?' She then persuades him to adopt the role of a knight in armour jousting with a rival to win a castle for his lady. The tournament, which Denis de Rougemont calls 'a physical representation of the myth' of Tristan, the 'great European myth of adultery' ([1940] 1983: 248, 18) is very appropriate to the 'stable-boy and the lady' myth as it develops later in the film, with the triangle situation between Edgar, Catherine and Heathcliff, and the children in this early scene are perceived as already joined in a sexual relation; their gender identity has been 'naturalized'. In the novel, however, Catherine's heterosexual orientation happens during her socialization in the Linton household, and it is this which *separates* her from Heathcliff.

The tournament scene in the film ends with Heathcliff, in his role as triumphant knight, raising Catherine from her role as his 'slave' to be 'the Princess Catherine of Yorkshire'. The class issue is thus neatly solved, in fantasy: she is allowed to be a princess, but only because he has raised her to that status; her gender status, on the other hand, is established as inferior to his. The visual image with which this scene ends, with Heathcliff looking out from Penistone Crag over the distant landscape and claiming his sovereignty over it, thus includes the gender construction of his sovereignty over Catherine. The later image of the adult Catherine and Heathcliff on Penistone Crag (Figure 4.8) might seem congruent with Cecil's Romantic reading of the lovers as elemental forces, unrelated to societies and codes of conduct, if we view it as an isolated still. Implicit in the film image, however, for the viewer who has already seen the knight-and-lady scene, is Catherine's subjugation by virtue of her sex to Heathcliff's dominance by virtue of his. The Catherine and Heathcliff pair are allowed to appear to transcend class differences at the cost of accepting gender difference as an essential part of the film's 'epic truth'. Viewers who believed themselves to be part of the classless society of the 1930s could identify sympathetically with the victims of the less enlightened days of costume drama, when stable-boys could not marry ladies, but the mythic status of the pair of lovers includes gender differences which have been naturalized as eternal truths, with a status which Kristeva calls, precisely, metaphysical (Moi 1986: 209).

It is perhaps significant that in Mooney and Stauffer's stage version of *Wuthering Heights* performed at Dublin Gate Theatre in 1939, the incidental music is no longer drawn from popular ballads and medleys, but includes Beethoven's 'Prometheus' overture, an aria from Tschaikovsky's *Eugène Onegin* and the theme from Wagner's *Tristan and Isolde*. Prometheus, the champion of humanity, who reached down fire from the gods, is a fitting symbol for the grander Romantic gestures of *Wuthering Heights*; the story of Tristan and Isolde, as de Rougemont verifies, provides the ultimate template for tragic heterosexual love in western culture; *Eugène Onegin*, a story of love for the wrong person or the right person at the wrong time, depends on the tragic ironies of love conceived as exclusive and ultimately subordinate to the economics of marriage. The use of these musical analogies confirms that *Wuthering Heights* has taken its place not only among the world's great love stories, but amidst our cultural heritage; the Hollywood hype, moreover, is not so far from the given structures of high culture. Olivier dying on Catherine's grave joins Tristan, who gains Isolde only in death, and Onegin, who dies for love of an inaccessible Tatiana; in each case the lamented woman is *la princesse lointaine*, held within the fastness of a husband's grasp. Sam Goldwyn may have been crude in expression, but he was in tune with the feeling of the age when he tried to call his film 'He Died for Her' (*BSG* 5: 1).[3]

Notes

1. According to Frank Kinkaid, 'the grandly passionate melody which represents the Jane/ Rochester relationship recurs in [Herrmann's opera] *Wuthering Heights* as Cathy's aria in Act 3, "I am burning"' (Kinkaid 1982: 16).
2. *The Times* 1.11.1939: 9, quoted in Cox 1992: 284. Philip Cox argues that the film was perceived as part of American culture as opposed to the English novel, so that the cool reception of the film in England repeats on a cultural level the political friction between Britain and America at this time. His argument is persuasive, but does not, I think, invalidate mine.
3. Wyler's film had ended with Heathcliff staggering onto Penistone Crag and dying there in the snow; Sam Goldwyn subsequently and against Wyler's wishes superimposed a ghostly pair of lovers walking towards the sky. See *Movie of the Week* (3.4.1939): 40 for a still of Heathcliff dead in the snow on what the caption describes as Catherine's grave.

Chapter 5

After the Second World War

Romance into Gothic: Jane Eyre *turns paranoid*

During the Second World War, the Hollywood films of *Jane Eyre* and *Wuthering Heights* gave unprecedented publicity to the Brontë stories while, as we saw in Chapter 4, assimilating their challenge to culturally acceptable norms. In the post-war era, as Elizabeth Wilson demonstrates, 'women's traditional role as a stabilising force – the ideology of the Victorians – was made a lynchpin of consensus now that women were citizens' (1980: 2). In this climate, these two novels, by way of their film versions, provided models of 'love' as a stabilizing force. A 1950s comicbook of *Jane Eyre* thus shows not the sensational failed wedding but the successful wedding, which is not represented in the novel. This reorientation seems derived directly from the 1944 film. The final words of the film are, 'as his first-born was put into his arms, he did see that his eyes were like his own, brilliant and black', and this heavy reinforcement of the reproductive family is repeated in the comicbook, whose final frame shows Rochester nursing his newborn son while Jane lies in her child-bed (Classics Illustrated No. 39).

During and after the war, the *Jane Eyre* plot became the formula of popular romance, and the staple of American television, but there was relatively little constructive interest in the novel before *Wide Sargasso Sea* in 1966. Existing stage plays continued to be performed, and a few new plays were performed at a local level. Most of these, especially those from the wartime period, reproduced the story in conventional gender terms. According to Donna Marie Nudd, Pauline Phelps's play, published in 1941 in Sioux City, Iowa, has a completely rewritten Ferndean scene which 'censors all of Brontë's feminism and replaces it entirely with sexist compromises' based on the following 'patriarchal' assumptions:

> 1) that a virile man, no matter how handicapped, would never allow himself to be dependent on a woman; 2) that it is alright for a woman to be deceitful if the goal is to help her man; and 3) that a woman will leave her lover, no matter how personally difficult it may be for her, if he wills it necessary.

Nudd reports that even women playwrights were still uneasy with Jane's declarations of equality, so that Jane Kendall's stage play, produced in Chicago in 1945, follows the Victorian melodramas and the 1920s Shomer play in having Rochester announce his marriage to Jane in public before any agreement has been reached between them (Nudd 1989: 180, 167). A Brontë Society exhibition in 1991 reported little post-war interest in *Jane Eyre* 'during this period of angry young men'. *Jane Eyre* needed, it seems, to be regarded as 'safe'.

Geoffrey Wagner describes *Jane Eyre* as 'probably *the* love story. It is so archetypal as to have made fortunes for women novelists, like Victoria Holt and Mary Stewart, who have used it as source' (1975: 244). Harriet Hawkins suggests that the phenomenally successful American soap opera, *Dynasty*, owes its structure to *Jane Eyre* (1990: 196), and women academics tell me that the same is true of the Spanish soap *Cristal*. Neil Sinyard suggests that *Jane Eyre* provided the plot for *The Sound of Music* (1965), in which 'a governess of independent spirit falls in love with her stern, domineering master whose forbidding façade is melted by her humane example . . .' (personal communication). The formula of mass market romance is also recognizably the plot of *Jane Eyre*. Tania Modleski describes the Harlequin formula as follows:

> a young, inexperienced, poor to moderately well-to-do woman encounters and becomes involved with a handsome, strong, experienced, wealthy man, older than herself by ten to fifteen years. The heroine is confused by the hero's behaviour since, though he is obviously interested in her, he is mocking, cynical, contemptuous, often hostile, and even somewhat brutal. By the end, however, all misunderstandings are cleared away, and the hero reveals his love for the heroine, who reciprocates. (1982: 36)

The formula represents a version of the Freudian paradigm – the Oedipal journey in which the young girl is kept from the desired father/lover by the rivalry of the bad mother until she is recognized as a sexual adult and rewarded by a father-like love. Juliet Mitchell and others have shown that Freud's model was descriptive rather than prescriptive; nevertheless because it was based on a nineteenth-century social pattern it has had a conservative effect in modern lives, being used to reinforce the ideology of femininity which Betty Friedan describes in *The Feminine Mystique*. Friedan shows that 'over and over women heard in voices of tradition and of Freudian sophistication that they could desire no greater destiny than to glory in their own femininity' ([1963] 1981: 13–14).

The large numbers of biographical works about the Brontës which continued to be produced during this period were also assimilated to this mystique, minimizing the distinctions between fiction and biography and emphasizing the 'love interest' (Braithwaite 1950; Raymond 1953; Day-Lewis 1954; Gérin 1954[–5]; Gittings [1955]; Carrington [1960]; Kyle 1963; Vipont 1966; Maurat 1969). Margaret Crompton, who published *Passionate Search: A Life of Charlotte Brontë* in 1955, also wrote a biographical play called *Shadows of Villette*, in which the situations of Charlotte Brontë's novel are used to reconstruct her life. Winifred Gérin, the biographer of all the Brontës, also wrote a play called *My Dear Master* in ?1954, containing a confrontation scene between Charlotte and Mme Heger and establishing the love triangle as the primary motivation in Charlotte's life. A reviewer of this play saw the dramatic contrast involved in this triangle as 'nothing but a trick of a playwright who understands the public's weakness', feeling that the 'story rises no higher than a woman's magazine story' (Gérin 1954[–5]).

Popular 'romance fiction' has a long history, and Mills and Boon, the publisher now most associated with this genre in Britain, was established in 1910, but this publishing field expanded rapidly in the post-war era with the new Canadian firm of Harlequin taking a lead in the field. According to Bridget Fowler, Harlequin sold 168 million copies worldwide in 1979, by which time they had absorbed most of their competitors, including Mills and Boon (1991: 27). The word 'romance' is difficult to define in literary terms. The popular meaning does not appear in the *Shorter Oxford English Dictionary*, for instance, and the word does not appear at all in M. H. Abrams's *A Glossary of Literary Terms* (1981). J. A. Cudden, in the Penguin *Dictionary of Literary Terms* (1979), gives eleven pages to medieval romance, the Romantic movement, the twentieth-century defeat of romance by realism, the Spanish romance, the French *romans* and Romanticism in general – but not a word about the meaning of the word as used in popular speech, meaning a love story. The entry in Maggie Humm's *Dictionary of Feminist Theory*, on the other hand, begins: 'early feminist theory generally denigrated romance as being a false construction of love' (1989: 194). For her, it is so obvious that a 'romance' is a love story that she does not find it necessary to say so. The difference between her assumptions and those of the Penguin Dictionary must be a difference of audience; romantic fiction in the modern, popular sense of a love story is mostly written by and for women. Humm's entry, however, is concerned with the argument which has gone on within feminism about whether reading romance fiction is a good or a bad thing for women; it does not help us with definitions or, really, with explanations. We must, therefore, turn directly to the Brontë novels to see what 'archetypal' features they offer.

Although *Jane Eyre* and *Wuthering Heights* are often bracketed together as archetypal romances, the pattern of romance they offer is actually quite different. Whereas *Jane Eyre* in essence accepts what Freud would see as the normal feminine path through the Oedipus complex, in which the young girl looks for a lover who is like her forbidden father, *Wuthering Heights* is based primarily on that earlier stage of psychological development in which children look for a confirmation of their own identity in a mirror-image of themselves, which can be provided metaphorically by the answering gaze of the mother, or of another child, a brother or sister. This type of love was, in the past, most characteristically expressed by men, whether medieval troubadors or the poets of the Romantic movement, and Emily Brontë's primary source within literature was the poetry of the male Romantics, who looked for ideal mirrors of themselves in mythological or divine women, spirits of beauty or truth, sometimes even conceived as sisters like Byron's half-sister Augusta or Shelley's Emilia Viviani, whom he imagines as his twin. It is a kind of love which finds its archetype in the myth of Narcissus, the youth who died for love of his own image in a pool. Psychoanalytic theory tells us that this kind of love is an attempt to recapture the pre-Oedipal child's blissful sense of wholeness, which actually derives from an unconscious union with its mother. The maternal element tends to be suppressed in statements of Romantic love, but it explains why the experience of Romantic love is more complete for men than for women. The element of the gaze, which is so important in masculine idealization of women, depends partly on the physical similarity between the desired woman and the lost mother. Women who try to recreate childish bliss in sexual love are usually frustrated by the fact that their masculine lovers are nothing like mothers, either in appearance or in behaviour (see Olivier 1989: 91; Dinnerstein [1976] 1987: 61).

Freud, however, described women's love rather than men's as narcissistic because he observed that women in the society he knew were often vain and obsessed with their appearance. Since this obsession is associated with the need to attract a lover, however, it does not derive from the mirror-like auto-eroticism of the Narcissus myth, but is an Oedipal manifestation – an effect of women's need to become the object of the 'father's' love. Men's love, on the other hand, he describes as anaclitic because men are assumed to be the active subjects of their desire, able to lay claim to the woman of their choice. Despite its inequality, Freud assumes that this pattern is more satisfying to the woman than the man, since it ends in the fulfilment of childbirth. The man, whose 'anaclitic' love is really a pursuit of his own ideal self, is not satisfied by domestication, and his frustrated desires have to be sublimated into the cultural products which constitute civilization. One form of sublimation is an intense, idealized love for a woman who is unattainable – for instance, because she is already married – and until the nineteenth century it was this kind of love, experienced exclusively by men and typically ending in death, which was called 'romantic' love. In literature, this tragic archetype of masculine, doomed love has been more highly valued than the feminine, domestic or 'comic' love which ends, like *Jane Eyre*, in marriage and procreation.

Superficially, *Wuthering Heights* seems to work within this archetype of tragic love, and, as we saw at the end of Chapter 4, Heathcliff in Wyler's film was assimilated to this pattern, represented by Tristan and Onegin. In the novel, however, as Heathcliff dies his lonely death twenty years after his Catherine, Catherine's daughter is about to marry her cousin who is in some ways a younger version of Heathcliff; what had been a tragic archetype for the older generation thus becomes a domestic love-and-marriage story for the younger. The existence of the younger generation complicates the tragic archetype in *Wuthering Heights*; but even if we concentrate on Catherine and Heathcliff, their story offers features which are different from medieval romances because we have almost equal access to the mental states of both lovers and their famous statements of their love are very similar. Catherine declares, 'Nelly, I *am* Heathcliff – he's always, always in my mind . . . – so, don't talk of our separation again – it is impracticable' (*WH* 82). Heathcliff laments Catherine's death by crying, 'Oh God! it is unutterable! I *cannot* live without my life! I *cannot* live without my soul!' (167). The novel offers a rare kind of narcissism in which each lover is both subject and object of their mirror-like love, but the unusual prominence of the female lover, and the modification offered by the second generation, are often ignored in reproductions.

Similarly, *Jane Eyre* cannot be read as conforming to an Oedipal structure in which the woman learns to be simply the passive object of masculine love. In *Jane Eyre*, the protagonist is vocal and active enough about her own subjective desires to destabilize her status as love-object. Much of the power of the novel lies in Jane's unconventional assertion of her own needs and independence, which Freud saw as 'masculine'. There are two climactic scenes in which Jane and Rochester negotiate terms on which their love might come to fruition. In the first proposal scene, in II viii, Rochester provokes Jane into a declaration by pretending to be about to marry someone else. Her response is,

> Do you think, because I am poor, obscure, plain, and little, I am soulless and heartless? – You think wrong? – I have as much soul as you, – and full as much heart! And if God had gifted me with some beauty, and much wealth, I should have made it as hard for you to leave me, as it is now for me to leave you. I am not talking to you now through the medium of custom, conventionalities, nor even of mortal flesh: – it is my spirit that addresses your spirit; just as if both had passed through the grave, and we stood at God's feet, equal, – as we are! (*JE* 265–6).

Later, in III i, when Rochester argues that she has no family to care what she does, she replies, '*I* care for myself. The more solitary, the more friendless, the more unsustained I am, the more I will respect myself' (334). In the last chapter, looking back on the happy conclusion to her trials, Jane describes her marriage:

> I have now been married ten years. I know what it is to live entirely for and with what I love best on earth. I hold myself supremely blest – blest beyond what language can express; because I am my husband's life as fully as he is mine. No woman was ever nearer to her mate than I am: ever more absolutely bone of his bone, and flesh of his flesh. I know no weariness of my Edward's society: he knows none of mine, any more than we each do of the pulsation of the heart that beats in our separate bosoms; consequently, we are ever together. To be together is for us to be at once as free as in solitude, as gay as in company. (475).

The novel thus gives us an ambiguous representation which conforms partly to the archetype of woman-as-object, but partly offers woman as subject of her desire and architect of an unconventional companionate marriage.

It can be argued that *Jane Eyre* is 'archetypal' not because its structure is simple, but because it reflects the tensions in female subjectivity which psychoanalysis itself recognizes as 'normal'. Freud himself confirmed that the woman's route through the Oedipus complex presents two particular sites of psychic difficulty. First, a girl must learn to give up the mother, the first object of desire, and substitute the relatively unknown and powerful father as a love object. This generates all those aspects of romance in which love is close to fear. In fictional terms, it is the source of the 'female Gothic' which Modleski identifies as the 'paranoid text' (1982: 33). Secondly, she must learn not actively to seek the object of love but to make herself into an object for an active, masculine desire. This generates self-doubt, since it is difficult to construct subjectivity from a passive position, and also anger, since active desire will not be easily repressed. If female Gothic is a 'paranoid text', then Julia

Kristeva, Juliet Mitchell and Tania Modleski agree that popular romance (for which *Jane Eyre* provides a paradigm) is a 'hysterical text'.

> The woman novelist must be an hysteric. Hysteria is the woman's simultaneous acceptance and refusal of the organisation of sexuality under patriarchal capitalism. It is simultaneously what a woman can do both to be feminine and to refuse femininity, within patriarchal discourse . . . the hysteric's voice . . . is *the woman's masculine language* . . . talking about feminine experience. It's both simultaneously the woman novelist's refusal of the woman's world . . . and her construction from within a masculine world of that woman's world. (Mitchell 1984: 289–90)

In Chapter 2 I argued that although *Jane Eyre* is a hysterical text in these terms, Jane Eyre is not (by comparison with the heroine of *The Turn of the Screw*, for instance), a hysterical heroine, because her access to the prevailing discourse about femininity offers her more power than a possible refusal of that discourse. Her situation within the dominant ideology is therefore alienated but not traumatic. The ways in which Jane negotiates her responses to Mr Rochester are repeated in 'women's romances' because Jane's response to Rochester is that of most 'normal' women within patriarchy. She accepts a father-figure in place of mother-love with a mixture of passion and suspicion, but she also intermittently takes up a pseudomasculine position herself, seeing herself from the outside, as the object of a masculine desire. This doubly alienating process creates in Jane, as in other women, an urgent need to diminish the gap between the father-figure and the lost mother, and between the masculine viewer and the feminine object of his gaze. Romance fictions written by women, therefore, often begin by emphasizing the gulf between men and women, but go on to show that the sexual lovers are really quite alike. This process of resolution is the simpler because, Modleski argues, the habitual romance reader, 'acquainted with the formula and hence in possession of what Wolfgang Iser calls "advance retrospection", is always able to interpret the hero's actions as the result of his increasingly intense love for the heroine'. At the same time, the hero's final confession of love comes to carry an element of revenge for the humiliations previously inflicted. Modleski argues that 'it is this element of revenge which must prevent us from analyzing the novels according to the Freudian paradigm of the young girl's maturation process' (Modleski 1982: 40).

Something of this 'revenge' can be felt in the transformation of Mr Rochester into a doting lover, especially when taken out of context. In 1962 Alfred Jepson published 'Rochester's Song to Jane Eyre', with 'lyrics by Charlotte Brontë'. The words sung by Rochester are so out of character with the brusque man we are first introduced to that when I first read these lyrics I thought they were not from the novel:

> The truest love, that ever heart
> felt at its kindled core;
> did thru each vein, in quickened start,
> The tide of being pour.
>
> Her coming was my hope each day

Her parting was my pain;
The chance that did her steps delay
was ice in every vein.
. . .

My love had placed her little hand
with noble faith in mine,
and vowed that wedlock's sacred band,
our nature should entwine.

My love has sworn, with sealing kiss,
with me to live to die.
I have at last my nameless bliss;
As I love, loved am I.

They are, of course, the words of the song Rochester sings during the engagement period, and in the novel they are placed in context by Jane's 'needle of repartee' which keeps him from the 'bathos of sentiment' (*JE* 286).

There is evidence, however, that by the 1950s male adaptors were smarting a little under Jane's treatment of Rochester. Sandra Gilbert and Susan Gubar argue that although, during the modernist era, women were perceived as 'winning' the sex war, 'male and female writers, working in the 1940s and 1950s, reimagined masculine victory' (1988: I 4–5). According to Donna Marie Nudd, Huntingdon Hartford's play, performed in New York in 1956, completely reorientates the story so as to remove Jane's spirited self-assertion and to focus instead on Rochester's inner torment; he is even given a new scene after the interrupted wedding, which 'could prove to be a true tour-de-force on the stage'. When Jane returns at the end to find Rochester blind, he completely controls the dialogue, proudly refusing to hear her confession of love even though she breaks down and confesses that she was wrong to have run away. Nudd reports that in a telephone interview, Hartford described the story of *Jane Eyre* as 'about "a man who's been around in the world . . . it's the same story as Rhett Butler and Scarlett O'Hara"' (1989: 105).

A gentler version of male victory can be seen in Hal Shaper's musical *Jane*, staged in 1961 at the Theatre Royal, Windsor, revived in London in 1966, in Canada in 1970–1 and again in Windsor in 1973. This version of *Jane Eyre* becomes, in Nudd's terms, 'a comic tale about the Master of Thornfield's love problems' (Nudd 1989: 114–18). Even gruff-an'-grim men like Rochester, it seems, can be shown as 'incurably romantic' inside, and their inadequately concealed needs become the stuff of romantic comedy as, for instance, we see Rochester's pre-wedding nerves. The titles of the songs indicate a basic romance structure. 'Thirty Pounds a Year' and 'Man's World' are followed by 'One Summer Evening' and 'If I'd Never Met You'. After complications involving the Ingrams and Rivers we conclude with 'Love Came By'. According to Nudd, Lowood in this musical is simply the location for the orphans to join enthusiastically in a chorus prefiguring how Jane will marry a duke, 'short and weighty' and 'very nearly eighty' who will leave her an heiress, free to marry for love. The whole ethos of the piece is determined by the assumption that Jane's pressing desire is to marry: 'It's sure to happen one day/That I'll be walking up the aisle' . . . (quoted in Nudd 1989: 109–10). Nudd describes Shaper's Rochester as 'a rather charming cad', and from her account he sounds rather like Henry Higgins in *My Fair Lady*, which had been on the West End stage since 1958. The Windsor programme note reminds us that 'few love stories are more well loved than "Jane Eyre"', and presumably Hal Shaper, the adaptor, was relying on the adage that all the world loves a lover. Charles Lemon of the Brontë Society was, however, churlish enough to wonder why it was decided

> to put Charlotte's novel to such a use and, for example, to portray Jane Eyre as a girl who falls in love with Mr Rochester at their first meeting in Hay Lane and who announces the fact to all and sundry on her return to Thornfield Hall. (*BST* 15.77.143 (1967))

A 1973 reviewer described the music as a 'Tin Pan Alley hash up'; perhaps the answer to Charles Lemon's wonder is that in the post-war era almost everyone had an interest in promoting 'love'. Elizabeth Wilson describes the effort which went into creating an ideology in which class struggle and the sex war were deemed to be outdated because their aims had been achieved. Since the welfare state and the emancipation of women had apparently made politics redundant, she argues, there was an unprecedented emphasis on private life (1980: 3–6).

The intensification of the domestic ideology of love and marriage produced, however, its own strains. Betty Friedan, in *The Feminine Mystique*, describes how women who had fought for independence in the 1930s now, in the 1950s, saw their daughters voluntarily giving up hard-won rights to education and employment and returning to the home under the impression that here was true feminine fulfilment. So much was invested in 'love' that it was bound to disappoint, and thus arose what Friedan calls 'the problem that has no name'. Her diagnosis is shocking: 'the feminine mystique has succeeded in burying millions of American women alive' ([1963] 1981: 293). Buried in the home, women 'finally are swallowed in an image of such passive dependence that they want men to make the decisions, even in the home' (44). Jacqueline Sarsby, working from a less affluent British situation where many women need to work, also describes how an unequal employment situation

> creates for women a dependence on marriage which puts them at a disadvantage within the relationship . . . No wonder, then, that what the fiction describes is a love-worship, not of women by men, as in the Middle Ages, but of men by women. (1983: 73)

Although dependence on marriage was the source of the problem, most women were unable to look outside marriage for the answer. As Sarsby puts it, 'as long as women perceive their career and their status as being achieved through marriage to a man, anxiety about that dependence is put into the idiom of romantic love' (108). The plot of *Jane Eyre* is, as we have seen, repeated in romance fiction to provide the reassurance that despite appearances, marriage does provide love, security and companionship. Simultaneously, however, the 'complications' of the *Jane Eyre* plot are exploited in the genre called woman's Gothic to give more emphatic expression to the heroine's repressed fears about the man she is involved with and/or the state of marriage towards which she is moving. Although *Jane Eyre* itself, with its 'comic' nuptial closure, conforms to the genre of romance, it also provides some major Gothic motifs – notably the incarcerated wife and the threatening mansion – and later reproducers of the Jane Eyre story have thus found it easy to tip the formal balance between romance and Gothic.

Christianna Brand's *Cat and Mouse* (*JE* 1950 Brand) suggests that the situation of post-war women made the Gothic mode particularly attractive to them. Katinka Jones, the heroine, is an agony aunt whose job depends on advising women conscious of 'hope passing, talents wasting away, beauty vanishing having blushed unseen' (22), mainly because of 'the war, darling . . . yours and my chaps were killed off' (12). Her jaunty advice is only a cover for her 'craving for cradles' (59); she knows that women in her situation must 'make do with a "career" and look as if you liked it' (21). Even those men who seem to be available, she complains, are always married already and probably keep 'a mad wife in the attic à la Jane Eyre' (12).

The situations of modern Gothics are similar to those of romance fiction, though in romances 'the preoccupation is with getting a man; in Gothics the concern is with understanding the relationship and the feelings involved once the union has been formed' (Modleski 1982: 61). Like romance, the 'Gothic' tale is able to draw on deep-seated psychological structures, but it invokes fear rather than desire. The formula of the romance is tipped so that the behaviour of the male can no longer be explained by hidden suffering, but becomes genuinely threatening. Joanna Russ, writing on the modern Gothic, thus entitles her article, 'Somebody's trying to kill me and I think it's my husband' (1973). Modleski explains that because the mother is for children of both sexes 'the first and strongest attachment', it is the father who is first perceived as '"the enemy" – the person capable of taking the mother away'. The boy deals with this situation by learning to identify with the former 'enemy' – a process which can be achieved even if the father is relatively distant; the girl, however, has the more difficult – because more intimate – task of making 'her "enemy" her "lover"' (73–4). Negotiating this process involves confronting the mother's own relationship to 'the enemy', since if the mother is perceived as threatened by the father, then the daughter will be unable to put herself in the mother's place. Modleski describes the Gothic as 'paranoid text' because its main project is to identify 'the enemy', but the Gothic heroine's anxiety is greatly increased because she suffers both 'the desperate need . . . to find out who her "enemy" is and the equally imperative desire to discover that the enemy is *not* the father (or the lover, who is the father substitute)' (74). Because in every western child's psychic history the father has in fact played the part of the enemy, Gothics cannot explain fear out of existence but can only divert it; moreover, since the heroines end by reinstating themselves in the situation of the mother, the potential for uncanny repetition is always reinscribed in the 'happy ending'.

Joanna Russ describes modern Gothics as 'a crossbreed of *Jane Eyre* and Daphne du Maurier's *Rebecca*'; this genealogy is conscious 'and most of them advertise themselves as "in the Du Maurier tradition", "in the Gothic tradition of *Rebecca*", and so on' (1973: 666). We have already seen how easily the elements of *Jane Eyre* can be re-emphasized to produce a chill of horror in works such as *The Turn of the Screw* (1898), *The Secret of Kyriels* (1899), *Vera* (1928), *Harriet* (1934), *Rebecca* (1938) and *I Walked with a Zombie* (1943). Russ describes the features of *Jane Eyre* which become essential to this later genre as 'the House, the Heroine, the Super-Male, the Other Woman, the Ominous Dialogue, the Secret and the Untangling' (670). The potential husband, like the romance hero, is

> an older man, a dark, magnetic, powerful brooding, sardonic *Super-Male*, who treats her brusquely, derogates her, scolds her, and otherwise shows anger or contempt for her. The Heroine is vehemently attracted to him and usually just as vehemently repelled or frightened – she is not sure of her feelings for him, his feelings for her, and whether he (1) loves her, (2) hates her, (3) is using her, or (4) is trying to kill her. (668)

The heroine of *Cat and Mouse*, for instance, falls in love with the husband of one of her correspondents, after which she produces wildly variant hypotheses to explain his behaviour, in which her perception of him swings from devoted husband to professional charmer to mass murderer; he proves to have killed three wives whose clothes are kept in the attic. This novel is thus a variant of the pattern described by Russ, in which the Untangling invariably reveals that the Super-Male is guiltless, though the superficially attractive man Russ calls the Shadow-Male may prove to be 'an insane mass-murderer of a whole string of previous wives' (669); in *Cat and Mouse* the Super-Male is the mass murderer and the Shadow-Male proves the reliable partner. The main difference between Gothic and romance is in the degree of threat experienced by the heroine (which often reaches extremes such as being buried alive or pushed over cliffs), and the confirmation that although she may have suspected the wrong person, the threat was in fact real. Moreover, the sensation experienced by the heroines in *Vera* and *Rebecca*, that '*it has all happened before*' becomes the staple of the modern Gothic. According to Russ, 'the eeriest plot element in these books is the constant "doubling" of the Heroine – she is always in some fashion a "stand-in" for someone else, usually someone who has been killed. This someone is often the Other Woman . . .' (683). Katinka, for instance, finds herself repeating a helpless retreat from Carlyon towards a cliff over which a previous wife has already fallen. Self-conscious literary reference extends this effect of iteration beyond the single text: the dedication to *Cat and Mouse* includes a long quotation from *Northanger Abbey* and Katinka finds herself visited in bed by a particularly gruesome version of the madwoman in the attic:

> something not human. A face and not a face. Two little pig-like eyes in a vast round disc of incredible patch-work . . . Something that drooled and dripped saliva on her upturned face, and slowly advanced towards her a clammy white claw, the crooked fingers glistening with wet blood . . . (*JE* 1950 Brand: 46)

Explicit allusion reminds the reader for the second time that in 1950 it is still possible for husbands to keep 'a mad wife in the attic, à la Jane Eyre' (184). It is this repetitive element in the Gothics, as Modleski argues, that explains why they have

proved very attractive to many women writers, including avowed feminists . . .
the Gothic has been used to drive home the 'core of truth' in feminine paranoid
fears and to connect the social with the psychological, the personal with the political.
It has been used to show how women are at least potentially 'pure victims', but how,
in coming to view themselves as such, they perpetuate the cycle of victimization
which occurs between fathers and mothers, mothers and daughters. (Modleski
1982: 83)

Eve Kosofsky-Sedgwick, in *The Coherence of Gothic Conventions*, offers a further
explanation, arguing that 'any dire knowledge that is shared but cannot be
acknowledged to be shared – that is, as it were, *shared separately* – has the effect of
rendering the people, whom it ought to bind together, into an irrevocable
doubleness' ([1980] 1986: 17).

This irrevocable doubleness is particularly evident in Victoria Holt's *Mistress of
Mellyn* (*JE* 1961 Holt), in which Martha Leigh arrives in Cornwall as governess to
Connan TreMellyn's daughter Alvean. 'Tragedy' seems to hang over the house;
she discovers that Alvean's mother, Alice, 'is dead, but somehow she remains'. As
in *Rebecca* and *South Riding*, Alice's riding-habit confers an inherited identity on
Martha when she borrows it; she looks in the mirror and sees Alice (81). Martha,
like Jane, resists her employer's embraces: 'Did he imagine he was an eastern
pasha?' (106). She awakes to find 'the dark shape of a woman' in her room, which
speaks to her, but it is only the riding-habit (107–8); later she sees Alice's portrait
and says, 'You are haunting me, Alice' (209). The story becomes complicated and
departs from the *Jane Eyre* paradigm when Martha, after suffering several attempts
on her life, finds herself locked in a priest's hole with the long-dead body of Alice.
Martha is rescued by an illegitimate girl-child who lurks in Alice's room, expecting
every female inhabitant to repeat Alice's story. The villain in this story turns out to
be another woman, Celestine, who is in love with the *house* and uses it against any
likely inhabitant; but before she can be tried for her crime 'she was a raving lunatic'
(254). The impact of the story is to make us feel that the world is indeed a dangerous
place for women, that threats are real and women's power small, yet that all the
threats can be evaded if only we choose the right man. As an old woman, Martha
remembers 'the day I felt Connan's arms about me and I knew he had brought me
back to life' (256).

One of the more uncanny moments in this formula story is when Martha, in the
priest's hole, tries to talk to the dead Alice. During this time 'I was not sure who I
was. Was I Martha? Was I Alice?' As in *Vera*, the two wives are potential allies;
Martha hears herself talking and believes it is Alice: 'I thought that at last I had
found her, and that we had comfort to offer each other as I waited to go with her
into the shadowy world' (247–8). After she is rescued she continues to talk to Alice,
believing they are both dead. The whole framing of the story, which is being told
by Martha as an old woman to her great-grandchildren, provides an illusion of
analysis, communication and warning, which nevertheless only encloses the female
hearers within the structure from which the danger derives. Eve Kosofsky-
Sedgwick argues that in the 'classic' Gothic tale

the important privation is the privation exactly of language, as though language were a sort of safety valve between the inside and the outside which being closed off, all knowledge, even when held in common, becomes solitary, furtive, and explosive. ([1980] 1986: 17)

The point about *The Mistress of Mellyn* and the other Gothics which so closely resemble it is that the speaker, like Jane Eyre, does have access to language. The language itself, however, is part of 'the law' of patriarchy which, while offering lucidity and escape, turns the speaker back into the prison. Jane Eyre, believing in the power of reason to revise social structures, shows Ferndean as a believable refuge from the world of the 'big house'. The Gothics are paranoid texts because, while pointing to the refuge, they also perpetuate the memory of the wife who was buried alive.

This cyclical, enclosing structure is crucial to the Gothic effect and is different from the merely frightening. As early as 1906 we find evidence that the madwoman from *Jane Eyre* proves frightening to a little boy. In L. Allen Harker's *Concerning Paul and Fiametta*, six-year-old Paul investigates the forbidden story of 'Jane, who lived "on the third shelf, right-hand corner bookcase near the door"'. That night, he wakens the house with 'the most dreadful heart-rending screams', which he explains by 'a long story about a "dreadful face – she looked in the glass – a dreadful purple face – and she tore the veil right in two – she tore it! Oh! is she gone? Send her away – oh, send her away!"' (in Cunliffe 1950: 333) On the other hand, Elizabeth Taylor's *At Mrs Lippincote's* (1945) includes a little boy who makes a friend of the first Mrs Rochester, whom he imagines shut in the tower of their house. The juxtaposition of these two texts reminds us that the 'effect' of a novel does not inhere within it, but is created in the dialogue of text and reader.

A number of Taylor's novels have explicit Brontë references, but her *Palladian* (1946) is a particularly penetrating analysis of the interface between romance and the Gothic. *Palladian* is a self-consciously 'literary' text with explicit references both to *Jane Eyre* and to the generic conventions of Gothic and romance. More interesting still, it merges the structures of *Jane Eyre* and *Wuthering Heights*. Despite the differences between *Jane Eyre* and *Wuthering Heights*, popular reproduction in the 1930s and 1940s had, as we saw in Chapter 4, already had the effect of assimilating the two texts to one another, both by stressing their common triangle structure, and by repeating material circumstances of reproduction such as the same actors playing parts in films and plays based on both texts. There was also a tendency to unify the geographical setting of the two novels: Helen Jerome's 1936 play of *Jane Eyre* has Jane hearing Rochester's voice in 'the wind wailing on the moors' (*JE* 1936 Jerome: 261), while comicbook versions from the 1950s stress Jane's wild life at Moor House, showing her with a short skirt and bare feet. The effect is to confuse Jane Eyre and Catherine Earnshaw, just as the swirling mist and wind-like music for Orson Welles's *Jane Eyre* creates an atmosphere similar to that of Olivier's *Wuthering Heights*, suggesting that what a 'wild woman' like Jane/ Catherine needed was the love of a passionate man, like Rochester/Heathcliff. Bernard Herrmann, who wrote the music for the 1944 film of *Jane Eyre*, was in fact to go on to write a full-scale opera, *Wuthering Heights* (1965). The general effect of these convergences is to produce the two stories as positive (comic) and negative (tragic) versions of the structure in which monogamous love excludes a third party.

Because popular fiction generally provides a happy ending for its love stories, it is the *Jane Eyre* plot which has been definitively associated with 'romance'. Jerry Palmer, commenting on the survival of melodrama into what Brooks calls a 'post-sacred' society, points out that in the twentieth century, 'the critical divide between "high" and "low" culture is located between . . . tragedy, on the one hand, and melodrama on the other; thus high culture is based upon masculine genres, and feminine ones are relegated to low culture' (1991: 167). *Wuthering Heights*, as we have seen, was slow to win popular approval, and the 'breakthrough' Olivier film was itself associated with 'high' culture. Nevertheless, this and other reproductions of the novel actually evade its real challenge, which lies in its focus on pre-Oedipal 'mirror' relationships rather than Oedipal triangles. What we might call the 'triangulation' of *Wuthering Heights* makes its story intelligible in the same way as *Jane Eyre*, bringing it into the category of the 'weepy', which is also built on a romance structure.

Palladian appears to follow this pattern, incorporating *Wuthering Heights* into a structure of overlapping triangles. The plot blatantly echoes *Jane Eyre*, showing us how Cassandra Dashwood goes to Cropthorne Manor as governess to Sophy, the daughter of Marion Vanbrugh. Marion, however, the figure who occupies the Rochester-slot, is in character like Edgar Linton, and is contrasted with his cousin, Tom, who has been made into 'a sort of glowering Heathcliff' by his dead mistress, Violet, who was also Marion's wife (*JE* [1946] 1985 Taylor: 166). Cassandra, the Jane-figure, has dreamt of 'the circle of her existence . . . one day becoming concentric' with another (134), and the novel does indeed end with her union with the 'Rochester' figure. It is not, however, a positive ending. While popular reproductions have 'domesticated' *Wuthering Heights* by association with *Jane Eyre*, *Palladian* uses *Wuthering Heights* to subvert *Jane Eyre*'s ideology. Juliet Mitchell points out that the pre-Oedipal mirror-love offered by *Wuthering Heights* is not a real alternative to what Lacan calls 'the law' of the Symbolic order. 'You cannot', Mitchell argues, 'choose the imaginary' (the pre-Oedipal) because 'it is set up by the law precisely as its own . . . imaginary alternative, but not as a symbolic alternative' (1984: 291). The idea of 'oneness' offered by *Wuthering Heights* is perennially attractive but practically unattainable:

> 'Oneness' is the symbolic notion of what happens before the symbolic; it is death and has to be death. The choices for the woman within the novel, within fiction, are either to survive by making the hysteric's ambiguous choice into a femininity which doesn't work (marrying Edgar) or to go for oneness and unity, by suffering death (walking the moors as a ghost with Heathcliff). (293)

Cassandra, the 'Jane'-figure in *Palladian*, seems to have settled for the first option; the 'ambiguity' of this option, however, is stressed in a way which the popular romances avoid.

As in *South Riding*, the 'big house' in *Palladian* is in a condition of decay which, again, recalls *To the Lighthouse*:

> as the life was gradually withdrawn, the house became a shell only, seeming to foreshadow its own strange future when leaves would come into the hall . . . Then the stone floor of the hall would heave up and erupt with dandelion and briar, the bats swing up the stairs and the dusty windows show dark stars of broken glass . . . (*JE* 1946 Taylor [1985: 187])

In *Jane Eyre*, *Rebecca* and *South Riding*, the heroine's future depends on the destruction of the grand house. The immediate post-war setting of *Palladian*, however, seems to intensify both the natural decay of the house, which there is no money to avert, and the nostalgia for the pre-war life it represents. Everyone in the novel is threatened by the imminent collapse of the conservatory, a 'great ruin of dusty glass' which 'might come down at any time' (44). On the other hand, they spend their lives reliving – even re-embodying – the past. Marion, like Maxim de Winter, has 'exaggeratedly long hands like hands in an Elizabethan portrait' (35) and spends his days reading the literature of past ages; even Nanny is addicted to film remakes of classic novels: 'That Elizabeth Bennet . . . That's a lovely place she's got up in Beverley Hills . . . Some of the old-fashioned stories make up into a nice film' (55). In *Palladian* the Jane and Rochester pair do not remove to Ferndean but return to the unchanged house which incorporates the past. Cassandra is perceived by the other characters as making 'the change from governess to mistress of the house very charmingly . . . like one of the fairy tales' (190). The first thing they do on returning from their honeymoon, however, is to inspect the conservatory, which has finally collapsed, and as they enter the crumbling mansion which is to be the scene of their domestic idyll, we are told that 'the dark shadows of indoors fell coldly . . . like a knife' (192). The novel thus chillingly suggests that Mitchell's apparent 'options' are identical; the heroine of romance chooses, not between life and death, but between one kind of death and another.

An added factor in *Palladian*'s critique of romance is Cassandra's consciousness of her proceedings. Modleski argues that the typical romance reader 'is superior in wisdom to the heroine' because she knows the formula and therefore 'does not have to suffer the heroine's confusion' (1982: 41). Cassandra, however, is a romance reader as well as a romance heroine, and accepts the Jane Eyre position with all the complacency of 'advance retrospection' (Wolfgang Iser, quoted in Modleski 1982: 40). John Hannay, in *The Intertextuality of Fate*, argues that the existence of generic plots like that of romance fiction constitutes a modern sense of 'fatedness'; 'we "know what comes next"', he says, 'because we recall analogous stories and so discern the proleptic logic of the one we are reading' – or living (1986: 1–2). Where Modleski describes the typical Gothic heroine as 'desperately struggl[ing] . . . against assuming the victim's role', Cassandra 'knows the plot beforehand'. Before she even meets Marion, we are told that she has 'a very proper willingness to fall in love, the more despairingly the better, with her employer' (*JE* 1946 Taylor [1985:

17]). After their first interview, she takes herself to task, knowing 'that Jane Eyre had answered up better than that to her Mr Rochester' (35). Cassandra, who identifies herself as a romance heroine, 'recognizes' her destiny with an expectation of bliss which is not disturbed by events. For us, the readers, however, this recognition only feeds a pattern of uncanny repetition. The novel's intertextual devices produce in us both the 'Gothic' terrors to which the heroine is immune, and the paranoid urge to 'identify the enemy'. *Palladian*, however, departs from the pattern of popular Gothics by identifying the enemy as neither the father/lover, nor the first wife/other woman, nor even the crumbling mansion, but as a literary structure incorporating a compulsion to repeat. Taylor's text plays with the categories of romance and Gothic in such a way that what the heroine perceives as romance the reader perceives as Gothic, in which 'the enemy' is identified as – romance. It is neither the plot nor the conventional motifs, but the self-referentiality of *Palladian* which forces us to read it as a Gothic text, in which the benign mirrorings of *Jane Eyre* and *Wuthering Heights* are inscribed as uncanny repetitions.

As in *South Riding* and *Mistress of Mellyn*, the daughter of the house in *Palladian* is obsessed with the portrait and the clothes of her dead mother, Violet, who, like Muriel Carne and Rebecca, was beautiful and temperamental and rode horses furiously (51, 55). In the *Jane Eyre* plot, Violet occupies the position of the madwoman who leaps to her death; in the *Wuthering Heights* structure she is the dead Catherine. In *Palladian*, however, as in Clemence Dane's *Regiment of Women*, it is the child that dies, killed by the falling statue of Pomona (148). The implication is that in these closed circles it is the future that is at risk, and that the crucial problem facing women is the daughter's relationship to her mother.

The story of *Palladian*, like *Rebecca* and *Mistress of Mellyn*, revolves around an absent centre constituted by the dead/mad wife/mother. John Crompton, in his thesis on Elizabeth Taylor, points out that for the other characters in the novel, 'Violet is . . . a repertoire of stories, texts by which they define their identities' (Crompton 1992: 215), and he has identified a similar structure in a text which otherwise has only a glancing relationship with *Jane Eyre*, namely Iris Murdoch's *The Unicorn* (1963). Marian Taylor, in *The Unicorn*, goes as governess/companion to Hannah Crean-Smith, who has been confined to Gaze Castle in a remote part of Scotland since she (perhaps) pushed her husband Peter over a cliff. He survives, maimed and mutilated, but stays off-scene in New York until the end. Hannah is (probably) not mad but it is difficult to ascertain what she is because her image is refracted by other people (a lover, Pip Lejour; his father Max, a Platonic scholar; Max's ex-student, now a senior civil servant; Effingham Cooper, who loves Hannah as *la princesse lointaine*; Denis Nolan, a local retainer; Gerald Sottow, her husband's stand-in and lover; Violet Evercreech, a distant cousin and housekeeper; and her young brother Jamesie who is also attached to Gerald). Each of these uses Hannah as the focus for some private fantasy or theory, so that she appears as everything from a perfected saint to a 'murderous, adulterous bitch'.

The text is self-consciously intertextual, with references to courtly love, the Virgin Mary, *la belle dame sans merci*, the Vampire, the Lady of Shalott and so on.

Although 'explanations' are sometimes offered for people's behaviour, they are always inadequate to the whole. Hannah is the 'absent centre' who keeps meaning moving in an endless process of deferral. She herself, however, is kept in place by the even more absent Peter, who is nothing but a name. When Hannah kills Gerald, she then has to kill herself; then Denis kills Peter and Pip kills himself – in other words, the whole interdependent structure collapses. 'Gaze Castle' clearly refers to the 'prison house' of the gaze for both gazer and gazed at. The Penguin cover picture shows a sixteenth-century French tapestry in which a lady shows a unicorn a mirror, and Hannah occupies the place of the unicorn, mythically beautiful and elusive. The relation between *The Unicorn* and *Jane Eyre* is tenuous except by way of a chain of texts, including *The Secret of Kyriels*, *Vera* and *Rebecca*, in which the 'madwoman' does not merely occupy a place in an Oedipal triangle, as an obstacle to true love, but constitutes a focus for the fears or desires of the other characters. *The Unicorn* is written in such a way that it is impossible to know 'the truth' about Hannah. By listening to different versions of her identity, we can read the whole story as, among many other things, a romance or a tale of terror. In conjunction with the other texts, it shows us that the difference between genres is less a matter of structure than of perspective. What the unicorn sees in the mirror we do not know.

Jane Eyre as mirror and monster: intertextual strategies in women's self-representation

Within the framework of the Gothic, the figure in the third storey changes from monster to mirror as our gaze shifts. It is, perhaps, even more disturbing to find that 'our heroine' – Jane Eyre herself – is subject to the same shifts of perception. By the late 1960s, in the beginnings of the women's liberation movement, we find women writers looking, as in the 1850s, for female heroines. Two such writers are A. S. Byatt and Margaret Drabble. The heroines of A. S. Byatt's *The Game* (1967) and Margaret Drabble's *The Waterfall* (1969) make extended use of literary 'mirrors'; *Jane Eyre* in particular appears as what Umberto Eco calls an 'intertextual archetype'. These latterday women, however, are much more ambivalent than their Victorian predecessors about Jane Eyre herself, the character who sometimes seems the mirror of our desires, and sometimes the horror-story of our frustrations. Despite their element of horror, these texts are not part of the Gothic genre but lean towards the *Bildungsroman*, dealing with women's self-knowledge and self-development. Because they foreground the intertextuality of both autobiography and fiction, however, they differ from those earlier texts referring back to *Jane Eyre*, such as *The Weather in the Streets* or *South Riding*, which discussed the proper object of women's desire – work or love – and are more like *The Brontës Went to Woolworth's* (Ferguson [1931] 1988) in being concerned with the control of the process of representation – of writing. Moreover, like Rachel Ferguson's novel, these later texts also suggest that women's control of self-representation is not always a process by which they find 'mirrors' of themselves in older texts or in other women, but is sometimes an unpleasantly aggressive process in which older texts and other women appear monstrous, so that the writer must at all costs separate herself from these mothers or sisters who are at the same time too much like themselves and too horribly unlike what they want to be.

Each of these texts refers explicitly to *Jane Eyre* and each was written by a woman who, like Charlotte Brontë, shared a childhood fantasy-world with siblings.[1] A. S. Byatt and Margaret Drabble are sisters who appear, fictionally transformed, in each other's novels; in Byatt's novel one of the fictional sisters also writes a novel about a fictional family-fantasy. The connections between 'life' and 'fiction' are here unusually convoluted, but it is commonly accepted that 'intertextuality' is not confined to the printed page. I referred above to John Hannay, who, in *The Intertextuality of Fate*, argues that the existence of generic plots like that of romance fiction constitutes a modern sense of 'fatedness' (1986: 1–2), so that Elizabeth Taylor can begin *Palladian* by saying, 'Cassandra, with all her novel-reading, could be sure of experiencing the proper emotions' (*JE* 1946 Taylor [1985: 5]). Patricia Duncker, in *Sisters and Strangers*, puts it more crudely: we 'interpret our experiences as we have been told to do' (1992: 13).

For Byatt and Drabble, *Jane Eyre* functions as a 'generic plot', transmitted both direct and by means of an intertextual chain, which for A. S. Byatt includes Rachel Ferguson.

> I read *The Brontës Went to Woolworths* [Byatt writes] when I was . . . a very well-read schoolgirl whose imaginary life was considerably livelier, more populated and more interesting than her real one. I was intrigued by the title, which seemed to suggest some impossible meeting of the urgent world of the romantic imagination and the everyday world of (in my case) Pontefract High Street. (in Ferguson [1931] 1988: iii).

For all these writers 'the urgent world of the romantic imagination' offered more than 'the everyday world'; moreover, it was a world shared with siblings. Charlotte Brontë describes *her* family-fantasy in a poem, 'We wove a web in childhood . . .' (epigraph to *JE* 1967 Byatt [1987: 6]); but the fantasy lasted into adult life. At the age of twenty, she knew her Angrian characters as well as her brother and sisters; her daydreams were a resource so valuable that she provides it for her heroine in *Jane Eyre*. As a governess in Thornfield Hall, Jane describes how 'my sole relief was . . . to open my inward ear to a tale that was never ended – a tale . . . quickened with all of incident, life, fire, feeling, that I desired and had not in my actual existence' (*JE* 114).

Like Antonia Byatt on Pontefract High Street, Jane Eyre's daydreaming stems from an unsatisfying life. In fact Freud, in *Creative Writers and Day-Dreaming* [1908], argues that 'every single phantasy is the fulfilment of a wish, a correction of unsatisfying reality' (1985: 134–5). Florence Nightingale made the same observation in the 1850s; in 'Cassandra', she imagines a Victorian family group and asks, 'Mothers, how many of your sons and daughters are *there*, do you think, while sitting round under your complacent eye? . . . Is not one fancying herself the nurse

of some new friend in sickness; another engaging in romantic dangers . . .?'
Nightingale sees that 'it is the want of interest in our life which produces'
daydreaming. Moreover, like Freud, she sees its connection with creative writing:
'what are novels? [she asks] What is the secret of the charm of every romance
. . . ?' Her answer is two-fold: novels provide scope for thoughts and feelings, and
they liberate the heroine from 'family ties' ([1852] 1978: 397).

Like Nightingale, Jane Eyre knows that 'human beings . . . must have action; and
they will make it if they cannot find it' (*JE* 114). On the other hand, Jane's dreams
seem to be satisfied by Mr Rochester, just as Elizabeth Barrett Browning writes,

> I lived with visions for my company,
> Instead of men and women, years ago . . .
> [x/ x/] . . . Then THOU didst come . . . to be,
> Belovéd, what they seemed . . . (*Sonnets from the Portuguese*, no. XXVI)

Freud, too, argues that while men's fantasies are mostly ambitious, women's are
mostly erotic. It is the interaction of erotic and ambitious dreams which these novels
investigate.

The sinister atmosphere of A. S. Byatt's *The Game* (*JE* 1967 Byatt) recalls *The
Brontës Went to Woolworth's*; but whereas in Ferguson's novel modern sisters use
their shared fantasy against a perceived Brontë threat, in Byatt's novel a childhood
game shared by sisters becomes an adult fight to the death. Freud suggests that

> a phantasy . . . hovers . . . between . . . the three moments of time which our ideation
> involves . . . some provoking occasion in the present . . . which . . . arouse[s] one of
> the subject's major wishes . . . a memory of an earlier experience . . . in which this
> wish was fulfilled; and . . . the future which represents a fulfilment of the wish. (1908
> [1985: 135])

In *The Game* the 'provoking occasion' is a television series, seen separately by both
sisters, presented by a man who had been part of their youthful game; but neither
their memories nor their 'wishes' are at all clear. Linda Anderson argues that
Freud's sense of connection between past and present was much more complex
than his 'Daydreaming' essay suggests; he 'came to believe that memories were
[themselves] . . . phantasies, constructed out of wishes and their repression'.
Thus 'the neurotic for Freud was someone who could not tell their own story'
(1986: 54–5).

In *The Game*, Cassandra, the elder sister, is an Oxford don; Julia a successful
novelist. Cassandra is celibate; Julia is married; but their desires cannot be reduced
to Freud's categories of erotic or ambitious wishes. Freud himself concedes that
the categories are 'often united', and Jacques Lacan argues that objects of desire
are always relatively arbitrary, since desire is a process of infinite deferral (Freud
1908 [1985: 135]).[2] Since the gap between the subject and the object of desire is
bridged, if at all, by language, it is appropriate that the sisters in *The Game* strive
not for specific objects but for transient victories in the battle for self-representation.

Judith Kegan Gardiner argues that 'literary identifications . . . derive some of
their undoubted power from analogy with earlier mental states' (1981: 356), and in

The Game, the academic Cassandra finds a literary 'mother' in Charlotte Brontë, who 'had seen the Duke of Zamorna leaning against a school mantel-shelf and had felt exhilarated and faint' (*JE* 1967 Byatt [1983: 24]). Her sister Julia, however, uses both Cassandra and Charlotte Brontë not as mothers but as daughters in her own novel, in the sense that Gardiner suggests, that 'the hero is her author's daughter' (1981: 349). Ironically, a fictional reviewer praises Julia's 'sympathy for her central character, Emily, the lady don', whose 'imaginative life' suggests 'Charlotte Brontë's passion for the Duke of Zamorna' (*JE* 1967 Byatt [1983: 219]). Julia's 'sympathy', however, has left no space for Cassandra to 'write herself'. If, as Gardiner argues, 'female identity is a process' (1981: 349), Cassandra's use of Charlotte Brontë had been a strategy in that process; but Julia's novel 'identifies' her sister in the sense of fixing her to that image. In a paper entitled 'The unfixed text', Judy Simons cites Felicity Nussbaum in *The Autobiographical Subject* as distinguishing 'between the fixed, finished and printed work, and the unfixed text, one that is continually in process, undergoing constant revision and apparently avoiding closure' (in Fortunati and Morisco [1993]: 1). This distinction exactly matches the difference between Cassandra's private use of Charlotte Brontë and Julia's public 'fixing' of her to that model. Cassandra's private mirror turns into a public monster. 'There is', she knows, 'nowhere I shall not drag this grotesque shadow' (*JE* 1967 Byatt [1983: 230]). So she kills herself. Julia is not unscathed – 'all her life Cassandra had been the mirror . . . that proved her existence; now, she had lost a space and a purpose' – but she has won the battle for reality, which proved to be a battle of words (235). Cassandra's real death comes in the final sentence where, 'closed into crates, unread, unopened, Cassandra's private papers bumped and slid' (238).

In *The Private Self*, Susan Stanford Friedman suggests that women's auto-biography is characterized by a sense of sharing. Drawing on Nancy Chodorow's theories, Friedman argues that whereas male autobiography requires 'a conscious awareness of the singularity of each individual life', women's autobiographies 'often explore their sense of shared identity with other women', feeling themselves 'very much *with* others in an interdependent existence'. This theoretical perspective raises a problem for the texts I am dealing with. Friedman acknowledges that women's 'sense of shared identity . . . exists in tension with a sense of their own uniqueness' (Benstock 1988: 34, 38, 44), and Gardiner points out that 'the word "identity" is paradoxical in itself, meaning both sameness and distinctiveness' (1981: 347). In Byatt and Drabble 'sameness' itself is the threat. In *The Waterfall*, Jane feels that her cousin Lucy is 'my sister, my fate, my example: her effect on me was incalculable' (*JE* 1969 Drabble [1971: 114]); but she is 'tired of all this Freudian family nexus' (130). Similarly Cassandra in *The Game* feels that she and Julia have been 'too real to each other, sharing the same thoughts . . . In an ideal state they should be no more and no less real to each other than anyone else' (*JE* 1967 Byatt [1983: 97]).

Carol Gilligan, in her book about women's ethical decision-making (1982), provides an explanation for this troubling unsisterliness. Like Susan Friedman, Gilligan uses Chodorow as her theoretical base, but unlike Friedman she argues that women, precisely because they have more fluid ego-boundaries than men, tend to experience ethical problems with individuation, whereas men experience problems with relationship. Interviews show that the women who feel happiest with their lives are those who feel that they have made their own decisions – even if afterwards they feel they were wrong – rather than being 'a character in someone else's story'. This could explain both the unpleasantly aggressive strategies by which my fictional sisters free themselves from the 'grotesque shadow' (*JE* 1967 Byatt [1983: 230]) of their monstrous symbioses (Creighton 1987), and the fact that the novels end on a fairly positive note. Even Jane Gray, in *The Waterfall*, who begins as 'the heroine of a life that *has no story*' (Gilbert and Gubar 1979: 39), stealing Charlotte Brontë's story to depict herself as suffering in 'some Brussels of the mind' (*JE* 1969 Drabble [1971: 84]), has 'the power of revision. As the narrator of the novel, she is able to rewrite the story of Jane Eyre' (Berg, T. 1985: 130). She ends by writing 'a very good sequence of poems' (*JE* 1969 Drabble [1971: 233]) from her fear that her lover was dying. The fact that he did not die underlines the extent to which our stories can be liberated from our lives – or vice versa. The generic texts of tragic love, of comic romance, are each susceptible to interception, and, like Derrida's postcard, can be diverted to other destinations.

The women in both Byatt's and Drabble's novels move from Jane Eyre to Charlotte Brontë and back with no sense of disparity. From this distance in time, of course, 'Charlotte Brontë' is just as much a textual construct as 'Jane Eyre', and there is no way of preventing our knowledge of the one influencing the way we read the other. Nevertheless there are important differences between them. Jane Eyre, a fictional heroine, writes her own life; she is happy with the decisions she has made and sees herself as a character in her own story. If Charlotte Brontë had written her autobiography, it is likely that she would have written not of her passionate desire but of her life as a dutiful daughter. When Robert Southey gave his famous advice that 'literature cannot be the business of a woman's life', Charlotte replied that her ambition had all been 'senseless trash' (Gaskell [1857] 1975: 173–4) – but she also began writing *Jane Eyre*. Stevie Davies describes this as a process 'whereby words (a sign in themselves of loss . . .) are liberated from their original conditions to be inscribed in the form of a homeopathic . . . remedy for the very conditions they record' (Davies 1988: 89–90).

Charlotte Brontë did not write her life, she wrote her daydream, composed of Freud's three elements; the memory of loss, of mother, sisters, lover; the present 'provoking' fear that her father too would die; and her future wish for a lover embodying mother, sisters, father. We may note, though, that in Charlotte's daydream Jane's 'sisters' (Diana and Mary) stay at a distance. Nancy Friday, in *My Mother My Self*, suggests that what we need is precisely sisters (or mothers) 'at a distance' ([1977] 1979: 67). We need the 'web' of relatedness but we also need to be authors of our own stories. Charlotte Brontë's daydream, anchored in the past but launched into the future, becomes our past, the mirror by which we know ourselves; but, read as our future, the mirror turns monstrous (cf. Drabble 1973: 6). 'We wove a web in childhood', Charlotte Brontë wrote; but 'the web is sticky', wrote Antonia Byatt (*JE* 1967 Byatt [1983: 230]). If female identity is a process (Gardiner 1981: 349), we must recognize that the moment when web turns to fly-trap and mirror to monster is also part of that process; the hope is that it forms a 'provoking occasion' for new daydreams, a new construction of past, present and future.

Romance into realism: Wuthering Heights *comes down to earth*

Bibliographic records suggest that after the 1939 film, *Wuthering Heights* suddenly passed into general circulation. *Brontë Society Transactions* for 1939 noted that 'more copies of *Wuthering Heights* were sold in the three weeks after the first showing of the film than in any five year period since the book was published' (Edgerley 1939: 239). By 1947, we learn that

> more than 220,000,000 people have seen the United Artists production of 'Wuthering Heights' since it was first released in April, 1939 . . . Since the release of 'Wuthering Heights' in America, a pocket edition of the book has sold 700,000 copies there and is continuing to sell. (A[ndrews] 1947: 175)

The Pocket Book edition printed in 1939 has as cover illustration a drawing taken from the scene in the film where Heathcliff carries Catherine to the open window to die (*WH* 1939). This scene, which does not appear in the novel, was nevertheless henceforth a part of the mythology of the story. Similarly, the film's representation of the adult Catherine and Heathcliff out of doors was henceforth emblematic of the novel's 'meaning'. A Penguin edition from 1946 has as cover illustration a sketch of Catherine and Heathcliff, large in the foreground, in a fierce embrace, against a background of stone walls and wide moors. The Camden Classics edition (1947) has a frontispiece by Anthony Gross showing Catherine and Heathcliff lying together deep in heather. A pen sketch by Ronald Searle for the cover of *Radio Times* (1948) shows a glowering Heathcliff leaning on a stone wall with a windswept moor behind him culminating in 'the Heights'. An original watercolour by Harry Turner entitled *Road to Wuthering Heights* (1958) shows a dramatic scene of towering cliffs.

Simultaneously with the 'lovers on the hilltop' mythology, however, these popular reproductions also reinforced what I have called the 'triangulation' of the plot of *Wuthering Heights*. The 1939 Pocket Book edition described above has as cover caption 'The vindicativeness [sic] of disappointed love'. An undated Mellifont Press edition, which looks from the style as if it dates from this period, has a cover illustration showing a whitewashed cottage in front of which stands a triangle of figures in Victorian dress. One man, who looks like Leslie Howard (further confusion with *Gone With the Wind*?) looks anguished up to heaven while the rather frilly woman takes his arm; the other man turns away. One odd feature of these pictures is that, despite their conventionality, the fact that Catherine is at the centre of the triangle gives her a new importance, and this is undoubtedly reinforced by the fact that the 1939 film gave her a Scarlett-O'Hara-like characterization, while Laurence Olivier's Heathcliff was not so strong as Clark Gable's Rhett Butler (also 1939). Like the Heathcliff in Balthus's 1933 drawings (see Figure 4.7) and Davison's 1937 stage play, Olivier is shown as browbeaten by a haughty Catherine who has to provoke him to revolt. Anthony Gross (1947) has a powerful picture of Catherine in the storm after Heathcliff's departure, and this scene also serves as the cover illustration for John Kennett's 'retold' version for Blackie (1959). Anthony Gross's illustrations also include one of Catherine and Heathcliff as children on Penistone Crag which shows him kneeling to her. This seems likely to derive not from Clare Leighton's 'feminist' version of 1931, but from the knight-and-lady scene in Wyler's film, which, as I argued in Chapter 4, confers a chivalrous superiority on Catherine at the expense of real subordination.

In 1966 an Indian film of the *Wuthering Heights* story gave full expression to all the romantic wish-fulfilment which lay behind the Hollywood version (*WH* 1966 Kadar). Instead of the moors this film gives us the restless sea, and the lovers (Roopa and Shankar) meet in an abandoned temple on a headland. Heathcliff/Shankar is found as a child in a wrecked boat, identified only by a strange medallion which, in the course of the story, enables him to claim his birthright as the son of a dead maharajah. Shankar returns from his absence (in which we follow him in this version) in time to prevent the marriage between Roopa and Mala/Edgar. Despite being shot by the dissolute and jealous Ravi (Hindley), Shankar recovers and the lovers are eventually married. The Indian title, *Dil Diya Dard Liya*, means 'give your heart and receive anguish'; because the anguish is only temporary, however, the film manages to recoup the tragic impossibilities of *Wuthering Heights* within the love-and-marriage archetype more properly represented by *Jane Eyre*; like the nineteenth-century versions of *Jane Eyre*, it is interspersed with songs and dances. Despite the attractions of anguish *and* a happy ending, however, the Brontë Society reviewer records that it was not particularly successful either in India or in Bradford, where it was screened without subtitles in the 1970s (Johnson, E. 1989).

Between 1947 and 1967 *Wuthering Heights* was broadcast on BBC Radio and in no fewer than four BBC television productions. Like the illustrations, these productions combine the 'hilltop' mythology with the domesticated triangle structure. In the days before outside broadcasts, television suffered from being studio-bound, and despite valiant use of the wind-machine, the Brontë Society observer reported that the performance broadcast in 1948 'seemed to be taking place on top of an occasional table' (Dunn 1948: 177). The dramatization for this 1948 broadcast was, however, John Davison's version from 1937 which, as we saw in Chapter 4, presented Catherine as using her relationship with Heathcliff as a weapon to make Edgar jealous. Surviving photographs from the television production show Katherine Blake and Kieron Moore (Catherine and Heathcliff) as a relentlessly housebound pair, dressed with an elaborate reproduction of eighteenth-century finery which would make scampering on the moors quite impractical. Cyril Dunn reports that both Moore and Blake had previously acted the same parts, in different productions, on the stage; probably these were also productions of the recent and popular Davison version (178). Publicity photographs for the 1953 television broadcast, with Yvonne Mitchell and Richard Todd, and the 1962 version with Keith Michell and Claire Bloom, show Catherine and Heathcliff together against the sky in what look like loose quotations from the 1939 film. Publicity material provided by the BBC describes the 1962 version as 'the passionate and illicit love story between Catherine Earnshaw and Heathcliff'; in other words, de Rougemont's 'myth of adultery' (de Rougemont [1940] 1983: 248, 18). In each of these versions, therefore, the potential exists for the novel to be turned either towards the 'metaphysical' oneness of the protagonists, represented by the 'elemental' setting, or towards the social situation of the love triangle.

In several illustrated editions there is a contrast between the cover and the inside pictures, which suggests that the 'outside' is an escape from the domestic situation. The cover of the Classics Illustrated edition, which I guess dates from the 1950s, shows a young Catherine standing above Heathcliff on the Crag. The inside pictures of this comicbook edition, however, show the young Heathcliff with a sulky expression and forward-falling quiff which make him look like Elvis Presley; there is a good deal of emphasis on his quarrel with young Hindley which again presents Heathcliff in a Presley-like role as the 'misunderstood' outsider. Apart from the cover, the illustrations to the 1959 Blackie edition also focus on interior scenes; despite the eighteenth-century costume, however, these are primarily scenes of domestic strife – Isabella smashing her wedding ring, Mr Lockwood and the 'tea-party' at the Heights, Heathcliff seizing young Catherine from the Grange after her father's funeral. Lynn Pykett points out that domestic space is itself ambiguous in Emily Brontë's novel:

> at the same time as *Wuthering Heights* traces the emergence of the modern family and its hegemonic fictional form of Domestic realism, other elements of the novel . . . work together to keep other versions of domestic life before the reader: the domestic space as prison, the family as site of primitive passions, violence, struggle and control. (Pykett 1989: 85)

Christine Gledhill points out that those films of the 1950s now called 'melodramas' share this ambiguity. She quotes Thomas Schatz to suggest that 'the 50s melodramas are actually among the most socially self-conscious and covertly "anti-American" films ever produced by the Hollywood studios' (1987: 5). Anne Kaplan, quoting Laura Mulvey, also argues that melodrama serves a useful function for women who lack any coherent culture of oppression. 'The simple fact of recognition has aesthetic importance,' she notes; 'there is a dizzy satisfaction in witnessing the way that sexual difference under patriarchy is fraught, explosive and erupts dramatically into violence within its own private stomping ground, the family' (Kaplan 1983: 26).

The most scathing presentation of *Wuthering Heights* as a drama deriving from bourgeois family values is Luis Buñuel's film, *Abismos de Pasión*, made in Mexico in 1953, yet strangely enough this too shows the ambiguous qualities which the critics have seen in the 1950s melodrama. Philip Strick, in the programme notes for the first British screening of the film in 1984, writes:

> At first glance, it's more Margaret Mitchell than Emily Brontë, as a girl in a wide-brimmed hat and flowing gown runs with a swirl of music into a Southern courtyard, and there are further unexpected echoes of Scarlett in the way that Cathy taunts and goads the two exasperated men to both of whom, after her own fashion, she has protested loyalty.

The characteristic Buñuel touch, however, emerges as 'her husband coolly transfixes a quivering moth so that it dies in the position of maximum elegance'. In this production '*L'amour fou*, the passion with too intense a blaze to be survived . . . symbolises an ironically futile romantic achievement the surrealists found glorious to contemplate'. At the end of Chapter 4, I argued that Davison and Wyler, in their pre-war versions of *Wuthering Heights*, helped to establish what Kristeva calls the 'metaphysical' status of masculinity and femininity in our culture (Moi 1986: 209). It is this status which allowed these reproducers implicitly to promote 'legitimate or married love', relying on what Ernest Baker called 'consummated union as eternal fact' without confronting marriage as either a sexual union or a social institution (in Lettis and Morris 1961: 50). Buñuel's transformation of *Wuthering Heights*, under the influence of Freud and Marx, focuses on the material conditions of 'consummation'. Every aspect of Buñuel's film seems designed to subvert the romantic idealism of 1930s Hollywood. The change of focus is welcome in that it resists the insidious incorporation of *Wuthering Heights* into the dominant ideology. It can, however, be depressingly deterministic.

Where Wyler shows Catherine and Heathcliff silhouetted against the sky (Figure 4.8), Buñuel's *Abismos de Pasión* confines all its characters to earth. His reversal of the title, from *Wuthering Heights* to *Depths of Passion*, seems abruptly to deny the mythical transcendence which the novel claims, at least at some level, for its protagonists. Made in 1953, it is, like other films of the 1950s, a film about adult sexuality, but its vaguely nineteenth-century setting, with the extrovert patriarchy of Latin countries, provides the codes of conduct that lead passion into the abyss. Significantly, there are no childhood scenes in this film – it begins with Alejandro/Heathcliff's return to find Catarina/Catherine married – and the outdoor scenes show the characters plunging into the earth rather than reaching for the sky. Alejandro's brutal and sardonic 'courtship' of Isabel takes place in an arid ravine which is only less fruitful, not less earthy, than the sunken wood where Alejandro and Catarina have a hiding-place in the roots of a tree. The film ends with the lovers dead in an underground tomb on which the heavy metal lid has just clanged shut. Visual echoes of *Romeo and Juliet* combine with the 'Liebestod' from *Tristan and Isolde* to emphasize that this story is, in Juliet Mitchell's terms, one of death-orientated love; but its imagery confines death to the tomb.

Cultural intertexts are here exploited to assert the place of *Wuthering Heights* in a masculine tradition in which women are the property of men. In the novel, however, the relationship between Catherine and Heathcliff is established before puberty, and is outside this kind of sexual economy. In I ix, when Nelly points out to the young Catherine that her marriage to Edgar Linton will divide her from Heathcliff, Catherine is bewildered: 'Who is to separate us, pray? . . . Oh, that's not what I intend – that's not what I mean!' (*WH* 81). If masculine love, within the sexual economy described by Freud, 'entails the desire to appropriate . . ., to contain and imprison the other', the love of Catherine and Heathcliff maintains a quality which Hélène Cixous describes as *jouissance*, in which each 'takes the other into the self and is taken into the other also', in 'a kind of mutual knowing or fluid mingling' (Still and Worton 1993: 27). In the novel, the later scenes between Catherine and Heathcliff, after Catherine's marriage, thus give us a curious sense of dissonance because we seem to be invited to interpret them both in terms of this earlier, non-proprietorial mirroring, and in terms of an adulterous triangle.

Abismos de Pasión, therefore, is more like *Romeo and Juliet* than *Wuthering Heights* itself in invoking an explicitly sexual rhetoric of social compulsion and judgement. Early in the film Catarina tells Isabel that she is carrying Eduardo/Edgar's child – 'What more does he want?' In later scenes her increasingly visible pregnancy serves as a sign of her sexual appropriation, and the birth is explicitly feared as the likely cause of her death. Eduardo complains that Catarina is unfaithful to him, not in her bedroom but in her thoughts, and Ricardo/Hindley later mocks Isabel, saying that her husband Alejandro 'cheats on [her] with a dead woman'. Like *Tristan and Isolde*, the film shows lovers whose tragedy derives from the transgressive (social) nature of their (adulterous) love. Lacking the childhood scenes and the second generation, it is focused on what de Rougemont calls the 'great European myth of adultery' ([1940] 1983: 18). Its very final deaths (Catarina stiff in her coffin, Alejandro shot through the head) disallow the perennially fascinating suggestion of Emily Brontë's novel – that our heart's desire, socially unattainable, might somehow, somewhere, be within our reach. Nor does it allow the consolation of Wyler's sweeter tragedy of 'star-crossed lovers', in which Catherine and Heathcliff are only unfortunate exceptions to the rule that finds our heart's desire in marriage. By contrast, Buñuel's film acts as a harsh critique of the norms which provide its tragic structure. Marriage can hardly be the lovers' goal in a world where Catarina and Isabel are the property of their husbands, and significant changes to the plot point to the robustness of this patriarchy. In the novel, Edgar and Hindley die, as well as Heathcliff, leaving an ambiguous promise of change for Catherine's daughter. In Buñuel's film, Eduardo and Ricardo live to close ranks over the lovers' expunged history, and as José/Joseph reads from the Bible that death is God's punishment for envy and that there is no return from the grave his voice has the dignity and resonance of accepted truth.[3]

In a complex article entitled 'Framing in *Wuthering Heights*', John T. Matthews argues that the structure of the novel causes us to pass from the frame narrative to the 'centre' and back, one incessantly dissolving into the other, because 'Catherine and Heathcliff's love is the ghost of the prohibitions that structure society' (Matthews 1985: 54). It is, therefore, sharply appropriate that in Buñuel's film the momentary vision of Catarina's ghost which Alejandro sees in the tomb dissolves as we watch, re-forming into the figure of Ricardo (Hindley) with a shotgun; it is Ricardo who lets the lid clang shut on the dead lovers as he repossesses the world in which Catarina's baby is 'a beautiful boy'. Buñuel's film, however, with its hard focus on the finality of power, resolves the restless movement of the novel and thus clangs shut the lid not only on the stiffening corpses of our lovers, but also on the transformative possibilities of Emily Brontë's text. In the introduction I quoted Annette Kuhn, who argues that 'a society's representations of itself . . . may be seen as a vital, pervasive and active element in the constitution of social structures and formations' and that 'interventions within culture have some independent potential to transform' them (Kuhn 1982: 5, 6). Buñuel's film is valuable in that it forces us to confront the power structures which are silently naturalized in a film like Wyler's. If Wyler's film tries to deny the social 'frame' by endorsing love as transcendence in images of sky, air, heaven (Figure 4.8), Buñuel's reinstates the frame as earth, prison, tomb. Both films, however, have the effect of halting what Matthews calls the 'incessant dissolving of figure into ground and back' which makes *Wuthering Heights* an open rather than a closed text, and thus they present us with meanings that are more limited than those of the original.

In the same year when Buñuel's Mexican film reminds us of the power of patriarchy, Henri-Pierre Roché's novel, *Jules et Jim* (*WH* 1953 Roché), explores a version of the *Wuthering Heights* plot in which the characters appear to escape from bourgeois conventions. Later made famous as a film by François Truffaut (1961), *Jules et Jim* shows us a liberated version of Catherine (played in the film by Jeanne Moreau), living, around the time of the First World War, in an uncertain *ménage à trois* with her two lovers. As Q. D. Leavis points out, however, 'it seems not to matter that, living in a sexually permissive society (twentieth-century Germany and France) she takes full licence, for she ends in Catherine's situation, and endures and causes similar suffering' (Leavis [1969] 1983: 241). Leavis believes that Roché's novel, 'a psychological drama written with an almost clinical detachment', provides an adequate 'explanation' for the events of *Wuthering Heights* as well as for its own; she finds it 'very unfortunate that the . . . "metaphysical" parts of *Wuthering Heights* should have been . . . universally seized on as a short cut to the meaning, the significance of the novel' (242). The superiority of *Wuthering Heights* as a text, Leavis argues, thus lies not in its mystical 'vision' but in 'its delicate annotation of behaviour' (248) and in the variations on its theme which prevent us from taking the elder Catherine as the inevitable epitome of womanhood. It is ironic that one of the very few reworkings of the *Wuthering Heights* story which acknowledges the possibility that Catherine intended to keep both her lovers should be written by a man who simply reverses the gender assumptions of Emily Brontë's novel. While Edgar and Heathcliff fall automatically into the antagonistic attitudes prescribed from antiquity for sexual rivals, Jules and Jim are bonded by shared intellectual pursuits into a friendship which survives their fighting on opposite sides in the war. On the other hand, where Emily Brontë's Catherine is a wilful but on the whole generous young woman, confused in her response to outside pressures rather than innately selfish, Roché's Kate is presented as an inevitable *femme fatale* – 'WOMAN in essence, a menace to masculine stability . . . yet indispensable to any life worth living' (244).

In both texts, the message seems to be that unconventional sexual arrangements are bound to fail – Roché's Kate ends by killing herself and the lover she is not married to. Traditional readings of *Wuthering Heights* have tended to blame Catherine for the way things turn out, pointing to a 'fatal flaw' which makes her susceptible to wealth and ease. My own reading of the novel would place the blame on our culture's concept of masculinity, which precipitates men into antagonistic postures and prevents them, in general, from even considering the kind of accommodation made in *Jules et Jim*. Roché's sympathetic menfolk seem, however, to have to have a scapegoat in their turn, and his novel thus presents Kate not as a human being whose confused responses can be traced to rational or even unconscious determinants, but rather as a 'force of nature' (245). In confirmation of this reading, and in contrast with *Wuthering Heights*, Leavis points out, 'Roché's novel and Truffaut's film with equal and unnecessary pessimism show Kate's daughter committed in childhood to an instinctive repetition of the mother's attitudes. Their message seems to be "*così fan tutte*"' (250).

Peter Holdsworth, writing in the *Telegraph and Argus* in 1964, describes a projected British film of *Wuthering Heights* which might have rivalled Buñuel's. This was to have been written by David Storey and directed by Lindsay Anderson, with Richard Harris as Heathcliff. This is the team that produced *This Sporting Life*, and, on the basis of this, Holdsworth predicts that their version of *Wuthering Heights* will make the Olivier version 'look like a fairy tale for children'. Unfortunately the film never came to fruition, but its planning is, perhaps, an indication that just as with *Jane Eyre*, the romance elements of *Wuthering Heights* seem constantly on the verge of giving way to something more threatening. Joyce Carol Oates, in her story, 'The Daughter' (1966), shows the fourteen-year-old protagonist reading from *Wuthering Heights* the scene where Catherine asks of Heathcliff, 'What new phase of this character is this? . . . you'll take revenge! How will you take it, ungrateful brute?' (*WH* 1966 Oates [1974: 52–3]). The child later seems about to slip into a sexual relationship with her estranged stepfather. Whose revenge this is against whom is not clear, but the atmosphere of broken family ties is very uncomfortable. The 1967 television version of *Wuthering Heights* also shows a much earthier image than the earlier productions; Angela Scoular and Ian McShane as Catherine and Heathcliff have a relationship whose physical quality is, as in the novel, more nursery violence than erotic dalliance. Whereas the threat in *Jane Eyre*, however, was felt to be a question of narrative, involving following threads of clues and 'identifying the enemy', the threat in *Wuthering Heights* is more instantaneous and unpredictable, flashing out in sudden bursts of violence which reveal the apparently known in unfamiliar lights. It is perhaps for this reason that whereas reproductions of *Jane Eyre* have taken predominantly narrative forms, *Wuthering Heights* has tended to be reproduced in other media – especially pictures and music.

During the same post-war period which emphasized both 'wild' and 'domesticated' illustrations of *Wuthering Heights*, there were also illustrations which tipped the domestic into the Gothic. Barnett Freedman's lithographs for the Heritage Press edition (1940) begin with an isolated representation of Catherine's and Lockwood's claw-like hands meeting through broken glass (*WH* 1940 Freedman: 26). His long-necked child Heathcliff seems to carry his own atmosphere of shadow (36), and although many of the subsequent pictures are ordinary enough portraits, Heathcliff on the night of Catherine's death has a maniacal air (164) and in the final frame, where Heathcliff looks out of the window to beg Catherine to return, he is represented as a gaunt, famine-stricken tramp (328). Nothing could be further from Olivier's tragic, white-haired dignity in the same scene, only a year before. Freedman's pictures are not attractive, but their predominant darkness reminds us that the family is the source of the deepest fears and pain. W. Stein's 1955 illustrations also begin with Heathcliff's agitation at the scene of Lockwood's nightmare, and though predominantly static, also present the scenes of the novel, whether inside or out, in an atmosphere of shadow which makes it difficult to discern, in the scene where Heathcliff digs in Catherine's grave, whether the figure of Heathcliff is substantially more material than that of the ghostly Catherine whom he feels but does not see. The cover illustration to the 1964 Everyman edition also shows Heathcliff leaning out of the window after Catherine's ghost, lit fitfully by a candle, and the 1965 Riverside edition shows a haunted Heathcliff on the front cover and on the back a Wuthering Heights with Gothic windows and a hint of a tower.

The most startling illustrations from this period, however, are those by Charles Keeping for the Folio Society, also in 1964. Keeping's pictures are made from a wash of grey and black on white. His frontispiece shows Heathcliff barbed around with spiky vegetation, against a lurid sky, in an attitude which seems to leave him headless. The picture of Heathcliff as a barefoot waif seems hardly human, with black pits for eyes, paw-like hands and bare, seemingly clawed feet (*WH* 1964 Keeping: 37). Catherine and Heathcliff on the moor race like manic marionettes (44) and the scene of Catherine's funeral (not described in the novel) draws again on the lurid sky and the spiked vegetation, this time reflected in a pool, or ice (141). These same features, monstrously enlarged, illustrate Nelly's fears for the younger Catherine (160); the contrast between this plate and the 1889 frontispiece captioned 'I entered, and beheld my stray lamb seated on the hearth' is that between fears rampant and fears allayed. The scene where Heathcliff takes the younger Catherine back to the Heights after her father's death is similar to the frontispiece, except that Heathcliff's head is now out of the frame (*WH* 1964 Keeping: 233). The final scene of the ghostly lovers' embrace shows Heathcliff as a black shape, holding a figure apparently composed of streaks of muddy water (274). Like Freedman's, Keeping's illustrations are shocking and painful, evoking not structures or linear patterns of relationship but sudden, raw states of emotion.

We might expect that some of these features might be repeated in the first colour film of *Wuthering Heights*, made in 1970, since its director, Robert Fuest, later became known as a director of horror stories such as *The Abominable Dr Phibes* (1971). The truncated plot does indeed open with the burial of the first Catherine, so that an atmosphere of death is created before the flashback to the arrival of Heathcliff; the moment when Heathcliff embraces the dead Catherine in her grave is, indeed, intense, as Timothy Dalton as Heathcliff fixes Anna Calder-Marshall with his gaze until her eyes appear to open under it. As in the Buñuel film, Heathcliff, immediately after this, is beguiled by Catherine's ghost into a position where he is shot dead by Hindley; in this version, however, the visible ghosts of the two lovers salve any anguish the viewers might be feeling.

As in Buñuel again, the motivations of most of Fuest's characters are explicitly sexual, so that Heathcliff is very probably Mr Earnshaw's illegitimate son, and Nelly, shown as young and *decolletée*, is very keen on Hindley, who is extremely keen on Frances; the romping scenes between the young adults are reminiscent, particularly in the revealing costumes, of the film version of *Tom Jones* (1963). Heathcliff is much given to rolling in the grass, whether happily with Catherine, or punitively with Isabella. The effect of making explicit many things that in the novel are mysterious or understated is to remove much of its fascination. David Drew, reviewing the film for *BST*, concludes that

> the juxtaposition of earthy sex and blanched ghosts simply becomes incongruous . . .
> The film presents the novel neither as a purely psychological drama nor as a Gothic
> tale of the supernatural, but rather equivocates uneasily between the two.

For Drew, 'the film of *Wuthering Heights* is a pleasant if light-weight love story . . .'; another reviewer found that 'you watch Anna Calder-Marshall rolling in the hay and exchanging sexy kisses with Timothy Dalton and you accept it as just another routine example of the permissive cinema exploiting its new freedom' (Drew 1971). Fuest apparently intended to treat the second generation story in a sequel to be called *Return to Wuthering Heights*, but this seems not to have materialized (*WH* 1972 [Fuest]).

Apart from the New Women of the 1890s, who were fascinated by Emily Brontë rather than her work, *Wuthering Heights* seems to have been appropriated by men, whose efforts have recuperated the novel into the structure of a jealous triangle – 'Cathy torn between Heathcliff's animal appeal and the security of marriage to the smooth Edgar Linton' (Wilson, *WH* 1970 Fuest). It comes as a shock to find, in the same year as Fuest's film, the Australian poet Judith Wright using Emily Brontë's poem, 'Cold in the Earth' to express her own grief, sifted to 'archaean levels' by 'living long'. As she calls, 'Come in, dead Emily', Wright's poem becomes a testament to the indestructibility of Emily's writing as well as of her own love, which Emily's writing, in an involution of time, seems to record. In the end, in the year of Fuest's film, the modern poem reinstates a testament to love, which survives, and to writing, which also survives:

> These gulping dry lines
> are not my song for you.
> That's made already.
> Come in, dead Emily . . .

I move through my present
gripping the steering-wheel,
repeating, repeating it.

The crossways fade; the freeway rushes forward.
'These days obscure but cannot do thee wrong.' (Wright [1971] 1985)

'Kinship with the proud': Wuthering Heights *canonized in music*

Virginia Woolf thought that we should make the women writers of the past into 'characters' in our own texts, and in Chapter 3 I described how Rachel Ferguson adopted this strategy, making the Brontë sisters into 'part of the family' in *The Brontës Went to Woolworth's*. Other women did the same. In Elizabeth Taylor's novel, *A Wreath of Roses* (1949), two young women on holiday together reminisce about how, as girls, they had had literary tea-parties:

> I think it was Charlotte who wrecked them, with her inverted snobbery. The time she told Ivy how much she gave for her lace shawl in Bradford.
> And said it was her best.
> Anne looked down in her lap. I saw her hands tremble.
> Virginia saw, too.
> Charlotte came too early, anyhow. Before we had chance to put a match to the parlour fire.
> Emily wouldn't come in at all. She stood up the road and eyed the gate . . . Who fetched her in the end? Emily, I mean.
> I think we sent George Eliot out for her.
> But she wouldn't co-operate. She wouldn't sit down. She ruined the party with her standing up . . .
> Virginia was right to feel wounded about the food. Women are not good enough to themselves. And indifferent food is the beginning of other indifferent things. (*WH* 1949 Taylor [1987: 30])

As in *The Brontës Went to Woolworth's*, the apparent whimsy of this conversation records women's efforts to create a kind of domestic pantheon of foremothers – something akin to E. M. Forster's vision of all the writers of all ages together in 'a circular room, a sort of British Museum reading-room'. Forster, however, is concerned to cut writers loose from the chronology of history: 'empires fall, votes are accorded, but to those people writing in the circular room it is the feel of the pen between their fingers that matters most' ([1927] 1962: 21, 27–8). Taylor's reference to the quality of the cakes, however, aligns her with Woolf in recognizing that 'intellectual freedom depends on material things' (Woolf [1928] 1970: 106). *A Wreath of Roses*, like Woolf's *Three Guineas*, denies that 'art' can be independent of 'history'. Published in 1949, the novel is permeated with death and the aftermath of the war.

The two young women who remember their literary tea-party are now staying with Frances, who is an artist and used to be their governess. For years she has painted calm interiors, but now is painting 'terrible' scenes prompted by world events. Persuaded by friends, she returns in a last picture to a wreath of roses, but does not finish it. The epigraph to the novel is from Woolf in *The Waves*: 'So terrible was life that I held up shade after shade . . . let there be rose leaves, let there be vine leaves . . .'. A young man befriended by Camilla, who proves to be a murderer and in the end kills himself, claims to be writing a book; Camilla asks if it is 'to exorcise [the war]? To drive it out of you, as Emily Brontë drove out Heathcliff, with her pen?' (*WH* 1949 Taylor [1987: 11]). This complex of literary fragments shows young women, uneasy with their present, using the women writers of their past to make sense of it, as imaginary friends, as models, as warnings. These writers are perceived as helpful because of their involvement with 'history', in shapes such as mundane as how much Charlotte's shawl cost and as insidious as Emily's need for exorcism. They are not perceived as having 'entered a common state' which Forster calls 'inspiration'; their writing is not '"consecrated"' either '"by time"' or '"beyond time"', in the phrases which he borrows from T. S. Eliot's *The Sacred Wood* (Forster [1927] 1962: 28–30).

One legacy of the pre-war critics T. S. Eliot and F. R. Leavis to the post-war world was the notion of the great tradition of literature which is now sometimes called 'the canon'. The word 'canon' is usefully metaphorical, since its primary meaning is the body of writing accepted as part of the Bible or other holy scripture; for a person to be canonized means to become a saint. For a work of literature to be part of the canon thus implies both orthodoxy and sublimity; it can be a way of both praising and containing it. In Chapter 4 I argued that Lord David Cecil's essay on *Wuthering Heights* had had the effect of receiving Emily Brontë into the company of saints, and Miriam Allott, writing in 1970, confirms that 'the critical attention which [her] single novel receives today contrasts dramatically in quantity and kind with the reception accorded to it by its first reviewers'. This change

> can be measured by looking at the six columns of close print devoted to the Brontës in *The New Cambridge Bibliography of English Literature*, [vol.] III (1969). Here the first three columns list most of the important studies written before 1940, while the remaining three represent the vast proliferation of Brontë criticism and commentary which has taken place since, the most striking feature of this later work being the enormous weight of attention now centred on Emily at the expense of Charlotte. (Allott 1970: 11, 27–8)

At the beginning of this chapter I referred to the phenomenon identified by Peter Brooks and others which, in the twentieth century, split high from low culture, leaving popular forms such as romance for women. One suspects that it was its status as romance which encouraged Cecil to exclude *Jane Eyre* from his pantheon, while *Wuthering Heights*, with its tragic ending and sublimity of tone, was accepted among the great. One aspect of the new status of *Wuthering Heights* was that it began to be regarded as appropriate material for musical settings, especially in the elevated and expensive form of opera. Although in the past few years there has been a movement to popularize opera, in Britain and America it has always been a relatively elitist form of art; for Emily Brontë's work to be adapted in this way corroborates, therefore, the canonization indicated by literary criticism.

Emily Brontë's poetry has always appealed to musicians, and the Brontë Parsonage Museum has an extensive collection of musical settings from all periods (see Voles (no date); Ballantine (1946); Jepson (1962); Stevenson (1969); Butterworth (1979)). In the years following the war, however, it was *Wuthering Heights* which attracted special attention. While some post-war reproducers tried to bring the novel down to earth by reducing its narrative to the 'myth of adultery', musicians were attracted by its general atmosphere of tumult and sublimity. Ernest Bradbury, writing in *The Yorkshire Post* in 1966, comments that

> Delius, who knew and loved the moors as well as the Brontës, composer of the wonderful 'North Country Sketches', was probably just the man for 'Wuthering Heights', and one must always regret that his operatic 'Wuthering Heights' remained only an idea.

Several other composers, however, took the idea to fruition, and it is interesting that they all have two things in common. First, they are all in the Delius/Butterworth tradition of neo-romantic, accessible music depending on dramatic and emotional effects rather than technical innovation. Secondly, they all seem to have been inspired by the William Wyler film rather than the novel itself. The result is that these operatic versions of *Wuthering Heights* confirm, at the level of 'high culture' (but not so high as to be rejected by their audiences), the message of the film; namely, that this is a tragedy entirely focused on Catherine and Heathcliff, deriving from a mistaken marriage choice and gaining its intensity from the association of the adult lovers with the realm of nature. Seen primarily from the point of view of the excluded male lover, the story becomes yet one more demonstration that 'the essential triangle (Father/Mother/Son) . . . is the poem of Western culture' (de Rougemont [1940] 1983: 371).

In October 1955, the *Telegraph and Argus* reported a Bradford performance of an excerpt from a new opera based on *Wuthering Heights* by the local pianist and composer, Gerald Gover. It is described as 'a major work, in three acts, with prologue and epilogue and employing full orchestra and a large chorus'. The composer claims to have been inspired by a dramatized television version 'some years ago'. Gover's music is praised for its lyrical, melodic beauty and lack of dissonance. Although he welcomed the idea of it being produced by the West Riding Opera Circle, this seems not to have happened.

Getting an opera produced is no easy feat. The American composer Carlisle Floyd was more fortunate; his 'music drama' based on *Wuthering Heights* was commissioned by the Santa Fe Opera and performed in New Mexico in 1958; it was staged again by New York City Opera in 1959, by the University of North Carolina in 1982 and by the Boston Lyric Opera Co. in 1993. This last revival was described by Mary Haigh in *Brontë Society Transactions*, and her account of the set, which included a double stairway to Penistone Crag, sounds very much like the set for the Northampton production of Michael Napier Brown's dramatic adaptation of the novel, later performed in York in 1994. Robert Sabin, in an article on Floyd's opera in *Tempo*, makes clear that, musically, it is a 'mainstream' composition, convincing because of its dramatic impact rather than innovative scoring (though Ray Chatelin (1982) comments on its 'un-hummable music'). Like Wyler, Floyd found the novel 'impossibly diffuse' and has 'condensed it in a masterly fashion', dropping many of the original characters, including the younger generation. 'He has transferred speeches from one character to another in an ingenious and effective fashion' and, again like Wyler, 'he has brought the whole action forward about 35 years, because he preferred the costumes . . .'. For Floyd, the central feature of the material he is working with is that Catherine and Heathcliff 'are true children of nature', and he 'gives us unforgettable portraits of Cathy and Heathcliff against the storm-tossed background of the wild countryside' (Sabin 1961: 23–4).

For Sabin, writing in 1961, the notion of 'storm-tossed lovers' appears to be a familiar, uncontentious and humanly 'central' idea, but we might pause a moment to consider its history. In 1855, Matthew Arnold had written of the Brontë sisters,

In the never idle workshop of nature,
In the eternal movement,
Ye shall find yourselves again. ('Haworth Parsonage' ll. 131–8)

In 1873, in *Literature and Dogma*, he foresaw that literature would take the place of a declining religion. Terry Eagleton points out that as 'literature works primarily by emotion and experience', it 'was admirably well-fitted to carry through the ideological task which religion left off' (1983: 26). In 1891, an educational policy-maker was arguing that people 'need to be impressed sentimentally by having the presentation in legend and history of heroic . . . examples brought vividly and attractively before them', to reinforce their essential instruction in 'political culture . . . that is to say, in . . . their duties as citizens' (in Eagleton 1983: 25). For Robert Sabin, Carlisle Floyd's opera represents something 'mainstream' and unsensational, deriving from a long and tested tradition; he adds in parenthesis that 'I am sure that the smart young serialists and post-serialists consider him positively medieval'. The context provided by Eagleton's comments on Arnold, however, brings into sharp focus what is involved when Sabin praises Floyd for writing 'honest, powerful, humanly expressive music about men and women experiencing the great joys and sorrows' (Sabin 1961: 26). Since Floyd's opera was first performed in 1958, and Sabin is writing in 1961, at the height of the Cold War, it is perhaps not too fanciful to see *Wuthering Heights* being here used to exemplify the values of 'the free world', not by prescription but by demonstration. In the post-war critical climate fostered by F. R. Leavis, Eagleton argues,

morality is no longer to be grasped as a formulated code or explicit ethical system: it is rather a sensitive preoccupation with the whole quality of life . . . the old religious ideologies have lost their force, and . . . a more subtle communication of moral values, one which works by 'dramatic enactment' rather than rebarbative abstraction, is thus in order. (Eagleton 1983: 27)

Sabin's highest praise, accordingly, goes to Floyd's 'bold, impassioned score', which creates 'a profound emotional experience in the theatre', leaving 'both performers and audience shaken with the elemental power of the Brontë story' (Sabin 1961: 23–4).

Bernard Herrmann's opera of *Wuthering Heights* ([1965]) had a longer gestation period than Floyd's but seems to share features of style and effect. Frank Kinkaid, writing in the programme to the first performance in 1982, calls it a 'grand tone poem that celebrates his love of England, the weather of Yorkshire and his identification with the Brontës' (Kinkaid 1982: 21). Ernest Bradbury confesses that

> my feelings have changed from an initially cold, superior, distant sniffing at the obvious Puccini-like sentimentalities of the piece to an interested, warm regard for how it might appear on the stage.
>
> Old-fashioned, in the grand operatic manner, it certainly is, calling for snowstorms, lightning, realistic scenery, 'strange and eerie' atmosphere . . . Yet this is inevitable. Is a symbolistic, 12-note 'Wuthering Heights' really feasible? (1966)

Other reviewers likened the style to Wagner, Puccini, Richard Strauss, Sibelius, Debussy and Vaughan Williams, though one found it 'ranging from early Schoenberg . . . to late Poulenc'. Several reviewers found the opera 'more atmospheric than dramatic, too much an extended tone-poem' (Estes 1982). A Californian reviewer found that such music did not soothe his savage breast, though it did, apparently, that of Brontë's characters: 'the pleasant music somehow makes the work's monstrous people appear positively NICE. Yes, a nice Heathcliff and a nice Cathy are singing nice duets'.

According to Herrmann's first wife and librettist, Lucille Fletcher, he first started work on the opera during the 1940s, inspired directly by Wyler's 1939 film. In a private letter to Stanley Johnson, Fletcher confirms that 'we more or less followed the adaptation used in the 1939 movie'. She used, she says, an 'old pocket-book version of the novel', which is presumably the Pocket Book edition of 1939 with the cover illustration showing Heathcliff carrying Catherine to the window to die – a scene from the Wyler film (not from the novel) which is repeated in the opera (Fletcher 1982). Herrmann is best known as a writer of music for such major films as Hitchcock's *Psycho* and Welles's *Citizen Kane* and *The Magnificent Ambersons*. The date on Herrmann's manuscript score for *Wuthering Heights* is 1943, which is, interestingly, the year in which he was working on the score for Robert Stevenson's film of *Jane Eyre*, and some interrelationships between the two pieces of music can be seen, as I shall argue below (Kinkaid 1982: 16). A printed score was published in 1965 and the full opera was recorded in 1966, but a stage production was only mounted in 1982, after Herrmann's death. The libretto itself went through several transformations, and the version printed in a limited edition to commemorate the 1982 premiere is shorter and differently structured from that provided with the reissue of the 1966 recording on CD in 1992.

Fletcher's preface to the 1982 libretto shows the extent to which the spirit of *Wuthering Heights*, rather than its literal text, was felt to represent its truth. With no sense of incongruity, she records first that her 'text remains a faithful transcript of the original story' and then, immediately, that

> many of Emily Brontë's poems and some of the poetic speeches from the second section of the novel have been interpolated. Both *Wuthering Heights* and the poems are of such a one-ness, that the use of the poems is not felt to be an anachronism [sic], but rather an intensification for the purpose of this musical setting.

It is ironic that one reviewer reproached Fletcher for having too great a 'reverence for the original novel' (Downey 1983: 27), since she makes, in fact, major changes, including the removal of most of the frame sequences and all the second generation. As in Floyd's opera, speeches are moved from one character to another; characters are also given bits of Emily Brontë's poems bridged by sections by Fletcher herself. The effect is to soften the distinctions between characters and to create, within the envelope provided by the music, an emotional 'world' in which subjectivities merge. In some cases this is appropriate and effective; for instance when Heathcliff runs away at the end of Act II, Catherine is given the words which, in the novel, Heathcliff speaks to the child ghost at the beginning – 'Oh my heart's darling hear me this time'.[4] In the 1966 recording, we have already heard this speech from Heathcliff in the prologue dealing with Lockwood's dream. The 1982 libretto splits the scene of Lockwood's dream into two, so that the prologue ends with Lockwood falling asleep, and Heathcliff's appeal to the ghost is deferred until the epilogue. The 1982 version thus ends with the much-publicized moment from the Wyler film when Heathcliff leans from the window to beg Catherine to return. This scene clearly made a great impact on Herrmann, and in the 1966 recording (which represents his wishes) we hear the words of Heathcliff's appeal three times, first from Heathcliff in the prologue at the time of Lockwood's dream, secondly from Catherine at the time of Heathcliff's flight, and thirdly from Heathcliff at the moment of Catherine's death (which in this version ends the opera, there being no epilogue). At this point, while her dead body lies before him, her ghostly voice comes to him from outside the window and echoes his own calls. The music fades with these repeated echoes, implying that the lovers are locked for ever in this agony of mirrored separation which in the end is nothing but a repetition of their names – 'Heathcliff. Heathcliff . . . Cathy. Cathy'. The 1982 libretto also stresses this 'fading' in its last words, although reviewers complain that in the production, director Malcolm Fraser 'gave us a corporal Cathy frolicking on the moors watching Heathcliff die, their spirits becoming mimes who walk off into the sunset'; 'a phantom Cathy and phantom Heathcliff vanished hand in hand and died happily ever after . . .'. Kinkaid notes that 'this hokey solution' was 'used in the 1939 movie'; Robert Fuest's 1970 film also gives us visible ghosts, though Herrmann's original intention seems more bleak than this (Kinkaid 1983; Lindstrom).

One interesting complication of Fletcher's 1982 libretto is that the printed version is illustrated by Fritz Eichenberg's wood engravings from the Random

House edition of 1943, though Fletcher has chosen only four of the original pictures: the 'mad' scene where Catherine, tearing the feathers from her pillow, is 'haunted' by the huge brooding figure of Heathcliff; the scene where the lovers cling together in a mirror-like embrace at Catherine's death-bed; the scene where Lockwood's wrist is seized by Catherine's ghost; and the small inset showing Heathcliff, 'like a savage beast', on all fours before Catherine's grave. In Chapter 4 (pages 119–21) I described the contrast between Eichenberg's 'mirror-embrace' picture (Figure 4.6), which is used to accompany Catherine's death in Fletcher's printed libretto, and his picture of Catherine's 'mad-scene', which appears in the libretto at the end of Act II (Act III in 1966). The opera repeats the contradiction implied by the illustrations, which, in Chapter 4, I explained as reflecting the contrast between the pre-Oedipal, 'imaginary' world of oneness, and the subsequent polarization of 'normal' masculinity and femininity.

The feathers which, in Eichenberg's 'mad' scene, float down before the huge face of Heathcliff, become a musical motif in Herrmann's opera. In the novel, of course, they are already ambiguous, reminding Catherine both of the carefree days when she was 'half savage and hardy, and free' on the moors, and also of Heathcliff's gratuitous cruelty in setting a trap for lapwings (*WH* 126, 122). In the prologue to the opera, a fluttering string passage, suggesting pattering leaves, becomes the snow which breaks through Lockwood's window (CD 1: band 2); this is echoed in Catherine's mad scene, in which 'scattery' music accompanies the scattered feathers (2: 16). The 1982 staging, moreover, included a scrim painted with a huge face which reviewers found hard to identify, though 'Portland Opera says it's supposed to be Heathcliff' (Cohen, J. 1982). Though not identical with the Eichenberg illustration (it has a screaming mouth, for instance), this huge face seems to have been inspired by it; the implication is that the 'scattering' of Catherine's wits, like her exile in the snowstorm, is the result of mental pressure deriving from Heathcliff. The visual and musical development of this picture, in which Heathcliff is a threatening and dominant figure, contrasts with the implications of the Eichenberg 'mirror-portrait' (Figure 4.6), which represents Heathcliff as Cathy's 'soul-mate', and in the opera neither is finally allowed to prevail. The final scene of the recorded opera is Catherine's death, enacted according to the 'mirror-embrace', and although their momentary union is marked by a brief reference back to the elegiac music of Act I, it is undercut at the moment of her death by the 'Let me in' phrase from the prologue (1966: 34; CD 3: 7). With the reassertion of Catherine's ghost-voice outside the window, the feather/snow music returns to remind us of their adult separation. If we ignore the visual additions of the 1982 staging, the effect of the ending is to suspend them in perpetual denial of the lost union of childhood.

Despite this tragic ending, it is the spiritual alliance of the lovers and their affinity with nature which is the strongest theme of Herrmann's opera. While Floyd simply reminded me of Matthew Arnold's 'Haworth Parsonage', lines from the poem appear as epigraph to Bernard Herrmann's 1965 score. The weather speaks even through the musical directions of the score, which begins with 'allegro tumultuoso' and goes on to 'adagio (tenebroso)'. The orchestral interludes representing the stormy weather, according to Kinkaid, 'contain Herrmann's finest measures, expressing the oneness of the characters and their environment' (1982: 19). Lucille Fletcher, in a letter to Stanley Johnson, records that Herrmann

> wanted in his music to . . . create something more awesome and eternal than the mere human tragedy . . . he wanted his music to *be* Nature, hovering always outside the walls of the houses, overshadowing the action, even moulding it at times – and finally fusing eternally with the savage torment of Heathcliff, who felt himself one with the elements, and hence doomed all the others in his life. (Fletcher 1982)

Robert Sabin notes that in Floyd's opera, Catherine and Heathcliff have 'superb monologues' describing natural effects such as clouds and sunsets, which do not derive from the novel (1961: 24). Similarly Herrmann, who describes his characters as 'passionate elemental beings' (Kinkaid 1982: 21), establishes Catherine and Heathcliff in Act I effectively as 'nature-spirits'; the music uses singing strings followed by bird-and-butterfly-like woodwind motifs to accompany their words about birdsong, heather and sunsets (1966: 16; CD 1: 7). At the end of Act I scene i they escape, in imagination, from Joseph's Bible-reading, to 'wander on through worlds of silver light'; the music here, which is very lyrical, with high strings, leads to an orchestral interlude ('Nocturne'), giving the clear impression that the 'children' are the voices of nature (1: 12–13).

The words here are near-quotations from Emily Brontë's poem (Hatfield 1941: 44; see Kinkaid 1982: 16, 19), but neither the writers nor the commentators on these operas appear to have reflected on the effects of making the characters actually speak words which seem to represent the 'message' of the whole novel or of the author's ethos – especially in a staged production, where the physical presence of the actors is insistent, and most particularly in an opera, where the actors' voices are reinforced by physical power, technique and all the devices of orchestral support. One of the most obvious problems is that Emily Brontë's characters are not serene metaphysical presences. At the end of the paragraph above, for instance, I was constrained to put the word 'children' in inverted commas, since, although Joseph refers to them in this scene as 'ill children', the singers are necessarily mature, and in fact the 1982 libretto replaces 'children' by 'people' (1966: 18; CD 1: 11; 1982: 18). One reviewer of the 1982 production reported that 'Victor Braun['s] . . . young Heathcliff looked inescapably middle-aged', but even if a more youthful actor were found, there is no escaping the fact that Herrmann's score requires a baritone. Making the lovers mouthpieces for philosophical statements about their relation to nature only reinforces the physical presence of the actors, giving them a dignity, even as 'children', which conflicts with the nursery violence of the novel. In the passage quoted above, Lucille Fletcher describes Herrmann's concept of 'Nature . . . fusing eternally with the savage torment of Heathcliff', and it is the figure of Heathcliff in particular which is dignified in this way by both Floyd and Herrmann. Terry Eagleton notes that one of Heathcliff's functions in the novel is to represent an 'opposing realm which can be adequately imaged only as

"Nature"' ([1975] 1988: 103), but the operas make him conscious and articulate about his position, like the speakers of Emily Brontë's poetry which is put into his mouth. Thus in Act I scene ii Heathcliff is presented not only as the self-dramatizing subject of 'I am the only being whose doom', but also as the mouthpiece of the author in 'I'm happiest, when most away' (1966: 20; CD 1: 16; 1982: 22; Hatfield 1941: 11, 44).

Dignifying Heathcliff in this way also has an effect on his relationship with Catherine. Although both Floyd and Herrmann have scenes representing the 'oneness' of the lovers *and* their joint 'oneness' with nature, in each case it is Heathcliff who is the primary spokesman for this joint position. In Floyd's opera, when Heathcliff dilates in a rhapsodic fashion on the 'curdled clouds' with 'scarlet and gold undersides', each phrase is addressed to Catherine and introduced by 'Can you see . . .? Can you see . . . ?'. Cathy adds 'Yes . . . Yes . . .' (quoted in Sabin 1961: 24), as if he were instructing her in proper appreciation of the landscape. Similarly, Act I of Herrmann's opera begins with arias for both lovers describing the landscape they have been wandering through, but whereas Catherine simply declares what she has been doing – 'I have been wandering through the green woods' – Heathcliff begins, with calm authority, 'Look, Cathy, . . .'. It is, moreover, left to Heathcliff to make metaphysical deductions about his sense of union with nature, and he uses the first person singular, not plural:

> I know not where I came, or who I am, but I was born to rule, and to be fierce and free. The hawks that wheel, the wind that blows all proclaim my kinship with the proud. I'm one with them. I'm the gaunt crag. I'm the radiant sky.

In the recording, this speech is delivered in broad, strong tones, accompanied by trombones, to which Catherine is allowed to reply, 'Oh Heathcliff. I am one with them. I too. I too'. Here her notes also soar, but are still secondary to Heathcliff's (1966: 16; CD 1: 7, 8; 1982: 15).

It is notable also that these nature rhapsodies are immediately followed, in Herrmann's opera, by completely conventional expressions of love: Cathy says '(*tenderly*) Heathcliff! You're very dear to me', to which Heathcliff replies, 'Dear Cathy . . .' with a positively sentimental cadence. Herrmann also goes on to repeat the suggestions of childish gender-role acting from the knight-and-lady scene of Wyler's film, which I discussed in Chapter 4. Catherine urges Heathcliff to 'defy them all', while rather childish music accompanies her 'mock-mysterious' speech about the Emperor of China and the Indian queen. The attempts at characterization of the lovers mostly derive from the film, and tend to undercut the tragic and elemental atmosphere created by the music. Catherine and Nelly, for instance, both repeat 'Poor Heathcliff', which first appears in Catherine's diary in the prologue, suggesting, as in the film, that he is a rather weak character needing encouragement and provocation; in the opera, however, this conflicts with the strength conferred on him by the power of his voice and of the philosophical statements given him to speak (I ii; CD 1: 18).

An interview with Barrie Smith, who sang Catherine in the 1982 production, shows that the cast conceived Catherine as a capricious character: '"We . . . were just discussing this morning that Cathy has a lot of Scarlett O'Hara in her", said Barrie Smith, . . . outspoken Southern Belle . . .' (Clark 1982). By comparison with the baritone spokesperson for nature, therefore, she comes to seem simply someone who does not know what she wants. When she tells Nelly of her proposed marriage to Edgar, Nelly asks 'how will *you* bear the separation' (my emphasis), whereas in the novel it is both 'you' and 'he' (1966: 25; CD 2: 7; cf. *WH* 81). When the characters are in a social situation, therefore, rather than representing nature, they seem to revert to the conventional triangle plot presented by the film. In Floyd's opera this is sexually explicit; Ray Chatelin says it is 'filled with lusty, robust seduction scenes', and Kinkaid more restrainedly reports a scene which ends as Catherine 'loosens her hair and opens her arms' (Chatelin 1982: 7; Kinkaid 1982: 29). This overt sexuality, however, is related to conventional gender definitions. Robert Sabin is very impressed with a 'terribly poignant' scene in Act II scene i, where 'Cathy bathes Heathcliff's wounds and lets her hair fall over him'. (I am not sure which episode of the novel this relates to.) Sabin comments: 'Such simplicity, and yet how tremendously effective!' (Sabin 1961: 25) He does not, however, notice that the 'intensely sensuous' scene reproduces Catherine as an icon of Mary Magdalene washing Christ's feet with her hair.

Herrmann still emphasizes the triangle situation but tends to dignify both of Catherine's relationships, providing languishing and expressive music for Catherine's statement of love for Edgar (which in the novel is conventional and perfunctory), so that her 'I love him' is soaring and emphatic (CD 2: 6). On the other hand, the music for 'in my heart and in my soul I am convinced I am wrong' has a tragic edge to it and 'queer dreams' is accompanied by long dreamy strings, and a melody recalling Elgar's 'Sea Songs', rising to a strong crescendo on 'sobbing for joy' (2: 7). In Act III, the scene of Heathcliff's return, Catherine's relationship with Edgar appears increasingly conventional: her 'My Dear Edgar' is almost cloying (1966: 26; CD 2: 9), while Edgar's song, 'Now Art Thou, Dear, My Golden June', is a traditional ballad (Kinkaid 1982: 19; 1966: 26; CD 2: 10). When Heathcliff returns, on the other hand, he immediately diagnoses what is wrong with Catherine – 'she lacks the moor wind' (1966: 28; CD 2: 12) and is thus identified as representing the realm of nature. Catherine is presented, therefore, as having to choose between Edgar (marital love) and Heathcliff (nature). Heathcliff's very explicit identification with nature, and the playing down of his financial manoeuvrings, tend to 'undo' the social/metaphysical paradox noted by Eagleton in *Myths of Power*, allowing Catherine's choice to be made as if it were a choice of lovers simply. When Heathcliff says 'I'm not *your* husband' in the novel, Catherine answers him smartly, saying that he can marry Isabella if he likes (*WH* 112); in the opera, however she cannot answer him but seems distraught, so that this appears to be the motivation for her decline (1966: 29; CD 2: 14).

According to Frank Kinkaid, Cathy's 'mad' aria in Act 3, 'I Am Burning' (1966: 30; CD 2: 15), repeats 'the grandly passionate melody [in Stevenson's *Jane Eyre* (1944)] which represents the Jane/Rochester relationship' (1982: 16).[5] This suggests that Herrmann sees the two novels as having similar triangular motivations. Act III, moreover, ends with Catherine seeing Heathcliff and Isabella together from the window, to which she responds with 'Heathcliff – you have betrayed me – And now – I'll break your heart by breaking mine' (1966: 31; 1982: 44; CD 2: 17). It is the 'great European myth of adultery' (de Rougemont [1940] 1983: 248, 11), dignified in the tradition of *Othello* or *Tristan and Isolde*, with the addition of Heathcliff as nature-spirit. In Act IV, after marrying Isabella, Heathcliff returns to the Heights carrying yellow crocuses which Isabella thinks he picked for Catherine. After an angry scene with Hindley and Isabella, Heathcliff sees the flowers on the ground and sings 'Poor blossoms . . . Blossoms that the west wind has never wooed to blow/ Scentless are your petals, your dew as cold as snow./ Wither, flowers, wither, you were vainly given./ Poor blossoms – wither' (1966: 32–3; 1982: 50, 52; CD 3: 5). The flowers are clearly meant to represent his love, born to blush unseen, as it were, but the moment is sentimental and conventional compared with Emily's Heathcliff, who is neither tender nor metaphorical about nature; in her novel it is Edgar who gives Catherine the crocuses (*WH* 134).

Herrmann's reliance on the Wyler script, and on various conventional devices such as the withered flowers, tend to recoup the story of his opera towards one of jealous love, in which one of the lovers just happens to represent 'nature'. The extent to which Wyler's film has structured people's memories and expectations of *Wuthering Heights* is indicated by the programme note by Stanley Johnson for the 1982 performance of Herrmann's *Wuthering Heights*. Although a Professor of English Literature at Portland State University, Johnson states in his plot summary of *Wuthering Heights* that Heathcliff 'forms an attachment to Cathy and shares her imaginary life as a princess' – a feature deriving from Wyler; this feature was repeated in a lecture series accompanying the premiere (Johnson 1982a: 32). One reviewer at least seems to think that there is only room for one 'dominant' version of a famous story at a time, doubting whether 'Herrmann's opera will supplant William Wyler's 1939 film' (Malitz 1982). The extensive collection of reviews of the 1982 performance held by the Brontë Parsonage Museum confirms that in the popular (educated) mind, *Wuthering Heights* had become assimilated with Wyler's film. The motivation of the characters was assumed to be sexual jealousy, and Joelle Cohen calls the novel 'Emily Brontë's classic melodrama of mismatched couples' (1982). Nevertheless, the repeated musical motifs and circular structure of Herrmann's original conception come near to representing the absent centre of *Wuthering Heights* – the fact that there is no mode in which the love of Catherine and Heathcliff can be consummated.

In the period between the recording and the first performance of Herrmann's opera, operas based on *Wuthering Heights* were published in France and Italy. Of the French work I know nothing but its title – *Les hauts de hurle-vent* (1961) – and composer – Philippe Hériat. A copy of Dino Milella's Italian opera, entitled *Una storia d'altri tempi* (*A History of Other Times*), is to be found in Haworth (1972). Like Kadar's Indian film of 1966, it is set by the sea, and shows on the front cover of the printed score a fierce sea with lighthouse and harbour wall. This sea, however, is in the north of England around the year 1800 and the cast list retains most of the original names of the characters. Wuthering Heights has been transformed into a 'castello', and the opera opens with Catherine's brother reviling Heathcliff, who is commonly called 'It'. 'It' replies that he is a man, not a beast, and cannot live by bread alone (*WH* 1972 Milella: 9–11). Without any intervening scene between Catherine and Heathcliff, we find her discussing with Meg (Nelly) whether she should marry Edgar. Meg warns her that her mother was unhappy after marrying without love, and Catherine replies that her mother once told her a strange thing; she searched for a twin soul and lived in vain hope of finding it. Catherine looks forward with joy to the splendour of that light, the infinite sweetness of the twin soul, the twin soul . . . (20–4).

When Edgar appears, she at first agrees to the wedding and then, seeing the men congratulating one another, suffers a revulsion against being used in a financial deal to settle her brother's gambling debts (30–3). She contemplates suicide, but decides she cannot send her soul to damnation (36–7). At this low point, 'It' declares his love, but Catherine cannot bring herself to marry a servant. Theirs is 'un amore impossibile' (an impossible love), it seems, on purely economic grounds (43–6). Nevertheless 'in questa sera di tempesta' (this stormy evening) they vow eternal love. As they part, Catherine vows that if she should die first, she will return to the lighthouse 'in una notte di tempesta' (a night of storm) (53–5). 'It' several times refers to Catherine as an 'angel' or 'quella santa creatura, sola luce in tanto buio' (that saintly creature, the only light in all this darkness) (49, 57). Act II scene ii shows 'It' declaring 'non posso continuare in quest'inferno!' (I cannot go on in this hell!) and looking for revenge (81–3). Even while marrying the sister of his enemy, he begs Catherine to haunt him; in scene iii the white figure of Catherine appears on the lighthouse, declaring eternal love. 'It' kills himself, Catherine descends from the tower and takes his hand. They walk away together, 'anime senza corpo, verso l'eternità' (souls without bodies, towards eternity) (84–95).

Milello's opera, like Buñuel's 1953 film, reads the motivations of Emily Brontë's characters through the medium of Latin patriarchal family structures, though it retains a conventional belief in the afterlife. Its most interesting innovation is that Catherine is forewarned by her mother and later laments that her accursed destiny has been a repetition of her mother's – a recognition more familiar from the Gothic derivatives of *Jane Eyre* discussed at the start of this chapter. The notion of love between Catherine and Heathcliff is, however, entirely conventional; Catherine is a sainted creature, and the 'twin soul' ideal is of marital perfection baulked of consummation by purely economic barriers. The atmosphere is tragic and high-minded; Milella, like the other operatic composers, clearly found in the story of *Wuthering Heights* a tragic myth to take its place in high culture.

In the inter-war period, the tendency to Brontë hagiography had been undercut by vigorous parody, but most reference to the Brontës during this post-war period were reverential – the musical reproductions particularly so. It is interesting first that the two exceptions I have found come from outside England, secondly that they have a musical dimension, and thirdly that their critical stance seems motivated by the enshrinement of the Brontë texts within the canon of high culture.

In 1955 the Canadian broadcaster Max Ferguson delighted audiences with his musical 'Rawhide' version of *Wuthering Heights*, 'highly recommended to English teachers for illustrating to unappreciative students the real meaning of tragedy in English literature'. In 1963 an even more outrageous publication, originally composed in Alexandria, appeared in New York. This was Bernard de Zogheb's *Le sorelle Brontë*. Like the 'Rawhide' version, *Le sorelle Brontë* seems to be motivated by impatience at the way in which the Brontës have been canonized within 'Eng. Lit.'. The foreword describes Zogheb's song cycle as a collection of 'works of high quality. On every page something is made clear about the tenacious inanity of human emotions . . .'. However, 'the reader will search in vain for the gloomy, introspective Brontës of his literature class. In their place, three wild extroverts ride the familiar Mediterranean pendulum between the most lavish endearments and the coarsest recriminations.' The frontispiece shows a pen version of Branwell's famous 'pillar portrait' with Anne droopy-eyed and wearing a very large cross, Emily very pretty and Charlotte extremely *decolletée* and come-hither. All three appear to be writing *Wuthering Heights* simultaneously – a nice reference to the pre-war authorship debates.

There are other indications that this work reacts not simply to the original texts, but to an intertextual chain including the Hollywood films. The cast list includes 'Emiglia, Carlotta and Anna' who are bracketed together as 'giovanissimi e bellissimi' (very young and beautiful) – no plain little heroines here – 'MacMillione, un editore avaro e ricco' (a rich and avaricious editor) and 'Thackeray' and 'Dickens', 'due scrivature famosi' (two famous writers). In Act III, Thackeray and Dickens have a duet, most of the words of which are 'Good morning' – clear reference to the farcical scene in *Devotion* where the two authors are introduced transparently for the purpose of indicating how Charlotte was now moving in literary society, by a film-maker who had no idea what literary people might say to one another (*WH* 1963 Zogheb: 19). Although *Le sorelle Brontë* is described as an 'opera' and all the words are set to music, the music is derived from miscellaneous popular sources, and considerable comic effect is derived from the would-be tragic characters delivering their rhymed verses in Alexandrian 'kitchen Italian' (with some unorthodox spelling!) to the tune of 'The Stars and Stripes', or 'Funiculi, Funicula'. In Act I scene iii Emily and Branwell have a scene, again referring back to such pre-war plays as *Wild Decembers*, in which she identifies the two of them with Catherine and Heathcliff: 'Tacci, tacci, non sentir la, Branwell, Dami bacci, io lo voglio quel. Sei mio Hisscliff, io son Kathi – ' (Be quiet, don't listen to her, give me kisses, that's what I want. You are my Heathcliff, I am Cathy); this is, however, sung to the tune of 'A Bicycle Made for Two' (7). In the next scene, Charlotte tries to persuade Emily to go to Brussels to the tune of 'Sing a Song of Sixpence', to which Emily replies, calling up the famous statements of her homesickness in innumerable biographies, 'Io non voglio lacciar 'l Yorkshire, Lacciar 'l Yorkshire, lacciar 'l Yorkshire – Mi ferà troppo soffrir, Mie sorelle' to the tune of 'London Bridge is Falling Down', followed by 'Io preferisco stare chui' to the tune of 'This is the Army, Mr Jones' ('I don't want to leave Yorkshire, I shall suffer too much, my sisters' and 'I want to stay here'; 10). My favourite, however, is in Act II scene ii, where 'Sig. Hegez' sings (to 'Music, Music, Music'), 'Dammi uno baccio chua Sulla bocca, Carlotta. Non vogl' che sentirti dirmi "Hegez, Hegez, Hegez"' ('Give me a kiss on the mouth, Charlotte. I only want to hear you saying 'Heger, Heger, Heger'; 11).

Terry Eagleton notes that the distinctively English project motivating 'English Studies' – 'the cultivation of "larger sympathies" . . . and the transmission of "moral" values' – is 'a frequent source of bemusement to intellectuals from other cultures' (1983: 25). It is perhaps because I was educated within the English tradition that while I am critical of the operatic elevation of *Wuthering Heights* to the realm of 'timeless truths', these 'foreign' parodies still provoke in me, alongside the smiles, a surge of fierce loyalty to the 'high seriousness' of the Brontë texts themselves. The next chapter calls into question the basis of that response.

Notes

1. Though Byatt claims that her fantasies were 'of their essence solitary' (Introduction, Ferguson [1931] 1987: v), she describes a shared family saga game in *The Game* (*JE* [1967] 1983); moreover her sister Margaret Drabble describes a joint imaginary world in 'The writer as recluse' (1974).
2. In a characteristic movement, Freud first distinguishes between the fantasies of men and women, then says they are 'often united', and then gives an example of how a *masculine* fantasy often 'contains' a feminine one – but neglects to give a counter-example, which in his terms would prove that a woman's erotic dream would contain an ambitious one. Lacan develops Freud's theory of 'displacement'.
3. The words spoken by José in the film include the following: 'death came into the world because of the devil's envy and his followers imitate his actions'. In *My Last Breath*, Buñuel explains that many of José's words are from the apocryphal book of Wisdom; nevertheless he describes them as 'from the bible' and adds 'of course, the author had to put these words into the mouth of unbelievers in order to get them printed' (Buñuel 1984: 205). I am grateful to Helen Hughes for bringing this book to my attention and for indicating the ambiguous source of José's words.
4. 1966 libretto, p. 26; CD 2: band 8. The 1966 version is in four acts; references, unless specified, are to this version; the end of Act II (1966) is the end of Act I in 1982. References to the CD recording are in the form (CD 1: band 1), later abbreviated to (1: 1).
5. Although Kinkaid's note is in the programme for 1982 performance, he must have been working from the record, because this aria does not feature in the 1982 libretto.

Chapter 6

Jane Eyre's other:
the emergence of Bertha

In previous chapters we have seen that the figure of Bertha Mason was initially perceived simply as a foil to the heroine. From the 1890s onwards, however, a fascination with the figure in the third storey led to an increase of sympathy – both in the sense of an extension of kindly feeling and, more importantly, of identification. The madwoman in *The Secret of Kyriels* and the first wife in *Vera* are shown to be victims of male dominance, occupying a position which the younger women in those stories could inherit. Even the wilful and selfish figures of Rebecca and Muriel Carne are not simple figures of revulsion. But the madwoman in the attic continued to provoke contradictory responses.

In Chapter 4, I quoted a review of Phyllis Birkett's stage adaptation of *Jane Eyre*, produced in Keighley in 1929 and in London in 1931. The Bradford reviewer of the London production objected not only to the 'shrieks and thuds' which accompanied the madwoman's appearance, but also to the fact that

> the mad woman is given a scene in her own room which takes nearly all the thrill from her famous appearance to Jane on the wedding night.
> Jane's relationship to Rochester has to be swallowed whole for the sake of the highly spiced tit-bits of sensation, and we find them engaged without seeing the intervening stages. ([Bradford] *Observer* 25.9.1931)

Although we cannot now react to the performance itself, we can detect the reviewer's assumption that the only reason for the madwoman to be present is to provide a 'sensation'. The *Observer* concurs with this, finding that 'while the drama creaked its way from crisis to crisis, capping sentiment with sensation; and the lunatic now moaned in the offing, now terrorized the fairway, Jane quietly shone' (27.9.1931). Yet another reviewer reported that

> Miss Phyllis Birkett has thrown Charlotte Brontë's plot out of balance by introducing Rochester's wife too early in the story, and repeating and over-stressing the mad scenes . . . We know all about the secret of the locked room from the first act . . . [Miss Birkett] played the lunatic with such tremendous gusto that one could not help suspecting her of improving on Charlotte Brontë in order to give herself a generous allowance of maniacal scenes. (*Yorkshire Post* 25.9.1931)

We have seen that in two of the male adaptations of *Jane Eyre* dating from this period, Rochester was given scenes to which Jane is not privy; it is a clear indication of the adaptor's interest and, often, a sign of sympathy with the character so isolated (*JE* 1956 Hartford and 1961 Shaper; see Nudd 1989: 109–10). Donna Marie Nudd's description of Birkett's 'extra' scene reveals, in fact, that it provides not only cause for sympathy with the madwoman, but a 'rational' explanation for her resentment and violence against Rochester and, more particularly, her brother. According to Nudd, the scene in the 'locked room' shows Mason reminding Bertha of her life in Jamaica, giving her gin to drink, telling her that their father is dead and giving her a paper to sign. It is when he reminds her that her name is now Rochester that she remembers how her brother had forced her to marry, and it is in this context that she attacks him. The scene finishes convincingly with the words which Charlotte Brontë gave to Bertha – "'I'll drain your heart'" – and in this new context both words and actions seem motivated and therefore less 'mad' and less 'bestial' than in the novel.

In 1931, when Birkett's play had its metropolitan staging, Jean Rhys was also living in London. It would be fascinating to know whether she saw Birkett's play; even hearing it discussed might have set the idea growing in her mind which would become *Wide Sargasso Sea* thirty-five years later (Rhys 1984: 14). Rhys, who was born in Dominica, knew all about the mad Creole heiresses; she also knew from first-hand the landscape and the culture of the West Indies which in Charlotte Brontë's novel provides a vague 'elsewhere' for Jane's story. It was 1939 when she wrote the first version of the story which, at that stage, she called *Le Revenant – The Ghost* (literally 'The one who returns') (Angier 1985: 67). By 1949 she is not only writing, but 'stuck' with the writing of a new version, now called "'the first Mrs Rochester'" (Rhys 1984: 50). Oddly, ten years later again she is trying to buy a copy of *Jane Eyre*; when she now reads its account of Bertha, she is 'a bit taken aback' to discover 'what a fat (and improbable) monster she was' (146, 149). In a later letter she says that she read *Jane Eyre* when she first came to England when she was 'between sixteen and seventeen' – that is, in 1907 (296). It is clear that the various readings had created different memories, quite apart from any different version – such as Birkett's play – which she might have come across, and had worked in her mind together with her personal memories to generate her new story. At the time of her last reading of the original, the new story was already some way away from it. She notes in a 'short-hand' letter: 'hadn't read "Jane Eyre" for years and nearly forgotten Creole' (153). This is a fascinating insight into the independence of famous texts from their printed sources.

In 1958 we find Rhys explaining that her book 'has no connection with any play, film or adaptation of "Jane Eyre" who does not appear at all' (153), but it is still possible that a play seen or heard almost thirty years before might be a forgotten impulse; in any case, Rhys is clearly concerned here with the change of focus from such plays or films as those of Jerome and Stevenson, both of which had appeared by this time. She insists that her book must not be 'just another adaptation of "Jane Eyre". There have been umpteen thousand and sixty already' (159). It is interesting, however, that Rhys expresses her sense of the change of focus involved in her book in theatrical terms:

The Creole in Charlotte Brontë's novel is a lay figure – repulsive which does not matter, and not once alive which does. She's necessary to the plot, but always she shrieks, howls, laughs horribly, attacks all and sundry – *off stage*. For me . . . she must be right *on stage*. She must be at least plausible with a past, the *reason* why Mr Rochester treats her so abominably and feels justified, the reason why he thinks she is mad and why of course she goes mad . . .

   I do not see how Charlotte Brontë's madwoman could possibly convey all this. It *might* be done but it would not be convincing. At least I doubt it. Another 'I' must talk, two others perhaps. Then the Creole's 'I' will come to life . . .

   That unfortunate death of a Creole! I'm fighting mad to write *her* story. (156–7)

For Rhys, the process of bringing the Creole 'on stage' involved emancipating herself from Charlotte Brontë's version, which she represents as a dominant discourse: 'One stupid thing I did was to read "Jane Eyre" too much. Then I found it was creeping into my writing. A bad imitation – quite dreadful. All had to be scrapped'. Fascinatingly, she finds a lever to separate herself from Charlotte in the writing of Charlotte's sister Emily. In 1959 Rhys finds *Wuthering Heights*: 'I'd never read it before. I start with a dream too in Mrs R. but no ghosts' (161). Twenty years before, of course, she had written a version which was to be called, precisely, *Le Revenant – The Ghost*. In the meantime she had also read another novel about ghosts. If we accept, as I argue in Chapter 2, that *The Turn of the Screw* throws into question the rationality of 'Jane Eyre' and her difference from the 'unmentionable relative kept in unsuspected confinement', it is very interesting to find Rhys in 1953 'reading "The Turn of the Screw" for the 6th time' (98). Her focus, however, is not on the presentable (if disturbed) governess, but on the previously unmentionable relative. Her first conception of the book that was to become *Wide Sargasso Sea* was that the whole book should be one 'long monologue'; Bertha was to be given her voice with a vengeance. But then she recollects criticism of the first version of her earlier novel, *Voyage in the Dark* (1934), and anticipates her readers saying '"A mad girl speaking all the time is too much!"' The novel is recast as 'a story, a romance, but keeping the dream feeling and working up to the madness' (233). In the process of creating a 'story' – which needs cause and effect, or what Barthes calls motivation – Rhys finds herself presenting as an alternative discourse to Bertha's that of Mr Rochester, who is, of course, also 'off-stage' for much of the 'motivating' hinterland of *Jane Eyre*.

   The interesting situation which arises here, therefore, is that as a result of being 'fighting mad' to tell the story of the 'off-stage' Creole (156–7), Rhys finds herself drawn into telling the story of Rochester, the feared/desired object of both women in Charlotte Brontë's novel. Nevertheless Rhys records that Part II of her novel, which is Rochester's story, 'has always been so much the worst and most difficult' (234). To some extent Rhys's text seems motivated by a desire to redress wrongs; Brontë's Bertha, for instance, is given back what seems to be her preferred, and more beautiful name, Antoinette – and this is more telling if we realize that for much of *Jane Eyre* she is referred to as 'Grace Poole', 'a form', 'a shape', 'a woman', 'it', 'a figure' (*JE* 296–7), 'the clothed hyena', 'the maniac', 'the lunatic' and '*my wife*' (307–8); and that in stage versions of Brontë's novel she is almost universally called The Maniac. Mr Rochester, on the other hand, whose name is repeated in *Jane Eyre* like a mantra representing economic and sexual power, in *Wide Sargasso Sea* becomes nameless, occupying a position like that of the nameless heroine in *Rebecca*, defined by his relationship to Antoinette, her country, her houses, her servants. The discomfiture of Rochester does not, however, work entirely against him. As in Browning's dramatic monologues, the textual adoption of Rochester's voice and of his self-analysis itself generates a consistently motivated 'story' which leads the reader, ironically, into a position of greater sympathy with Rochester than is offered by *Jane Eyre*.

In a letter written in 1964, Rhys explains how her initial conception of the story, motivated by being 'vexed at [Brontë's] portrait of the "paper tiger" lunatic, the all wrong creole scenes, and above all the real cruelty of Mr Rochester', nevertheless 'didn't click. It wasn't there' until she wrote a poem from the position of Mr Rochester; 'then it clicked – and all was there and always had been' (1984: 262). In her note to this poem, called 'Obeah Night', Paula Burnett writes:

> By substituting for the materialist Mr Rochester of the first draft a man consumed by very real passion for Antoinette, a passion which is plausibly channelled to the 'angry love' of the poem, she was able to make the book true to her first impulse to write. (Burnett 1986: 403)

In a letter to another correspondent, Rhys expands on the impulse which made her revise the Mr Rochester who was motivated by '*lovely* mun' and realize that 'Mr Rochester is *not* a heel'. The explanation is that

> he is a fierce and violent (Heathcliff) man who marries an alien creature . . . My Mr Rochester as I see him becomes as fierce as Heathcliff and as jealous as Othello . . . I have tried to show this man being magicked by the place which is (or was) a lovely, lost *and magic* place but, if you understand, a *violent* place. (Rhys 1984: 269)

This was written in 1964, when the book was nearly complete. Five years earlier, when she first read *Wuthering Heights*, she describes Emily's novel as 'So magnificent in parts. But none of this probability nonsense. Still a hurricane isn't *probable* is it?'. The later references to Rochester as 'fierce as Heathcliff' might lead us to see him as the 'hurricane' figure in Rhys's novel, and it is relevant here to look at Terry Eagleton's shrewd analysis of Heathcliff in *Myths of Power*. Eagleton accepts that for Catherine, Heathcliff represents the equivalent of Rhys's 'hurricane': something which takes her 'outside the family and society into an opposing realm which can be adequately imaged only as "Nature"' ([1975] 1988: 103). Moreover, Eagleton makes large claims for the kind of Romantic alternative which Heathcliff represents; his version of Heathcliff makes him sound quite akin to the *communal* spirituality represented in *Wide Sargasso Sea* by the combination of landscape, black people and obeah:

> The force Heathcliff symbolises can be truly realised only in some more than merely individualist form; *Wuthering Heights* has its roots not in that narrowed, simplified

Romanticism which pits the lonely rebel against an anonymous order, but in that earlier, more authentic Romantic impulse which posits its own kind of 'transindividual' order of value, its own totality, against the order which forces it into exile. Heathcliff may be Byronic, but not in the way Rochester is: the novel counterposes social convention not merely with contrasting personal life-styles but with an alternative world of meaning. Yet it is here that the limits of 'possible consciousness' assert themselves: the offered totalities of nature, myth and cosmic energy are forced to figure as asocial worlds unable to engage in more than idealist ways with the society they subject to judgement. The price of universality is to be fixed eternally at a point extrinsic to social life – fixed, indeed, at the moment of death. (109–10)

Heathcliff, however, is not an unproblematic Romantic 'symbol'. Eagleton argues that as a historically situated character he embodies a contradiction in 'that he combines Heights violence with Grange methods to gain power over both properties' (115); this also applies well to Rhys's conception of Rochester, who uses both his own sexual force and his father's legal manoevrings to gain power over Antoinette. Eagleton, however, goes further, distinguishing this contradiction within Heathcliff as a character from 'the contradiction of the *novel*', which is

that Heathcliff cannot represent at once an absolute metaphysical refusal of an inhuman society and a class which is intrinsically part of it. Heathcliff is both metaphysical hero, spiritually marooned from all material concern in his obsessional love for Catherine, and a skilful exploiter who cannily expropriates the wealth of others. It is a limit of the novel's 'possible consciousness' that its absolute metaphysical protest can be socially articulated only in such terms – that its 'outside' is in this sense an 'inside'. (116)

Bearing all this in mind, it is instructive to look back at Rhys's letters and find that it is not in fact Heathcliff/Rochester whom she likens to a hurricane but the Creole: 'now she is angry too. Like a hurricane' (Rhys 1984: 263). Susan Meyer, moreover, in 'Colonialism and the figurative strategy of *Jane Eyre*', points out that tropical storms function not only in Charlotte Brontë's work (as in the storm which kills M. Paul Emanuel, for instance) but in 'writers as diverse as Monk Lewis and Harriet Martineau' as metaphors for 'the rage and revenge of the black West Indians' (1991: 159–60). It is also interesting in this respect that Eagleton, in the passage quoted above, describes Heathcliff as 'spiritually marooned from all material concern', using the word 'marooned', now commonly used in the sense of 'shipwrecked by a storm', which originated in the experiences of rebel Caribs (maroon or chestnut-coloured) who found themselves outlawed in their own land. The implication of all this is that in Rhys's novel, Rochester's passion – the quality contrasted with his pursuit of 'lovely mun' – aligns him on the metaphysical plane with Antoinette, who represents an 'opposing realm which can be adequately imaged only as "Nature"' with its threat of leaving them marooned (Eagleton [1975] 1988: 103). On the material plane, however, Antoinette *embodies* the lovely mun acquired through marriage, which constitutes social status. As in *Wuthering Heights*, therefore, Rhys's Rochester finds that the outside of his society (love, passion, beauty, magic) is also its inside (legality, kinship, exploitation, possession).

Unlike *Wuthering Heights*, however, *Wide Sargasso Sea* does not keep Heathcliff/ Rochester 'fixed eternally at a point extrinsic to social life'; instead it shows us his choice: to ally himself either with Antoinette ('My lunatic. My mad girl') or with her keepers ('a memory to be avoided, locked away') (*JE* 1966 Rhys [1983: 136,142]). In the poem, 'Obeah Night', Rochester provides a concise account of his motivation and reaction to his marriage to Antoinette. Under the influence of obeah – magic – he gives way to 'Love's dark face . . . cruel as he is', but is too cowardly to look next morning 'at what I'd done'. Instead 'I turned away – Traitor/ Too sane to face my madness (or despair)'. For a moment he asks

How can I forget you Antoinette
    When the spring is here?
Where did you hide yourself

After that shameless, shameful night? . . .
Did I ever see you again?

No. I'll lock that door
Forget it.

The process of repression described here ('lock that door. Forget it') and in the novel ('a memory to be avoided, locked away') is the process which, in Henry James's governess, produces the hysteria of divided consciousness, in which 'shameful' knowledge is projected in the form of 'unmentionable relative[s]'. Rhys, however, decided that her novel would have 'no ghosts' (1984: 161). Rochester need not suffer in this way because he has the power to redefine reality. The Antoinette who comes back after the shameful night is less than human ('Where did you hide yourself . . . (*What* did you send instead?')) and the loved Antoinette can be divorced from 'what I'd done': 'I'll never see you now/ I'll never know/ For you left me – my truest Love/ Long ago' (264–6). Rochester, in fact, does not need to project his repressed recognition in the form of hallucinations because he can define the real Antoinette in terms which make her a ghost to herself. At the end of the novel, before she sets fire to Thornfield, she sees herself in a mirror: 'It was then that I saw her – the ghost. The woman with streaming hair. She was surrounded by a gilt frame but I knew her' (*JE* 1966 Rhys [1983: 154]). In the year of publication, Rhys still speculates about Antoinette's inheritance: 'perhaps . . . the seeds of madness, at any rate hysteria' (Rhys 1984: 297). If, like Anna O and Lucy R, Antoinette was pushed towards hysteria by her education in modesty, then Rochester, with his sexual initiation, acts as potential therapist and confessor, removing inhibitions and encouraging transference. This 'talking', however, does not effect a 'cure' because instead of validating her experience Rochester repudiates it, casting her into a world where words and appearances are treacherous and must be charmed by magic.

Unlike Jane, Antoinette does not gain access to the Symbolic by the process of writing her story – perhaps because for communication to take place there must be a sense of a hearer. 'Reader, I married him!' is one of the most famous sentences in *Jane Eyre*, announcing Jane's arrival at a status which allows her to join the 'reader' as a full member of society. Antoinette's lack of an audience, on the other hand, gives her words the status of a 'dead letter', launched into air and apparently 'unclaimed'. In the last pages of the novel, she first 'dreams' her own death and then resolves to enact it, thus also enacting the 'fate' already inscribed in *Jane Eyre*. Because her words have no material status, as speech or writing confirmed by a recipient, and because in the end they merge with the already written testament of a confident 'rational' speaker (Jane), the final effect of *Wide Sargasso Sea* is to reinstate Antoinette's ghostly marginality. Interestingly, Rhys herself seems to have no sense of an audience, and throughout her letters describes how her neighbours, who cannot read or write, think her mad. On the same page where she describes writing 'Obeah Night', she says, 'I'm sure the neighbours think I'm potty but after all – they can hardly haul me off to the bin for scribble scribble scribble' (Rhys 1984: 239, 263). This reading of Antoinette's 'hysteria' is indirectly confirmed by Diane Price Herndl (1988). Herndl points out that Breuer's claim that Anna O was completely cured by his 'treatment' was not strictly true; milder symptoms persisted for seven years after the treatment was ended. Bertha Pappenheim, the real Anna, was not completely cured until 1890, when she published a volume of short stories. She went on to translate Mary Wollstonecraft's *Vindication of the Rights of Woman*, wrote plays and essays and became a prominent member of the Judischer Frauenbund (the German Jewish Women's League). Herndl also applies her theory to Charlotte Perkins Gilman, whose heroine in *The Yellow Wallpaper* is not, she argues, cured by writing her story (for/to whom?), though Gilman was cured by publishing it. In other words, women are not cured, but cure themselves by claiming a place in the Symbolic.

Jane Eyre, apart from the physical descriptions of Bertha which mostly deny her humanity, gives us two articulated attitudes towards her. On the one hand, there is Rochester's deep resentment deriving from the trick played on him by his father and brother: 'a nature the most gross, impure, depraved I ever saw, was associated with mine, and called by the law and by society a part of me' (*JE* 323). On the other, there is Jane's 'humane' response to this 'unfortunate lady' who 'cannot help being mad' (317). In addition, the 'unconscious' of the text, by means of juxtapositions, metaphors, and so on, suggests parallels between Jane and Bertha which form the basis of later Gothic reproductions.

Jean Rhys's novel was not the first to exploit the suggestions of sympathy in Charlotte Brontë's text, but it was qualitatively different from the rest. Phyllis Birkett's rather startling interpolation in her 1929 play indicates sympathy for Bertha, but it is focused on the economic wrong done to her through her marriage. There were also indications during the 1950s that popular audiences were ready to react sympathetically to parallels between Bertha and Jane. Even the comicbook versions of this period, while retaining the horrific contrast of the scene after the failed marriage, suggest some similarity between Jane and the Bertha who falls from the roof. The comicbook described in Chapter 5 (page 146 above), in which Jane is shown barefoot on the moor, also shows Bertha in this final scene as slim and girlish, and dressed in a short dress with bare feet. Earlier in Chapter 5, I presented

Tania Modleski's argument that 'in the classic female Gothic, part of the heroine's progress involves . . . a more or less gradual understanding of the "mother's" situation' (1982: 68). In *Jane Eyre*, it is Bertha who occupies the Oedipal position of mother, and, as if this process of 'understanding' were becoming general, it is also observable in a film of this period made by a man.

Douglas Sirk's *Interlude* (1957) is a remake of John M. Stahl's 1939 film, *When Tomorrow Comes*, and gives us a version of the *Jane Eyre* story without its original happy ending. Although the film does not basically challenge the love-and-marriage imperative, it does show a softened version of the first wife. *Interlude* shows a love ? between a young American woman (played by June Allyson) and a half-Italian ?r (Rossano Brazzi) who has a mad wife. Initially, the Jane figure promises ?er 'Rochester', but the mad wife, who is beautiful, young and appealing (? ?tently out of control), appeals to her not to take the husband who is al? ? version, it is 'Jane' who rescues the madwoman (from water, not fire), ? 'St John Rivers'. Some of the tension is removed from the *Ja*? ?spense, and, more interestingly, all the characte? ?le for his wife's condition; the madwoman is ? ?ficing. Although some film critics have seen an iro? ? excess of costumes, interiors and landscapes in this film (Gleu?? ?ny unsophisticated viewer it confirms the self-repression tradition? ? women without either rewarding its heroine with the object of desir? ?g her with a proud independence. There is, however, a suggestion that honour between women can override the imperatives of marriage; where Jane Eyre runs away because she cares for her*self*, this heroine retreats for the good of the 'other woman'.

Interlude, despite its air of sad rationality, is in effect a conservative film, endorsing female self-sacrifice and a sentimental view of marriage. It serves by contrast to emphasize the radical ideological breakthrough represented by Rhys's novel, which focuses neither on the wrong constituted by marriage itself, like Birkett's play, nor on the adventitious sadness of Bertha's madness, but on Rochester's behaviour after the marriage, which forms a paradigm for nineteenth-century sexual ideology. The immense revision which Jean Rhys's novel makes to *Jane Eyre* is first to give Bertha her voice – and, moreover, to let us hear Rochester corroborate her story – and then to show exactly why this voice cannot be heard. Antoinette, an innocent, convent-educated girl, reluctant to marry, nevertheless gives herself trustingly enough to her husband who initiates her into sexuality. Her behaviour, interpreted as shameful abandon, then nauseates its perpetrator, who uses his power to distance himself from the result he has produced. The story, thus exposed, stands like a recognition of the economic basis of nineteenth-century sexual ideology, in which men deplored the existence of saleable sex for which they themselves formed the market.

Published just a few years before the women's liberation movement, *Wide Sargasso Sea* was ready to hand for feminist critics to work on. Since *Jane Eyre* rapidly became a canonized text of the movement, there was an uneasy negotiation of the relationship between the two novels, which was seen as everything from corroboration to critique. *Jane Eyre* had, as we have seen, been read from the beginning as a revolutionary text in terms of class and gender, and from this point of view *Wide Sargasso Sea* seemed to corroborate its insights, suggesting that all women shared their subordinate economic and legal status within marriage. Nancy Pell's fine essay, published in 1977, for instance, refers back to Virginia Woolf's criticism of Jane's 'feminist manifesto' in I xii, about how women 'suffer from too rigid a restraint, too absolute a stagnation' – a speech which is interrupted by 'Grace Poole's' laugh (*JE* 115). For Woolf, concerned with the quality of the writing, this transition had seemed abrupt and inartistic; Pell, however, points out the thematic appropriateness of this juxtaposition:

> Here at the center of a novel about one woman's struggle for independence and love is a woman who is utterly restrained and considered socially dead, who, nevertheless, breaks through her restraints and occasionally wreaks havoc in the house of which she is the hidden, titular mistress: . . . Woman under too rigid a restraint – a woman offered as an object in a marriage settlement – displays in perverse ways the power that she is continually denied. (Pell 1977: 419)

A further development of this position came in 1979 with Gilbert and Gubar's famous book, *The Madwoman in the Attic*. Subtitled *The Woman Writer and the Nineteenth-century Literary Imagination*, this critical work argues that Bertha Mason functions as the textual representative of the social and sexual rage which could not be tolerated in the decorous heroines of nineteenth-century writing by women. Locked away in the attic, Bertha's tumult can be overtly repudiated by the female speaker, but her presence in the text nevertheless serves to destabilize the apparently endorsed social order. The impact of *The Madwoman in the Attic* can be gauged not only by its ubiquitous presence in undergraduate essays, and by changes such as 'the maniac' in the cast list to John Cannon's 1973 play, which by 1982 had become 'the madwoman', but also in such incidental references as a recent television crime thriller series whose first episode was entitled 'The Madwoman in the Attic', and which explained the process of repression in a possible murderer by saying, 'Nobody ever loses their memory. It just gets locked away, like the madwoman in the attic. You hear a scream now and then but don't dare unlock the door to see what's going on' (*JE* 1993 McGovern; see also 1991 B[ennett]).

It now seems probable, as Shirley Foster argues, that Gilbert and Gubar overstated the enforced 'silence' of heroines such as Jane Eyre in order to develop their argument (1985: 14–15). The 'revolutionary' aspects of *Jane Eyre* as a feminist text had for a long time been not only located in Jane's own words (e.g. by [Eastlake] 1848), but also associated with other statements of 'grievance'. Virginia Woolf, reacting in 1929 to what she saw as Charlotte Brontë's over-emphatic statement of her wrongs, argues that this resentment 'brings into women's writing an element which is entirely absent from a man's, unless, indeed, he happens to be a working-man, a Negro, or one who for some other reason is conscious of disability' (Woolf 1979: 47). Ellen Moers, writing in 1963, turns Woolf's point into a positive, identifying *Jane Eyre* as 'the prime source . . . for the language of rage and the metaphors of slavery as they permeated the literary imagination of Victorian women' ([1963] 1978: 165). Both these critics, however, register the primary meaning of the text as Jane's anger, for which the anger of other oppressed people serves as an analogy, surfacing only through the textual devices – metaphor, juxtaposition – which constitute the 'unconscious' of the text. Susan Meyer, in fact, argues that 'the figurative strategy of *Jane Eyre*', with its extensive, if unconscious, reliance on metaphors drawn from colonialism, is itself an extension of colonial thinking:

> Like colonial exploitation itself, bringing home the spoils of other countries to become commodities such as Indian ink, the use of the racial 'other' as a metaphor for class and gender struggles in England commodifies colonial subjects as they exist in historical actuality and transforms them into East or West 'Indian ink', ink with which to write a novel about ending oppression in England. (Meyer 1991: 180)

Wide Sargasso Sea helped to change the focus of this discussion, since its madwoman is no longer confined and unmentionable but has, precariously, the status of a speaking subject. She is, moreover, not just a generalized symbol of oppression, interchangeable with the 'working man', but precisely located in historical and geographical terms. Antoinette is inescapably an early nineteenth century Creole – a white West Indian of European descent – and this aspect of her identity, together with her wish to be black, and her close association with her black nurse, Christophine, and her black friend Tia, raises the question of colonial relationships in a new and insistent form. *Wide Sargasso Sea* forced readers to acknowledge the existence of a colonial woman within the text of *Jane Eyre* – a woman, who, though conceivably once articulate, is now denied access to the rational discourse which is Jane's salvation from hysteria, and can only manifest her anger 'in perverse ways'.

The celebration of *Wide Sargasso Sea*, however, observable in some feminist critics of the 1970s and 1980s, colludes with what Meyer calls the 'commodification' of colonial subjects. Elizabeth Baer, for instance, writes of 'The sisterhood of Jane Eyre and Antoinette Cosway', arguing that 'Antoinette/Bertha . . . and Jane are not polar opposites, nor a handy dichotomy, but sisters, doubles, orphans in the patriarchy'. Antoinette's function in *Jane Eyre*, she argues, is to provide 'the story from which Jane learns'. According to Baer, Rhys 'forces us to examine . . . how Jane survived, and to conclude that it is Antoinette's warning that makes Jane's marriage to Rochester possible, that the real meaning of sisterhood is the courage of one generation to empower the next' (Baer 1983: 147–8, 133). Baer's reading, which calmly accepts the sacrifice of Antoinette in the cause of Jane, does not acknowledge the racial dimension to their relationship. Selma James, however, in *The Ladies and the Mammies*, also sees Antoinette as a sacrificial heroine, but this time in the interests of Tia, her black friend, who in Antoinette's final dream waits for her as she jumps from the battlements:

> Jean Rhys has said her heroine, a West Indian, a white woman, was 'brought here' to burn Rochester's England down. And when she does, there is another West Indian,

woman, waiting for her because that's what she wants to do too . . . Jean Rhys's
.ie works out her conflicts with Rochester always in the consciousness of where
⸱ has come from, always drawing on the power, at least in imagination and dream,
of Christophine and Tia. In the end, that is why she can convincingly win against him.
(James 1983: 74)

Into this euphoria Gayatri Chakravorty Spivak's essay, 'Three women's texts and a critique of imperialism', breaks like a dose of acid. On the one hand, Spivak reminds us that the western feminism which is providing these readings of *Jane Eyre* and *Wide Sargasso Sea* is concerned above all with

> the making of human beings, the constitution and 'interpellation' of the subject not only as individual but as 'individualist' . . . As the female individualist, not-quite/not-male, articulates herself in shifting relationship to what is at stake, the 'native female' as such . . . is excluded from any share in this emerging norm. If we read this account from an isolationist perspective in a 'metropolitan' context, we see nothing there but the psychobiography of the militant female subject. (Spivak 1985: 244–5)

Spivak's reading of Bertha's sacrificial role differs markedly from both Baer and James: 'Bertha's function in *Jane Eyre* is to render indeterminate the boundary between human and animal and thereby to weaken her entitlement under the spirit . . . of the Law' (249). According to Spivak, moreover, *Wide Sargasso Sea*, far from challenging the ethos of *Jane Eyre*, corroborates and reinforces it; in Rhys's novel, Antoinette must 'kill herself, so that *Jane Eyre* can become the feminist individualist heroine of British fiction . . . an allegory . . . of a self-immolating colonial subject for the glorification of the social mission of the colonizer' (251). Spivak sees Christophine, rather than Antoinette, as the potential voice of the colonized woman, but argues that her 'tangential' position in the narrative is inevitable because 'she cannot be contained by a novel which rewrites a canonical English text within the European novelistic tradition in the interest of a white Creole rather than the native' (253).

Spivak's is a sophisticated contribution to a debate which has more commonly been conducted in terms of reader-identification with the characters. However, there are other critics who see *Jane Eyre* as ripe for critique on racial grounds. Patricia Duncker, quoting a Jamaican woman who identified with Bertha rather than Jane, argues against reading *Jane Eyre* as a 'celebratory feminist text' because 'the heterosexual nexus of passion, power and force is the sexist basis of rapist ideology and this is, in the end, all the action Jane ever finds'. Duncker's argument moves towards recommending that we 'should write the gaps in each other's texts', but her disparaging account of *Jane Eyre* ignores the extent to which our imaginings, as well as our lives, are structured by our past. Charlotte Brontë's imaginary experience of other races was drawn from contemporary accounts of colonization, written from the colonists' point of view, so that we do now need to augment her story (see Azim 1993: chapter 5). Her white individualist feminism is not, however, without resonance for black women. The black child Marguerite in Maya Angelou's *I Know Why the Caged Bird Sings* sees similarities between her friend Louise and

Jane Eyre, though Louise is 'dark chocolate brown' (*JE* 1970 Angelou: 136)), and
Barbara T. Christian, as a black woman, affirms that she sees points of identification
in both Jane Eyre and Bertha Mason. Adopting a stance of reconciliation, Christian
suggests that

> language is one means by which we sound out the sameness/difference that we all
> are. And if we cannot grapple with that sameness/difference in texts and see it as a
> creative possibility rather than a threat, how are we to effect any lasting change beyond
> the text? (Christian 1988: 36)

The problem of 'grappling with difference', however, requires more sophisticated
tools than the notion of identification. The theory underlying Spivak's acerbic thesis
makes important advances towards this process, and is explained and developed in
Firdous Azim's admirably lucid book *The Colonial Rise of the Novel* (1993). Azim
follows Homi Bhabha in adapting Lacan's mirror-phase theory to provide a model
for the colonial process in the construction of subjectivities. The crucial point is
that although the mirror-image is sought as a perfect 'identity', what it provides is
always a (mis)recognition which provides the necessary basis for both a sense of
identity *and* a sense of separateness or difference (24, 175). The image must be
recognized as both self and other. In a brilliant examination of the Brontë juvenilia,
Azim goes on to show how the identity of the powerful white male is defined in
relation to the subjected black races of Africa. 'Angria', of course, the country of
Charlotte Brontë's youthful writing, is an African colony, and Charlotte's early
story, 'The African Queen's Lament' serves as an object lesson in the exclusion of
the black woman from European culture. In this story, written in 1833, the Duke
of Wellington, after the war in which the African nation of the Quaminas has been
defeated, finds a dying black woman, richly dressed, singing what he takes to be a
lament. As Azim says,

> Sexuality, race and the hierarchies of power and domination are starkly represented
> in this image. The position of the gaze is strongly delineated: the Black woman is the
> passive object of the white man's gaze. This man takes away her child, using his power
> to separate child and mother. The Black mother is associated with the lost territory,
> which can never be recovered, and remains as representative of the ideal and blissful
> state of the mother/child dyad . . .

The narrative now follows the child, not the mother, and, Azim argues, 'this
novelistic effacement may be symptomatic of the effacement of the Black woman's
voice from all representative forms' (129–30). Wellington adopts the child, Quashia,
and educates him at his court, and Azim takes this 'adoption' as representative of
the process of colonization in general, which alters the subjectivity of the colonized
so that the status of 'innocent' native, like the mother/child dyad, becomes
inaccessible (126, 129). Colonization creates instead both fear of and desire for the
position of the colonizer as the child/colonized moves from the 'imaginary' pre-
Oedipal relationship with the mother/homeland to the 'Symbolic' Oedipal
relationship with the father/empire.

Another early story by Charlotte Brontë tells of how a white girl is lost and adopted in turn by Quashia. Azim points out that the positions of the two adopted children are not identical, since the girl can return to her 'homeland', while Quashia is 'homeless' in his own country: 'his country is lost, and the only position he can occupy is that of the envious and desiring Other subject of colonialism' (135). There are, however, some analogies between them, since the white woman's gender denies her full access to the status of autonomous subject. By contrast with both white woman and black man, moreover, the black woman is denied a speaking position. The final irony of 'The African Queen's Lament' is that her song proves to be not a lament but a curse and a call to arms, which is remembered by her infant son, but even here she is denied direct expression, since he enacts it not by recourse to some 'essential' heritage, but according to the desire which he has 'adopted' with his education, for 'the seizure of colonial power' (135, 132). Similarly, Azim argues, the black woman is absent in *Jane Eyre*, and

> Bertha Mason provides the site for the colonial encounter in the text . . . the savage Other is represented by a Creole, a figure brought into being by the hierarchising and dominating processes of commercial colonisation. *Wide Sargasso Sea* . . . , written as a correction of *Jane Eyre* and as an effort to bring the discourse of the Other woman to the forefront, best shows how the Other is mediated and created by the processes of colonisation, and does not represent an 'essential' or original moment. Crucially, in *Wide Sargasso Sea* it is a *white* Creole woman who represents the figure of the colonised double. (Azim 1993: 183)

In a further revision of Spivak's reading, Azim argues that Jane herself is not 'triumphally' incorporated into English society. Spivak reads 'the final pages [of *Jane Eyre*] as a bringing back of the female protagonist into the fold, as a demarginalisation which places her firmly as a homogeneous and autonomous subject. This interpretation', Azim comments, 'ignores the processes of displacement' which render Jane's subject-status tenuous and disrupt her attempts at coherent linear narrative. At the end of *Jane Eyre*, Azim argues, Jane's 'adoption' into full subject status depends on colonial possessions; her wealth and social identity derive from a subjugated land and 'Creolise, as it were, the central figure [of the novel], whose inscription within English society remains heterogeneous'. Like Antoinette, Jane derives riches from plantations worked by slaves; unlike Antoinette, she lives at a distance which enables her to separate herself from this process. It is in this sense that Jane's position 'remains heterogeneous'. This reading reveals Bertha as Jane's other not in the sense of the early feminists (such as Showalter in *Literary Women*), as a dark passion which must be eliminated, but as an inevitable adopted self for the woman whose claim to equality lies in other lands (177, 101).

Post-colonial theory is one of the fastest-growing areas of academic discourse and its revision of *Jane Eyre*, in relation to *Wide Sargasso Sea*, will surely become a new academic orthodoxy. It is well, however, to remind ourselves that Jean Rhys's novel has had a gentler, more dispersed and yet recognizable impact on popular perceptions of the earlier text. Delbert Mann's 1970 film of *Jane Eyre* marks the end of a period which began with Stevenson's 1944 version. Like the earlier version, Mann's film makes extensive use of wild moorland scenery and makes Thornfield into a kind of moorland fortress. Hay Lane, where Jane and Rochester first meet, is a moorland track between granite crags, and in the final scene at Ferndean, the camera draws away from the tree-lined walk where Jane and Rochester are reunited and fades into the same empty moorland with which the film began. The effect, once more, is to invoke the atmosphere of *Wuthering Heights*. In every other way, the two films are very different; the later version is in particular very alert to the beginnings of the women's movement. Whereas Orson Welles had taken over the Stevenson film as a vehicle for his dominant masculine persona, the later film is much more egalitarian, particularly in the dialogue, which stresses the equality of the lovers even more explicitly than the original.

After the young Jane has delivered her defiant speech to her aunt, Aunt Reed in Mann's film replies, 'You have ever thought yourself our equal. Perhaps at Lowood you will learn your place'. Jane is left alone, repeating in a fierce whisper, 'I *am* equal. I *am*. I *am*.' This not only recalls the class defiance of the old melodramas, but also prepares the way for Jane's 'equal, as we are' speech to Rochester in the garden, giving it a new resonance. The theme is then taken up in the scene after the failed marriage, where Jane explains her motives much more explicitly than in the novel:

Jane: I will not live as your mistress . . . What would I be as your mistress? A hanger-on, a dependent with no place of my own, no right to be here. All rights would be on your side, none on mine.
Rochester: Rights! you talk like a lawyer! Everything that's mine is yours. What more can I give you?
Jane: I want nothing, nothing – only you.
Rochester: Then stay, Jane.
Jane: When I come to you, Edward, I come to you as an equal. I *will not* be less, even for the man I love.

The scene as a whole is less explosive than earlier versions and has more of the air of rational equals negotiating real problems. Similarly, in the final scene at Ferndean, although Jane ends like all other Janes in an embrace in which Rochester is physically dominant, this time she clearly chooses to take up this position; 'I'm come home, Edward; let me stay' – and she rests her head on his shoulder. He does not envelope her, like the Fritz Eichenberg woodcuts, for instance, but remains still, pleased with her voluntary closeness. It is, therefore, on the whole a film which tries hard to represent Jane as making a bid for rational, autonomous subjectivity.

Donna Marie Nudd, however, contests the makers' claim that the film is shot from Jane's point of view. Even when he is absent, she argues, Rochester's absence dictates the scene, as when Jane stares from a rainy window after his sudden departure, or in the use of a musical leitmotif to indicate the direction of her thoughts. In several scenes, moreover, our sympathies are directed towards

Rochester's sufferings. The most notable instance of this is a scene which could not be presented in the novel, since it happens in Jane's absence, when he lingers after the failed wedding for a poignant few moments with his wife. Although Nudd sees this scene as diverting our attention from Jane's reaction, she concedes that it is 'well done'. Nudd, however, bases her search for 'feminism', in the various adaptations she considers, entirely on their representation of what Spivak calls 'the psychobiography of the militant female subject' (1985: 244–5). From this perspective, the scene between Rochester and Bertha is a scene from which the male antagonist gains sympathy. Nudd does not consider its effect on our perception of Bertha, particularly in conjunction with the other scenes in which she appears. Altogether it seems probable that *Wide Sargasso Sea* has influenced the makers of this film towards a softer and more sympathetic representation of 'the madwoman' and a closer identification of her position and that of Jane.

In the veil-tearing scene, for instance, Bertha makes little cooing noises to herself which are almost echoed by Jane as she murmurs in her sleep. Similarly, when the wedding party enters Bertha's room, she is seen from the front, with her hair hanging all round her face; behind her and a little to the right we see Jane, also facing the front, with her veil framing her face in the same shape as Bertha's hair. The film, like Ethel Gabain's 1923 lithograph (Figure 4.2), is emphasizing continuities not disparities between them. When Bertha grapples Rochester to the ground, they lie for a moment together, almost like lovers, while she pants slightly, increasing the illusion of a bedroom scene. When they get up, he strokes the hair from her face, revealing a sweet, pretty young woman. The scene which Jane could not have narrated, since it takes place after she leaves the attic, emphasizes still further the fact that this woman has been and is still in name his wife. Rochester, addressing Bertha, asks in a quiet way how they should spend the evening; should he play? will she sit with him and tell him the story of her day? Bertha's blank face reveals the poignancy of these requests, increasing our sympathy both for her, since she is clearly a sad victim of her condition, and for him, since he has clearly behaved 'well' (not sending her to an asylum, for instance). Oddly, this scene seems to create the same effect as was registered by Jean Rhys in the writing of *Wide Sargasso Sea*, namely that in order to 'motivate' her story, she had to accept that 'Mr Rochester is *not* a heel' (Rhys 1984: 269).

Consciousness of Bertha's existence as a human being, not just a technical obstacle to their marriage, is evident in this film in Jane's reply to Rochester's invitation to her to stay as his mistress. Brontë's Rochester asks who will care what *Jane* does, to which she replies, '*I* care for myself'. In Mann's film Rochester asks, 'Who in the world will care what *we* do?' (my emphasis) and Jane replies,

> *I* care. You have a wife still living. She still lives, and whatever state God has seen fit to visit on her, she still lives. She cannot help what she is. I will not slip past her slyly in the night to take her place in your bed.

As with the speech about equality, this is much more explicit than the novel or any previous reproduction. It moves Jane's resistance from the arena of Victorian prudery to that of women's liberation and solidarity. It is interesting, moreover, that what follows relates to the debates about male chastity discussed in Chapter 2 (above). When Jane stands firm, Rochester retorts, 'You fling me back, then, upon the life I lived before?' and Jane answers, 'You need no more choose that than I. We are born to strive and endure. You will forget me before I forget you.' Charlotte Brontë's text here provides the 1970 film-makers with words with which to repudiate the Victorian belief in woman's 'influence' in favour of an insistence on each person's responsibility for his or her own actions. The Moor House section of the film, however, departs from its original to establish this as an alternative, humanistic morality. St John's fanatical devotion to God is shown, not as the option of a choice elite, but as absolutely wrong. When Jane refuses to marry him, St John says, 'You are rejecting God', but Jane replies, with great certainty, '*No!* I am finding him, in his people and the love they have for each other – for each other, St John, each other. You cannot love just God alone . . .'

This film constructs an explicitly negotiated version of Charlotte Brontë's companionate marriage, removing in the process some of the 'fireworks' of its original. David Drew prefers Orson Welles's Gothic version, because '*Jane Eyre* is a story of human passion and the interaction of strong personalities and Mann's film does Brontë an injustice by diluting these themes to such an extent' (Drew 1971: 60). Kate Ellis and E. Anne Kaplan, however, argue that the reason why Brontë's Gothic trappings are robbed of their bite in this film is that 'the gothic is premised on the father's being distant, unknown, unapproachable, commanding', whereas George C. Scott's Rochester is 'a vulnerable, open, accessible father who is not afraid to reveal his weakness or the depth of his needs' (Ellis and Kaplan 1981: 93). Nudd sees the 'feminization' of Rochester in this film as analogous to the Henry-Higgins-like Rochester of Hal Shaper's musical, the two productions being tragic and comic versions of the same strategy. In explanation, she quotes Ellis and Kaplan, who write:

> One cannot help but see both the musical and the film as responses to the feminist movement. In the optimistic early seventies, many believed that all would be well with the world if men could just acknowledge their burdensome defenses. (Nudd 1989: 131–2, quoting Ellis and Kaplan 1981: 94)

The corollary to this humanization of 'the enemy', however, is that we lose Jean Rhys's sharp perception of Rochester's collusion in the sexual and colonial ideology which contributes to Bertha's condition. Whereas *Wide Sargasso Sea* shows Rochester choosing to 'turn away [from] what I'd done', Mann's *Jane Eyre*, like Douglas Sirk's *Interlude*, shows Bertha's madness as given – a merely unfortunate accident.

In John Cannon's stage play, *Jane Eyre*, produced in Crewe in 1973, three years after Mann's film, we see how this softening of Rochester and humanization of attitudes to Bertha can tip the balance of sympathy decisively towards Rochester. In this play, 'the maniac' is described as

> a pitiful broken wretch of a woman with straggling hair and deep haunted eyes. As yet

she gives no sign of violence, rather the reverse in fact she is docile and smiling a little. Then her mouth opens foolishly and saliva runs from it. She picks up the hem of her long dress and wipes her mouth, incidentally exposing her legs. Mrs Fairfax and Jane turn from the sight.

Later Rochester explains to Jane:

> I've tried everything. Everything! I thought of an asylum. Years ago. I went to several. Money would have been no object, but the best that money can provide are . . . awful places. They are treated worse than animals, beaten; half drowned sometimes. Chained. It is beyond belief to see what we provide for such people.
> *Jane:*   Poor woman.
> *Rochester:*   We fear the insane, because we know how thin the border twixt them and ourselves. (II i)

A Japanese stage production of *Jane Eyre* in 1978 also treated Bertha sympathetically; she appears in the programme design as young and pretty and in a photograph as attractive and well-dressed; the Japanese correspondent who comments on the production for the Brontë Society was clearly sympathetic towards Rochester. The programme for Lionel Hamilton's dramatization of *Jane Eyre* in 1989 explicitly acknowledges its debt to *Wide Sargasso Sea*:

> No longer can one dismiss the broken wreck of a woman locked in the attics of Thornfield Hall as an outsize manic–depressive, just a period piece of Gothic melodrama. Touchingly she haunts us, investing the triangle with a tragic dimension, as real as Rochester's tormented sexuality and Jane's untutored honesty.

The impact of *Wide Sargasso Sea* on readings and reproduction of *Jane Eyre* is enormous – it is interesting, for instance, to find a dramatized reading of *Jane Eyre* by Joan E. Morgan being performed in Bermuda in 1972 – and it has itself produced derivatives. In 1985 the feminist poet Michelene Wandor produced 'a feature' for Radio 4 called 'A consoling blue', which the *Radio Times* describes as 'based on the letters of Jean Rhys'; the cast list includes Antoinette, Jane Eyre and Mr Rochester, and the accompanying line drawing shows an Antoinette with a hint of Hispanic plus negroid features. The colonial dimension is becoming, literally, broadcast. In 1988 the Sherman Theatre Postgraduate Company in Cardiff produced a play by Valerie Lucas and David Cottis called *Shadow in the Glass*, which is described as 'based on *Jane Eyre* . . . and *Wide Sargasso Sea*'. The title is explained in the epigraph, 'The Other Side of the Mirror' by Mary Elizabeth Coleridge:

> Shade of a shadow in the glass,
>   O set the crystal surface free!
> Pass – as the fairer visions pass –
>   Nor ever more return, to be
> The ghost of a distracted hour,
>   That heard me whisper, 'I am she!'

The play has a complete cast including Ingrams and Eshtons on the one hand, and Cosways and Masons on the other; it begins with Grace Poole singing 'The Poor

Orphan Child' and ends with Antoinette saying 'Now I know why I was brought here and what I must do'. Act II, set in the West Indies and based on Jean Rhys, serves as explanation, critique and eerie doubling of the familiar *Jane Eyre* scenes in Act I, which are largely unaltered except for an encounter between Jane and Antoinette in which Antoinette holds a piece of a broken mirror, with which she cuts Rochester. The title poem and the simple juxtaposition of the two perspectives makes the scene very resonant and suggests that the idea of Jane and Bertha/Antoinette as mirror-images has become widely accepted.

Robbie Kydd's novel, *The Quiet Stranger* (*JE* 1991 Kydd), on the other hand, gives us a picture of Antoinette's life which is almost independent of *Jane Eyre*. In his author's notes, Kydd tells us that he read *Wide Sargasso Sea*

> some fifteen years after it was published. During those years I read many reviews of it, and references to it, and formed a mental picture of the kind of novel it must be. The real novel turned out to be entirely different – so different indeed that I was left with this other novel fermenting away and demanding to be written. (*JE* 1991 Kydd: 375)

Although he acknowledges a debt to Jean Rhys, therefore, the sources of his book are independent. The cover shows a striking young black woman in eighteenth-century costume, and the dedication shows that Kydd's information and motivation come partly from his Trinidadian wife. The novel is in a way different from other treatments of Antoinette, focused in the West Indies, so that it is England and Jane which appear marginal. Kydd's title is, however, derived from *Jane Eyre* and refers to Richard Mason. In *Jane Eyre* II v, where Richard is injured, Jane asks herself: 'this common-place, quiet stranger – how had he become involved in the web of horror?' (*JE* 221); Kydd's novel is Richard's answer to this question, written in extreme old age. In the author's notes Kydd tells us that

> unlike Jean Rhys, who set her novel in post-Emancipation times (that is, after 1834) I have tried to make the dates of the events in mine coincide precisely with those in *Jane Eyre* by using the one clue provided by Charlotte Brontë. In Chapter XXXII [III vi] St John Rivers presents Jane with 'a new publication, a poem'. This turns out to be [Scott's] *Marmion*, which was published in 1808. (*JE* 1991 Kydd: 375)

Richard Mason describes himself as born in Tobago in 1767, the son of a Scottish Royalist (exiled after '45 and turned sugar-planter) and a French aristocrat. He is a fat, studious boy who hates the active life but eventually becomes rich and influential by being very good with money. His older sister Antoinette by contrast is fearless, active and passionately devoted to horses. At seventeen she is running her own plantation including hundreds of slaves. She is given to fits of violent temper and is hectically excited by the annual cane-burning. Against her will, and to save her father's fortune, she is married to Rochester, a brutal man who will not tolerate her unfeminine ways (she wears her riding breeches under her wedding dress!) He locks her up, beats her and eventually takes her to England. When Richard visits her there she is quite sane, if slightly confused, surviving only because Grace Poole allows her out at dead of night to talk to the horses. Richard's injury in the attic is in this version presented as accidental; Rochester bullies the doctor into confirming the account in Brontë's novel. Richard does not understand Rochester's relationship with Jane and puts it down to fortune-hunting on her side and lust on his. She seems to him like a witch who has Rochester spellbound – but the focus of this novel makes Jane (and eventually Antoinette) peripheral to the main interest, which is firmly in the Caribbean.

One unexpected feature of Richard's story is that from childhood he has had an intense friendship with a black slave girl called Betsy, who in middle age becomes his acknowledged mistress and they have a son; in old age they are legally able to marry. Her family are the West Indian equivalents of Charlotte Brontë's Quaminas – dispossessed royalty now leading slave uprisings. Richard's granddaughter, Francisca Maria, is the daughter of a high Hidalgo whose Castilian ancestors had captured and married an Inca princess; she therefore has

> in her veins the blood of African Chiefs and an Inca Princess, as well as that of Highland Chieftains, French Seigneurs and Spanish Grandees. Surely she would need all the pride gained from this knowledge to live happily in Trinidad, which, whilst beginning to proclaim tolerance as a virtue, nevertheless still valued a white skin above – [Richard's manuscript breaks off here] (369)

Francisca is an enchanting child, revelling in her mixed blood, and her grandmother Betsy is a truly formidable woman, strong, intelligent and courageous.

Kydd's novel is full of capable women. His version of Antoinette is the reverse of Rhys's malleable victim – brave, energetic and independent, if volatile and unpredictable. The main problem with *The Quiet Stranger* is its dissonance with *Jane Eyre*'s version of Mr Rochester. Even Rhys's Rochester is 'not a heel'; Kydd's is a totally heartless brute. Despite Kydd's scrupulousness about dates and places, his unrecognizable Rochester and his forced explanation of the events in the attic loosen the links between his text and *Jane Eyre*. Whereas *Wide Sargasso Sea* lives like another dimension to the older text, *The Quiet Stranger* gives us an alternative version. Its strongest point is not exactly its reading of Antoinette but rather the change of focus, which diverts our attention from the Eurocentrism of both Brontë's and Rhys's novels and reminds us that elsewhere, the story continues – differently.

In 1958, before the breakthrough represented by 'Obeah Night', Jean Rhys also wrote to a friend about her troublesome novel, 'It might be possible to unhitch the whole thing from Charlotte Brontë's novel, but I don't want to do that. It is that particular mad Creole I want to write about, not any of the other mad Creoles' (Rhys 1984: 153). In 1964, however, when *Wide Sargasso Sea* was nearly finished, she wrote, 'I think there were several Antoinettes and Mr Rochesters. Indeed I am sure. Mine is *not* Miss Brontë's, though much suggested by "Jane Eyre"' (263). Debbie Shewell's play, *More Than One Antoinette*, written and produced for the Young Vic in 1990, advertises in its title the critical implication which I have argued is crucial to Jean Rhys's novel, that Bertha's story is exemplary rather than unique. Shewell's play allows the later novel to reflect back on the earlier in a more critical way than *Shadow in the Glass*. According to Heather Neill's review in *The Times*, 'the romantic ending of *Jane Eyre*' becomes, in Shewell's version, 'self-punishment' as Jane, 'obsessed by the suffering of Antoinette, . . . condemns herself by marriage to Rochester's hatred'.

The emergence of Bertha has thus not only focused new attention on the colonial woman within Charlotte Brontë's text; it has also called into question the whole status of *Jane Eyre* as '*the* love story'. It is now possible to write such a poem as Jane Barry's 'Mr Rochester', describing how 'he', waiting for 'the 8.15 to Woking', lures the 'little girl' with tales of how

> 'I have no wife, she doesn't understand me'.

> Was it her nature, bestial, corrupt,
> That rendered joy extinct and love profane?

Or was it, the poem asks, that she 'slipped into madness' from being 'always found wanting'? The poem ends with a warning that

> Unless you put out that often-smiling never-laughing eye
> Yours will be the laughter
> That echoes nightly round the West Wing,
> Not the happy ever after. (*JE* [undated] Barry: 18)

Chapter 7

Recent developments

'*Women's books, aren't they?*': illustrations, musicals, stage, film and television

In David Lodge's 1988 novel, *Nice Work*, the old-fashioned industrialist Victor drives the feminist university lecturer Robyn past a signpost to Haworth. To her the word means 'The Brontës!' but he has never read *Jane Eyre* or *Wuthering Heights*, though he has heard of them: 'Women's books, aren't they?' His response sets her wondering what it was like

> never to have shivered with Jane Eyre at Lowood school, or throbbed in the arms of Heathcliff with Cathy . . . 'Of course', she added, 'they're often read simply as wish-fulfilment romances, *Jane Eyre* especially. You have to deconstruct the texts to bring out the political and psychological contradictions inscribed in them.' (*JE* and *WH* 1988: Lodge: 202–3)

The scene beautifully conveys the complex responses elicited by the famous Brontë texts in the post-1968 world. On the one hand, *Jane Eyre* and *Wuthering Heights* are now almost universally known, even to those who have no more than heard of them. To a large audience, including sophisticated readers like Robyn, their first appeal is one of identification with the characters and their emotional neediness. Simultaneous with this, however, there is a growing body of self-consciously analytical reading – including reproductive 'readings' as well as academic criticism – which sets out to deconstruct the contradictions of the texts from stated or implied positions such as feminism, Marxism or psychoanalysis.

Even where such intentions are not overt, reproductions from this period are inevitably received in the context of sexual politics – though critics feel freer, it seems, to be familiar and irreverent with *Jane Eyre* than with *Wuthering Heights*. Peter Fiddick, reviewing Robin Chapman's 1973 adaptation of *Jane Eyre* for BBC2, calls the novel 'undeniably one of the most enduring of schoolgirl romances (albeit for an audience far wider than schoolgirls)' (*Guardian* 29.10.1973). Reacting to the bra-burning phase of women's liberation, where the phrase invoked free sex rather than female autonomy, Bernard Davies explains that 'one would have expected a rake of Rochester's experience to have attempted a casual seduction, even if plain

198

little Jane didn't seem to offer much in the way of excitement . . .' (*Broadcast* 12.10.1973) Patricia Smith, however, congratulates Jane on getting her man:

> in these days of feminine emancipation in its most ultra-form, it really is quite a remarkable thing to discover that the poor, down-trodden Jane does rather better in all her petticoats than most women do in their bra-less tank-tops. (*Southern Evening Echo* 26.10.1973)

A 'public school mistress of English', writes to the *Radio Times* to say how refreshing it was to see 'Jane as a real woman, instead of the usual pathetic creature who wouldn't have attracted a blind hippo let alone a man of Rochester's calibre' (8.11.1973). John Cannon's stage play, *Jane Eyre*, also produced in 1973, also foregrounds Jane's sexuality, introducing a scene of explicit rivalry between her and Blanche Ingram. The programme note introduces the play as 'a secret, sensitive and compelling story of a love affair which the society of Brontë's day could not approve'. By 1982, the emphasis had markedly changed; the programme for a later production of the same play presents Jane as 'plain, courageous, determined . . . In her view, women were entitled to as fulfilling and active a life as men, and she refused to compromise or settle for second best'.

A year later, in 1983, there was a new television dramatization for BBC1 by Alexander Baron, with Zelah Clarke as Jane and Timothy Dalton as Rochester. Maire Messenger Davies, in a *Radio Times* preview, faces head-on the contradictory appeal of *Jane Eyre* as

> a fairly predictable romantic novel. It has a *Cinderella* plot; Charlotte Brontë's prose is occasionally purple; the hero has provoked derision as a Freudian wish-fulfilment figure . . . Yet *Jane Eyre* is a classic as popular on the bookstalls as in the universities (it has never been out of print) . . . (8–14.10.1983)

The contradictions of this popular/academic success are embodied in Timothy Dalton, whose presence in *Jane Eyre*, according to the Bradford *Telegraph and Argus*, makes sure that 'Sunday teatime is weak-at-the-knees time. Just ask the ladies!' (26.11.1983) When BBC Enterprises sold the film abroad in 1987, the *Daily Mail* carried a headline, '*Bond is a wow in Moscow, but not as 007*', explaining,

> the new James Bond actor, Timothy Dalton, is being hailed as a new star in Russia – but not for his exploits as 007. It is his role in the BBC film Jane Eyre that has made him a heart-throb behind the Iron Curtain. (9.2.1987)

In rather different language, Peter Kemp in the *Times Literary Supplement* agrees, finding Dalton 'a potently saturnine, Byronically erotic Rochester'. Yet Dalton, who played Heathcliff as a sexual romp in Robert Fuest's 1970 film of *Wuthering Heights*, is much more than a romantic lead as Rochester – physically rather too tall and slender, but with a craggy, expressive face and the right mixture of explosive impatience, lurking humour and real tenderness. His muttered asides about atonement, for instance, convince us that his regard for God and morality are genuine. Zelah Clarke, a tiny Jane who is several inches short of Rochester's shoulder, similarly embodies the repressed passion which is Jane's major characteristic. Her impassive 'Yes, sir' becomes so familiar that the few moments of unrestrained joy – as when, on the morning after the proposal, she literally leaps off the ground into Rochester's arms – are stunning in their impact.

These effects are not simply the result of good acting, but depend on careful direction. The television series of eleven episodes lasts for a total of four hours, giving time for the inclusion of most of the major speeches from the novel. Jane's speech on the roof, the gypsy scene, the scene after Mason's wounding, Rochester's proposal, his explanation of his first marriage and so on are rendered in detail. Perhaps even more important is the slow, relatively static camera work, which allows dialogue, rather than action, to figure as the crucial means of 'development'. 'Action' scenes which were given prominence in previous (shorter) film versions, such as the fall in Hay Lane or Jane's wanderings on the moor, are treated glancingly by director Julian Amyes to make room for the conversations which carry the weight of the drama. Interestingly, in the shot-reverse sequences normal for the visual representation of dialogue, Amyes's direction allows the gaze to rest at least as much on the listener as on the speaker (see Kuhn 1982: 53–6). For Jane this is crucial, since we hear Rochester's voice – often brutal or provocative – while seeing Jane's plain and apparently unresponsive face. Forced to contemplate this controlled exterior, we become sensitive to minute changes – a compression of the lips, a widening of the eyes – which are the only visible signs of inner turmoil.

This point is interesting since some commentators on film or television adaptations of novels have argued that visual representation is necessarily less subtle than writing. Robert Giddings, Keith Selby and Chris Wensley, in their book, *Screening the Novel*, argue that a process of simplification is inevitable, because 'the film or television image is predominantly iconic whereas words in a novel are symbolic; in other words, the film or television image implies a close relationship between signifier and signified, compared to the arbitrary relationship of verbal language' (1990: 6). There is thus, they argue, much less room for ambiguity in a visual image, less work for the reader to do and less opportunity for the kind of 'divided' reading which Gilbert and Gubar, for instance, encourage us to make of *Jane Eyre*. This argument seems to me to underestimate the degree of ambiguity which arises in the juxtaposition of visual and verbal signs, especially in the extended treatment possible in television. Modleski, in fact, argues against adapting film theory to television because the dynamics of viewing are different. Feminist film criticism, for instance, deriving from Laura Mulvey, has assumed that films are produced within a male-orientated industry, placing women on screen as objects for a masculine viewer. Television, on the other hand, with a more female audience and a more intimate mode of procedure, can, according to Modleski, be understood as 'training [viewers] to become, like women in the home, "ideal readers" – not of texts but of people' (1982: 34). In Charlotte Brontë's novel, the first-person narrator 'teaches' her readers how to 'read' the enigmatic Rochester, while revealing to us her inner thoughts in silent narrative. The Dalton/Clarke serial, reducing the narrative voice to occasional linking passages, compensates by extending its tutelage to both protagonists. We not only see with Jane that 'Mr Rochester *is* peculiar'

(*JE* 140); we also see with Rochester the tiny signs which reveal that Jane is 'cast in a different mould to the majority'. Though the television's reduction of the narrative voice may seem a departure from the original, this mutual recognition process is very true to it, established from their earliest conversations: 'My eye met his as the idea crossed my mind: he seemed to read the glance, answering as if its import had been spoken' (141). If, as Judith Thurman argues, the generic function of the Rochester-figure in popular romance fiction is as 'the great Recogniser' (1989: 122), then television, which unlike pulp romance has a large male audience, may be the very thing to teach men how to do it.

The whole question of faithfulness in screen adaptations has been much debated in recent years as a cynical awareness of commercial priorities shapes people's responses to the BBC 'classic serial', while a growing postmodernist consciousness suggests that representation always introduces historically specific change. Giddings, Selby and Wensley, for instance, point out that while classic serials are scrupulous about costumes and props, they normally make an effort with regional accents only when the characters are working class.

> In a society where the cultural goodies are mainly consumed by the well-to-do must all creative/cultivated persons speak 'good' standard English? If so, it must follow that if Dr Johnson was a scholar and a writer and an Oxford man, then he must speak good South-Eastern English. The media, then, are unwittingly part of an ideological conspiracy in which we are invited to look back at our past through the distortions of our present culture. (Giddings, *et al.* 1990: xi)

(Dr Johnson, it seems, was notorious in his own day for a Staffordshire accent impenetrable to Londoners.) It is notable, in fact, that Zelah Clarke in the 1983 television version of *Jane Eyre* does speak in the way Giddings *et al.* describe as the norm for such reproductions – as if she had been a 'star pupil[] at [a] singularly severe elocution class' (x–xi). It is hard to evaluate the potential effect of making her speak Yorkshire. Probably, since her claim to distinction lies in her education (as opposed to wealth or beauty), a pronounced regional accent would confuse the signs for a modern audience who are, as Giddings *et al.* point out, used to associating refinement with received pronunciation.

If television and film reproductions in general aim at 'a synthetic "historical" realism in which everything must seem authentic and true to period' (x; see also Taylor 1993), workers in more limited media continue to allow themselves more interpretative space. Simon Brett's wood engravings for the 1991 Folio Society edition of *Jane Eyre* begin with what looks like a deliberate allusion to Fritz Eichenberg's 1943 Random House edition (Figure 4.4) – a tiny linked couple stroll beneath huge trees. Compared with Eichenberg, however, Brett's illustrations focus much more on Jane, and show her, moreover, in the role of saviour, lifting the fallen Rochester in Hay Lane (*JE* 1991 Brett: 115) and appearing beside his burning bed like a Botticelli angel (148). Interestingly, however, the stylized representation of flames in this bedroom scene are strikingly similar to the stylized water which Jane flings over Rochester, implying that her 'rescue' only feeds the ardour which consumes them both. Brett also chooses to pick up the textual metaphors describing Jane's joy after Rochester's proposal, showing her literally thigh-deep 'under surges of joy' (151), while after the spoiled wedding relentless waves of 'deep waters' carry the snowy 'drifts' which 'crushed the blowing roses' (287–8). On the other hand, where Eichenberg shows an inspired St John gazing at the beyond while Jane inspects a posy of flowers, Brett emphasizes St John's power to rivet her attention (388) and to enlist her to his purpose as they stand in black bars of shadow which suggest Jane's 'iron shroud' (404). The extreme contrast between the 'flames' and 'surges' of Jane's desire and the 'fetters' offered by St John give added force to Brett's final picture of the reunited Jane and Rochester: she sits on his knee, feet swinging, dressed in a girlish sprigged muslin, drawing his head down to be kissed; they are seated on a felled tree-stump and the living trees in the background no longer dominate but form a fresh environment for a pairing which seems to have escaped the extremes produced by repression.

Some recent musical versions of *Jane Eyre* have had considerable pretensions, such as Nils Vigeland's opera, *False Love/True Love*, performed by the Almeida Opera (ENO) in 1992. John Joubert is also planning an opera to coincide with the 150th anniversary of the publication of *Jane Eyre* in 1997. Ted Davis's musical *Jane Eyre*, however, presents a queer mixture; music by David Clark, who wrote the music for *Miss Saigon*, is used to give prominence to unequivocally feminist views. According to the 1990 programme, 'Ted Davis originally conceived a non-musical dramatization for the Theatre at Monmouth (Maine) in 1984 using fragments of Chopin's music'. He subsequently enlisted the aid of David Clark and the musical *Jane Eyre* was produced in Maine in 1988, and in New York State in 1990. The 1990 programme includes an intelligent note by Kathryn Long quoting Victorian reviews, discouraging too biographical an interpretation of the novel and suggesting Jane's authorship of her story, her artwork and her independent morality as focus points for reading (*JE* 1990 Davis: 11–17). The songs, moreover, foreground material from the novel which might have been chosen by a feminist critic: 'Time Never Changes' includes 'women are supposed to be very calm', and goes on, 'I long for motion, something more vivid than living the still doom that millions of women feel waiting at home. All they can hope for is endless dependence, silent revolt, then mindless surrender'. Similarly, when Rochester and Jane sing a conventional-sounding song, 'Wild Birds', as a response to the birds in her paintings, he sings 'a long way to fall' while she corrects him: 'a long way to fly'. The pervasive syrupy cadences of the music are, however, disturbing; one has to listen hard to the words and in songs like 'Moon Ages', where the words are invented ('All you know is that you must sing and dance for him'), the music imposes its own atmosphere – very like 'I Could Have Danced All Night'. The effect of having Jane sing, to soupy music, of her wish for 'something designed to be new to my mind' is debatable; as in the melodramas, Jane stands centre-stage and articulates her desire, but the power of the medium to constitute its own message may well mean that Jane's 'vague ideal' is read as what George Eliot calls 'the common yearning of womanhood' ([1871–2] 1930: xiii).

Stage adaptations of *Jane Eyre* by Christopher Martin (1983), Jonathan Myerson (1984), Sheila Haughey (1985) and Peter Coe (1986) tend to move away from the 'core story' to allow room for 'neglected' aspects of the text. Myerson's play was perceived (wrongly) by one reviewer as being 'the first on stage to include Jane's traumatic childhood', while Haughey's play foregrounds Jane's individualistic Christianity. Peter Coe's play emphasizes the narrative framework of the novel, using

> Peter Rice's sparse but workable set on three levels to give us a sense of the manner in which Jane's adult behaviour is informed by the nature of her childhood experiences. The structure also lends added emphasis to the role of St John Rivers. (*Plays and Players* 10.86: 27)

While these changes of emphasis register an increasing awareness of the textuality of Charlotte Brontë's novel, they also tend to dissipate its power. Even Coe's madwoman, presented 'with much rattling of chains and ominous thuds . . . never acquires real dramatic force' (27). (Interestingly, Alexander Baron's powerful television version makes no concessions to a post-Rhysian perception of Bertha but gives us a savage and sudden madwoman, almost beyond human communication, who constitutes (as in Brontë's novel) a legal obstacle to Jane and Rochester's wedding rather than a recognizable centre of consciousness.)

In Fay Weldon's adaptation, self-conscious textuality is combined with a dramatic force which derives, like that of her novels, from a feminist orientation. First performed at Birmingham Repertory Theatre in 1986, this play has acquired major stature and a revised version of it was subsequently produced in Leeds (1988), Dublin (1990), Pitlochry (1992) and London (1993). The 1988 programme includes a lengthy, academic-feeling biography of Charlotte Brontë by Juliet Barker, then librarian/curator of the Brontë Parsonage Museum; the flier for this production, however, bills Fay Weldon as 'author of "Life and Loves of a She-Devil" (recently serialized on BBC TV)'; the combination produces a review headline, 'Brontës Haunt She-Devil Writer'. While the prospect produced 'trepidation' in the (Bradford) *Telegraph and Argus* (5.4.1988), Carol Wilks, reviewing for the *Guardian*, praised Weldon and her producer, Helena Kaut-Howson, for tackling this 'dangerous territory' and 'put[ting] the danger where it should be – on stage'. Wilks's review makes it plain that this 'rare and compelling theatrical treat' combines a 'serious' treatment of the text, including Jane's 'naive' claim for 'heaven on earth . . . with God's blessing', with the popular appeal of 'melodrama': 'David Gwillim's half-human half-satanic Rochester is quite enough to set most female knees aquiver . . . True love rears its purified head through the ashes – Mills and Boon eat your heart out' (16.4.1988). In an interview for the (American) *Brontë Newsletter*, Fay Weldon confirms that this combination of feminist with romantic appeal was deliberate, deriving from the novel: 'It is the timeless predicament of all women – the struggle to be independent, but then looking to men for emotional fulfillment' (Weldon 1988: 1). Oddly, the *Daily Telegraph* objected to the melodramatic elements of the staging because they gestured towards aspects 'better left to academics and psychologists – the tale is worth telling plain and true' (20.4.1988). But what is 'true'? The reviewer for the *Rothwell Advertiser* thought it a pity that 'David Gwillim [Rochester] did not have the handsome looks that Charlotte Brontë endowed him with' (21.4.1988). The 'hideous' Rochester of the text (*JE* 461) has, it seems, been replaced in at least some minds by a mythical Romantic hero.

The staging of Fay Weldon's play did add a great deal to the spoken words. A cyclorama provided floating clouds; dramatic lighting provided storms, ominous shadows, apparitions and alarming fires; music merged with galloping hooves and thunder; a grey set included doors which opened onto the past, and the silhouette of Thornfield Hall provided a shorthand reminder of a complex of Gothic elements. Bertha's fiery appearance in a red swirling dress combined traditional melodrama with a post-Rhysian consciousness, though in an interview for the *Yorkshire Post*, Fay Weldon confirms that her conception of Bertha comes straight out of *The Madwoman in the Attic*:

> 'What she is, of course, is sexually insatiable . . . And that's why she's in the attic. Sexual appetite in women was seen as a mental disorder . . . Indulgence led to uncontrolled desire and to chaos . . . She's the self who breaks in upon order, who shrieks, who moans, who makes demands.' (13.4.1988)

By 1990, this explanation has become widespread. In an interview for the *Sunday Independent*, producer Helena Kaut-Howson states categorically that 'the mad woman in the attic is a metaphor for repressed sex, when she is banished only then is Jane free'. Conceding that 'madness as sexuality is slightly obscure', she points to 'the description of the deranged female – "her full lips, purple face, heavy breathing"' (2.12.1990). By 1993, reviewers were describing the play as 'a feminist fairytale' (*Daily Express* 8.12.1993), which 'rightly brings out the novel's proto-feminist leanings' (*The Stage* 23.12.1993).

The most innovative aspect of the staging, however, only appeared for the Leeds production in 1988, for which Fay Weldon completely rewrote the play after a suggestion from her producer, Helena Kaut-Howson. This version includes not just Jane's story, but also the story of how it was written. Although foregrounded gravestones remind us that they are long dead, Branwell, Emily and Anne are on stage throughout, helping Charlotte to write her story. Charlotte becomes Jane from time to time and the staging also identifies young Jane with her pupil, Adèle, and with all the orphans of Lowood, represented by life-sized dolls (see Weldon 1988). Fritz Eichenberg's 1943 illustration had shown rows of identical Lowood orphans, as did the 1944 film; in each case the effect is to emphasize Jane's isolation from a uniform mass. Jane's story is certainly that of a woman who feels acutely lonely; but Fay Weldon, rewriting *Jane Eyre* after the Women's Liberation Movement, sees sisters everywhere, and her play foregrounds this paradox by representing to us as interchangeable girls and women who, in the 'mother-text' are distinct (like Jane and Adèle), so that we feel that each of the 'dummies' also has the potential to assume life. Jane's sense of isolation is thus shown to be an illusion, for all round her are girls and women each separately sharing the same experience. The paradox is perhaps explained by Eve Kosofsky-Sedgwick's perception that 'any dire knowledge that is shared but cannot be acknowledged to be shared – that is, as it were, *shared separately* – has the effect of rendering the people, whom it ought to bind together, into an irrevocable doubleness' ([1980] 1986: 17). Weldon's staging allows us, as modern viewers, to perceive both Jane's experiential isolation and its status as socially engineered. The effect combines some of the impact of Gothic with the more hopeful imposition of an explanatory metanarrative.

Despite the 'frame' staging of Weldon's play, most critics and commentators outside academia still focus on the content of the story rather than its process, finding 'the true flavour of the book' (*Irish Times* 5.12.1990) in the 'relationship between the[] two principals' (*Sunday Press* 9.12.1990). Although the female reviewer for the Irish *Sunday Tribune* saw that Charlotte, Emily and Anne were there on stage to 'tell us how the book might have been written' (9.12.1990), other reviewers found 'the device of the peripheral Brontë family observing the action . . . an irrelevant intrusion' (20.4.1988), 'a disturbance to the audience's "willing suspension of disbelief"' (*Sunday Press* 9.12.1990), 'clever but useless' (*Irish Times* 5.12.1990). Nevertheless, in academic circles textual process is now foregrounded in readings of *Jane Eyre*, perhaps influenced by such treatments as Maggie Berg's *Jane Eyre: Portrait of a Life* (1987). The programme to the 1992 Pitlochry performance of Weldon's play carried quotations familiar to feminist critics; Robert Southey's advice to Charlotte Brontë that 'literature cannot be the business of a woman's life', and Jane's declaration in I xii, that 'women feel just as men feel' (115). Moreover, *Jane Eyre* continues to be adapted for academic as well as commercial theatre (e.g. *JE* 1989 Marten) and at least one such production foregrounds textual process. Judy Yordon's 1989 *Jane Eyre*, according to the director's programme notes, includes three Jane Eyres: 'Jane in the Present tells her story, Jane in the Past relives it, and Jane the Dancer symbolizes Jane's passionate inner life that Victorian convention does not allow her to reveal or express' (in Nudd 1989: 222). Willis Hall's 1993 dramatization had Jane's opening words spoken by a chorus of women, one by one, and this chorus re-emerges at the end to speak as one the words 'Reader, I married him!' Several features of this production were, however, incongruously funny (raising audience laughter).

One perhaps unintended effect of Weldon's treatment of *Jane Eyre* was to reintroduce the confusion of life with works (and with Emily's works) which, as we have seen, has dogged the Brontë texts since the authors' identity became known. The 1990 Dublin production of Weldon's *Jane Eyre* is set on the Yorkshire Moors and its programme shows a faint but recognizable photograph of Top Withins behind the cast-list. One reviewer thought that the actor playing Branwell looked 'like Olivier' (presumably in his 1939 role as Heathcliff) (10.12.1990) and another, under the title, 'Throbbing Heights', quotes Helena Kaut-Howson explaining the 'novel's epic love story in relation to the strange repressed sexuality of the sisters' (*In Dublin* 5.12.1990). The programme for Willis Hall's 1992 *Jane Eyre* also features a picture of Top Withins, and an advertisement for the 1993 London production of Weldon's play shows Jane silhouetted against mist, with a huge brooding face reminiscent of Eichenberg's illustration for *Wuthering Heights*. As the 'Brontë story' becomes more widely, but vaguely, known, this confusion becomes more extreme, prompting comments such as one overheard in the Parsonage Museum in 1992 – 'which of the Brontë sisters married Heathcliff?' (*BSG* 6: 14).

Wuthering Heights itself continues to increase its exposure. Since 1972 it has been serialized on BBC Radio 4 (1972), Bengali Radio (1974) and BBC television (1978). There have been nearly a dozen new stage adaptations, a recorded musical (1991) and a major film (1991). In contrast to *Jane Eyre*, however, most of these reproductions are written and directed by men and betray little feminist or other theoretical consciousness. There is, in fact, an extraordinary discrepancy between the academic reception of *Wuthering Heights* during this period and its popular reproduction. The text which nineteenth-century readers found opaque and repellent found its ideal readership in the post-structuralist revolution following 1968. Some indication of the range and sophistication of such readings can be found in the anthologies of critical essays which have been published since 1987 (e.g. Bloom 1987; Stoneman 1993), and in the fact that *Wuthering Heights* features as the exemplary text in three chapters of *Feminist Readings/Feminists Reading* (Mills *et al.* 1989). During this period, Marxist critics, following Terry Eagleton's *Myths of Power: A Marxist Study of the Brontës* ([1975] 1988), have deconstructed the mythical status of the text in terms of its historically specific representation of class struggle; feminist critics, including Gilbert and Gubar, who had such a massive influence on popular readings of *Jane Eyre*, have shifted the general focus of readers away from Heathcliff towards Catherine (see Stoneman 1992a); post-structuralist readers have established that the core story cannot be detached from its frame, that what seem to be extreme Gothic experiences are paradigmatic of normal perceptions of identity, and that the famous indeterminacy of the text mirrors our postmodernist perception that 'communication' is only ever a process of endless deferral of meaning. Yet these revolutionary perceptions have had almost no impact on reproductions of the novel. Claire Tomalin writes a learned and intelligent preview of the 1978 television serial for *Radio Times*, ending with an acknowledgement of the variety of critical positions now available to readers of *Wuthering Heights*. Her conclusion, however, is that despite being 'loaded with all these possible interpretations, it springs up again directly as popular art, like a ballad, a song or a story that invites only the simple question, what next?' (24.9.1978)

After surveying stage and film adaptations of *Wuthering Heights* over the last twenty years, however, my conclusion is that if they have avoided postmodernist deconstructions, this is not because they are reading the novel in a fresh, unmediated way. The indications are that, far from assuming folk art status, stage reproductions in particular have vigorously continued the work of canonization discussed in Chapter 5. Roland Petit's 1982 ballet, 'Les Hauts de Hurlevant: histoire d'une passion' was produced in the same year as Bernard Herrmann's opera and promulgates very much the same atmosphere. Photographs of the dancers show intense, anguished gestures; the plot is truncated and both Catherine and Heathcliff die visibly for love. David Dougill's review in *Dance and Dancers* suggests an animated, dramatic performance, with Jean-Charles Gil as Heathcliff 'throbbing with manic, animal passion' and 'finely-made . . . frenzied pas de deux' (4.83: 20); as with many narrative vehicles for opera and ballet, however, we are asked to accept as given the clean lines of the tragic love story, intense but non-contradictory. It is worth noting that just as Herrmann was used to working in Hollywood, Marcel Landowski, who wrote the music for Petit's ballet, made his name with *The Phantom of the Opera*.

Audience preconception means that even where efforts are made at a different reading, they are quickly assimilated to an epic norm. The playbill for John Boyd's 1988 adaptation of *Wuthering Heights* promises that the play 'pays faithful attention to the social background of the gallery of characters surrounding the protagonists', but two different reviewers choose to compare it with *King Lear* (*Belfast Telegraph* and *Belfast Newsletter* 18.12.1988) and the latter also comments on the 'clever use of Mahler's Fifth Symphony' to create 'an epic of Wagnerian proportions'. In many cases it is clear that the plays themselves encourage this response. Like the operas, Vince Foxall's 1984 adaptation attempts to heighten the text by introducing Emily Brontë's poetry into the script. The August 1988 programme for Charles Vance's play gives the last word to Lord David Cecil, who finds *Wuthering Heights* 'undimmed . . . by the dust of time' (11), while the November programme is even more ecstatic, finding the union of Catherine and Heathcliff 'so volcanic that the world cannot contain it'. Michael Parker, reviewing a Buxton production of Vance's play, compares it unfavourably with 'the naturalism of Chris Martin's' (6.5.1989); the same reviewer, however, finds Martin's play lacking according to some gold standard in which Heathcliff should bring together 'the tragic grandeur and passion of Othello and infinite malevolence of Iago' (28.4.1989). Eunice Skirrow, on the other hand, found Julia Ormond's performance as Catherine in Sheffield (1989) reminiscent of Ophelia (*BST* 19.7.328).

A contradiction is evident in this process of canonization. On the one hand *Wuthering Heights* is claimed as unique and timeless; on the other hand its stature is established by extensive citation of comparable works. Claire Tomalin's *Radio Times* article is accompanied by photographs of four previous reproductions of the novel, notably the Olivier film, proving its persistent life, but not, surely, its immutability. Similarly the reviewers invoke Lear, Othello, Wagner, establishing the cultural status of the novel, but not its incomparability. What is going on here is a process of iteration which establishes which other texts can properly be mentioned together with *Wuthering Heights*.

There are, however, peculiar aspects to this process, which can be seen most clearly in relation to Peter Kosminsky's 1991 film, *Emily Brontë's Wuthering Heights*. On the one hand, the film is promoted explicitly as a 'classic' – a serious piece of high culture; on the other hand, the 'timeless' qualities invoked as evidence of its classic status are precisely those which are being denied by current academic analysis, so that the division between high and low culture becomes confused. The classic, it seems, is not so much real high culture as a popular notion of high culture.

Paramount's preliminary production notes for *Emily Brontë's Wuthering Heights* begin with a flurry of adjectives: "'incredible . . . powerful, elemental. It is, quite simply, timeless", said producer Mary Selway as she embarked on a new production of Emily Brontë's immortal classic'. *The Yorkshire Post* rejoices as diverse eminences converge: the singer Sinead O'Connor 'is starring alongside the Shakespearian actor, Ralph Fiennes, a Laurence Olivier lookalike who plays Heathcliff in the remake of the 1939 Hollywood epic' (30.10.1991). The *Daily Telegraph* similarly foregrounds Fiennes's previous role as Lawrence of Arabia, 'which made a screen icon of Peter O'Toole' (11.4.1992). A reviewer who thinks little of the film uses the same evaluative process with different cultural content: the set looks like 'a cross between Dracula's castle, Arnley Jail and Norman Bates's house in Psycho' (2.10.1991) – in other words, the set is misconceived because it invokes the generic rhetoric of Gothic, not of grand tragedy. It is significant that while the *Financial Times* reviewer is apoplectic about the film's departure from the patterns of greatness – 'Wuthering Heights itself might have strayed in from a 1960s Edgar Allan Poe film: a crenellated carbuncle teetering over a comic-book chasm' (15.10.1991) – the academic critic Lucasta Miller finds that 'the quest for visual authenticity ends up cramping the story's emotional impact. *Wuthering Heights* is strong enough to withstand a less cautious, more melodramatic approach' (16.10.1992: 34). To be confined to a category of greatness may, it seems, nevertheless be confinement.

To be a classic has explicit market value; in an interview for a study guide to the making of the film, UIP's marketing director, Ken Green, refers to market research showing that 'a lot of people' were already aware of the novel and of Olivier's previous film, though

> not everyone who knew about the book had read it, nor had all people seen the Olivier film. They remembered the image of the scene on the moors, which they have probably seen on the television . . . Most people remember that it is a romantic novel and also a classic. (Wall [1991])

The continuing appeal of the classic suggests that the ideological motivation behind the 'verbal icon' of the 1930s is still active, presenting works of art as 'the heart of a heartless world, promising to reconcile . . . universal and particular, necessity and freedom' (Easthope 1991: 13). The marketing response to the public recognition of *Wuthering Heights* as a classic was to play up the 'recognized' element of romance:

> because we felt that women were an important part of the audience we made two decisions – firstly to make the character of Heathcliff and the actor who plays him, Ralph Fiennes, central to the campaign and secondly, when it came to putting the trailer together, we would use a woman's voice for the trailer. If you think of all the trailers that you see you will realise how different an approach this is. We wanted to present the character of Heathcliff to be charismatic and intriguing to the audience. On the poster design, Heathcliff (Fiennes) is the main visual element. (Wall [1991]: 22)

Despite the claim to an original orientation, the recognition of women's importance is therefore not of their importance as an active readership but as a body of consumers, and its effect is to reverse the feminist critical perception that *Wuthering Heights* can be read as *Catherine's* story, and to reinstate Heathcliff as the focus of attention. The film text itself, moreover, corroborates pre-war perceptions of romance as adulterous triangle, reducing Catherine to the bone of contention. The implicit claim of the classic to transcend time is thus collapsed into a particular (albeit long-enduring) paradigm of romance.

In accordance with this paradigm, however, Catherine's relationship with Heathcliff is shown as less rooted in childhood; they are aged ten and twelve at the time of Heathcliff's arrival, and by the time of Joseph's scripture lesson the parts have been taken by the adult actors, making them at least eighteen years old. When, therefore, they are revealed embracing on their shared bed there is no possibility of interpreting the scene as one of childish innocence, so that Joseph's scandalized response to their intimacy is less unreasonable than in the novel. Although the film follows the written text at many points, significant changes shift the relationships towards a conventional sexual triangle. After Heathcliff's return, he tells Catherine, 'I love you', whereupon she weeps and begs him to go away, since if he stays she would have to leave Edgar, which she would not survive. After the scene in the kitchen, Catherine's illness is made to appear simply and directly the result of grief at Heathcliff's departure, removing the complexity of her anger against both men in the novel; while Nelly warns Catherine that her behaviour might be dangerous 'with the baby due'. As in Buñuel's 1953 film, Catherine's pregnancy and childbirth are visible and noisy, demonstrating how she 'belongs' to Edgar. Whereas in the novel Catherine on her death-bed blames both men for having 'broken her heart' (leaving open the possibility that she hoped to keep them both) here she blames only Heathcliff – though whether for going away or for coming back is not clear.

Kosminsky's full portrayal of the second generation, with its opportunities for repetition and confusion, does give a more complex rendering of the original than previous truncated films. Juliet Binoche plays both Catherines, with enough difference in her appearance to play on identity and difference. Film techniques are also exploited to suggest the identity of Emily Brontë with the older Catherine, and Catherine and Heathcliff with young Catherine and Hareton. The final union of the lovers, however, is not left open. Lockwood's dream sequence, with which the film began, is replayed at the end, making Catherine's ghostly presence explicit and seductive to Heathcliff, who dies in the moment of embracing her, repeating the 'curtain scene' of the 1920 film. The final voice-over, however, reverses not only the soothing certainties of 1920 but also the alternatives offered by the novel, ending not with the 'sleepers in that quiet earth' but with the 'country folk who swear that he still walks'.

Taking the country folks' conviction that 'he walks' out of context in this way reinforces the publicity campaign which places Heathcliff at the centre of interest; and this is not the only way in which the film grants him a privileged position. As in the operas discussed in Chapter 5, it is Heathcliff who becomes the spokesperson for Romantic pantheism when he says he will send Catherine's spirit into a tree which will then talk to them. More dramatically, Kosminsky introduces a scene –

widely used for publicity purposes – in which Heathcliff prophesies that Catherine's life will follow the pattern of the weather. His words are clearly perceived as apophthegmatic, since they are reproduced as epigraph to the preliminary production notes for the film:

> 'If when you open your eyes, the day is sunny and bright, so shall your future be. But if the day is full of storms, so shall be your life.' Heathcliff to Cathy in 'Wuthering Heights' (Paramount [1991])

Yet this scene, which has no precedent in Emily Brontë's text, undermines the famed oneness of the lovers by making it appear that Heathcliff has 'written' Catherine's life.

On the other hand, Kosminsky's film includes the figure of Emily Brontë herself as author, and it might seem that this layering of authors is similar to Fay Weldon's framing of *Jane Eyre* within the process of its writing; the effect, however, is the opposite. In Fay Weldon's play Charlotte is shown not only writing but also talking about her writing, trying out possibilities, discussing her plans with her siblings. The process shown is one of intellectual labour, in which raw materials (partly biographical) are worked up into a fictional text. In Kosminsky's film, the lone figure of Emily is shown happening upon a (real) house (Wuthering Heights) which appears already to contain its history, just waiting for Emily to 'imagine' it. Although producer Mary Selway says that 'the aim is to convey something of the creative process', what we get is 'a great deal of Emily clutching her forehead, staring wild-eyed into the middle-distance, and scribbling feverishly while the storm rages' – a 'wonderfully hammy vision of the Great Writer At Work' (Heller 10.11.1991: 17). Like Mary Shelley's idea for *Frankenstein*, which she explains as having come to her in a dream, the idea for *Wuthering Heights* appears to involve no work, no labour of thought or of craft, but only what Antony Easthope calls the wonderfully ectoplasmic process of imagination (1991: 13). This Emily reinforces the idea of author as inspired genius: 'cloaked in mystery, she stands alone in an untamed landscape', as the *Daily Mirror* puts it (5.12.1991: 3). One reason for this may be that while Jane Eyre, as both narrator of and character in her story, can easily be identified as the focus of meaning in *Jane Eyre*, the meaning of *Wuthering Heights* is notoriously elusive. One movement towards closure of this slippery text is, as we have seen, the invention of the hilltop lovers motif. Another, however, is the projection of meaning onto the figure of the author. While academia acknowledges 'the death of the author', therefore, stage and film are still investing in the Romantic genius: the flier for S. Robertson-Brown's 1994 biographical play, *Emily*, draws on pictures and poetry to present Emily as a 'lone, dark figure of the moors'.

In the same year as Kosminsky's film, Bernard Taylor recorded his musical version of *Wuthering Heights* (1991). Like the film, the musical draws on input from 'high culture' (the operatic soprano Lesley Garrett, the Philharmonia Orchestra and Cantorum Choir) together with the more popular appeal of Dave Willetts, star of *Phantom of the Opera*, and a musical style reminiscent of Andrew Lloyd Webber. The plot, simplified for musical purposes, sharpens to its essence the myth of star-crossed lovers. To this end the second musical number, 'Wuthering Heights', with its refrain, 'our house on the hill', paints a cosy picture of lost childhood; the accompanying booklet tells us that Catherine and Heathcliff are in the habit of escaping to their 'kingdom' on Peniston [sic] Crag, suggesting a direct ancestry from the 1939 film. There are dramatic performances from both Garrett and Willetts, especially in the quarrel song ('I See a Change in You') and occasional felicities such as the emphasis on Heathcliff's gypsy origins, which allows Catherine to avow her preference for the exotic ('My soul rides out on a gypsy caravan/To a strange and wonderful land') while recognizing the real social significance of such a preference ('My heart gives no recognition/To distinctions of colour or creed'). As in the Kosminsky film, however, the motivation of the lovers after Heathcliff's return is rationalized according to the adulterous triangle:

> Heathcliff . . . begs Cathy to leave Edgar and join him at Wuthering Heights. Though her love for him is strong, Cathy's sense of duty prevails; she rejects Heathcliff's entreaties. He vows to wait each night at Peniston Crag until she returns to him . . . she is drawn from her sickbed onto the wild moorland to seek him . . . Cathy dies in Heathcliff's arms.

The cover picture shows Heathcliff carrying Catherine's inert body literally into the sunset where, we are given to understand, he dies soon after. The final duet, 'Up Here With You', leaves it unclear whether the lovers are 'up here' on the top of the moor or 'up here' in heaven; all we know is that they are no longer 'down there below in that dark world'. Although Cathy's words here – 'down there . . . I felt somehow that I was . . . Pulled by the flow In a direction I had no wish to go' – are a good way of representing her contradictory behaviour, 'Up Here With You' does not rise to the challenge of the earlier song in which Cathy recounts her dream of heaven and asserts, in strong major harmonies, that 'I Belong to the Earth'.

Michael Napier-Brown's 1994 dramatization of *Wuthering Heights* also shares some of the qualities of the Kosminsky film. It is a long production including the second generation and many speeches direct from the novel. The York production had fine individual performances and unlike the Kosminsky film, which notoriously suffered from Juliet Binoche's French accent, these characters were Yorkshire speakers dressed with appropriate shabbiness. This drive towards authenticity, however, coexisted with devices tending to mythologize the 'immortal lovers'. There was generous use of recorded music to reinforce an emotional atmosphere. The set, which sounds similar to the 1993 Boston production of Carlisle Floyd's opera, consisted of two converging stairways leading to Penistone Crag; the revolving domestic interiors were contained in the space between them, and Catherine's bedroom coincided with the moor-top. The scene-painting was reminiscent of John Martin's apocalyptic landscapes, and the lighting created dramatic effects of sun and cloud. The staging thus exploited the iconic currency of the hilltop lovers motif established by the 1939 film, filling what Jay Clayton calls the novel's 'representational void' with a vengeance (1987: 84). The play opens with a tableau showing Catherine and Heathcliff embracing on Penistone Crag against the sunset before the action with Lockwood begins; Heathcliff also stands motionless on the Crag while Mr Earnshaw dies and Catherine runs to join him in an embrace; an account of Hindley's persecution of the children is followed by a picnic on the Crag, showing them clearly as adults. When Catherine reports Nelly's description of Heathcliff as a 'child of storm' he retorts that he is not a child and tries to kiss her – this invented scene precedes their scramble to Thrushcross Grange, which in the novel takes place when Catherine is twelve. What we have here is yet another repetition of the pre-war assimilation of Lord David Cecil's metaphysical 'children of storm' argument (here explicitly quoted) to William Wyler's 'star-crossed lovers' presentation which I discussed in Chapter 4. In addition, we have an emphasis on visual tableaux which recalls the moral universe of the Victorian melodrama.

On his return from exile this Heathcliff immediately climbs to Penistone Crag where Catherine follows him; they embrace but she pulls away before he can kiss her. As in the Kosminsky film and the Taylor musical, it is her status as a married woman which divides them – yet the social explanation coexists with an explicit other-worldliness. When Heathcliff tells Nelly that he does what he does because he is what he is, she repeats, 'a child of the storm'. A lurid sunset grows during Catherine's death and Heathcliff's curse is shrieked from the Crag; the scene ends with him on his knees with arms outstretched in an iconic pose. In the second act much of this visual material is repeated for the younger generation, suggesting more strongly than usual that the pattern will be repeated rather than changed; but the focus is still on Heathcliff, who climbs to the Crag to die. During Nelly's description of the churchyard, three figures finally appear on the Crag against a brilliant sunset and swelling music; Catherine and Heathcliff are dressed as they were as children yet, given the 'triangle' treatment, the third figure must perpetuate the idea of their separation rather than suggesting their possible coexistence. None of these productions confronts the fact that Catherine does not wish to give up either of her lovers (cf. *WH* xxx).

The emphasis given to Cecil's 'children of storm' phrase in Napier-Brown's play suggests that despite the growing popular interest in *Wuthering Heights*, and the mountain of criticism deconstructing precisely the humanist/transcendent reading offered by Cecil's essay, it is still that 1934 reading which predominates sixty years later. Even where the medium and style seem innovatory, as with Kate Bush's famous 1978 song, 'Wuthering Heights', the structure of emotional response is unchanged. Kate Bush's sound is extraordinary, and one can understand why devotees were 'spellbound' by what Charlotte Soares describes as 'the shriek of a banshee' (*BSG* 5). The underlying emotion, however, is simple: 'I've lost my man'. Cathy wanders the moors remembering a love compounded of love and hate, just as in Roland Petit's ballet, 'leurs jeux sont amour et bataille' ('their games are love and war'; 1982 programme note). Her refrain is 'I've come home and I'm so cold, let me in', but the price she pays for coming back from 'the other side' where 'it gets lonely' is to acknowledge 'cruel Heathcliff' as 'my only master'. Ideologically, it is retrograde and unappealing; emotionally it rivets its audience. Theodore Adorno offers an argument which explains not only the appeal of this remarkably successful song but also the tendency of the Wuthering Heights industry to project the meaning of the text into a pair of lovers welded into an iconic whole by their very separation.

> when the audience at a sentimental film or sentimental music become aware of the overwhelming possibility of happiness, they dare to confess to themselves what the whole order of contemporary life ordinarily forbids them to admit, namely, that they have no part in happiness . . . The actual function of sentimental music lies rather in the temporary release given to the awareness that one has missed fulfilment . . . Emotional music has become the image of the mother who says, 'Come and weep, my child'. (quoted in Easthope 1991: 100)

The current compulsion to repeat what we might call the icon of loss embodied in the lovers on the hilltop suggests that *Wuthering Heights* occupies a place in the popular imagination of the present comparable to that of *Jane Eyre* in the melodramatic imagination of the nineteenth century. *Jane Eyre* was reproduced predominantly as a social drama, the story of the orphan denied her place in family and class. *Wuthering Heights*, it seems, has come to represent the more existential loss of the twentieth century, the fantasy of those orphaned by a non-existent God and alienated from a society which pretends to belong to us all.

There are, however, belated indications of resistance to the 'weepy' reading. Lynn Robertson Hay, who adapted *Wuthering Heights* for the Snap Theatre Company (1993), hates the thought of 'turning out a glossy tear-jerker', while with only four actors performing in school halls with minimal props, the company is forced to expose the mechanics of representation. With scenery doubling as domestic interior and moortop, and fast-moving cuts and fades as characters turn into other people, this production forces the audience to work hard, considering whether there are intrinsic links between the different locations, or between different characters played by the same actor. Paul Kavanagh, for instance, doubling as Heathcliff and Linton Heathcliff, allowed us to recognize Linton's petulance as a version of Heathcliff's obstinacy. In the absence of elaborate sets and lighting, an enforced focus on the actors' bodies sometimes glosses the text in interesting ways. During Catherine's last scene with Heathcliff, for instance, she behaved as if heavily pregnant (although no padding is used) so that her words must be interpreted in that knowledge. The second generation are fully and interestingly represented, repeating the older pair's games but with poignant attention to young Catherine's weary role as nurse to the dying Linton; her final call to Ellen from behind a screen is framed in such a way as to suggest that she is a ghost, forcing us to reconsider the nature of haunting, repetition and change.

William Ash's casting for his dramatization of *Wuthering Heights* (Good Company, 1994) is a deliberate affront to the 'high culture' associations fostered by other reproducers. Martin Spence, reviewing the play for the *Brontë Society Gazette*, announces gleefully: 'It had to happen: *Wuthering Heights* performed by half the cast of Britain's best-loved soap' (*BSG* 12). The associations of Nigel Pivaro and Caroline Milmoe (who play Terry and Lisa Duckworth in *Coronation*

Street) as Catherine and Hindley, and Jason Riddington (who played a young doctor in *Casualty*) as Heathcliff are quite different from the Shakespearian echoes raised by Olivier or Fiennes. Caroline Milmoe is compared to Vivien Leigh (who did *not* get the part opposite Olivier) and Riddington's Heathcliff was sexy enough to raise wolf-whistles from the audience (3), but Spence also comments that 'accents in this production are rightly from The Street rather than RADA. These are real, not beautiful people' (2). Another distinctive feature of the production is that, 'uniquely among dramatised versions, it brings out Emily's wit and humour' (2). Like the Kosminsky film, this play has Emily herself on stage, but its interpretation of her 'free spirit' is evidently very different from the inspired genius of the film. Spence describes how 'she confesses to being a right-on feminist, annoyed at having to cloak her real identity under a pseudonym' (2); 'in this politically correct production . . . under Emily's civilised surface, there's a Wuthering Heights self just dying to get out . . .' (3). It is difficult to gauge from the irony of Spence's review how convincing the right-on emphasis was, but it is clear that this production has at least acknowledged critical and ideological developments since 1934.

Another star from *Casualty* played Heathcliff in Jeremy Raison's adaptation of *Wuthering Heights* for the Chester Gateway Theatre (1994). Again the reviewers made much of this departure from tradition, but this time the focus was on the fact that Patrick Robinson, who plays Ash in *Casualty*, is a black actor. Tracey Harrison, under the headline, 'Casualty star to be a black Heathcliff', guesses that 'It may be the first time a black actor has taken on one of the greatest romantic roles in English literature'; while Gerry Dempsey proclaims, 'Dreadlocked Heathcliff triumphs' (29.3.1994). The emphasis is more than sensational. Gerry Dempsey goes on to describe Robinson as 'an actor of towering presence', whose

> dreadlocked presence subtly alters the tone and emphasis of the play . . . lines like 'Why educate a blackamoor?' and 'I'm master here and don't you forget that, Gipsy!' take on a new ugliness . . . The conflict is suddenly racial, not social, and Heathcliff is a different kind of victim . . .

Post-colonial criticism of *Wuthering Heights* is slower to get into circulation than that of *Jane Eyre*, though Christopher Heywood's 'Yorkshire slavery in *Wuthering Heights*' (1987) has opened the door. Jeremy Raison's casting is important in showing how a single, simple change in representation can prompt radical rereading.

The unsettling effects of Raison's play can already be found, albeit for an elite audience, in Peter Forster's wood engravings for the 1991 Folio Society edition of *Wuthering Heights*. Heathcliff, as he receives Lockwood's visit, is represented as fleshy, thick-lipped and dark-skinned, though dressed as a Victorian bourgeois with neck-cloth and watch-chain, lounging in the doorway to Wuthering Heights complete with statues and inscription (*WH* 1991 Forster: 13). In the flashback to childhood, as Nelly 'makes him tidy', the background suggests Heathcliff's possible Indian/Chinese origins, though his dark, blunt features and woolly hair, in conjunction with a high-necked shirt, suggest the American plantations. The handwritten representation of Isabella's questions, 'Is Mr Heathcliff a man? And if not, is he a devil?' has pinned to it, however, a portrait of a handsome European face, suggesting Lord Byron, making visible her misconception of him (136). This slippage of identity forms the interpretative focus for Forster's engravings. The frontispiece shows Branwell's famous profile portrait of Emily, but with her left hand shielding her face; later, after the various pictures of Heathcliff, we find both of Branwell's portraits with the heavy, bearded, explicitly African face which we now identify as Heathcliff between them. Shockingly, though the portraits are not much changed, both show Emily with thick, prominent lips (250). Similarly, when Catherine looks at herself and Nelly in a mirror, the lower part of her face is concealed by her curly hair (114); in her last embrace with Heathcliff, however, her short hair (possibly cropped during fever) curls to resemble his, while her half-closed eyes and open lips also mirror his (unseen) face (144). Shortly before Heathcliff's death, when he warns young Catherine not to provoke him, Forster shows him flinging a black, muscle-bound arm across his eyes while a sharp-eyed Emily watches from a picture-frame on the wall; her gaze and (thick-lipped) features are exactly replicated in Hareton and Catherine who stand under the picture (278: Figure 7.1).

These suggestions of racial instability are, however, only one aspect of Forster's radical destabilization of the usual certainties of identity. The illustration to Lockwood's dream, for instance, gives us a box-like structure of which one side is window-panes showing the moon and another is carved panelling. Every surface is covered with the name 'Catherine', carved at right angles to itself so that letters coincide. It is not clear, however, whether the rectangle formed by the four sides of the enclosure is the bottom or the top of the window-embrasure; moreover, the hands, casting several shadows, which reach into it do not come through the glass panes, so that they appear to be Lockwood's. The result is to cast doubt on Lockwood's account of the ghost hands which come through the window.

The engravings repeatedly draw attention to the textual fabrication of the novel; the text is interspersed with childish drawings – for instance of a crenellated house with a frieze of two-dimensional people (39) – reminding us that the core of the story (Catherine's diary) is put together by a young child. On the other hand, Catherine's caricature of Joseph as a saint is delayed to accompany the moment when Joseph demands that Edgar should release Linton Heathcliff to his father, where it acts as a telling comment on Joseph's Christian kindness (180). The childish handwriting of her marginal 'diary', moreover, forms a pointed gloss on the beautiful gothic letters of the testament, from which Forster has chosen to select the words: 'Surely I am more brutish than any man and have not the understanding of a man . . . I neither learned wisdom, nor . . .'. Against this, Catherine writes, 'little did I dream that Hindley would make me cry so! My head aches . . . I cannot keep it on the pillow; and still I can't give over . . . POOR HEATHCLIFF!' (52). The juxtaposition makes us wonder whether the brutish man is Heathcliff, deprived of learning, or Hindley, whose learning has not given him wisdom. Throughout, these engravings perform the opposite function from those stage plays which

Figure 7.1   Peter Forster's wood engraving from the 1991 Folio edition of *Wuthering Heights*, p. 278.

reinforce received meanings; they force us to reconsider the conjunctions and patterns of words and images from which we have habitually constructed the meaning of *Wuthering Heights*. As Heathcliff recounts his attempts to re-establish contact with the dead Catherine, we are offered an engraving in which his hands force apart two gravestones on which we can read 'ORY OF | | IN MEM'. As he widens the breach, it seems to fill with the black moorland behind – or is it merely earth? The black void can be filled with what we will. Simultaneously, however, the breach suggests the possibility that his interference is simply allowing the interrupted text to re-establish itself elsewhere as 'IN MEMORY OF' – but of whom? of Catherine, or of Catherine and Edgar? *Wuthering Heights* has always demanded such a reading, which raises more questions than it answers.

Jane Eyre *and* Wuthering Heights *as popular currency*

'What do Gary Lineker, Charlotte Brontë, the Milan police force and the "dreaming Spires" of Oxford have in common? They're all part of the summer package at York Theatre Royal' (*JE* 1993 Hall: flier). As the Brontë texts become more widely known, such bizarre conjunctions proliferate. Umberto Eco has argued that 'in order to transform a work into a cult object one must be able to break, dislocate, unhinge it so that one can remember only parts of it, irrespective of their original relationship with the whole' (1988: 447). Readers are now invited to join in the fun of selecting memorable features, as in the *Daily Telegraph*'s 'Novel in a nutshell' (13.8.1994). *Jane Eyre* and *Wuthering Heights* are also regularly subjected to a further process, in which the dislocated parts are extracted for purposes unconnected with the original text. Apart from the innumerable puns used in reviews, such as 'wuthering flats' (*WH* 1988 Foxall: 28.5.1989) and headlines on Brontë issues such as 'Brontë wrangles sink to wuthering depths' (Furbisher and Rayment 1992), or 'Brontë Society imitates Heathcliff and Cathy' (Lonsdale 1992), headline writers appropriate the title of *Wuthering Heights* for use in quite alien contexts, as in the *New Statesman*'s 'Swithering heights', where 'swithering' refers to 'voters who regularly switch between parties' (Howe 1989). The very fame of the famous sisters can now be exploited to fix interest on issues which might otherwise escape readers' attention, as in 'Report reveals Patten paradox of Charlotte Brontë', in which a *Guardian* writer shows that although *Jane Eyre* is now on the National Curriculum, its author would not have shown well according to its system of testing (Weale 1993).

Such rivetting power can be harnessed to more simply commercial purposes, as you can see by walking through Haworth's modern array of Brontë biscuits and Heathcliff bed and breakfast houses; but big names are worthy of big business. In August 1991

> the Bradford-based British Wool Marketing Board was surprised to discover that a plan to display their products in Japan was accompanied by a request to base their presentation on Emily's novel *Wuthering Heights*! To meet the Japanese request Board staff worked with [Brontë] Museum staff to produce the drama, music and dance spectacle, *The Romance of Wool*. Cathy, Heathcliff and the others duly appeared at the British Fair in Tokyo's Mitsukoshi store last October. (*BSG* 5: 3)

Yorkshire copywriters go into punning overdrive as they report how actors 'reach new heights . . . in Japan' (*Yorkshire Post* 24.8.1991), 'wool team gives Japan its money's Haworth' (15.8.1991), 'Boost for those with yen for Brontës' (15.8.1991: 9) and 'new Brontë yarn set for trade spin-off' (*Telegraph and Argus* 30.8.1991). The process, however, works both ways; Jane Sellars, the director of the Brontë Parsonage Museum, was reported in the *Keighley News* as saying that 'Japanese tourists . . . may be attracted' to Haworth by the Tokyo performance. The Brontë Society now has over three thousand members, nearly a third of whom are from outside Great Britain, and the Museum has over one hundred thousand visitors a year (see Lemon 1993 appx 3). Although steps have been taken to reduce the number of visitors since the 1970s, and its commercial initiatives are severely overseen by the membership, nevertheless the museum is now run as a modern enterprise in which publicity plays an important part. In Jane Gardam's novel, *The Summer After the Funeral*, two characters wait for 'the Brontë bus' which goes every day –

'and not from here only?' 'Oh no – from Harrogate, York and Leeds and Scarborough
I suppose. They come from London, Americans, and back for supper. From Rome,
Tibet, Afghanistan. Hurrah for the three weird sisters.' . . .

    '*Every* day?'

    'Well – a lot of days. Only twice a week from Tibet'. (*WH* 1973 Gardam [1977:
129–30])

In reality, signposts to Brontë beauty spots are now in Japanese (Wainwright 1991).

Japanese interest in the Brontës covers the whole span from commercial spin-
off to high culture. In 1989 a Japanese comicbook version of *Wuthering Heights*
appeared, showing Catherine and Heathcliff as wide-eyed juveniles dressed in
pantomime style with frilly pantaloons for Cathy and ragged knee-breeches for
Heathcliff (Figure 7.2). The pictures of Catherine, all blonde curls and ribbons
and bows, locked in an embrace with a very youthful Heathcliff on the pinnacle of
a conical Japanese Penistone Crag, or of Catherine's Disney-style wedding to a
Fauntleroy-Edgar in an explosion of flowers and lace jabots, encompass the
combined sentimentalities of Japanese and American culture; Catherine's ghost
descends at the end with widespread arms and rippling hair worthy of an art
nouveau flower-fairy. On the other hand, *Wuthering Heights* seems to have been an
influence on Ayako Miura's prize-winning novel *Hyoten* (*c*. 1970); the 1939 film was
shown in Tokyo in Japanese in 1981 and the Japanese director Yoshige Yoshida
derived his famous film *Onimaru* (1988) from Emily Brontë's novel. According to
the Brontë Society exhibition of 1990–1, *Onimaru* is

> a Samurai version of *Wuthering Heights*. The Japanese director was inspired to make
> his film by reading Georges Bataille's essay on the novel in his book *La Litterature et
> le Mal* (1957) which concentrates on the dramatisation of sexuality and death.

Chris Peachment, reporting on *Onimaru* at the 1988 Cannes Film Festival,
comments that 'as so often happens with our novels, it takes a foreign sensibility to
illuminate their darker corners'. The Brontë Parsonage Museum also holds the
typescript and programme of a Japanese stage version of *Jane Eyre* which was
produced in 1978 by Kazue Kontaibo. The young woman who sent the information
writes that she has seen both the Orson Welles and the Delbert Mann films as well
as a BBC television film of *Jane Eyre* and is dissatisfied with all of them, as with
the Japanese play, because it 'was performed as a simple love story'.

Japanese interest in the Brontës is indicative of their increasing fame at home
and abroad, which includes the Brontë lives as well as their works. In 1973, BBC
television broadcast a series of plays entitled *The Brontës of Haworth* by the eminent
playwright Christopher Fry, and during the past twenty years formal biographies
have been written by Winifred Gérin (1967, 1978), Margot Peters (1975), Lynne
Reid Banks (1976, 1977), Helen Moglen (1978), Edward Chitham (1987), Rebecca
Fraser (1988), Katherine Frank ([1990] 1992), Lyndall Gordon (1994) and Juliet
Barker (1994). There is also, however, an unslackening stream of biographical
performances of various kinds (Robinson, N. 1974; Mantkelow 1977; Cross 1978;
Jackson [1978]; Nash 1979; Hunt 1985; Lesley [1988, 1989]; Bollinger 1989;

Figure 7.2   Catherine and Heathcliff on the hilltop, from a 1989 Japanese picture-book version.

Voices Go Round 1990; Wild Workshop 1992; Snow Storm Theatre 1993; Gondal Theatre 1994; Robertson-Brown 1994; Fowler, J. (n.d.)). Some of these treatments are quite old-fashioned and adulatory – Douglas Jackson's 1978 *Episode* has Emily acquiescing in Branwell's theft of *Wuthering Heights* quite in the manner of the inter-war apologists, and his four Brontës are described as 'good-looking . . . pretty . . . attractive' and 'very pretty'. When Charlotte Cory attempted, in a light-hearted context, to tell the 'awful truth' about Charlotte in 1993, she attracted a storm of protest. In 1980 Charlotte and Emily appeared on British postage stamps and in 1985 a British Rail locomotive was named 'The Brontës of Haworth' (Lemon 1993: 92, 102).

The prevalence of the myth means that there is a market for works which claim to be 'lost' texts by the famous writers, or works related in some indirect way, such as Louise Brindley's *In the Shadow of the Brontës* (1982), a story about a friendship between Anne Brontë and (the fictitious?) Lizzie Godolphin, Pamela Haines's *Daughter of the Northern Fields* (1987), which claims to be the story of Branwell Brontë's illegitimate daughter, or Caroline L. Grinnell's *Try to Remember* (1992), in which the heroine relives a previous life in which she was Maria Branwell. Robert Barnard's *The Missing Brontë* (1983) is one of a series about the detective Perry Trethowan; the missing Brontë is a manuscript which may be Emily Brontë's missing novel. Since Robert Barnard has for many years been a prominent member of the Brontë Society, he is well placed to write a detective story which involves many of the type-characters of current Brontëana – 'a crazy collector of literary relics, a dislikeable academic, a very smooth millionaire, and a shifty cleric from the wilder fringes of American religious life' (cover).

As well as the biographical myth, however, the novels themselves have received such wide exposure that the Brontë Society was prompted to mount exhibitions of stage and film versions of *Wuthering Heights* and *Jane Eyre* in 1990 and 1991. In British public libraries in 1991–2 *Wuthering Heights* and *Jane Eyre* were the third and fourth most borrowed books (*BSG* 9: 25–6); by 1994 *Jane Eyre* had been translated into twenty-four languages and *Wuthering Heights* into twenty-six; *Jane Eyre* is currently available in the UK in twenty-three different editions and *Wuthering Heights* in twenty-seven. The Brontë fame means that there is always a market for 'spin-off' products such as Paul Reade's suite, *Jane Eyre* [1987], which began life as the music accompanying the BBC television adaptation. It also means that the Brontë names can be used wherever the signification is merely 'famous'. In Barbara Taylor Bradford's *Voice of the Heart* (1989), for instance, the heroine, actress Katherine Tempest, is 'doing a re-make of a great classic, probably the greatest love story ever written, *Wuthering Heights*'. Despite the apparent significance of Katherine's name, *Wuthering Heights* appears simply as an indicator that she has 'made it' as an actress. Similarly, Miriam Darce Frenier's book on recent romance fiction is called *Good-bye Heathcliffe* [sic] (1988), not because it contains the slightest reference to *Wuthering Heights*, but because Heathcliff has come to represent a certain kind of romantic hero.

In the 1990s it is *Wuthering Heights*, to a much greater extent than *Jane Eyre*, which is the focus for commercial exploitation. Bernard J. Taylor's 1991 musical (discussed above) and Paul Dick's 1992 *Romantic Musical* are part of an almost farcical current competition to get there first with material based on *Wuthering Heights*. Franco Zeffirelli is reported as planning to film both *Jane Eyre* and

Wuthering Heights, while the Northern Ballet Company has discussed plans for a *Wuthering Heights* ballet and is mounting a ballet called *The Brontës* in March 1995. In 1991 disc-jockey Mike Read announced his intention to produce a West End musical starring Cliff Richard. Cliff Richard, an apparently incongruous choice for Heathcliff because of his well-publicized religious views, says that he has 'been obsessed with the character since I was a kid because he is everything I am not. I am struck by how much evil and hate he has' (*Daily Mail* 27.4.1991). At the time of writing, these plans had been postponed several times (*Yorkshire Post* 30.12.1993 and 13.5.1994), but the *Yorkshire Post* revealed late in 1993 that the music was to be written by John Farrar, who wrote the hit songs from *Grease*. Alek Keshishian was also reported in 1991 to be planning what he called a 'popera', possibly with songs by George Michael and a performance from Madonna. Well may the *Daily Mail* describe these various entrepreneurs as 'racing to the moors' (19.7.1991). Fame has brought to the Brontës not just devoted readers but also, it seems, plenty of people ready to cash in on fame.

Where there is fame there are also, however, people ready to deflate it, and it is perhaps inevitable that as the Brontë fame increases, so does the number of parodies. I have not been able to see James Prideaux's unpublished musical *Jane Heights* (1980), but it is clear that its comic focus is on those unthinking enthusiasts who can scarcely distinguish one novel from the other. David Toothill's *Brontë Follies* (1988) presents the three famous sisters as a brash and sexy music-hall act whose sickly brother Branwell writes all the novels, reversing the implications of all those inter-war fictions which suggested that they had not the wit to do it themselves. John Sessions's *Travelling Tales* is also impatient with the mythical fragility of the sisters:

> Sessions plays Emily Brontë as a lewd Yorkshire thug . . . reading the opening lines of *Wuthering Heights* to her sisters. 'It was a wet night', says Sessions, sounding like an irritable Geoffrey Boycott. 'It was a *bastard* wet night'. (*Independent on Sunday* 1.9.1991)

The *New Yorker* (1992) provides a more refined version of this joke in the form of a cartoon by Ronald Searle entitled 'Crossed Paths: The Brontë Sisters Meet Paris' (?1992). The drawing shows Paris, in sandals and tunic, attempting to award the golden apple to one of the three ringletted Brontës, who have sprung up in a fury; one throws a book at his head, another spatters him with ink, the third magisterially points the way out. It is intriguing to find the students of Szeged University in Hungary performing a parody based on the Brontë lives in 1992, but since I do not read Hungarian I am unable to comment on its import (Zsolt and Csaba 1992).

Most recent parodies are directed either, like these, at the whole Brontë myth or at the canonical status of *Wuthering Heights* as an archetype of (R)romantic love. Monty Python's semaphore version of *Wuthering Heights* wittily reduces the novel to its mythical skeleton; its minimalist representation of Catherine and Heathcliff on separate hilltops, signalling their desire with semaphore flags, points up the sheer impracticality of tragic love (*WH* 1989 Chapman). The Radio Rentals advertisement similarly shows their communication interrupted by electrical interference. Noreen Kershaw's stage entertainment, *Withering Looks*, performed by Lip Service in Buxton in 1989 and in York in 1993, finds its comic inspiration in the dual effects of most recent reproductions of the Brontë lives and works, in which a drive to authenticity of dress and behaviour coexists uneasily with a wish to find transcendent values. *Withering Looks* gives us a ramshackle stage parsonage, doubling as *Wuthering Heights*, which shelters an elaborately costumed Brontë/ Earnshaw family who periodically venture out to be blasted by stage winds and lightning, re-entering with dishevelled wigs and bonnets while keeping up a rapid double-act patter recounting the deep and tragic events which are mostly happening off-stage. The incongruity between daily life and the turbulence of the 'beyond' is immortalized in the final line of the nutshell summary of *Wuthering Heights*, 'So everyone was happy but some of them were dead'. The inconvenience of Romantic love as a way of life also underlies a sketch by Ian Frazier entitled 'Linton's whatnots'. This *New Yorker* parody (1992) hinges around the discovery that Edgar Linton is an eminent collector of nutcrackers. In the context of 'Sunset. The moors. A strong gale blowing', Catherine and Heathcliff embrace and assert their love, Cathy vowing that 'Edgar Linton's spirit is to mine as a small bedchamber washbasin is to a great, deep millpond . . .' The narrative shifts to Edgar's contribution to the nutcracker-collectors' newsletter; the comedy lies in the fact that although at first he seems insufferably boring in the way of suburban collectors everywhere, in the end Catherine concedes a little interest in 'the ones with the little huntsman . . . and the ones in the shape of pug dogs. And the little banty roosters . . .' Eventually Heathcliff is drawn to protest that 'the wretched huntsman' holds 'a crossbow, unmistakably . . .' Through the newsletter, Heathcliff now begins a 'lively correspondence with Mr Ulrich Link, of Ulm' while 'Cathy died, but not seriously'. As for Edgar, 'after a reasonable period of mourning, he began to look for a companion whose interests more closely matched his own'.

Wuthering Heights According to Spike Milligan (1994) employs a repetitive formula which either literalizes the original text ('I was thrown into the company of a fascinating creature; two men took me by the limbs and hurled me through the window') or fantasizes it in a random fashion ('Mr Heathcliff has reasons for keeping his hand behind him when he meets an acquaintance. It had two thumbs and six fingers' (*WH* 1994 Milligan: 3)). In common with the other recent parodies, however, it highlights the conflict between Romantic love and the normal conveniences of life; Catherine runs 'barefooted on the moor in the wind and the rain . . . stopping now and then to pull thorns from the soles of her feet' (50). When asked what she gets out of this habit, she replies, 'bronchitis' (36). The pervasive metaphors of the novel, drawn from the landscape and the weather, are also literalized ('Hareton grew black as thunder. "Look", said Catherine, "he's about to start raining"' (83)). One unpleasant aspect of this rather puerile book, however, is that Heathcliff's 'exotic' origins are presented in stereotyped racial terms; the 'gibberish' he speaks as a child is 'Pakistani' (21) and he lives 'a free, wild life on the moors making chapattis and tandoori on the wood fire' (23). On the occasion of Heathcliff's return, Edgar orders tea and 'a curry' for Heathcliff (48). Later, Heathcliff's enforcement of the marriage between young Catherine and Linton is described as 'an old Asian custom' (109). Heathcliff's charisma is reduced to crude sex; his advantage over Edgar is a matter of six inches (43) and the text ends with the shepherd lad who has seen 'Heathcliff, and a woman yonder . . . and they're doing it' (118). It is perhaps significant that the illustrations for Milligan's book are those by Balthus (discussed in Chapter 4 above), which also present the story as a sexual battleground; unlike Balthus, however, Milligan shows Heathcliff as a stud who literally carries all before him. The general import of the book is confused; are we meant to feel superior to the oriental who betrays his presence by 'a whiff of garlic, ghee and dung' (41) or to rejoice in the fabulous 'heat in his trousers' (69)? Either way, the text offers no position for a female reader.

Jane Eyre, which is receiving a more lively and less adulatory treatment in the context of recent feminist concerns, has been much less the butt of parodic critique. One parody comparable with those on *Wuthering Heights* is a cartoon by Neil Bennett, showing a butler greeting a plumber at the door of a stately home. The caption reads, 'You'll find the cold water tank in the attic, along with the mad woman'. The implication that Gilbert and Gubar have reached the stage of notoriety in which 'every home must have one' is only mildly critical. On the other hand, there is evidence that *Jane Eyre* itself is still subversive enough to call forth genuine attack. In 1991 BBC TV's Russ Abbot Show featured a sketch in which the blind Rochester sits in a drawing room with an immensely fat and ugly Jane. 'Remind me once more', he says, 'what you look like'. 'Well,' she replies, 'to begin with I am very slender, and I have long blonde hair and blue eyes'. 'Oh', says Rochester, 'I am expecting Sir Harley Wimpole, the famous eye surgeon, to come and restore my sight. I can't wait to see you with my own eyes'. The door-bell rings, Jane goes out, there is an explosion and Jane returns with a smoking blunderbuss and a satisfied expression; loud audience laughter (*JE* 1991 Davis). Charlotte Brontë's vision of a woman 'poor, obscure, plain, and little' (*JE* 265) who nevertheless becomes her 'husband's life as fully as he is' hers (475), is clearly still dangerous enough to need expensive deflation.

Catching them young: the Brontë heroines as female role models

The young Jeanette, in Winterson's *Oranges Are Not the Only Fruit*, is encouraged to look to the example of 'Jane Eyre, who faced many trials and was always brave' (*JE* 1985 Winterson: 28). It is only later that she discovers 'that Jane doesn't marry St John at all, that she goes back to Mr Rochester'. Jeanette's missionary mother 'had rewritten the ending' when she 'read it to me over and over again, when I was very small' (74). To modern readers this seems like comic exaggeration, yet, in a talk entitled 'The imperialism of eternity: race and missionaries', Judith

Rowbotham described how the version of *Jane Eyre* used by missionaries was 'expurgated such that Rochester became virtually invisible!'

As early as 1877 the Brontë sisters themselves were being used as role models. The suffrage campaigner Millicent Garrett Fawcett has a chapter on Charlotte and Emily Brontë in her book, *Some Eminent Women of Our Times*, which originally appeared in sections in *The Mother's Companion*. Fawcett explains that 'the sketches were intended chiefly for working women and young people; it was hoped it would be an encouragement to them to be reminded how much good work had been done in various ways by women' ([1877] 1889: preface). Charlotte and Emily, however, appear mainly as victims. Fawcett hints, ever so gently, that Patrick Brontë should have had fewer children if he was not prepared to play his part in their upbringing; she laments that boys like Branwell 'are not sufficiently guarded from temptation', while the Brontë girls, despite their 'inexorable fidelity to duty', were subject to 'conventional propriety' (103–4).

Although much of the biographical material dealt with in Chapter 3 implicitly presents the Brontës as role models, there has during the past twenty years been a more explicit tendency to present Brontë material for young readers. Richard Crane's play *Thunder: A Play of the Brontës* (1976) was, for instance, published by Heinemann Educational Books, and Florence Sturges's *A Brontë Tapestry* is advertised as 'by a Children's Librarian'. There are also a number of biographical studies specifically about the young Brontës. Some of these are very lively, such as Pauline Clarke's *The Twelve and the Genii* (1962) or Jane Amster's *Dream Keepers: The Young Brontës* (1973). The cover blurb describes Amster's young Brontës as 'a spirited band of sceptics who question orthodoxy and probe the essential meanings of good and evil in a self-determined endeavour for self-realization'. Postma *et al.*'s *Glasstown Confederacy* (1993) is a stage dramatization of the juvenile writings.

The novels have also been packaged for juvenile consumption. Academic Industries' Pocket Classics edition of *Wuthering Heights* (1984) is a small black-and-white comic-strip. Longman's Movieworld easy reading edition (1985), Longman's Classics (simplified) edition (1989) and Macmillan's Students' Novels edition (1982) of *Wuthering Heights* are all illustrated by pictures from the 1978 BBC television serial with Ken Hutchinson and Kay Adshead. Lee Paul's adaptation of *Wuthering Heights* is subtitled 'The Story of Catherine and Heathcliff' (NYPL: no details), while Isis publish *Wuthering Heights* in a large-print edition (no date). Similarly, a 1960s comicstrip version of *Jane Eyre* is updated by the addition of Timothy Dalton on the cover; Longman's Movieworld *Jane Eyre* (an 'easy reading edition': 1985) and Longman's Classics (simplified) edition (1987) are both illustrated by pictures from the Dalton/Clarke television serial. Stills from Delbert Mann's 1970 film were used to illustrate OUP's Bookworms edition (1990). These simplified versions reduce the text to its story outline and sometimes make explicit the implications of the text: for instance, in the Movieworld *Jane Eyre*, when Jane first contemplates Rochester she finds 'something in his eyes that was not hard. "Something in the past has hurt him badly", I thought' (1985: 16). Editions described as 'abridged', however, can make more insidious changes. The Bancroft

Classics abridged edition, for instance, appears to use only Charlotte Brontë's words, but crucial sections of her text are missing, such as the 'feminist manifesto' in I xii. On the other hand, the Longman Movieworld and Classics editions include exercises and questions to promote more alert reading ('The horseman was (a) a neighbour (b) Adèle's father (c) Mr Rochester'; 1985: 32). Sylvia Wharton's play, *The Childhood of Jane Eyre* (1985) was clearly aimed at children, parents and teachers, as was *young jane eyre* by the Children's Theatre Company, Minneapolis (1988). Charles Vance's Touring Production of *Jane Eyre* (1985) has an elaborate scholarly programme apparently aimed specifically at schoolchildren, 'to help you in your studies'.

In 1990 the Educational Unit of the National Museum of Photography, Film and Television at Bradford held a dayschool on *Wuthering Heights* for school pupils, accompanied by a twenty-eight-page workbook called 'Visual Responses to "Wuthering Heights"'. The workbook included material on several film versions as well as the novel itself and encouraged an active involvement with 'reading' visual aspects and versions of the text. The educational package produced by Literary Images Limited also encourages students to move from the visual images embedded in Emily Brontë's text to film shots of the real landscape of Yorkshire and back again, considering the social and metaphorical processes at work. Their material includes a copy of the text, a videotape including landscape sequences chosen to fit the text, a student worksheet and a worksheet guide for the teacher (no date). Film Education produced a study guide, 'The Making of the Film' to accompany Kosminsky's *Emily Brontë's Wuthering Heights*; it includes questions about the decision to adapt classic texts as well as statements from the producer and scriptwriter, and information about budget, timetable and marketing as well as casting, design and the techniques of *mise en scène* (Wall [1991]). Snap Theatre Company ('founded in the belief that the Arts could be more accessible') have also made a point of directing their stage version of *Wuthering Heights* towards sixth-form audiences, joining in discussions about the novel and its adaptations (1993).

Much of this educational material is laudably designed to prompt young readers to question what they read; evidence from readers themselves, however, especially women, suggests that a relatively naive process of identification is the most common response of children to works of fiction, especially works like *Jane Eyre* with a strong first-person narrative. Rachel Brownstein, in *Becoming a Heroine*, argues that this process of fictional identification is specifically feminine.

> Girls, enjoined from thinking about becoming generals and emperors, tend to live more in novels than boys do, and to live longer in them. It is not megalomaniacal to want to be significant; it is only human. And to suspect that one can be significant only in the fantasy of fiction, to look for significance in a concentrated essence of character, in an image of oneself, rather than in action or achievement, is, historically, only feminine. ([1982] 1984: xv)

Donna Marie Nudd, moreover, reports that 'when Dr Carol MacKay conducted a workshop on *Jane Eyre* for advanced placement teachers, "a great many of them had only been teaching it to their 'girls', assuming of course that the 'boys' wouldn't be interested"' (Nudd 1989: 141 n6). This may be done with the best of motives; Brownstein goes on to argue that

> to want to become a heroine, to have a sense of the possibility of being one, is to develop the beginnings of what feminists call a 'raised' consciousness: it liberates a woman from feeling . . . a victim or a dependent or a drudge. The domestic novel can be credited with strengthening and shaping the female reader's aspirations to matter, to make something special of herself. ([1982] 1984: xix)

Where young readers are involved, therefore, we may properly ask ourselves whether *Jane Eyre*, and to a lesser extent *Wuthering Heights*, offer female role models to their readers, or whether readers' responses are more complex than this.

The Brontë novels were written in a climate where heroines were expected to be beautiful, accomplished and good – an ideal to be aspired to. Charlotte was therefore consciously revolutionary when she protested to her sisters that she would take a 'real' heroine – as small and plain as herself – and make her as interesting as the heroines of conventional fiction (see Gaskell [1857] 1975: 308). Jane Eyre, moreover, proves to be more of a challenge to convention than simply being small and plain. As a child she is 'a picture of passion', a 'fury'; as she is hauled off to the Red Room as a punishment, Bessie warns her fellow servant to 'hold her arms, Miss Abbot; she's like a mad cat' (*JE* 12). Both the idealist and the realist concepts of literature, however, are based on a mirror-like concept of the reading process. The idealists assumed that the reader, by identifying with an image of perfection, would become more perfect herself. The realists, on the other hand, assumed that readers needed above all confirmation of their own imperfect existence.

Ideals, of course, are subject to historical change; Charlotte Brontë's 'realist' heroine has become an ideal of non-conformity for later readers. Valerie Grosvenor Myer argues that 'Jane Eyre has been an inspiration and example to generations of clever girls . . . She is the first defiantly intellectual heroine in English literature' (1987: 108). Her defiance, moreover, is as important as her intellect. The playbill for the Children's Theatre Company production of *young jane eyre* in Minneapolis (1988) reads:

> ten-year-old Jane is thrust into a frightening . . . orphanage. But the waif's spirit does not succumb. A passionate testament to the courage and fortitude of youth, the power of love, and the eternal promise of a brighter tomorrow.

In Stevie Davies's *Arms and the Girl*, the abused child January seems to draw courage from an example which we recognize, though she does not: '*I care for myself*, she seems to be saying, from behind her customary screen of mutinous defiance', and from her state of extremity she reaches out, like Jane, to the 'kind eye' of the moon (*JE* 1992 Davies: 144, 162). Jane's 'testament', moreover, speaks beyond the white Anglo-Saxon world. As women in the real world begin to make their experiences known to one another, it appears that *Jane Eyre* has been an influence in very diverse lives. Patricia Duncker quotes O. C. Ogunyemi as evidence that *Jane Eyre* as a 'feminist utopia is for white women only' (Duncker 1992: 24–7); but Maya Angelou writes,

> when I read the Brontës, I was a small black girl in the dirt roads of Arkansas during the depression. The society was against me surviving at all, but when I read about Heathcliffe [sic] and Jane Eyre, white society in that mean town had no power against me. (Angelou 1991; see also *JE* 1970 Angelou)

Tsitsi Dangarembga's heroine Tambudzai, a black child in Rhodesia, writes, 'I read everything from Enid Blyton to the Brontë sisters, and responded to them all . . . Thus began the period of my reincarnation' (*JE* 1988 Dangarembga). In the Brontë Parsonage Museum at Haworth there is a handwritten comment from a Japanese woman called Hideko Maki on a Japanese stage production of *Jane Eyre*; she says that the woman director, Kazue Kontaibo, 'has the same feeling on Jane Eyre, Charlotte Brontë as I have: She respects and loves Jane (Charlotte)'s dauntless, bracing way of life' (*JE* 1978 Kontaibo). A Japanese woman professor tells me that 'it is no exaggeration to say that "Jane Eyre" is read by almost all Japanese women and this novel greatly influenced their way towards a life of self-support. Even very young girls, . . . teen-agers read "Jane Eyre" sometimes recommended by their mothers' (Yuriko Yamawaki, personal communication 28.2.90). Barbara T. Christian, a black Caribbean woman, writes,

> Disturbed as I was by Brontë's portrayal of Bertha, I nonetheless loved *Jane Eyre* and identified with plain Jane . . . Despite the cultural differences between her world and mine . . . I saw that her life too was sharply constrained . . . Jane and I shared something in common, even as the mores of her society, even as the physical geography of her world were alien to me. (1988: 32–3)

The need for identification with literary models lies behind the 1970s phase of feminist literary criticism known as 'images of women' criticism. Arlyn Diamond, in *The Authority of Experience*, asks for 'authentic' pictures of women's lives, because she cannot 'recognise [her]self, or the women I know' in the female characters of male writers (quoted in Mills *et al.* 1989: 57). 'Authenticity', however, easily shades into idealism: by 1975, Cheri Register asks that 'A literary work should provide *role-models*, instill a positive sense of feminine identity by portraying women who are "self-actualising, whose identities are not dependent on men"' (quoted in Moi 1985: 47; see also Austen, Z. 1976: 551). Maurianne Adams, in *The Authority of Experience*, actually quotes a famous passage of *Jane Eyre* – 'women feel just as men feel; they need exercise for their faculties and a field for their efforts as much as their brothers do' – to prove precisely this point (quoted in Mills *et al.* 1989: 51). This authentic realism movement was partly discredited in the 1980s by post-structuralist critics who found the mirror theory of literature naive. Toril Moi, for instance, compares it with the misguided aims of socialist realism: 'instead of strong happy tractor drivers . . . , we are now presumably, to demand strong happy *women* tractor drivers' (1985: 8).

Maurianne Adams's model of reading is not, however, a static one: 'Every time we rethink and reassimilate Jane Eyre', she writes, 'we bring to it a new orientation' (in Mills *et al.* 1989: 55). Adult rereading of *Jane Eyre* is unnerving, she says, because we do not encounter the same novel 'we were engrossed by in our teens or preteens, when we saw in Jane's dreadful childhood . . . our own fantasies of feeling unloved and forever unloveable' (in Myer 1987: 108). As adult women, for instance, we have to come to terms with the precise kind of 'happy ending' offered by the novel. Each of the women I quoted as making Jane Eyre their heroine has, in fact, made a complicated negotiation between recognition and 'unnerving' difference. Pat Macpherson thus asks herself how Jane can be a 'heroine' both for her and her students twenty years later:

> I myself, at the age of thirteen looked down the years and refused my mother's desperate flirtation with the madwoman in the attic, and fashioned myself as watchful governess; Esther and Anna looked at me, a married feminist twenty years older, and at Jane's final deal with Rochester, and thought: 'It can be done'.
> In 1964, I had looked to fiction and romance (and later, to my career) as free space, a real escape from the power relations skewering my family. By 1984, those easy exits were closed. All gender relations and women's work were on the map of power relations, all fictional endings of romantic transcendence made 'corny' by the real lives of real mothers. (Macpherson 1989: xii, xi)

She concludes that

> what [my students] and I shared in *Jane Eyre* was a reading of ourselves, present-to-future, that half-described and half-prescribed our course out of lost girlhood to the resting place of fulfilled womanhood . . . From real women we learn . . . the limits of female space and power in the world as it presently is constituted . . . From fiction, we learn how far we might push the limits of our own space and power.' (xii).

For Barbara T. Christian this negotiation of sameness and difference extends over race and culture as well as over time:

> to read is not only to validate the self but also to participate in 'the other's' view of the world, the writer's view. Or why read? Writing and reading are means by which we communicate with one another, as Audre Lorde would say, 'bridge the joinings'. (1988: 34–5)

Maggie Berg, in her book, *Jane Eyre, Portrait of a Life*, argues that *Jane Eyre* itself provides a model for this process of negotiation. 'In the red-room', Berg argues, 'Jane sees herself as a rebellious slave, a hunger striker, the "scapegoat of the nursery" . . . "No doubt", says [Jane] the autobiographer in retrospect, "I was a precocious actress"'. Jane's self-dramatization here is equivalent to her looking into literary mirrors for an image of herself, just as Angelou, Dangarembga, Maki, Kontaibo, Christian and Macpherson look into *Jane Eyre*. 'This first identification of oneself in a mirror', Berg goes on,

> is regarded by Jacques Lacan as the most decisive stage in human development, constituting the awareness of oneself as an object of knowledge. Although the reflection is a misrepresentation, because static, it nevertheless confers the mark of adulthood: self-consciousness. (Berg, M. 1987: 37–8)

It is from this position of self-consciousness, achieved through repeated part-mirrorings of her self, that Jane is able to contribute to the symbolic construction of her identity. As Berg puts it, 'that Jane is the author of her own story is the single most important yet most neglected aspect of the novel' (24).

Many of the reproductions of *Jane Eyre* discussed in this book have tended to domesticate Jane's story, to emphasize its closure and to focus on her childhood experience, if at all, not as 'mad cat' but as victim. Recent attempts to interest children in the Brontë texts, however, have focused on the writing process. In 1988 the Brontë Parsonage Museum sponsored a national essay competition for schoolchildren, and more recently parties of children have been encouraged to write little books of their own after being shown round the parsonage by actors dressed as the Brontës (*BSG* 6: 1). Individual teachers have also encouraged children to use the Brontë texts as an impetus to their own writing, for instance in creating Heathcliff's missing years from *Wuthering Heights*. Even the Movieworld edition of *Wuthering Heights* includes among its final exercises the question, 'Do you like the end of the story? If you answer "Yes", can you say why? If you say "No", what changes do you want?' Adult writers have also been encouraged by the Brontë Society. When the novelist Charlotte Cory conducted a writers' workshop as part of the 1993 Ilkley Literature Festival, one of the exercises was to write a letter describing a visit to Haworth as in 1893, 1916, 1935 or 1950; the (actual) writers then constructed dialogues between the (supposed) writers. The result was to foreground the historical specificity of versions of the Brontë myth – a way of actively deconstructing current mythologies (*BSG* 9: 27–8). Recognition of the writing process also appears in unexpected places; in 1990 *Good Housekeeping* magazine launched a competition to rewrite the end of *Jane Eyre*, recognizing its force as a catalyst for new writing rather than as a role model. The result of this activity, whatever the quality of writing, must be to dispel the more passive aspects of identification by fostering an awareness of the constructed nature of the text.

The sixteen-year-old winner of the 1988 Brontë Society writing competition enacts the negotiation described by Maggie Berg between the mirror-phase of literary identification and writing. Her essay, 'A Brontë childhood', begins by impersonating Charlotte Brontë, but shifts at the end to the third person:

> Charlotte put down her pen . . . She thought of all the dreams and aspirations they had had, and of her governess sisters and broken brother. As she thought a new emotion swept her tiny body, and fired by a new wave of hope she resolved to urge herself and sisters and brother to follow their common passion: the written word. (Tillotson 1988)

The shift in narrative position here from first to third person indicates the developing 'self-consciousness' which enables the writer to recognize the distance between herself and Charlotte, albeit bridged by writing. This same process is explored in published work for young people. Sheila Greenwald's novel for teenage girls is entitled *It All Began With Jane Eyre* (1980). It begins,

> Franny tapped her pen impatiently on her desk and pulled at her lip. What was she to

do? Then it came to her. Just because nothing had happened in her life didn't mean she couldn't *make* something happen. She wrote, 'I will make something happen . . . I will go at least two steps further than any girl I've read about lately'.

Nevertheless this first stage of her endeavour is one of identification. Because her life is less interesting than fiction, Franny tries to fit the people in her life into roles provided first by *Jane Eyre*, and later by modern stories, scandalizing her family by imagining passion, incest and abortion among her relations:

> For Franny was convinced that her life could be guided by all the rules of novels. She fervently believed that if she was clever and careful and quick, she would find in her daily life a plot complete with heroes, heroines, minor characters, dramatic situations, calamities, and coincidences that would structure themselves into the form of a novel similar to the ones she had just read. (*JE* 1980 Greenwald: 47)

Eventually a literary friend persuades her to read *Jane Eyre* not just for its story but for its author's commentary: 'It is vain', Franny reads at last, 'to say human beings ought to be satisfied with tranquility: they must have action; and they will make it if they cannot find it' (122). Forced to confront this description of what she has done, she also realizes that writing is a kind of action; the last line of the novel repeats the first as she sits down to write, 'My mother thinks it all began with *Jane Eyre* . . .' (123). Sheila Greenwald's novel is not subtle, but it suggests that the processes familiar to feminist academics as writing the self, or searching for subjectivity, are proceeding on a broad front. The Franny Dillman who writes her own story occupies the same position as the critic Pat Macpherson, who affirms that

> my reading of Jane Eyre, and my feminism, started from the questions of my own adolescence. In identifying with Jane Eyre as the subject, the narrator, the moral agent of her own experience, I practised how to become the nervy heroine, rather than the confused victim, of my own experience. (1989: xiii)

Even a Mills and Boon novel which completely misreads *Jane Eyre* nevertheless shows its heroine in this active negotiation with the (misunderstood) earlier text. In *Devil Within*, by Catherine George (1984), the heroine conceives Jane Eyre to be a timid Victorian spinster:

> The fictional Mr Rochester in Jane Eyre was a pussycat compared with the dour, unfriendly man who had met her today without a word of welcome. Not that she was any Jane Eyre, either, decided Claudia – it would take more than a bit of boorish behaviour to put her off life in this idyllic spot. (*JE* 1984 George: 37)

Claudia's self-construction involves rejection of what, to her, is the *Jane Eyre* image of sexual propriety: 'her attitude had been one of antediluvian rectitude, like some Victorian prunes-and-prisms spinster drawing her skirts aside from contact with man's baser instincts' (171). If one reads for the outcome of the story, *Devil Within* is a reactionary story in feminist terms, ending with Claudia being deeply satisfied with the prospect of marrying 'one of those chauvinists who consider woman's place is in the home' (191). There is no doubt, however, that Claudia does go through the process described by Maurianne Adams and Pat Macpherson, of matching herself against a partially accurate mirror-image. For her, liberation and change is constituted by a less 'Victorian' attitude to sex, and although sophisticated feminists may feel that we have 'seen through' the permissiveness of the 1970s, there is still a measure of self-assertion to be read in Claudia's recognition of advance from an earlier model: 'It was hard to recognise the grim, dour Mr Rochester in this elated male creature who was occupying her bed in such flagrant nudity' (190).

Whether Claudia's Jane Eyre is a paper tiger, or whether for her and her readers emancipation from a Victorian mirror-image is still a real necessity is difficult to tell. Perhaps the important thing is that the process of emerging from misrecognition in order to write one's own story can be observed in novels as different as *Devil Within* and *Oranges Are Not the Only Fruit*. Jeanette Winterson's heroine ends by rewriting *Jane Eyre* as a love story between women:

> Romantic love has been diluted into paperback form and has sold thousands and millions of copies. Somewhere it is still in the original, written on tablets of stone. I would cross seas and suffer sunstroke and give away all I have, but not for a man, because they want to be the destroyer and never the destroyed. That is why they are unfit for romantic love. There are exceptions and I hope they are happy. (*JE* 1985 Winterson)

The missionary texts referred to at the beginning of this section rewrote *Jane Eyre* so as to show Jane 'drawing her skirts aside from contact with man's baser instincts' and joining St John in the quest for the New Jerusalem. The Russ Abbot sketch (described on page 223) rewrites *Jane Eyre* in terms of dominant gender relations determined precisely by 'man's baser instincts'. Jeanette Winterson refuses this alternative by refusing men as romantic partners. The *Good Housekeeping* competition described above included a version of *Jane Eyre* by Clare Boylan in which Jane discovers that she is to be the latest in a whole series of wives each of whom has been locked up in the attic and called mad. This version, which obviously suggests a feminist critique of marriage and the romance hero, ends with Jane going off to India to join St John in the spirit of 'adventure' (*JE* 1990 Boylan: 140). Clare Boylan's ending is thus, at the level of story, the same as the expurgated missionary texts – yet the import of the two versions is different because of the context of reception. Although these examples are extreme in that they actually rewrite their original, they still demonstrate the more general proposition that meaning is always a process of interaction between the original text and its historically specific readers. Because each reading differs according to the needs of the readers, *Jane Eyre* does not exactly provide a role model but rather a point of departure, so that many women who have taken courage from Jane's example can say, like Franny Dillman, that 'It all began with *Jane Eyre*' (*JE* 1990 Greenwald).

Temma Berg writes: 'Like Brownstein, I see the history of the English novel as a series of re-constructions or re-inventions of feminine possibility' (1985: 135 n6). Catherine Earnshaw, however, has not functioned for women readers in the same way as Jane Eyre, and there are several possible reasons for this. One is that

Catherine's waywardness goes well beyond defiance, verging on hysteria. Nelly Dean tells us that 'her spirits were always at high-water mark . . . A wild, wick slip she was . . . At fifteen she was the queen of the country-side . . .: and she did turn out a haughty, headstrong creature!' (*WH* 40, 65). In I viii, not getting her own way, she pinches Nelly, shakes little Hareton, boxes Edgar's ear and then threatens to 'cry – I'll cry myself sick!'. Nelly warns Edgar: '"Miss is dreadfully wayward, sir! . . . As bad as any marred child – you'd better be riding home, or else she will be sick, only to grieve us"' (70–2). Feminist writers on nineteenth-century hysteria point out that 'the hysterical fit, for many women, must have been the only acceptable outburst – of rage, of despair, or simply of *energy* – possible' (Ehrenreich and English 1979: 124); nevertheless it seems the desperate ploy of the victim rather than the chosen exercise of power. In another essay I have argued that Catherine's apparent self-destruction – her turning her fits of passion to account – has to be seen not as wilful egotism but as her despairing response to her two lovers' failure to love her enough to share her attention (*WH* xxxviii). Whatever our explanation, the outcome to her story is enviable only to the few who feel the world well lost for love; the uneasiness expressed by Maurianne Adams about the 'happy ending' to *Jane Eyre* is nothing compared with Catherine Earnshaw's fate. The decisive reason that Catherine is not imitated, however, may be that because she does not tell her own story, readers cannot make the same movement as in *Jane Eyre* from identification to writing. *Wuthering Heights* seems to offer no departure point for later women, and has, as we have seen, been reproduced mostly by men.

Nevertheless there are women who include *Wuthering Heights* in their list of influential books. H.D., writing in 1927, uses the name as a shorthand for everything which is not London and the *avant garde* when Julia experiences a kind of rebirth in Cornwall: 'wind from *Wuthering Heights* lifted a very visible dark wing from the sea . . .'. Fifty years later, in *Lady Oracle*, the focus has come to rest on Heathcliff, who represents everything dangerous and exotic in a lover. Seeing the Royal Porcupine subside into dull Chuck Brewer, Joan Foster asks, 'Was every Heathcliff a Linton in disguise?' (*WH* 1976 Atwood [1982: 269]). Rachel Brownstein, in *Becoming a Heroine*, sees life as a battle. On one side, there is the 'tyranny' of 'submission to "The Right Thing"' – what Creon, convention, and one's mother advised'.

> On the other side were massed the forces of Emily Brontë. Heathcliff, in 1956, was as he always had been, dark and indefinably dissolute, angry and sullen; he drank Scotch and smoked a little reefer, when he could get it, and hung out with Negroes and homosexuals in the West End Bar. Sexually, he meant business. He was a writer. What you would be was his woman. You would get up in the morning, after going to bed with him in his apartment, and you would be able to say, like Cathy, 'I am Heathcliff'. No, you could write it, and then everyone else would say, 'She is Heathcliff'. If there was paper in the house. If he let you get out of bed. If there was a bed. (Brownstein [1982] 1984: 17, 18)

Though not a very positive or attractive picture, the forces of Emily Brontë are opposed to what is dull, conventional and predictable, and sometimes this is just what women need – even very young women.

It is notable, however, that this quoted paragraph begins not with Catherine or Heathcliff, but with 'the massed forces of Emily Brontë'. As with the New Women of the 1890s, recent women are happier to identify with the writer than with her character; Brownstein's enthusiasm for being 'Heathcliff's woman' seems to run into the sand at the end of her paragraph. Tabitha, a student in Penelope Lively's novel, *Perfect Happiness*, is also one of those young women who

> had lived, she realized, ever since she could confidently read, through the pages of books. She had been Tess and Natasha and Catherine Earnshaw and the girl in *Rebecca* and later and more ambitiously Madame Bovary and Anna Karenina. She knew all about passion and suffering and the complexity of things . . . she was prepared for anything . . . (*JE* 1983 Lively: 187).

Nevertheless, facing the death of her father, she finds that 'when it comes to the point they have led you up the garden path: Catherine Earnshaw and Tess and Jane Eyre and Dorothea and Anna and the rest of them. Whatever you thought you knew about it, you do not' (91).

Emily Brontë is a figure who seems to be invoked especially in novels confronting death. In Stephanie Dowrick's novel, *Running Backwards Over Sand*, Zoe is an independent and successful woman who nevertheless has difficulty coming to terms with the death of her mother when she was nine. In the midst of an obsessive love affair, she searches the Brontë texts 'for some understanding of how those women dealt with the imminence, and presence, of death through – or was it while maintaining? – their creativity' (*WH* 1985 Dowrick: 312]). Her lover, Gabriel, begins to comment on her plans to write a novel involving the Brontës and she is oppressed by the old idea 'that whatever she knew Gabriel would know more and better' (314); they have an argument, which she wins. The point seems to be that the Brontës – Emily especially – have given her the strength, which she needed, to assert herself against his too dominant presence.

Jane Gardam's novel for teenage girls, *The Summer After the Funeral* (1973), also proffers Emily, not Catherine, as a focus of fascination for her heroine, Athene Price. Athene is a parson's daughter, both beautiful and dutiful but afflicted by a 'private madness' (*WH* 1973 Gardam: 21). She realizes the potential impact of saying to her teacher, 'Please, Miss Beecroft, I've just discovered that I am Emily Brontë' (25), but nevertheless it is her own likeness that looks back from Branwell's portrait (22), and the cover illustration by Graham Dean shows the familiar Emily Brontë of that portrait holding a book containing the portrait. The moment of visual identification is swiftly followed by reading Emily's work, after which 'she discovered that she had lived before' (23). Unlike the saintly Emily of the 1890s, however, this Emily means trouble.

> 'I mean, she was violent. Flinging those vicars out! Holding open those great iron gates and shouting!' (She had read *Shirley* now and knew that Shirley and Emily were one person.) 'And being so difficult, and everyone being worried about whether she'd

behave properly. 'Was Emily all right?' – Charlotte dashing out to ask someone if Emily had been unbearable on a walk on the moors . . .'.

   'I'm not like that. I am the absolute opposite . . .'

   'And then – Heathcliff?' (23–4)

After the death of her beloved father Athene is confronted by Heathcliff in a summer-house during a duty visit to an aunt. Rather like Brownstein's Heathcliff, 'he said nothing but continued to stand watching her, leaning against the tree-trunk door frame, smoking a cigarette. His eyes were heavy and sleepy, his hair very thick and long, his mouth discontented, rather curly, clear cut' (39). Later she surprises him with a girl in the tennis pavilion but nevertheless writes, 'My darling, Oh my darling. I love you, I adore you. I want you. My darling my darling my darling my darling my darling my darling my darling my darling. Always – Athene' (50). She tears the letter up, but from now on, appalled by the available patterns of female life, she becomes 'dreadfully wayward' – the 'absolute opposite' of her usual self. She is rude to her father's friend, fears she has absent-mindedly lost her virginity and falls in love with a married schoolteacher who declares his love in Haworth Parsonage (134). Her 'being so difficult' ends with her climbing the church tower where the spectacle of all her friends and relatives gathered below, 'thinking only about her' (151) brings her down again. She returns to her brisk and practical mother, becoming herself brisk and outspoken, less conventionally pretty and well-behaved, more political and also 'more fun' (154). The Heathcliff-figure also proves to be accessible through her family, not an escape from it. As a female *Bildungsroman*, the novel is an oddity in that what the heroine has to learn initially is not to come down to earth but to leave it. Athene's revolt is not, however, the fruitless hysteria of Catherine Earnshaw, but provides a critique of Oedipal orthodoxy, allowing her to recognize both her own sexuality and her previously unvalued mother. The Emily Brontë projected by Gardam's novel is a heroine not victimized by but able to contain the contradictions of her text.

   Placing *The Summer After the Funeral* next to *Becoming a Heroine*, we can see that Emily Brontë has taught one young woman to come home to mother, and another to dare to evade her; there is no way of prescribing or predicting the endless dialogue of the text with successive readers. For Barbara T. Christian it is this, and not any concept of role models, which is the point of reading as a woman:

> Language is one means by which we sound out the sameness/difference that we all are. And if we cannot grapple with that sameness/difference in texts and see it as a creative possibility rather than a threat, how are we to effect any lasting change beyond the text? In the world? (Christian 1988: 36)

The sequels syndrome: writing beyond the ending?

At the end of this huge book I hardly need assert that one of the prime effects of the Brontë texts is to prompt people to write new texts. Robert Duckett, editor of the *Brontë Society Gazette,* comments on the large amount of poetry received from members (*BSG* 6); much of this, however, offers rhyme and emotion as substitute for metre, syntax and history. One difference between such poems and Sylvia Plath's 'Wuthering Heights' (1961) is that while her poem is conscious of the seduction of the Brontë myth and of the contrast between the then and the now (in which the present always seems inadequate), it is also aware of the delusory nature of myths and of the fact that passion, made romantic by time, is related semantically to suffering. Standing on the moortop, Plath perceives that

> . . . the wind
> Pours by like destiny, bending
> Everything in one direction . . .
> The sky leans on me, me, the one upright
> Among all horizontals.

The particularities of the scene (wind, sky), while recalling Emily Brontë's words ('thorns all stretching their limbs one way' (*WH* 2)) are so presented as to offer an explanation of what less stringent writers call, without explanation, Fate, or elemental forces. Plath's verbs (pours, bending, leans), acting upon the speaker, reveal the elemental as entropy, the tendency of nature to reduce the exceptional to the state of common inertia; 'the roots of the heather . . . invite me /To whiten my bones among them'. Nevertheless,

> The horizons ring me . . .
> Like a series of promises, as I step forward

– their prospects, even though they 'dissolve and dissolve', contrast alluringly with the life below, where

> Now, in valleys narrow
> And black as purses, the house lights
> Gleam like small change.

What constitutes the small change of the valleys is ambiguous: the life of Thrushcross Grange (as opposed to Wuthering Heights)? Present-day values in general? Or, more specifically, the Brontë industry, including the writer and reader of the poem? The values of this currency, quantified by textbooks and tourist guides, intervene between valley and horizon, precluding even while feeding the impulse to realize the dissolving promises of the landscape.

With the Derridean perception that absence is a kind of presence, the (unfulfillable) imperative to revisit the Brontës still gives rise to genuine, if self-ironizing, anguish. In Ursula Bentley's novel, *The Natural Order* (1982), the heroine declares,

> Reader, I was born in Kingston Hospital (Alight at Norbiton) and brought up in Worcester Park. It follows that well into adolescence my close friends – equally disadvantaged – and I were never without the bitter taste of not having been one of the Brontë sisters . . . In a recent biography of Charlotte, Ms. Margot Peters has

written, 'What 20th-century city dweller would not like to undergo the torments of solitude in a moorland village?' I knew torment all right – but the torment of giving one's address as 53 Forsythe Gardens, the torment of a complete dearth of torment. (cover)

More seriously, Nicole Ward Jouve writes that 'I, a French woman, had settled in Yorkshire, because myths like the Brontës, spaces like the moors, had appealed to me as deeply nurturing, promising freedom and scope'. One of the motivations behind her search to understand the Yorkshire Ripper is that 'I had to reclaim those landscapes'. Throughout her brilliant and wide-ranging book the Brontë texts remain as a kind of fixed star to orientate the present (Jouve 1986: 18; see also 52, 69, 156). It is, however, a process which in other hands becomes sentimental. An unidentified poem called 'A Visit to Brontëland' compares the present Haworth, where 'the television aerial aspires' with that sterner time when 'No idle toy would have tempted Branwell /From the "Bull" and brandy; or kept that sister /From her tragic poems'. The equation of pub and poetry suggests a glamorizing of the past which Plath might well have called 'small change'. Merle Collins also erects 'the Brontës' into a standard of 'art /that had no colour /of pleasure that existed /for its artistic self'. In comparison with that mythical time, Collins finds that 'Yorkshire when I visited, later, /was not exactly as I remembered it'. Stan Barstow also uses the then-and-now dialogue to raise questions about colour. His novel, *A Brother's Tale*, begins in Haworth, which reminds his characters of nineteenth-century social conditions; they compare the lazy car-borne present and 'those famous young women who themselves thought nothing of walking four miles to Keighley'. The contrast is problematized, however, when, sitting in the Black Bull, watching some National Front supporters, they hear a black man compare England in the nineteenth century with the present-day third world. The narrator then shows his wife a page of *Jane Eyre* in which he has marked the passage: 'It is weak and silly to say you *cannot bear* what it is your fate to bear' (Barstow 1980: 65, 71).

Uncomfortable racial echoes are also found in V. S Naipaul's novel, *The Guerrillas* (1975). Set in Trinidad, the novel nevertheless opens with the disorientating words, 'After lunch Jane and Roche left their house to drive to Thrushcross Grange' (*WH* 1975 Naipaul: 9). The literary place-name, it seems, has been chosen by Jimmy Ahmed for his agricultural commune, and later Jane finds the manuscript of a novel which Jimmy is writing, in which a fictional version of herself has a conversation with Jimmy about *Wuthering Heights*. At first it seems that he values it simply as a sign of culture – '"Ah", he said . . ., "you are looking at that great work of the Brontës. What a gifted family, it makes you believe in heredity. Would you like some tea?"' (40). Later, still in Jimmy's novel, we find that the Brontë reference has a more pointed significance. The Jane of the novel speaks about Jimmy:

'He's the leader they're waiting for and the day will come of that I'm convinced when they will parade in the streets and offer him the crown, everybody will say then "This man was born in the back room of a Chinese grocery, but as Catherine said to Heathcliff 'Your mother was a Indian princess and your father was the Emperor of

China', we knew it all along" and that was in the middle of England mark you, in the days when they had no racial feeling before all those people from Jamaica and Pakistan came and spoiled the country for a man like him. They will see him then like a prince, with his gold colour.' (62)

According to John Thieme, Jimmy Ahmed

> is based on the figure of Abdul Malik (Michael X) . . .: like Malik, Jimmy is a self-styled 'black' radical of mixed parentage, who, after rising to fame in England, has been deported as a criminal . . ., has rather futilely tried to set up an agricultural commune in his home island; and . . . his love/hate relationship with the white world . . . lead[s] to his involvement in the killing an English girl. (Thieme 1979: 125)

As Thieme points out, there are a number of ironies involved in Jimmy's fantasy – not least the idea of a prelapsarian England free from racial prejudice – but nevertheless this 'view from the island' gives a startling perspective on the Heathcliff of Emily Brontë's novel built on its own hints that he might be 'a little Lascar, or an American or Spanish castaway' (*WH* 48). Jimmy's dream of power is, however, like that of Peter Sutcliffe, the Yorkshire Ripper, a nastier and more fleshly affair than Heathcliff's cruelty. Nicole Ward Jouve writes, 'Wuthering Heights may be dead, and all the nobility it entailed. Dreams of taking the top by storm stay around. The methods get worse' (Jouve 1986: 52). Jimmy, baulked of genuine revolution, enacts his resentment against white power by raping and killing Jane. As in *Devil Within*, Jimmy's concept of Jane is a misrecognition of Jane Eyre, 'a type of the passive, sexually chaste heroine of the traditional English novel' (Thieme 1979: 127). In fact the Jane of Naipaul's novel is an independent and sexually experienced woman, looking to Roche, a white liberal refugee from South Africa, to suggest a meaningful life. Ironically, Roche is a spent force, who in effect colludes in Jane's death. Wherever you look in Naipaul's novel, the Victorian names reverse or disappoint the expectations they arouse, a 'series of promises' that 'dissolve and dissolve'. Thieme's article, which pursues these false parallels in detail, ends by quoting Naipaul's comment on *Wide Sargasso Sea*, equally apt to his own novel: 'an order has collapsed and some people are "marooned" . . . a world that appeared simple is now seen to be diseased, and is no longer habitable' (Thieme 1979: 124, 130).

On the other side of the world, in New Zealand, Janet Frame invokes the Brontës in an effort to inhabit the uninhabitable world. In her autobiographical essay, 'Beginnings', she writes,

> Sometimes, when it seemed to us that our family was doomed, we would console ourselves by remembering the Brontës and drawing between them and us a grandiose dramatic parallel . . . With a background of poverty, drunkenness, attempted murder and near-madness, it was inevitable that we should feel close to the Brontës. (quoted in Delbaere-Garant 1979: 704–5)

She and her two sisters 'became' Charlotte, Emily and Anne. Commenting on Janet Frame's response to Emily Brontë, Jeanne Delbaere-Garant overstates Emily's ability to contain the contradictions of her novel, so that 'the world of vision and the world of fact live side by side in benevolent tolerance' (708). It is startling, however, to find this critic using, to discuss Janet Frame's intensely personal accounts of madness, the vocabulary of Naipaul's *Guerrillas*. As in Naipaul, the Brontës provide an emblem against which to measure the present

> cosmic pessimism of a whole generation. The disintegration of the traditional values and the scientific organization of the mass culture have left the individual self stranded on a solipsistic beach at the edge of the world . . . The wide spaces of the Yorkshire moors . . . had contracted . . . into a cleft in the deepest recesses of the mind. (710)

Janet Frame, Delbaere-Garant argues, 'is as romantic as Emily Brontë but she is forced to resort to the guerrilla tactics and total war threats of her age' because the bridge 'between "this" world and "that" world . . . has been blown up' (710). In Doris Lessing's *The Four-Gated City* (*JE* 1972 Lessing), Lynda Goldridge is also a 'madwoman' who has a privileged perception of the disintegration of the modern world through war, famine and disease. Inhabiting the basement rather than the attic of her Thornfield Hall, she emerges at the end not to die but to form one of a tiny band of survivors of a world catastrophe, united by their ability for psychic telecommunication.

The cool tone of Muriel Spark's novel, *Not To Disturb* (*JE*: 1971), appears at first to contrast with these apocalyptic echoes; its outcome, however, is as potentially revolutionary. The novel has no overt Brontë references, but a number of features ironically gesture towards *Jane Eyre*. Without summarizing the story, we can note that within a 'big house' setting, the servants lay claim to money and power not primarily by 'marrying into' a higher class but by easing its self-destruction – carrying out to the letter the instruction 'not to disturb' – and selling the story to the press. The unemotional present-tense narrative reads like a play script with stage directions; the servants are at ease with the procedures of law, finance and telecommunication which in this text is not telepathic but electronic. The lunatic is a young man, not a madwoman; his cries are of lustful delight; and the wedding with which the story ends is between 'Jane' (here pregnant to an indeterminate father) and the lunatic who is the unwitting but legal heir to wealth and status. The final irony is that when the butler tries to telephone the ostensible heir, he is answered by *his* butler, who is most scrupulously obeying orders 'not to disturb'. In this version of 'then and now', the lower orders who are coming into ascendancy are as cultured and intelligent as their 'betters'; they are the natural inheritors of an age of commerce and technology; they are, moreover, much more successful in avoiding the destructive consequences of passion.

The texts dealt with so far in this section have suggested Brontë parallels by allusion or structural echoes which exploit the ironic or tragic distance between then and now. There has also, however, been a crop of texts, intensifying in the 1990s, which attempt to 'grapple with that sameness/difference' by extending the original stories of a variety of famous texts by Jane Austen, the Brontës and Thomas Hardy among others (e.g. Martin, V. [1990] 1991; Ripley [1991] 1992; Hill 1993; Tennant

1993, [1993] 1994; Bigsby 1994; *WH* 1990 Urquhart, 1992 Haire-Sargeant; *JE* 1991 Kydd; see Stoneman 1995b). Some of these authors themselves recognize that they are part of a syndrome; Alexandra Ripley, Lin Haire-Sargeant, Emma Tennant, Chris Bigsby and Susan Hill all took part in a discussion entitled 'Sequels by another hand' at the 1993 Cheltenham Literature Festival. Most readers regard sequels as secondary not just in the neutral sense of 'coming after' their originals but also in the qualitative sense of being inferior, even ludicrous. 'Son of Heathcliff' is bound to raise a smile. There is, however, considerable formal variation between texts loosely grouped under this title. Not all of them form a *continuation* of a preceding narrative; most bear some more complicated relationship to their originating text. This makes it useful to adopt the term 'incremental literature', used by Christopher Richards in his thesis 'The idea of the sequel' (1989). 'Incremental literature' includes all literature which builds on a previously existing text, without defining the nature of the relationship. It includes stories of what happens *before* the originating text, such as Jean Rhys's *Wide Sargasso Sea*; or stories which are 'missed out' of the original, like Heathcliff's missing years in Lin Haire-Sargeant's *Heathcliff*; stories of marginal figures, such as Robbie Kydd's *The Quiet Stranger*, which tells the life history of Richard Mason, Bertha's brother in *Jane Eyre*; or stories which give a new perspective on known events, like Geoffrey Wheatcroft's *Catherine, Her Book*, in which Catherine, after her marriage, elaborates upon her childish diary paper. Perhaps most interesting are the texts which acknowledge the fictionality of the original and show us their effects in the real lives of later readers; Jane Urquhart's *Changing Heaven* bears this relationship to *Wuthering Heights*. The inclusiveness of the term 'incremental literature' leads us to question whether the sequel is, in fact, either marginal or inferior, since it performs an intertextual function accepted as culturally central where the originating text is *Electra*, *Prometheus Bound*, or *The Metamorphoses* of Ovid. I am also attracted by a subsidiary *Shorter Oxford English Dictionary* definition of sequel as 'the remaining part of a narrative'. This suggests a *necessary* rather than arbitrary continuation, implying Macherey's perception that texts are not completed while 'they have not finished being read' ([1966] 1978: 70). What is regarded as constituting *the* remaining part depends on ideological priorities. As feminists we might argue that women's meanings are the remaining part left out of many mainstream texts.

In a literal sense, sequels attempt writing beyond the ending of their originals; but this phrase has acquired evaluative critical meanings. John Stokes, in his book, *Fin de Siècle, Fin du Globe* (1992), assumes that all critical considerations of 'endings' now inevitably look back to Frank Kermode's *The Sense of an Ending* (1967). Subtitled *Studies in the Theory of Fiction*, Kermode's book makes connections between our sense of epoch and the structure of novels, suggesting that 'we project ourselves – a small, humble elect, perhaps – past the End, so as to see the structure whole, a thing we cannot do from our spot of time in the middle' (1967: 8). The sense of a novel ending, he implies, depends paradoxically on a sense of social life continuing; as Barthes was later to write, the design of traditional novels 'implies a return to order' (quoted in Modleski 1982: 88). Historically, Kermode points to the opposite paradox that the apocalyptic sense of an ending produced by the Cold War was accompanied by reluctance in post-war fiction writers to bring their narratives to an end. Kermode's analysis has been seminal, but his assumptions that his audience is an elite, that fiction always aims to create a whole and that history is always masculine, all beg 'the remaining part of the narrative'. Some of this is told by Rachel Blau du Plessis's book, *Writing Beyond the Ending* (1985).

Du Plessis's argument is that, in nineteenth-century texts dealing with women, 'the romance plot . . . is a trope for the sex-gender system as a whole' (5). Nineteenth-century novels dealing with women, she argues, often combine a romance plot with a quest or *Bildung* plot despite some element of contradiction between them. This contradiction has, she argues,

> one main mode of resolution: an ending in which one part of that contradiction, usually quest or *Bildung*, is set aside or repressed, whether by marriage or by death. It is the project of twentieth-century women writers to solve the contradiction between love and quest . . . by offering a different set of choices. They invent a complex of narrative acts with psychosocial meanings, which will be studied here as 'writing beyond the ending'. (3–4)

The twentieth-century writers dealt with by du Plessis include well-known innovators such as Olive Schreiner, Virginia Woolf and H.D., in whose works it is easy to perceive revolution at the level of the plot, and even at the level of the sentence. The late twentieth century sequel writers discussed here are not all conscious innovators, but sequels in themselves imply a revisionist intention. Incremental writing has to involve more than imitation of an original; the act of looking back from the 1990s to a text from a previous age provides a double perspective which does not simply reinscribe its original. I want to consider whether these writers tell 'the remaining part' of their source narrative in a way which has political significance; whether the merely technical act of 'writing beyond the ending' can be construed in the constructive sense of Rachel Blau du Plessis's book.

It is interesting that while the previous section of this chapter, which dealt with feminist revisions, was largely devoted to *Jane Eyre*, the sequels, which aim at a more general readership, have overwhelmingly focused on *Wuthering Heights*, and this seems to be because, while the female protagonist of *Wuthering Heights* seems to resist identification, the 'open' nature of the story invites completion. The first pair of incremental novels I have found predate the current millennial syndrome. One is Jeffrey Caine's *Heathcliff* (*WH* 1977 Caine), which tells the story of Heathcliff's missing years; the other Anna L'Estrange's *Return to Wuthering Heights* (*WH* 1978 L'Estrange), which tells the story of Catherine and Hareton and their descendants. The interesting thing about this pair of novels, aimed at a general paperback market, is that they reproduce the world of *Wuthering Heights* transformed in gender-specific genres. Jeffrey Caine's *Heathcliff* is a fast-moving, hard-hitting picaresque story of fist-fights, card-games, amorous intrigues, tangles with the law and breathtaking ruses. In this version of Heathcliff's missing years he has hardly left Gimmerton before he is adopted by a highwayman, hardly arrives in London before becoming toy-boy to a lady of fashion, and ends by cheating the gallows literally, appearing to be hanged but escaping by bribery and clever medication.

It is not, however, a thoughtless book. The detailed descriptions of violence (for instance, in chapter 3) establish a masculine culture into which Heathcliff has little option but to fit. In chapter 5 he allies himself with rioters who destroy upper-class property, just as Naipaul's Jimmy Ahmed sees Heathcliff as the natural hero of the dispossessed. On the other hand, the first phase of his self-education takes place in a *lady's* library, including Gothic novels and Romantic poets. He likens himself to Byron's Manfred (possibly one of Emily Brontë's sources) and this reflects back on Emily Brontë's novel, making us consider whether Heathcliff's behaviour in the latter part of the novel might be conscious self-dramatization. The mediation of layers of scholarship, even in a popular novel like this one, thus precludes a subsequent innocent response to the Brontë texts. The fact that the literary sources of Gothic imagery are spelled out in this novel also has the effect of 'denaturalizing' the Gothic effects of *Wuthering Heights*, revealing them in particular as effects of the power which men have historically wielded over women. In chapter 6 of Caine's *Heathcliff*, Heathcliff ransacks the library of Lord Mansfield (Lord Chief Justice of England, famous for the judgement in 1772 that slavery is illegal on British soil), and carries away a copy of Blackstone's *Commentaries on the English Law* (1765). This not only explains how Heathcliff is later able to go so unerringly about his plot to become master of both houses, but also highlights the gender-dominance which, by endorsing the legal slavery of women, opens the path of revenge. Feminist historians have made Blackstone famous outside legal circles for his summary of the status of married women: 'By marriage the very being or legal existence of a woman is suspended, or at least it is incorporated or consolidated into that of the husband, under whose wing, protection and cover she performs everything'. Commenting on this statement, Ray Strachey writes:

> This, in plainer language, meant that the property, the earnings, the liberty, and even the conscience of a wife all belonged to her husband, as did also the children she might bear. The incorporation and consolidation were complete, 'my wife and I are one, and I am he'; and since there was no divorce obtainable for a woman before 1857, there was no way of escape save death. ([1928] 1978: 15)

Gilbert and Gubar argue that in *Wuthering Heights*, Heathcliff and Edgar represent two different types of masculine power – one depending on physical force, and the other on the legally documented ownership of property (1979: 281). Jeffrey Caine's Heathcliff cleverly amalgamates the two, ready for any fray which offers, but also studying Blackstone 'as the pious do their Bibles' (*WH* 1977 Caine: 175). Commenting on *Jules et Jim* in Chapter 5 (above), I called it ironic that the sworn enemies in Emily Brontë's novel should, in Roché's, be sworn friends. Caine's novel, rooted in popular conceptions of masculine bonding, shows that friends and enemies may not be so far apart; Durrant and Heathcliff are like 'two small boys daring each other to a contest and becoming firm friends in the process' (161). The adventures of these three years, as shown by Jeffrey Caine, reflect back onto Emily

Brontë's book, making us see Heathcliff's long revenge in the context of a world in which men establish themselves in one another's eyes by competing, among other things, for women. Catherine thus becomes not a soul-mate but an item in a transaction which is essentially between men. Judged as 'the remaining part' of *Wuthering Heights, Heathcliff* is both shrewd and limiting, offering explanations of Heathcliff's behaviour which are only too plausible in terms of gender ideology, but failing to suggest the promise of escape which forms the main appeal of the earlier novel.

Anna L'Estrange, on the other hand, adopts the popular 'family saga' format to show the second Catherine haunted by that promise, represented by her unknown mother. Although L'Estrange rejects much literary criticism, she understands that the romantic/sexual quest is psychologically linked with the quest for the lost mother (*WH* 1978 L'Estrange: v, ix–x). In *Return to Wuthering Heights*, the younger Catherine becomes ill, explaining to Nelly's niece, 'You know what ails me, Agnes. I must go to Wuthering Heights where my mother awaits me' (47). What she finds at the Heights, however, is Heathcliff's illegitimate son, Jack. Her affair with him, enacted in her mother's bed, is both an escape from her conventional marriage with Hareton and an expression of desire for something beyond: 'It is not only Jack but the *place* that gives me freedom. Jack has the spirit of Wuthering Heights about him; the love of the moors. He is at home there, he told me; and he is at home in my arms' (103–4). There is a hint here of Dorothy Dinnerstein's vision of sexuality as 'a wild place to be visited for pleasure, a special preserve where old, primitive regions of human personality can be rediscovered' ([1976] 1987: 113–14). The characters do not, however, escape the historical constructions of sexuality. The story extends beyond the young Catherine to her legitimate daughter, Margaret, who thinks that Jack is like 'Lord Byron . . . or some romantic knight from the novels of Sir Walter Scott' (223). Like Isabella in *Wuthering Heights*, Margaret is first seduced and then ill-treated by Jack. The men, meanwhile, are partaking in History, Jack fighting with the Duke of Wellington, Hareton investing in industry, his son Rainton going off on the Beagle as a botanist and others becoming rich in South America or India. Margaret eventually marries well and becomes a society hostess and mistress of Lord Palmerston – in other words theirs becomes a story of dynasty, while the brutal and unhappy Anthony Heathcliff, illegitimate son of Jack and the younger Catherine, retires to Wuthering Heights to provide the 'dissolving promise' of the 'beyond' for later generations.

Edward Said defines the classic realist text as 'dynastic in form, concerned with ideas of genesis and family continuity' and hence 'mimetic, bound to sources and origins' (summarized by Shuttleworth 1984: 54). We might object, therefore, that L'Estrange reduces Emily Brontë's proto-modernist text to the shape of classic realism. Her family saga, however, reminds us that the continuity Said speaks of extends forward into the future as well as back into the past, and can be a way of evading closure. Roland Barthes defined the classic realist text as structured by the hermeneutic code which keeps readers looking for clues to strategic enigmas; expectation thus becomes 'the basic condition for truth: truth, these narratives tell us, is what is *at the end* of expectation' (quoted in Modleski 1982: 88). In L'Estrange's novel, however, the teleological impulse is not resolved by a final revelation. Unlike Caine's novel, L'Estrange's keeps the structure of the original, having Nelly Dean's niece tell the story to Lockwood's son, for along with the notion of dynasty goes the notion of serial storytelling; Tom Lockwood finds that writing this story has given purpose to his life, and he will return because 'in a decade or two there would be another story for me to hear' (*WH* 1978 L'Estrange: 365).

This emphasis on narrative process means that the novel is less like the classic realism of post-structuralist myth and more like popular soap opera, for, as Tania Modleski points out, 'soap operas do not end'. In so far as soap operas (and dynasty novels) have a specifically female audience, Modleski argues that 'truth for women is seen to lie not "at the end of expectation" but *in* expectation, not in the "return to order" but in (familial) disorder' (1982: 88). Moreover, because such serials 'can offer us depictions of people in situations which grow and change over time', they encourage a greater '"audience involvement, a sense of becoming a part of the lives and actions of the characters"' (Modleski 1982: 87, quoting Horace Newcomb). Anna L'Estrange is quite conscious that her book is of a different kind from *Wuthering Heights*:

> Emily was a poet and a mystic and I am neither . . . The marvellous imagery, the facility of detail and expression is what has made *Wuthering Heights* a work of art and it would be quite impossible for me to emulate it and foolish for me to try. And this realisation became my moment of truth. I wouldn't attempt to be like Emily. I would write a completely different kind of novel merely taking on her two main characters where she left off – Hareton and Cathy – and my interest would be solely in the interplay of human relationships, the development of character, and the influence of natural and unnatural forces on human destiny. (*WH* 1978 L'Estrange: ix)

Not only does her choice of genre enable her literally to 'write beyond the ending', but its evolving story also alerts us to the processes of history. Like Caine's Heathcliff, L'Estrange's Jack Heathcliff knows that 'a man's wife is his chattel . . . He owns her, and short of murder, can dispose of her how he likes' (281). In this and similar ways *Return to Wuthering Heights* shows that the economic, legal and political situations of *Wuthering Heights*, as well as its psychology, provide a determining mechanism which can, almost automatically, run forward into the future.

John Wheatcroft's novel, *Catherine, Her Book* (*WH* 1983 Wheatcroft), builds on *Wuthering Heights* in quite a different way. Instead of looking from the frame inwards, like L'Estrange, it is formally equivalent to Caine's book in giving the narrative to one of the protagonists. The jacket blurb to Wheatcroft's novel places Catherine and Heathcliff in company 'with Tristan and Isolde, Romeo and Juliet, Mellors and Lady Chatterley', suggesting the inevitable triangle discussed in previous chapters. Wheatcroft's first-person narrative, however, is unique in giving Catherine's perspective on the story; its material detail, moreover, acts against a facile mythologizing of the love story. The novel consists of Catherine's diary notes from *Wuthering Heights* expanded by Catherine four months after her marriage. Its entries are precisely dated, running from August 1 to September 30, 1783, and within that from July 24, 1774 to September 15, 1780. The style is also scrupulously appropriate to a girl who has grown up with little formal education, in close proximity to a young boy and a farmyard. Catherine describes, sensitively and probably, how childhood intimacy leads without embarrassment to early sexual union between herself and Heathcliff which she describes, biblically, as 'cleaving'. They also invent a version of the Brontë childhood 'plays', derived, with greater probability than Wyler's chivalric fantasies, from *The Pilgrim's Progress* (*WH* 1983 Wheatcroft: 29). The novel shows considerable research into local dialect (there is a glossary) and eighteenth-century dictionaries, as well as the Bible which provides the fatal framework of moral penalties. It also, however, includes compelling accounts of the physical sensations of contact with water, stone, wind, intensified to the point where consciousness is almost lost, and flowing without much distinction into descriptions of orgasm, after which Catherine desperately tries 'to prevent the feel of my flesh from returning' (73) – a description which recalls, without diminishing, Emily's poem, 'The Prisoner', which has normally been read as describing a purely spiritual trance state.

The sequence of events shows how Catherine and Heathcliff first make love when she is twelve, having accidentally seen Nelly and Hindley 'cleaving', though she has already guessed that Nelly is their half-sister and that this is why Hindley is to be sent away. Thereafter, reading the Bible convinces Catherine that her first menstruation and her father's illness and death are punishments for their act; this conviction is unbearably intensified when she realizes that Heathcliff is also her father's illegitimate son and when, during a sermon on 'the helmet of salvation', she reads in 2 Samuel xiii the story of Amnon, who raped his sister and then rejected her (123). Further researches in the library reveal that Heathcliff's 'pizzle' should properly be called his 'penis' and that her favourite word 'cleave' can mean divide as well as cling. In one of the more fanciful sections, she realizes that Penistone Crag is 'a monumental landscape replica of Heathcliff and me as we cleaved, Heathcliff the penis-stone, I the gorge' (133). 'Cleaved or clove or cleft, akin to cliff', she reads, and thinks, 'the very name HEATHCLIFF contained us both! I, the SHAW, the thicket, a part of the heath that was CLEFT by him' (135).

The complex education Catherine thus suffers, compounded of physical, genealogical, biblical and semantic knowledge, provides the explanation for what Heathcliff, like most readers of *Wuthering Heights*, found inexplicable: '*Why* did you betray your own heart, Cathy? . . . Because misery, and degradation, and death, and nothing that God or Satan could inflict would have parted us, *you*, of your own will, did it' (161). In *Catherine, Her Book*, Catherine denies Heathcliff because she believes that their incestuous union will bring an apocalyptic judgement on them both. She plans to use Nelly to pass on to Heathcliff the difference between her love for him and for Edgar, but Heathcliff runs away. Her journal ends with his return; the last words of the novel are 'when he whispered my name, I heard a sound like the rush of water, or the heave of the wind' (170). These words return us to the events of *Wuthering Heights* with a changed consciousness of Catherine's hitherto unspoken life. In one way this opens up the text of *Wuthering Heights*, revealing a richness of experience underlying the laconic accounts of Emily Brontë's children and filling what Jay Clayton calls 'the void of representation' more convincingly than the iconic 'hilltop lovers' motif used in film and stage versions (1987: 93, 83, 84). It also gives tragic dignity to Catherine, presenting her not simply as confused and wilful but as deliberately taking upon herself a great moral responsibility together with the pain of having her motives misjudged. Perversely, however, I found that even while being convinced by this filling of the void, I nevertheless resisted its being filled. While fruitfully turning us back into the original text, Wheatcroft's explicit Freudian/Levi-Straussian explanation still effectively closes it by precluding other explanations.

Most of the transformations of *Wuthering Heights* discussed in this book have tried to make the novel into what Roland Barthes called a 'readerly' text – a text which would yield its secrets if we could just hit on the right interpretative strategy. Thus, Bernard Herrmann interprets the novel as a mystical elegy to nature, Jeffrey Caine as a macho tale of revenge, and John Wheatcroft as a Freudian case study. All these strategies render the text intelligible, but by so doing limit its elusive fascination. In academic criticism, *Wuthering Heights* only came into its own when it was recognized not as a readerly but as a 'writerly' text – one which invites the reader to participate in its construction rather than to solve its mystery. It is, therefore, interesting that Lin Haire-Sargeant's novel *Heathcliff* (1992) originated in one of those writing exercises described above. Her acknowledgements describe 'an extraordinary graduate seminar' which conjured 'three slight female forms . . . outside the classroom windows, and someone dark and brooding in the shadow', so that 'when Professor Gezari asked what Heathcliff had done in those years he was gone from Wuthering Heights, I thought I knew' (*WH* 1992 Haire-Sargeant: ix).

Rather than 'filling the void' with extraneous material, like Jeffrey Caine, Haire-Sargeant opts for an ingenious interweaving of both our famous texts, explaining that when Heathcliff runs away to Liverpool in search of his origins, he is adopted by a 'Mr Are' and educated as a gentleman. Eventually it emerges that Mr Are is Mr Rochester from *Jane Eyre*, and that Heathcliff is his son by Bertha Mason, placed in a mad-house in Liverpool at an early age, from which he escaped to be found by Mr Earnshaw. In this story it is Jane's disappearance from Thornfield which keeps Heathcliff searching for her instead of returning to Wuthering Heights to rescue Catherine before her wedding to Edgar; Jane returns to occupy with Rochester the very Ferndean which Heathcliff had furnished to receive Catherine, highlighting the linked status of the two novels as 'comic' and tragic versions of the romance plot. The linking of the two novels, however, is not the only interweaving involved, since *Heathcliff* also links fictional and historical people. The book opens with Charlotte Brontë meeting Mr Lockwood on a train, where he asks her to read Heathcliff's narrative of his missing years, originally written for Catherine but kept from her by Nelly Dean. The novel ends with Charlotte and Emily being invited to visit Nelly Dean at Thrushcross Grange, where the younger Catherine, now a widow, is about to marry Mr Lockwood.

Because my main interest in incremental literature is ideological, I have in this book largely avoided the question of aesthetic value. To the question, 'but is it any *good*?' I have implicitly answered, 'good *for what*?' Under this formula it is possible to recognize that books whose ideological purpose one disagrees with, or which fail to meet traditional criteria such as complexity or coherence, can nevertheless be well written for that purpose. Thus I feel no need to disparage Anna L'Estrange's *Return to Wuthering Heights* by comparison with Geoffrey Wheatcroft's *Catherine, Her Book*, although the latter is a more sophisticated text in terms of language play, intertextuality and evocative description; both are well written for their purpose. Lin Haire-Sargeant's *Heathcliff*, however, fails to live up to its own 'writerly' promise.

Informed readers will know that Charlotte Brontë is a real person (with a death certificate, for instance) and that Mr Lockwood is a character in a novel. When Charlotte Brontë meets Mr Lockwood on a train, therefore, we are invited either to read Mr Lockwood as a real person, or Charlotte Brontë as a fictional one. The situation is different from that in, say, *War and Peace*, where real and fictional figures mingle; in that case, the fictional characters are presented as if they are real people who happen not to have been documented. Lockwood, on the other hand, is known to exist only inside *Wuthering Heights*, so that his conjunction with Charlotte Brontë makes the reader uneasy about the proper strategies for reading. According to Rosemary Jackson, this kind of uneasiness is generically exploited by fantasy writers: 'by presenting discrete elements which are juxtaposed and reassembled in unexpected, apparently impossible combinations, fantastic art draws explicit attention to the *process* of representation' (1981: 84). In Haire-Sargeant's text, however, the apparently impossible combinations do not readily induce insights about the textuality of reality because the boundary between the normally 'discrete elements' of history and fiction is muddied by what can only be read as mistakes. Good fantasy writers know that challenges to a 'commonsense perspective' (Jackson 1981: 48) must earn belief by a more scrupulous attention than usual to verisimilitude; in Haire-Sargeant's text a hazy invention serves in place of history. Although her novel, like *Wuthering Heights*, begins with a date – January 3rd, 1844 – she does not provide us with the historical substance which the date invites us to look for. She does not, for instance, know that trains did not have corridors until a long time after 1844, and could not therefore have been patrolled by the 'train employee' whose repeated arrival punctuates Charlotte's conversation with Lockwood (*WH* 1992 Haire-Sargeant: 3–13); more pedantically, we might note that the old lady with the knitting would indeed be 'in time to catch the Ipswich train' (since she would have had to wait for the line to be constructed), but that she would not even then have found it by 'crossing the platform' at King's Cross (4), since trains for Ipswich left (several years later) from Liverpool Street Station, on the other side of London. These trivial mistakes give the reader, not an exciting sense of destabilization, but a merely uncomfortable sense of insecurity.

The problem is confounded by the complex dove-tailing of the two pre-existing fictions. Haire-Sargeant agrees (218) with Geoffrey Wheatcroft's dating of

Catherine Earnshaw's marriage as in 1783 – but this entails her Mr Rochester attempting to marry Jane Eyre in that same year. Even the dating (1808) suggested by St John Rivers's gift of *Marmion* as a 'new publication' (*JE* 390) offers problems for the careful reader, since the evangelical atmosphere surrounding Brocklehurst and St John belongs to a later generation. Haire-Sargeant's text, however, asks us to put the date of *Jane Eyre* back another twenty-five years. Undaunted by these difficulties, she introduces extra complications: Charlotte, reading Heathcliff's sixty-year-old manuscript, recognizes him as a young friend of Emily's in present time (*WH* 1992 Haire-Sargeant: 47), and although the novel gives Heathcliff a genealogy, this question about his identity in time is left as one of those stories which 'can never be told' (291).

Heathcliff's story, as told in his manuscript, gives us elements not included in *Jane Eyre* or *Wuthering Heights*; it also changes their perspective, making Heathcliff the centre of consciousness. The cover illustration to the American edition, showing a cloaked Heathcliff contemplating a distant mist-shrouded crag, presents him in the tradition of the questing knight facing difficulties to reach *la princesse lointaine*. His manuscript, moreover, includes Catherine's 'voice' only in the form of poetic snatches which Heathcliff 'hears', giving the effect, as in Kosminsky's film (1991), that she has no consciousness independent of him. At the end of the novel, Emily is not satisfied with Nelly Dean's account of Catherine's death and Heathcliff's subsequent decline, and suggests to Charlotte what might really have happened. Her narrative, however, reverses only the outcome of Heathcliff's, not its gendered focus, conjuring up a scene in which Heathcliff seizes Catherine from her blood-soaked child-bed, revives her with a phial of scarlet liquid and carries her off to a Louisiana plantation (*WH* 1992 Haire-Sargeant: 282).

Wuthering Heights itself is notable for its evasion of conventional endings, and Haire-Sargeant's Emily offers this story as a gesture towards a higher truth than Charlotte's pedantic historicism ('but did it *happen?*' (291)). Its only claim to evade history, however, lies in its palpable improbability; as a narrative structure it cancels the ambiguity of the original (replacing the question, 'in what sense is Catherine "dead"?' with the statement, 'Catherine is not dead') and reinscribes it as conventional romance. Although the rescue story is presented as Emily's fantasy, it is in line with the impulse to romantic closure in Haire-Sargeant's 'parent' text which gives us the marriage of that charming old gentleman, Mr Lockwood, to the gracious Mrs Catherine Earnshaw. When the Lockwood of Emily Brontë's text imagines that young Catherine would receive his proposal of marriage as 'something more romantic than a fairy tale' (*WH* 304), his words are heavy with ironies carried over from the first chapters; Haire-Sargeant not only takes them literally but makes them literally come true. It is only surprising that the novel does not provide some charming suitor for Charlotte, who is shown on her last journey home from Brussels quite diverted from her 'wistful memories of Monsieur Heger' (1). To anyone with even a casual acquaintance with Charlotte Brontë's life the word 'wistful' is as painfully inadequate to the torture she suffered at that time as are the words in which Haire-Sargeant's Emily paints the scene of Catherine's rescue:

What is that? A rustle in the ivy outside? The curtain blows out and in. A hand gains hold on the sill. Yes. A shadowed face; eyes blaze from shadow. Ripple of powerful, dark-clad shoulder, white flash of lace, thrust of shining black boot into candlelight.
    'Heathcliff!' (282)

When, after hearing this story, Charlotte challenges Emily about the relation between 'truth' and 'historical fact' (291), Emily is scornful of Charlotte's limited vision. This conversation between Charlotte and Emily is reminiscent of Virginia Woolf's imaginary conversation with the Edwardian novelists who told her she could capture Mrs Brown if she would only 'describe cancer. Describe calico' (1966: 332), while she wanted to render the 'luminous halo' (1929: 189) which is the experienced quality of life. The trouble is that Haire-Sargeant's Emily writes her fantasy in words which are as historically specific and limited as anything written by Arnold Bennett. These direct visual images ('white flash of lace . . . shining black boot') of a masculine rescuer ('ripple of powerful . . . shoulder') seen as by a woman who waits for rescue ('Yes') are drawn, not from the tradition of verbal complexity suggested by the writerly debate, but from the tradition of popular romance which, 'with its dependence on visualisation and the idea of the expressivity of the body, is formally predisposed towards wish-fulfilment instead of duty' (Easthope 1991: 95, 93). What Haire-Sargeant's *Heathcliff* offers us as the apogee of liberating imagination, available only to the inspired few ('you will never understand' (1992: 291)), is the irresponsible fantasy of pleasurable escape; what is wrong with this is not that it evades duty, but that it is offered, with a sneer at history, under the guise of truth.

    One of the many remarkable things about *Wuthering Heights* is that it has what Stevie Davies calls 'a *trompe l'oeil* cunning to persuade us to believe we have seen what we have not been shown . . . Few readers emerge aware of how little the moorlands have been described in the first half of the novel' (1994: 181). After his definition of 'wuthering', Lockwood goes on: 'one may guess the power of the north wind, blowing over the edge, by the excessive slant of a few, stunted firs at the end of the house; and by a range of gaunt thorns all stretching their limbs one way, as if craving alms of the sun' (*WH* 2), but more characteristic are what we might call functional references; when the snowstorm forces Lockwood to stay the night at the Heights, the focus is not on the storm, which is there as part of the story, just as the wind that makes the fir-tree tap on the window is the necessary but taken-for-granted cause of Lockwood's dream. The impression that the moor is all-present does not come from formal descriptions such as we find in the novels of Thomas Hardy, but from incidental references, such as Isabella's one-sentence account of her flight from the Heights, 'rolling over banks, and wading through marshes' (181), or, more typically, in metaphors; Catherine describes Heathcliff's mind as an 'arid wilderness of furze and whinstone' (102) and when young Catherine and Linton describe their ideal heaven, they contrast a breezy, rocking tree-top, alive with bird-song, with a murmurous, bee-ridden heath, hot with sunshine (248). Thus the landscape does not appear like a 'background' to the events of the novel, but is more like part of the characterization.

In the final words of Haire-Sargeant's novel, her Charlotte undergoes a kind of conversion, recognizing in 'the rushing of the spring-swollen beck . . . the very murmur of life, strong and insistent, continuous beneath the hardened surface of everyday existence' (*WH* 1992 Haire-Sargeant: 292). This belated recognition of the local landscape does not suffice to erase the New Orleans idyll on the previous page, but contrasts with Wheatcroft's book in relation not only to *Wuthering Heights* but to Emily Brontë's poetry. When Wheatcroft's child Catherine, lying perilously along the jutting top of Penistone Crag, sees Nelly and Hindley 'cleaving' far below in the ravine, her responses include the physical landscape:

> All of whatever my innards are made of had turned to water, warm water. Though I told myself to keep my fingers clamped on the ridge of rock and though my body lay stretched full-length on the rough hard jut, I could scarcely feel the stone. I wanted to flow. The idea of rushing over the side and dropping like water down the cataract into the pool below now prompted no fear . . . With my inner eye, in the golden haze of the sun filtering through my lashes and lids, I beheld circles of pure color, pinks and reds and purples, growing out of points until the circles swelled so large they dissolved. Now the wind was a voice, crying and sighing about my head. I lay within a huge warm drop of water. I was gone out of the world. I was the water. (*WH* 1983 Wheatcroft: 34–5)

Unlike Haire-Sargeant's easy metaphor (water equals life), Wheatcroft's description gives us the process of interaction between human body and physical elements, heightened by sexual excitement, which leads to the illusion of reaching the 'beyond'.

This fascination with wind and water is the starting point for the Canadian novelist Jane Urquhart's novel, *Changing Heaven* (*WH* 1990 Urquhart). Its modern heroine, Ann, looks at the cover of what must be Fritz Eichenberg's illustrated edition of *Wuthering Heights* and sees that 'the wood engraver has drafted the weather so intricately it looks like the sea. Swirling currents lift the man's dark curls' (*WH* 1990 Urquhart: 47–8). *Changing Heaven*, however, resists the temptation to explain its original, neither offering truth nor resolving enigmas, but playing with place, time, words and history in such a way as to offer what Douglas Barbour calls 'an extraordinary contemporary fiction floated on the emotional weather of Emily Brontë's *Wuthering Heights*' (17.3.1990). *Changing Heaven* takes its title from one of Emily Brontë's poems,

> I loved the plashing of the surge,
> The changing Heaven, the breezy weather. (Hatfield 1941: 96)

In one way it is a novel about the weather. It begins with an undefined 'she' (who may be Emily Brontë or may be the modern woman writer, Ann), who 'wants to write a novel about the wind, about the weather . . . She wants the again and again of that revenant, the wind' (*WH* 1990 Urquhart: 1). So much is contained in these simple sentences that the book demands a reading like poetry, with attention to single words. The wind as 'revenant' lifts the idea of haunting easily into the text, while 'the again and again' raises the question, as with running water, of whether a repeated action is the same or different. This wind, moreover,

> has been around for a long, long, time . . . born about the same time as chaos; or that other semi-human, a Cyclops called Brontë – the Greek word for thunder. And what is thunder, hereabouts, but a strong voice making itself heard in a rough wind? (*WH* 1990 Urquhart: 2)

The movement here, from physical to mythical to semantic registers and back, is not confusing but exhilarating, like encountering 'elements that change shape but never substance' (2).

The reader of this novel is surprised, but never confused, because its devotion to mutability is combined with a remarkable sense of history. Not only does it present Haworth as a place of industry, 'the air filled with the sound of banging shuttles' (171); its three-part structure also recapitulates a history of women. Part One, entitled, 'Wind', has an epigraph from Emily Brontë – 'This is my home, where whirlwinds blow' (3) – and is to do with Romantic escapism, the kind of identification with nature which Geoffrey Wheatcroft attributes to Catherine and which Simone de Beauvoir, in *The Second Sex*, sees as a panic-retreat from womanhood (de Beauvoir [1949] 1970: 104). Part Two, called, 'The Upstairs Room', has an epigraph from Emily Dickinson – 'I am looking oppositely /For the site of the Kingdom of Heaven' (*WH* 1990 Urquhart: 121) – and suggests the trapped existence of the Victorian madwoman in the attic. Part Three, called 'Revenants', has an epigraph from Stevie Smith and suggests twentieth-century ambitions – 'Oh would that I were a reliable spirit careering around /Congenially employed and no longer by *feebleness* bound . . .' (193) – while simultaneously reminding us that to be 'a reliable spirit' is also to be a 'revenant', a revisiting spirit.

In accordance with its aim to be 'a novel about the weather', *Changing Heaven* takes place largely out of doors. Much of the novel is devoted to a conversation on Haworth Moor between the ghost of Emily Brontë and the ghost of a lady balloonist called Arianna Ether who was killed on Haworth Moor at the turn of the century. There is also a modern Canadian woman academic who is obsessed with *Wuthering Heights* and goes to live near Haworth. In relation to each of these speakers (and Branwell Brontë, and the male lovers of the balloonist and the academic), the title, *Changing Heaven*, has a significance apart from the weather; each, like young Catherine and Linton, has their own idea of heaven, and most of them are heavens of love. For readers raised on William Wyler's film, *Changing Heaven* offers a *reductio ad absurdum* of the dual skyward gaze of Wyler's lovers (Figure 4.8), vividly and wittily demonstrating Juliet Mitchell's perception that romantic love, 'the triumph of death over life, . . . does not have a sexual object that is ultimately different from itself' (1984: 111). Emily tells Arianna how her brother Branwell constructed the image of his lost mistress so that she became

> silent and motionless and reaching for him only with her eyes, which he said were just like his eyes . . . She drank and took opium and wrote long, desperate, undeliverable messages. She had shut everyone else out of herself.

Branwell's true spirit-breaker, his perfect prison. An exact reproduction of himself one week before he died. (*WH* 1990 Urquhart: 139)

Arianna in turn tells Emily how her lover required that she lose her name, her job, her family, to become the white, ethereal image of his ideal, rising into the sky as 'the very spirit of British womanhood ascending to her rightful place with the angels in the clouds. Remote, untouchable, apart'. It is 'the apotheosis of Arianna' (25– 26). Not content, however, with constructing her aerial persona and her skyey habitat, he cannot rest until he has caused her death, when she is perfected, the unattainable object of his obsessive desire. In Wyler's film, Heathcliff follows the ghost of Catherine to a snowy death on Penistone Crag; in *Changing Heaven* the balloonist pursues his creation, like Frankenstein his monster, into the frozen wastes of the Arctic, dropping messages of love from his balloon.

Changing Heaven deconstructs 'eternal truth', so that not only ideals of love, or the 'very spirit of . . . womanhood', but even the 'elemental' landscape of the Yorkshire moors is seen as a construction in words. Arianna objects, 'You could not possibly have built this landscape!' but Emily insists:

> 'But I did, I did! I invented, I built it all! . . . I knew it the day I finished my book. My dog Keeper and I set out on our daily walk and, suddenly, the landscape had altered. There it was, the landscape of my novel! I could never see it any other way again. It was mine, mine! I'd made it mine! And I'd changed it, forever. It is hard work, too, building landscape. The rocks were particularly difficult, and that is what Mr Capital H was made out of – different shapes of black stone. And he was obdurate, unyielding, fixed, unchanging, difficult to describe, and originating God knows where. Practically unkillable!' (179–80).

Despite its light-hearted tone, this is a believable account of how, as Oscar Wilde puts it, 'Life imitates Art far more than Art imitates Life' (1966: III 284). It also suggests intriguing relations between the 'rock' which Catherine uses as a metaphor for her love for Heathcliff (*WH* 82), the 'granite block' which Charlotte Brontë describes as Emily's raw material for Heathcliff (*WH* 370), and the 'obdurate' myth of the romance hero. The American edition of Lin Haire-Sargeant's *Heathcliff* (1992) is called *H*, and the cover shows a huge black capital H containing the figure of Heathcliff gazing at a black rock. Haire-Sargeant's novel consolidates the myth which Urquhart seeks to fragment. For *Changing Heaven* shows not only landscapes and myths to be mutable, but also authors. If this version of Emily Brontë claims responsibility for having made a practically unkillable myth, she is also shown as having changed her mind. By the end of the novel even her ghostly presence is wearing thin, and the present-day heroine, Ann, learns that Mr Capital H will no longer serve as her ideal of love.

Ann's childhood fantasies are unlike the adolescent fixation on Heathcliff described by Rachel Brownstein ([1982] 1984; see page 232 above); 'Ann is storm-driven instead by the distant winds of *Wuthering Heights*' and 'the child Heathcliff, a demonic baby god with the sea in his eyes and foreign ports submerged in his unconscious' (*WH* 1990 Urquhart: 18). In adulthood her obsession gains the dignity of academic research while simultaneously being projected onto her lover until he makes her see that, like Branwell, she sees not him but herself; 'it wasn't that she wanted *him* so much as that she wanted him to become her . . . She wanted him to feel only what she felt. A rush of moorland wind – the weather – and all the real details swept away' (236–7). The danger of her ideal is represented in a feverish dream in which 'winged lovers beating and beating up against the mirror of their opposite selves' become monstrous in union; 'they have become one during the night and the new beast they are is prowling' (142–3). Emily explains to Arianna, 'Absence was essential, after childhood, to the hallucination. Desperate departures, absences, reversals, withdrawals – the ongoing war. A permanent state of unfulfilled desire. And, weirdly enough, longing itself was what they desired' (84).

In different language, John T. Matthews argues that in *Wuthering Heights*, 'each of the lovers seeks to supplement an interior lack by representing it as an other who becomes the "all in all"' (1985: 56). However, to attempt union with this other reveals that 'all that beckons to us as the beyond is the blank inverse of what is within' (54). Matthews's argument is that it is impossible to detach this ideal love from the society which appears to prevent it because 'Catherine and Heathcliff's love is the ghost of the prohibitions that structure society'. Not only is it impossible to realize a love which is a 'hallucination' born of desire, it is also impossible to escape from this desire, because 'the oppressions of society not only compromise our present, they condition the dreams of its reversal'. This is not such a pessimistic position as it may sound, for two reasons. One is that if desires and prohibitions, as Matthews claims, 'incessantly dissolve' into one another (54), there is no way of assigning primacy to either. Our dreams may be shaped by 'the oppressions of society', but this is a reciprocal interaction, in which the discourse of dreams can 'shape forms of consciousness and unconsciousness' which in turn can motivate 'transformation of our existing systems of power' (Eagleton 1983: 210). Secondly, therefore, 'the oppressions of society' are not themselves immutable. The rhetoric of our desires, the intensity with which we tell ourselves stories of tragic love, is a social force which erodes the prohibitions that structure tragedy, just as weather, as it 'wuthers' round obstructive crags, makes new shapes of 'obdurate' landscape. Society, like landscape, changes slowly, but our weathered crags no longer have quite the contours seen by Emily Brontë. As we read old stories, we half recognize the landscape of past prohibitions, but our pleasure comes from moving with the narrative as it wuthers through to its appropriate heaven.

The danger of *Wuthering Heights*, for modern readers, is that we locate our pleasure, not in its restless movement, but in its specific heaven. Ann, in *Changing Heaven*, longs to say 'I *am* Arthur!', but the social landscape has changed since *Wuthering Heights*, eroded in part by the force of desire in the texts described in this book. She thinks of Catherine's dream, in which she is thrown out of heaven, and 'all through the night Ann falls, falls to earth, just as if certain angels had taken it upon themselves to toss her out of an inappropriate heaven' (*WH* 1990 Urquhart: 238). Instead she finds love in a new shape, neither Romantic nor 'legitimate', between adults with separate identities, who do not belong to each other, who do not mirror each other, whose love does not require the death of either. And their intercourse begins in discourse – telling stories about the weather.

Listening to one of John's more fantastic stories, Ann asks the question given to Haire-Sargeant's Charlotte: 'Is it . . . true?' (170). Instead of asserting a higher truth than history, Urquhart's storyteller tells a story about a storyteller which shows how all truth is a process of endless deferral which is not, however, unrelated to history:

> as time went by the lad began telling himself stories that were not quite like the original. And since he often told himself the stories at night before he went to sleep, his dreams crept into them and, as time went by, some of his own memories. And because he lived here, on the moors, it were impossible – you'll like this – to keep the weather out of the stories . . .
>
> Eventually, the stories were all his. A bit borrowed, true, from the Greek and a bit from the Bible . . . a bit from his father, a bit from his mother . . . More, much more, from the silently mouthed rumours of the mill . . . and the persistent surrounding weather that nudged its way into his mental narrations whether he wanted it to or not. (*WH* 1990 Urquhart: 177)

Urquhart's novel tells the story of the death of the author as timeless myth, but reinstates the story of the storyteller as craftworker: 'only he himself knew the agony of it, the loneliness: telling the stories, often ones of lies, betrayals, injustices, and broken hearts, over and over to himself in the dark until they came to be just right' (177). And part of his getting it just right must be related to his occupation as a moor-edger – someone who 'push[es] the moor back to where it belongs' (134–5), who knows the boundary between valley and dissolving horizons which allows life to be sustained, but not confined to 'small change'.

In the polyvocal textures of *Changing Heaven*, 'eternal truths' become stories and the 'timeless' Emily Brontë a whimsical ghost who vanishes into landscape. 'When ghosts become landscape, weather alters, the wind shifts, and heaven changes' (258). As we listen to the new storytellers giving new shapes to old desires, we must be content to let go of the ghost of the author, knowing that in her text the dialogue of crag and weather wuthers on.

Jane Eyre *derivatives listed chronologically*

Sources and abbreviations

Barclay	Barclay, Janet (1989) *Emily Brontë Criticism 1900–1980: An Annotated Check List*, Westport, Conn.: Meckler
b/w	black and white
BFI	British Film Institute
BL	British Library
BPM	Brontë Parsonage Museum (numbers are acquisition numbers)
BS	Brontë Society
BSG	*Brontë Society Gazette*
BST	*Brontë Society Transactions* (references take the form (vol.part.page (date))
Halliwell	Halliwell, Leslie (1986) *Halliwell's Film Guide*, 5th edn, London: Paladin Grafton
Hodgkins	Ian Hodgkins (Booksellers) Catalogues
LCP	Lord Chamberlain's Plays, British Library (ms plays are identified by additional manuscript ('Add. ms') numbers)
LCO	Lord Chamberlain's Office (responsible for licensing plays)
ms	manuscript
NYPL	New York Public Library of the Performing Arts
Nudd	Nudd, Donna Marie, 'Bibliography of Film, Television and Stage Adaptations of *Jane Eyre*', *BST* 20.3.169–72. (1991) [Note Nudd (1989) and Nudd (1992) refer to the general bibliography]
Rauth	Rauth, Heidemarie (1971), 'Dramatisierungen von Leben und Werk der Brontë-Schwestern', dissertation
ts	typescript
v	verso; where ms pages are written on both sides of the paper but only one is numbered, 1v indicates the reverse of p. 1.
vol.	volume
Wagner	Wagner, Geoffrey (1975) *The Novel and the Cinema*, London: Associated University Presses
Y & T	Yablon, G. Anthony and John R. Turner (1978) *A Brontë Bibliography*, London: Ian Hodgkins (Connecticut: Meckler Books)

Notes

1. All versions of *Jane Eyre* are listed under the name of the adaptor, illustrator, etc., and not under Brontë.
2. Where bibliographic details are in brackets, this indicates an edition other than the original.
3. Parenthetic references in the form 'Myer 1987: 106' refer to the general bibliography.
4. Where an author, date, etc. is in square brackets, this indicates that the information has been supplied from a later source; where a whole entry is in square brackets, this indicates a subsequent edition, performance, etc. of an item from a previous date.
5. Some additional illustrated editions of *Jane Eyre* which form part of multi-volume *Works* of the Brontë sisters will be found under *Wuthering Heights* derivatives below.

Jane Eyre *derivatives listed chronologically*

Undated
Films
Brontë, Charlotte, *I Take This Woman*, 'The film title of the famous novel *Jane Eyre*', published for Collins by the London Book Co.

> BPM has copy (SB: 2271); appears to be 'the book of the film'. Editor's preface (no author) refers to Ann Harding as 'Jane Eyre in the film version of Charlotte Brontë's novel'. BPM and Nudd have no record of a film with Ann Harding. Halliwell lists two and Milne one film[s] with this title, but they do not have a *Jane Eyre* plot or Ann Harding.

Illustrations, paintings, etc.
Lamb, Lynton (illus.), Charlotte Brontë, *Jane Eyre*, Janet Adam Smith (intro.), London: Macdonald.

> Page 130 shows Rochester on horse.

BPM has four undated comicstrip versions listed below under 1930–9, 1950–9 and 1980–9. The relationship between these is complicated and it may help to list them together here. (1) Thriller Comics No 31 ('ear-muff' hair-style suggests 1930s). (2) *Jane Eyre*, illustrated by Harley M. Griffiths (BPM SB: 1439); 'Cast-list' cover; includes Moor House; 1950s? (3) Classics Illustrated No. 39 (no BPM No.); 'That is *my wife*' cover; inside pictures same as (2). (4) Classics Illustrated No. 39 (BPM SB: 3011c); Timothy Dalton cover (1980s); different inside pictures; omits Moor House; 1960s?

> *Note:* Myer dates (3) and (4) as 1947 and 1968 but gives no evidence (1987: 106).

Novels, poems, etc.
Barry, Jane, 'Mr Rochester'.

> Poem, source unidentified.

1848

Musical settings

Turner, Joseph W. (arr.), (1848) 'The Little Orphan's Song', Ballad. The Words from *Jane Eyre* . . . , Boston: Oliver Ditson.
  Copy in BPM: SB: 3133.

Stage plays

Courtney, John (adapt.) (1848), *Jane Eyre or The Secrets of Thornfield Manor*. BL: Licensed by LCO 1848; Add. ms 43009, ff. 595–629.
  Nudd (1991: 171) establishes that ms 43009 had previously been wrongly attributed to John Brougham. NYPL has programme for 'Jane Eyre; or, The Secrets of Thornfield Manor: 1848. By Charlotte Brontë. Adapted by J. Courtney. London: Victoria Theatre.' Charlotte Brontë knew of this performance, though she did not see it; see letters to William Smith Williams, 5.2.1848, 15.2.1848. *See also 1849, 1856, 1866, 1910.*

1849

Novels, poems, etc.

Brontë, Anne (1849) *The Tenant of Wildfell Hall*, London: Newby.
  Possibly an answer to *Jane Eyre*'s suggestion that 'a reformed rake makes the best husband'.

Stage plays

Brougham, John (1849) *Jane Eyre*.
  BS exhibition, 1991: '1849 John Brougham's version performed in New York 26.3.1849. Miss Wemys and Mr J. Gilbert. Revised 1856 with Laura Keene as Jane'. NYPL has a clipping; also review of performance identified as Brougham's at Bowery Theatre, March 1849: *Spirit of the Times*, vol. 19 p. 72, 31.3.1849. Nudd does not record this performance. *See also 1856, 1866, 1910.*

1850

Novels, poems, etc.

Craik, Dinah Mulock [1850] *Olive*, London: Richard Edward King.
  Small plain heroine; hero injured in a fire.
Kavanagh, Julia (1850) *Nathalie: A Tale*, 3 vols, London: Henry Colburn.
  See Foster (1982). Review: *Athenaeum* no. 1203, 16.11.1850, pp. 1184–5.

1852

Novels, poems, etc.

Craik, Dinah Mulock [1852] *The Head of the Family*, London & Newcastle: Walter Scott.
  Oliphant (1855: 560): 'the author of *the Head of the Family*' is one of 'the host of followers or imitators' of *Jane Eyre*. See Foster (1985).

1853

Novels, poems, etc.

Craik, Dinah Mulock [1853] *Agatha's Husband*, London: Nicholson (Portway Bath: Cedric Chivers, 1969).

> Oliphant (1855: 560): 'the author of *the Head of the Family*', who also wrote *Agatha's Husband*, is one of 'the host of followers or imitators' of *Jane Eyre*'. See Foster (1985).

Kavanagh, Julia (1853) *Daisy Burns*, 3 vols, London: Bentley.

> Oliphant (1855: 559): 'the last novel of this author exaggerates the repetition [of the *Jane Eyre* story] beyond all toleration'.

1854

Stage plays

Birch-Pfeiffer, Charlotte (1854) *Die Waise Von Lowood* performed in New York in German.

> Nudd (1989: 73): 'records of the 1854, 1856, 1882 & 1884 productions can be found in William Torbert Leonard's *Theatre: Stage to Screen to Television*, Metuchen, N. J. & London: Scarecrow, 1981, pp. 765–8'. *See also 1856, 1867, 1870, 1871, 1882, 1884, 1910.*

1855

Musical settings

Charleton, W. H. (1855) 'To the Memory of the Author of "Jane Eyre"', Hesleyside.

> Printed on reverse of Alfred Jepson, 'The Orphan Child' (song), New York: Etnorb, 1962. Copy in BPM.

Novels, poems etc.

Gaskell, Elizabeth (1855) *North and South* (Harmondsworth: Penguin, 1970).

> Oliphant (1855: 559): Gaskell is one of 'the host of followers or imitators of *Jane Eyre*'.

Kavanagh, Julia (1855) *Grace Lee*, 3 vols, London: [no publisher].

> Oliphant (1855: 559): 'from *Nathalie* to *Grace Lee*, [Kavanagh] has done little else than repeat the attractive story of this conflict and combat of love and war' [i.e. as shown in *Jane Eyre*]. Summarizes plot.

1856

Stage plays

[Birch-Pfeiffer, Charlotte (1854) *Die Waise Von Lowood*.]

> Performed 1856 in New York in German (Nudd 1989: 73)] *See also 1854, 1867, 1870, 1871, 1882, 1884, 1910.*

Brougham, John (1856) *Jane Eyre: A Drama in five Acts . . . as performed at Laura Keene's varieties*, New York: Samuel French, French's American Drama. The

Acting Edition No. 136 [1856?], London: John Dicks, Dicks' standard plays series No. 400 (Y & T).

BPM has copy: SB: 500S. *See also 1849, 1866, 1867, 1910.*

1857

Novels, poems, etc.

Browning, Elizabeth Barrett (1857) *Aurora Leigh.*

Hero is blinded in a fire. Barrett Browning sent for *JE* 'to refresh her memory' when the similarity was remarked on (see Kenyon 1897: II 245–6).

1858

Incidental references

Victoria Regina, comments on *Jane Eyre*: see *BSG* 6: 7.

Novels, poems, etc.

Kavanagh, Julia (1858) *Adèle: A Tale*, London, Hurst & Blackett.

Some plot and psychological similarities.

1861

Incidental references

Jenkin, Henrietta Camilla (1861) *Who Breaks, Pays.*

Showalter (1976: 1) quotes the heroine as saying, 'Jane Eyre's Mr Rochester! . . . If I had been Jane Eyre I would have killed him'.

1862

Novels, poems, etc.

Braddon, Mary Elizabeth (1862) *Lady Audley's Secret* (London: Virago, 1985).

1865

Novels, poems, etc.

Warboise, Emma (1865) *Thorneycroft Hall*, London: Jackson, Walford & Hodder.

Author was at Clergy Daughters' School ten years after Charlotte Brontë.

1866

Stage plays

Bell, Currer (1866) *Jane Eyre.*

NYPL has a review of a performance of *Jane Eyre* (no adaptor) in 'St Louis – Olympic Theatre, October 1866': *New York Clipper* vol. 14, p. 246, 5.11.1866. *See also 1849, 1867, 1910.*

1867

Novels, poems, etc.

Broughton, Rhoda (1867) *Cometh Up As a Flower* (London & New York: Macmillan, 1899).

Broughton is one of the 'fleshly' writers mentioned by Oliphant (1867) as influenced by *Jane Eyre*.

Stage plays

[Birch-Pfeiffer, Charlotte (1854) *Jane Eyre*.]

LCP Add. ms 53063 F., Nov.–Dec. 1867 (no author cited in catalogue or on ms). Nudd: 'appears to be a plagiarized version of Charlotte Birch-Pfeiffer's *Jane Eyre*'. *See also 1854, 1856, 1868, 1870, 1871, 1882, 1884, 1910.*

[[Brougham, J.] (1849) *Jane Eyre*].

NYPL has programme 'London, New Surrey Theatre' which it identifies as '(J. Brougham) 1867'. (But see Birch-Pfeiffer, 1867.) *See also 1849, 1866.*

1868

Stage plays

(1868) *Jane Eyre*.

NYPL has programme for a performance of '*Jane Eyre*. London: New Surrey Theatre'. (But see also 1867.) *See also 1854, 1856, 1870, 1871, 1882, 1884, 1910.*

1870

Stage plays

Birch-Pfeiffer, Charlotte (1870) *Jane Eyre, or, The Orphan of Lowood*, 'A Drama in Two Parts and Four Acts . . . as performed by Mme Marie Seebach, and her dramatic company in New York and all the principal cities of the US, under the direction of J. Grau, New York Fourteenth Street Theatre 1870'. (First printed edition of play performed in 1854.)

Y & T: 'Dramat *Jane Eyre* Text in German and English'. NYPL has review of 'Dram. by Charlotte Birch-Pfeiffer. Fourteenth Street Theatre, October 1870': *Spirit of the Times* n.s. vol. 23 p. 144, 15.10.1870. *See also 1854, 1856, 1866, 1867, 1870, 1871, 1882, 1884, 1920, 1993.*

1871

Stage plays

Tayleure, Clifton W. (1871) *Jane Eyre, or The Orphan of Lowood*.

Nudd: 'Cited in *Dramatic Compositions Copyrighted in the United States 1870–1916*, US Copyright Office, entry 22457. Tayleure's play is an English adaptation of Charlotte Birch-Pfeiffer's German version, *Die Waise Von Lowood*'. NYPL has programmes for performances in: St Louis, Olympic Theatre (undated), stars Maggie Mitchell and Wm Harris; Washington, Gaiety Theatre (undated), star Maggie Mitchell. *See also 1873, 1874, 1875, 1882.*

1872

Illustrations, paintings, etc.

Wimperis, E.M (illus.), (1872) *Jane Eyre*, Charlotte Brontë, London: Smith, Elder.

Illustrations show Gateshead Hall, Thornfield Hall, Lowood and Ferndean Manor (with massive avenue and dappled deer). BPM has copy.

1873

Stage plays

[Tayleure, Clifton W. (1871) *Jane Eyre, or The Orphan of Lowood*.]
  NYPL has review of unidentified adaptation at Union Square Theatre June 1873: *Spirit of the Times* n.s. (3) vol. 28 p. 314, 21.6.1873; see production at this theatre 1874.

1874

Stage plays

Houghton, J.S. (adapt.) (1874) *Jane Eyre*, Philadelphia.
  Nudd: 'Cited in *Dramatic Compositions Copyrighted in the United States 1870–1916*, US Copyright Office, entry 22458'.
[Tayleure, Clifton W. (1871), *Jane Eyre, or The Orphan of Lowood*.]
  NYPL has programmes for performances in: Boston (1874), Boston Theatre, stars Maggie Mitchell and L. R. Shewell; New York (1874) Union Square Theatre, star Miss Charlotte Thompson [but no adaptor named; could this be Thompson? (See 1883)]. *See also 1875.*

1875

Stage plays

[Tayleure, Clifton W. (1871) *Jane Eyre, or The Orphan of Lowood*.]
  BPM (SB 2030) and NYPL have programme for performance at Boston (1875) Globe Theatre, directed by Mr D. W. Waller, stars Charlotte Thompson and Frederic Robinson. NYPL has programmes for performances at Chicago (1875) McVicker's Theatre [sic], stars Maggie Mitchell and Wm Harris; St Louis (1875) DeBar's Grand Opera House, stars Maggie Mitchell and Wm Harris. *See also 1871, 1873, 1874, 1876, 1881, 1882, 1883.*

1876

Stage plays

Dickinson, Anna (adapt.) (1876) *Jane Eyre*, New York.
  Nudd: 'Cited in *Dramatic Compositions Copyrighted in the United States 1870–1916*, US Copyright Office, entry 26437'.
[Tayleure, Clifton W. (1871) *Jane Eyre, or The Orphan of Lowood*.]
  NYPL has programmes for performances at Buffalo (1876) Academy of Music, star Charlotte Thompson [but no adaptor; is this Thompson? (See 1883)]. *See also 1871, 1873, 1874, 1875, 1881, 1882, 1883.*

1877

Stage plays

von Hering, Mme Heringen (trans.) (1877) *Jane Eyre*, LCP Add. ms 53182 N.; Lic. No. 45, Feb/Mar 1877.

LCP Add. ms 53182 N. has Mme von Hering's name plus '*Jane Eyre: A Drama in two Acts* An adaptation from a Danish Play To be performed at the Theatre Royal Coventry'.

Nudd: 'Translated or plagiarized version of Charlotte Birch-Pfeiffer's *Jane Eyre*'.

1879

Stage plays

[Paul, T. H. (adapt.)] (1879) *Jane Eyre*, LCP Add. ms 53224.A., Lic. No. 181, October 1879.]

Identified by Nudd: Licence ticket: '*Jane Eyre* Drama 3 Acts Adelphi Oldham October 1879'.

Willing, James [J. T. Douglass] and Leonard Rae (adapts) (1879) *Jane Eyre or Poor Relations*, LCP Add. ms 53222.B.; Lic. No. 149, Sept. 1879.

Ms title page reads: '*Jane Eyre or Poor Relations* A Drama in a Prologue and 4 Acts founded on Charlotte Brontë's novel *Jane Eyre* By James Willing and Leonard Rae. From J. Douglass. Park Theatre August 20th 1879'.

Mentioned in BS exhibition 1991–2; BPM has playbill for Royal Park Theatre, Camden Town, 27 August 1879 (SB: 2031); NYPL has programme for 'London, Royal Park Theatre, Camden Town, 1879'. *See also 1883, 1888.*

1881

Stage plays

[Tayleure, Clifton W. (1871) *Jane Eyre, or The Orphan of Lowood*.]

NYPL has programme for performance at New York (1881) Grand Opera House, star Maggie Mitchell. *See also 1871, 1873, 1874, 1875, 1876, 1882, 1883.*

1882

Stage plays

[Tayleure, Clifton W. (1871) *Jane Eyre, or The Orphan of Lowood*.]

NYPL has reviews: 11.9.1882, star Maggie Mitchell (no adaptor); *NYDM* 16.9.1882.

[Wills, W. G. (adapt.)] (1882) *Jane Eyre*, LCP Add. ms 53285.E.; Lic. No. 265, December 1882.

Identified by Nudd. Licence ticket: *Jane Eyre* Drama Globe Decr 18th 1882.

BS exhibition 1991–2 showed 'Globe Theatre production with Mrs Bernard-Breere as Jane', 1882. BPM has playbill for London, Globe Theatre (n. d.). *See also 1883.*

1883

Stage plays

Thompson, Charlotte (adapt.) (1883) *Jane Eyre*.

NYPL has clipping and programme: 'Star Charlotte Thompson, New York, 23rd St Theatre'. Note: Charlotte Thompson played Jane in Tayleure's version in New York, 1874, Boston 1875, Buffalo 1876; two productions listed under

'Tayleure' 1874 and 1876 could be Thompson's adaptation. *See also 1884, 1887, 1936.*

[[Wills, W. G. (adapt.)] (1882) *Jane Eyre*]
   BPM has playbill for performance at Theatre Royal, Manningham Lane, Bradford: 'the Celebrated Play in 4 Acts, founded on Miss Charlotte Brontë's Novel of the same name, lately acted with Great Success at the Globe Theatre, London, – *Jane Eyre*. By W. G. Wills, Esq.' BS exhibition 1991–2 showed '1883 27 & 29 Sept, Theatre Royal Bradford'.

1884
Stage plays
[Thompson, Charlotte (adapt.) (1883) *Jane Eyre*.]
   NYPL has reviews: 'star Charlotte Thompson, Star Theatre O. D. 8 December 1884: *New York Times* 9 December 1884, p. 9'; 'By Thompson, 8 December 1884, *NYDM* 13 December 1884.' *See also 1887, 1936.*

1887
Stage plays
[Thompson, Charlotte (adapt.) (1883) *Jane Eyre*.]
   NYPL has clipping and programme: '1887 Philadelphia, Forepaugh's Theatre and Museum'. *See also 1936.*

1888
Stage plays
[[Willing, James [J. T. Douglass] and Leonard Rae (adapts)] (1879) *Jane Eyre or Poor Relations*]
   NYPL has programme for London, Globe Theatre, dated ?1888.

1890
Illustrations, paintings, etc.
Brontë, Charlotte (1890) *Jane Eyre* (illus.), 2 vols, New York: Thomas Y. Crowell. Frontis., title vignette and 23 illustrations. (These illustrations, though not attributed, are the same as those by Edmund H. Garrett for the 1897 Walter Scott edition.)

1892
Novels, poems, etc.
Doyle, Arthur Conan, (1892) 'The Copper Beeches' (in *The Adventures of Sherlock Holmes*, London: John Murray, 1968)
   Sherlock Holmes story; see White (1992).

1897
Illustrations, paintings, etc.
Garrett, Edmund H. (illus.) (1897) *Jane Eyre*, Charlotte Brontë, London and Felling-on-Tyne: Walter Scott.

BPM has copy: p. 132 shows Jane on the heath; p. 280 Bertha in the fire. [See 1890]

Townsend, F. H. (illus.) (1897) *Jane Eyre*, Charlotte Brontë, London: Service & Paton.

BPM has copy. (Figure 4.1 above.)

1898

Novels, poems, etc.

James, Henry (1898) *The Turn of the Screw* (Kenneth B. Murdock (intro.), London: Everyman, 1964.)

Plot similarities. See Cargill (1963); Tintner (1976); Felman (1977); Passow (1979); Petry (1983).

1899

Novels, poems, etc.

Nesbit, E. (1899) *The Secret of Kyriels*, London: Hurst & Blackett.

See Briggs (1987: 193–5): a *Jane Eyre* derivative. Copy in Bodleian Library; also City of Westminster Public Libraries.

1900–9

Illustrations, paintings, etc.

Davidson, Thomas, *The First Meeting of Jane Eyre and Mr Rochester* (oil painting).

Kathryn White (personal communication 31.8.1993): 'The original painting was donated to the Brontë Parsonage Museum by the artist in 1907, and presumably was painted not long before then. We do not have a precise date' (BPM No. P56).

1904

Novels, poems, etc.

Ramal, Walter [Walter de la Mare] (1904) *Henry Brocken: His Travels and Adventures* (London: Faber & Faber, 1944).

Travelling hero meets Jane and Rochester after their marriage.

1905

Illustrations, paintings, etc.

Dulac, Edmund (illus.) (1905) *The Novels of the Brontë Sisters*, 10 vols, London: Dent.

BPM has copy.

1906

Incidental references

Harker, L. Allen (1906) *Concerning Paul and Fiametta*.

Quoted in Cunliffe (1950: 333); a small boy is frightened by 'Mrs Rochester'.

1909

Films

Jane Eyre (1909) Italian silent film.

BS exhibition 1991–2.

Stage plays

Leffingwell, Miron (adapt.) (1909) *Jane Eyre*, Morton Collection ts 316, University of Chicago, 1909.

1910

Films

Italian film (1910).

> From Pinion (1975: 386).

Marston, Theodore (adapt. and dir.) (1910) *Jane Eyre*, 1 reel b/w film with Irma Taylor and Frank Crane, Thanhauser Pictures.

> From Nudd. NYPL has review: *Motion Picture Herald*, vol. 6, 7.5.1910: 755.

Stage plays

Blaney, Charles E. (adapt.) (1910) *Jane Eyre*. (Unpublished play; ts Library of Congress).

> Nudd: 'Appears to be a plagiarized version of John Brougham's adaptation'.

1914

Films

Crane, Frank H. (dir.) (1914) *Jane Eyre*, 2 reels, b/w, with Ethel Grandin and Irving Cummings, Imp-Universal Pictures.

> From Nudd.

Kellette, John William (adapt.) (1914) Martin J Faust (dir.) *Jane Eyre*, 4 reels, b/w, with Alberta Ray, Blinkhorn Photoplays Corporation, New York, Whitman Productions.

> From Nudd. BPM has photocopies of stills (showing modern dress) and plot summary; this is fairly faithful except that Adèle is the legitimate daughter of Rochester and Bertha. The film ends with Jane saving the blind Rochester from a precipice.

Stage plays

Haswell, Percy (1914) [*Jane Eyre?*].

> NYPL has reviews from 'Robinson Locke collection of dramatic scrapbooks', Toronto, 1914. NAFR ser. 2 vol. 242 pp. 140, 150.

1915

Films

(1915) *The Castle of Thornfield* (Italian film).

> From Pinion (1975: 386).

(1915) *Jane Eyre* with Alan Hale as Rochester.

> BS exhibition 1991–2.

(1915) *Jane Eyre* with Richard Tucker as Rochester.

> BS exhibition 1991–2.

(1915) *Jane Eyre* with Conway Teale as Rochester.

> BS exhibition 1991–2.

(1915) Percy Haswell.

> NYPL has reviews from 'Robinson Locke collection of dramatic scrapbooks', New Orleans, 1915. NAFR ser. 2 vol. 242 pp. 140, 150.

Kirkbride, W. H. Churchman (adapt.) (1915) *The Master of Thornfield*, ts Maryland.

> Nudd: 'Cited in *Dramatic Compositions Copyrighted in the United States 1870–1916*, United States Copyright Office, Entry 28717a. *See also Shomer 192?, Brandon 1944.*

Vale, Travers (adapt. and dir.) (1915) *Jane Eyre*, 3 reels b/w, with Louise Vale and Franklin Ritchie, Biograph Company.

> From Nudd.

1917

Novels, poems, etc.

Dane, Clemence [Winifred Ashton] (1917) *Regiment of Women* (London: Heinemann, 1927).

> Plot similarities.

1918

Films

(1918) Italian film.

> From Pinion (1975: 386).

West, Paul (adapt.) (1918) *Woman and Wife*, 5 reels, b/w, dir. Edward Jose with Alice Brady and Eliott Dexter, Select Pictures.

> Listed in Nudd. BPM has photocopies of stills and a review: Robert C. McElravy, '"Woman and Wife"', *Moving Picture World*, 26.1.1918, p. 528, including plot summary. The distinctive feature here is that Rochester believes his insane wife to be dead until his brother-in-law reveals her existence for purposes of blackmail. She finally drowns, allowing Jane and Rochester to marry.

1920–9

Stage plays

Shomer, Rose Bachelis and Miriam Shomer-Zunser (adapts), *The Master of Thornfield*, ts Performing Arts Research Council NYPL 192?

> From Nudd. *See also 1915, 1944.*

1920

Films

The Orphan of Lowood (1920) Hungarian film.

> BS exhibition 1991–2. *See 1870, 1993.*

1921

Films

Ballin, Hugo (adapt., dir. and prod.) (1921) *Jane Eyre*, 7 reels b/w, with Mabel Ballin and Norman Trevor, W. W. Hodkinson Corporation.

From Nudd. BFI has stills. BS exhibition 1991–2 showed stills.

Novels, poems, etc.
von Arnim, Elizabeth (1921) *Vera*, Basingstoke: Macmillan (London: Virago, 1983).
  Plot similarities.

1922
Illustrations, paintings, etc.
Dulac, Edmund (illus.) (1922) *The Novels of the Brontë sisters*, May Sinclair (intro.),
6 vols, London: Dent; New York: Dutton.
  Hodgkins: Frontis. each vol. and 43 illus. BL (Boston Spa) does not have copy.

1923
Illustrations, paintings, etc.
Gabain, Ethel (illus.) (1923) *Jane Eyre*, Charlotte Brontë, Paris: Editions du
Souvenir et de l'Amitié.
  Quarto edition interleaved with tissue. Eight full-page lithographs: p. 64
  Rochester leans on Jane; p. 78 Rochester with Jane and Adèle; p. 140 Rochester
  and Jane in the garden; p. 160 Bertha tears the veil (Figure 4.2, above); p. 182
  Jane on the run; p. 189 Jane on the moor; p. 248 Jane lights the blind Rochester;
  p. 254 Jane serves Rochester at Ferndean. BPM has copy.

1926
Films
Bernhardt, Curtis [Kurt] (dir.) (1926) *Die Waise von Lowood*, German film.
  BPM, from Katz (1980). Note Charlotte Birch-Pfeiffer's stage adaptation had
  this title (1970); also Tayleure (1871); also Hungarian film 1920.

1929
Stage plays
Birkett, P[hyllis] (1929) *Jane Eyre*, BL LCP Add. ms 1929, Box 52.
  In Nudd. BPM has letter from Ann Wilton (who played Jane in London, 1931)
  to Mrs Edgerley, 29.12.1929, showing the 1929 production as 'prior to London'.
  Wilton is one half of 'Birkwill Productions', who staged the play. BPM has
  playbill for Hippodrome, Keighley, week commencing Monday 16 December
  with Phyllis Birkett as Jane 'with full London cast' (16 December was a Monday
  in 1929). NYPL has clipping. *See also 1931.*
Stone, Phyllis M. [1929] *Parish Plays* No. 24, Dramatic Readings from 'Jane Eyre'
(Charlotte Brontë) arranged by P. M. Stone, London: Sheldon Press.
  From Y & T.

1930–9
Illustrations, paintings, etc.
Sewell, Helen (illus.) *Jane Eyre*.

According to the dust-jacket of M. L. Jarden's *The Three Brontës* (1938), Helen Sewell had 'recently completed a wonderful set of drawings for *Jane Eyre*'. BPM has no information (personal communication 31.8.1993).

Jane Eyre told in pictures, Thriller Comics No. 31.
BPM has copy (SB: 1650). Large format comicbook; style suggests 1930s; plot begins with Thornfield.

Brontë, Charlotte, *The Romance of Jane Eyre*, Woman's World Library No. 347.
Cover shows head of Jane smiling; ruins in background. BPM has copy. Style suggests date.

Novels, poems, etc.
Webb, Mary
Brontë Society Reports for 1991–2, Centenary Sub-Committee: Mary Webb wrote an essay on *Jane Eyre* (I have not traced this).

1930
Radio
(1930) *Jane Eyre*, radio.
BPM has cutting from *Radio Times* 25.7.1930: 'The three demon-haunted sisters: Richard Church tells the story of the three Brontë sisters . . . Readings from "Jane Eyre", Charlotte Brontë's great novel, have been broadcast on Thursday evenings'.

1931
Illustrations, paintings, etc.
(1931–3) Brontë Sisters, *The Complete Works*, illus., in 11 vols, Oxford: Basil Blackwell & Houghton Mifflin (Shakespeare Head edition).
Hodgkins Cat. 48 No. 118. *Jane Eyre* volume has illustration p. 46. 'Rydings Hall, Birstall "Thornfield Hall" from a drawing by Jack Hewer'.

Radio
(1931) Couper, Barbara and Howard Rose (adapts), *Jane Eyre*, prod. Howard Rose, radio.
BPM has cutting from *Radio Times* 6.11.1931. *See also 1932, 1936, 1946, 1972.*

Stage plays
[Birkett, P[hyllis] (1929) *Jane Eyre*.]
BPM has playbill for Kingsway Theatre (London) with Phyllis Birkett as Bertha and Ann Wilton as Jane, September, 1931. BS exhibition 1991–2: '1931. Phyllis Birkett produced her own adaptation for Kingsway Theatre, London, with Anne Wilton and Basil Gill.' Reviews: *Yorkshire Post* 25.9.1931; [Bradford] *Observer* 25.9.1931, 27.9.1931.

1932
Radio
[Couper, Barbara and Howard Rose (adapts) (1931) *Jane Eyre*, prod. Howard Rose, radio.]

BPM has cutting from *Radio Times* 30.12.1932; same cast-list as for 1931. BS exhibition 1991–2: '1932 BBC Radio adapt[ation] . . . (broadcast several times up to the early 1940s). 1932 version had Milton Rosmer (who played Heathcliff in the 1920 silent film of *Wuthering Heights*) as Rochester'. *Note:* Couper adapted *Wuthering Heights* for Radio in 1934. *See also 1936, 1946, 1972.*

1933
Films
(1933) *Jane Eyre*.

NYPL has 'a collection of pressbooks for non-United Artists productions'.

1934
Films
Comandini, Adèle (adapt.) (1934) *Jane Eyre*, 16 mm-sound-b/w, dir. Christy Cabanne, prod. Ben Verschleiser, Monogram Pictures, starring Virginia Bruce, Colin Clive, Olaf Hytten and Edith Fellowes.

In Nudd. BPM have some film strips and stills. BFI have stills. NYPL have photographs and press book. See Wagner (1975: 248). *Note:* Colin Clive, who played Rochester, played Frankenstein in the 1931 Boris Karloff film (BS exhibition 1991–2).

Novels, poems, etc.
Jenkins, Elizabeth (1934) *Harriet*.

See Rhys (1984: 68, 69 n.): Rhys's editors find 'obvious affinities' with '"the first Mrs Rochester" in *Jane Eyre* and *Wide Sargasso Sea*.' I do not find the similarities striking.

1936
Novels, poems, etc.
Holtby, Winifred (1936) *South Riding* (Glasgow: Fontana, 1974).

Plot similarities and explicit references (1974: 137–8). *See also 1937, 1974.*

Lehmann, Rosamond (1936) *The Weather in the Streets* (London: Virago, 1981).

Plot similarities.

Stage plays
Carleton, Marjorie Chalmers (adapt.) (1936) *Jane Eyre by Charlotte Brontë: A Dramatisation in Three Acts*, Baker's Plays, New York, Boston, Los Angeles.

Y & T: Baker's professional plays series. In Nudd. *See also 1938.*

Jerome, Helen (1936) *Jane Eyre: A Drama of Passion in Three Acts . . . dramatised from Charlotte Brontë's novel*, Hamish Hamilton, London 1936. Printed text defined as 'Produced by Athole Stewart, Queen's Theatre Shaftesbury Avenue, 1936, with Curigwen Lewis as Jane, Reginald Tate as Rochester, Dorothy Hamilton as The Maniac'.

Y & T. BPM has playbill for the first performance, at Birmingham Repertory, for three weeks from Feb. 1936, produced by Herbert M. Prentice, with Curigwen Lewis and Stephen Murray, with musical interludes (piano) by Schumann, Grieg, Chopin, Liszt, Schubert; also programme for Eighth Malvern Festival, August 1936, including Helen Jerome's *Jane Eyre* produced by Herbert M. Prentice; also review of same production (now with Reginald Tate) at Theatre Royal [Brighton?]: *Brighton and Hove Herald* 26.9.1936. *Play Pictorial*, vol. 69 (143) has photographs of Shaftesbury Avenue production (see Figure 4.3, above). BPM has copy. *See also 1937, 1938, 1940, 1943, 1944, 1946, 1961, 1966, 1989.*

[Jerome (1936)]: US stage production with Katharine Hepburn, ? Theresa Helburn (dir.).

See Higham (1975: 82–3). NYPL has souvenir programme and 'several on-stage scenes with Katharine Hepburn', New York 1936–7, Theatre Guild Collection; also Boston, Colonial Theatre 1936; also uncatalogued programmes; also undated 'Souvenir programme: Stars, Sylvia Sidney and Luther Adler'; Shreveport, La. [sic], Little Theatre of Shreveport; Denver, Denver Auditorium, with Sylvia Sidney and Luther Adler.

[Thompson, Charlotte (adapt.) (1883) *Jane Eyre*.]

NYPL has photographs; 'Road Tour Production 1936–7'.

1937
Films
Saville, Victor (dir. and prod.) (1937) *South Riding*, prod. Alexander Korda, written by Ian Dalrymple from the novel by Winifred Holtby, with Ann Todd as Sarah and Ralph Richardson as Carne.

Hull City Library Holtby Archive has small and large prints. Halliwell quotes *Variety*: 'Another artistic Korda film . . . lacking in a story of popular appeal'. *See also 1936, 1974.*

Stage plays
[Jerome, Helen (1936) *Jane Eyre: A Drama of Passion*.]

Doubleday, New York, 1937. BPM and NYPL have playbills for Aldwych Theatre, London, April 1937; 'the play first produced at the Malvern Festival by Herbert M. Prentice' (but see 1936), produced by Athole Stewart with Curigwen Lewis. BPM has programme and publicity leaflets for a performance at the Grand Theatre, Leeds, produced by Emile Littler, 1937, with Myrtle Richardson as Jane and Donald Mather as Rochester (England Touring production); the pictures, however, are of Curigwen Lewis and Reginald Tate.

[Jerome (1936): US stage production with Katharine Hepburn.]

NYPL has programmes for performances with Katharine Hepburn in Chicago,

Erlanger Theatre, 1937 and Washington (DC), National Theatre, 1937. According to Higham (1975: 83), Hepburn played Jane in Chicago, Cleveland and Pittsburgh. *See also 1938, 1940, 1943, 1944, 1946, 1961, 1966, 1989.*

Television
[Jerome, Helen (1936) *Jane Eyre: A Drama of Passion.*]
Televised with Curigwen Lewis as Jane 8.3.1937 (BPM). See *Radio Times* 20.9.1973: 11.

1938
Novels, poems, etc.
Du Maurier, Daphne (1938) *Rebecca* (London: Pan, 1975).
Plot similarities with *Jane Eyre*. See Hawkins (1990: 139–49). *See also 1940.*

Stage plays
[Carleton, Marjorie Chalmers (adapt.) (1936) *Jane Eyre.*]
NYPL has programme for performance in New York City Friends' Meeting House, 1938.
[Jerome, Helen (1936) *Jane Eyre: A Drama of Passion*]
Published (1938), London: Samuel French. BPM has programme for and unidentified review of performance by the Arthur Brough Players at Prince's Theatre, Bradford, week commencing 10.1.1938, with Pamela Titheradge as Jane and Allan Goford as Rochester, produced by Oswald Dale Roberts; also review by P. R., *Liverpool Echo* 11.3.1938 about 'Playhouse' production produced by Charles Thomas, with Ruth Lodge as Jane and Roderick Lovell as Rochester; also programme for performance at Birchcliffe Sunday School, Hebden Bridge, 1.11.1938 and 5.11.1938, produced by F. T. Pickles with Gertrude Crabtree and Herbert Sutcliffe. *See also 1937, 1940, 1943, 1944, 1946, 1961, 1966, 1989.*

1939
Films
Ratoff, Gregory (dir.) (1939), *Intermezzo* (UK title *Escape to Happiness*), written by George O'Neill, original scenario Gosta Stevens, Gustav Molander, with Leslie Howard and Ingrid Bergman.
Halliwell: 'A renowned, married violinist has an affair with his musical protegee. Archetypal cinema love story . . . William Wyler is said to have assisted in the direction'.
Sobol, Edward (dir.) (1939) *Jane Eyre*, 95 min. film with Flora Campbell and Dennis Hoey, NCB 12.10.1939.
From Nudd.
Stahl, John M. (dir.) (1939) *When Tomorrow Comes*, written by Dwight Taylor from James M. Cain short story, with Charles Boyer, Irene Dunne, Barbara O'Neill.
Plot similarities with *Jane Eyre*. Halliwell: 'The same story was remade twice in 1956, as *Serenade* and *Interlude*, and in 1968 as *Interlude*'. (*Note*: *Interlude* was released in 1957.)

1940–9
Radio
[Couper, Barbara and Howard Rose (adapts) (1931) *Jane Eyre*, prod. Howard Rose, radio.]

BS exhibition 1991–2: '1932 BBC Radio adapted by Barbara Couper and Howard Rose (broadcast several times up to the early 1940s)'. *Note*: Couper adapted *Wuthering Heights* for Radio in 1934. *See also 1932, 1936, 1946, 1972.*

1940
Films
Hitchcock, Alfred (dir.) (1940) *Rebecca*, written by Robert E. Sherwood and Joan Harrison from the novel by Daphne du Maurier, with Laurence Olivier and Joan Fontaine.

Novel published 1938. Halliwell quotes Maxim (Olivier): 'She was incapable of love, or tenderness, or decency'. *Note*: Joan Fontaine, who played the girl in this film, was to play Jane in the 1944 film. Olivier played Heathcliff in 1939. *See also 1944, 1956.*

Stage plays
[Jerome, Helen (1936)] – *Jane Eyre*, Little Theatre Bristol, 4.3.1940, directed by Ronald Russell with Peggy Ann Wood as Jane, Richard Hinton as Rochester.

BPM has playbill (SB 1298b). *See also 1962, 1966, 1989.*

1941
Stage plays
Phelps, Pauline (1941) *Jane Eyre, A Drama adapted from Charlotte Brontë's book of the same name* (published by Wetmore Declamation Bureau, Sioux City, Iowa).

Y & T; Nudd.

1942
Illustrations, paintings, etc.
Freedman, Barnett (illus.) (1942) *Jane Eyre*, Charlotte Brontë, G. T. Wintereich (intro.), New York: Heritage.

Hodgkins Cat. 48 No. 20: 16 coloured lithographs.

1943
Films
Tourneur, Jacques (dir.) (1943) *I Walked With a Zombie*, produced by Val Lewton, screenplay by Curt Siodmak and Ardel Wray, based on an original story by Inez Wallace, with James Ellison, Frances Dee, Tom Conway.

Plot similarities with *Jane Eyre*. BPM has stills and poster from BFI. Film featured in BS exhibition 1991–2. See Drake ([1967]: 212–13; BPM has photocopy); also Wagner (1975: 250). Halliwell: 'A nurse is retained by a Caribbean planter to care for his voodoo-sick wife. Mild horror from the famous

Lewton package ... generally thin stuff, the plot having been mirthfully borrowed from *Jane Eyre*'.

Illustrations, paintings, etc.

Eichenberg, Fritz (illus.) (1943) *Jane Eyre*, Charlotte Brontë, New York: Random House.

Sixteen wood engravings, and front and back covers. BPM has copy. *Note*: Eichenberg also illustrated *Wuthering Heights* for Random House 1943. See Figure 4.4, above.

Stage plays

[Jerome, Helen (1936) *Jane Eyre: A Drama of Passion*.]

Published (1943) New York: Samuel French. BPM has playbill and programme for Theatre Royal Leeds, 5.7.[1943], produced by Eric Howard with June Daunt as Jane and Michael Gover as Rochester, described as 'From the Queen's Theatre London' (i.e. 1936 production). NYPL has review of performance at Brooklyn, Flatbush Theatre, 11.5.1943; also clippings, halftones, reviews, Denver, Detroit, San Francisco, 1943. *See also 1937, 1938, 1944, 1946, 1961, 1966, 1989.*

1944

Films

Stevenson, Robert (dir.) (1944) *Jane Eyre*, film adapted by Robert Stevenson, Aldous Huxley and John Houseman, produced by William Goetz, with music by Bernard Herrmann (who wrote the opera, *Wuthering Heights*, in 1965), Orson Welles as Rochester, Joan Fontaine as Jane and Elizabeth Taylor as Helen, Twentieth Century Fox.

BPM has stills from BFI; also pictures and review in *Picture Post* 15.1.1944; also Japanese publicity stills 1953, from 2 vol. edn of *Jane Eyre* (SB 3426). Reviews: see Andrews (1944); Lemon (1944). See Nudd, Wagner (1975: 244–51). NYPL has clippings, photographs and pressbooks (English and American). Review: New York Radio City Music Hall, *[New York?] Times* 4.2.1944. *Note*: Joan Fontaine played the vulnerable heroine in 1940 film of *Rebecca* and in *Serenade* (1956), both plots with *Jane Eyre* similarities. *Note*: Wyler is said to have assisted in the direction of *Intermezzo* (1939).

Stage plays

Brandon, Dorothy (adapt.) (1944) *The Master of Thornfield*; ts British Theatre Play Library, British Theatre Association, produced 1944.

In Nudd. BPM has playbill for 'Dorothy Brandon's new dramatization of *Jane Eyre*', New Theatre Oxford, produced by Keneth Kent with Rosalinde Fuller as Jane and Henry Edwards as Rochester, week commencing 14.2.1944. NYPL has programme. See Kirkbride, 1915 (same title); also Shomer 1920s.

[Jerome, Helen (1936) *Jane Eyre: A Drama of Passion*.]
> BPM has playbill for performance at Garrick Playhouse, Altrincham, week commencing 23.10.1944, produced by Maxwell Colburn with Dallas Yorke as Jane and John Hardinge as Rochester. *See also 1961, 1966, 1989.*

1945

Films

Bennett, Compton (dir.) (1945) *The Seventh Veil*, written by Muriel and Sydney Box with James Mason, Ann Todd, Herbert Lom.
> Halliwell (870): 'A splendid modern melodrama in the tradition of *Jane Eyre* and *Rebecca* . . . the most utter tosh.' Quotes Richard Mallen, *Punch*: 'An odd, artificial, best sellerish kind of story, with reminiscences of *Trilby* and *Jane Eyre* and all their imitations down to *Rebecca*'.

Novels, poems, etc.

Allingham, Margery (1945) 'Wanted: someone innocent', in *Deadly Duo*.
> *Jane Eyre* similarities.

Taylor, Elizabeth (1945) *At Mrs Lippincote's* (London: Virago, 1988).
> Small boy imagines Mrs Rochester lives upstairs.

Stage plays

Kendall, Jane [Anne Martens] (adapt.) (1945) *Jane Eyre* adapted from Charlotte Brontë's novel, Dramatic Publishing Company, Chicago.
> Y & T; Nudd. NYPL has undated programme.

1946

Illustrations, paintings, etc.

Booker, Nell (illus.) (1946) *Jane Eyre*, Charlotte Brontë, Mary Lamberton Becker (intro.), New York: World Publishers.
> Hodgkins Cat. 48 No. 22: coloured and b/w illus.

Novels, poems, etc.

Taylor, Elizabeth (1946) *Palladian*, Peter Davies (London: Virago, 1985).
> *JE* plot plus explicit reference (1985: 35). See Crompton, J. (1992: 59) for Rosamond Lehmann's comment on *Palladian* (referring to *JE*).

Radio

[Couper, Barbara and Howard Rose (adapts) (1931), *Jane Eyre*, produced by Howard Rose, radio.]
> Broadcast in eleven weekly parts from February 1946. BS exhibition 1991–2: '1946 version had Reginald Tate (who played Rochester in the 1936 Jerome version)'. *Note*: Couper adapted *Wuthering Heights* for Radio in 1934. See Raleigh [1946]: Belle Crystal as Jane. *See also 1932, 1936, 1972.*

Television

29.9.1946: BBC Television; Mary Mackenzie, Anthony Hawtrey.
   From Pinion (1975: 386).

1947

Illustrations, paintings, etc.

Classics Illustrated No. 39 (no BPM No.); comicstrip booklet; 'That is *my wife*'
cover.
   Myer (1987: 106) dates this as 1947.

Incidental references

Taylor, Elizabeth (1947) *A View of the Harbour* (London: Virago 1987).
   Reference to *Jane Eyre* [1987: 33–4].

1948

Television

26.9.1948; BBC Television; Barbara Mullen, Reginald Tate.
   From Pinion (1975: 386).

1949

Television

Jane Eyre, Studio One [CBS], with Charlton Heston, 1949.
   From Nudd.

1950-9

Illustrations, paintings, etc.

Brontë, Charlotte, *Jane Eyre*, Classics Illustrated No 39, 'Featuring stories by the
world's greatest authors', 15c in Canada and Foreign.
   BPM has copy but it has no number. Large format comicstrip including Moor
   House episode; cover has 'that is *my wife*' scene; inside pictures are the same as
   Jane Eyre illustrated by Harley M. Griffiths (BPM SB: 1439), which has 'cast-
   list' cover. Style suggests 1950s. Another copy in BPM (SB: 3011c) has same
   title material as unnumbered copy, but different cover, text and illustrations and
   omits Moor House episode; since cover shows a Timothy Dalton-like Rochester,
   this was presumably produced after the 1983 film with Timothy Dalton.
Griffiths, Harley M. (illus.) *Jane Eyre*, Charlotte Brontë, Classics Illustrated.
   Copy in BPM (SB: 1439): large format comicstrip; inside pictures are the same
   as 'Classics Illustrated No. 39' (version with no BPM No., including Moor
   House episodes, showing Jane with bare feet and short skirt), but front cover is
   different – this one has 'cast-list' portraits. Style suggests 1950s.

1950

Novels, poems, etc.

Brand, Christianna (1950) *Cat and Mouse* (London and Edinburgh: Ian Hendry,
1982).
   Some plot similarities and explicit allusion [1982: 12, 184].

Stage plays

[Jerome, Helen (1936) *Jane Eyre: A Drama of Passion.*]

BPM has playbill for Brontë Festival held in Church School Theatre, Haworth, including Jerome's *Jane Eyre* (30 June–4 July) with Davison's *Wuthering Heights* and *The Brontës. See also 1989.*

1952

Illustrations, paintings, etc.

Brontë, Charlotte, *Jane Eyre*, Regents Classics, 1952.

BPM has copy; front cover shows Jane and Rochester about to open an arched door, Rochester holding a candle; atmosphere of a girl's school story.

Television

Nickell, Paul (dir.) (1952) *Jane Eyre*, 1 hour, prod. Worthington Miner with Katherine Bard and Kevin McCarthy, Studio One, CBS, 4 August 1952.

From Nudd.

1953

Film

[Stevenson, Robert (dir.) (1944) *Jane Eyre.*]

BPM has Japanese publicity stills 1953, from 2 vol. edition of *Jane Eyre.*

1955

Stage plays

Jane Eyre, play performed at Oakwell Hall by the Dewsbury Pioneers Amateur Operatic Society, with Desmond Hettle as Rochester and Joan Swift as Jane.

BPM has unidentified cutting and review from [Bradford] *Telegraph and Argus*, 30.9.1955.

1956

Films

Mann, Anthony (dir.) (1956) *Serenade*, written by Ivan Goff, Ben Roberts and John Twist with Mario Lanza and Joan Fontaine.

Halliwell: 'opera singer . . . is desired by two women' [but he sees it as related to *Interlude* (1939 and 1957]. *Note*: Fontaine played the girl in *Rebecca* (1940) and Jane Eyre in 1944.

Stage plays

Hartford, Huntingdon (adapt.) (1956) *Jane Eyre*, ts Performing Arts Research Center, NYPL, produced 1956.

From Nudd. NYPL has clipping. *See also 1958.*

Television

Cox, Constance (adapt.) (1956) *Jane Eyre*, BBC TV serial in six parts, February and March 1956, with Stanley Baker as Rochester and Daphne Slater as Jane.

BPM has cutting from *TV Mirror* 25.2.1956, vol. 6 (8), p. 8. See Nudd. *See also 1946, 1948, 1959, 1963, 1965, 1972.*

1957
Films
Sirk, Douglas (1957) *Interlude*, film written by Daniel Fuchs from a James M. Cain short story, with Rossano Brazzi, June Allyson (filmed by John M. Stahl in 1939 as *When Tomorrow Comes*).

Plot has *Jane Eyre* similarities. Halliwell: 'American girl in Munich falls in love with an orchestral conductor but leaves him because of his insane wife'; quotes *MFB*: 'contains every cliché known to romantic fiction'. *See also 'Intermezzo', 1939; 1968.*

Television
Esson, Robert (adapt.) (1957) *Jane Eyre*, colour, 1 hour, with Joan Elan and Patrick Macnee, Matinee Theatre, NBC 16.5.1957.

From Nudd.

1958
Stage plays
[Hartford, Huntingdon (adapt.) (1956) *Jane Eyre*, ts Performing Arts Research Center, NYPL, produced 1956.]

NYPL has review of performance at New York Belasco Theatre, 1.5.1958.

1959
Stage plays
Cox, Constance (1959) *Jane Eyre, A Play from the Novel by Charlotte Brontë*, London: J. Garnet Miller.

Y & T; Nudd. *See also 1956, 1972, 1984.*

1960–9
Novels, poems, etc.
Brontë, Charlotte, *The Orphan of Lowood*, 1960s(?).

According to a Hungarian academic in Debrecen, Hungary, a bowdlerized Hungarian version of *Jane Eyre* was published under this name in the 1960s. *Note*: this title originated with Charlotte Birch-Pfeiffer's 1870 adaptation in English and German; a Hungarian film was made under this title in 1920, and a German film in 1926.

1961
Musical settings
Shaper, Hal and Roy Harley Lewis (adapts) (1961) *Jane* (musical), lyrics by Hal Shaper, music by Monty Stevens, London, 1961; first performed Theatre Royal,

Windsor, 1961, Starring Diane Todd and Terence Cooper, and attended by members of the Royal family (BS exhibition, 1991–2).

Nudd: ts courtesy of Confederation Centre of the Arts, Charlottetown, Prince Edward Island, Canada. *See also 1966, 1970, 1973.*

Novels, poems, etc.
Holt, Victoria (1961) *Mistress of Mellyn*, London: Collins.
Plot similarities; modern Gothic.

Stage plays
[Jerome, Helen (1936) *Jane Eyre: A Drama of Passion.*]
Published New York: Samuel French. *See also 1937, 1938, 1943, 1946, 1962, 1966, 1989.*

Television
Dyne, Michael (adapt.) (1961) *Jane Eyre*, 1 hour, produced by David Susskind, directed by Marc Daniels, with Zachary Scott and Sally Ann Howes, Family Classics, CBS 27 April.
From Nudd.

1962
Musical settings
Jepson, Alfred (1962) 'Rochester's Song to Jane Eyre', 'lyrics by Charlotte Brontë, music by Alfred Jepson', New York: Etnorb.
BPM has copy; in twelve stanzas, beginning 'The truest love, that ever heart'

Stage plays
[Jerome, Helen (1936) *Jane Eyre: A Drama of Passion.*]
BPM has signed playbill for performance at Little Theatre, Bristol, 15 October for two weeks, produced by Ronald Russell with Pauline Taylor as Jane and Giles Phibbs as Rochester. *Note*: Ronald Russell produced this play at this theatre in 1940, but on different dates and with different cast. *See also 1989.*

1963
Novels, poems, etc.
Murdoch, Iris (1963) *The Unicorn*, London: Chatto & Windus (Harmondsworth: Penguin, 1966).
Generic similarities only. See Scholes (1967).

Television
[Cox, Constance (adapt.) (1956) *Jane Eyre*, BBC TV serial in six parts.]
New production broadcast in 1963, directed by Rex Tucker, with Ann Bell and Richard Leech. BPM has cutting from *Radio Times*, 11.4.1963, with cast list and picture.

1964

Stage plays

Holroyd, George Henry (1964) *Plays from Literature . . . Jane Eyre from the Novel by Charlotte Brontë*, London: George Philip.

Y & T.

Tyler, Brian (1964) *Jane Eyre*, England Touring Production.

BPM has playbill for performance at Theatre Royal, Nottingham, produced by Patrick Desmond with Barry Sinclair as Rochester and Josephine Stuart as Jane. Nudd cites BPM and NYPL as source for 'London, 1964'.

1965

Films

Wise, Robert (dir) (1965) *The Sound of Music*, Argyle.

Plot similarities.

1966

Musical settings

[Shaper, Hal and Roy Harley Lewis (adapts) (1961) *Jane*.]

BPM has playbill for second production, directed by Stanley Hawkins, musical director Howard Robinson, with Valerie Evans as Jane and Nicol Thorogood as Rochester, produced by Finchley and Friern Barnet Operatic and Dramatic Society, Hornsey Theatre, The Broadway, London, 26 September–1 October [1966]; also programme for performance in Finchley, 1966: *Jane Eyre: A Musical*, 'a new musical play adapted from Charlotte Brontë's *Jane Eyre*. Book by Hal Shaper and Roy Harley Lewis'. Nudd: 'Produced in London, 1966'. See L[emon] (1967). *See also 1970, 1973*.

Novels, poems, etc.

Rhys, Jean (1966) *Wide Sargasso Sea* (Harmondsworth: Penguin, 1983).

Story of first Mrs Rochester; see Baer (1983); James (1983); Angier (1985); Spivak (1985); Azim (1993).

See also 1993.

Stage plays

[Jerome, Helen (1936) *Jane Eyre: A Drama of Passion*.]

BPM has playbill for performance by the Arthur Brough Players, directed by Elizabeth Addyman, at Leas Pavilion, Folkestone, 23.5.1966 with Sally Goldie as Jane and Louis Halser as Rochester. *Note:* The Arthur Brough Players performed this play at Prince's Theatre, Bradford, week commencing 10.1.1938. *See also 1989.*

1967

Illustrations, paintings, etc.

Brontë, Charlotte, *Jane Eyre*, Storm Jameson (intro. and notes), London: Pan Books.

BPM has copy: front cover shows woman with bonnet and crinoline *c.* 1840.

Novels, poems, etc.
Byatt, A. S. (1967) *The Game* (Harmondsworth: Penguin, 1983).
Mostly biographical references to Charlotte Brontë; see Creighton (1987).

1968
Films
Billington, Kevin (dir.) (1968) *Interlude*, written by Lee Langley with Oscar Werner, Virginia Maskell, John Cleese.
Seems to be a remake of Sirk, Douglas, *Interlude*, film based on a James M. Cain short story filmed by John M. Stahl in 1939 as *When Tomorrow Comes*; but Halliwell sees it as '*Intermezzo* remade'. *See also 'Intermezzo' (1939); 1957.*

Illustrations, paintings, etc.
Classics Illustrated No. 39 (BPM SB: 3011c); 'Timothy Dalton' cover (1980s); inside pictures 1960s?
Myer (1987: 106) dates this as 1968.

1969
Novels, poems, etc.
Drabble, Margaret (1969) *The Waterfall* (Harmondsworth: Penguin, 1971).
Explicit references to *JE*; see Creighton (1987).

1970
Films
Mann, Delbert (dir.) (1970) *Jane Eyre*, Frederick Brogger (prod.), Jack Pulman (screenplay), with George C. Scott as Rochester and Susannah York as Jane, British Lion Pictures, 16 mm colour, released UK and Europe 1970.
BPM has BFI stills; also Chinese publicity pamphlet. Review: *Yorkshire Post* 16.3.1971. See *BST* 16.81.59-61 (1971). *See also 1971, 1982, 1990.*

Incidental references, etc.
Angelou, Maya (1970) *I Know Why the Caged Bird Sings*, New York: Bantam (London: Virago, 1984).
Heroine finds an analogy between Jane Eyre and one of her friends [1984: 136].

Musical settings
[Shaper, Hal and Roy Harley Lewis (adapts) (1961) *Jane.*]
Nudd: 'produced . . . in Canada 1970–1'. *See also 1966, 1973.*

1971
Films
[Mann, Delbert (dir) (1970) *Jane Eyre*; shortened version of British Lion Film version, NBC 24.3.1971; Jack Pulman (adapt.).]

From Nudd. BS exhibition pictures the 'TV movie with Jack Hawkins as Brocklehurst and music by John Williams'. *See 1982.*

Novels, poems, etc.
Spark, Muriel (1971) *Not To Disturb* (Harmondsworth, Penguin, 1974).
   Has a 'mad[man] in the attic'. *Note:* Spark collaborated with Derek Stanford on *Emily Brontë* (1953) and *The Brontë Letters* (1953).

1972
Novels, poems, etc.
Lessing, Doris (1972) *The Four-Gated City*, London: Granada.
   'Madwoman' pattern.

Radio
Couper, Barbara (adapt.), *Jane Eyre*, Radio 4 serial, produced by Betty Davies with Meg Wynne Owen as Jane and Patrick Allen as Rochester.
   Note: Couper first adapted *Jane Eyre* for radio in 1931 (qv). BPM has review: *The Scotsman* 8.5.1972.

Stage plays
[Cox, Constance (1959) *Jane Eyre.*]
   BPM: performed by Canterbury Players with Denise Woolley as Jane and Roy Wallwork as Rochester, 1972. *See also 1956, 1959, 1973, 1984.*
Morgan, Joan E. (1972) *Jane Eyre*, Bermuda Library, City Hall.
   BPM has playbill for performance of 'an adaptation for dramatized reading' with male narrator, Jill Hopwood as Jane and Leonard McDonald as Rochester. Review: *Royal Gazette*, Bermuda, 12.7.1972 (BPM).

1973
Musical settings
[Shaper, Hal and Roy Harley Lewis (adapts) (1961) *Jane.*]
   BPM has press cutting: *Ruislip Weekly Post* 25.7.1973: 'Jane Eyre is to return to the Theatre Royal Windsor after twelve years, and Diane Todd will again take the star role'; Gordon Clyde as Rochester. Review: *Bracknell News*, 19.7.1973: 'unfortunately the management have seen fit to exhume "Jane Eyre"'. *See also 1961, 1966, 1970, 1973.*

Sound recording
(1973) *Jane Eyre*, a dramatic reading of the novel by Claire Bloom, Anthony Quayle, Cathleen Nesbitt, George Rose, Maria Lennard, John Malcolm and Anna Steiger, Caedmon Spoken Word Records.
   See *BST* 16.83.237.

Stage plays

Cannon, John (1973) *Jane Eyre*.

BPM has typescript; also playbill for 'World Premiere', Charles Savage (dir.), with Jacquie Dubin as Jane, Charles McKeown as Rochester and Philippa Howell as 'the maniac' at Crewe Theatre, 18–29 September [1973]. BPM has unidentified review; also press cutting: *Bury Times* 27.7.1973. See 1982, 1984.

[Cox, Constance (1959) *Jane Eyre*.]

BPM: produced by Mary McKeown with Pat Richmond as Jane at Wigan Little Theatre, 21–8.4.1973. *See also 1956, 1959, 1972, 1984*.

Television

Chapman, Robin (adapt.) (1973) *Jane Eyre*, BBC serial 1973, five 60-minute episodes, Joan Craft (dir.), John McRae (prod.), with Sorcha Cusack as Jane and Michael Jayston as Rochester.

In Nudd. BPM has copies of the scripts for episodes 1, 2, 4 and 5; also *Radio Times* 22–8.9.1973; also letter from (Mrs) Veronica White, *Radio Times* 8.11.1973; also press cutting: *Sheffield Star* 16.4.1973 [account of filming at Chatsworth]; also reviews: [Southend] *Evening Echo* 4.10.1973; *Bournemouth Evening Echo* 22.9.1973; *Daily Telegraph* 24.9.1973 and 28.9.1973; *Scunthorpe Evening Telegraph* 27.9.1973; *Daily Mail* 28.9.1973; [Ipswich] *Evening Star* 28.9.1973; *Derbyshire Times* 28.9.1973; *The Times* 28.9.1973 and 29.9.1973 (identical): *Colchester Evening Gazette* 1.10.1973; *Shields Gazette* 3.10.1973; *Lancashire Evening Post* 4.10.1973 and 16.11.1973; *Banstead Herald* 4.10.1973; *Croydon Advertiser* 5.10.1973 (musical introduction is Elgar's Introduction and Allegro for strings); Bernard Davies, *Broadcast* 12.10.1973; *Sunday Times* 21.10.1973 (picture only); Patricia Smith, *Southern Evening Echo* 26.10.1973; Peter Fiddick, *Guardian* 29.10.1973; *Justice of the Peace* 3.11.1973.

1974

Television

Holtby, Winifred [1936] (1974) *South Riding*, Yorkshire Television serial.

Hull City Library has seven colour prints; *JE* plot similarities.

1975

Novels, poems, etc.

Jhabvala, Ruth Prawer (1975) *Heat and Dust* (London: Sphere, 1991).

Has a first (mad) wife and female narrator.

Naipaul, V. S. (1975) *Guerillas* (Harmondsworth: Penguin 1976).

Implied reference to *JE* (1976: 9).

1978

Stage plays

Hamilton, Lionel (adapt.) (1978) *Jane Eyre*, England.

Nudd: Cited in *British Theatrelog*, Autumn 1978, p. 17. *See also 1989*.

Kontaibo, Miss Kazue (dir.) (1978) *Jane Eyre*, Japanese play, with Miss Fumie Kashiyama as Jane and Mr Hiroshi Iwashita as Rochester.

BPM has programme with photograph of Top Withens, etc., accompanied by letter from Japanese member of audience, with typescript note attached: 'performed by Mingei Theatre Co. Three Acts, Eight Scenes'. Featured in BS exhibition 1991-2.

1980–9
Illustrations, paintings, etc.
Brontë, Charlotte, *Jane Eyre*, Classics Illustrated No. 39, 'Featuring stories by the world's greatest authors', Classics Illustrated, New York (n.d.).

BPM has copy (SB: 3011c): large format comicstrip; omits Moor House episode. Cover shows a Timothy Dalton-like Rochester and is presumably post-1983 Dalton film, though the style of the inside pictures suggests the 1960s (*see 1968*). Another copy in BPM (no number) has same title material but different cover, text and illustrations; it emphasizes childhood episodes and includes Moor House; style suggests 1950s.

Television
Dynasty, American Television soap opera series.

See Hawkins (1990: 196, n.4 to Ch. 4): *Dynasty* owes its structure to *Jane Eyre*.

1980
Novels, poems, etc.
Greenwald, Sheila (1980) *It All Began with Jane Eyre or The Secret Life of Franny Dillman*, New York: Laurel-Leaf Books, Dell Publishing (Harmondsworth: Penguin, 1988).

BPM has copy of US edition. Front cover: 'Would Franny's life ever be as exciting as the books she loved to read?'

Parodies
Prideaux, James (1980) *Jane Heights*, A Parody of *Jane Eyre* and *Wuthering Heights*, produced in Los Angeles, California, music by Arthur B. Rubinstein, lyrics by James Prideaux, 1980.

From Nudd: ts Courtesy of the William Morris Agency, Beverley Hills. See Nudd (1992).

1982
Stage plays
[Cannon, John (1973) *Jane Eyre*.]

Performed by the Wyvern [Community] Theatre, Shelley Sutton (dir.) with Suzanne Alford as Jane, David Abery as Rochester and Kate Goodall as 'Madwoman' at Swindon, 1982. BPM has programme; also review: *The Stage* 22.4.1982: 'This version of "Jane Eyre", an adaptation by writer John Cannon from Charlotte Brontë's novel, was originally commissioned by Wyvern director Charles Savage on behalf of the Arts Council and Crewe Repertory Theatre, where it was first performed'; BPM has two photographs. *See also 1984.*

Television
[Mann, Delbert (dir.) (1970) *Jane Eyre.*]
   BPM has *Radio Times* cutting 31.10.1982, BBC1. *See also 1971.*

1983
Illustrations, paintings, etc.
Jane Eyre, easy reading edition illustrated by pictures from 1983 BBC TV serial with Timothy Dalton and Zelah Clarke, Longman Movieworld (n.d.).

Incidental references
Lively, Penelope (1983) *Perfect Happiness*, Harmondsworth: Penguin.
   Jane Eyre reference (91).

Novels, poems, etc.
Weldon, Fay (1983) *The Life and Loves of a She-Devil*, London: Hodder & Stoughton.
   John Crompton (personal communication 8.5.1991): 'the hulking Bertha figure turns into the little Jane figure, the princess in the tower'. Note many commentators on Weldon's adaptation of *Jane Eyre* noted the fact that she was the author of *LLSD*.

Stage plays
Martin, Christopher (adapt.) (1983) *Jane Eyre*, ts Courtesy of Victoria Theatre, Stoke-on-Trent; produced 1983.
   From Nudd.

Television
Amyes, Julian (dir.) (1983) *Jane Eyre*, BBC TV serial dramatized by Alexander Baron in eleven episodes, colour, 239 minutes, with Timothy Dalton as Rochester and Zelah Clarke as Jane, 1983; BBC video presentation, 1983.
   BPM has Maire Messenger Davies, *Radio Times* 8–14.10.83; also video sleeve (BBC V 4382); also press cutting: Steve Absalom, *Daily Mail* 9.2.1987: 'Bond is a wow with Moscow, but not as 007' (reference to the fact that Dalton played James Bond ('007') before Rochester). Reviews: Peter Kemp, *Times Literary Supplement* (n.d.); Barry Letts, *The Stage* 17.3.1983; *Daily Telegraph* 10.10.83; Peter Holdsworth, [Bradford] *Telegraph and Argus* 26.11.83. *See also 1870, 1985, 1987.*

1984
Musical settings
Davis, Ted (1984) *Jane Eyre* (musical) produced at the Theatre Monmouth (Maine).

BPM has programme for 1990: 'Ted Davis . . . originally conceived a non-musical dramatization for the Theatre at Monmouth (Maine) in 1984 using fragments of Chopin's piano music to underscore the piece . . .' *See also 1988, 1990.*

Novels, poems, etc.
George, Catherine (1984) *Devil Within*, London: Mills & Boon.
  Plot similarities and explicit references (37, 190).

Stage plays
[Cannon, John (1973) *Jane Eyre*.]
  Performed in Swindon, 1984 (BPM).
[Cox, Constance (1959) *Jane Eyre*.]
  Performed in Bolton, 1984; directed by Felicity Taylor with Charmion Gradwell as Cathy and Mark Lindsay as Heathcliff (BPM).
Myerson, Jonathan (adapt.) (1984) *Jane Eyre*, Mark Piper (dir.), with Jenny Seagrove as Jane, Harrogate Theatre
  Nudd: 'ts Courtesy of the adaptor; produced in York, England, 1984'. BPM has playbill for 'World Premiere' at Harrogate Theatre, 12–29 September [1984]; also unidentified review by W.H.W. Mentioned in BS exhibition, 1991–2. *See also Coe, 1986.*

1985
Illustrations, paintings, etc.
Jane Eyre, Movieworld easy reading edition (London: Longman).
  Illustrated by pictures from the Dalton/Clarke 1983 television serial.

Incidental references
Winterson, Jeanette (1985) *Oranges Are Not the Only Fruit*, London: Pandora.
  Explicit references pp. 28, 74.

Novels, poems, etc.
Comyns, Barbara (1985) *The Juniper Tree*, London: Methuen.
  From John Crompton (personal communication 8.5.1991).

Radio
Wandor, Michelene (1985) *A Consoling Blue*, Radio 4, 18.8.1985.
  BPM has *Radio Times* 18.8.1985: 'a feature by Michelene Wandor based on the letters of Jean Rhys, edited by Francis Wyndham and Diana Melly with Brenda Bruce as Jean Rhys, Mia Soteriou as Antoinette, Janet Maw as Jane Eyre, John Church as Mr Rochester'. Produced by Cherry Cookson.

Stage plays
Haughey, Sheila (dram.) (1985) *Jane Eyre*, Cheltenham.

Nudd: 'ts Courtesy of Harvest Arts Group, Cheltenham'. BPM has programme for performance by Harvest Arts Group, Shirley Collins (prod.) with Sheila Haughey as Charlotte Brontë, Shirley Collins as Jane Eyre, Barry Linney as Rochester and Norma Collins as Bertha Rochester at the Parish Centre of SS Philip and James, Suffolk Square, Cheltenham, 4–5 May 1985; also review: *Gloucestershire Echo* 14.5.1985.

Vance, Charles (adapt.) (1985) *Jane Eyre*, England Touring Production.

Nudd: 'ts courtesy of the adaptor'. BPM has list of eleven venues 16.9–2.12.[1985]; also playbill: 'Bill Simpson (Doctor Finlay from BBC TV's 'Doctor Finlay's Casebook') as Rochester. Tessa Wyatt (from ITV's 'Robins' Nest') as Jane Eyre'; also *Clue Notes for Jane Eyre*, produced by the British Theatre Association.

Wharton, Sylvia (1985) *The Childhood of Jane Eyre*, Belgrade Theatre, Coventry Studio Production, Keighley Playhouse, 16.3.1985.

BPM has ticket; also review: [Bradford] *Telegraph and Argus* 18.6.1985.

Television
[Amyes, Julian (dir.) (1983) *Jane Eyre*, BBC TV serial.]
CBS Fox Video, 1985.

1986
Stage plays
Coe, Peter (adapt. and dir.) (1986) *Jane Eyre*, with Jenny Seagrove as Jane and Keith Michell as Rochester, Chichester Festival.

Nudd: 'Revised ts courtesy of Chichester Festival Theatre'. BPM has Festival Programme; also reviews: unidentified; *Brighton and Hove Express* 26.7.1986; Mick Martin, *Plays and Players* October 1986. *Note:* Jenny Seagrove played Jane in Myerson version, 1984.

Weldon, Fay (adapt.) (1986?) *Jane Eyre*, directed by Helena Kaut-Howson.

BPM has programme for performances at Leeds Playhouse, 1988, and Pitlochry Festival Theatre, 1992, both of which report that '*Jane Eyre* was first presented at Birmingham Repertory Theatre in 1986' (but see 1987, 1988). *See also 1990, 1992, 1993.*

1987
Illustrations, paintings, etc.
Brontë, Charlotte, *Jane Eyre*, Longman's Classics.
Illustrated by pictures from the Dalton/Clarke 1983 BBC TV serial.

Musical settings
Reade, Paul [1987] *Jane Eyre* Suite, oboe, piano, Sussex: Nova Music, *c.*1987: NM 388.

From the music for BBC TV's adaptation of Charlotte Brontë's novel, *Jane Eyre*; duration *c.* 9:00; Prelude – Jane and Rochester – Blanche Ingram – Adèle – On the moors – Reconciliation (from NYPL).

Stage plays

Weldon, Fay (adapt.) (1987) *Jane Eyre*, directed by Helena Kaut-Howson.
BS exhibition 1991–2: 'first produced Birmingham Rep 1987'. *See also 1986, 1988, 1990, 1992.*

1988

Incidental references

Dangarembga, Tsitsi (1988) *Nervous Conditions*, London: Women's Press.
Lodge, David (1988) *Nice Work*, Harmondsworth: Penguin.
　　Explicit references (202–3).

Musical settings

[Davis, Ted (1984) *Jane Eyre*, (musical).]
　　BPM has programme for 1990 production: 'in the summer of 1988, the first musical version of *Jane Eyre* was produced at the Theatre at Monmouth'; I have personal communication describing the 1988 production in Maine. *See also 1990.*

Stage plays

Lucas, Valerie and David Cottis [1988] *Shadow in the Glass*, play based on *Jane Eyre* and *Wide Sargasso Sea* by Jean Rhys, presented by The Sherman Theatre Postgraduate Company, Sherman Arena [Cardiff], 12–23 Jan.
　　BPM has typescript; also playbill.
Weldon, Fay, (adapt.) (1988) *Jane Eyre*, directed by Helena Kaut-Howson, Leeds Playhouse, with Wendy Nottingham as Jane, David Gwillim as Rochester and Judy Damass as 'Mrs Rochester', 14.4.–7.5.1988.
　　BPM has programme; also playbill; also photographs; also reviews: [Bradford] *Telegraph and Argus* 5.4.1988, 8.4.1988 (Janet Buckton) 14.4.1988, 15.4.1988 and 16.4.1988; [Aire Valley] *Target* 7.4.1988; Jill Parkin, *Yorkshire Post* 13.4.1988 and 14.4.1988; *Yorkshire Evening Post* 15.4.1988; *Guardian* 8.4.1988, 16.4.1988 & 23.4.1988; *Leeds Guardian* 16.4.1988; Peter Mortimer, *Daily Telegraph* 20.4.1988; *Rothwell Advertiser* 21.4.1988; *Leeds Weekly News* 21.4.1988 & n.d.; *Stage and Television Today* 26.5.1988. See *Brontë Newsletter*, no. 7 (1988) for interview with Fay Weldon. *See also 1986, 1987, 1990, 1992.*
young jane eyre (1988) Children's Theatre Company, South Minneapolis, 8.1–27.2.1988.
　　BPM has playbill and poster.

1989

Novels, poems, etc.

Swindells, Robert (1989) *Follow A Shadow*, Harmondsworth: Penguin.
　　Novel for teenagers. Mostly about an identification with Branwell, but see p. 145: hero is 'doing' *Jane Eyre* at school but 'it's taking me all my time to get through *Jane Eyre*'. Note p. 49: the red room in *Jane Eyre* reminds him of *The Shining*

(film starring Jack Nicholson) where the word REDRUM appears in mirrors (= MURDER).

Stage plays

[Hamilton, Lionel (adapt.) (1978) *Jane Eyre*, England.]

Performed by Northampton Repertory Players Ltd, Michael Napier Brown (dir.), with Charlotte Harvey as Jane, Richard Warwick as Rochester and Cynthia Cherry as 'Bertha', at Royal Theatre, Northampton, prior to National Tour, 1989. BPM has programme; also photographs; also tour dates: Swindon Wyvern (25.9); Croydon Ashcroft (2.10); Warwick Arts Centre (9.10); Billington Forum (16.10); Liverpool Neptune (23.10); York Opera House (6.11); Harlow Playhouse (13.11); Winchester Theatre Royal (20.11); Eastbourne Devonshire Park (27.11); Peterborough Key Theatre (4.12).

[Jerome, Helen (1936) *Jane Eyre: A Drama of Passion*.]

Directed by Sybil Cooke with Jane Loignon as Jane and Geoffrey Gruson as Rochester, Ottawa Little Theatre 9–28 January 1989. BPM has review: *Ottawa Citizen* [1989].

Marten, Annette (adapt. and dir.) (1989) *Jane Eyre*, Eastern Michigan University Theatre Production, Michigan, Ypsilanti, Michigan.

Nudd: 'ts Courtesy of the adaptor'.

Yordon, Judy (adapt. and dir.) (1989) *Jane Eyre*, Ball State University Theatre Production, Muncie, Indiana.

Nudd: 'ts Courtesy of the adaptor'.

1990-9

Translations

Brontë, Charlotte, *The Orphan of Lowood*.

University lecturer, Debrecen, Hungary 1993 confirmed that a 'bowdlerised child's version of *Jane Eyre*' is still currently available in Hungary under this title. *See also 1867, 1868, 1870, 1920.*

1990

Illustrations, paintings, etc.

West, Clare, retells *Jane Eyre*, OUP Bookworms

Illustrated with stills from Delbert Mann's 1970 film.

Musical settings

[Davis, Ted, *Jane Eyre* (1984) (musical).]

BPM has programme for 1990 production, with book and lyrics by Ted Davis based on the novel by Charlotte Brontë, music by David Clark, with Charles Pistone as Rochester, Maryann Plunkett as Charlotte Brontë/Jane Eyre and Cecile Mann as Bertha Mason, at the Studio Arena Theatre, 23 October–18 November 1990: 'This newly developing version is a co-production between GeVa Theatre in Rochester and Studio Arena.' *Note*: Ted Davis directed the American premiere of *Saigon Rose* among many others. *See also 1988.*

Novels, poems, etc.
Boylan, Clare (1990) 'Jane Eyre revisited: an alternative ending', *Good Housekeeping* (January), pp. 136–40.

Competition to write new endings for *Jane Eyre* (141).

Stage plays
Shewell, Debbie (1990) *More Than One Antoinette*, Monstrous Regiment, Debbie Shewell (dir.), Young Vic Studio.

BPM has review: Heather Neill, *The Times* 30.3.1990: combines *Jane Eyre* and *Wide Sargasso Sea*.

[Weldon, Fay, (adapt.) (1987) *Jane Eyre*.]

Helena Kaut-Howson (dir.) with Jane Brennan as Jane, Alan Stanford as Rochester and Anna Healy as Mrs Rochester, Dublin Gate Theatre, 4.12.1990. BPM has programme with new programme note by Fay Weldon; also photographs: also reviews: Madeleine Keane, *Sunday Independent* 2.12.1990 and 9.12.1990; *In Dublin* 5.12.1990; *Irish Independent* 5.12.1990; *Irish Times* 29.11.1990 and (Gerry Colgan) 5.12.1990; *Evening Press* 5.12.1990; *Evening Herald* 5.12.1990; *Sunday Business Post* 9.12.1990; Mary O'Donnell, *Sunday Tribune* 9.12.1990; Tim Harding, *Sunday Press* 9.12.1990; Kay Hingerty, *Cork Examiner* 10.12.1990. *See also 1986, 1987, 1988, 1992.*

1991
Exhibitions
Brontë Society Exhibition of Dramatic Adaptations of *Jane Eyre*, Brontë Parsonage Museum, February 1991–January 1992.

Illustrations, paintings, etc.
B[ennett], N[eil], 'You'll find the cold water tank in the attic, along with the madwoman' (n.d.).

Cartoon, pen and ink, reproduced in Hodgkins, Cat 60, Winter 1991–2: original source unknown.

Brett, Simon (illus.) *Jane Eyre*, Charlotte Brontë, London: Folio Society.

Frontis. and 31 wood engravings. BPM has copy.

Musical settings
Shelmerdine, Roger (1991) *Jane Eyre: The New Musical*, Stage One AOS, Sale Civic Theatre, Altrincham, 25–7 April.

BPM has playbill.

Novels, poems, etc.
Kydd, Robbie (1991) *The Quiet Stranger*, Edinburgh: Mainstream.

Stage plays
Loki Theatre Co-operative, *The Haunting of Jane Eyre*.

BPM has typescript, letter and photographs of performance in Wakefield, 1991. Letter from Emma Gee describes it as 'a devised piece based on Charlotte Brontë's novel and "The Wide Sargasso Sea" [sic] by Jean Rhys'.

Madigan, Timothy (dram.) (1991) *Jane Eyre*, Life-Line Theatre of Chicago [Buffalo?].

Reported by Mary Haigh, USA Report, BS AGM 6.91 Haworth.

Television

Davis, Tudor (dir.) (1991) *The Russ Abbot Show*, John Bishop (prod.), with Russ Abbot, BBC 1, 18.10.1991: *Radio Times* 12–18.10.1991, p. 80: 'More madcap humour involving Jane Eyre and Mr Rochester . . . With Sherrie Hewson, Bella Emberg and guest star Les Dennis'.

Sketch in which hugely fat and ugly Jane shoots the doctor who is to restore Rochester's sight.

1992

Incidental references

Davies, Stevie (1992) *Arms and the Girl*, London: Women's Press, pp. 144, 162.

Musical settings

Vigeland, Nils and Charlotte Brontë (1992) *False Love/ True Love*, music and text by Nils Vigeland, a chamber opera in two scenes based on *Jane Eyre*, commissioned for Almeida Opera (ENO) and first performed at the Almeida Theatre, Islington, 17.7.1992.

Stage plays

Hall, Willis, (adapt.) (1992) *Jane Eyre*, Crucible Theatre, Sheffield, 5–28 November, Annie Castledine (dir.).

BPM has playbill and programme with picture of Top Withens; also review: *Daily Telegraph* 6.11.1992. *See also 1993.*

[Weldon, Fay (adapt.) (1987) *Jane Eyre.*] Performed Pitlochry Festival Theatre, 1992, John Harrison (dir.) with Rosaleen Pelan as Jane and Graham McTavish as Rochester.

BPM has programme.

1993

Films

Potter, Sally (dir.) (1993) *Orlando*.

Has *Jane Eyre* scene.

[Rhys, Jean (1966) *Wide Sargasso Sea.*]

Film version shown at Bradford Film Theatre 30.8–2.9.1993. Reviewed *BSG* 9: 24. *See also 1966.*

Incidental references

Weale, Sally (1993) 'Report reveals Patten paradox of Charlotte Brontë', *Guardian* 17.4.1993.

> Article showing that although *Jane Eyre* is on the National Curriculum, Charlotte Brontë did not come up to standard as tested by Cowan Bridge.

Musical settings

Thompson, David (1993), *Jane Eyre*, a musical, music by Brian Knowles, performed Royal Naval School, Farnham Lane, Haslemere, Surrey, 17, 19, 20 November.
> *BSG* 8: 14.

Stage plays

[Hall, Willis, (adapt.) (1992) *Jane Eyre*.]
> Directed by John Adams with Monica Dolan as Jane and Michael Irving as Rochester, Theatre Royal, York, 24.6–17.7.1993.
> BPM has flier and poster; also review: *Yorkshire Post* 30.6.1993.

Hunt, Sally (adapt.) (1993) *Jane Eyre*, Proscenium Players, Ian Rattee (dir.), Leeds Civic Theatre, October.
> BPM has flier.

[Jerome, Helen (1936) *Jane Eyre*.] Produced by Fay Higgins, Holywood Players, St Patrick's Hall, Holywood, Co. Down, 1–4.12.1993, with Lynn Barr as Jane, Irwin Murphy as Rochester and Josephine Anderson as Bertha.
> BPM has programme and photographs.

Jones, Nick (adapt.) (1993) *Jane Eyre*, Everyman Theatre, Gloucestershire; Martin Houghton (dir.), with Kate Paul as Jane, Ken Shorter as Rochester and Nikki Slade as Bertha.
> BPM has programme.

Schooling, Margaret (1993) *Lowood*, Stowmarket High School, Onehouse Road, Stowmarket, Suffolk, 9–11 December.
> *BSG* 9: 25. Play written by head of English, music by sixth form, costumes by Year 10, performed by Year 9.

[Weldon, Fay, (adapt.) (1987) *Jane Eyre*.]
> Performed Theatr Clwyd, Mold, 23.4.–15.5.1993 (from *BSG* 8: 14); performed Theatr Clwyd/Thorndike Theatre Production, The Playhouse, Northumberland Avenue, London, with Tim Pigott-Smith and Alexandra Mathie. Advertisement in *The Observer* 21.11.1993: 'A major new production of Charlotte Brontë's sweeping romantic epic'; design recalls *WH* 1943 Eichenberg: 81. Reviews: Maureen Paton, *Daily Express* 8.12.1993; Peter Hepple, *The Stage* 23.12.1993. BPM has playbill and notice: *Daily Mail* 19.11.1993.

Television

McGovern, Jimmie (1993) *Cracker*, 'The Madwoman in the Attic', 27.9.1993 and 4.10.1993, ITV series; Michael Winterbottom (dir.), Gub Neal (prod.) with Robbie Coltrane as Fitz.

1994

Radio

Cookson, Cherry (dir.) (1994) *Jane Eyre*, Radio 4 classic serial, from 21.8.1994, with Sophie Thompson as Jane and Ciaran Hinds as Rochester.

BPM has review: *Stage and Television Today* 25.8.1994.

Stage plays

Brontë Society and Gondal Theatre (1994) *Portrait of a Governess, Disconnected, Poor and Plain*, 26 March, BPM.

1995

Zeffirelli, Franco [1995] *Jane Eyre*.

BPM has cuttings: *Daily Mail* 3.9.1993: 'Franco Zeffirelli . . . arrives in London in November to begin casting, with producer Dyson Lovell, his film of Jane Eyre at Shepperton Studios. The British dramatist Hugh Whitemore has written the screenplay'; *Daily Mail* 29.10.1994: Charlotte Gainsbourg will play Jane, William Hurt Rochester and Elle Macpherson, '6ft Australian supermodel nicknamed The Body', will play Blanche Ingram.

Incidental references

Brittan, Samuel (1995) 'Beware of the new Victorians', *Financial Times* 5.6.1995, p. 14.

Quotes from 'Mr Brocklehurst nodded' to 'their immortal souls' (*JE* 65–6) to support argument against the revival of 'Victorian values'.

1997

Musical settings

Joubert, John [1997] *Jane Eyre*, opera.

See *BSG* 7: 16: Joubert is finishing an opera on *Jane Eyre* in time for the 150th anniversary of publication [1997].

Wuthering Heights *derivatives listed chronologically*

Sources and abbreviations

Barclay Barclay, Janet (1989) *Emily Brontë Criticism 1900–1980: An Annotated Check List*, Westport, Conn.: Meckler
b/w black and white
BFI British Film Institute
BL British Library
BPM Brontë Parsonage Museum (numbers are acquisition numbers)
BS Brontë Society
BSG *Brontë Society Gazette*
BST *Brontë Society Transactions* (references take the form (vol.part.page (date))
Halliwell Halliwell, Leslie (1986) *Halliwell's Film Guide*, 5th edn, London: Paladin Grafton
Hughes Hughes, Helen (1991) '*Wuthering Heights*: the challenge of dramatic adaptation', MA thesis, Brigham Young University
Hodgkins Ian Hodgkins (Booksellers) Catalogues
LCP Lord Chamberlain's Plays, British Library (ms plays are identified by additional manuscript ('Add. ms') numbers)
NYPL New York Public Library of the Performing Arts
Rauth Rauth, Heidemarie (1971), 'Dramatisierungen von Leben und Werk der Brontë-Schwestern', dissertation
Wagner Wagner, Geoffrey (1975) *The Novel and the Cinema*, London: Associated University Presses
Y & T Yablon, G. Anthony and John R. Turner (1978) *A Brontë Bibliography*, London: Ian Hodgkins (Connecticut: Meckler Books)

Notes

1. All versions of *Wuthering Heights* are listed under the name of the adaptor, illustrator, etc., and not under Brontë.

2. Where bibliographic details are in brackets, this indicates an edition other than the original.
3. Parenthetic references in the form 'Myer 1987: 106' refer to the general bibliography.
4. Where an author, date, etc. is in square brackets, this indicates that the information has been supplied from a later source; where a whole entry is in square brackets, this indicates a subsequent edition, performance, etc. of an item from a previous date.

Wuthering Heights *derivatives listed chronologically*

Undated
Illustrations, paintings, etc.
Davidson, Thomas, *'Mr Heathcliff?' I said, a nod was the answer* (oil painting).
  BPM sells postcard reproduction, photograph by Simon Warner.
Mellifont Press edition (London).
  Cover illustration.

Translations
Linh, Nhat (unfinished) Japanese translation of *Wuthering Heights*.
  See *BSG* 5: obituary of Mr Mguyen Tuong Vu: 'His uncle, Nhat Linh, was a famous writer who began a translation of *Wuthering Heights*': information from Patricia Marshall, Canadian Representative of the Brontë Society.

1847–59
Stage plays
LCP: nothing under 'Wuthering' for 1824–99; nothing under 'Heathcliff' or 'Cathy' for 1824–1968.

1851
Translations
Barclay (91–2) gives list of German translations: 'German translation of *Wuthering Heights* began in 1851, together with the appearance of the English edition of the German publisher Tauchnitz in Leipzig. *Wuthering Heights* in Germany, however, did not have a lasting impact'.
  See also Ganner (1980).

1873
Illustrations, paintings, etc.
Wimperis, E. M. (illus.) (1873) *Life and Works of Charlotte Brontë and Her Sisters*, 7 vols, vol. 5 *Wuthering Heights* by Ellis Bell, and *Agnes Grey* by Acton Bell, London: Smith, Elder.

Topographical etchings; BPM has copy and photographs. See also Emily Brontë and Anne Brontë (n.d.) *Wuthering Heights* and *Agnes Grey*, London: Smith, Elder, with frontis. 'Valley of Gimmerton', identical to Wimperis illustration.

1883
Novels and poems
Schreiner, Olive (1883) *The Story of an African Farm*, London: Hutchinson.
See Haynes (1981); also Barclay: '*The Story of an African Farm* has striking similarities to *Wuthering Heights*'

1890–9
Illustrations, paintings, etc.
Bell, Ellis and Acton Bell [*c.* 1889–95] *Wuthering Heights* and *Agnes Grey*, London: W. Nicholson.
Frontispiece and title page illustration. BPM has copy.

1892
Translations
de Wyzewa, Theodore (1892) *L'Amant* (first French translation of *Wuthering Heights*).
Barclay (105): 'The Brontë Society recently purchased a copy of this edition, with the title translated as "L'Amant", reputedly the first French translation'. See Lemon (1976).

1893
Illustrations, paintings, etc.
Greig, H. S. (illus.) (1893), *The Works of the Brontë Sisters*, 12 vols, London: Dent.
Frontis. and 24 illustrations. BPM has copy; vol. 9 is *Wuthering Heights*.

Novels and poems
Grand, Sarah [Frances Elizabeth Clarke, later McFall] (1893) *The Heavenly Twins*, London: Heinemann.
'Twin' theme and some thematic similarities.

1900
Illustrations, paintings, etc.
[Greig, H. S. (illus.) (1893) *The Works of the Brontë Sisters*, 12 vols, London: Dent.]
Ward, Mrs Humphrey (introd.) (1900–2) *The Novels of the Brontë Sisters*, 7 vols, New York: Harper (Haworth edition). Frontis. to each vol. and 59 illus.
Ian Hodgkins Cat. 48 No. 113. 1920 edition has photographic illustrations.

1905
Illustrations, paintings, etc.
Dulac, Edmund (illus.) (1905) *The Novels of the Brontë Sisters*, 10 vols, London: Dent.

BPM has copy; BL (Boston Spa) does not.

1907

Illustrations, paintings, etc.

(1907) *The Novels of the Brontë Sisters*, 12 vols, Edinburgh: John Grant (Thornton edition).

Frontis. each vol. and other illus. (Ian Hodgkins Cat. 48 No. 114). BPM has edition of 1924.

1914

Stage plays

Lovell, Catherine Couper (1914) *Wuthering Heights: A Drama in Five Acts, from the novel by Emily Brontë*, plays by Alabama Authors 21, Birmingham, AL (no publisher).

From Hughes.

1915

Novels and poems

Woolf, Virginia (1915) *The Voyage Out*.

Topographical and thematic similarities. See Delbaere-Garant (1979).

1920–9

Illustrations, paintings, etc.

Buckland, A. H. (illus.) (no date) *Wuthering Heights*, Emily Brontë, London and Glasgow: Collins Clear-Type Press.

Style of illustrations suggests 1920s. BPM has copy: SB: 2306. Frontis. and 6 illus.

1920

Films

Bramble, A. V. (dir.) (1920) *Wuthering Heights*, The Ideal Film Renting Co., London.

Starring Milton Rosmer as Heathcliff, Anne Trevor as Cathy, Warwick Ward as Hindley, John L. Alderson as Linton and Colette Bretel as Cathy 2; screenwriter Eliot Stannard. Nowlan and Nowlan (1989) claim that it was filmed on location at Top Withens and High Sunderland Hall, but Twinks Kenyon, who played the child Catherine, confirms that Haworth Old Hall was used for *Wuthering Heights* and Kildwick Hall for Thrushcross Grange; these buildings are recognizable in the photographs in the complimentary eight-page pro-gramme for the film which includes synopsis of plot and cast-list (copy in BPM courtesy of Mrs Kenyon). No print of the film is known to exist, but stills are available from BFI (see Figure 4.5, above); BPM also has a large number of small stills. BPM also has pictures of the filming in Haworth; also an invitation to private viewing at Kinema Exchange, Leeds, 5.8.[1920]. Review: *Yorkshire Observer* 5.5.1920 (BPM). *See also BST* 6.31.67–8 (1921); *BSG* 1; *Yorkshire Post*

25.7.1991 (BPM). *Note*: Milton Rosmer played Rochester in the 1932 radio version of *Jane Eyre*.

Illustrations, paintings, etc.
[Ward, Mrs Humphrey (introd.) (1900–2) *The Novels of the Brontë Sisters*.]
   (1920) London: John Murray. This edition has photographic illustrations of places. BPM: SB 2293.

1921
Incidental references
von Arnim, Elizabeth (1921) *Vera*, Basingstoke: Macmillan (London: Virago, 1983).
   Heroine reads *Wuthering Heights* [1983: 210].

1922
Illustrations, paintings, etc.
Dulac, Edmund (illus.) (1922) *Wuthering Heights*, Emily Brontë, May Sinclair (introd.), London: Dent. 6 colour plates.
   Ian Hodgkins Cat. 48 No. 87. BL (Boston Spa) does not have copy.
Dulac, Edmund (illus.) (1922) *Wuthering Heights*, Emily Brontë, 6 vols, May Sinclair (intro. to each vol.), New York: Dutton. Frontis. each vol. and 43 illus.
   Ian Hodgkins Cat. 48 No. 116: 'Illustrations first issued 1905; introductions by May Sinclair appear here for the first time'. BL (Boston Spa) does not have copy.

1924
Illustrations, paintings, etc.
[(1907) *The Novels of the Brontë Sisters*, 12 vols, Edinburgh: John Grant (Thornton edition).]
   Frontis. each vol. and other illus. BPM has edition of 1924: SB: 37. *Wuthering Heights* volume has frontis., 'Gateway to Wuthering Heights' and photograph facing p. 498, 'Ruins of Old Bell Chapel, Thornton'.
Tarrant, Percy (illus.) (1924) *Wuthering Heights*, Emily Brontë, Harrap. 16 coloured illus.
   Ian Hodgkins Cat. 48 No. 88. BL (Boston Spa) does not have copy.

1927
Incidental references
H. D. (1960) *Bid Me To Live* (begun 1927; London: Virago, 1984).
   'A wind from *Wuthering Heights*' (1984: 158).

1929
Stage plays
[1929] Birkett Phyllis, adaptor of *Jane Eyre*, is contemplating a dramatization of *Wuthering Heights* (letter from Ann Wilton, who played Jane in 1931, 29.12.1929 – BPM).
   No further information.

1930–9

Illustrations, paintings, etc.

(n.d.) *Brontë, Charlotte and her Sisters, The Complete Works*, with 9 full-page illustrations, Gresham Publishing.

BPM has copy: SB: 439; illustrated by photographs.

Novels and poems

Brontë Society Reports for 1991–2, Centenary Sub-Committee: the influence of Emily Brontë can be seen in Mary Webb's novels and poetry (see also de Beauvoir ([1949] 1970), who quotes from Emily Brontë and Mary Webb on the same page).

Stage plays

Wuthering Heights; performed at The Little Theatre, Sheffield.

BPM has undated programme, printed at the Sheffield Educational Settlement, Shipton St, Sheffield, signed by cast; this includes a quotation from Charles Simpson's *Emily Brontë* (1929).

1931

Illustrations, paintings, etc.

Leighton, Clare (illus.) (1931) *Wuthering Heights*, Emily Brontë, New York: Random House.

12 wood engravings. BPM has copy. For frontis. see cover of this book.

1932

Illustrations, paintings, etc.

Balthus [Balthasar Klossowski], (?1932) *Les Enfants* (painting).

See Knoepflmacher (1989); he claims it is based on one of a set of 14 drawings intended as illustrations for *Wuthering Heights*, begun in 1932 and finished in 1934–5. For Balthus's drawings for *Wuthering Heights*, see Lemon 1969. BPM has copies of drawings (source unknown).

1933

Illustrations, paintings, etc.

Balthus [Balthasar Klossowski] (1933) *La Toilette de Cathy*, Musée National d'Art Moderne, Centre Georges Pompidou, Paris; oil painting (see Figure 4.7, above).

BS exhibition 1990–1 showed copy reproduced from the catalogue, *La France: Images of Women and Ideas of Nation, 1789–1989*, with permission of the Musée National d'Art Moderne. *See 1985 Rivette.*

Balthus [Balthasar Klossowski] (1933–5) 14 drawings to illustrate *Wuthering Heights*.

See 1968 Tate Gallery exhibition catalogue; also Lemon (1969).

Stage plays

Carter, Randolph (1933) *Wuthering Heights: A Drama in Three Acts . . . based on the* novel by Emily Brontë, copyright 1933 Randolph Carter, 1939, Samuel French, New York, Los Angeles, London, Toronto (information from Y & T).

   Performed Longacre Theatre, New York, 27 April 1939 (Hughes). *See 1934, 1937, 1938, 1939, 1943, 1990.*

Pakington, Mary and Olive Walter (1933) *Wuthering Heights: A Play in Three Acts, A Prologue and an Epilogue.* LCP 1933/43; 9.12.1933, 14.12.1934. (N.d.) London: Nelson (Hughes).

   BPM has a programme for a performance in Croydon (1933), produced by Henry Cass with R. Eric Lee as Heathcliff and Myrtle Richardson as Catherine. See Rauth. *See also 1934, 1935, 1937, 1938, 1947.*

1934
Radio
Couper, Barbara [1934] *Wuthering Heights*, Radio Play.

   BPM has copy of Barbara Couper, 'Adapting "Wuthering Heights" as a Radio Play', *Radio Times* (23.11.[1934]), p. 636, including the words 'three years ago . . . *Jane Eyre* . . . was broadcast'. Barbara Couper adapted *Jane Eyre* for radio in 1931. The review includes a photograph of Milton Rosmer, who played Heathcliff in A. V. Bramble's 1920 film (see Figure 4.5, above). Caption: 'The monster Heathcliff'. *Note*: Rosmer also read the part of Rochester in Couper's 1932 radio adaptation of Jane Eyre.

Stage plays
[Carter, Randolph (1933) *Wuthering Heights*.]
   NYPL: Woodstock, NY, Maverick Theatre, 1934.
[Pakington, Mary and Olive Walter (1933) *Wuthering Heights*.]
   BPM has programme for the Royalty Theatre, Dean St, London (3.6.1934) produced by Olive Walter; also the Prince's Theatre, Bradford (week commencing 29.10.1934) (review: *Yorkshire Observer* 30.10.1934); also review of performance by Leeds Repertory Players at the Little Theatre, Leeds (*Yorkshire Post* 25.10.1934).

1935
Stage plays
[Pakington, Mary and Olive Walter (1933) *Wuthering Heights*.]
   BPM has programme for the England Touring Production (1935); also signed programme for the Manchester Repertory Theatre, Rusholme, with Joan Littlewood as Assistant Stage Manager, Keith Pyott as Heathcliff and Enid Hewit as Catherine (includes orchestral overture and five ballads); also evidence of performance by the Terence Byron Repertory Company (1935 and 1937).

1937
Stage plays
[Carter, Randolph (1933) *Wuthering Heights*.]

NYPL: 1937; Tamworth, NH: Barnstormers Theatre.

Davison, John (1937) *Wuthering Heights: A Play from the Novel by Emily Brontë*, London: Frederick Muller. LCP 1937/7; 26.1.1937. Little Theatre, Strand, London, February 1937 (Hughes).

> BPM has undated programme for performance at the Royalty Theatre, Morecambe, produced by Alfred Richards, with Lawrence Storm as Heathcliff and Muriel North as Catherine, including a programme of music. See Rauth. See Stoneman (1992b). *See also 1938, 1939, 1942, 1943, 1948, 1950, 1951, 1957, 1986.*

[Pakington, Mary and Olive Walter (1933) *Wuthering Heights*.]

> BPM has programme for the Theatre Royal, Huddersfield (week from 21.6.1937), produced by John Izon with Hugh Latimer as Heathcliff, Judi Lipscomb as Catharine [sic] (with programme of music); also evidence of performance by the Terence Byron Repertory Company (1935 and 1937); also reviews: *The Times* 9.12.1937 and *The Observer* 14.2.1937.

1938

Stage plays

[Carter, Randolph (1933) *Wuthering Heights*.]

> NYPL: clipping for Lichfield (Conn): Lichfield Summer Theatre, 1938.

[Davison, John (1937) *Wuthering Heights*.]

> BPM has programme, signed by performers, of performance at Prince's Theatre, Bradford (week beginning 31.10.1938); the Arthur Brough Players, produced by Frank Barnes, with Allan Goford as Heathcliff and Daphne Maddox as Catherine, including a programme of music.

[Pakington, Mary and Olive Walter (1933) *Wuthering Heights*.]

> BPM has programme for a performance at the Victoria Theatre, Burnley (1938), produced by Dominic Roche, with John Scott as Heathcliff and Barbara Reynolds as both Catherines.

1939

Films

Wyler, William (dir.) (1939) *Wuthering Heights*, United Artists: A Samuel Goldwyn presentation starring Merle Oberon, Laurence Olivier and David Niven, Geraldine Fitzgerald and Flora Robson; screenplay by Ben Hecht and Charles MacArthur; music by Alfred Newman.

> *Cinegram* no. 81 (Pilot Press) has information about casting, etc. (BPM). BFI has stills (see Figure 4.8 above); BPM has stills, Regal Films and Videos International poster and *Wuthering Heights* press book. Reviews: BPM has pp. 78-80 (source unidentified) of comments, cuttings; 'Merle Oberon learns of 1840 England via film', 4.15.1939 (source unidentified); *Kinematograph Weekly*; *Monthly Film Bulletin*; *New Republic*; *New Statesman*; *New York Times* 4.16.1939; *Tatler*; *New York World Telegram*, 4.14.1939; *New York Post* 14.4.1939; *New York Sun* 14.4.1939; Howard Barnes (source unidentified) 14.4.1939; *Daily News*

15.4.1939; 16.4.1939; *Daily Mail*, 28.4.1939; supplement to *Farmer and Stock-Breeder* 16.5.1939. See Cox (1992); Edgerley (1939); Wagner (1975: 232-43); *BSG* 5: 1; 'Film Notes' from National Museum of Photography, Film and Television at Bradford. See Hughes, Rauth. Halliwell quotes *Variety*: 'Sombre dramatic tragedy, productionally fine, but with limited appeal'. NYPL: New York, Rivoli Theatre; reviewed 14.4.1939; NYPL has pressbook, English pressbook, programme; review in French: *Cinema* (Paris), no. 301, January, p. 49. *See also 1981, 1991, 1993.*

Illustrations, paintings, etc.

Brontë, Emily, *Wuthering Heights*, New York: Pocket Book.
> Reprinted 24 times up to 1945. BPM no. 1431. Front cover shows Heathcliff carrying a slender Catherine to open window (i.e. a scene from Wyler's film, not in the novel). Top caption: 'The vndicativeness [sic] of disappointed love'. (*Note*: This was probably the edition used by Fletcher in writing libretto for Herrmann's opera: see 1982.)

Stage plays

(1939) *Wuthering Heights*: new play 'under the management of Robert Henderson and Harry Young' (*New York Herald Tribune* 16.4.1939).
[Carter, Randolph (1933) *Wuthering Heights*.]
> BS AGM 2.6.1990: American representative Mary Haigh reported a production by the Actors Co. of Pennsylvania January 1990 at Fulton Opera House, Lancaster, Pennsylvania, of Randolph Carter's play, 'first performed on Broadway in 1939'. BPM has review of unidentified play: [New York] *Herald Tribune* 16.4.1939, with Edith Barrett as Catherine. NYPL: New York, Longacre Theatre, 27.4.1939; production by Cothurnus of State University Teachers College, Geneseo (NY): Speech Auditorium.
[Davison, John (1937) *Wuthering Heights*.]
> BPM has programme, signed by producer, of performance by the Arthur Brough Players at the Theatre Royal, Leeds (1939), produced by Frederick Tripp, with Ursula Strachey as Catherine and Peter Walter as Heathcliff; also programme signed by performers at the Little Theatre, Bristol, Peggy Ann Wood (prod.), Ronald Russell (dir.), with Margaret Fry as Catherine and Richard Hinton as Heathcliff; also undated programme, with no town specified, for 'Little Theatre, John St., Adelphi, Sun. Jan 31st & Mon. Feb 1st', with Reginald Tate as Heathcliff (*note*: he played Rochester in Helen Jerome's adaptation of *Jane Eyre*, 1936).
Mooney, Ria and Donald Stauffer (1939) *Wuthering Heights*, directed by Hilton Edwards, Dublin Gate Theatre.
> BPM has programme: Micheal MacLiammoir as Heathcliffe [sic], Meriel Moore as Catherine; musical interludes (Beethoven, Tschaikowsky, Bach, Wagner).

1940–9

Illustrations, paintings, etc.

[Brontë, Emily (1939) *Wuthering Heights*, New York: Pocket Book.]
    Reprinted 24 times up to 1945. BPM SB: 1431.
Brontë, Emily (n.d.) *Wuthering Heights*, London: Mellifont Press.
    BPM: SB: 2618: dust-jacket shows cosy cottage with triangle of characters; style
    suggests 1940s.

Radio

Lawrence, Jerome and Robert E. Lee (adapts), *Little Women*; *Wuthering Heights*,
with Janet Waldo and Conrad [sic], introduced by Ronald Colman, recorded
Cincinnati; OH: Ziv, 194-. (Hughes).
Vidor, King (dir.), with James Mason, Dorothy McGuire and Pamela Colino, NBC
series: Screen Director's Playhouse, recorded North Hollywood, CA: Center for
Cassette Studies, ?1970, 1979 (Hughes).
    See Hughes for account. In NYPL list.

1940

Illustrations, paintings, etc.

Freedman, Barnett (illus.) (1940) *Wuthering Heights*, Emily Brontë, John Winterich
(intro.), New York: Heritage.
    15 lithographs. Ian Hodgkins Cat. 48 No. 92; BPM SB: 60.

Radio

DeMille, Cecil B. (1940) *Wuthering Heights*, with Basil Rathbone and Ida Lupino,
Lux Radio Theatre 15, broadcast 4.11.1940, recorded Houston, TX: Pastime,
?1970, 1975 (Hughes).
    See also 1951, 1978.

1941

Stage plays

[Davison, John (1937) *Wuthering Heights*.]
    New edition (1941) [Ian Hodgkins]
Mynhardt, C. F. (*c.* 1941–2) *Helshoogte*, Emily Brontë se Liefdesdrama 'Wuthering
Heights' in Drie Bedrywe. Afrikaanse vertaling deur ds. C. F. Mynhardt.
    BPM has programme sent from Pretoria 16.3.1942.
[Pakington, Mary and Olive Walter (1933) *Wuthering Heights*.]
    Published [1941] London, Edinburgh, Paris, Melbourne, Toronto and New
    York: Nelson. Y & T: 'Dramat. *WH* no. 7 in Nelson's "Plays for amateurs"
    series, general editor Nora Ratcliff'.

1943

Illustrations, paintings, etc.

Eichenberg, Fritz (illus.) (1943) *Wuthering Heights*, Emily Brontë, New York:
Random House.

BPM SB: 2759. 16 wood engravings and front and back covers and end-papers (see Figure 4.6, above). *Note*: Eichenberg also illustrated *Jane Eyre* for Random House in 1943. *Note*: Jane Urquhart confirms (private communication) that this was the edition she had in mind when writing *Changing Heaven* (1990). See *JE* 1993 Weldon.

Stage plays
[Carter, Randolph (1933) *Wuthering Heights*.]
    LCP 1943/35; 29.12.1943.
[Davison, John (1937) *Wuthering Heights*.]
    BPM has programme of performance at Royal Lyceum Theatre, Edinburgh, produced by Reginald Long, with Roger Snowdon as Heathcliff and Mary Morris as Cathy. Review: *Scotsman c.* 7.8.1943 (BPM).

1945
Novels and poems
Taylor, Elizabeth (1945) *At Mrs Lippincote's*.
    Contains references to *Wuthering Heights*.

1946
Illustrations, paintings, etc.
Brontë, Emily (1946) *Wuthering Heights*, Harmondsworth: Penguin.
    BPM SB: 1972. Front cover: Heathcliff and Catherine embrace before a stone wall.

Novels, poems, etc.
Taylor, Elizabeth (1946) *Palladian*, Peter Davies (London: Virago, 1985).
    Plot echoes and explicit reference [1985: 166].

1947
Illustrations, paintings, etc.
Gross, Anthony (illus.) (1947) *Wuthering Heights*, Emily Brontë, Norman Nicholson (intro.), London: Elek (Camden Classics series).
    Frontis. and 15 b/w illus. (Ian Hodgkins Cat. 48 No. 95.)

Radio
Gregson, James R. (adapt. and prod.), with Carl Bernard as Heathcliff and Valerie Skardon as Catherine, BBC Leeds, 23 and 30 October, 6 November 1947 (Hughes).
    See Hughes for account. See Gregson (1947).

Stage plays
[Pakington, Mary and Olive Walter (1933) *Wuthering Heights*.]
    BPM has programme for a performance by the Tudor Players at the Ashford

Theatre, Kent (1947), produced by Colin Kent, with Maxwell Franck as Heathcliff and Marie Dale as Catherine.

1948

Illustrations, paintings, etc.

Searle, Ronald (1948) *Wuthering Heights* (pen and ink sketch).
> BPM has original ink drawing of Heathcliff outside Wuthering Heights marked 'Radio Times. Cover. (Wuthering Heights) Ronald Searle [signature]'.

Stage plays

[Davison, John (1937) *Wuthering Heights.*]
> BPM has programme for performance in Manchester (week beginning 5 July, 1948), 'with additional dialogue by Alfred Sangster', produced by Noel Morris, with Terence de Marney as Heathcliff and Anne Trego as Catherine.

Television

O'Ferrall, George (adapt.) (1948) *Wuthering Heights*, dram. John Davison with additional dialogue by Alfred Sangster; with Kieron Moore and Katharine Blake as Catherine and Heathcliff, and Vivien Pickles as the younger Catherine, BBC 7.3.1948. (BPM exhibition, 1990–1, Hughes).
> BBC has still photograph; also original ink drawing of Heathcliff outside Wuthering Heights marked 'Radio Times. Cover. (Wuthering Heights) Ronald Searle [signature]'. See Hughes. Note both main actors had appeared in the roles on stage, Kieron Moore with the Richmond Repertory Company during the war, Katharine Blake with the Repertory Company, Perth; see Dunn (1948).

1949

Novels and poems

Taylor, Elizabeth (1949) *A Wreath of Roses* (Harmondsworth: Penguin, 1987).
> References to biography (1987: 30) and *WH* (11).

1950–9

Illustrations, paintings, etc.

Brontë, Emily (n.d.) *Wuthering Heights*, Classics Illustrated No. 59, 'Featuring stories by the world's greatest authors', New York: Gilberton.
> Comicstrip, large format. BPM SB: 1487. Style suggests 1950s.

Musical settings

Barri, Richard, *Wuthering Heights*, opera in three acts (four scenes).
> Hughes: 'listed in Northouse'.

Stage plays

Fenoglio, Beppe [before 1960] *La Voce nella Tempesta* [*The Voice in the Storm*]
> See Bruce Merry, 'An unknown Italian dramatisation of "Wuthering Heights"',

BST 16.81.31–9 (1971) (includes Merry's translation of an unpublished essay by Fenoglio on *Wuthering Heights*). According to Merry, Fenoglio's play was written before 1960 (31). Also in Hughes.

1950
Radio
(1950); Hughes: 'listed by Rauth'.

Stage plays
(1950) *Wuthering Heights*, Shrewsbury.
  BPM: see Bonnell drawers for photographs.
[Davison, John (1937) *Wuthering Heights*.]
  Performed in Haworth with *The Brontës*, 5–8.7.1950 as part of Brontë Festival. BPM has various unidentified reviews.

1951
Radio
(?1951) *Wuthering Heights*, prod. Lux Radio Theatre, Merle Oberon and Cameron Mitchell, recorded Bakersfield, CA: Radio Tape Library ?1951.
  Hughes: 'this may be the same adaptation as the 1940 one, with different actors'. *See also 1954, 1978, 1986.*

1953
Films
Buñuel, Luis *et al.* (screenplay) (1953) *Abismos de Pasión*, Mexico: Producciones Tepeyac; Oscar Dancigers (prod.), Abelardo Rodriguez (dir.); Jorge Mistral as Alejandro [Heathcliff]; Irasema Dilian as Catarina, Tamarelles International Films (Hughes).
  Stills available from BFI; BPM has copies. First UK screening 14.2.1984; National Theatre Programme notes by Philip Strick (BPM has copy). See Thomson (1975: 69–71); *BST* 18.94.310 (1984). See Knoepflmacher (1989); Stoneman (1992b). *See also 1954, 1983.*

Novels and poems
Roché, Henri-Pierre (1953) *Jules et Jim*.
  See Leavis [1969] 1983: 241: 'I should have thought the resemblance of the plot and theme of the film to the core of the first half of *Wuthering Heights* was very striking'. See Knoepflmacher (1989). *See also Truffaut 1961.*
Taylor, Elizabeth (1953) *The Sleeping Beauty* (London: Virago, 1982).
  Contains references to *Wuthering Heights*.

Television
(1953) Richard Todd as Heathcliff; Yvonne Mitchell as Cathy.
  Radio Times North of England edition, 4.12.1953; cover photograph of Catherine and Heathcliff (BPM has copy).

1954
Films
[Buñuel, Luis (1953) *Abismos de Pasión.*]
NYPL: 1954: New York; opened 27.12.1983.

Radio
[(1951) *Wuthering Heights*, Merle Oberon.]
Recorded Sandy Hook, CT: Radio Yesteryear, 1954, 1986 (Hughes).

1955
Illustrations, paintings, etc.
Stein W. (illus.) (1955) *Wuthering Heights*, Emily Brontë, Daphne du Maurier (intro.), London: Macdonald Illustrated Classics.
BPM SB: 1699B. Frontis. and 5 illustrations.

Musical settings
Gover, Gerald [1955], *Wuthering Heights* (opera).
BPM: [Bradford] *Telegraph and Argus* 6.10.1955: performed at St George's Hall, Bradford; 'a major work, in three acts, with prologue and epilogue and employing full orchestra and a large chorus. London will hear the first performance of excerpts at the Royal Festival Hall, London, in December . . .' (no evidence that this performance took place).

Parodies
Ferguson, Max, (1955) 'Rawhide', Folkways Records, New York, fp 86–2. (Album no.). Copyright 1955, Folkways Records and Service Corp. 117 W.46 St NYC USA. I: Wuthering Heights.

Radio
Ferguson, Max (1955) *Wuthering Heights*, comedy sketch written and read by Ferguson, CBS radio programme no. 2: Rawhide, 1955. Folkways Records.
See Hughes for account.

1956
Stage plays
Winch, Jurneman (dram.) (1956) *Wuthering Heights*, presented by Studio Theatre Limited, Library Theatre, Vernon Road, Scarborough.
BPM has typescript: 1743. *See also 1961.*

1957
Stage plays
[Davison, John (1937) *Wuthering Heights.*]
Performed Prince's Theatre, Bradford (week beginning 2.12.1957), produced by Doel Luscombe, with Brian Cullis as Heathcliff and Jean Kitson as Catherine (BPM).

1958
Illustrations, paintings, etc.
Turner, Harry (1958) *Road to Wuthering Heights* (water-colour).
> Ian Hodgkins Cat. 48 No. 124 contains reproduction: 'original water-colour of an Imaginary dramatic scene of towering cliffs for Emily Brontë's novel *Wuthering Heights*. Signed and dated 1958'.

Musical settings
Floyd, Carlisle (1958) *Wuthering Heights*, A musical drama in a prologue and 3 acts. Dramatization and text by the composer after the novel by Emily Brontë Commissioned by the Santa Fe Opera, Boosey and Hawkes. Vocal [piano] score, Boosey, New York, 1958. World premiere, Santa Fe Opera, Opera House, Santa Fe, NM, 16 July 1958 (Hughes).
> See Chatelin (1982); Sabin (1961). See Rauth. *BSG* 9: 21 describes the 1993 performance, followed by a forum with 'Phyllis Cutin, who was the first Cathy in the premier performance held 35 years ago [i.e. 1958]'. *See also 1982, 1993.*

1959
Illustrations, paintings, etc.
Brontë, Emily (1959) *Wuthering Heights* retold by John Kennet, London and Glasgow: Blackie.
> BPM SB 3065b. Frontis. and 3 illustrations.

Stage plays
Cox, Constance (1959) *Heathcliff*, 1959.
> Hughes: 'listed by Rauth'.

1960–9
Illustrations, paintings, etc.
Brontë, Emily (n.d.) *Wuthering Heights*, James William Johnson (intro.), Boston: Houghton Mifflin Duraflex.
> BPM: cover illustration shows Catherine and Heathcliff looking like something from *Gone With the Wind*.

Stage plays
Bernard, Paul, *Wuthering Heights*
> NYPL: Stars: Carolyn McDaniel, Eben Henson; Danville (KY): Pioneer Playhouse.
Vance, Charles (adapt.), *Wuthering Heights*, Buxton.
> Review: *Guardian* 6.5.1989 ('Vance's adaptation dates from the 1960s') (BPM)

1961
Films
Truffaut, François (1961) *Jules et Jim*, written by François Truffaut and Jean

Gruault, based on 1953 novel by Henri-Pierre Roché, with Oskar Werner, Jeanne Moreau and Henri Serre.

See Leavis ([1969] 1983: 241): 'I should have thought the resemblance of the plot and theme of the film to the core of the first half of *Wuthering Heights* was very striking'; also Knoepflmacher (1989). Halliwell: 'Before World War I, in Paris, a girl alternates between a French and a German student, and after the war they meet again to form a constantly shifting triangle'.

Musical settings

Hériat, Philippe (1961) *Les Hauts de Hurle-Vent*: Livret d'opera en trois actes, un prologue et sept tableaux, Paris: Gallimard.

I have been able to discover no information about performances or recordings. Stubbs, Thomas (1961) *Les hauts de hurlevant*. Libretto by Philippe Hériat: *Les hauts de hurlevant: Livret d'opera en trois actes, un prologue et sept tableaux*, Paris: Gallimard.

See Rauth. *See also 1967.*

Novels and poems

Frame, Janet (1961) *Faces in the Water*.

See Delbaere-Garant (1979).

Sylvia Plath (1961) 'Wuthering Heights' in *Collected Poems*, Ted Hughes (ed.), London: Faber and Faber, pp. 167–8.

Quoted in programme note for Ivan Charles's adaptation, 1988.

Stage plays

[Winch, Jurneman (dram.) (1956) *Wuthering Heights*.]

Also performed at Grand Theatre, Llandudno, 1961 (Hughes: 'listed by Rauth').

1962

Television

Serial with Keith Michell and Claire Bloom (11.5.1962).

BPM exhibition, 1990–1. BBC has still photographs.

1963

Musical settings

Zogheb, Bernard de (1963) *Le Sorelle Brontë*, opera in 4 acts, New York: Fibor de Nagy (foreword by James Merrill).

Frontis. shows pen version of Branwell group portrait with Anne droopy-eyed and wearing a cross, Emily very pretty and Charlotte extremely *decolletée* and come-hither. All three appear to be writing *Wuthering Heights*. Foreword: 'a libretto set to popular tunes of variable vintage and familiarity . . . concerned with money, food, sex and renown . . . It has never been performed for more than a handful of its Alexandria born poet's friends'.

1964

Films

Storey, David [1964] *Wuthering Heights*; proposed film dir. Lindsay Anderson starring Richard Harris.

See Bradford *Telegraph and Argus* 2.7.1964 (BPM has copy).

Illustrations, paintings, etc.

Brontë, Emily (1964) *Wuthering Heights*, London: Everyman.

BPM: front cover illus: Heathcliff begs Cathy to return.

Keeping, Charles (illus.) (1964) *Wuthering Heights*, Emily Brontë, London: Folio Society.

Frontis. and 11 three-colour lithographs. Ian Hodgkins Cat. 48 No. 96; BPM SB: 1959.

Stage plays

Croft, Stephen (1964) *Wuthering Heights*, Everyman Theatre, Cheltenham.

Hughes: 'listed by Rauth'.

Tyler, Brian (1964) *Wuthering Heights*, Wimbledon Theatre, Week beginning 31.8.1964, produced by Patrick Desmond, with Raymond Armstrong and Janet Hargreaves.

BPM has programme. Listed NYPL.

1965

Illustrations, paintings, etc.

Brontë, Emily (1965) *Wuthering Heights*, Boston, New York: Houghton Mifflin Riverside Literature series.

BPM SB: 2040: front and back cover illustrations.

Musical settings

Herrmann, Bernard [1965] *Wuthering Heights*, opera in four Acts and a prologue; libretto adapted from the novel of Emily Brontë by Lucille Fletcher; music by Bernard Herrmann; vocal [piano] score, London: Novello. Libretto in English and German also published separately, London: Novello.

BPM has copies of both score and libretto: SB: 2225. *See also 1966, 1982, 1992.*

1966

Films

Kardar, A. R. (1966) *Dil Diya Dard Liya*, Kary Productions, Bombay; Dilip Kumar as Heathcliff/Shankar, Waheeda Rehman as Catherine/Roopa.

See Johnson, E. (1989): title means 'give your heart and receive anguish'. See Hughes.

Incidental references

Oates, Joyce Carol (1966) 'The daughter', in *The Goddess and Other Women*, New York: Vanguard (1974, pp. 51–71), 1974, pp. 52–3.

Musical settings

Herrmann, Bernard (1966) *Wuthering Heights*, opera, libretto by Lucille Fletcher, Pro Art Orchestra conducted by the composer with Morag Beaton, Donald Bell, John Kitchener and Pamela Bowden, recorded Pye stereo CSCL 30173/1–4 and mono CCL 30173/1–4.

This version is in 4 acts and lasts three and a half hours; it seems that its length was one of the obstacles to its being performed on stage. During his life Herrmann refused to cut it, but Fletcher cut about thirty minutes from the 1982 version (Johnson, 1982a: 34).

See L[emon] (1967): 'still awaiting stage performance'. See Bradbury (1966). *See also 1982, 1992.*

Stage plays

Hall, John (1966) *Wuthering Heights*, Northampton Repertory Theatre.
Hughes: 'listed by Rauth'.
Smithson, Norman (1966) *Wuthering Heights*, Victoria Theatre, Stoke-on-Trent.
Hughes: 'listed by Rauth'.

1967

Musical settings

[Stubbs, Thomas (1961) *Les hauts de hurlevant.* Libretto by Philippe Hériat: *Les hauts de hurlevant: Livret d'opera en trois actes, un prologue et sept tableaux*, Paris: Gallimard.]

World premiere: Théâtre des Arts, Rouen, France, 16.4.1967 (Hughes). See Lemon (1967).

Radio

(1967); Hughes: 'listed by Rauth'.

Television

Leonard, Hugh (adapt.) (1967) *Wuthering Heights*, BBC2 TV serial, Peter Sasdy (dir.), with Ian McShane and Angela Scoular, 28.10.1967; four part serial (Hughes).
BPM has cutting by John Stevenson, 27.7.1967.
(1967); RTB, publication for the Belgian television programme by Rodolph Cartier.
Hughes: 'listed by Rauth'.

1968

Television

(1967); ORTF, publication for the French television programme. Hughes: 'listed by Rauth'.

1970–9

Television

Morecambe, Eric and Ernie Wise (*c.* 1970?), sketch on Cathy and Heathcliff.
BBC archive has no stills.

1970
Films
Fuest, Robert (dir.) (1970) *Wuthering Heights*, American International Pictures, prod. James H. Nicholson and Samuel Z. Arkoff, screenplay by Patrick Tilley, with Timothy Dalton as Heathcliff and Anna Calder-Marshall as Cathy. Royal premiere ABC-2, Shaftesbury Avenue, London, 9.6.1970 (Hughes).

From BS exhibition 1990–1; first colour film. BFI has stills; BPM has copies; also eight cinema front-of-house stills. See Drew, *BST* 16.18.59–61 (1971). Reviews: four unidentified, including Cecil Wilson; 'Forecast of staggering Brontë film success'; and 'printed by D. C. Thomson & Co'; *Daily Express* 23.4.1970; *Cork Evening Echo* 26.5.1973 (BPM). See Luhr (1978). NYPL: press releases 1971–2; New York: Radio City Music Hall; reviewed 19.2.1971. *See also 1972.*

Novels and poems
Miura, Ayako (*c.* 1970) *Hyoten* (*Freezing Point*).

Personal communication from Yuriko Yamawaki, 3.3.1990: 'People say Miss Miura the author of the novel got influence from "Wuthering Heights" but I don't know in what way'.

Radio
[DeMille, Cecil B. (1940) *Wuthering Heights*.]

Recorded Houston, TX: Pastime, ?1970, 1975; also Allentown, PA: Old Time Radio, ?1970, 1975. (Hughes). *See also 1951, 1978.*

[Vidor, King (dir.), with James Mason, Dorothy McGuire and Pamela Colino, NBC series: Screen Director's Playhouse.]

Recorded North Hollywood, CA: Center for Cassette Studies, ?1970, 1979 (Hughes).

1971
Stage plays
Taylor, Markland J. (1971) *Wuthering Heights: A Full-length Play*, Chicago: Dramatic Publishing Co. (Hughes)

1972
Films
[Fuest, Robert (dir.) (1970) *Wuthering Heights*.]

BPM has unidentified article, 'Shades of Emily – now a return to Wuthering Heights', 4.12.1972, promising that American International Pictures are about to film the second-generation story from a screenplay by Anthony Friedman.

Musical settings
Milella, Dino (1972) *Una Storia D'Altri Tempi*, Opera drammatica in 2 atti tratto dal Romanzo 'Wuthering Heights' (*Cime Tempestose*) di Emily Brontë, riduzione per canto e pianoforte dell'autore, Milano: Edizioni Curci.

BPM has copy: cover picture of woman on cliffs(?) harbour wall(?) with fierce sea and lighthouse. Listed NYPL. I have been able to discover no information about performances or recordings.

Radio
Macdonald, Nan (abridged) (1972); Radio 4 serial reading read by Ronald Harvi and Marah Stohl.
> Source: *Southern Evening Echo* 1972 (BPM).

1973
Novels and poems
Jane Gardam (1973) *The Summer After the Funeral*, London: Hamish Hamilton (Peacock 1977; Puffin 1983).
> Young heroine fears she is a reincarnation of Emily Brontë and is haunted by 'Heathcliff'.

1974
Radio
Rahman, Serajur (trans., adapt. and prod.) (1974) *Wuthering Heights*, serialization in sixteen episodes, BBC Bengali service, beginning 6.4.1974 (Hughes); read by Kazi Nurus Subhan and Taleya Rehman (BPM).

1975
Novels and poems
Naipaul, V. S. (1975) *Guerillas* (Harmondsworth: Penguin 1976).
> Reference to *Wuthering Heights* (1976: 9, 62). See Thieme (1979: 116–33).

Radio
[DeMille, Cecil B. (1940) *Wuthering Heights*.]
> Recorded Houston, TX: Pastime, ?1970, 1975. (Hughes). *See also 1951, 1978.*

Stage plays
Nivison, Jay (1975) *Wuthering Heights*, Lagoon Players Theatre Company, Durban, SA, 13–23.8.1975, with Andre Gialarakis as Heathcliff and Margaret Carter as Catherine.
> BPM has programme.

1976
Incidental references
Atwood, Margaret (1976) *Lady Oracle* (London: Virago, 1982).
> 'Was every Heathcliff a Linton in disguise?' (1982: 269).

1977
Novels and poems
Caine, Jeffrey (1977) *Heathcliff*, London: W. H. Allen.
> Novel based on 'missing years'.

1978

Musical settings

Bush, Kate (1978) *'Wuthering Heights'* (song; recording).
    See *BSG* 5 for a poem on Kate Bush's song. *See 1979.*

Novels and poems

L'Estrange, Anna (1978) *Return to Wuthering Heights*, London: Corgi.
    Novel, sequel to *Wuthering Heights*. Review: *Yorkshire Post* 30.1.1978 (BPM).

Radio

[Lux Radio Theatre (1951) *Wuthering Heights*, Merle Oberon and Cameron Mitchell.]
    Recorded Bakersfield, CA: Radio Tape Library 1978. Hughes: 'this may be the same adaptation as the 1940 one, with different actors'.

Stage plays

Bland, Joellen (1978) *Scenes from Classic Stories* (includes *Wuthering Heights*). Capsule Classics, Colorado Springs, CO: Meriwether (from Hughes).

Television

Hammond, Peter (dir.) (1978) *Wuthering Heights*; BBC 2 classic serial, Hugh Leonard (adapt.), Jonathan Powell (prod.) with music by Carl Davis; Ken Hutchison as Heathcliff and Kay Adshead as Catherine, in five parts beginning 24.9.1978.
    See *Radio Times*, 23–29.9.1978: cover; Claire Tomalin, 'The Height of Romance', pp. 4–7 (includes illustration from Wyler film and three previous TV serials); p. 33 has programme note with picture of young Catherine and Heathcliff. (BPM has copy.) *See also 1982, 1983, 1985, 1989.*

1979

Illustrations

Reingold, Alan (1979) (illus.) *Wuthering Heights*, Emily Brontë, Pennsylvania: Franklin Library.
    5 double page b/w illus. (Ian Hodgkins Cat. 48 No. 99). BL (Boston Spa) does not have copy.

Musical settings

[Bush, Kate (1978) *'Wuthering Heights'* (song).]
    Single from the LP *Kick Inside*, EMI London, 1979. *See 1992.*

Radio

[Vidor, King (dir.) (1979) with James Mason, Dorothy McGuire and Pamela Colino, NBC series: Screen Director's Playhouse.]
    Recorded North Hollywood, CA: Center for Cassette Studies, 1979 (Hughes).

1980

Incidental references

Barstow, Stan (1980) *A Brother's Tale*, London: Michael Joseph.

Some scenes in Haworth; characters buy *Wuthering Heights* p. 65.

Parodies

Prideaux, James (1980) *Jane Heights*, A Parody of *Jane Eyre* and *Wuthering Heights*, produced in Los Angeles, California, music by Arthur B. Rubinstein, lyrics by James Prideaux.

From Nudd: ts courtesy of the William Morris Agency, Beverley Hills. See Nudd (1992).

Radio

(1980); radio adaptation of the novel by Emily Brontë, recorded San Francisco: Jabberwocky (Hughes).

1981

Films

[Wyler, William (dir.) (1939) *Wuthering Heights*.]

Revival presented in Tokyo (August, 1981). BPM has programme in Japanese (SB: 3044).

1982

Illustrations

Brontë, Emily (1982) *Wuthering Heights*, Macmillan Students' Novels.

BPM SB 3323: front cover: Ken Hutchison as Heathcliff (under avenue of trees). *(See Television, 1978)*

Musical settings

Fletcher, Lucille (1982) *Wuthering Heights: Libretto of the Opera by Bernard Herrmann*, Fritz Eichenberg (illus.). Printed for the world premiere in Portland, Oregon, November, 1982 by the Portland Opera Assoc.

Eichenberg illustrations are from the 1943 Random House edition of *Wuthering Heights* (see Figure 4.6 above). *See 1982 Herrmann, below.*

[Floyd, Carlisle (1958) *Wuthering Heights*.]

Performed University of North Carolina, April 1982. BPM file on Bernard Herrmann includes Michael Mott: '"Wuthering Heights" top opera event of 1982', *San Antonio Express*, 10.11.1982: 6, reporting 'a revival of composer Carlisle Floyd's 1958 opera of the same name at the University of North Carolina this past April'. See Chatelin (1982). See Rauth. *See also 1993.*

Herrmann, Bernard (1982) *Wuthering Heights*, opera performed by Portland Opera, Oregon, November 1982, libretto by Lucille Fletcher.

BPM has world premiere programme, including Frank Kinkaid, 'Benny's *Wuthering Heights* at last' and Stanley Johnson, 'The making of *Wuthering*

Heights'; also 'World premiere *Wuthering Heights* lecture series' (small leaflet) with titles of lectures on 'The opera', 'The novel', 'The libretto' and 'Other compositions of Bernard Herrmann'; also photocopy of 'The libretto' by Stanley Johnson. Reviews: Robert Lindstrom, 'Heights staging fails to reach anticipated level', *The Oregonian* (n.d.); Dan Rodgers, *Portland State University Vanguard*, 12.11.1982: 7; Robert Lindstrom, 'World premiere hits the Heights', *The Oregonian* 5.11.1982; Martin Clark, *The Oregonian* 11.7.1982 and 5.11.1982; Dave Jewett, *The Columbian* [Vancouver, Wash.] 8.11.1982; [Oregon City] *USA Today* 8.11.1982; *The Seattle Times*, 9.11.1982; William Dunlop, '"Carmen" and "Wuthering Heights" . . .' unidentified source; stamp on copy reads 10.11.1982; Michael Mott [Texas] *San Antonio Express* 10.11.1982: 6; *Salem Statesman/Journal* 11.10.1982; Mary Hoffman, *Enterprise-Courier* 12.11.1982; *Northwest Arts* 12.11.1982: 2; *the province* 14.11.1982: 7; *Los Angeles Times* 15.11.1982; *Opera News* 15.1.1983: 43; [Oakland, California] *The Post* 17.11.1982: 11; *Newsweek* 29.11.1982; (BPM). See Cariaga (1982); Chatelin (1982); Cohen (1982); Downey (1983); Estes (1982); Kinkaid (1982, 1983); Lindstrom (n.d.); Malitz (1982); Swan (1982). BPM has ms letter from Lucille Fletcher to Stanley Johnson concerning the composition of the opera. See also *BST* 15.77.143 (1967); 18.91.39 (1981); 18.93.233 (1983).

Petit, Roland (dir.) (1982) *Les Hauts de Hurlevant: histoire d'une passion*. Ballet National de Marseilles, December 1982, music by Marcel Landowski, scenario Edmonde Charles-Roux. Sound recording: *Les hauts de hurlevant: Ballet en deux actes d'apres un argument d'Edmonde Charles Roux*, Marcel Landowski, Paris: Voix de son maitre, 1982 (Hughes).

BPM has programme: SB: 2768b: 'Ballet de Roland Petit. Sur un argument d'Edmond Charles-Roux. Musique de Marcel Landowski. 26.12.1982–2.1.1983. See Hughes for account. Reviews: David Dougill, *Dance and Dancers* April 1983 pp. 19–20 (BPM). BPM has two ballet stills from 1983 *Dance and Dancers*. See also *BST* 18.93.233 (1983).

1983

Films

[Buñuel, Luis (1953) Abismos de Pasión.]
    NYPL: 1954: New York; opened 27.12.1983.

Illustrations, paintings, etc.

Brontë, Emily (1983) *Wuthering Heights*, simplified by Celia Turvey, London: Longman.
    BPM SB: 2835: frontis.: Ken Hutchison as Heathcliff. *See Television 1978.*

Incidental references

Chatwin, Bruce (1983) *On the Black Hill*, Picador.
    John Goodridge (personal communication 2.9.1989 points to references to a ballad called 'The Unquiet Grave' (p. 83) and topographical similarities with *Wuthering Heights* plus an 'Earnshaw' reference (p. 48).

Lively, Penelope (1983) *Perfect Happiness*, Harmondsworth: Penguin.
Wuthering Heights references (91, 187).

Musical settings
[Petit, Roland (dir.) (1982) *Les Hauts de Hurlevant: histoire d'une passion*. Ballet National de Marseilles.]
> *BST* 18.93.233 (1983): notice of a recording 'of a two-act ballet *Les Hauts de Hurlement – Histoire d'une Passion* by Roland Petit, with music by Marcel Landowski . . . first performed in December 1982. The music is provided by L'Orchestre Colonne . . . conducted by Marcel Landowski . . . French EMI record C 069-73140 issued under the auspices of the Ministère de la Culture et de la Communication in co-operation with Radio France'.

Novels and poems
Wheatcroft, John (1985) *Catherine, Her Book*, New York and London: Cornwall.
> Catherine's version of *Wuthering Heights*. Copy in BPM: SB: 3575.

1984
Films
[Buñuel, Luis (1953) *Abismos de Pasión*.]
> First UK screening 14.2.1984: National Theatre programme notes by Philip Strick (BPM has copy). See Buñuel (1984); also *BST* 18.94.310.

Illustrations, paintings, etc.
Brontë, Emily (1984) *Wuthering Heights*, Pocket Classics, West Haven, Conn.: Academic Industries.
> BPM SB: 3008: small b/w comicstrip; retains Lockwood as narrator.

Stage plays
Cox, Constance (1984) *Wuthering Heights*, directed by Felicity Taylor with Mark Lindsay as Heathcliff and Charmian Gradwell as Cathy, Octagon Theatre, Bolton, 3–28 April 1984.
> BPM has programme.

Foxall, Vince (1984) *Wuthering Heights*.
> Produced by Ted Craig, with Charlotte Attenborough as Catherine and Jonathan Morris as Heathcliff. Performances: Cambridge Theatre Company (1984), (review: *Guardian* 9.11.1984); Theatre Royal, Bury St Edmunds (1984); Theatre Royal, York (review: *Yorkshire Post* 4.12.1984). *See BST* 19.7.327–8 (1989). NYPL: see *London Theatre Round*, vol. 4 (23), p. 1048. *See 1985, 1986, 1988, 1990.*

1985
Films
Rivette, Jacques (1985) *Hurlevant*, with Lucas Belvaux, Fabienne Babe, Olivier

Torres, Alice de Poncheville, Sandra Montaigu, Olivier Cruveiller. Screenplay by Jacques Rivette, Pascal Bonitzer and Suzanne Schiffman (Hughes).
French film inspired by the painter Balthus (from BS exhibition, 1990–1). See Hughes for comment. See Figure 4.7, above, for Balthus's painting, *La Toilette de Cathy*.

Illustrations, paintings, etc.
(1985) Longman Movieworld Easy Reading edition, illus. from Peter Hammond (dir.), *Wuthering Heights*; BBC2 classic serial.

Incidental references
Dowrick, Stephanie (1985) *Running Backwards Over Sand*, Harmondsworth: Penguin.
Contains *Wuthering Heights* references (312–17).

Musical settings
Keshishian, Alek (dir.) [1985] *Wuthering Heights* ('popera').
News and Notes 25.10.1991: 'a "popera" (or "pop opera") version, directed by Alek Keshishian (*Truth or Dare*) will add music to Brontë mix. Keshishian, who staged the material as a Harvard undergrad in 1985, is approaching Madonna and George Michael to write songs and appear in the film' (BPM). NYPL: *Wuthering Heights: A Pop Myth* (multimedia presentation) adapted by Alek Keshishian from the novel by Emily Brontë; music by Sting, Kate Bush *et al.*

Stage plays
[Foxall, Vince (1984) *Wuthering Heights*.]
Performance: Harrogate Theatre Company, directed by Andrew Manley, with Mari Rowland Hughes as Catherine and Maurice Thorogood as Heathcliff (1985). BPM has programme.

1986
Radio
[(1951) *Wuthering Heights*, Merle Oberon.]
Recorded Sandy Hook, Conn.: Radio Yesteryear, 1954, 1986 (Hughes).

Stage plays
[Davison, John (1937) *Wuthering Heights*.]
BPM has programme for a performance by Stantonbury Campus Drama Group, Milton Keynes (1986) directed by Jo Foster-Powell.

1988
Films
Yoshida, Yoshige (dir.) (1988) *Onimaru*.
Japanese film (also book of the film) derived from *Wuthering Heights*. Source: BS exhibition 1990–1: 'The Japanese film director was inspired to make his film by

reading Georges Bataille's essay on the novel in his book *La litterature et le mal* (1957) which concentrates on the dramatization of sexuality and death. The actor Yusaku Matsada plays the Heathcliff role as a grunting Samurai of murderous inclination, and the young actress Yuko Tanaka is Kinu or Catherine'. BPM has stills. Reviews: *Figaro-Magazine* 14.5.1988 pp. 164–5; Chris Peachment, *Films and Filming* 1988 (BPM). Title means 'demon' (Hughes).

Novels and poems
Lodge, David (1988) *Nice Work*, Harmondsworth: Penguin.
Brontë references pp. 202–3.

Stage plays
Boyd, John, (dram.) (1988) *Wuthering Heights*, produced Lyric Theatre, Belfast 17.2–19.3.1988; Roy Heayberd (prod.), with Richard Croxford as Heathcliff and Emma Lewis as Cathy.
BPM has playbill, programme and photographs. Reviews: Grania McFadden, *Belfast Telegraph* 18.2.1988; Charles Fitzgerald, *Belfast Newsletter* 18.2.1988; Lena Ferguson, *Sunday News* 21.2.1988; *Ulster Tatler* March 1988 (BPM).
Charles, Ivan [Charles Vance] (adapt.) (1988–9) *Wuthering Heights*, dir. David Horlock.
Performances: Alhambra Theatre, Bradford, 1988–9, directed by David Horlock, with Ralph Arliss and Lynn Clayton; same production, Salisbury Playhouse 18.8–10.9.1988 (BPM has programmes); also David Horlock, 'Emily Brontë and Wuthering Heights' (18.8.1988); the play is advertised as by Ivan Charles, but the November programme explains that this is a pseudonym for Charles Vance. BPM also has poster for Theatre Royal, Lincoln, 26.9–1.10. Hughes: 'also performed at Hayes'.
[Foxall, Vince (1984) *Wuthering Heights*.]
Performances: Beck Theatre, Grange Road, Hayes, Middlesex, (5–10.9.1988) (BPM has playbill); Crucible Theatre Sheffield, produced by Jane Collins, with Rory Edwards as Heathcliff and Julia Ormond as Catherine; music by Matthew Scott [1988]–9 (BPM has programme and typescript of 'this version'). Reviews: *BST* 19.7.327–8 (1989); *Guardian* 28.5.1989.

1989
Illustrations, paintings, etc.
Bell, Steve (1989), cartoon accompanying Clancy Sigal, 'Shaker of the slot machine', *Guardian*, 21.9.1989, p. 27.
Cartoon shows film poster for *Withering Heights* in which both Catherine and Heathcliff have Sam Goldwyn's face. (This was his name for *Wuthering Heights*.) Article has no other reference to *Wuthering Heights*. See Stoneman (1992b).
Suzuka, Reni (illus.) (1989), Famous love comics no. 2, Tokyo: Telehouse.
BPM SB: 3370: Disney-like characters, blonde Catherine in frilly bloomers, on conical Japanese Penistone Crag (see Figure 7.2 above).

Turvey, Celia (1989) *Wuthering Heights* (simplified version), London: Longman Classics.

Uses illustrations from Peter Hammond (dir.) (1978) *Wuthering Heights*; BBC2 classic serial.

Incidental references

Howe, Stephen (1989) 'Swithering heights', *New Statesman and Society*, 24.11.1989, p. 14.

'Swithering' refers to 'voters who switch and dither between parties', p. 15.

Parodies

Chapman, Graham *et al.* (1989) 'The semaphore version of Wuthering Heights' in *Monty Python's Flying Circus: Just the Words*, 2 vols, London: Methuen, vol. 1, pp. 198–9.

Kershaw, Noreen (dir.) (1989) *Withering Looks*, Lip Service, Buxton Festival.

Pastiche on *Wuthering Heights*. BPM has playbill. *See also 1993*.

Stage plays

Martin, Chris, (adapt. and dir.) (1989) *Wuthering Heights*, New Victoria Theatre, Stoke, with Jeremy Clay as Heathcliff and Carol Holt as Cathy, from 26.4.1989.

Source: *What's On Staffordshire* May [1989]. BPM has programme. Reviews: *The Express and Star* 4.5.1989; Michael Parker, *Guardian* 28.4.1989. Also touring production, Gatehouse Theatre Stafford (reviewed *Evening Sentinel* 22.4.1989); New Victoria Theatre, Newcastle. NYPL: Newcastle-under-Lyme Staffordshire (England): New Victoria Theatre: cast includes Jeremy Clay, Carol Holt.

Vance, Charles (adapt.) (1989) *Wuthering Heights*, Buxton.

Review: Michael Parker, *Guardian* 6.5.1989 ('Vance's adaptation dates from the 1960s') (BPM).

Television

Bradford, Barbara Taylor (1989) *Voice of the Heart*, ITV adaptation in four one-hourly parts, March.

Heroine, actress Katharine Tempest, is starring in Victor Mason's remake of *Wuthering Heights*.

Chapman, Graham *et al.* (1989) 'The semaphore version of Wuthering Heights', in *Monty Python's Flying Circus: Just the Words*, London: Methuen, vol. 1, pp. 188–9.

1990–9

Films and videos

[Before 1992] *Wuthering Heights by Emily Brontë*, Literary Images Limited.

Video plus worksheet and copy of Penguin edition of *Wuthering Heights*.

Musical settings

Penn, Michael, 'No Myth', *March* LP.

Pop song containing 'lines about Heathcliff'.

1990

Films and videos
(1990); *Visual Responses to 'Wuthering Heights': Notes for the Dayschool*, Educational Unit, National Museum of Photography, Film and Television, Bradford.

Illustrations, paintings, etc.
Brontë Parsonage Museum Exhibition of stage and film versions of *Wuthering Heights*, February 1990–January 1991.

Novels and poems
Urquhart, Jane (1990) *Changing Heaven*, Sevenoaks: Hodder & Stoughton.
   Novel full of references to *Wuthering Heights*. Review: Douglas Barbour, *The Edmonton Journal*, 17.3.1990. See Stoneman (1992b). *Note*: the author confirms that it is Eichenberg's 1943 engravings that she had in mind (personal communication).

Stage plays
[Carter, Randolph (1939) *Wuthering Heights*.]
   BS AGM 2.6.1990: American representative Mary Haigh reported a production by the Actors Co. of Pennsylvania Jan 1990 at Fulton Opera House, Lancaster, Pennsylvania, of Randolph Carter's play, 'first performed on Broadway in 1939'.
[Foxall, Vince (1984) *Wuthering Heights*.]
   Performed York Theatre Royal 7–24.11.1990, dir. Derek Nicholls, with Silas Carson as Heathcliff and Trilby Harris as Catherine (review: *Yorkshire Post* 9.11.1990, repeated in *Stage and Television Today* 15.11.1990). BPM has programme.

1991

Films and videos
[Wyler, William (dir.) (1939) *Wuthering Heights*.]
See *Daily Mail* 22.11.1991, '*Wuthering Heights*? Over my dead body says Goldwyn' [son of Samuel Goldwyn will not allow Kosminsky to use title for new film]

Illustrations, paintings, etc.
Forster, Peter (illus.) (1991) *Wuthering Heights*, Emily Brontë, London: Folio Society.
   Frontis. and 27 wood engravings; BPM has copy (see Figure 7.1. above).

Incidental references
Angelou, Maya (1991) Virago publicity leaflet for *Reading Women Writers*, a learning resource produced by the National Extension College, September.
Wainwright, Martin (1991) 'Help for wuthering tourists lost in the delights of Brontës', *Guardian* 6.8.1991: 18.
   Brontë footpaths signposted in Japanese; copy in BPM.

Musical settings
British Wool Marketing Board (1991); *The Romance of Wool*, Trade Fair Exhibition, Tokyo, with Paul Henly as Heathcliff and Ann Lloyd as Catherine.

> *BSG* 5: 3: 'To meet the Japanese request Board staff worked with our Museum staff to produce the drama, music and dance spectacle'. Comment: *Keighley News* 6.9.1991; *Yorkshire Post* 15.8.1991; 24.8.1991; [Bradford] *Telegraph and Argus* 30.8.1991.

Keshishian, Alek [1991] *Wuthering Heights*.

> *BSG* 25.10.1991 reports him to be planning what he called a 'popera', possibly with songs by George Michael and a performance from Madonna; NYPL lists a clipping referring to *Wuthering Heights: A Pop Myth*, with music by Sting, Kate Bush, etc., but I am unable to discover whether this is a projected or an achieved work.

Read, Mike [1991] *Wuthering Heights* (musical).

> *Musical Express* 27.4.1991: 'Radio 1 disc-jockey Mike Read is completing a new musical based on *Wuthering Heights*, which he aims to bring to the West End . . . Cliff Richard . . . has already shown interest in playing Heathcliff . . . before the show is mounted, Mike will record an album of his Wuthering Heights songs recorded by well-known artists – a treatment he used for his last musical about John Betjeman'. cf. [Bradford] *Telegraph and Argus* (n.d.) p. 23: 'Cliff Richard is said to be seeking a writer for his own *Wuthering Heights* musical' (BPM). See *Daily Mail* (27.4.1991). *See 1994.*

Taylor, Bernard (1991) *Wuthering Heights: The Musical*, based on the novel by Emily Brontë. CD and Cassette 1991: Philharmonia Orchestra, leader Hugh Bean, Cantorum Choir, conductor Nic Raine, produced by Nic Raine for Silva Screen Records Ltd, Digitally recorded at The Hit Factory (London) July–September 1991.

> Cast: Heathcliff: Dave Willetts; Catherine: Lesley Garrett; Isabella: Bonnie Langford; Hindley: Clive Carter: Nellie: Sharon Campbell; Edgar: James Staddon. BPM has photocopy of libretto. The [Bradford] *Telegraph and Argus* reported that 'the show is aimed to hit the West End stage in the spring after a four-week tour of the provinces' (4.9.1991), but this seems not to have happened. *BSG* 5 repeats this, adding: 'BBC TV have been making a documentary of the progress for screening soon, and Radio 2 have recorded a special session of the performance'. See also *BSG* 7: 16: 'no news yet'. See [Bradford] *Telegraph and Argus* (n.d.) p. 23; *Keighley News* 6.9.1991 (BPM). Reviews: *Daily Mail* 9.7.1991; [Bradford] *Telegraph and Argus* 4.9.1991; *Keighley News* 6.9.1991 (BPM).

Novels and poems
Higden, David Leon [1991] *Emily Brontë Rocks*.

> Poem (?) referred to in *BSG* 5 (February 1992).

Television
Zeffirelli, Franco [1991] *Wuthering Heights*.

Leonard Klady and Lawrence O'Toole, *News and Notes* 25.10.1991: 'With financing from Britain's Granada TV and Italy's Berlusconi media group, Zeffirelli is trying to get his TV movie on CBS by the spring'; *Daily Mail* 19.7.1991: Joanne Whalley Kilmer & Val Kilmer are offering to play Catherine & Heathcliff in Granada TV film for transmission Christmas ITV (BPM).

1992

Films and videos

Kosminsky, Peter (dir.) (1992) *Emily Brontë's Wuthering Heights*, Paramount, Mary Selway (prod.), screenplay by Anne Devlin with Ralph Fiennes as Heathcliff and Juliet Binoche as Catherine.

BPM has early draft of screenplay, stills, Paramount Press Release and Study Guide. Reviews: *Keighley News* 6.9.1991; [Bradford] *Telegraph and Argus* 1.10.1991: p. 7; 2.10.1991; 15.7.1991: p. 1; *Daily Mail* 16.10.1991 p. 40; *News and Notes* 25.10.1991; *Yorkshire Post* 30.10.1991, 24 and 28.9.1992 (BPM); Zoe Heller, *Independent on Sunday* 10.11.1991: 16–17; *Daily Mirror* 5.12.1991; David Gritten, *Daily Telegraph* 30.9.1991 and Supplement 11.4.1992; *Elle* August 1992; *Mail on Sunday* 4.10.1992; Nigel Andrews, *Financial Times* 15.10.1992; Lucasta Miller, *New Statesman and Society* 16.12.1992: 33-4. BPM also has many cuttings of ephemeral interest. See Paramount [1991].

Incidental references

(1992); *Birmingham Post* television guide, quoted Leslie J. McDonald, *BSG* 6: 4: '*Wuthering Heights*: "The daughter of an unhappy middle-class Yorkshire family falls passionately in love with a gypsy'.

(1992); 'Brontë wrangles sink to wuthering depths', *Sunday Times* 31.5.1992.

Account of Brontë Society dispute over parsonage extension. BPM has copy.

BSG 6: 14: Overheard in the Parsonage: 'Which of the Brontë sisters married Heathcliff?'

Lonsdale, Sarah (1992) 'Brontë Society imitates Heathcliff and Cathy', *Observer*, 7.6.1992.

Article about Brontë Society AGM.

Musical settings

Dick, Paul (1992) *Wuthering Heights* (Broadway musical); book, music and lyrics by Paul Dick, performed in the McGinn/Kazale Theatre, directed by Jack Horner, with John LaLonde as Heathcliff and Beth Thompson as Cathy.

NYPL has clippings and programmes; BPM has programme.

[Herrmann, Bernard (1966) *Wuthering Heights*.]

Unicorn-Kanchara Records 3-CD set UKCD 2050/51/52 1992. *See also 1982*.

Keshishian, Alek (dir.) [1992] *Wuthering Heights* ('popera').

News and Notes 25.10.1991: 'a "popera" (or "pop opera") version, directed by Alek Keshishian (*Truth or Dare*) will add music to Brontë mix. Keshishian, who staged the material as a Harvard undergrad in 1985, is approaching Madonna and George Michael to write songs and appear in the film' (BPM).

Northern Ballet Company [1992].

> *BSG* 7: 'discussion with the Northern Ballet Company in progress. The Society is considering sponsorship'; it is not clear whether this is the project which became 'The Brontës' (March 1995).

Novels

Haire-Sargeant, Lin (1992) *Heathcliff: The Return to Wuthering Heights*, London: Century.

> American title: *H: the Story of Heathcliff's Journey Back to Wuthering Heights*, New York: Pocket Books (NYPL list). Reviews: *BSG* 7: 16; Lucasta Miller, *New Statesman and Society* 16.12.1992: 33–4. *The Buffalo News* 24.6.1992 reports that the novel may be filmed with Kenneth Branagh as Heathcliff.

Parodies

Frazier, Ian (1992) 'Linton's Whatnots', *The New Yorker*, 11.5.1992, pp. 32–3.

Poems

Soares, Charlotte (1992) untitled poem, *BSG* 5 February.

> Poem inspired by Kate Bush's *Wuthering Heights*.

1993

Films and videos

[Wyler, William (dir.) (1939) *Wuthering Heights*.]

> Shown with revival of Carlisle Floyd's 1958 opera, Boston, March 1993. *BSG* 6.

Musical settings

[Floyd, Carlisle (1958) *Wuthering Heights*.]

> Performed by Boston Lyric Opera Co., Boston, MA, March 1993 (*BSG* 9: 21; 'all parts, both singing and acting, were performed by students from Boston University . . . The music was atonal . . . A forum followed . . . with Mr Floyd and Phyllis Cutin, who was the first Cathy in the premier held 35 years ago. Also present was the conductor Stephen Lord [1993 or 1958?] . . . The 1939 film . . . was shown at the Boston Public Library'. BPM has programme and typescript report by Mary Haigh: SB: 4016. *See also 1958.*

Parodies

[Lip Service (1989) *Withering Looks*.]

> Pastiche on *Wuthering Heights* performed Theatre Royal, York, July 1993.

Stage plays

Hay, Lynn Robertson (adapt.) (1993) *Wuthering Heights*, Jeremy James (dir.), Snap Theatre Company.

> Performed Wyke Sixth-Form College, Hull, 18.11.1993.

1994
Musical settings
Richard, Cliff: 'Cliff Richard . . . plans to be Heathcliff in a new London musical' (Spivey [1994]) (no more details; *see 1991).*

Parodies
Milligan, Spike (1994) *Wuthering Heights According to Spike Milligan*, Balthasar Klossowski de Rola ['Balthus'] (illus.), London: Michael Joseph.
    See Figure 4.7, above, for Balthus's *La Toilette de Cathy.*

Stage plays
Ash, William (dram.) (1994) *Wuthering Heights*, Good Company, directed by Sue Pomeroy, with Caroline Milmoe as Cathy and Jason Riddington as Heathcliff, Theatre Royal, Nottingham 26.9–1.10.1994.
    Reviewed Martin Spence, 'Cathy, it's me, Terry!', *BSG* 12: 2–3. BPM has review: *Stage and Television Today* 29.9.1994.
Napier-Brown, Michael (dram. & dir.) (1994) *Emily Brontë's Wuthering Heights*, Royal Theatre, Northampton 26.1–26.2.1994, with Keith Woodason as Heathcliff and Tara Woodward as Catherine; Grand Opera House, York, with Andrew Scarborough as Heathcliff and Emma Jay as both Catherines.
    BPM has programmes, information pack, photographs and reviews: *Leicester Mercury* 21.1.1994; *Chronicle and Echo* 26, 28 and 31.1.1994; *Herald and Post* 27.1.1994; *Northampton Mercury* 3.2.1994; *The Mail* [Harborough] 3.2.1994; *M. K. Gazette* 4.2.1994.
Raison, Jeremy (adapt. and dir.) (1994) *Wuthering Heights*, Chester Gateway Theatre 18.3-16.4, with Miranda Pleasence as Cathy and Patrick Robinson as Heathcliff; music by Corin Buckridge.
    Reviewed Tracey Harrison, 'Casualty star to be a black Heathcliff', *Daily Mail* 1.3.1994; Gerry Dempsey, 'Dreadlocked Heathcliff triumphs', *Daily Express* 29.3.1994. BPM has copies.
[Vance, Charles (1960s) *Wuthering Heights*]
    Performed by Stourbridge Theatre Company, Georgian Theatre Royal, Richmond, 16–19.8.1994, directed by Lyn Williams, with Philip Hemming as Heathcliff and Helen Young as Catherine. BPM has programme, photographs and unidentified reviews (9.8.1994).

1995
Musical settings
Gable, Christopher and Gillian Lynne (1995) *The Brontës* (ballet), Northern Ballet Theatre, March–June 1995.
    Music by Dominic Muldowney; includes sequence with Catherine and Heathcliff.

Stage plays
[Ash, William (dram.) (1994) *Wuthering Heights*, Good Company]
   Sue Pomeroy (dir.), New Theatre, Hull, 10–15 April; Billy Geraghty as Heathcliff and Jacqueline Leonard as Catherine.

General bibliography

For abbreviations see Chronological Lists.

Abrams, M. H. (1988) *A Glossary of Literary Terms*, 5th edn, London & New York: Holt, Rinehart and Winston.

Adams, W. H. Davenport (1891) *Stories of the Lives of Noble Women*, London: Nelson.

Alexander, Christine (1983) *The Early Writings of Charlotte Brontë*, Oxford: Blackwell.

Allott, Miriam (ed.) (1970) *Wuthering Heights, A Casebook*, Basingstoke: Macmillan.

Allott, Miriam (ed.) (1973) *Charlotte Brontë: 'Jane Eyre' and 'Villette', A Casebook*, Basingstoke: Macmillan.

Allott, Miriam (ed.) (1974) *The Brontës: The Critical Heritage*, Routledge & Kegan Paul: London.

Amster, Jane (1973) *Dream Keepers: The Young Brontës*, P. J. Franklin (illus.), New York: William-Frederick.

Anderson, Linda (1986) 'At the threshold of the self: women and autobiography', in Monteith (1986).

Andrews, W. L. (1944) 'Is this film the real "Jane Eyre"?', *BST* 10.54.225–8.

A[ndrews], W. L. (1947) 'On the cinema screen', *BST* 11.57.175.

Angelou, Maya (1991) in *Reading Women Writers*, National Extension College & Virago Press (press release for open learning course; no source cited).

Angier, Carole (1985) *Jean Rhys*, Harmondsworth: Penguin.

Athenaeum (1850) Review of Julia Kavanagh's *Nathalie*, no. 1203 (16 November), pp. 1184–5.

Austen, Jane ([1818] 1953) *Northanger Abbey*, London: Collins.

Austen, Zelda (1976) 'Why feminists are angry with George Eliot', *College English*, vol. 37 (6), pp. 549–61.

Azim, Firdous (1993) *The Colonial Rise of the Novel*, London: Routledge.

Baer, Elizabeth R. (1983) 'The sisterhood of Jane Eyre and Antoinette Cosway', in *The Voyage In*, Elizabeth Abel *et al.* (eds), Hanover, NH: University Press of New England, pp. 131–48.

Baldick, Chris (1987a) *In Frankenstein's Shadow: Myth, Monstrosity and Nineteenth-century Writing*, Clarendon Press: Oxford.

Baldick, Chris (1987b) *The Social Mission of English Criticism*, Clarendon Press: Oxford.

Ballantine, Edward (1946) 'Lake Werna's Water' (song), Witmore: New York.

Banks, Lynne Reid (1976) *Dark Quartet*, Harmondsworth: Penguin.

Banks, Lynne Reid (1977) *Path to the Silent Country*, Harmondsworth: Penguin.

Barker, Juliet (1994) *The Brontës*, London: Weidenfeld & Nicolson.

Barnard, Robert (1983) *The Missing Brontë, A Perry Trethowan Novel*, London: Collins.

Barstow, Stan (1980) *A Brother's Tale*, London: Michael Joseph.

Barthes, Roland ([1972] 1981) *Mythologies*, London: Granada.

Beauman, Nicola (1983) *A Very Great Profession: The Woman's Novel 1914–39*, London: Virago.

Bennett, Tony (1982) 'Text and history', in *Re-reading English*, Peter Widdowson (ed.), London: Methuen.

Benstock, Shari (1988) (ed.) *The Private Self: Theory and Practice of Women's Autobiographical Writings*, London: Routledge.

Bentley, Eric (1964) *The Life of the Drama*, New York; Atheneum.

Bentley, Phyllis (1947) *The Brontës*, London: Arthur Barker.

Bentley, Ursula (1982) *The Natural Order*, London: Secker and Warburg.

Berg, Maggie (1987) *Jane Eyre: Portrait of a Life*, Boston: Twayne.

Berg, Temma F. (1985) 'From Pamela to Jane Gray; or how not to become the heroine of your own text', *Studies in the Novel*, vol. 17 (2), pp. 115–37.

B[ickley], F[rancis] (1935) 'Christmas dinner at Haworth Parsonage', *Punch*, 25 December, p. 708.

Bigsby, Christopher (1994) *Hester: A Romance*, London: Weidenfeld & Nicolson.

Blain, Virginia *et al.* (eds) (1990) *The Feminist Companion to Literature in English*, London: Batsford.

Bloom, Harold (ed.) (1987) *Emily Brontë's Wuthering Heights*, Modern Critical Interpretations series, New York: Chelsea.

Bollinger, Lee (1989) *The Gales of March*, Hampton, NH: Wave Productions.

Boyle, Thomas F. (1983) 'Fishy extremities', *Literature and History*, vol. 9 (1), pp. 92–6.

Bradbury, Ernest (1966) '"Wuthering Heights" as opera', *The Yorkshire Post*, 27 September.

Bradford, Barbara Taylor (1989) *Voice of the Heart*, ITV adaptation, March.

Braithwaite, W. S. (1950) *The Bewitched Parsonage: The Story of the Brontës*, New York: Coward-McCann.

Briggs, Julia (1987) *A Woman of Passion: the Life of E. Nesbit 1858–1924*, London: Hutchinson.

Brindley, Louise (1982) *In the Shadow of the Brontës*, London: Frederick Muller.

Brontë, Charlotte ([1847] 1967) *Jane Eyre* (abridged), Bancroft Classics edn, Maidenhead: Purnell Books.

Brooks, Peter (1976) *The Melodramatic Imagination*, New York & London: Yale University Press.

Brown, Ivor (preface) (1936) *Jane Eyre, A Drama of Passion* in Three Acts . . . dramatised from Charlotte Brontë's novel by Helen Jerome, London: Hamish Hamilton.

Browning, Elizabeth Barrett (1850) *Sonnets from the Portuguese*, London: ?, No. XXVI.

Brownstein, Rachel M. ([1982] 1984) *Becoming a Heroine*, Harmondsworth: Penguin.

Bryson, Norman (1983) *Vision and Painting: The Logic of the Gaze*, Basingstoke: Macmillan.

Buñuel, Luis (1984) *My Last Breath*, Abigail Israel (trans.), London: Jonathan Cape.

Burnett, Paula (ed.) (1986) *The Penguin Book of Caribbean Verse in English*, Harmondsworth: Penguin.

Butterworth, Arthur (1979) 'Night Wind' (song; performed at The Grail, Pinner).

Cariaga, Daniel (1982) 'An opera premiere in Portland', *Los Angeles Times*, 15 November, part IV, p. 1.

Cargill, Oscar (1963) 'The Turn of the Screw and Alice James', *PMLA*, vol. 78, 238–49.

Carrington, Norman Thomas ([1960]) *The Brontës of Haworth Parsonage*, London: James Brodie.

Cecil, Lord David (1934) 'Emily Brontë and *Wuthering Heights*', in *Early Victorian Novelists*, London: Constable.

Chapple, J. A. V. and Arthur Pollard (eds) (1966) *The Letters of Mrs Gaskell*, Manchester: Manchester University Press. [*Note:* numbers refer to letters and not pages.]

Chatelin, Ray (1982) '*Wuthering Heights*: an opera's debut', *the province*, 14 November, p. 7.

Chitham, Edward (1987) *A Life of Emily Brontë*, Oxford: Basil Blackwell.

Christian, Barbara T. (1988) 'Response to "Black women's texts"', *NWSA Journal*, vol. 1 (1), 32–6.

Cixous, Hélène (1981) 'Sorties', in *New French Feminisms*, Elaine Marks and Isabelle de Courtivron (eds), Hemel Hempstead: Harvester Wheatsheaf, pp. 90–8.

Clark, Martin (1982) 'Soprano strives for devilment in "Wuthering Heights" heroine', *The Oregonian*, 5 November, p. F1.

Clarke, Pauline (1962) *The Twelve and the Genii*, Cecil Leslie (illus.), London: Faber & Faber.

Clayton, Jay (1987) *Romantic Vision and the Novel*, Cambridge: Cambridge University Press.

Cohen, Joelle (1982) *Seattle Times*, 9 November.

Cohen, Paula Marantz (1986) 'Freud's *Dora* and James's *Turn of the Screw*: two treatments of the female "case"', *Criticism*, vol. 28 (1), pp. 73–87.

Collins, Merle (1992) 'Visiting Yorkshire – Again', *Rotten Pomerade*, London: Virago, p. 17–18.

Cominos, Peter (1974) 'Innocent femina sensualis in unconscious conflict', in Vicinus (1972), pp. 155–72.

Conrad, Joseph ([1902] n.d.) 'The heart of darkness', in *Youth: A Narrative; and Two Other Stories*, London: Nelson.

Cook, E. T. (1935) *They Lived: A Brontë Novel*, London: John Murray.

Cory, Charlotte (1993) 'Back bites', *The Independent Magazine*, 29 May, p. 59.

Couper, Barbara ([1934]) 'Adapting "Wuthering Heights" as a radio play', *Radio Times*, 23 November, p. 636.

Cox, Philip T. (1992) 'Wuthering Heights in 1939: novel, film and propaganda', *BST* 20.5.283–8.

Crane, Richard (1976) *Thunder: A Play of the Brontës*, London: Heinemann Educational Books.

Creighton, Joanne V. (1987) 'Sisterly symbiosis: Margaret Drabble's *The Waterfall* and A. S. Byatt's *The Game*', Mosaic, vol. 20/1, pp. 15–29.

Crompton, John (1992) 'All done by mirrors: reflectivity in the novels of Elizabeth Taylor', PhD thesis, University of Hull.

Crompton, Margaret (1955) *Passionate Search: A Life of Charlotte Brontë*, London: Cassell.

Crompton, Margaret (n.d.) *Shadows of Villette: A One-act Play*, New Playwright's Network (copy in BPM).

Cross, Beverley (1978) *Haworth: A Portrait of the Brontës*, Toronto: Theatrebooks.

Cross, Gilbert (1977) *Next Week – 'East Lynne': Domestic Drama in Performance*, London: Associated University Presses.

Cudden, J. A. (1979) *Dictionary of Literary Terms*, Harmondsworth: Penguin.

Cunliffe, Walter R. (1950) 'The Brontës in other people's books', *BST* 11.60.332–6.

Dane, Clemence (Winifred Ashton) ([1917] 1927) *Regiment of Women*, London: Heinemann.

Dane, Clemence (Winifred Ashton) (1932) *Wild Decembers: A Play about the Brontë Family in 3 Acts*, London: Heinemann.

Davison, John (1934) *The Brontës of Haworth Parsonage*, London: Frederick Muller.

Davies, Stevie (1988) *Emily Brontë*, Hemel Hempstead: Harvester Wheatsheaf.

Davies, Stevie (1994) *Emily Brontë: Heretic*, London, Women's Press.

Day-Lewis, C. (1954) *Notable Images of Virtue: Emily Brontë*, Toronto: Ryerson Press.

de Beauvoir, Simone ([1949] 1970) *The Second Sex*, London: New English Library.

de Rougemont, Denis ([1940] 1983) *Love in the Western World*, Princeton: Princeton University Press.

Delafield, E. M. (1935) *The Brontës: Their Lives Recorded by their Contemporaries*, London: Hogarth Press.

Delbaere-Garant, Jeanne (1979) 'The divided worlds of Emily Brontë, Virginia Woolf and Janet Frame', *English Studies*, vol. 60, pp. 699–711.

Dickinson, Emily (1955) *The Poems of Emily Dickinson*, Thomas Johnson (ed.), 3 vols, Cambridge, Mass.: Belknap Press.

Dinnerstein, Dorothy ([1976] 1987) *The Rocking of the Cradle and the Ruling of the World*, London: Women's Press.

Downey, Roger (1983) 'Portland Opera: Herrmann "Wuthering Heights"', *High Fidelity*, March, p. 27.

Drabble, Margaret (1973) 'A woman writer', *Books*, vol. 11, pp. 4–6.

Drabble, Margaret (1974) 'The writer as recluse: the theme of solitude in the works of the Brontës', *BST* 16.84.259–69.

Drake, Douglas ([1967]) *Horrors*, London: John Baker.

Drew, David (1971) 'Two new Brontë films', *BST* 16.81.59–61.

Drotner, Kirsten (1983) 'Schoolgirls, madcaps, and air aces: English girls and their magazine reading between the wars', *Feminist Studies*, 9 (1), (Spring) pp. 33–52.

du Plessis, Rachel Blau (1985) *Writing Beyond the Ending: Narrative Strategies of Twentieth-century Women Writers*, Bloomington: Indiana University Press.

Duncker, Patricia (1992) *Sisters and Strangers: An Introduction to Contemporary Feminist Fiction*, Oxford: Basil Blackwell.

Dunn, Cyril (1948) 'The first television broadcast of "Wuthering Heights"', *BST* 11.58.176–9.

Eagleton, Terry ([1975] 1988) *Myths of Power: A Marxist Study of the Brontës*, Basingstoke: Macmillan.

Eagleton, Terry (1983) *Literary Theory*, Oxford: Basil Blackwell.

Easthope, Antony (1991) *Literary into Cultural Studies*, London: Routledge.

[Eastlake, Lady] (1848) *Quarterly Review*, vol. 84, (December), pp. 153–85.

Eco, Umberto (1988) 'Casablanca: cult movies and intertextual collage', in *Modern Criticism and Theory*, David Lodge (ed.), Longman: London.

Edgerley, C. M. (1939) '*Wuthering Heights* as a film', *BST* 9.49.239–41.

Ehrenreich, Barbara and Deirdre English (1979) *For Her Own Good: 150 Years of the Experts' Advice to Women*, London: Pluto Press.

Eliot, George ([1871–2] 1930) *Middlemarch*, London: Everyman.

Ellis, Kate and E. Ann Kaplan (1981) 'Feminism in Brontë's novel and its film versions' in *The English Novel and the Movies*, Michael Klein and Gillian Parker (eds), New York: Frederick Ungar.

Ellis, Mrs [Sarah] (1845) *The Daughters of England: Their Position in Society, Character and Responsibilities*, London & Paris: Fisher.

Elshtain, Jean Bethke (1982) in *Feminist Theory: A Critique of Ideology*, Nannerl O. Keohane, Michelle Z. Rosaldo and Barbara C. Gelpi (eds), Hemel Hempstead: Harvester Wheatsheaf.

Estes, Jim (1982) 'Somber opera grips audience in world premiere' *Salem Statesman/Journal*, 10 November.

Fawcett, Millicent Garrett ([1877] 1889) 'Charlotte and Emily Brontë', in *Some Eminent Women of Our Times: Short Biographical Sketches*, London: Macmillan.

Federer, C.A. (1906) 'The Bradford Mechanics' Institute Library', in *Library Association Record*, vol. 15.

Felman, Shoshana (1977) 'Turning the screw of interpretation', *Yale French Studies*, vol. 55 (6), pp. 94–207.

Ferguson, Rachel ([1931] 1988) *The Brontës Went to Woolworth's*, London: Virago.

Ferguson, Rachel (1933) *Charlotte Brontë: A Play in Three Acts*, London: Ernest Benn.

Firkins, Oscar W. (1932) 'Empurpled Moors', in *The Bride of Quietness*, Minneapolis: University of Minnesota.

Fletcher, Lucille (1982) Letter to Mr Stanley Johnson (31 August), BPM.

Flowerdew, Margaret (1933) *The Lonely Road*, London: John Hamilton.

Forster, E. M. ([1927] 1962) *Aspects of the Novel*, Harmondsworth: Penguin.

Fortunati, Vita and Gabriella Morisco (eds) [1993] *The Representation of the Self in Women's Autobiography*, Bologna: University of Bologna.

Foster, Shirley (1982) '"A suggestive book": a source for *Villette*', *Etudes Anglaises*, tome XXV (2), pp. 177–84.

Foster, Shirley (1985) *Victorian Women's Fiction: Marriage, Freedom and the Individual*, London & Sydney: Croom Helm.

Fowler, Bridget (1991) *The Alienated Reader: Women and Popular Romantic Literature in the Twentieth Century*, Hemel Hempstead: Harvester Wheatsheaf.

Fowler, Jennifer (n.d.) 'Letter from Haworth' for mezzo, clarinet, cello and piano (ms in BPM).

Frank, Katherine ([1990] 1992) *Emily Brontë: A Chainless Soul*, Harmondsworth: Penguin.

Fraser, Rebecca (1988) *Charlotte Brontë*, London: Methuen.

Frenier, Miriam Darce (1988) *Good-bye Heathcliffe: Changing Heroes, Heroines, Roles and Values in Women's Category Romances*, London: Greenwood.

Freud, Sigmund ([1908] 1985) *Creative Writers and Day-dreaming*, The Pelican Freud Library, vol. 14, James Strachey (ed.), Harmondsworth: Penguin.

Freud, Sigmund ([1933] 1973) 'Femininity', in *New Introductory Lectures on Psychoanalysis*, Harmondsworth: Penguin.

Freud, Sigmund and Joseph Breuer ([1893–5] 1991) *Studies on Hysteria*, The Pelican Freud Library, vol. 3, James Strachey (ed.), Harmondsworth: Penguin.

Friday, Nancy ([1977] 1979) *My Mother My Self*, Glasgow: Fontana.

Friedan, Betty ([1963] 1981) *The Feminine Mystique*, Harmondsworth: Penguin.

Fry, Christopher (1975) *The Brontës of Haworth*, Davis-Poynter TV script, 2 vols.

Furbisher, John and Tim Rayment (1992) 'Brontë wrangles sink to wuthering depths', *Sunday Times*, 31 May.

Ganner, Heidemarie (1980) 'Wuthering Heights in German translation', *BST* 17.90.375–8.

Gardiner, Judith Kegan (1981) 'On female identity and writing by women', *Critical Inquiry*, vol. 8, pp. 347–61.

Gaskell, Elizabeth ([1857] 1975) *Life of Charlotte Brontë*, Harmondsworth: Penguin.

Gérin, Winifred (1954[–5]) *My Dear Master*, performed Leeds Civic Theatre (BPM has *Telegraph and Argus* review of unidentified play performed in this theatre in 1954).

Gérin, Winifred (1967) *Charlotte Brontë*, Oxford: Oxford University Press.

Gérin, Winifred (1978) *Emily Brontë*, Oxford: Oxford University Press.

Gibbons, Stella ([1932] 1978) *Cold Comfort Farm*, Harmondsworth: Penguin.

Giddings, Robert, Keith Selby and Chris Wensley (1990) *Screening the Novel: The Theory and Practice of Literary Dramatization*, Basingstoke: Macmillan.

Gilbert, Sandra and Susan Gubar (1979) *The Madwoman in the Attic: the Woman Writer and the Nineteenth-century Literary Imagination*, New Haven, Conn.: Yale University Press.

Gilbert, Sandra M. and Susan Gubar (1988) *No Man's Land: The Place of the Woman Writer in the Twentieth Century*, vol. 1, The War of the Words, New Haven and London: Yale University Press.

Gilligan, Carol (1982) *In a Different Voice: Psychological Theory and Women's Development*, Cambridge, Mass.: Harvard University Press.

Gittings, Robert ([1955]) *The Brontë Sisters: A Play in One Act*, London: Heinemann.

Gledhill, Christine (1987) *Home is Where the Heart Is: Studies in Melodrama and the Woman's Film*, London: British Film Institute.

Gondal Theatre and Brontë Society (1994) 'Portrait of a governess, disconnected, poor, and plain', performed Haworth, 26 March.

Gordon, Lyndall (1994) *Charlotte Brontë: A Passionate Life*, London: Chatto & Windus.

Goudge, Elizabeth (1939) *The Brontës of Haworth*, in *Three Plays*, London: Duckworth.

Graves, C. L. (1917) 'To Charlotte Brontë' in *War's Surprises*, London: Sidgwick & Jackson.

Gregson, J. R. (1947) '"Wuthering Heights" on the air', *BST* 11.58.179–83.

Grinnell, Caroline L. (1992) *Try to Remember*, Northampton, Mass.: Purple Star Press.

Haines, Pamela (1987) *Daughter of the Northern Fields*, London: Collins.

Halliwell, Leslie (1986) *Halliwell's Film Guide*, 5th edn, London: Paladin.

Hannay, John (1986) *The Intertextuality of Fate: A Study of Margaret Drabble*, Columbia: University of Missouri Press.

Harland, Marion (1899) *Charlotte Brontë at Home*, Literary Hearthstones series, New York: Putnam.

Haskell, Molly (1974) *From Reverence to Rape: The Treatment of Women in the Movies*, New York: Holt, Rinehart & Winston.

Hatfield, C. W. (ed.) (1941) *The Complete Poems of Emily Jane Brontë*, New York Morningside: Columbia University Press (note reference is to poem numbers and not page numbers).

Hawkes, Terence (1986) *That Shakespeherian Rag*, London: Methuen.

Hawkins, Harriet (1990) *Classics and Trash*, Hemel Hempstead: Harvester Wheatsheaf.

Haynes, R. D. (1981) 'Elements of Romanticism in *The Story of an African Farm*', *English Literature in Transition 1880–1920*, vol. 24 (2), pp. 59–79.

Herndl, Diane Price (1988) 'The writing cure: Charlotte Perkins Gilman, Anna O, and "hysterical" writing', *NWSA Journal*, vol. 1 (1), pp. 52–74.

Heywood, Christopher (1987) 'Yorkshire slavery in Wuthering Heights', *Review of English Studies*, vol. 38, pp. 184–98.

Heywood, Christopher (1989) 'Africa and slavery in the Brontë children's novels', *Hitotsuhashi Journal of Arts and Sciences* vol. 30 (1), pp. 75–87.

Higashi, Sumiko (1977) 'Jane Eyre: Charlotte Brontë vs. the Hollywood myth of romance', *Journal of Popular Film*, vol. 6 (1), pp. 13–31.

Higham, Charles (1975) *Kate*, London: W. H. Allen.

Hill, Susan (1993) *Mrs de Winter: The Sequel to Daphne du Maurier's Rebecca*, London: Sinclair-Stevenson.

Hoeveler, Diane Long (1990) *Romantic Androgyny: The Women Within*, University Park & London: Pennsylvania State University Press.

Holdsworth, Peter (1964) 'Another "Wuthering Heights" film', *Telegraph and Argus*, 2 July, p. 8.

Holloway, Laura Carter (1882) *An Hour with Charlotte Brontë or Flowers from a Yorkshire Moor*, Philadelphia: J. W. Bradley.

Holtby, Winifred ([1924] 1981) *The Crowded Street*, London: Virago.

[Hope, Eva] (1886) 'Charlotte Brontë, the moorland romancist', in *Queens of Literature of the Victorian Era*, London: Walter Scott.

Howe, Stephen (1989) 'Swithering heights', *New Statesman and Society*, 24 November, p. 14.

Hughes, Helen (1991) '*Wuthering Heights*: The challenge of dramatic adaptation', MA thesis, Brigham Young University.

Hughes, Winifred (1980) *The Maniac in the Cellar: Sensation Novels of the 1860s*, Princeton: Princeton University Press.

Humm, Maggie (1989) *A Dictionary of Feminist Theory*, Hemel Hempstead: Harvester Wheatsheaf.

Hunt, Anthony (1985) *Brontë Seasons*, Macclesfield: New Playwright's Network.

Jackson, Douglas ([1978]) *Episode: A Moment in the Lives of the Brontës*, New Playwrights network (ts in BPM).

Jackson, Rosemary (1981) *Fantasy: The Literature of Subversion*, London: Methuen.

James, Selma (1983) *The Ladies and the Mammies*, Bristol: Falling Wall Press.

Jepson, Alfred (1962) 'Rochester's song to Jane Eyre', New York: Etnorb Music.

Jerome, Helen (1923) *The Secret of Woman*, London: Chapman & Hall.

Johnson, Edward Hotspur (1989) '*Wuthering Heights*: Bombay style', *BST* 19.7.325–7.

Johnson, Joseph [1860] *Heroines of our Time: Being Sketches of the Lives of Eminent Women with examples of their benevolent works, truthful lives and noble deeds*, London: Darton.

Johnson, Stanley (1982a) 'The making of Wuthering Heights', programme to performance of Herrmann's *Wuthering Heights*, Portland, Oregon.

Johnson, Stanley (1982b) '*Wuthering Heights* Lecture Series: II: "The novel on which the opera is based"' (copy in BPM).

Jouve, Nicole Ward (1986) *The Street-cleaner: The Yorkshire Ripper Case on Trial*, London & New York: Marion Boyars.

Kaplan, E. Ann (1983) *Women and Film: Both Sides of the Camera*, New York & London: Methuen.

Katz, Ephraim (1980) *The International Film Encyclopaedia*, Basingstoke: Macmillan.

Kenyon, Frederic G. (ed.) (1897) *The Letters of Elizabeth Barrett Browning*, 2nd edn, 2 vols, London: Smith, Elder.

Kermode, Frank (1967) *The Sense of an Ending: Studies in the Theory of Fiction*, New York: Oxford University Press.

Kinkaid, Frank (1982) 'Benny's Wuthering Heights . . . at last', programme for Portland Opera performance of Bernard Herrmann's *Wuthering Heights*, November, pp. 16–21.

Kinkaid, Frank (1983) 'Portland, Ore.', *Opera News*, 15 January, p. 43.

Kosofsky-Sedgwick, Eve ([1980] 1986) *The Coherence of Gothic Conventions*, London: Methuen.

Knoepflmacher, U. C. (1989) *Wuthering Heights*, Basingstoke: Macmillan.

Kristeva, Julia (1986) *The Kristeva Reader*, Toril Moi (ed.), Oxford: Blackwell.

Kuhn, Annette (1982) *Women's Pictures: Feminism and the Cinema*, London: Pandora Press.

Kyle, E. (1963) *Girl with a Pen*, London: Evans Bros; 1964, New York: Holt, Rinehart.

Langbridge, Rosamond (1929) *Charlotte Brontë: A Psychological Study*, London: Heinemann.

Leavis, Q. D. (1966) *Jane Eyre*, Harmondsworth: Penguin, introduction.

Leavis, Q. D. ([1969] 1983) 'A fresh approach to Wuthering Heights, in *Collected Essays*, vol. 1 (2 vols), G. Singh (ed.), Cambridge: Cambridge University Press.

Lehmann, Rosamond ([1936] 1981) *The Weather in the Streets*, London: Virago.

Lehmann, Rosamond ([1967] 1982) *The Swan in the Evening*, London: Virago.

Lemon, Charles H. (1944) 'Another opinion of the film', *BST* 10.54.229–30.

L[emon], C. L. (1967) 'A musical *Jane Eyre* and *Wuthering Heights* as opera', *BST* 15.77.143–4.

Lemon, C. H. (1969) 'Balthus and "Wuthering Heights"', *BST* 15.79.337.

[Lemon, Charles H.] (1976), A note on the preface to the French translation by Theodore de Wyzewa, *BST* 17.86.29–30.

Lemon, Charles (1993) *A Centenary History of the Brontë Society 1893–1993*, supplement to *BST* vol. 20.

Lesley, Alexandra ([1988, 1989]) *A Tender Fire: A Portrait of Emily Jane Brontë*, performed Salisbury and Haworth.

Lettis, R. and W. E. Morris (eds) (1961) *A Wuthering Heights Handbook*, New York: Odyssey Press.

Lewis, Jane (1984) *Women in England, 1870–1950: Sexual Divisions and Social Change*, Hemel Hempstead: Harvester Wheatsheaf.

Lindstrom, Robert (n.d.) '"Heights" staging fails to reach anticipated level', *The Oregonian*.

Linton, M. B. ([1926]) *The Tragic Race: A Play about the Brontës*, Aberdeen: Lindsay.

Lodge, David (ed.), (1988) *Literary Criticism and Theory: A Reader*, London: Routledge.

Lonsdale, Sarah (1992) 'Brontë Society imitates Heathcliff and Cathy', *Observer*, 7 June.

Luhr, William George (1978) 'Victorian novels on film', dissertation, New York University.

Macdonald, F. (1914) *The Secret of Charlotte Brontë*, London: Jack.

MacFarlane, Kathryn Jean (1936) *Divide the Desolation: Based on the Life of Emily Jane Brontë*, New York: Simon & Schuster.

Macherey, Pierre ([1966] 1978) *A Theory of Literary Production*, G. Wall (trans.), London: Routledge & Kegan Paul.

Mackereth, J. A. (1927) *Storm-Wrack: A Night with the Brontës*, London: Lane.

Macpherson, Pat (1989) *Reflecting on Jane Eyre*, London: Routledge.

Mair, Mary (1946) (poem from *The Small Voice*) reprinted in *BST* 11.56.39.

Malham-Dembleby, J. (1911) *The Key to the Brontë Works*, London: Walter Scott.

Malitz, Nancy (1982) '"Wuthering Heights" storms into Portland', *USA Today*, 8 November.

Mannon, W. (1946) *Devotion: The Book of the Film about the Brontës*, Hollywood Publications.

Manktelow, Bettine (1977) *Branwell: A Play*, London: Samuel French.

Martin, John (1964) 'Satan addressing the Infernal Council' (painting), reproduced in Jean Seznec, *John Martin in France*, London: Faber & Faber.

Martin, Valerie ([1990] 1991) *Mary Reilly: A Dramatic Retelling of the Classic Horror Story, Dr Jekyll and Mr Hyde*, London: Black Swan.

Marxist-Feminist Literature Collective, (1978) 'Women's writing', in *The Sociology of Literature: 1848*, Francis Barker *et al.* (eds), Colchester: Essex University.

Matthews, John T. (1985) 'Framing in *Wuthering Heights*', *Texas Studies in Literature and Language*, vol. 27, 25–61.

Maurat, Charlotte (1969) *The Brontë's Secret*, M. Meldrun (trans.), London: Constable.

Maynard, John (1984) *Charlotte Brontë and Sexuality*, Cambridge: Cambridge University Press.

Merry, Bruce (1971) 'An unknown Italian dramatisation of "*Wuthering Heights*"', *BST* 16.81.31–9.

Mew, Charlotte (1981) *Collected Poems and Prose*, V. Warner (ed. and intro.), Manchester: Carcanet.

Meyer, Susan (1991) 'Colonialism and the figurative strategy of *Jane Eyre*', in *Macropolitics of Nineteenth-century Literature*, Jonathan Arac *et al.* (eds), Philadelphia: University of Pennsylvania Press, pp. 159–83.

Meynell, Alice ([1926] 1947) 'The Brontës', in *Essays of Today and Yesterday*, Vita Sackville-West (ed.), London: Jonathan Cape.

Michie, Helena (1989) 'There is no friend like a sister', *ELH* vol. 56 (2), pp. 401–21.

Mills, Sara, Elaine Millard and Lynne Pearce (eds) (1989) *Feminist Readings/Feminists Reading*, Hemel Hempstead: Harvester Wheatsheaf.

Mitchell, Juliet (1984) *Women: The Longest Revolution*, London: Virago.

Mitchell, Sally (1977) 'Sentiment and suffering: women's recreational reading in the 1860s', *Victorian Studies* 21 (1), pp. 29–46.

Modleski, Tania (1982) *Loving With A Vengeance: Mass-produced Fantasy for Women*, London: Routledge.

Moers, Ellen ([1963] 1978) *Literary Women*, London: Women's Press.

Moglen, Helen (1978) *Charlotte Brontë: The Self Conceived*, New York: Norton.

Moi, Toril (1985) *Sexual/Textual Politics*, London: Methuen.

Moi, Toril (ed.) (1986) *The Kristeva Reader*, Oxford: Blackwell.

Monteith, Moira (ed.) (1986), *Women's Writing: A Challenge to Theory*, Hemel Hempstead: Harvester Wheatsheaf.

Moore, George (1924) *Conversations in Ebury Street*, London: Heinemann.

Moorhouse, Ella (1936) *Stone Walls: A Play About the Brontës*, London: Epworth Press.

Morgan, Charles (1932) 'Emily Brontë', in *Great Victorians*, H. J. and Hugh Massingham (eds), London: Nicholson & Watson, pp. 59–74.

Morris, Claud (1957) 'Purple Heather Bell' (song), London: Doric Music.

Myer, Valerie Grosvenor (1987) *Charlotte Brontë: Truculent Spirit*, London: Vision Press.

Nash Ensemble (1979), 'World Within', performed Leeds Playhouse.

Nightingale, Florence ([1852] 1978) 'Cassandra', in Strachey ([1928] 1978), pp. 395–418.

Nowlan, Robert A. and Gwendolen Wright Nowlan (1989) *Cinema Sequels and Remakes, 1903–87*, US: McFarland.

Nudd, Donna Marie (1989) '"Jane Eyre" and what adaptors have done to her', PhD thesis, University of Texas at Austin.

Nudd, Donna Marie, (1991) 'Bibliography of film, television and stage adaptations of *Jane Eyre*', *BST* 20.3.169–72.

Nudd, Donna Marie (1992) 'Rediscovering *Jane Eyre* through its adaptations', in *Approaches to Teaching Jane Eyre*, Diane Hoeveler and Beth Lau (eds), New York: Modern Language Association.

Oliphant, Mrs (1855) 'Modern novels – great and small', *Blackwood's Magazine*, vol. 77, pp. 554–68.

Oliphant, Mrs (1867) 'Novels', *Blackwood's Magazine*, vol. 102, pp. 257–80.

Olivier, Christiane (1989) *Jocasta's Children: The Imprint of the Mother*, London: Routledge.

Palmer, Jerry (1991) *Potboilers: Methods, Concepts and Case Studies in Popular Fiction*, London: Routledge.

Paramount [1991] '*Wuthering Heights*: preliminary production notes' (to Kosminsky's film), London: Paramount (unpublished; BPM has copy).

Passow, Emilie S. (1979) 'Orphans and aliens', *Dissertation Abstracts International*, vol. 40, 2698A.

Pell, Nancy (1977) 'Resistance, rebellion, and marriage: the economics of *Jane Eyre*', *Nineteenth-century Fiction*, vol. 31 (4), pp. 397–420.

Peters, Margot (1975) *Unquiet Soul: A Biography of Charlotte Brontë*, New York: Doubleday.

Petersen, William S. (1971) 'Henry James on "Jane Eyre"', *Times Literary Supplement*, vol. 30, 7 July, pp. 919–20.

Petry, Alice Hall (1983) 'Jamesian parody, *Jane Eyre* and The Turn of the Screw', *Modern Language Studies*, vol. 13 (4), pp. 61–78.

Pinion, F. B. (1975) *A Brontë Companion*, Basingstoke: Macmillan.

Pollock, Griselda (1988) *Vision and Difference: Femininity, Feminism and Histories of Art*, London & New York: Routledge.

Postma, Melanie, Sally Dunbar and Timothy Clarke (1993) *Glasstown Confederacy*, performed Chichester Festival.

Purchase, Edward (1937) *The White Flame: A Play in Three Acts Based on the Life of Branwell Brontë* (ts in BPM).

Pykett, Lyn (1989) *Emily Brontë*, Basingstoke: Macmillan.

Pykett, Lyn (1992) *The Improper Feminine: Women's Sensation Novel and the New Woman Writing*, London: Routledge.

Rainwater, Mary J. (1976) 'Emily Dickinson and six contemporary writers: her poetry in relation to her reading', *Dissertation Abstracts International*, vol. 36, January 1976, 4479A.

Raleigh, H. M. [1946] 'The broadcast version of "Jane Eyre"', *BST* 11.56.35–7.

Ramal, Walter [Walter de la Mare] ([1904] 1944) *Henry Brocken: His Travels and Adventures*, London: Faber & Faber.

Ratchford, Fanny (1941) *The Brontës' Web of Childhood*, Columbia University Press: New York.

Raymond, E. (1953) *The Brontë Legend*, Oxford: Oxford University Press.

Reiss, Erna (1934) *Rights and Duties of Englishwomen*, Manchester: Sherratt & Hughes.

Rewald, John (1963) *Drawings by Balthus*, New York: E. V. Thaw.

Rhys, Jean (1984) *Letters (1931–66)*, Francis Wyndham and Diana Melly (eds), Harmondsworth: Penguin.

Rich, Adrienne (1979) 'Jane Eyre: The temptations of a motherless woman', in *Of Lies, Secrets and Silence*, New York: Norton.

Richards, Christopher (1989) 'The idea of the sequel', PhD thesis, University of Leeds.

Richards, Martyn [Aline Mary Campion Richards] (1948) *Branwell: A Play in Five Acts*, Dorchester: Longman.

Ripley, Alexandra ([1991] 1992) *Scarlett: The Sequel to Margaret Mitchell's Gone With the Wind*, London: Pan.

Roberts, Helène (1974) 'Marriage, redundancy or sin: the painter's view of women in the first twenty-five years of Victoria's Reign', in Vicinus (1972).

Robertson-Brown, S. (1994) *Emily*, Alchemy Theatre Company National Tour.

Robinson, A. Mary F. ([1883] 1890) *Emily Brontë* (Eminent Women series), 3rd edn, London: W. H. Allen.

Robinson, Noel (1974) *Glasstown: A Play*, London: Samuel French.

Romieu, Georges and Emilie (1930) *Three Virgins of Haworth*, Robert Tapley (trans.), New York: Dutton.

Romieu, Emilie and Georges (1931) *The Brontë Sisters*, London: Skeffington; quoted in *BSG* 9 (July 1993); first published as *La Vie des Soeurs Brontë*, Paris: Galimard, 1929.

Rose, Jacqueline (1983) 'Femininity and its discontents', *Feminist Review*, vol. 14, pp. 5–21.

Rossetti, Christina and Dinah Mulock Craik (1993) *Maude, On Sisterhoods and A Woman's Thoughts about Women*, Elaine Showalter (ed.), London: Pickering.

Rowan, Nicole (ed.) (1995), *(W)righting the Nineties*, Gent: University of Gent.

Rubinstein, David (1986) *Before the Suffragettes: Women's Emancipation in the 1890s*, Hemel Hempstead: Harvester Wheatsheaf.

Ruskin, John ([1865] 1905) 'Of Queens' gardens', in *Sesame and Lilies*, London: George Allen.

Russ, Joanna (1973) 'Somebody's trying to kill me and I think it's my husband: the modern gothic', *Journal of Popular Culture*, vol. 6 (4), pp. 666–91.

Russell, Elizabeth and Aranzazu Usandizaga (eds), (1995) *Wayward Girls and Wicked Women*, Barcelona: University of Barcelona Press.

Sabin, Robert (1961) 'Carlisle Floyd's "Wuthering Heights"', *Tempo*, vol. 59, pp. 23–6.

St John, Susan E. (1984) 'A study of the opera *Wuthering Heights* by Bernard Herrmann', DMA thesis, University of Oregon; Ann Arbor, MI: University Microfilms International (microfilm).

Sarsby, Jacqueline (1983) *Romantic Love and Society: Its Place in the Modern World*, Harmondsworth: Penguin.

Schneewind, J. B. (1970) *Background of English Victorian Literature*, New York: Random House.

Scholes, Robert (1967) *The Fabulators*, New York: Oxford University Press.

Searle, Ronald (?1992) 'Crossed paths', *New Yorker*, p. 35.

Selden, Raman (1985) *A Reader's Guide to Contemporary Literary Theory*, Hemel Hempstead: Harvester Wheatsheaf.

Shaw, Marion (1986) 'Feminism and fiction between the wars: Winifred Holtby and *Virginia Woolf*', in Monteith (1986), pp. 175–91.

Shelley, Mary ([1831] 1968) *Frankenstein*, in *Three Gothic Tales*, Harmondsworth: Penguin.

Sheridan, Mary D. (1933) *The Parson's Children : A Play in Four Acts* (ts in BPM).

Shorter, Clement (1896) *Charlotte Brontë and Her Circle*, London: Hodder & Stoughton.

Showalter, Elaine (1975) 'Dinah Mulock Craik and the tactics of sentiment: a case study in Victorian female authorship', *Feminist Studies*, vol. 2, pp. 5–23.

Showalter, Elaine (1976) 'Desperate remedies: sensation novels of the 1860s', *Victorian Newsletter*, vol. 49, pp. 1–5.

Showalter, Elaine (1977) *A Literature of Their Own*, London: Virago.

Showalter, Elaine (1978) 'Family secrets and domestic subversion: rebellion in the novels of the eighteen-sixties', in *The Victorian Family: Structure and Stresses*, Anthony Wohl (ed.), London: Croom Helm.

Showalter, Elaine (1982) 'Feminist criticism in the wilderness', in *Writing and Sexual Difference*, Elizabeth Abel (ed.), Hemel Hempstead: Harvester Wheatsheaf.

Showalter, Elaine (1984) 'Looking forward: American feminists, Victorian sages', *Victorian Newsletter*, vol. 65, pp. 6–10.

Showalter, Elaine (1987) *The Female Malady: Women, Madness and English Culture, 1830–1980*, London: Virago.

Showalter, Elaine (1992) *Sexual Anarchy: Gender and Culture at the Fin de Siècle*, London: Virago.

Shuttleworth, Sally (1984) *George Eliot and Nineteenth-century Science*, Cambridge: Cambridge University Press.

Simons, Judy (1992) *Rosamond Lehmann*, Basingstoke: Macmillan.

Sinclair, May (intro.) (1908) *Jane Eyre, Shirley*; (1909) *Villette*; (1910) *The Professor*; (1914) *The Tenant of Wildfell Hall*, London: Dent.

Sinclair, May (1912) *The Three Brontës*, London: Hutchinson.

Sinclair, May ([1914] 1982) *The Three Sisters*, London: Virago.

Sitwell, Edith (1942) *English Women*, London: William Collins.

Smith, Barbara Herrstein (1980) 'Narrative versions, narrative theories,' *Critical Inquiry*, vol. 7 (1) (1980).

Snow Storm Theatre Co., (1993) (one-woman play about Charlotte Brontë), performed Haworth, 21–7 August.

Spivak, Gayatri Chakravorty (1985) 'Three women's texts and a critique of imperialism', *Critical Inquiry*, vol. 12, pp. 243–61.

Spivey, Nigel [1994] 'Brontë country can go with the wind', *Financial Times*, 26/27.2.1994.

Spofford, Harriet Prescott (1897) 'Brontë', in *In Titian's Garden and Other Poems*, Boston: Copeland & Day.

Stephen, Sir Leslie (1879) *Hours in a Library*, London: Smith, Elder.

Stevenson, Ronald (1969) 'No Coward Soul is Mine' (song), London: Novello.

Still, Judith and Michael Worton (eds) (1993) *Textuality and Sexuality*, Manchester: Manchester University Press.

Stokes, John (1992) *Fin de Siècle, Fin du Globe*, Basingstoke, Macmillan.

Stoneman, Patsy (1987) *Elizabeth Gaskell*, Hemel Hempstead: Harvester Wheatsheaf.

Stoneman, Patsy (1989) 'From Glass Town to Thornfield: the difference of view', Erasmus occasional paper no. 12, Department of English, University of Hull.

Stoneman, Patsy (1992a), 'Feminist criticism of Wuthering Heights', *Critical Survey* (June) pp. 147–53.

Stoneman, Patsy (1992b) 'Reading across media: the case of *Wuthering Heights*', in *Rebirth of Rhetoric*, Richard Andrews (ed.), London: Routledge.

Stoneman, Patsy (ed.) (1993) *Wuthering Heights, A New Casebook*, Basingstoke: Macmillan.

Stoneman, Patsy (1995a) '"Mad Cat" and "Marred Child": the Brontë heroines as female role models', in Russell and Usandizaga (1995), *op. cit.*

Stoneman, Patsy (1995b) 'The sequels syndrome', in Rowan (1995).

Strachey, Ray ((1928) 1978) *The Cause*, London: Virago.

(Sturges, Florence), (1981) *A Brontë Tapestry*, by a Children's Librarian (privately published).

Swan, Annalyn (1982) 'Rare adventures in opera', *Newsweek*, 29 November.

Swinburne, Algernon (1883) 'Emily Brontë', *Athenaeum*, 16 June, pp. 762–3.

Taylor, D. J. (1993) 'Serial fillers', *Sunday Times*, 29 September, p. 18.

Tennant, Emma (1993) *Pemberley: A Sequel to Pride and Prejudice*, London: Hodder & Stoughton.

Tennant, Emma ((1993) 1994) *Tess*, London: Flamingo.

Thieme, John (1979) 'Apparitions of disaster: Brontëan parallels in *Wide Sargasso Sea* and *Guerrillas*', *Journal of Commonwealth Literature*, vol. 14 (1), pp. 116–32.

Thomson, David (1975) *A Biographical Dictionary of the Cinema*, London: Secker & Warburg.

Thurman, Judith (1989) 'Reader I married him', *New Yorker*, 20 March, pp. 109–14.

Tillotson, Catherine (1988) 'A Brontë childhood', Brontë Parsonage Museum Haworth National Essay Competition for Schoolchildren, printed by the Brontë Society.

Tintner, Adeline R. (1976) 'Henry James's use of "Jane Eyre" in "The Turn of the Screw"' *BST* 17.86.42–5.

Tomalin, Claire (1978) 'Height of romance', *Radio Times*, 24 September, pp. 4–7.

Toothill, Derek (1988) *Brontë Follies*, performed Railway Institute, York.

Totheroh, Dan (1934) *Moor Born: A Play*, New York: Samuel French.

Vicinus, Martha (ed.) (1972) *Suffer and Be Still: Women in the Victorian Age*, Bloomington: Indiana University Press.

Vicinus, Martha (1981) '"Helpless and unfriended": Nineteenth-century domestic melodrama', *New Literary History*, vol. 13 (1), pp. 127–43.

Vipont, Elfrida (1966) *Weaver of Dreams: The Girlhood of Charlotte Brontë*, New York: Henry Z. Walck.

Voices Go Round (1990) 'No coward soul is mine: an evocation of the Brontë sisters', performed by Virginia Rushton (soprano), Vanessa Rosenthal (reader) and Ann Bond (piano), performed Haworth.

Voles, Wm. (n.d.) 'Loneliness' (song).

Wagner, Geoffrey (1975) *The Novel and the Cinema*, London: Associated University Presses.

Wainwright, Martin (1991) 'Help for wuthering tourists lost in the delights of Brontës', *Guardian*, 6 August, p. 18.

Wall, Ian ((1991)) *The Making of the Film Emily Brontë's Wuthering Heights*, Film Education Study Guide, Film Education for UIP.

Ward, Mrs Humphrey (intro.) (1900–02) *The Novels of the Brontë Sisters*, 7 vols (The Haworth edition), New York: Harper.

Weale, Sally (1993) 'Report reveals Patten paradox of Charlotte Brontë', *Guardian*, 17 April.

Weldon, Fay (1988) 'An interview with Fay Weldon', *Brontë Newsletter*, no. 7.

West, Rebecca (1932) 'Charlotte Brontë' in *Great Victorians*, H. J. and Hugh Massingham (eds), London: Nicholson & Watson.

White, Kathryn (1992) 'Literary antecedents in the canon: a consideration of *The Copper Beeches*', *The Ritual* No. 10, pp. 225–48.

Widdowson, Peter (1983) 'Hardy in history: a case-study in the sociology of literature', *Literature and History*, vol. 9 (1), pp. 3–16.

Widdowson, Peter (1989) *Hardy in History*, London: Routledge.

(1992), *Wild Workshop: Yorkshire and the Brontës*, Wilmslow, Cheshire: Videolink.

Wilde, Oscar (1966) 'The decay of lying', in *The Complete Works of Oscar Wilde*, 3 vols, London: Collins.

Wilson, Elizabeth (1980) *Only Halfway to Paradise: Women in Postwar Britain: 1945–1968*, London: Tavistock.

Wilson, Edmund ((1934) 1938) 'The ambiguity of Henry James', in *The Triple Thinkers*, New York: Harcourt, Brace.

Wilton, Ann (1929) Letter to Mrs Edgerley, 29 December, BPM.

Wollstonecraft, Mary ((1792) 1929) *A Vindication of the Rights of Woman*, London: Everyman.

Woolf, Virginia ((1928) 1970) *A Room of One's Own*, Harmondsworth: Penguin.

Woolf, Virginia (1929) 'Modern fiction', in *The Common Reader*, London: Hogarth Press.

Woolf, Virginia ((1938) 1977) *Three Guineas*, Harmondsworth: Penguin.

Woolf, Virginia (1966) 'Mr Bennett and Mr Brown', in *Collected Essays*, London: Hogarth Press.

Woolf, Virginia (1979) *Women and Writing*, Michèle Barrett (ed.), London: Women's Press.

Worton, Michael and Judith Still (eds) (1990), *Intertextuality: Theories and Practices*, Manchester: Manchester University Press.

Wright, Judith ((1971) 1985) '"Rosina Alcona to Julius Brenzaida"', in *Collected Poems*, London & Sydney: Angus & Robertson, pp. 286–8.

Zsolt, Gyorei and Schlachtovszky Csaba (1992) *Brontë-K*, Szegedi Ifjusagi Has (in Hungarian).

Sources and acknowledgements

The still from William Wyler's 1939 film, *Wuthering Heights*, is reproduced by permission of the Samuel Goldwyn Company (© MCMXXXIX by Samuel Goldwyn; all rights reserved); 'La Toilette de Cathy', by Balthus, by permission of the Musée National d'Art Moderne, Centre Georges Pompidou, Paris (© DACS 1995).

The photographs of illustrations by Ethel Gabain and Peter Forster, of the Helen Jerome play and the Japanese picturebook, were kindly supplied by the Brontë Society. The photograph of Balthus' 'La Toilette de Cathy' appears by courtesy of Photographie Musée Nationale d'Art Moderne, Centre Georges Pompidou, Paris, and the stills from A. V. Bramble's film of *Wuthering Heights* (1920), and William Wyler's film of *Wuthering Heights* (1939) by courtesy of BFI Stills, Posters and Designs, 21, Stephen St, London W1P 1PL. Photographs of the wood engravings by Clare Leighton and Fritz Eichenberg were made by the photographic service of the University of Hull from originals in the possession of the author.

The author and publishers wish to offer acknowledgement to Mrs Antonie Eichenberg for the reproduction of Fritz Eichenberg's wood engravings from the 1943 Random House editions of *Jane Eyre* and *Wuthering Heights*, to Peter Forster and the Folio Society for Peter Forster's wood engraving from the 1991 Folio edition of *Wuthering Heights*, to Reni Suzuka and Telehouse, Tokyo, for the drawing from the 1989 Japanese picturebook edition of *Wuthering Heights*, and to Lucille Fletcher for the extracts from a letter quoted on pp. 168 and 171.

Considerable efforts have been made to contact these and other copyright holders, and anyone claiming copyright should contact the publishers.

Index

Dane, Clemence (*continued*)
  Wild Decembers, 54, 73, 76–7, 80, 84–5, 176
Dangarembga, Tsitsi, 227–8, **286**
Darwin, Charles, 32, 41, 70
Davidson, Thomas, **263**, **293**
Davies, Bernard, 198, **281**
Davies, Maire Messenger, 199, **283**
Davies, Stevie, 154, 248
  Arms and the Girl, 226, **289**
Davis, Carl, **312**
Davis, Ted, 202, **283–4**, **286–7**
Davis, Tudor, 223, **289**
Davison, John, 72, 124–7, 131–2, 156–8, **275**, **299–305**, **316**
daydreams, 16–18, 21, 24, 47, 94, 112, 151–2, 154–5
de Beauvoir, Simone, 118, 250, **297**
de la Mare, Walter, 54, 91, **263**
de Rougemont, Denis, 132–3, 157, 159, 166, 174
de Wyzewa, Theodore: *L'Amant*, **294**
death of the author, 4, 6, 210, 253
deconstruction, 32, 46, 198, 206, 212, 229, 251
deferral, 150, 152, 206, 253
Delbaere-Garant, Jeanne, 114, 237–8, **295**, **307**
Delius, 166
DENVER, **269**, **272**
Derrida, Jacques, 2–3, 154, 235
Desmond, Patrick, **278**, **308**
detective stories, 41–2, 220
DETROIT, **272**
Devotion, 77, 176
DEWSBURY, **275**
Dick, Paul, 220, **321**
Dickinson, Anna, **260**
Dickinson, Emily, 78, 250
Dinnerstein, Dorothy, 138, 242
discourse, 3, 8, 26, 53, 59, 74, 99, 130–1, 140, 180, 187, 190, 252–3
  double-voiced, 50
  reverse, 69
doubleness, 17, 31, 34, 50, 52, 64, 103, 140, 144–5, 187, 190, 195, 205, 213, 222, 240
  doppelgänger, 42
Downey, Roger, 169, **314**
Dowrick, Stephanie, 233, **316**
Doyle, Conan 41–3, **262**
Drabble, Margaret, 151, 177n1
  The Waterfall, 150–1, 153–4, **279**

dream, 12, 14, 17, 19, 25, 51, 52, 56, 75, 82, 94–5, 147, 152, 173, 177n2, 180, 184, 187–8, 210, 211, 215, 224, 229, 237, 252, 253
Drew, David, 163, 193, **310**
Drotner, Kirsten, 118
du Maurier, Daphne, **305**
  Rebecca, 92, 94, 99–104, 106–8, 110, 143–5, 148–50, 178, 181, 233, **270–3**, **275**
du Plessis, Rachel Blau, 61, 240
Dublin, 133, 203, 205, **288**, **300**
Dulac, Edmund, **263**, **266**, **294**, **296**
Duncker, Patricia, 151, 188, 226–7
Dunn, Cyril, 156, **303**
DURBAN, **311**
Dynasty, 136, **282**
Dyne, Michael, **277**

Eagleton, Terry, 2, 5, 74, 76, 117, 129, 167–8, 171, 173, 177, 181–2, 206, 252
EASTBOURNE, **287**
Easthope, Antony, 2–3, 6, 208, 210, 213, 248
Eastlake, Lady, 7, 186
Eco, Umberto, 3, 127, 150, 217
economics, 2, 5, 8, 30, 57, 63, 95, 112, 120, 133, 175, 181, 184–6, 243
Edgerley, C. M., 155, **266**, **300**
Ehrenreich, Barbara and Deirdre English, 46, 120, 232
Eichenberg, Fritz, 37, 89, 109–10, *111*, 118, 119, 121, *122*, 124, 127, 169–70, 191, 201–2, 204, 206, 249, **272**, **290**, **301– 2**, **313**, **319**
Eliot, George, 79, 97, 164, 202
Eliot, T. S., 165
Ellis, Kate and Ann Kaplan, 112–13, 193
Elshtain, Jean Bethke, 2
ENGLISHness, 7–8, 28, 73, 177, 188, 190, 199, 201, 237, 241
  'Eng. Lit.', 57, 117, 129–30, 165, 174, 176, 214, 226, 231, **290**
  English studies, 74–6, 177
epic, 75, 83, 129–30, 132–3, 205, 207–8, **290**
Esson, Robert, **276**
Eugène Onegin, 133, 138
existential loss, 213

fairy tales, 19, 148, 247
fallen woman, 37, 51